Airpower ...

SMALL WARS

Airpower in SMALL WARS

Fighting Insurgents and Terrorists

James S. Corum *&* Wray R. Johnson

 UNIVERSITY PRESS OF KANSAS

Published by the University Press of Kansas (Lawrence, Kansas 66049), which was
organized by the Kansas Board of Regents and is operated and funded by Emporia
State University, Fort Hays State University, Kansas State University, Pittsburg
State University, the University of Kansas, and Wichita State University

Library of Congress Cataloging-in-Publication Data
Corum, James S.
  Airpower in small wars : fighting insurgents and terrorists / James S.
Corum, Wray R. Johnson.
    p. cm. — (Modern war studies)
Includes index.
  ISBN 0-7006-1239-4 (cloth : alk. paper) — ISBN 0-7006-1240-8 (pbk. : alk. paper)
  1. Air warfare — History — 20th century.   2. Low-intensity conflicts
(Military science)   3. Close air support — History — 20th century.
  I. Johnson, Wray R.   II. Title.   III. Series.
  UG700.C67 2003
  358.4 — dc21   2003000115

British Library Cataloguing in Publication Data is available.

Printed in the United States of America

10   9   8   7   6   5   4   3

The paper used in this publication meets the minimum requirements of the
American National Standard for Permanence of Paper for Printed Library
Materials z39.48-1984.

CONTENTS

Maps and Illustrations, *vii*

Preface, *xi*

Acknowledgments, *xiii*

Introduction, *1*

1 Biplanes and Bandits:
    The Early U.S. Airpower Experience in Small Wars, *11*

2 Colonial Air Control:
    The European Powers Develop New Concepts of Air Warfare, *51*

3 The Greek Civil War and the Philippine Anti-Huk Campaign, *93*

4 The French Colonial Wars, 1946–1962:
    Indochina and Algeria, *139*

5 The British Colonial Wars, 1945–1975:
    Malaya, South Arabia, and Oman, *179*

6 Airpower in South Vietnam, 1954–1965, *225*

7 Airpower and Counterinsurgency in Southern Africa, *279*

8 Protracted Insurgencies:
    Latin American Air Forces in Counterguerrilla Operations, *325*

9 Intervention in the Mideast, 1962–2000:
    Three Counterinsurgency Campaigns, *379*

10 Conclusion, *423*

    Notes, *441*

    Bibliographical Essay, *495*

    Index, *497*

    About the Authors, *507*

MAPS AND ILLUSTRATIONS

Maps

Southern United States and Mexico, ca. 1917, *13*
Haiti and the Dominican Republic, ca. 1919, *22*
Nicaragua, ca. 1927, *30*
Iraq, ca. 1922, *56*
Spanish Morocco, ca. 1912, *67*
The Greek Civil War, 1943–1949, *94*
The Hukbalahap Insurgency, the Philippines, 1946–1956, *111*
Vietnam, ca. 1954, *140*
The War in Algeria, 1954–1962, *162*
The Malayan Emergency, 1948–1960, *185*
Aden and Protectorate of South Arabia, ca. 1964, *200*
Oman, ca. 1970, *209*
Republic of Vietnam, ca. 1961, *226*
Rhodesia, ca. 1965, *293*
Namibia, ca. 1962, *303*
Angola, ca. 1971, *310*
The War in El Salvador, 1980–1992, *328*
The War in Guatemala, 1960–1996, *350*
Colombia, ca. 1998, *360*
North Yemen, ca. 1962, *381*
The Soviet Invasion of Afghanistan, 1979–1989, *388*
Northern Israel and Lebanon, ca. 1982, *399*

Illustrations

U.S. Army JN-3 at Chihuahua City, Mexico, April 1916, *45*
U.S. Army "Jenny" during the Punitive Expedition, *45*
Vought 02U-1 "Corsair" at McHugh Airdrome in Managua,
    Nicaragua, *46*
U.S. Marine Corps aviators with TA-2 Atlantic-Fokker
    trimotor transport, *46*

Augusto C. Sandino, a Nicaraguan nationalist who at one time lived in
    Mexico and served under Pancho Villa, 47
U.S. Marines preparing to embark for the voyage to Nicaragua, 48
Marine Corps DH-4B over Monotumbo Volcano near Managua,
    Nicaragua, 48
U.S. Marine Corps Fokker trimotor and officer aviators, ca. 1930, 49
McHugh Airfield, Managua, Nicaragua, 49
Standard patrol gear for Marine Corps aircraft, 50
RAF planes bombing Chabaish Village, northern Iraq, December 1924, 87
RAF DH-9 modified for medical evacuation in Somaliland campaign, 87
RAF DH-9s in Waziristan, Northwest Frontier of India, 1925, 88
Bristol Fighter of the RAF's No. 20 Squadron over the Northwest
    Frontier, 1925, 88
RAF "Z Force" DH-9 light bomber modified for medical evacuation, 89
Tuareg chiefs visiting an Italian air force Caproni heavy bomber squadron
    in Tripoli, Libya, 1922, 89
Eritrean infantry Askaris (Italian colonial troops) with a Caproni bomber
    and crew, Tripoli, Libya, 1922, 90
Italian light reconnaissance plane loaded with food supplies for the
    besieged town of Azizia, 1921, 90
Italian pilots and an RO 1 aircraft, ready to take off, North Africa, 1924, 91
Italian air force Caproni bomber squadron waiting to take off for a
    bombing mission, Libya, 1925, 91
RAF Vickers Victoria bomber over Egypt, ca. early 1930s, 92
RAF Vimy bombers over Egypt, late 1920s, 92
A squadron of F-8 Bearcats at Dien Bien Phu airfield, late 1953, 175
French B-26 bombers being readied for a mission, 175
French C-47 transport squadron at Do Son airfield, 1954, 176
Ms 500 "Criquet" light reconnaissance planes of the First South Vietnamese
    Air Force Squadron, flying in support of the French army, 1954, 177
French airborne operation, North Vietnam, 1953, 178
French paratroops in Algeria, 178
Royal Air Force Squadron No. 84 Brigand in Malaya, 219
No. 1 Squadron Lincoln bombers of the Royal Australian Air Force at
    Tengah airfield, Singapore, 219

Royal Air Force Venom fighters of No. 8 Squadron, Khormaksar airfield, Aden, *220*

Royal Air Force Whirlwind helicopter over Malaya, *220*

British army Gurkha soldiers disembarking from a Royal Air Force Westland Whirlwind helicopter of No. 155 Squadron in Malaya, *221*

Royal Air Force "Valetta" transport over Malaya, *221*

Royal Air Force Dakota dropping supplies to government forces in Malaya, *222*

General Sir Gerald Templer, appointed by Prime Minister Winston Churchill as high commissioner in Malaya, *224*

Royal Air Force Bristol Airfreighter, one of the more modern transport aircraft that augmented C-47 Dakotas late in the Malayan Emergency, *224*

South Vietnamese Air Vice Marshal Nguyen Cao Ky and U.S. Air Force Colonel William Bethea, commander of the Thirty-fourth Tactical Group, *275*

South Vietnamese paratroops boarding U.S. Air Force C-123 transports at Tan Son Nhut airfield, *275*

U.S. Air Force Sikorsky H-19 helicopter at Tan Son Nhut airfield, *276*

Former French air force F-8F "Bearcat" in South Vietnamese markings, *276*

Farm Gate aircrews and ground personnel in South Vietnam, *277*

U.S. Air Force and South Vietnamese airmen standing before a T28D, *277*

A-1E and T-28D fighter-bombers, *278*

U.S. Air Force H-19 helicopter at Tan Son Nhut airfield, *278*

A Portuguese AF Fiat G.91R trainer, *317*

One of the B-26s bought clandestinely by the Portuguese in the mid-1960s to reinforce their handful of old PV-2 Harpoon bombers, *317*

U.S.-built DC-6 transport of the Portuguese air force, *318*

FAP C-47 transport, the primary short-distance transport of the Portuguese forces, *318*

T-6 "Harvard" of the SAAF, *319*

Member of Rhodesian Army Grey's Scouts, *319*

First Rhodesian Light Infantry in a fireforce operation, 1973, *320*

Rhodesian fireforce deploying from an Alouette III, *321*

SAAF Mirage F-1 CZ, *321*

Sud Aviation Super Frelon helicopter of the SAAF, *322*

C-130 Hercules of the SAAF, 322

SAAF "Bosbok" light utility plane, 323

SAAF "Impala" light strike fighter, 323

RVLK attack helicopter developed by the South Africans in the late 1980s, 324

Crash site in El Salvador of an aircraft carrying Soviet-made SA-18 antiaircraft missiles for the FMLN from Nicaragua's Sandinista government, 373

Author James Corum in front of an FAS AC-47 gunship, 373

O-2A "Super Skymaster" twin engine (fore and rear) reconnaissance plane, 374

FAS UH-1 helicopter modified as rocket-carrying gunship, 374

A-37B counterinsurgency strike fighter of the FAS during the civil war of 1980–1992, 375

Ouragan fighter-bomber of the FAS, 375

UH-60 Blackhawk demonstrating the operating power of its two General Electric T-700 turboshaft engines at Colombia's high altitudes, 376

A-37 attack plane of the FAG, 377

Colombian Kfir fighter-bomber bought from Israel, 377

Colombian A-37 attack planes, 377

U.S. State Department contract crop duster (Ayers Turbo Thrush) spraying a coca field in northeastern Colombia, 2001, 378

Afghan Mujahideen fighters, early 1980s, 419

The Mi-8 Hip, primary transport helicopter of the Soviet army in Afghanistan, 419

The Soviet army Mi-24 Hind with rocket pods and a twin 23 mm cannon in Afghanistan, 420

Israeli F-4 fighter-bomber, workhorse attack plane of the IAF since the late 1960s, 421

Israeli F-16 employed against Hizbullah and the PLO in the 1990s and in the West Bank rebellion of 2000 to 2002, 421

IAF AH-1 Cobra helicopter gunship, 422

PREFACE

During the three years we taught a course at the School of Advanced Airpower Studies (SAAS) entitled Airpower and Small Wars, one of our prime difficulties in the course was finding good readings that covered the history of airpower in counterinsurgency and counterterrorism. Simply to provide our students with some historical background, we ended up writing several essays on the history of airpower in small wars. This book is largely an outgrowth of that course, those essays, and our conviction that a comprehensive history of airpower in small wars is urgently needed to provide American military officers and policymakers, as well as the military professionals and policymakers of friendly and allied nations, with a useful analysis of the historical experience of airpower in conflict less than general war.

Good fortune brought us together on the faculty of the SAAS. Both of us had done a lot of research on the history of airpower and small wars. In teaching together we found that we fundamentally agreed on our understanding of small wars theory and operational doctrine. It is a big task for one person to write a comprehensive history of airpower in small wars and provide adequate research and detailed analysis of all the major small wars operations. We found that the task was manageable for two people: we simply divided up the work per our own research interests, and each of us wrote several chapters. We both wrote the introduction and conclusion as a joint effort. Wray Johnson wrote chapters 1, 3, 5, and 6, and James Corum wrote chapters 2, 4, 7, 8, and 9. Although there are some differences in writing style between the chapters, we fully agree on the method of analysis of each small war and in the conclusions that we provide.

The objective of this book is to provide a comprehensive history of airpower in small wars through the twentieth century up to the present. In this book we examine dozens of conflicts — mostly insurgencies — and briefly outline the nature of the conflict, the strategies employed by the insurgent and counterinsurgent forces, and the air forces (by that we include army and other forms of aviation) that took part in the conflict; and then we discuss the specific airpower operations themselves. Finally, in each case we comment on the effectiveness of the aircraft, equipment, and tactics employed as well as judge the utility of airpower in its broadest sense. Unfortunately, our treatment of most of these campaigns is much too brief. In only a few cases have we been able to examine the role of airpower in a specific setting in any depth. In truth, the role of airpower in each of these conflicts deserves book-length treatment. In that regard, we do not contend that this work is the final word on the subject. However, if our effort serves to inspire other writers to take any one of our case studies as a starting point to more fully examine airpower in a specific conflict in much greater depth, then we will consider our own book to be a very positive contribution to military and airpower history.

Counterinsurgency and counterterrorism campaigns are, by their nature, joint operations, and airpower has generally been employed as a support arm of the police and surface military and paramilitary forces. Although we focus primarily upon the airpower side of campaigns, some discussion of the ground campaigns and the political background is necessary to provide context for the historical discussion. We have attempted to look at the history of airpower in small wars as broadly as possible. This book is not just about the American or European experience in fighting small wars. We have included several studies of non-Western states using airpower against irregular enemies. For example, Egypt conducted a large counterinsurgency operation in Yemen in the 1960s. Rhodesia and South Africa used airpower in long counterinsurgency campaigns. We also examine the role of airpower in several Latin American insurgencies. By looking at airpower in small wars in a broad fashion, we hope to prompt certain inferences from which certain conclusions about the nature of airpower in these campaigns can be drawn and, perhaps, make some general assessments about the most effective and least effective use of airpower thereby. We hope that our book, by accurately relating the history of airpower in small wars, will be of some practical use to U.S. decision-makers as well as to the military forces of America's friends and allies in framing the discussion about the employment of airpower in future conflicts against insurgents and terrorists.

ACKNOWLEDGMENTS

We had considerable assistance from many people in researching and writing this book. Indeed, some of the top airpower historians and experts on small wars have freely offered their valuable time and expertise in the most generous fashion simply because they liked the idea of the project and wanted to see this gap in airpower history filled. The people who have helped us have demonstrated the real meaning of scholarly cooperation. We really could not have done this book without their help.

We would first like to thank Colonel Steve Chiabotti, commandant of the USAF School of Advanced Airpower Studies. Colonel Chiabotti not only encouraged us to write this book, but also was always willing to support our research trips and attendance at conferences where we were able to gather much of our data. Dr. Conrad Crane, one of America's top airpower historians, reviewed our manuscript and gave us a long list of revisions to make this a better book. Throughout the process we received superb support from the staff of the USAF Historical Research Agency (USAF Archives). The Historical Research Agency is, by far, the best-organized and most user-friendly major archive in the U.S. government system. If a document existed, they could find it in minutes. They were always helpful in suggesting places to look to find obscure material. Likewise, the comprehensive collection available at the U.S. Marine Corps Historical Research Center proved invaluable. It is always a pleasure to do research with such professionals.

Because our book covers the operations in several countries, the list of those who have helped us has an international flavor. Mr. Sebastian Cox, chief of the Royal Air Force History Branch, and his colleagues in the RAF were helpful in every research request we made of them. We especially appreciate being able to use a variety of photos from the RAF collection. Dr. Ciro Paoletti, president of the Italian Military History Society, delved into the Italian military archives and found some wonderful material for us, including some rare photos. Several South Africans reviewed the chapter on counterinsurgency in Southern Africa and made some helpful comments. Brigadier General "Monster" Wilkins, who spent many years flying helicopters in Angola, Namibia, and Rhodesia, checked for accuracy and made useful comments. Stephan Botha and Dean Wingrin, keeper of the unofficial South African Air

Force website (one of the better historical websites we've found), commented on the draft and allowed us to use their photos. The chapter on airpower in Latin America owes a lot to the assistance of colleagues in the Latin America Aviation Historical Society. Tulio Soto provided a lot of information on the Guatemalan Air Force Reserve, one of the more obscure issues we examined. Mario Overall, Gary Kuhn, and Tulio Soto carefully reviewed the sections on Guatemala and El Salvador and made several helpful comments and corrections from their own personal experience. It's awfully hard to keep all the events straight in these small and confusing wars, and such help is invaluable. Dr. Russell Ramsey, professor at the Western Hemisphere Institute for Security Cooperation (WHINSEC) and one of America's leading scholars on counterinsurgency in Latin America, was kind enough to review the sections on El Salvador and Colombia. We would also like to thank Ray Farley for his hard work in producing the maps for this book.

Finally, but most significant, our families have been wonderfully patient and supportive during the three years it took to write this book. We send our special thanks to Lynn and Tommy Corum as well as Marcia, Erica, and Christine Johnson.

Airpower in
SMALL WARS

Almost from the moment the airplane was invented a century ago, Western powers found it to be an exceptionally useful weapon for fighting rebellious tribesmen in the colonies. In 1913, only a decade after man first took flight in a motor-driven, heavier than air machine, the French army deployed a flight of aircraft to Morocco to support military operations against native peoples resisting French authority. Ever since that first deployment of airplanes, the role of airpower in small wars has broadened. First airplanes were used, then helicopters, and today unmanned aircraft see increasing use. Airpower in its many forms has long since become an indispensable tool for any military force fighting against guerrillas, terrorists, and other irregular forces.

By the 1920s the airplane had matured into a formidable means to deliver firepower, conduct reconnaissance, transport personnel and supplies, and even evacuate wounded soldiers from battle. As a result, every major power that conducted colonial operations or military interventions between the world wars found airplanes to be indispensable in suppressing the many colonial rebellions of the era (1919–1939). Britain, France, Italy, and Spain used airpower extensively in policing their colonial empires. Following the rather dismal showing of U.S. Army aviation in the punitive expedition against Pancho Villa, the U.S. Marine Corps deftly used more modern aircraft to help put down insurgents in Haiti, the Dominican Republic, and Nicaragua.

After World War II there emerged a new era of large-scale nationalist and communist-led insurgencies. These small wars required new strategies, operational solutions, and tactics fundamentally different from prewar colonial operations. France and Britain found themselves battling several nationalist and communist-inspired insurgencies in their empires. Although not saddled with similar colonial burdens, the United States nonetheless provided aircraft, training, and support to threatened states, including the Greek government in their fight against communist guerrillas, and the Philippine government fighting against the Huks. Advanced aircraft technology, developed during World War II, played a major role in all of these conflicts.

From the 1960s to the 1980s, the Cold War often ran pretty hot as the Soviet Union alternately inspired, financed, armed, and supported numerous leftist and nationalist insurgencies in Africa and Latin America. The last remaining colonial power, Portugal, found itself fighting three insurgencies at once in its African colonies. Britain aided its Mideast allies in fighting indigenous Marxist rebels. Rhodesia and South Africa found themselves battling insurgents in their home territories. In Central America, Guatemala and El Salvador engaged in long and bloody civil wars, and their governments received aircraft, training, and other support from the United States. In each conflict, airpower played a major role.

The fall of the Soviet Union in the early 1990s did not bring an end to communist and other insurgencies. In fact, since the end of the Cold War, the world has become an even more dangerous and unstable place. Maoist insurgents in Peru and Marxist-Leninist insurgents in Colombia found that they did not need outside support from the Soviet Union or Cuba to sustain their cause. They could simply take a large share of the highly lucrative illicit drug trade and purchase advanced weapons on the world market with the proceeds. Israel found itself in an eighteen-year war against Islamic terrorist groups — generously supported by Iran and other Islamic states — in southern Lebanon. When Israel withdrew from the occupied zone of southern Lebanon in 1999, the fighting did not end. Since then Israel has found itself in a desperate battle with Palestinian terrorists within the Israeli-occupied West Bank and Gaza Strip. On September 11, 2001, the United States found itself propelled into a global war to preserve its own national security as Islamic terrorists attacked the World Trade Center and the Pentagon, killing some three thousand people and wounding thousands more. In November 2001, U.S. forces deployed to Afghanistan to topple the terrorist-friendly Taliban regime and then to hunt down members of the al-Qaeda terrorist organization. At the same time, the United States accelerated its military aid to the Colombian government's campaign against Marxist insurgents there, as well as to the Philippine government in its years-long struggle against Muslim extremists. Airpower has played and will continue to play a central role in these military operations.

Given the extensive employment of airpower in small wars for almost a century (that is, wars involving nonstate entities such as guerrillas and terrorists), it is surprising that no comprehensive history of the subject has been written. Of course it makes sense that the major books on airpower history would emphasize the great air campaigns of the two world wars and the role of strategic airpower in the Cold War. These were conflicts in which the survival of major powers was at stake. From the perspective of an American observer, victory or defeat in a Third World insurgency is relatively insignificant if one weighs it in terms of national survival. Nothing that happened to U.S. allies in Central America, to the Russians in Afghanistan, or to the British in Malaya could approach the same historical significance of any major campaign of World War II or a major shift in the balance of airpower and military power during the Cold War. Losing the "big one" meant the end of American civilization; losing the occasional small war did not hold similar prospects. For the many small nations involved, these wars were, in fact, a matter of national survival — but comprehensive histories are seldom written from the perspective of these smaller powers.

Nevertheless, if none of the dozens of small wars waged against insurgents and terrorists in the last century counts as much in grand strategic terms as a World War II air campaign, these many small wars still amount to a very important part of the military history of the last century. For example, since at least 1915 (when the U.S. Navy employed aircraft in the Dominican Republic), the United States has used airpower in more than a dozen conflicts against guerrillas, so-called bandits, and other irregulars. At times, for example in Nicaragua in the 1920s and in South Vietnam in the early 1960s, American air units have been directly employed in combat against insurgents. In many other cases, starting with Greece and the Philippines in the 1940s and in Latin America from the 1950s through the 1990s, the United States built up, advised, trained, and sustained foreign air forces in their fight against insurgents and other internal threats. We predict that, unless human nature undergoes a sudden, dramatic, and unexpected change for the better, the United States will continue to employ its armed forces or support the armed forces of other states in similar conflicts, and airpower — whether U.S. or host-nation assets — will be used to take the battle to the enemy. For this reason, a comprehensive history of the use of airpower in small wars is relevant and useful to the airman, the soldier, and the military and political leader.

Many theories are circulating today in top military and defense policy circles about how the United States can use military force against insurgents and terrorists. However, the application of theory, when not firmly grounded in historical experience, can often lead to disastrous results. The U.S. forces that were first committed to Vietnam from 1960 to 1964 were equipped with plenty of theories about how to fight an insurgency, but U.S. military and political leaders appear to have been woefully ignorant of the many useful lessons available from the history of earlier counterinsurgency campaigns that could have been used to modify or even discard some of the popular theories guiding the use of American military force in the early years of that war.

This book highlights the often negative role played by the institutional culture of the U.S. military and, more pointedly, the U.S. Air Force in terms of exploiting airpower in small wars. The air force is the least historically minded of all the U.S. armed services. In contrast to the army, the navy, and the Marine Corps, there are huge gaps in the history of American airpower in World War II, not to mention the Korean and Vietnam wars.[1] Indeed, air force involvement in small wars often does not even rate a long foot-note in official histories. For example, the air force equipped, trained, ad-vised, and supported El Salvador's air force during the long and bloody counterinsurgency effort there between 1981 and 1992. Yet not even a short monograph has since been produced by the air force to record the operational experience or the broader contribution of airpower to a military campaign that was very important for U.S. national security and foreign policy inter-ests in Latin America. That U.S. Air Force aircraft were not involved in the effort is not the point. The air force played a major role in shaping the devel-opment of the El Salvadoran air force, and American airpower thought greatly informed its employment. Yet the experience remains marginal to U.S. Air Force history, if not ignored altogether.

Another issue that drove us to write this book is the utterly inadequate discussion of airpower in small wars in the U.S. armed forces' joint and ser-vice professional military education and in doctrine. Considering that the U.S. military has extensive experience in using airpower against insurgents, and that the United States will almost certainly be involved in fighting insurgents and terrorists and will no doubt assist other nations in their own fights against irregular opponents in the future, the lack of attention in military colleges and in doctrine regarding this subject is scandalous. The U.S. Air Force, in particular, has tended to ignore and downplay air operations in small wars in its education system and in its doctrine.[2] Neither of us would advocate that the U.S. military should reorient its primary focus from fighting major con-ventional wars to fighting counterinsurgency campaigns, counterterrorism, or peace operations. We clearly recognize and approve of the primacy of conventional war in U.S. military organization and doctrine. We are merely making a modest proposal that some serious consideration be given to the small wars operations in joint and service education and doctrine.

Finally, in the few cases where writers have addressed the history of airpower in small wars, they have tended to get the history wrong. One common theme is to misinterpret the British "air policing" experience as being an example of airpower going it alone. As a result, some analysts have accepted this view and subsequently advocated that the United States consider a similar unilateral airpower approach, in which U.S. aircraft, unsupported by surface forces, would control events on the ground.[3] This book sets the record straight. As we hope to show, such a view of historical events constitutes far more myth than history. The employment of airpower in small wars in the future should be based solidly in fact, not myth.

By beginning with the general theory and history of small wars, we want to emphasize the very different nature of these wars from conventional state-on-state conflict. The very structure of small wars is different. Whereas military operations become the focus of any conventional war, in a small war the military dimension of the conflict is generally overshadowed by political, social, economic, and psychological concerns. As the authors of the Marine Corps *Small Wars Manual* well understood,[4] in countering an insurgency, systemic political and economic reforms are likely to have as much or more value in gaining victory over the insurgents as success on the battlefield. One can view the structure in vertical as well as in horizontal terms. Vertically, small wars, especially those of the insurgent variety, are different from conventional wars at the strategic, operational, and tactical levels. Horizontally, success in small wars requires the integration of all aspects of national power. In more than a few cases, governments have enjoyed military success in countering insurgents but lost the war in the political and economic spheres.

For the purposes of this book, airpower is defined as all forms of aviation employed to combat insurgents and terrorists. In this sense, airpower includes the aircraft of air forces and of armies and navies, police helicopter and light aircraft units, military unmanned aerial vehicles, and aircraft of the civil air reserve. In combating insurgencies there is usually little useful distinction between the aircraft of the air force, army, navy, and the police, and we see no need to make any such distinctions.

To describe the conflicts covered in this book, we prefer the term "small wars," which first came into use in the late nineteenth century to describe any conflict against nonregular forces such as guerrillas, bandits, rebellious tribes, or insurgents of various stripes.[5] The term soon came to mean any conflict waged against a nonstate entity by regular military forces. The primary nonstate enemies engaged in wars of the twentieth century have been insurgents and terrorists.

Although small wars remains an archaic term, it saw widespread use in the first half of the twentieth century. In 1940 the U.S. Marine Corps published the *Small Wars Manual*, which outlined a comprehensive doctrine for dealing with the various rebels, insurgents, bandits, and warring factions commonly encountered by the Marines during their numerous intervention operations before World War II. The *Small Wars Manual* emerged from the collective experience of the Marine Corps in conducting pacification operations in China and throughout the Caribbean and Central America from 1898 to 1934. Such operations included counterinsurgency, suppressing banditry, peacekeeping, supervising and supporting elections, and training foreign forces.[6] In the post–World War II era, the term "small wars" was replaced by "counterinsurgency" and later by "low-intensity conflict" (LIC).[7] LIC was defined in U.S. military doctrine at the time as "a limited politico-military struggle to achieve political, social, economic or psychological objectives." Such struggles were regarded as being generally confined to the Third World and were characterized by "constraints on the weaponry, tactics and the level of violence."[8] However, the definition of LIC was so vague it could apparently encompass everything from terrorism to nonnuclear conventional war (e.g., the Korean War). Terms without clear meaning are not a good foundation for any military doctrine.

In the mid-1990s, the Defense Department introduced a new term that confused matters even more than LIC. Low-intensity conflict evolved into "Military Operations Other Than War," or MOOTW — a term meant to describe a range of operations that includes combat but avoids using the terms "war" or "conflict." Such an appellation proved useful to the Clinton administration as it deployed U.S. forces around the globe and yet denied that such operations had anything to do with war. It is, frankly, a bizarre term when one considers that U.S. combat operations in Somalia in 1993, the U.S. bombing campaign in Bosnia in 1995, and the U.S. air war against Serbia in 1999 were all, under official doctrine, military operations other than war. By the late 1990s, MOOTW lost favor and new euphemisms such as "stability operations" (actually not a new term, since it was used during the Vietnam War) came into vogue. Again, these new terms have continued to fall short of any doctrinal usefulness simply because they are carefully crafted to obscure rather than clarify the nature of conflict less than major war — certainly most would never pass muster in terms of Clausewitz's definition of war.

Along with some other defense policy thinkers of the 1990s, namely the late Colonel Harry Summers and Professor Eliot Cohen, we wish to see the term "small wars" revived in the military lexicon.[9] The term "small wars" is clear and blunt. Simply put, military operations against insurgents and terrorists involve combat and by definition are a form of warfare. The term itself does not necessarily refer to the scale of the war but rather to its nature: a war waged against a nonstate entity and nonregular forces is a form of war very different from a war waged against a state with regular armed forces. This is a point we wish to emphasize. States possess capital cities, a formal government organization, regular armed forces, and an economic infrastructure and war industries. If a state uses airpower in a military conflict, the distinction between a state and nonstate entity is essential. In a war against an enemy state, all of the attributes and assets of a formally recognized state listed above become legitimate targets for aerial attack. A strategic bombing campaign against enemy government centers, war industries, transportation infrastructure, and the armed forces makes perfect sense in a conventional war ("conventional war" being defined as a major nonnuclear war between states).

In contrast with a conventional state-on-state war, insurgents and terrorists rarely possess a capital city, a formal government infrastructure, regular fielded armed forces, or war industries. Insurgents are commonly organized as guerrilla forces that hide within the civilian population. Insurgent organizations and leadership commonly operate underground or have sanctuary in another country that is not openly part of the conflict. Insurgent forces are likely to be law-abiding, pro-government peasants by day and anti-government guerrillas by night. Insurgents generally fight in small units to exploit their inherent advantages in surprise, mobility, and initiative. On occasion, insurgent forces may combine into a large force and wage a conventional battle against government forces. When this occurs, the direct and lethal employment of airpower can be applied with great effectiveness. However,

generally speaking, guerrillas and terrorists rarely present lucrative targets for
aerial attack, and even more rarely is there ever a chance for airpower to be
employed in a strategic bombing campaign or even in attack operations on
any large scale. As a result, it is the indirect application of airpower — that
is, the use of aviation resources for reconnaissance, transportation, psychological operations, and communications — that proves most useful.

Insurgents are typically organized into a political group that engages in
military conflict with the purpose of replacing the government of its country
with its own group. Insurgencies normally begin with the creation of a political organization that sets forth a clear political agenda as the ultimate goal
of the insurgent group. Insurgents seek to mobilize popular support from the
citizenry and carry out military action as part of a larger political strategy.
The most common form of small war in this regard is an insurgency — essentially an internal rebellion in which one or more factions within a country seek the violent overthrow of the existing government. Insurgencies often
include external as well as internal participants. For reasons of their own, other
countries become involved by providing support to the insurgents (usually
clandestine) or providing support to the extant regime. It is important to note
that insurgents commonly use terror as a tool to undermine the legitimacy
of the government, but terrorist tactics do not make an insurgent group a
terrorist organization (though the government may characterize them in this
fashion, as the British did in Malaya). The distinguishing feature between
insurgents and terrorists is whether and to what extent the group in question seeks to organize a mass base. (This allows for ineptitude and doctrinal
misfires. For example, Ché Guevara's *foco* theory viewed the guerrilla army
as the engine of revolution that seeks to foment mass uprising by its own
success. Guevarists simply cannot be bothered, however, with the tedious
political organization required in the Maoist approach.)

Whereas insurgents seek to mobilize a mass base, terrorists generally do
not concern themselves with mass mobilization. Their aim is to destabilize
and demoralize a nation by acts of terror, that is, acts of violence often aimed
at civilians, with the goal of demoralizing and destabilizing the state. Terrorists, in contrast to insurgents, normally do not have a clear, long-term political program beyond simply killing and damaging their enemies. Terrorist
groups, such as the Red Brigades of Italy or the Red Army Fraktion of Germany during the 1970s and 1980s, are generally small organizations with little

interest in winning broad popular support. Carrying out acts of indiscriminate violence becomes an end in and of itself. Admittedly, Islamic terrorist groups often have broad popular appeal and even seek the kind of popular support that most terrorist groups in the West eschew, and as a result have received considerable financial and other support from individuals, whole communities, and even Islamic regimes. However, terrorists in the Mideast are distinguished from insurgents in that their movement is not geared to bringing about any clear, precise, long-term political goal, other than the realization of a vague "Islamic state." Insurgent groups use terrorist tactics (assassination, kidnapping, bombing, and hijacking aircraft) within the context of achieving their larger political goals; terrorists, as a rule, commit acts of terror for terror's sake.

One can argue that the new Islamic terrorism, which enjoys strong popular support, best fits into a definitional gray area. In this case we have movements that started as terrorist groups but are slowly evolving into insurgencies as their political organization and political goals become more clear. This is certainly the case of some Palestinian organizations, such as Hamas, and of Hizbullah, which is taking a more open role in Lebanese politics. As to overthrowing a specific government, Islamic radicals seem less interested in conducting insurgencies against their own governments (although that is likely to change) but in somehow toppling Israel, the United States, and the Western nations in general.

Partisan operations properly belong to any study of small wars. Partisans are usually irregular forces, sometimes regulars, who conduct guerrilla operations behind enemy lines in support of conventional armies waging a conventional war. There are numerous cases of airpower being employed in support of and against partisan forces. For example, Allied Chindit irregulars and locally recruited guerrillas who fought behind the Japanese lines in Burma in World War II were supplied and supported by British and American airpower. The Soviets used airpower to support partisans behind German lines on the eastern front, and the Royal Air Force and the U.S. Army Air Forces supported French and Yugoslav partisans fighting behind German lines as well. Conversely, the Luftwaffe and Germany's allied air forces devoted considerable resources to fighting these partisans during World War II. After the war, U.S. airpower was employed against North Korean partisans and at the same time conducted extensive aerial unconventional operations, including the insertion and support of partisan forces behind North Korean lines. More recently, airpower was used in support of the Northern Alliance fighting against the Taliban regime in Afghanistan, arguably an example of using airpower in support of partisan forces.

Nevertheless, we have decided to leave the history of airpower and partisan operations out of this book. Part of our reason is simply to keep the book manageable; to cover the subject of airpower and partisan operations in any depth would require several hundred additional pages. We have already done considerable research on this subject and expect to deal with partisan operations and airpower in a future book. For the same reason, we have not included airpower in peace operations. The use of airpower by the United Nations in suppressing rebel factions in the Congo from 1960 to 1964 and the use of airpower by the United States and United Nations in fighting hostile factions in Somalia in 1993 would certainly count as small wars under the definition of a conflict against a nonstate entity. However, we believe that the use of airpower in peace operations is a large enough subset of the small wars category that it is best addressed in a separate volume.

Biplanes and Bandits
The Early U.S. Airpower Experience in Small Wars

The U.S. Army has the distinction of being the first American armed service to employ airpower in a small war setting, but it was the U.S. Marine Corps that first took the role of airpower in small wars seriously. The army's first use of airplanes against an irregular opponent occurred during the Mexican Punitive Expedition of 1916, when President Woodrow Wilson ordered Brigadier General John J. Pershing to pursue and disperse rebel forces led by Francisco "Pancho" Villa.[1] From 15 March to 15 August 1916, the First Aero Squadron, under the command of Captain Benjamin D. Foulois, flew 540 sorties, covered over nineteen thousand miles, and logged over 340 flying hours in support of Pershing's troops on the ground.[2] But with the end of the expedition in February 1917 and America's entry into World War I, the army's interest in small wars quickly evaporated, and with it any interest in airpower in small wars.

The Marines, on the other hand, were so closely identified with military intervention as an instrument of American foreign policy that they were sometimes referred to as "State Department Troops in small wars."[3] The Marines participated in the pacification of the Philippines at the turn of the century and were very active in China following the Boxer Rebellion, averaging twelve landings a year between 1911 and 1914, and clashing some fifty-seven times with Chinese forces in 1926 and 1927 during the Chinese Civil War.[4] But it was in the Caribbean and Central America that the Marines realized their raison d'être. Between the close of the Spanish-American War and the "Sandino Affair" in Nicaragua in 1927, the Marines intervened in Nicaragua ten times (nine times before 1912); in Panama in 1903; Cuba in 1906, 1912, and from 1917 to 1922; in Haiti from 1915 to 1916, and again from 1919 to

1920; and in Santo Domingo from 1916 to 1917 and again in 1919.[5] For Marine aviators, fighting "bandits" in the Dominican Republic and *cacos* in Haiti was a formative experience, but Nicaragua was the proving ground for the Marines' concept of airpower in small wars, a laboratory that also provided the basic formula for Marine air-ground teams in World War II and up to the present.

Chasing Pancho Villa

Revolution broke out in Mexico in 1910 when the government of Porfirio Díaz Mory collapsed. What began as a coup d'état degenerated into a long and bloody civil war characterized by a guerrilla campaign in northern Mexico led by Pancho Villa, and another in the south led by Emiliano Zapata. The "Great Revolution" had begun with a general uprising to oust Díaz. The broadly based movement was led initially by Francisco I. Madero — a wealthy cotton planter who became a popular hero for challenging Díaz. When the Mexican federal army was unable to put down the rebellion, Díaz capitulated (the treaty of Ciudad Juárez), to be replaced in succession by Madero and General Victoriano Huerta, who allegedly had Madero murdered. Another popular movement led by a wealthy former senator, Venustiano Carranza, arose to avenge Madero's death and oust Huerta, who ultimately resigned and fled to Spain, whereupon Carranza assumed the presidency in August 1914. Chaos followed, however, with armed struggles between Carranza, Villa, Zapata, and various freebooters. In the end, the Carrancista forces, led by General Álvaro Obregón, defeated the Villistas and Zapatistas in succession.[6]

Ten days after Madero's death, Thomas Woodrow Wilson was inaugurated as the twenty-eighth president of the United States. During his campaign, Wilson had closely followed the developments in Mexico, and although he had hoped to devote his attention primarily to domestic social issues, he was soon faced with the same thorny diplomatic problems concerning Mexico that had plagued his predecessor, William Howard Taft. Neither Wilson nor his secretary of state, William Jennings Bryan, had any direct experience in foreign affairs, but they both agreed upon a need to promote a higher standard of morality in international relations and that America had been called to advance the cause of democracy.

Such "missionary diplomacy" did not, however, eschew military intervention. Confronted with a man he believed to be no less than a murderous thug

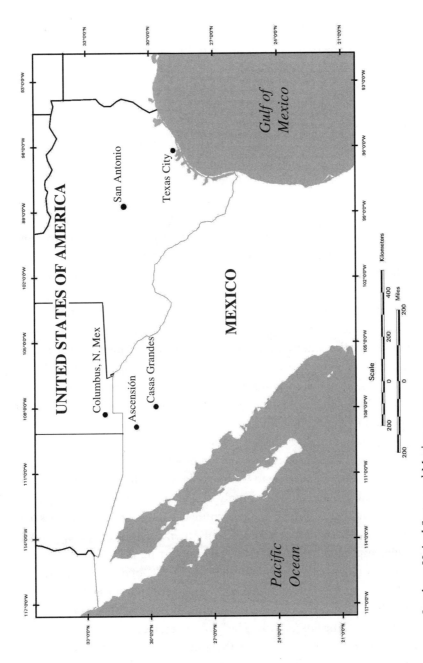

Southern United States and Mexico, ca. 1917

in General Huerta, Wilson enunciated a new doctrine of "nonrecognition," refusing to acknowledge the legitimacy of the Huerta government. Wilson removed an embargo on arms to Mexico in order to help the revolutionary forces of Carranza and then stationed warships off Mexico to halt arms shipments — originating mostly in Germany — from reaching Huerta's government. The dictator's hold on power was tenuous, and Wilson used the arrest of several American sailors at Tampico in April 1914 to justify military occupation of the port of Veracruz. The moral effect was to sufficiently weaken Huerta's government so that he resigned in July, to be succeeded by Carranza. Wilson's subsequent recognition and support of the Carranza government embittered Villa, who regarded himself as the rightful heir to the presidency. He also considered American recognition of Carranza to be an intolerable meddling in Mexican internal affairs. In January 1916, Villa and his men boarded a train at Santa Isabel and murdered sixteen American mining engineers in a deliberate attempt to provoke American military intervention, thereby discrediting Carranza and raising himself as the "liberator" of the Mexican people. That failing, Villa wrote a letter to Zapata stating his intention to "attack the Americans in their own dens" and requesting that Zapata send troops north to assist in the endeavor.[7] Zapata apparently declined; nevertheless, on 9 March 1916, Villa's guerrillas struck at Columbus, New Mexico, killing seventeen American citizens, after which Villa withdrew to the mountains of northern Mexico.

Villa's attack outraged the American public, and President Wilson concluded that he had to use military force in order to discourage future incursions by Villa as well as respond to the public's demand that reprisal action be taken. But Wilson could not simply invade Mexico given his recognition of the Carranza government as the legitimate ruling authority. A workable protocol was necessary that would permit American troops to pursue and, if possible, apprehend Villa. To that end, an existing 1882 treaty permitted American forces to cross the border in "hot pursuit" of hostile Indians. Wilson used this treaty as his authority to order American troops into Mexico to pursue Villa. But in a statement given to journalists on 10 March 1916, Wilson maintained that the pursuit would be "done in entire friendly aid of the constituted authorities of Mexico and with scrupulous respect for the sovereignty of that republic."[8] In effect, the military action to be taken would be limited in scope.

The officer chosen to bring Villa to heel was fifty-five-year-old Brigadier General John Joseph Pershing. Posted as the garrison commander in El Paso, Texas, Pershing had taken part in the army's final campaigns to subdue the Apaches under Geronimo and had also participated in the army's successful pacification campaign against Filipino guerrillas. Albeit seemingly well suited for the mission, Pershing faced daunting obstacles. Northern Mexico was an inhospitable environment with featureless plains overlooked by the soaring mountains of the Sierra Madre Occidental. The Mexican people in the region were not friendly toward Americans, and President Wilson forbade the use of towns and villages as temporary or semipermanent base camps. The president did not want even the hint of "occupation." Moreover, there was the problem of Carrancista troops in the area also in pursuit of Villa. Pershing was instructed to exercise great caution in that regard and to avoid any armed clashes with troops of the de facto government of Mexico.

As Pershing assembled his forces, primarily elements of the Seventh, Tenth, Eleventh, and Thirteenth Cavalry, as well as the Sixth and Sixteenth Infantry Regiments, the mission changed. In his statement to the press on 10 March, Wilson had claimed the "single object" of American military intervention to be the capture of Villa and putting a stop to his forays into the United States. However, the final instructions to the expedition called simply for Villa's forces to be "broken up."[9] Pershing, his immediate superior, Frederick J. Funston, and U.S. Army Chief of Staff Hugh Scott were uncomfortable with this limited aim, but Wilson was constrained by his own supposedly noninterventionist ideology and the difficult diplomatic relationship that existed between the United States and Mexico. Consequently, Pershing was forced to devise an operational scheme that would at once reduce the Villista threat to the United States but avoid precipitating a war between the two countries. The operational plan was fairly simple. The guerrillas would be encircled between two fast-moving cavalry columns. On 16 March 1916, the first column entered Mexico, comprising cavalry, infantry, artillery, and eight airplanes from the First Aero Squadron.

When President Wilson ordered Pershing into Mexico, the First Aero Squadron was located at Fort Sam Houston in San Antonio, Texas. The squadron had been unofficially organized in March 1913 in Texas City, near Galveston, Texas, but only became official in December 1913 after the unit was disbanded in Texas City and reformed at North Island near San Diego, California, as part of the Signal Corps School of Aviation. In July 1915 the squadron moved to Fort Sill, Oklahoma, for joint duty with the artillery School of Fire, and in November moved once again to Fort Sam Houston.[10] At the time the squadron was dispatched to support the expedition, it included ten officers and eighty-two enlisted men, and was equipped with eight JN-3s.[11] The JN-3 "Jenny" was a two-place biplane with a top speed of less than eighty miles per hour. With a crew of two, the airplane could reach a maximum altitude of only ten thousand feet. Although the Jenny would perform yeoman service as a trainer during World War I and would gain additional fame during the 1920s as a "barnstorming" airplane, it would prove woefully inadequate as a combat platform. Nevertheless, the JN-3-equipped First Aero Squadron represented the entire tactical airpower of the U.S. Army prior to 1917.[12]

Participation in the expedition by the First Aero Squadron was directed by the secretary of war, Newton Baker, who instructed Pershing "to make all practical use of the aeroplanes at San Antonio, Texas, for observation."[13] Baker's instructions to use the airplanes for observation were interpreted as restricting the squadron from conducting offensive combat operations against the Villistas.[14] Rather, the squadron would perform reconnaissance, scouting, and other duties in support of the ground troops. In this fashion, the squadron would protect the expedition from surprise attack as well as aid in the location of Villa's guerrillas. In short, the JN-3s would be General Pershing's "eyes."

Owing to the arguably "defensive" role for the squadron, there is some debate as to whether the aircraft were ever armed. A 1958 study claimed that the squadron's JN-3s were equipped with machine guns, but there are no surviving photos of any aircraft with mounted weapons and no specific reference in official records.[15] Moreover, General Carl A. Spaatz, who served with the squadron late in the expedition and ultimately retired as the first chief of staff of the U.S. Air Force, denied that any machine guns had ever been mounted on the Jennies or any other airplanes used in the expedition. He did, however, state that the crews would occasionally carry machine guns for self-defense on the ground should they be forced down, but only when weight and altitude limitations permitted.[16] Regardless, the squadron performed a decidedly limited mission in an already limited endeavor.

Shortly before noon on 13 March 1916, the squadron departed Fort Sam Houston for Columbus, New Mexico, under the command of Captain Foulois. Foulois was a veteran pilot who later rose to the rank of major general and retired in 1935 as chief of the Army Air Corps. In his memoirs, Foulois recounted that, following Villa's raid on Columbus, he began to visualize the attack from an "airman's point of view."

In my mind's eye I saw the locale, the raid, the defense of the town by the 13th Cavalry, and the scattering of Villa's guerrillas afterward as though I were hovering above the scene. In short, I realized that I was thinking about a ground battle from the vantage point of the sky. Although I had forced myself to think this way previously, I found that I was doing it subconsciously now. It is this third-dimensional point of view of ground events that sets the airman apart from his earth-bound colleagues.[17]

Notwithstanding his "airman's" perspective and the potential value added by their support of the expedition, Foulois and his men faced a considerable challenge in simply bringing the squadron into action. One of the pilots, Lieutenant Edgar S. Gorrell, recalled that the squadron "was in horrible shape."[18]

The [eight] airplanes were not fit for military service, especially along the border. . . . The squadron had no machine guns, no bombs, and none of the utensils of warfare later known to World War I flyers. . . . It wasn't until about sixty days after reaching Columbus that we got our hands on about sixteen machine guns which represented, according to Captain Walsh, the Ordnance Officer, about 50 percent of the total number of army machine guns then in existence.
The bombs arrived in April and were but three-inch artillery shells and nobody knew how to use them. They were sent, not for use, but so that certain authorities in Washington could tell the newspapers that we were equipped with bombs.[19]

The airplanes themselves had seen extensive service and were plagued with mechanical problems. The dry climate caused the wooden propellers to crack, so that they had to be removed after each flight and stored in a specially constructed humidor.[20] After receiving a request for assistance from Foulois, the Curtiss Aeroplane Company sent three of its own mechanics to Columbus to help maintain the squadron's airplanes.[21]

Flying presented its own unique dangers. Much of the topography of northern Mexico was at twelve thousand feet. Unable to coax the 90 hp airplanes over even some of the foothills of the Sierra Madre, the squadron's pilots were generally relegated to passes and gorges where high winds, vicious crosscurrents, and downdrafts made controlling the aircraft extremely difficult. Even if the pilots were successful in getting airborne and reaching their assigned areas for observation, distinguishing between Villistas and Carrancistas from the air was very nearly impossible. Consequently, the pilots were instructed to note those areas with troop concentrations of any sort and then fly to the nearest American column and report the whereabouts of the suspicious formation. Beyond that, the squadron mostly carried the mail and dispatches and assisted in maintaining communications with friendly troops in forward positions.

The first day of flight operations set the pattern for the remainder of the expedition. On 19 March, Foulois was ordered by General Pershing to leave the main operating base at Columbus and join him at Casas Grandes, Mexico. Despite the fact that only one of the pilots had ever flown at night, the squadron took off at 5:15 P.M. for the two-hour flight. One plane was forced to turn back almost immediately with engine problems. Around six o'clock, Foulois concluded that the danger was too great to continue a night journey and set down with three others at La Ascensión, halfway to Casas Grandes. The other three airplanes did not notice Foulois and his companions descending and pressed ahead. Noticing lights he believed to be Casas Grandes, one pilot landed his airplane on a road in the small village of Janos, ten miles beyond La Ascensión. Another airplane ran out of fuel and crash-landed about twenty miles southeast of Casas Grandes. The last pilot turned north in an attempt to return to Columbus but made a forced landing in the wilderness due to engine problems. Over the course of several days all three of the pilots managed to return to the squadron, and two of the three aircraft were recovered and rejoined Foulois at Casas Grandes. The airplane left behind in Columbus was also repaired and flew uneventfully to Casas Grandes as well.[22]

At Casas Grandes, Foulois set about to perform reconnaissance missions with his remaining airplanes in support of Pershing's troops. A second aircraft was destroyed while landing in high winds. The remaining six aircraft continued to perform reconnaissance, dispatch, and communications missions, but the JN-3's poor performance and the difficult operating environment limited the squadron's effectiveness as the American columns pushed farther south into the Sierra Madre. Within two months only three of the original aircraft remained operable.

Earlier in Columbus, Foulois had requested better aircraft and at Casas Grandes he insisted that the squadron be reequipped with airplanes with better performance. In a lengthy memorandum, Foulois requested two airplanes each from several manufacturers (Martin, Curtiss, Sturtevant, Thomas, and Sloane), all of which had engines rated at 125 hp or higher. He also requested spare parts, including propellers, wings, landing gear, magnetos, and radiators. Pershing endorsed the request and Funston placed an order for eight new aircraft, but Secretary Baker denied the request.[23] However, following a scandalous press report in which the plight of the squadron was described as "criminal," Congress passed the Urgent Deficiency Act, which provided $500,000 to the Air Service for, among other things, the purchase of twenty-four new airplanes. Secretary Baker subsequently authorized eight of these airplanes to be delivered to the First Aero Squadron.

The last operational flight of JN-3s occurred at Namiquipa on 17 April. During a photo reconnaissance mission employing a new type of camera, one airplane made a forced landing, was wrecked, and burned by its crew of two, who subsequently walked over forty miles to the small town of San Antonio de los Arenales. They rejoined the expedition two days later.[24] With only two aircraft remaining — and these practically unserviceable — the squadron retired from the field and returned to Columbus on 22 April. The two surviving JN-3s were declared unsafe and destroyed. The arrival of new Curtiss R-2s did little, however, to improve the squadron's operational capability, the airplanes suffering from engine problems and structural defects.[25] But it little mattered — field service with the Punitive Expedition was over. With their withdrawal from the interior of Mexico, the squadron's contribution to the expedition was effectively ended, albeit the unit remained officially attached until the middle of August 1917 when it embarked for service in France. Moreover, none of the new aircraft ventured farther south into Mexico than ten miles, and the squadron personnel busied themselves trying to keep the airplanes flying and performing limited experiments with the Lewis machine gun and bombing techniques.

The First Aero Squadron's contribution to the Mexican Punitive Expedition cannot be described as anything more than marginal, despite heroic efforts on the part of Foulois and his men to overcome the obstacles placed in their path. The squadron was never permitted to take on an offensive role in the effort and was relegated mostly to reconnaissance and communications. Nevertheless, the squadron accomplished these missions to the extent possible given the equipment available. In his final report, Foulois noted the sacrifice and courage of his fellow airmen: "Due to a lack of aeroplanes with greater carrying capacity, all flying officers were continually called upon to take extraordinary risks in every reconnaissance flight made while on duty in Mexico. . . . The earnest and willing spirit, shown by every officer in the command, in performing this new and perilous service, with inadequate equipment, and under very severe conditions, is deserving of the highest commendation."[26] He also commended the enlisted mechanics and other soldiers, stating, "Without the willing and efficient cooperation of the enlisted men of this command, the flying service of the Punitive Expedition would have ended at Columbus, New Mexico."[27]

The long-term impact of this first use of American airpower in a small war was to point out the glaring inadequacy of U.S. Army aviation. At a time when European air arms were using airplanes in a variety of combat roles and with considerable success, and were producing machines with impressive speeds, climbing ability, and ceilings, the degree to which American airplanes were deficient became all too obvious. But press accounts of the struggles of the First Aero Squadron in Mexico brought about a public awareness that ultimately persuaded the Congress to authorize over thirteen million dollars for military aviation.[28]

Perhaps more important, many of the aviators that cut their teeth in Mexico went on to gain distinction in World War I and later provided the intellectual grist for the formative years of the U.S. Army Air Corps in the 1920s and 1930s. For example, Lieutenant William C. Sherman, one of the founding members of the squadron, later became chief of staff of the First Army Air Service in 1918, where he earned the Distinguished Service Medal. While in France he wrote both the "Tactical History of the Air Service" (considered by some to be a seminal work) and the "Tentative Manual for the Employment of the Air Service." The army published the latter as Training Regulation 440-15, *Air Tactics,* arguably the first formal manual of air theory and doctrine in the U.S. Army Air Service. At its publication, Sherman was the assistant to the commander of the Air Service Tactical School at Langley Field, Virginia, the predecessor of the more famous Air Corps Tactical School. A strong believer in airpower and an acolyte of Billy Mitchell, Sherman left the school in 1923 and attended the army's Command and General Staff School at Fort Leavenworth, Kansas, after which he served on the faculty. In 1926 he published *Air Warfare* (New York: Ronald Press Company), detailing the principles of airpower and its utility in modern war. The book was syncretic, examining the full spectrum of tactical and strategic applications of airpower, and marked Sherman as one of the more intellectually flexible of the early airpower theorists. Tragically, at age thirty-nine, he died after a long illness on 22 November 1927.

In the end, the First Aero Squadron's contribution to the expedition was far less than the expedition's contribution to the evolution of American airpower. Much of what Foulois and the fledgling Air Service had learned in Mexico paid dividends during World War I, particularly the need for first-rate aircraft, but also the need for adequate training and a sound logistical infrastructure. The expedition was a galvanizing experience for American airpower and was recalled fondly by many of its participants, including General Spaatz. Reflecting on his long career in military aviation in 1968, Spaatz described his brief tour with the First Aero Squadron in New Mexico as "very satisfactory — if not the most satisfactory" period of his career.[29] Thus, the first use of American airpower was in a small war, but other than shaping the character of airmen who would themselves shape the Army Air Corps, the experience was marginal to the interests of the U.S. Army. The same cannot be said for the Marines' experience with airpower in the Caribbean and Central America between 1919 and 1933.

Cacos *and Bandits*

The first Marine to fly solo under official orders was Lieutenant Alfred A. Cunningham, on 20 August 1912, after two hours of instruction at the Burgess Company and Curtis aircraft factory at Marblehead, Massachusetts.[30] Cunningham had been enthralled with the idea of flight ever since he'd flown in a balloon in 1903, the year the Wright Brothers first flew.[31] In an essay published four years after his solo flight, Cunningham extolled the virtues of aviation as having "revolutionized tactics in land fighting."[32] Cunningham would later put his ideas to the test in World War I and in the Caribbean where the Marines first employed the airplane in a direct support role of troops on the ground.

The first airplane acquired by the Marines was an AX-1 flying boat, manufactured by the Curtiss Company, delivered to the navy in 1911, and handed over to the Marines in 1913. The second airplane, a Curtiss Jenny, would not be acquired until 1917.[33] Although the number of airplanes owned and operated by the Marine Corps was small, the number of Marine aviators grew. As

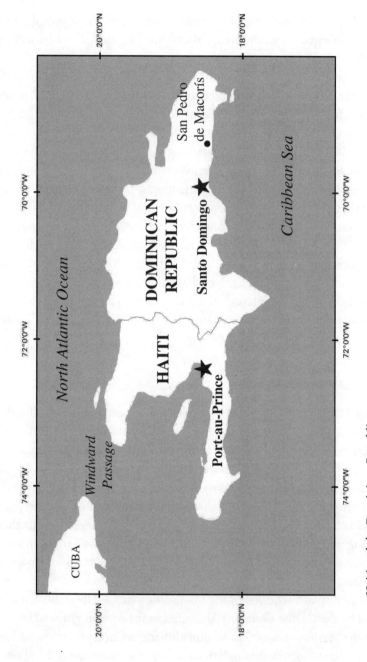

Haiti and the Dominican Republic, ca. 1919

the ranks of Marine Corps aviation swelled, separation from naval aviation was avidly sought and in 1914 became official when a Marine section of the Navy Flying School was established.[34]

Marine aviators served with distinction in World War I. Trained mostly in Jennies, the Marines soon acquired the British DeHavilland DH-4 bomber, which would become a mainstay of Marine Corps aviation following the war. The DH-4 was a two-seat biplane not unlike the Jenny, but it had a ceiling of nineteen thousand feet, with a top speed of about 124 miles per hour, and could climb to fourteen thousand feet in fourteen minutes with a load of roughly twelve hundred pounds. The three squadrons of the First Marine Aviation Force, commanded by then Major Cunningham, conducted their first combat operation in force on 14 October 1918. By the end of the war, several Marine aviators recorded air-to-air kills, and collectively the Marines had dropped over fourteen tons of bombs. Marine pilots also supported Allied troops on the ground. In October 1918, three Marine DH-4s dropped supplies to an isolated French regiment in the face of heavy German ground fire. The three pilots were awarded the Distinguished Service Cross and the Navy Cross was awarded to their enlisted observers. As the war continued, a number of Marine aviators received similar awards, and two Marine aviators, Lieutenant Ralph Talbot and Corporal Robert Guy Robinson, received the Medal of Honor.[35]

With the conclusion of World War I and up to the outbreak of World War II, the Marine Corps emerged as the preferred force for military intervention in foreign affairs. Victory in the Spanish-American War had been a turning point in American history as the United States embraced the role of a global power and the Marines found themselves in the forefront, particularly in Central America and the Caribbean. The idea of an interoceanic canal across the isthmus of Panama had been a dream ever since Balboa made his crossing in 1513. Admiral Alfred Thayer Mahan, a principal architect of American imperialism, regarded a canal as crucial to American commerce and naval power. Following a successful revolt led by Manuel Amador, and supported by the U.S. Navy, the newly independent Panama leased the Canal Zone to the United States. On 15 August 1914, the canal opened, less than two weeks after the outbreak of World War I. With its opening, the security of the canal became the key strategic consideration in the region and the proximate cause of intervention by the Marines on several occasions.

The issue of the canal aside, Washington had always been concerned about the Caribbean area. Since the Monroe Doctrine, first promulgated in 1823, the United States had meddled in the affairs of her southern neighbors, ostensibly to prevent intervention by other powers, particularly European states. Another useful rationale for intervention was to force the collection of debts owed to American citizens. In 1904, President Theodore Roosevelt set forth what has become known as the Roosevelt Corollary to the Monroe Doctrine: that is, since the Monroe Doctrine enjoined intervention in the hemisphere by the European powers, the United States was justified in intervening first to prevent the same. The Roosevelt Corollary was soon followed by a policy of "dollar diplomacy" during the presidency of William Howard Taft. The policy encouraged American bankers to financially underwrite unstable governments throughout Latin America. Several of these banks invested in Haiti, the Dominican Republic, and Nicaragua, among others. But when internal conflict in these countries threatened American capital, American forces intervened — usually the Marines. And where the Marines intervened, so, too, went Marine Corps Aviation.

Marine aviation received its first small wars baptism in the Dominican Republic and later in Haiti. Six Jennies of the First Air Squadron, commanded by Captain Walter E. McCaughtry, deployed to San Pedro de Macorís, the Dominican Republic, in February 1919. Six more Jennies and six HS-2L flying boats of the Fourth Air Squadron, commanded by Captain Harvey B. Mims, began operations at Port-au-Prince, Haiti, on 31 March. The First Squadron remained in the Dominican Republic until 1924, and the Fourth Squadron departed Haiti in 1934.

The Dominican Republic has had a long and tortured history. Ruled for almost three hundred years by the Spanish, then briefly by the French, and again by the Spanish, the Dominican Republic achieved independence in 1821. But the newly independent country was almost immediately invaded by Haiti, which ruled there until 1844 when the Dominican people reestablished their national sovereignty. A succession of corrupt and inept rulers held sway in the Dominican Republic throughout the remainder of the nineteenth century. During this period, the national debt was vastly enlarged and the government borrowed extensively from American and European lenders. Economic disorder led to political disorder, which finally provoked the United States to intervene. The Dominican Republic was of strategic value to the United States not only because of its ties to American financial institutions, but also because it lay astride the approaches to the Panama Canal. The Dominicans' financial entanglements with European powers seemed especially threatening to the United States. When the political situation unraveled in April 1916, President Wilson ordered the Marines to Santo Domingo City to protect the American legation and secure American interests in the country.[36]

The first Marines arrived on 5 May 1916, numbering some 150 men in two companies. The Marines soon found themselves in the midst of civil war. Opposing groups comprising Dominican army soldiers and civilian irregulars fought with one another for control of the countryside. The ostensible president of the country, Juan Isidro Jiminez, had received firm guarantees of American support. But Jiminez resigned not long after the Marines arrived and the country continued to descend into chaos. More Marines arrived as it became clear to the commander of the operation, Rear Admiral William B. Caperton, that military occupation of the whole country would be necessary to restore order. Shortly afterward, the Fourth Marine Regiment, under the command of Colonel Joseph H. Pendleton, arrived in the Dominican Republic. Within weeks after their arrival, the Marines secured the capital city, and Captain Harry S. Knapp (later rear admiral), who had succeeded Caperton, declared the Dominican Republic to be under the military jurisdiction of the United States. The First Provisional Regiment, which had made the first landing in May, returned home in December 1916, but left behind its headquarters and staff as the Third Provisional Regiment. Together, the Third and Fourth Regiments became the Second Provisional Brigade under the newly promoted Brigadier General Pendleton. From late 1916 until withdrawal in 1924, the Second Brigade served as an army of occupation. Throughout its service, the brigade battled constantly with various irregulars collectively labeled by the Americans as "bandits."[37] It was during the pacification campaign waged by the Second Brigade, from 1917 to 1922, that Marine aviators were first employed in the Dominican Republic.[38]

Upon its arrival on 27 February 1919, the First Air Squadron and its six JN-6 Jennies began operations from a rough airstrip carved out of the jungle at Consuelo, twelve miles from the town of San Pedro de Macorís. In 1920, the squadron was moved to another improvised airfield near Santo Domingo City where it was reequipped with DH-4Bs. An improved version of the DH-4 used by the Marines in World War I, the DH-4B was sturdy, maneuverable, and versatile, serving as an observation platform, light transport, ambulance, and bomber.[39] From the beginning, the role of the squadron was principally one of support, including communications and transport. But not long after receiving the DH-4Bs, the squadron also received a new commander — Major Alfred Cunningham — who arrived in the Dominican Republic after having served as the head of Marine Corps Aviation in Washington, D.C. With the arrival of new airplanes and a new commander, the squadron's mission soon took on a new complexion.

Initially, the Jennies performed duties not unlike those of the First Aero Squadron during the Mexican Punitive Expedition, but with the arrival of the DH-4Bs, Cunningham's air crews soon took part in active combat, guiding patrols to contact with the guerrillas and bombing and strafing bandit formations. However, the lack of current intelligence and reliable air-to-ground communications limited the value of the squadron in its attack role, and its greatest contribution remained that of support. But even in support, the Marines on the ground recognized the new dimension that aviation brought to antibandit operations. As one Marine aviator concluded afterward, "We were there and they used us, and they used us to their advantage, and consequently we became a useful and integral part of the Marine Corps."[40] In neighboring Haiti, Marine aviators would experiment with a tactic that would have significant consequences for the future of Marine Corps aviation.

The Republic of Haiti occupies the western third of the island of Hispaniola, shared with the Dominican Republic. Like the Dominican Republic, Haiti's location on the Windward Passage has given that country a strategic significance to the United States out of proportion to its size and resources. During the first half of the nineteenth century, the issue of slavery dominated relations between the United States and Haiti, but since that time considerations of naval strategy centered around the defense of interoceanic communications — in particular, the Panama Canal — have dominated.

Haiti achieved its independence during the French Revolution after a protracted slave revolt led by Jean Jacques Dessalines and Toussaint-Louverture, making Haiti the oldest independent state in the Western Hemisphere after the United States. Unlike the United States, however, which emerged from revolution with stable political institutions and a fundamentally sound economy, Haiti enjoyed no such stability and prosperity. Like the Dominican Republic, Haiti has experienced a tortured history since independence.

Segregated by what amounted to a "caste" system between the wealthy *gens de couleur* (wealthier, educated mulattoes and blacks who had embraced French cultural values) and the black peasantry, Haiti has been subjected to a seemingly endless series of revolutions.[41] By the beginning of the twentieth century, these revolutions followed a well-established pattern. A military strongman would form a *caco* army, consisting mostly of military adventurers and conscripts.[42] The *caco* army would seize the capital city of Port-au-Prince, surround the legislature, and oversee the election of the insurgent leader as the new president. When the Marines landed in July 1915, a *caco* army supporting Dr. Rosalvo Bobo, who had overthrown the government of Vilbrun Guillaume Sam, resisted the American intervention.

On 28 July 1915, some 330 sailors and Marines under the command of Marine Captain George Van Orden, occupied Port-au-Prince and were quickly reinforced by additional Marines dispatched from Guantánamo Bay, Cuba.[43] It is unlikely that authorities in Washington, D.C., anticipated a twenty-year occupation of Haiti; Admiral Caperton's initial instructions were simply to protect life and property. But as would occur in the Dominican Republic a year later, an American military government was soon installed to rule the country until stability could be restored. To achieve stability across the whole of the country, Admiral Caperton believed it necessary to clear the countryside of the *cacos* as well as occupy the hill country from which the *cacos* were generally raised. With that end in mind, Admiral Caperton formally proclaimed the subordination of Haitian civil authority to American martial rule. The immediate effect was to force the *cacos* to disperse into the countryside. The long-term effect was to engender considerable hostility toward the occupation force, even from those who had harbored no ill will toward the American troops in the beginning and were wholly unsympathetic toward the *cacos*. There had been little organized military opposition to the initial occupation by the Marines in 1915. But with the institution of military rule, those Haitians determined to resist withdrew to the interior of the country where a number of *caco* armies were still operating. Putting down these various bands became the principal military objective of the occupation and it was during this pacification campaign that the Marines began to experiment with coordinated air-ground tactics.

Roughly one month after the First Air Squadron arrived in the Dominican Republic, elements of the Fourth Squadron, designated at the time as the

First Division, Flight E, arrived in Port-au-Prince. For the next fifteen years, the aviators supported a Marine brigade of roughly 80 officers and 1,200 enlisted men as well as an American-trained gendarmerie of about 2,700 men.[44] As was the case in the Dominican Republic, the squadron's aircraft proved most useful in indirect roles, such as ferrying personnel and supplies to remote posts, carrying dispatches and the mail, other communications missions, reconnoitering, and aerial mapping. However, in Haiti the Marines began to develop a tactic that became fundamental to their principal future role of close air support — dive-bombing.

It is difficult to pinpoint the origin of dive-bombing, since aviators in World War I on both sides used steep bomb deliveries on occasion and U.S. Army fliers are said to have experimented with the technique as early as 1917.[45] But it was the Marines who embraced dive-bombing and advanced the technique following the war, as well as incorporated it into their tactical doctrine.[46] Up until the intervention in Haiti, however, the Marines had followed the standard technique developed in World War I of allowing the observer in the rear of the aircraft to release bombs from horizontal flight using a crude bombsight. But dropping bombs was one thing, dropping them accurately on guerrillas in close proximity to Marines on the ground was quite another. Searching for a more accurate method of delivery, Lieutenant Lawson H. M. Sanderson developed the idea of entering the airplane into a forty-five-degree dive with the pilot releasing the bomb from a makeshift bomb rack at approximately 250 feet above the ground. Sanderson recalled, "The dive bombing idea was more or less forced on us. We were required to bomb the hostile forces in the immediate vicinity of our Marines. Fifty to 100 yards in front of friendly troops. We could not do this with safety to our troops when employing horizontal bombing."[47]

Although more accurately described as "glide bombing," a powered dive of forty-five degrees was considered at the time to be quite steep, and the technique was invariably described as dive-bombing. Only when sturdier aircraft such as the Curtiss F6C entered the inventory did true dive-bombing in excess of forty-five degrees begin to take shape.

Pilots in Haiti and the Dominican Republic quickly adopted dive-bombing as a standard maneuver for supporting Marines in close contact with the enemy. By late 1920, Sanderson had returned to the United States and was training Marine aviators in the new maneuver at Quantico Marine Corps Base,

Virginia. In 1923, Marine aviators on the West Coast also adopted dive-bombing after their commander, Major Ross "Rusty" Rowell, introduced the technique following training with U.S. Army fliers at the Advanced Flying School at Kelly Field in San Antonio, Texas. The Army's Third Attack Group had fitted their DH-4s with the new A-3 bomb rack, capable of holding up to five small bombs under each wing. There were no bombsights; the pilots simply "eyeballed" the target over the top of the airplane's engine after entering into a shallow dive and released the bombs from roughly six hundred feet.[48] Rowell was impressed with the accuracy of this technique, claiming: "I immediately visualized the certain naval employment of such tactics where accuracy against small moving targets is paramount." More important, Rowell concluded, "It also seemed . . . that it would be an excellent form of tactics for use in guerrilla warfare."[49]

After completing his training at Kelly Field, Rowell was given command of Marine Observation Squadron One (VO-1M) at San Diego in August 1924.[50] Upon his arrival, Rowell set about to train his pilots in dive-bombing. Small bomb racks were fabricated locally and attached to the fuselage of the squadron's venerable DH-4s. But with the arrival of more advanced U.S. Army A-3 bomb racks, Rowell and his pilots were able to employ standard navy practice bombs as they continued to experiment with dive-bombing tactics. By the spring of the following year, the squadron was putting on dive-bombing demonstrations up and down the West Coast.[51] Two years later, Rowell would test his ideas regarding the utility of dive-bombing in counterguerrilla warfare in Nicaragua.

Lanzabombas *Against the Sandinistas*

Not unlike Haiti and the Dominican Republic, Nicaragua has had a tortured history. It was first seen by European eyes in 1522. During the Spanish colonial period, it was part of the Captaincy General of Guatemala, but in 1821 declared its independence from Spain and joined the Mexican empire. In 1823, Nicaragua joined the United Provinces of Central America, but a long civil war resulted in the collapse of the Federal Union in 1838. At that point Nicaragua became fully sovereign. But an independent Nicaragua was no less troubled than other independent Latin American states. A dispute with Great Britain in 1841 garnered the attention of the United States and, in keeping with

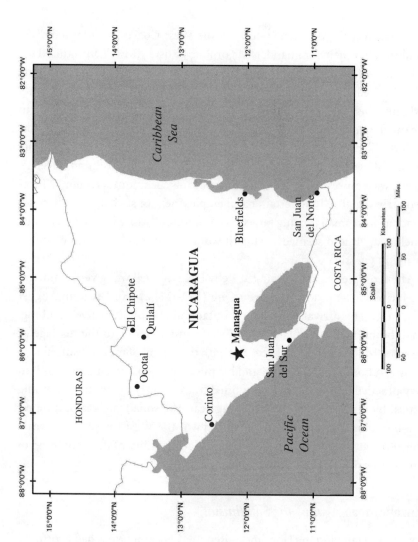

Nicaragua, ca. 1927

the Monroe Doctrine, the United States intervened militarily in 1854 for the first time to secure American interests. U.S. naval forces and Marines also figured prominently during the "Walker Affair" in 1855 through 1857.[52] Between 1854 and 1912, the Marines would intervene in Nicaragua a total of nine times.

Thus, United States interests in Nicaragua did not arise suddenly with the emergence of the revolutionary disturbances of the 1920s. Indeed, the small country had become of strategic importance to American interests following the war with Mexico when, along with the Isthmus of Panama, Nicaragua became vital to transcontinental communications. Two years after Nicaragua gained its independence from Spain, Dewitt Clinton, a one-time Republican presidential candidate, governor of New York, and the promotional genius behind the Erie Canal, expressed an interest in building a canal across Nicaragua from the Atlantic to the Pacific. Ultimately, the canal was constructed in Panama as a result of the Hays-Pauncefote Treaty of 1901; nevertheless, economic penetration of Nicaragua began in anticipation of a canal being built there. American diplomats quickly secured transit rights across Nicaragua, and American businessmen promptly organized an interoceanic company to transport freight and passengers from San Juan del Norte (Greytown) on the Atlantic Coast to San Juan del Sur on the Pacific Coast. It was when the native dictator José Santos Zelaya revoked concessions granted to American businessmen that the United States government began to consider more pronounced intervention in Nicaraguan internal affairs. Zelaya was deposed in 1909, whereupon American investment in Nicaragua soared. But political conditions in Nicaragua were fraught with conflict and violence, and the country was close to anarchy and collapse in 1911. In August 1912, impending civil war and the concomitant threat to American commercial interests prompted the first large-scale intervention by the U.S. Marines. As a result of American intervention, the extant government survived and a modicum of peace was restored to Nicaragua.

But after a decade of military occupation, the United States began to grow weary of her role in Nicaragua, and the State Department hoped the national elections in 1924 would create conditions favorable for withdrawal of the Marines. Crucial to the American plan was the creation and training of an indigenous constabulary to keep the peace. Although the elections were not entirely satisfactory to American interests, the organization of a native constabulary, the Guardia Nacional de Nicaragua, prepared the way for complete withdrawal. On 3 August 1925, the Marines embarked on the USS *Henderson* and departed for home.

But within a month, Emiliano Chamorro, an aristocrat and former general who had failed to gain the presidency in the 1924 elections, seized power in a coup d'état. The United States refused to recognize the new government under Chamorro. Civil war soon followed, with the opposition headed by Dr. Juan Sacasa, the former vice president. Mexico, which had only just emerged from its own revolution, recognized Sacasa as the legitimate heir to the presidency and began supplying Sacasa's forces, led by General José Moncada, with arms and ammunition. In October 1926, the United States secured a temporary armistice and conference between the warring factions, but failed to secure a lasting peace. As a result, reinforcements were dispatched to bolster the Marine security guards at the American legation in the capital city of Managua. In May of that same year, the first detachment of Marines arrived from the United States to protect American lives and property and occupied the town of Bluefields on the east coast of Nicaragua.

The United States government did not want to intervene a second time; when the Marines had left in 1925, it was hoped for good. But a bond had emerged between those Nicaraguans opposed to the Chamorro government and Mexican Marxists. In fact, the material support from Mexico had enabled the opposition forces to garner considerable military success in the field. Consequently, when Chamorro resigned on 30 October 1926, the United States promptly recognized his successor, Adolfo Diaz, who had served as chief executive during the 1912 intervention, to serve until the 1928 elections. Sacasa, however, refused to accept this turn of events and the bloody impasse continued. President Diaz subsequently requested full-scale American intervention and the Marines began to arrive in force in December 1926, including aviation elements attached to the initial intervention force.

The Second Nicaraguan Campaign officially lasted between 27 August 1926 and 31 March 1930. What distinguished American intervention in Nicaragua during this period from the earlier interventions in the Dominican Republic and Haiti was the fact that U.S. forces never occupied the country as a military government. Whereas in Port-au-Prince and in Santo Domingo martial law was invoked and the Marines conducted operations as they saw fit to restore order, in Nicaragua the Marines were initially dispatched to support the Diaz government and to mediate between warring factions.

American forces in Nicaragua were strengthened in January 1927 when the Second Battalion, Fifth Marines (less one company) arrived at Bluefields aboard the USS *Argonne*. Throughout the following weeks more Marines arrived, including the Marine Battalion of the Scouting Fleet, composed of detachments from the USS *Texas*, USS *Florida*, and USS *Arkansas*, which arrived on 21 January.[53] On 26 February, VO-1M, under the command of Major Rowell, with eight officers, eighty-one enlisted men, and six DH-4B aircraft, arrived at Corinto on the west coast, alongside the First Provisional Company (Rifle).[54] On 7 March, the Fifth Regiment (less the Second Battalion) and the staff of the Second Brigade, under the command of Brigadier General Logan Feland, also arrived.[55]

The situation in the major towns and cities, including Managua, improved somewhat with the arrival of Marine reinforcements. However, the countryside was another matter altogether. Although the opposition leadership under Sacasa had agreed to a cease-fire and disarmament according to the terms of the Tipitata agreement, various irregular units under General Moncada refused to comply, including a small band led by Augusto C. Sandino, a Nicaraguan nationalist who had at one time lived in Mexico and served under Pancho Villa. When Sandino disobeyed General Moncada's order to disarm and withdrew to the wilderness of northern Nicaragua to carry on the fight, President Diaz issued an appeal for additional Marines to disarm them.[56] Between 17 and 22 May, the Eleventh Regiment (less one battalion) arrived along with an additional observation squadron, VO-4M, with seven officers, seventy-eight enlisted Marines, and six Boeing 02B-1s (a metal-fuselaged derivative of the DH-4B). VO-4M was also placed under Major Rowell's command. Combined, the two units were designated Aircraft Squadrons, Second Brigade.[57] The arrival of these additional forces gave the brigade a total strength of 178 officers and 2,725 enlisted men.[58]

The mission of the two squadrons was to support the ground forces of the Second Brigade "by providing observation aviation, ground attack aviation, and transport service."[59] From February until the end of May, VO-1M and VO-4M flew patrols over a neutral zone established by the Marines. But owing to a perceived lessening in hostilities, most of VO-1M returned to San Diego in June. Before their departure, however, VO-1M handed over two aircraft to VO-4M, which was redesignated VO-7M on 1 July 1927. Major Rowell remained in Nicaragua to command VO-7M.[60]

In his privately published classic regarding American intervention in Nicaragua between 1912 and 1934, *Quijote on a Burro,* Lejeune Cummins wrote: "Perhaps the only subject regarding the American intervention . . . upon which all authorities are able to agree is the efficacy with which the marines [*sic*] employed the air power at their disposal."[61] Indeed, Navy Secretary Curtis D. Wilbur in his annual report in 1929 declared that Marine Corps aviation in Nicaragua was "of inestimable value."[62] Thus, Cummins was moved to note: "It is probably not an exaggeration to say that the marine occupation . . . could not have been accomplished" without Marine Corps aviation.[63]

VO-1M actually arrived ten days ahead of the main body of the Second Brigade and during a period in which U.S. forces were expected to remain entirely neutral with respect to the contesting factions. The squadron occupied an airdrome in Managua then used by the government air force, consisting of two Laird Swallow aircraft flown by two American mercenaries named Mason and Brooks. The two Americans dropped crude homemade bombs on opposition forces, made of iron pipes and sticks of dynamite lit by the pilots' cigars. The use of these airplanes in Nicaragua was so novel that during the battle of Chinandega the effect was to "stampede" opposition forces from the field. But having recovered from their initial shock, these same opposition forces largely ignored the efforts of Mason and Brooks during the battle of Muy Muy, driving off government forces despite their air support.[64] The net effect was to convince opposition troops that airplanes invariably belonged to the enemy, but that they were of little consequence anyway. This attitude would be proved sorely mistaken weeks later when Marine Corps aircraft struck their first concerted blow at former opposition troops led by Sandino.

Although the Marines were ostensibly neutrals at the outset of the intervention, and General Moncada had instructed his forces to refrain from shooting at the Americans, Marine aircraft were fired upon routinely and holed on almost every flight.[65] According to Major Rowell, "We carried only front machine guns; we had no rear guns or bombs. We had authority to return hostile fire, but the American mission was to stop the war — not to become involved in it. I appealed to all pilots to avoid hostilities and to return fire only when necessary to save their own lives. During the period of observation our planes were hit twenty-three times."[66]

But neutrality soon gave way to active combat operations as Sandino deliberately attacked Marine patrols and garrisons as well as other Americans and their property. As the American role in Nicaragua became wider and deeper, operational constraints on the Marines were loosened, but never approximating the freedom Marine aviators enjoyed in the Caribbean. Nevertheless, during the period of American neutrality, Rowell and his crews observed the tactical methods of opposition troops, noting where they placed their command posts, how they deployed, and how they dug in. As Rowell would later write, "It was splendid training for the campaign which followed."[67]

Sandino's base of operations was the remote province of Nueva Segovia. The nearest railroad was over one hundred miles away, and the roads were barely passable by oxcart. As one Marine veteran of the conflict noted, "This was quite a different matter from operations conducted a few miles inland from coast towns, which usually distinguished the West Indian expeditions."[68] Regardless, the Marines occupied the capital of the province, Ocatal, with a small garrison of thirty-nine Marines under the command of Captain G. D. Hatfield, along with a forty-seven-man platoon of the Guardia Nacional. But on 15 July 1927, over four hundred guerrillas led by Sandino attacked the garrison at first daylight.[69] The Marines were outnumbered almost five to one, but Marine airpower soon proved its worth.

A regular patrol by two aircraft discovered that the Marines in Ocatal were in desperate circumstances. Both planes attacked the guerrillas but exhausted their ammunition and returned to Managua. The nearest available ground reinforcements were some six days away by overland march. VO-7M was therefore the only unit capable of providing immediate assistance to the beleaguered garrison, and Rowell was ordered to provide whatever support he could. At the time, the squadron had a mix of only five DH-4Bs and 02B-1s. Nonetheless, Rowell had trained his pilots in dive-bombing and he decided to attack the guerrillas using this maneuver.

Ocatal was over one hundred miles from Managua and the weather was bad. But within an hour after first receiving news of the battle, all five of the aircraft took off for Ocatal with Rowell in the lead. Each airplane carried six hundred rounds of machine-gun ammunition, but only a partial load of bombs — the long flight necessitating a heavy load of fuel. Navigat-

ing between thunderstorms, the formation arrived over Ocatal around two
o'clock in the afternoon. After making one pass to reconnoiter the situation, Rowell attacked.

On our second approach we went at them. It was our first engagement but it was
the most dramatic fight we ever fought. The setting was theatrical in the extreme.
On the ground our men were fighting for their lives, and they had been fighting
for sixteen hours without sleep or food. They did not know how much assistance
we could give them, and we ourselves were none too sure. I went in first, leading
the attack. As I went down I could see enemy troops firing in groups. They were
absolutely unconcerned. Just before I dropped the first bomb I saw a puff of smoke
come from a man sitting on a horse and smoking a cigar. After the first bomb
dropped the whole picture changed. We could see enemy groups milling around.
Then they seemed to hesitate as if they were too surprised to know what to do.
Complete panic followed the second and third attacks. Men threw away their rifles,
jumped over fences and raced wildly through the streets. Everywhere they went
planes were diving at them. After we finished our bombing my men became so
interested in chasing enemy groups out of town and down the road that I could
hardly assemble them to return before our gas was exhausted. It was a complete
rout for Sandino.[70]

Sandino and his men had suffered a devastating setback with significant
casualties.[71] In fact, Sandino never made another attack on Ocatal. But
Sandino was not finished and several months later, having reconstituted his
forces, entrenched himself in a strong mountain redoubt known as El Chipote.
The Marines planned a joint air-ground operation against the stronghold. By
this time the DH-4Bs had been augmented by much more capable Vought
02U-1 "Corsairs," an airplane that would prove invaluable to air-ground
operations for the remainder of the campaign.[72] The ground column and its
ration train never made it to El Chipote. It was ambushed by a strong guerrilla force at Quilalí, was surrounded, and suffered numerous casualties, including all of the officers. A desperate plea for air support was made by the
acting commander: "A full concentration of planes, with a thorough searching of all trails and a thorough bombing of Chipote . . . is most *urgently* recommended [emphasis in original]. . . . If humanly possible, I recommend that
a Corsair land here to evacuate the wounded."[73]

While a plan was being developed to relieve the column, First Lieutenant
Christian F. Schilt volunteered to bring out the wounded. Quilalí is located
in a deep valley surrounded on all sides by high mountains. The only level

ground was a narrow road with a three-foot ditch down the middle that led into the town. Flying a Vought Corsair, Lieutenant Schilt and a second airplane dropped picks and shovels to the desperate Marines on the ground, who promptly demolished houses on one side of the road, making a rough runway seventy feet wide and three hundred feet long. Lieutenant Schilt then replaced the Corsair's undercarriage with the much larger wheels and tires from a DH-4B. After a failed first attempt, Lieutenant Schilt dropped his unarmed airplane through withering small arms fire onto the improvised runway, bouncing thirty feet into the air before being brought to a stop by Marines grabbing onto the wings, the Corsair not having any brakes. After loading up a wounded Marine officer, Schilt took off under the covering fire from the escort plane flown by Lieutenant Lamson Scribner. Over the course of three days (6–8 January 1928), Schilt returned nine more times, retrieving another wounded officer and sixteen wounded enlisted men.[74] In addition, Schilt delivered a relief commander and fourteen hundred pounds of provisions and medical supplies.[75] For his heroism, Schilt was awarded the Medal of Honor, the third such award made to a Marine aviator. [76] Following this action, the battered column was extricated from Quilalí under continuous air escort. Three guerrilla ambushes were discovered by observation planes and in each case were driven off by the air escort. The column withdrew to safety without any further casualties.[77]

But Sandino's stronghold at El Chipote remained intact. The guerrillas were dug in and well armed with rifles and machine guns. El Chipote is three thousand feet high with the only approaches being deep narrow ravines. Although the original ground column had been reinforced with an additional two hundred men, the brigade commander considered a ground assault to be too risky and ordered Rowell to attack the stronghold from the air. Heralded as the "first independent and unsupported air attack ever made against a fortified position held by ground troops,"[78] Rowell's airplanes bombarded El Chipote using "17-pound fragmentation bombs, 50-pound demolition bombs, machine guns, and [White Phosphorous] hand grenades."[79]

A swift approach was made from an unexpected direction, attacking in two columns without reconnoitering. The attack was met by a barrage of incendiary sky rockets. We came down with the front guns wide open and opened up with light bombs at 600 feet. The rifle and machine gun fire was heavy and most of the planes stopped some bullets. The following ships came in with heavier bombs. After the second dive, the enemy broke cover and there was a wild stampede. . . . On the following day the mountain was devoid of bandits. According to Sandino's own statement, his entire army deserted him except about 150 of his old reliables.[80]

Sandino never again attempted to contest the American Marines in positional warfare. In fact, Rowell noted that "the loss of this much vaunted stronghold was a severe blow to the prestige of Sandino" and afterward he "never occupied a position of any sort."[81] Thereafter, fearing the firepower of the Marine *lanzabombas* (as they were called by the Sandinistas), Sandino and his men resorted to more traditional guerrilla tactics.[82] They moved mostly at night, camouflaged their encampments and stables, and confined their operations to terrain offering cover from aerial observation and protection from aerial attack. As a result, attack aviation no longer enjoyed the spectacular successes experienced at Ocotal and El Chipote, whereas observation, reconnaissance, "infantry missions" (air escort and liaison), aerial resupply, and air transport gained in importance.

Following his defeat at El Chipote, Sandino largely abandoned Neuva Segovia and withdrew to the even more rugged interior of Nicaragua in an area known as Prinzapolca. Marine patrols into this province, as well as the whole of northeastern and north central Nicaragua, were routinely escorted by airplanes to provide cover as well as scout ahead for possible guerrillas lying in ambush. As ground patrols pushed deeper into the countryside, Marine aircraft maintained communications between the base camps and the patrols. Aircraft also delivered supplies to these far-flung units. When Captain Merritt "Red" Edson led a series of patrols 350 miles up the Coco River along the border between Nicaragua and Honduras, a base of air operations was established at Puerto Cabezas. From this remote location, three officers and thirty enlisted men operated five amphibian observation aircraft maintaining regular contact with Edson and other patrols.[83] The amphibians would search for guerrillas and ensure that the patrols were never surprised by ambuscade. They would also land on quiet stretches of the river or on sandbars to off-load supplies, or otherwise drop packages and weapons from the air.[84] Throughout the interior of Nicaragua, the Marines established outposts, most of which could be resupplied only by air, and it was in support of these outposts that airpower proved of immense worth.

At the beginning of the campaign, transportation of supplies and personnel was accomplished by the light observation airplanes then operated by the squadrons under Rowell's command. But with the arrival of the first TA-2 Atlantic-Fokker trimotor transport in December 1927, the air transport mission evolved to a new level. During its first six weeks of operation, this one airplane ferried twenty-seven thousand pounds of freight and 204 passengers. The trip between Managua and Ocatal normally required ten days to three weeks by oxcart and mule train, but the Fokker could accomplish the same mission in under two hours.[85] Additional trimotors were immediately requested, and two more Fokkers arrived nonstop from Miami, Florida, in January and February 1928.[86] These airplanes were subsequently reinforced by the more easily maintained all-metal Ford RR-2 trimotor transports, and a utility squadron was formed.

Able to fly six tons of supplies per day, Rowell regarded the contributions of the Fokker and Ford trimotors to the brigade's mission to have been "immeasurable." In his annual report submitted in 1928, Rowell wrote:

The list of serious emergencies that have been met by these airplanes is too long to include in this report. Entire garrisons in the most remote localities depend wholly upon the transports for supply, an entire regimental headquarters was transported to the front, minor troop movements are effected, the sick and wounded evacuated, casual officers and enlisted men are carried, the mail is delivered and emergency articles and materials of every conceivable nature are delivered with the greatest speed and efficiency. . . . Although the transports have only been operating during the latter part of the period covered by this report, it is worthy of note to record that the amount of material transported amounts to approximately 900,000 lbs., and that the number of passengers transported by air assumes the surprising total of one thousand five hundred. All of this has been accomplished without the slightest accident.[87]

The transports not only carried supplies, the mail, and the payroll to Marines at the various crude airstrips constructed around the country, they also air-dropped ammunition, medical supplies, and rations to the deep-penetration patrols. In addition, they provided air mobility for combat forces. In November and December 1931, a large group of guerrillas operating in the Chinandega, Leon, and Esteli provinces threatened to overwhelm the local Guardia troops. Prompt movement of additional Guardia soldiers and the rapid concentration of these forces at key points by air kept the guerrillas constantly on the move and off-balance. The guerrillas ultimately quit the area.[88]

As the hard fighting of 1927 and 1928 slackened, the Marine squadrons in Nicaragua concentrated on observation, communications, and logistical support.[89] But not only did Marine aircraft prove a useful weapon in counter-guerrilla warfare, they also proved a valuable tool in the political process crucial to counterrevolutionary warfare. To that end, Marine aircraft conducted psychological operations and served in a variety of support roles during the national elections in 1928 at the height of the guerrilla war, especially in remote areas of the country. Thousands of propaganda circulars were dropped by Marine aircraft, sometimes over enemy encampments. According to Major Rowell, "They were really effective."[90] But more important than simply conveying propaganda, aviation played a part in the democratic process itself.

It was necessary to ferry by plane most of the American personnel to outlying districts, to supply them there, to maintain communication with them, to patrol the towns and mesas on registration and election days, and, finally, to bring to Managua the ballots. In order to accomplish this work, flying time generally reached its peak during the weeks immediately before and after the election periods. . . . [In 1928] on election day 237 cantons were visited by airplanes.[91]

As the war wound down, leading to eventual withdrawal of the Marines in 1933, aviation continued to play a significant role in the political life of Nicaragua. Owing to an earlier agreement with the government and the insurgents, the United States agreed to oversee national elections again in 1932. The assistance provided by Marine aviators during this election was invaluable and the most extensive use of aviation in a political support role during the whole of the intervention in Nicaragua.[92]

In August 1928, Major Rowell left Nicaragua, to be replaced in succession by Major Louis Bourne Jr., Major Ralph Mitchell, and Captain Francis Mulcahy. Captain Mulcahy commanded the aviation element until it was withdrawn from Nicaragua in January 1933. At the end, Marine aviators could look back on a period of significant achievement. In the Caribbean, and in particular in Nicaragua, Marine aviators had developed and refined their organization and tactics to fulfill their primary mission of supporting their fellow Marines on the ground. Major Rowell would subsequently write: "Probably no broader experience has been gained, or greater success achieved through the employment of aircraft in minor warfare, than that which attended the operations of our own Marines during the Nicaraguan campaign of 1927 and 1928."[93]

Lessons Learned and Unlearned

The lessons to be taken from the earliest American experiences with airpower in small wars were considerable, but for the U.S. Army they were fleeting at best. The army's First Aero Squadron, which had accompanied Pershing's Punitive Expedition into Mexico, saw service in World War I as an observation unit. It remained active after the war, at a time when many army aero squadrons were demobilized, but like the army in general during the 1920s and 1930s, it suffered from lack of personnel and material. In 1935, the squadron was redesignated as the First Bombardment Squadron, and although the unit was sent to Panama in 1940, the purpose was to strengthen the defense of the Canal Zone, not to participate in interventionary operations of any sort. A year later, the United States entered World War II, and the squadron served mostly in a training capacity at the Army Air Force School of Applied Tactics at Orlando, Florida, albeit the unit did see some combat in the latter stages of the war.[94]

Outside of the First Aero Squadron, the only U.S. Army airplanes stationed outside of the United States that could have participated in counterguerrilla operations were a 1911 Type B Wright Flyer shipped to the Philippines in 1911 and two Type C airplanes that arrived in 1912. These airplanes were exclusively engaged in training new pilots at Fort William McKinley, and by the end of 1912 all three machines had been destroyed in accidents. A Burgess-Wright "hydro-plane" was subsequently assigned to Corregidor Island, but it was employed solely to provide spotting for the large caliber guns and mortars used in the defense of Manila harbor.[95]

Thus, U.S. Army aviation had little experience with airpower in small wars, and the U.S. Army was not particularly interested in the topic. For one thing the army existed primarily for the defense of the United States, not to participate in exercises of imperial reach — the navy and Marines being by custom and legal opinion the instrument of choice in that regard. Other than the counterguerrilla campaign in the Philippines that took place following the Spanish-American War and the Mexican Punitive Expedition, the U.S. government was generally loath to employ the army outside of the United States except in times of war. As a navy rear admiral stated in 1909, "You can land a Sailor or Marine and it is not considered war; but if you land one section of the Army that is war."[96]

The interwar years were nevertheless a time of great ferment for the Army Air Corps. During this period, Billy Mitchell, Ken Walker, Larry Kuter, "Possum" Hansell, and Muir Fairchild, among others, articulated a theory of strategic airpower based on bombardment aviation as opposed to tactical aviation in a small wars setting. At the same time, deep rifts emerged between many air-minded army officers and their more traditionally minded brethren. Army aviators tended to emphasize strategic bombardment, not ground attack. Moreover, the court-martial of Brigadier General Billy Mitchell served to isolate and to some extent alienate a number of army air thinkers from the mainstream of the army's intellectual processes. The more visible "Mitchellites," such as "Hap" Arnold and "Tooey" Spaatz, were effectively grounded, and the Air Corps Tactical School — which had provided Mitchell with willing accomplices to his "mischief" — was exiled from Langley, Virginia, to the wilderness that was Montgomery, Alabama. But the diaspora served to provide a near "monastic" environment in which young air-minded officers could think and write about strategic airpower. As a result, airpower thought in the army emanated from two different sources. Official thinking originated at the General Staff, the Army Staff, and at the War College. Not surprisingly, airpower thought from these sources viewed airpower in terms largely subordinate to ground combat forces in major war. The unofficial yet ultimately dominant source of airpower thought emerged, however, from the Air Corps Tactical School in the form of staff comments on doctrinal proposals, curricula, and unsanctioned articles published by insurgent thinkers at the school. Not surprisingly, writers at the Air Corps Tactical School emphasized the strategic utility of airpower as an independent instrument of modern major war.

Interestingly, many of the Marine Corps aviators who had served in Nicaragua attended the Air Corps Tactical School, including Rusty Rowell, Francis Mulcahy, and Christian Schilt, all of whom went on to become general officers in the Marine Corps. It was Christian Schilt, of course, who had won the Congressional Medal of Honor in Nicaragua. The Tactical School faculty took note of the Marines' experience. During his stay there, Rusty Rowell, who was first to command the aviation squadrons of the Second Brigade, wrote a monograph entitled "Aircraft in Bush Warfare," which served as the basic text for the "minor warfare" block of the air force course, the foundation curriculum of the school. Later, the monograph appeared as an article in the *Marine Corps Gazette*. But as General Vernon McGee, another Nicaragua veteran, later recalled, the army aviators had little interest in small wars or the role of aviation therein, concentrating instead on bombardment aviation and the strategic role of airpower.[97]

The same could not be said of the U.S. Marine Corps. Although the emphasis on small wars in the Marine Corps was greatly reduced in consonance with the inward focus of American isolationism, much of what the Marines had learned in Nicaragua was synthesized and codified in the *Small Wars Manual,* first published in 1935 and revised in 1940.[98] Several of the Marine aviators who had served in Nicaragua participated in this effort, and an entire chapter of the manual was devoted to aviation.[99] The *Small Wars Manual* was a major departure in the history of American military doctrine, and its treatment of revolutionary guerrilla warfare was groundbreaking. Regarding the role of aviation in small wars, numerous articles also appeared in the *Marine Corps Gazette* and other publications after the Second Nicaraguan Campaign on the role of airpower in small wars. Marine aviators clearly believed that airpower could play a significant if not a decisive role in fighting guerrillas and other irregulars.

Although some Marines recognized the strategic potential of airpower, it was clear that Marine aviators understood that their role would be largely one of support within the Marine Corps itself. Thus, as the Marines shifted their emphasis from small wars to amphibious conventional warfare, Marine Corps aviation settled into its already comfortable role of close air support. According to General McGee: "Undeterred by any necessity for counterair operations, and untempted by any 'wild blue yonder' schemes of semi-independent strategical forays, the Marines buckled down to their primary mission of supporting Marine ground forces."[100]

In 1931 Marine aviation units were assigned to duty with the carriers of the U.S. Fleet and by 1933 were fully integrated into the amphibious warfare mission of the Fleet Marine Force. By 1935, the Marine Corps' *Tentative Landing Operations Manual* described the Marine air arm's role as "progressive relief of Naval aviation supporting a landing operation as well as attack in support of ground operations."[101] Once the skies had been cleared of enemy opposition, Marine air units would concentrate on their primary reason for existence — support of the Marines on the ground, especially during the critical ship-to-shore phase of a landing attack.[102]

In retrospect, the Marine air-ground team that took its first steps in the Caribbean reached maturity in Nicaragua, and the concept of close-in air support developed during that period crystallized between the world wars as

Marine aviation adapted to its new role in support of amphibious warfare. As General Megee wrote:

It may be said that Marine aviation came of age during the Nicaraguan campaign. The lessons learned were incorporated in the training manuals later concocted for the guidance of a younger generation; the officers and men who flew in Nicaragua were destined to be leaders in the great Pacific war; the doctrine of close air support was refined to an exact science through the medium of instant and reliable radio communications; new and far more effective aircraft were made available under the impetus of all-out war to meet the conditions of major amphibious operations. All this spilled over, of course, into the subsequent Korean hostilities.[103]

In the end, the conclusions reached by the army and Marine Corps regarding the utility of airpower in small wars were largely shaped by the respective service cultures and their worldviews. As an institution, the army considered its role to be defense of the United States in a major war with an aggressor and saw little of consequence in the Mexican Punitive Expedition and therefore derived few if any lessons regarding airpower in small wars. On the other hand, airmen attached to the expedition rightfully regarded their lack of a solid contribution to the effort to have been the result of inadequate equipment and other obstacles. As a result, aviators attached to the expedition expressed some of the earliest complaints about hidebound army thinking regarding the future promise of airpower. In that sense, the first cracks that ultimately widened into the chasm that divided air-minded army officers from their more mainstream brethren appeared long before the 1920s when the likes of Billy Mitchell took up the cudgel of "victory through airpower." The rift that fully emerged in the 1920s and 1930s remains discernible today between the U.S. Army and the U.S. Air Force.

With the exception of the role they played in the two world wars, the Marines have generally regarded small wars and expeditionary warfare as their *historie raisonnée*. So it is not surprising that the Marines were more open to exploring the full potential of airpower in small wars and capitalized on their experiences in the Caribbean and Central America to fully develop the modern concept of close air support. Although their interest in small wars has waxed and waned over the years since that time, the Marine aviators' commitment to close support of their earthbound comrades remains undiminished. In the final analysis, the roots of that commitment are to be found in Marine Corps aviation's first experiences in small wars.

U.S. Army JN-3 at Chihuahua City, Mexico, April 1916. At the time of the Punitive Expedition against Pancho Villa, the JN-3–equipped First Aero Squadron represented the entire tactical airpower of the U.S. Army. (USAF)

U.S. Army "Jenny" during the Punitive Expedition. Secretary of War Newton Baker ordered General Pershing "to make all practical use of the aeroplanes at San Antonio, Texas, for observation." As a result, the First Aero Squadron became the "eyes" of the army during the pursuit of Pancho Villa. (USAF)

Vought 02U-1 "Corsair" at McHugh Airdrome in Managua, Nicaragua. The two-seat Corsair was powered by a Pratt and Whitney Wasp radial engine with a top speed of over 150 miles per hour, but a low landing speed of only about 50 miles per hour, which proved crucial to operations from unimproved airstrips. Christian F. Schilt, who was awarded the Medal of Honor in Nicaragua, called the Corsair an "outstanding combat plane," owing to its performance, ease of handling, and rough field capability. (USMC Historical Research Center, Quantico, Virginia)

U.S. Marine Corps aviators with TA-2 Atlantic-Fokker trimotor transport. At the beginning of the Nicaraguan campaign, transportation of supplies and personnel was accomplished by the light observation airplanes then operated by the squadrons. But with the arrival of the first trimotor transport in December 1927, the air transport mission evolved to a new level. Additional trimotors were immediately requested, and two more Fokkers arrived nonstop from Miami, Florida, in January and February 1928. These airplanes were subsequently reinforced by the more easily maintained all-metal Ford RR-2 trimotor transports, and a utility squadron was formed. (USMC Historical Research Center, Quantico, Virginia)

Augusto C. Sandino was a Nicaraguan nationalist who had at one
time lived in Mexico and served under Pancho Villa. Following the
battle of El Chipote, in which Marine Corps aircraft forced the
Sandinistas to abandon a fortified and well-defended position,
Sandino and his men resorted to more traditional guerrilla tactics.
(James Corum)

U.S. Marines preparing to embark for the voyage to Nicaragua. The Second
Nicaraguan Campaign officially lasted between 27 August 1926 and 31 March 1930.
What distinguished American intervention in Nicaragua during this period from
the earlier interventions in the Dominican Republic and Haiti was the fact that
U.S. forces never occupied the country as a military government.

Marine Corps DH-4B over Monotumbo Volcano near Managua, Nicaragua. The
DH-4 was the principal combat aircraft employed by the Marines in World War I
and in the following decade and served well in the Caribbean and in Nicaragua
until replaced by the more capable Vought o2U-1 "Corsair," an airplane that
would prove invaluable to air-ground operations for the remainder of the
campaign. (USMC Historical Research Center, Quantico, Virginia)

U.S. Marine Corps Fokker trimotor and officer aviators, circa 1930. The Marines used enlisted pilots in Nicaragua. Quite often the pilot of an observation aircraft was an enlisted Marine, and the observer would be a better-educated officer who could more aptly interpret what he saw on the ground. (USMC Historical Research Center, Quantico, Virginia)

McHugh Airfield, Managua, Nicaragua. Marine Corps Squadron VO-1M arrived ten days ahead of the main body of the Second Brigade and during a period in which U.S. forces were expected to remain entirely neutral with respect to the contesting factions. The squadron occupied the airdrome in Managua then used by the government air force, consisting of two Laird Swallow aircraft flown by two American mercenaries named Mason and Brooks. (USMC Historical Research Center, Quantico, Virginia)

Standard patrol gear for Marine Corps aircraft operating in Nicaragua, including a Thompson .45 caliber submachine gun, water, food, a machete, maps, poncho, ammunition, flares, and rope. The Marines often conducted search and rescue missions to recover aircraft and crews forced down by hostile fire and poor weather, and it was necessary that the crews be provisioned to survive a force-down.

2

Colonial Air Control

The European Powers Develop New Concepts of Air Warfare

The airplane came of age as an important weapon of war during World War I. By the end of the war, the airplane was a fairly sophisticated weapon. The Allies and Germans had all carried out strategic air attacks against the enemy's homeland using heavy bombers capable of carrying up to a ton of bombs. By 1918 the combatants on the western front were using thousands of aircraft in reconnaissance, bombing, ground attack, and air superiority missions. The major powers all developed large air forces during the war, and all the formal military doctrines recognized aviation as an essential part of employing military force.

After World War I, the beginnings of nationalist sentiments and the disorder in the Mideast left by the collapse of the Ottoman Empire meant that the major European colonial powers, Britain and France, would have to use military forces to keep the peace in their colonies and to establish order in their new mandates. One challenge was how aviation organization and doctrine could be adapted to the urgent demands of colonial operations. Europe's smaller colonial powers, Italy and Spain, had also built up their air forces and were ready to employ military aviation in their colonial wars.

During the colonial campaigns of the European powers in the interwar period, 1919 to 1939, air forces became a prominent and integral part of fighting small wars. The British used airpower more extensively in their colonial campaigns, and the Royal Air Force (RAF) developed a doctrine of "air control" in which it asserted that airpower ought to be the primary force in colonial military operations. The French were also interested in the concept of air control, but the nature of their colonial conflicts pushed them to use airpower in a conventional war setting. Despite differences in doctrine, all of the colonial powers used airpower extensively in the colonial wars — with varying degrees of success. A great many lessons were learned about using airpower in small wars. However, there were also many lessons that were not learned. Whether the British concept of air control was successful or whether the colonial air war experience can provide lessons for the contemporary use of airpower in small wars is an issue still in dispute.

The British Colonial Air Campaigns

In the aftermath of World War I, a financially strapped Britain had to face up to several expensive new colonial obligations in the form of League of Nations mandates to govern Palestine, Transjordan, and Iraq. At the same time that the armed forces were ordered to assume a costly burden of military occupation in regions rife with violent internal conflicts, the government moved to demobilize the wartime forces and to economize by any means possible. This meant that the new imperial obligations had to be policed on the cheap.

The RAF, which had only become a separate service in April 1918, was fighting for its institutional existence. Both the army and navy argued that the RAF ought to revert to its position as a subordinate arm of the two senior services. Air Marshal Hugh Trenchard, RAF chief of staff, was in search of a mission that would justify his service's independence. The effectiveness of a few aircraft in putting down a minor rebellion in British Somaliland from 1919 to 1920 provided Trenchard and the air staff with the concept of an independent mission for the RAF. Trenchard proposed that the RAF be given the full responsibility for conducting military operations in Britain's most troublesome new mandate, the former Ottoman provinces of Mesopotamia.[1]

Trenchard promised that the RAF could police the mandate with air squadrons and a few armored car squadrons, supported by a few British and locally recruited troops, at a fraction of the cost of a large army garrison. That argument was irresistible to Whitehall, so in October 1922, RAF Air Marshal John Salmond took over military command and assumed military responsibility for Iraq. Initially, the RAF's garrison for Iraq was eight squadrons of fighters and light bombers such as the DH-9. As the RAF's account goes, the air control doctrine worked remarkably well. All through the 1920s and 1930s the RAF was able to quell minor rebellions and tribal banditry by swiftly punishing the culprits from the air. Bombing and the threat of bombings seemed to work to keep Iraq relatively quiet. Policing the empire by means of airpower was popular in other colonies as well. RAF bombing raids largely replaced the traditional army punitive expeditions that had been mounted against troublesome tribes on India's Northwest Frontier. In Aden, trouble in the interior was also dealt with swiftly by air attack on numerous occasions.

The Genesis of Air Control

The concept of air control was first employed in the wastes of Somaliland, one of the most primitive backwaters of the British Empire. Since the 1890s Mohammed bin Abdullah Hassan, a charismatic tribal leader known as "the Mad Mullah," had caused trouble in the British protectorate raiding tribes friendly to the British. From 1900 to 1904 the British mounted several punitive expeditions against him and took fairly heavy losses. In 1904 the British finally brought the Mad Mullah's main force to battle, defeated it, and drove Abdullah Hassan out of British territory. However, in 1909 Abdullah Hassan started raiding again, and in 1913 he shot up a party of the British constabulary. During World War I the British ignored the problems in Somaliland, but after the war, in the autumn of 1919, the British government decided to reinforce the protectorate with a RAF squadron of DH-9 reconnaissance/light bomber aircraft. Eight aircraft arrived by January 1920, and the British set to work with surprise bombing raids on the Abdullah Hassan's forts. Several days of bombing inflicted heavy casualties and forced the Mad Mullah to abandon his forts. The army field force consisting of detachments from the King's African Rifles, Somaliland Camel Corps, and Indian Army moved in pursuit of the Mullah's force. Over the next weeks, the RAF reverted to supporting the ground force by reconnaissance and bombing. The Mullah escaped and took his remaining forces over the border into Ethiopia where he died the next year.[2] For the astoundingly low price of eighty thousand pounds, airpower had played a central role in defeating a force that had irritated the British colony for many years.

The RAF, fighting for institutional survival, made much of this case of airpower in colonial policing. That most RAF sorties had been in support of ground forces was not stressed. Indeed, the most significant part of the outcome for the British government was the low cost of the whole affair. With the successful operation in Somaliland behind them, in March 1921 at the Cairo Conference on Mideast Affairs chaired by Colonial Secretary Winston Churchill, Air Marshal Trenchard formally proposed that the RAF take over the task of directing military operations in Iraq and that the primary British force to be employed in that troublesome country be RAF squadrons.[3]

While Somaliland had been a very small operation, the problems in Iraq were enormous and the military situation was grim. The British army had seen heavy fighting in Iraq throughout World War I as British expeditionary forces, mostly from the Indian army, fought for four years trying to push the Turks out of the region. Iraq was the scene of one of Britain's most humiliating defeats when a British army of nine thousand men was cut off and forced to surrender by the Turks at Kut in April 1916. The British reinforced their army in Mesopotamia, counterattacked, and in 1917 took Baghdad.[4] By the end of the war, the Turks had been pushed to Mosul and the British occupied most of the country. In 1918 the British had 420,000 men in Iraq.[5]

After the war the British Foreign Office and Colonial Office had little idea of what to do with Iraq. It was a poor and backward part of the Ottoman Empire, and the British had no major strategic interest in the area (the extent of the oil reserves was not yet known). However, various wartime deals had allocated responsibility for Mesopotamia, Jordan, Arabia, and Palestine to Britain and had given France the responsibility for Lebanon and Syria. During the war, the British-occupied portions of Iraq had been placed under military rule and Indian Civil Service political officers were brought in to administer the territory. This arrangement persisted after the end of the war.

If the British government had had a carefully crafted grand strategic plan to alienate the three major groups in Iraq (Kurds, Shiite Muslims, and Sunni Muslims) and to force the whole country into rebellion against their British occupiers, they could not have succeeded more handily. The Indian political officers tried to impose a very alien Indian-style administration upon the Arabs and Kurds. Under the Turks, the administration might have been inefficient, but at least the Turks spoke Arabic and left the tribes largely alone.[6] On top of this new and irritating administration, the British and French governments had issued a declaration on November 7, 1918, assuring Arabs of freedom and self-government after the war.[7] Not only the Arabs but also the Kurds had been given hopes for self-government.[8] Such promises were quickly forgotten by the imperial powers as the British moved to create an Iraqi monarchy and put a Sunni Muslim on the throne. None of the major groups in Iraq were consulted by the British administration, and the Kurds and Shiites, the majority of the population, were especially offended.[9] By 1920 Iraq was ready to blow up — and it did. The rebellion began in Kurdistan and quickly spread throughout the country.

There were 60,200 British troops in Iraq when the rebellion began, and they were hard-pressed to simply hold on. Small British garrisons in the hinterlands were wiped out. The Kurd and Arab rebels were not the primitive and poorly armed tribesmen that the British had faced in Somaliland. When the Turkish Empire had collapsed and the Turks retreated, stocks of modern arms and ammunition throughout Syria and Mesopotamia fell into the hands of local tribesmen.[10] Thus, the rebels were equipped with large quantities of modern rifles and machine guns. Many of the leaders of the revolt had served in the Ottoman and Arab armies during the war and had a good understanding of modern warfare. They were not likely to be overawed by British aircraft and technology as the Somalis had been.[11]

The hard-pressed British garrison called for army and air force reinforcements. Nineteen battalions (4,883 British and 24,508 Indian army troops) were dispatched to Iraq as well as two additional RAF squadrons to reinforce the two squadrons already in the country.[12] By August the British were able to mount a counteroffensive that stamped the rebellion out by the end of the year. The RAF squadrons performed sterling service in evacuating British personnel, dropping supplies on besieged outposts, and in constant reconnaissance and bombing missions in support of the ground forces. The 1920 rebellion amounted to a fairly large conventional war including some major pitched battles between the rebels and British forces. At Rumaitha on 13 October, a three-thousand-man rebel force dug in and stood up to a daylong attack by a British brigade. Starting at 0800 the British pummeled the Iraqis with artillery, and RAF aircraft relentlessly bombed the defenders. Finally, under the weight of a brigade attack the rebels finally broke and retreated in disorder at 1700.[13] The rebellion was suppressed at the British cost of 1,040 killed and missing soldiers and 1,228 wounded and an estimated 8,450 dead Iraqi rebels.[14] The financial cost of the enterprise shocked the British government. To maintain control of a minor colonial mandate with little strategic value, military operations had cost the treasury forty million pounds — con-

Iraq, ca. 1922

siderably more than Britain had spent in supporting the Arab revolt in World
War I.

Iraq was such a drain of British personnel and resources that when the RAF
offered to garrison the country at a minimal cost, the idea was welcomed. On
1 October 1922, when the military forces in Iraq were turned over to RAF
control, it was the first time that an airman had been placed in control of all
military operations in a country.[15] The British government was able to an-
nounce that all British army forces had been pulled out of Iraq at great savings to the taxpayer. Henceforth, the military garrison in Iraq would consist
of eight RAF squadrons and four RAF armored car companies.[16] There were
fifteen thousand local Iraqi levies and police, five thousand of whom were
under British command and organized as the core of an Iraqi army. These
local forces would be British equipped, officered, and trained and supported
by the revenues of the Iraqi state.[17]

When the government announced that all *British* forces had been withdrawn from Iraq, it was technically correct. However, there was little mention that the departing British forces were replaced by Indian army brigades and supporting troops. Since the Indian army troops were paid for out of the Indian state military budget and not out of the British War Department budget, the British taxpayer and politicians got a pretty good deal, and the only player unhappy with the arrangement was the government of India.[18] Although Iraq was held up as an example of a country garrisoned by airpower, there was a significant army force on hand throughout the whole period of the British mandate until Iraq was granted full independence in 1932. By 1926, the framework of an Iraqi army had been created by the British. The Iraqi army had a military college, training center, and cavalry school, and the regular army had grown to a force of six infantry battalions, four cavalry regiments, four artillery batteries, and various supporting units.[19] The British also maintained at least a brigade of Indian army troops in the country until the 1930s.

The Air Control Policy

The British Empire had long relied upon the punitive expedition to bring rebellious natives back into line. When a border tribe on India's Northwest Frontier violated a treaty or when a band in Aden took a British official hostage, the standard response was to put together a military expedition, march on the tribal center, burn some villages, destroy crops, and kill any tribesmen who offered resistance. Then the army column would return to garrison knowing that the natives had been taught a lesson and would not likely defy British power again. The lesson and deterrent effect would last for a short time, sometimes months, sometimes years, and then the tribe would commit another outrage necessitating another British expedition to punish them.[20] Punitive expeditions ranged in size from a platoon of the Camel Corps riding against one village to months-long operations mounted on the Northwest Frontier by thousands of soldiers. A comprehensive list of punitive expeditions mounted by Britain at the height of empire, between 1840 and 1940 from Burma to India to the Sudan, would certainly number in the hundreds, probably in the thousands. In short, it was a brutal but indispensable means of keeping the empire in hand.

To put it simply, air control meant substituting aerial bombardment for the traditional ground punitive expedition. Airplanes could reach the object of the punitive expedition (i.e., the tribal headquarters or main village) very quickly. Airplanes had an impressive amount of firepower and the capability to inflict serious harm upon rebellious natives. Since disruption and destruction was the goal of a punitive expedition, a small force of airplanes was cheaper and more efficient, as it could inflict as much damage as a large and cumbersome ground force expedition.

The early RAF statements on air control stress its effectiveness and lethality. In the sprit of the empire, it was acknowledged that strong and forceful action was the best means to keep natives under control. As pointed out by RAF Wing Commander J. A. Chamier in 1921:

To establish a tradition, therefore which will prove effective, if only a threat of what is to follow afterwards, is displayed, the Air Force must, if called upon to administer punishment, do it with all its might and in the proper manner. One objective must be selected — preferably the most inaccessible village of the most prominent tribe which it is desired to punish. All available aircraft must be collected. . . .

The attack with bombs and machine guns must be relentless and unremitting and carried on continuously by day and night, on houses, inhabitants, crops and cattle. . . . This sounds brutal, I know, but it must be made brutal to start with. The threat alone in the future will prove efficacious if the lesson is once properly learnt.[21]

The draft of the RAF's *Notes on the Method of Employment of the Air Arm in Iraq* proudly pointed out that "within 45 minutes a full-sized village . . . can be practically wiped out and a third of its inhabitants killed or injured by four or five planes which offer them no real target and no opportunity for glory or avarice."[22] Although such tactics expressed the common military view on how the empire needed to be policed against the rebellious tribes and bandits that threatened good order, such policies came under increasing attack in the British Parliament during the 1920s. The RAF had to defend itself against the charge of inhumane warfare when a labor government came to power in 1924. That year Colonial Secretary James Thomas wrote to the high commissioner in Iraq and complained that critical press stories had appeared about bombing rebellious tribesmen and that heavy casualties "will not be easily explained or defended in Parliament by me."[23] To make air control more palatable to the politicians, later drafts of the RAF's notes on air control stressed the humanitarian aspects of air control. Per the new RAF doctrine, rebellious villages would be first warned that they would be bombed if they did not accede to government demands. Villagers would be given time to evacuate their village, then aircraft would demolish the houses with bombs, not with the intention of destroying the village, but with the aim of disrupting daily life.[24]

The War Ministry, which resisted the idea of RAF control of military operations in any colony, also chimed in and criticized the inhumanity of the RAF doctrine of bombing women and children.[25] The argument, however, falls a bit flat when one considers that army punitive expeditions had routinely burned the crops and food stores of rebellious tribes and fired artillery into villages.[26] In fact, most of the army officers out in the colonies heartily approved of immediate and forceful action by the RAF as a means of keeping incipient native rebellions in check. After the 1919 massacre, when army troops under General Dyer killed four hundred unarmed civilians at a protest meeting at Amritsar, India, the armed forces policing the empire were directed to operate under the doctrine of "minimum necessary force." The RAF learned to report the casualties of air control on vague terms, and enthusiastic supporters of the policy, such as military commentator Basil Liddell Hart, argued that by prompt action by the air force at the first sign of trouble, "tribal insubordination has been calmed before it could grow dangerous and there has been an immense saving of blood and treasure to the British and Iraqi governments."[27]

While the RAF officially acknowledged the humanitarian policy of minimum necessary force and the proponents of air control could point out that the RAF stayed its hand on occasion to avoid inflicting casualties on women and children, one suspects that in the far reaches of the empire, out of the reach of nosey correspondents and against people without any direct communication to the British government or League of Nations, humanitarian sentiments gave way to the practical mission of running an empire. The true view of the average British officer in the empire was probably expressed by Major General Sir Charles Gwynn, who argued against the minimum necessary force policy in his 1936 book *Imperial Policing.* "The far-reaching effects of General Dyer's action at Amritsar should be noted by soldiers. The government of India appears to have allowed itself to be drawn into the common error of altering well-recognized and tested procedure in consequence of one exceptional incident."[28] A RAF flight commander based on India's Northwest Frontier in the 1930s recalled the fairly constant action against tribes in that part of the empire. "If they went on being troublesome, we would warn them that we would bomb an assembly of people. An assembly was normally defined as ten people. . . . Indeed, in my case I can remember actually finding nine people and saying 'That's within ten per cent and that's good enough,' so I blew them up."[29]

The Reality of Air Control

From the start, air control was used quite enthusiastically in Iraq as a basic means of keeping the population in line. The RAF found that a few airplanes, without support from the other arms, could deal with a myriad of police problems common to violent, tribal societies. Tribes that persisted in raiding caravans found themselves under air attack and were soon coerced into changing their ways. The air control methods were widely applied in other colonies to include Aden, Sudan, Transjordan, and India's Northwest Frontier. Indeed, the Northwest Frontier Province, home to numerous warrior tribes with a long history of hostility against British India, saw more instances of air control operations than Iraq in the period between the world wars. A typical operation occurred in March 1921 when a band of one hundred Mahsud tribe raiders stole fifty camels. Later, the same band got in a firefight with an Indian army detachment, wounding a British officer and inflicting thirty-six casualties. The RAF responded with a series of raids and dropped 154 bombs on the Mahud capital. The area soon quieted down.[30]

Aden was the scene of numerous air control operations. A typical example of the coercive power of air attack, or the threat of attack, dealt with deterring Yemeni rustlers. In July and September 1933, Yemeni tribesmen raided the territory of the Aden Protectorate and made off with livestock from a tribe under British rule. Moreover, the Yemenis took some hostages from the tribe and held them for ransom — fairly typical behavior for the Arab tribes in that part of the world. The small British garrison at Aden got word of the incident and promptly threatened the Yemenis with a bombing raid unless the livestock were returned along with all the remaining hostages and ransom money. The British threat was taken seriously and the looted property was promptly returned.[31]

In Iraq, the air control tactic was used as a means of enforcing revenue collection. At the outset of the air control program, the RAF in several instances bombed tribes that refused to pay their taxes. The Colonial Office in London considered this policy to be a bit heavy-handed, but the high commissioner in Iraq insisted it was necessary, as nonpayment of taxes was seen as defying the authority of the British regime. So, although it was not widely publicized, bombing tax evaders continued.[32] Once the tribes got the word that the British were *really* serious about collecting taxes, fiscal cooperation seems to have been the order of the day and the tax compliance in Iraq reached a satisfactory level.

Although one gets the impression from the RAF reports to London and articles written by sympathizers such as Basil Liddell Hart that the RAF operations in the colonies consisted primarily of airpower policing operations, the reality was quite different. Most of the RAF operations in the colonies in the interwar years were in support of, and in cooperation with, ground troops. Although a RAF officer was in command in Iraq, significant ground forces were also required to keep order. Any banditry or rebellion on a larger scale than the minor instances noted above required a force of ground troops to engage the enemy. Sizable Iraqi and Indian army forces were available to deal with serious rebellions and, from 1922 to Iraqi independence in 1932, they saw considerable fighting.

In 1920 Sheik Mahmud, a tribal leader with his capital at Suliamania, was one of the first Kurdish nationalist leaders to rebel against the British regime. He was forced into exile after the rebellion but allowed home in 1923 with the agreement that he would support British rule of Kurdistan and oppose the Turkish attempts to encroach on the province. However, Mahmud began to secretly negotiate with the Turks, and open conflict began between the British and the Kurdish tribes supporting Mahmud. For three years Mahmud carried on a guerrilla campaign against the British and Iraqi forces.[33] The RAF bombed his capital for several months without any noticeable effect on the morale of Mahmud and his supporters. In operations against Mahmud, the air force cooperated with army and police columns trying to corner the rebels. Army columns were often mounted and made as light as possible. In this type of counterinsurgency operations the primary role of the RAF was reconnaissance, and in this role the aircraft proved to be fairly effective. When rebels were cornered by British/Iraqi troops, the RAF provided the heavy firepower in the form of close air support.

One army officer who participated in the campaign against Mahmud noted that the effect of airpower had been overestimated against tough guerrillas like Mahmud's Kurds. First, the air force claims of casualties inflicted by air attack appeared to have been consistently exaggerated.[34] Furthermore, aerial reconnaissance often failed to spot rebel forces, as the rebels had learned to cleverly camouflage their camps and positions and generally moved by night.[35] Supply of ground columns by aircraft was tried in the campaign against Mahmud, but proved unsuccessful.[36] It took a three-year combined air and ground campaign to finally force Mahmud into exile in Iran.

In September 1930 an election in Kurdistan turned into an antigovernment riot. Antigovernment protests soon turned into a demand for a united Kurdistan. In October Mahmud returned from exile and mounted a guerrilla campaign against the British.[37] From October 1930 to May 1931 the Iraqi army put two mounted columns in the field against him. The RAF's role in this campaign was purely one of support, providing reconnaissance for the ground forces and attacking Mahmud's forces only if they had been found and fixed by army units. In this campaign, bombing villages was prohibited, as it was likely that such actions would generate support for Mahmud.[38] For a campaign against another Kurdish rebel leader, Sheik Ahmed of Barzan, carried out between December 1931 and June 1932, the British assembled a ground force of three infantry battalions, a machine-gun company, an artillery battery, and two hundred police. The RAF supported the ground troops in several battles and conducted an extensive bombing campaign against Sheik Ahmed's territory. Ahmed was forced into exile in Turkey.[39]

Creating the Myth

In the early years of air control, the RAF leadership was careful not to offend the army or slight the ground forces while advocating an air control doctrine. One RAF officer wrote in 1922, "It is not for one moment to suggest that aircraft alone can garrison any country without military assistance, but rather to show that economy in military strength and in money may be effected by a more extensive employment of aircraft."[40] Air Marshal Sir John Salmon, writing of his campaigns against Kurdish rebels in Iraq and his operations to drive back Turkish incursions on the northern border, gave full credit to the many British and Iraqi army units that had participated in the campaigns.[41]

However, by 1929, after a decade of fairly successful air operations, RAF chief of staff Trenchard was so confident in the effectiveness of air control that he proposed that the RAF take over the defense responsibilities for Kenya, Uganda, Tanganyika, and Nyasaland. He argued that airplanes could replace six battalions of King's African Rifles in East Africa.[42] The army opposed this scheme as well as Trenchard's proposal to have the RAF take responsibility for the Northwest Frontier of India.

Once the future of the RAF as an independent service was assured, largely due to the perceived success of the air control program, the RAF and its supporters began to assert their views with considerably more boldness. It is not surprising that RAF accounts of air control operations written in the 1930s tended to minimize the army part of the operations and magnify the role of airpower.[43] The role of the army in the RAF's account of air control gradually faded. One account of air control in Iraq written in 1945 completely excludes any mention of the army in the colonial campaigns of the 1920s and 1930s.[44]

The primary criticism of air control was that it was a blunt instrument that operated on the basis of group accountability. A village or whole tribe would be indiscriminately targeted by the RAF for the transgressions of a small bandit gang or clan. Field Marshal Milne, chief of the Imperial General Staff, criticized the RAF for its air control techniques in Aden, arguing that constantly bombing the tribesmen would not create conditions for a peaceful administration.[45] Senior British officials in India, including the viceroy, disliked the airpower concept for similar reasons. They believed that bombing villages and attacking civilians to punish a tribe for the actions of some of its bandits was not only morally doubtful but also politically risky, as it would likely increase the hatred that the border tribes felt for the British.[46]

The RAF replied by emphasizing the humanitarian nature of the air control doctrine. Since the tribes were warned that they would be bombed, the air attacks were mostly destroying property and certainly not killing many innocents. However, the warning policy was never very consistent. Often, the officers in the field preferred that bombing take place without warning so as to get the maximum effect from an air attack. Indian Air Headquarters reluctantly accepted the requirement to warn in 1923 but argued that inflicting heavy casualties caused the greatest moral effect.[47] Although the Air Ministry maintained that warnings were always issued, in practice this was not true. Tribes were bombed on the Northwest Frontier in the 1920s without warning.[48]

Another RAF argument asserting the humanity of its air control operations was the assertion that aerial bombardment was a precision instrument. The RAF Air Staff pointed out that the air operations on the Northwest Frontier in November 1928 proved that the RAF could single out the specific houses of tribal leaders for destruction while leaving the rest of the village unharmed. This claim was true in a few cases. Carefully selected pilots and aircrew could hit a target with some accuracy at low level. However, for the most part, the RAF claim that airpower was a precision instrument was frankly ludicrous. RAF bombing accuracy in the interwar period was, for the most part, appallingly bad. Of the 182 bombs dropped on tribesmen on the Northwest Frontier in November 1928, 102 completely missed the target villages.[49] The Bristol fighters that equipped many of the units flying air control lacked bombsights, so only very low-level attacks came close to the target. In the March 1932 border campaign, only half the bombs dropped fell within the target villages.[50]

More embarrassing than not being able to hit the target was the problem of hitting the wrong target. If interwar gunnery and bombing training in the RAF were poor, then the service's navigation skills were no better.[51] In the hills of Kurdistan or on the wild Northwest Frontier of India, one valley and village looked very much like another. Coupled with often mediocre intelligence and the fact that one group of tribesmen looks very much like another at seven thousand feet, it is understandable that villages of friendly tribesmen were sometimes attacked by mistake.[52] One cannot be sure just how often this kind of "imperial friendly fire" occurred. The victims had no means of reporting their outrage to Parliament, and the RAF was not likely to publicly report mistakes. In any case, the official reports of the RAF and the writings of its supporters continued to maintain that the RAF's air control methods were very humane, resulted in very little loss of life, and were always carried out with full warning.[53] If air control did not win the goodwill of various native peoples, it did a pretty effective job in keeping many of them in line, at least for a time.

In general, air control by itself seems to have had only very temporary effects. A tribe would steal cattle or raid a police outpost, get bombed, and desist, and then the whole cycle would repeat itself in the next year or so. The

RAF was never able to handle anything but the smallest rebellion by its own efforts, but when it flew in support of army columns, it certainly made military operations more efficient. A couple of aircraft could provide the same level of support as a cavalry battalion for the army. The heavy firepower that the aircraft could bring to the battle was a psychological shock to the enemy and a great morale boost for the British troops. However, that is not the way that the RAF wanted air control remembered. While the critiques of air control circulated mostly within the closed circles of the government and the military, the RAF's version of the success story was pushed in military journals, in parliamentary reports, and to the general public. Eventually, the RAF view of air control became well established in the public mind.

The reason for the acceptance of the air control doctrine by the public and the government was not its fairly modest success; it was the low cost. Journal and newspaper articles by RAF officers and supporters of air control invariably pointed to the much lower cost of conducting colonial police operations from the air. At a time when the defense and colonial expenditures had to be kept low, air control was cost-effective. The true limits of the air control doctrine were displayed during the Arab revolt in Palestine from 1936 to 1939. When the revolt started there were an estimated five thousand insurgents. By 1938 the insurgents had grown to a force of fifteen thousand. Although most of the fighting occurred in the countryside, much of the combat was in urban areas.[54] The British rushed thousands of troops to the colony, and the fighting consisted of small skirmishes and ambushes. In 1938 alone, 486 Arab civilians, 292 Jews, 69 British, and 1,138 rebels were killed.[55]

Air Commodore Arthur Harris (later known as "Bomber Harris") was commanding officer of the RAF in Palestine and proffered a characteristic solution to the revolt that foreshadows his strategy as chief of Bomber Command in World War II. The solution to Arab unrest was to drop "one 250-pound or 500-pound bomb in each village that speaks out of turn. . . . The only thing the Arab understands is the heavy hand, and sooner or later it will have to be applied."[56] To the dismay of the RAF, the army rejected this approach of dealing with the revolt in Palestine. Air control was not applied, and the RAF was restricted to missions such as flying cover for convoys in ambush-prone rural areas.[57] The army wisely decided that air control had reached its limits and that the political reaction to employing airpower in largely urban areas would have exacerbated an already ugly situation and brought strong international protests. Unlike Iraq and the Northwest Frontier, Palestine was more urban and developed and had good communications with the outside world. Given the bombing accuracy of the RAF in this era, it would not have been long before the RAF leveled the wrong Arab village. Such an event would have been well publicized and the RAF's policy of air control brought under intense criticism. The army, by turning down the RAF's advice in dealing with the Palestinian revolt, saved the RAF and the air control policy from a grand failure. By keeping air control to the more isolated reaches of the empire, one could portray the policy in a romanticized, if inaccurate, way.

The Spanish Experience

At the start of the twentieth century, Spain, once a mighty empire, was demoralized and impoverished. Spain had lost virtually all of its considerable overseas empire to the Americans in 1898 when the Spanish army and fleet had been humiliated in battle. In an era in which national power and prestige were largely measured in colonial possessions, Spain sought to expand its small coastal enclaves on the Atlantic and Mediterranean coasts of Morocco into a large colonial holding. Colonial conquest not only would acquire some prestige for Spain, but also would provide a field where the Spanish armed forces could win victory on the battlefield and remove some of the humiliation from the defeat of 1898.

In the years just before World War I, the Spanish made some small efforts to expand the Moroccan colony. As with most colonial enterprises, the conquest was accomplished by a mixture of treaties and alliances with some tribes and military action against others. As long as the Moroccan tribes remained divided, this fairly standard means of European colonization could be conducted by a mix of European and locally raised troops. Fighting either with or against the Spanish, the Moroccan tribes were composed of tough and fierce warriors. By the start of World War I, Spain had expanded its power into a small strip of land along the Atlantic coast and the city of Melilla on the Mediterranean coast. In 1912 the Spanish made a territorial agreement with the French, who had also been conducting their own conquest of Morocco since the start of the century. The Spanish territory would consist of the northern tenth of the country, a mineral-rich terri-

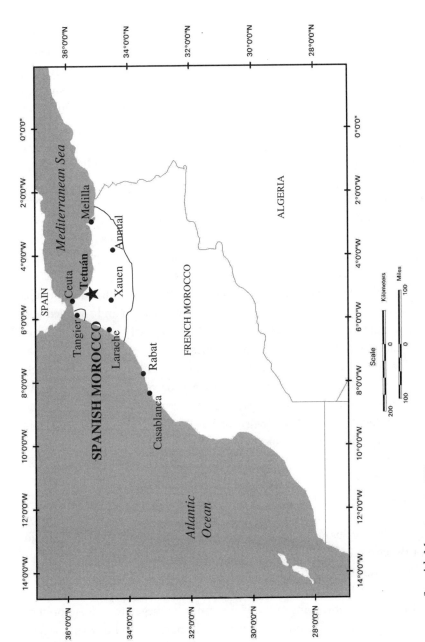

Spanish Morocco, ca. 1912

tory (large iron ore, zinc, silver, coal and phosphate deposits) 360 kilometers long and 80 kilometers wide with 760,000 people divided into 66 tribes. The border between Spanish and French territory was drawn on the map and looked good on paper. But neither the French nor the Spanish could verify the border and mark it on the ground because neither country controlled the mountainous interior of the country.

The Spanish were one of the first powers to use airpower in colonial warfare. A small air detachment equipped with Austrian-made Lohner biplanes dropped a few German-made shrapnel bombs in December 1913 on the village of Beni Hozmar south of Tetuán during one of the many skirmishes with the Moroccans.[58] During World War I the colony remained fairly quiet. It was not to last. While the rest of Europe was at war, the Spanish drew up plans for the full conquest of their part of Morocco and began a program of aerial mapping and reconnaissance in 1919.[59] In that year, the Spanish air service was equipped with modern bomber and fighter aircraft bought from France and Britain. The air corps in North Africa was built up and supplied with French Farman and Bréguet-14 bombers, British DeHavilland DH-4 and DH-9 light bomber/reconnaissance planes, and Bristol fighters. Small air groups operated out of the three main Spanish airfields located at Lareche and Tetuán, in the western part of Spanish Morocco and at the small enclave of Melilla in the east.[60] The Spanish aircraft were rugged and capable aircraft for their day and had proven their worth in combat from 1917 to 1918. However, all were hampered by short range.

The Spanish expanded their holdings in 1920 in a major campaign in the west in which an army of more than twenty-five thousand troops advanced south from Tetuán and, with little fighting, captured the Moroccan holy city of Xauen in the central mountain range (elevation twenty-five hundred meters).[61] The Spanish scattered blockhouses and small garrisons throughout the conquered territory to secure the roads and enforce the rule of the colonial administration. A large part of the Spanish army was tied down in this fashion.

In the meantime, some of the Moroccan tribes began to unite to preserve their independence from the French and Spanish. Abd el Krim, a well-educated forty-year-old Berber (educated at the University of Fez) from the largest tribe in the Rif Mountains, convinced several other tribes to join under his leadership to fight the Spanish. Abd el Krim was on good terms with the Spanish until 1920, but the tone of the Spanish rule and their indifference toward the idea of sharing power with the Moroccans soured Abd el Krim on the Spanish.[62]

Disaster at Annual, 1921

In 1921 General Silvestre advanced an army of approximately twenty-five thousand Spanish troops and Moroccan auxiliaries west from the enclave of Melilla with the intention of finishing the conquest of Morocco's interior and uniting the two halves of the Spanish colony. Silvestre's force met heavy resistance from a small force of three thousand to six thousand Berber warriors led by Abd el Krim throughout June and July. On 17–20 July, part of the Spanish force was overrun at the village of Annual and Silvestre ordered a retreat back to Melilla. The retreat turned into a complete rout. Silvestre was killed and virtually the whole Spanish army was destroyed with only a few survivors straggling into Melilla. The Spanish official figure for losses, including the garrisons wiped out by the Berbers, was 14,772 killed. In the brief campaign the Spanish also lost 29,504 rifles, 392 machine guns, and 129 artillery pieces.[63] It was one of the worst disasters to ever befall a colonial army. There were almost no prisoners taken as the war in Morocco was literally a "war to the death." In the aftermath of the battle, the small Spanish garrisons throughout the interior of the country, none capable of supporting the others, were efficiently cut off and wiped out as the Spanish were pushed back to the enclaves they had held prior to World War I. Abd el Krim's only mistake in this spectacular campaign was his failure to capture the city of Melilla, which was in no state to effectively defend itself after the destruction of Silvestre's army. Taking Melilla would have deprived the Spanish of their only foothold in the eastern half of the country. Because of this strategic mistake, the Spanish were left with a base for the reconquest of Spanish Morocco.

After the victory at Annual, other tribes rushed to join Abd el Krim. Thanks to the equipment captured at Annual, he was in a position to equip a sizable army with the modern weapons. In addition, Abd el Krim found international arms dealers ready and willing to supply arms and ammunition to the rebels.

In 1922 Abd el Krim established a formal government and formally declared the Rif to be an independent republic. However, under diplomatic pressure from France and Spain, the major powers prevented any recognition of the Rif Republic, although the Rif army did receive the help of a Russian artillery colonel, sent by the Soviet government, to train the Rif forces in the use of the artillery captured at Annual.[64]

The Spanish reacted energetically to the disaster at Annual. A Spanish government commission found that the Spanish colonial army had been poorly equipped, led, and trained. After the battle of Annual the war became, for the Spanish, a no-quarter war of revenge. The Spanish would spare no effort to rebuild their forces and eventually destroy the Rif Republic. Emphasis was put on building up elite formations, such as the Spanish Foreign Legion, and capable and aggressive young commanders, such as Francisco Franco, would be found and promoted to lead the combat troops.

One of the Spanish initiatives in their war of revenge was to send a secret delegation to Germany to negotiate the sale of poison gas to be used on the Rif army. After World War I, poison gas was seen by most of the world as a barbaric weapon, and treaties would soon be drawn up outlawing the use of poison gas in war. However, the Spanish desire for victory and revenge proved to be far stronger than any international legal scruples. The Spanish army's selection of Germany as a secret ally in the war against the Rif was a sound one. The Germans had proven to be masters of gas warfare during the First World War, and the German army, despite the provisions of the Versailles treaty, maintained secret facilities for production of poison gas as well as a cadre of gas warfare experts. The Spanish were willing to pay top dollar for a large quantity of the most effective poison gas they could find, and the Germans were happy to accept secret Spanish funding to keep their poison gas facilities active and were also willing to provide expert advice on the tactical use of gas.

In December 1923 the German and Spanish armed forces signed a secret agreement for Germany to provide poison gas artillery shells and airplane bombs to the Spanish army.[65] The Spanish preference was for a large quantity of "yellow cross" (mustard gas), for which the Spanish were willing to pay the Germans' price of twenty-five thousand marks (over five thousand dollars) per ton.[66]

The Campaign Against the Rif Rebels, 1922–1925

After the news of Annual broke, the Spanish sent 150,000 men to North Africa to ensure that their last enclaves were not overrun. The Spanish air force was reinforced. A commission set up to investigate the Annual disaster concluded that the Spanish air force had performed incompetently in the campaign and that the accuracy of air attacks had been poor.[67] The air command at Melilla was expanded to a three-squadron group (sixteen aircraft), which was kept busy by constant reconnaissance and bombing missions in order to protect Melilla itself.[68] In 1922 the Spanish began a systematic campaign to advance their border west from Melilla and regain the territory lost in 1921. The Spanish air force did its best to support the ground troops, but the small bombs available did relatively little harm to hardened warriors dug into the mountains, and there was little evidence that the Spanish air force had improved much since Annual. As the Rif warriors moved by night and had learned to conceal themselves by day, air reconnaissance rarely spotted them or was able to successfully engage them. Most of the fighting in Morocco was close-range infantry fighting, something at which the Rif warriors excelled. Thus, by 1923 the Spanish airmen took to bombing the Rif villages to break the morale of the population as a primary mission of their force.[69] The German army sent two experienced aviation officers to Spanish Morocco in 1925 to report on the war there. Captain Ulrich Grauert and Lieutenant Hans Jeschonnek (both became Luftwaffe generals, Jeschonnek the chief of staff of the Luftwaffe) visited the Spanish forces between April and July 1925 and reported on the air campaign.[70] The two Germans were not impressed with the Spanish air force or its bombing campaign. They reported that the inhabitants of the Rif mountain villages had long become accustomed to bombing by the Spanish and had built numerous trenches and shelters for protection in bombing raids.[71] Even bombing with poison gas had not broken the will of the tough mountain tribesmen. The German officers concluded that bombing the population would not have a decisive effect in the war.[72]

In 1923 the Spanish air force in Africa was considerably enlarged. The Melilla air group was expanded to three squadrons of DH-4s, two squadrons of Bristol fighters, one squadron of British Martinsyde fighters, and two squadrons of navy seaplanes for a total of sixty aircraft. On the other side of the colony the air force had two squadrons of Bréguet-14s at Laranche (twenty-four planes) and two squadrons of Bréguets at Tetuán (twenty-four planes).[73] The Spanish continued to procure the best aircraft available from European manufacturers. As the Germans had earned a reputation for building first-rate aircraft during the First World War, the Spanish bought several large twin-engine German Dornier flying boats for use of the naval air arm. The Dorniers, the best flying boats of the day, were able to carry out long-range reconnaissance and bombing missions and were ideal for operations in Morocco with its long coastline.

In the summer of 1924 Abd el Krim's forces went on the offensive and cut the Tangier-Tetuán road and threatened Tetuán. The Spanish force at Xauen was put under siege. A large relief force, including Lieutenant Colonel Francisco Franco and his Spanish Foreign Legion, fought their way through to Xauen in October and evacuated all of the Spanish and Berbers friendly to Spain. It took a month for the Spanish army to fight its way out of Xauen to Spanish-held territory.[74] The incompetence of many of the Spanish officers in this campaign was notable. When the relief force arrived at Xauen, they noted that the army's fortifications were in name only. Military posts defending the city had no barbed wire or reserve defense positions, and the outposts had been sited so that they were unable to support each other.[75]

With the fall of Xauen to Abd el Krim's troops, the Rif Republic was at the height of its power. Abd el Krim could field a force of twenty thousand to thirty thousand well-armed regular troops, fully equal to European troops, and perhaps one hundred thousand irregular warriors.[76] However, French forces operating out of France's Moroccan colony carried out a methodical advance north of Fez into territory claimed by the Rif Republic. Abd el Krim turned his forces on the French in the spring of 1925 and in a rapid offensive, drove the French army back to within twenty miles of Fez, the French capital of Morocco. This, in turn, pushed the French and Spanish to develop a joint strategy to deal with Abd el Krim. In June 1925, the Spanish dictator, Primo de Rivera, and the French commander in North Africa, Marshal Lyautey, agreed to coordinate a grand offensive against the Rif Republic. The first part of the offensive would be an amphibious landing by a large Spanish army at the Bay of Alhucemas, a strategic position in the middle of Rif territory. The Spanish forces would drive south while the French prepared an offensive to drive north.[77]

Alhucemas Landing and the Final Offensive

The Spanish amphibious landing of twelve thousand troops at Alhucemas on 7 September 1925 went badly. The operation was poorly planned and landing boats hit shoals, the naval gunfire was badly coordinated, and the men wading ashore faced heavy resistance from entrenched Rif soldiers.[78] A hundred aircraft supported the operation — eighty land-based airplanes and twenty seaplanes — but they seem to have had little effect on the defenders. Yet, some of the Spanish troops clawed their way ashore and successfully established a beachhead. Once ashore the Spanish prepared for a methodical offensive to sweep south into the heart of Rif territory. The Spanish air force was ready to use poison gas as a primary means of dislodging the Rif defenders. The German Stoltzenberg Chemical Firm, working with the approval and support of the German army, set up facilities in Spain during late 1924 and early 1925 for the production of poison gas bombs and artillery shells. The Germans complained that the Spanish had a poor understanding of poison gas production, but the shells and bombs were made and ready for the grand offensive after the Alhucemas landing.[79]

The Spanish air force used gas bombs extensively during the 1925 to 1926 campaign. It was, for the most part, a pure terror campaign that made villages and the civilian population the primary target.[80] The Spanish preferred to use mustard gas, which tended to blind and cripple rather than kill its victims. Mustard gas, because of its toxicity and persistence, also poisoned and destroyed crops and wells and made life unbearable for the villagers.[81] Under the cover of artillery and aircraft, the Spanish force moved slowly south while a large French force moved north in 1926. Abd el Krim faced a combined Spanish and French offensive in 1926 that put over three hundred thousand soldiers into the field armed with aircraft and artillery, against his twenty thousand regular troops. On 27 May 1926, the inevitable came and Abd el Krim surrendered to the French. Although resistance by some tribes would continue for years, particularly in the French part of Morocco, the Rif War was concluded.

The French in Morocco

The French had maintained a large force in Morocco since the turn of the century. Legally, the French held Morocco as a protectorate in the name of the sultan of Fez but in reality ruled Morocco as a colony. The French deployed an airplane squadron to provide reconnaissance support for their forces in 1912. Although military aviation was still in the experimental stage, Marshal Lyautey, commander in chief of the French forces in Morocco, directed in 1913 that the aircraft would also be used for aerial bombardment.[82] The army's planes performed well in the reconnaissance role and in April 1914 carried out their first bombing mission against rebel tribesmen. According to the French, the bombing produced a "great moral effect" upon the tribesmen.[83]

After World War I, the French were ready to resume their systematic conquest of Morocco and began to push deep into the Atlas Mountains. The French approach was much like that of the Spaniards. As the French advanced, roads were built and blockhouses, each containing one or two platoons of infantry, were left to maintain control of the countryside.[84] These small garrisons saturating the country were effective against small bands of tribesmen or bandits, but were not designed to hold off attacks by large forces. By 1924, the French had expanded their line of occupation north of Fez into territory claimed by Abd el Krim, who did not recognize any artificial European boundaries of French and Spanish Morocco. The Ouerrha Valley was a major source of food for the Rif Republic, and the French occupation of the area posed a serious threat to Abd el Krim.

In the spring of 1925 Marshal Lyautey had sixty thousand troops in Morocco, equipped with modern artillery and supported by eighty aircraft organized into ten squadrons under command of the Thirty-seventh Air Regiment.[85] The French were confident that what had happened to the Spanish at Annual in 1921 could not happen to their forces. Thus, despite some warnings, the French were generally unprepared when Abd el Krim launched eight thousand of his soldiers in an offensive against the French position north of Fez on 13 April 1925. The Rif warriors relied on offensive tactics and concentrated on destroying enemy forces. The Rif troops moved in highly mobile bands and avoided concentrating their forces to hold defensive positions where French firepower could be brought to bear with the most effect.[86] Abd el Krim's offensive turned into a French disaster. Within two months, forty-four of sixty-six French outposts had been overrun by Rif warriors, usually accompanied by the massacre of the French garrison.[87] Rif forces soon advanced to within twenty miles of Fez. Although the French had placed a great deal of confidence in their air superiority, the air units proved to be fairly ineffectual during the first two weeks of the campaign because of the lack of advanced landing fields in that sector of Morocco. Marshal Lyautey was only able to concentrate most of the Thirty-seventh Air Regiment at the end of April.[88]

The French, shocked by their defeat in Morocco, chose to massively reinforce the colony with fifty battalions of troops from France. Marshal Pétain, who had never served outside of France, took over as the commander of military forces in Morocco while Marshal Lyautey retained the post of resident general. True to character, Pétain methodically built up his forces and prepared for a massive counteroffensive against Abd el Krim. The Thirty-seventh Air Regiment was reinforced with additional squadrons and by autumn 1925 had reached a strength of twenty-two squadrons with 160 aircraft.[89]

The French army air service (the air force would not become an independent service until 1932) performed a wide variety of support duties in Morocco. One of the major missions of the air squadrons was aerial resupply of small garrisons by airdrop. Throughout the campaign the French relied heavily upon aerial resupply to maintain isolated garrisons, and several aircraft were detailed to this duty alone. By this means, the French were able to maintain isolated small forces for long periods in the rugged country of the Rif.[90] The use of aerial photography for mapping was also an important part of French air operations.[91] Aircraft were also regularly used in the liaison role of dropping and picking up messages.[92] One of the most important innovations of the French air service in Morocco was the use of aircraft in medical evacuation of wounded or sick soldiers. After World War I the French developed special models of Farman and Bréguet bombers for exclusive use as medical evacuation aircraft. Such aircraft could land on rough fields close to the front lines and get wounded and sick soldiers quickly back to well-equipped base hospitals in the rear. Several of these aircraft were in use in Morocco by 1921.[93] By the major campaigns of 1925, the French had established the first large-scale aerial medevac system. The French air service specially modified twenty-two Bloch 81, Potez 29, and Hanriot 431 airplanes to carry the wounded and sick (the medevac version of the Hanriot was named the Hanriot 437) and formed flights with the exclusive mission of evacuating the sick and wounded to the rear.[94] A regular system of collection points at forward landing fields was established, and the aerial ambulances flew a regular schedule of flights to get the wounded and sick soldiers from the battle lines to central military hospitals in an hour or less.[95] During the heavy fighting against the Rif troops in 1925, the French evacuated 987 wounded and sick soldiers to rear hospitals by air.[96]

Like the Spanish, the French initiated a program of heavily bombing the Rif villages. In July 1925 the French air service flew 1,219 bombing sorties against Rif villages and forces.[97] In 1925 the undefended Rif town of Chechaouen was heavily bombed, with heavy casualties to the civilian population. Most of the casualties were women and children, as the men were off at the front fighting the French.[98] One British observer commented that the French carried out heavy bombing of the Rif villages and crops and "conduct of these operations was drastic in the extreme."[99] Coming from the British, who were not squeamish about bombing villages in Iraq and on the Northwest Frontier of India, this says a lot about the French approach to colonial warfare. During the campaign against the Rif Republic between 1925 and 1926, the French air service had considerably less success in inflicting casualties upon the Rif warriors than upon Moroccan civilians. The Rif regular troops and irregular warriors were highly mobile and avoided establishing strongpoints that could become targets for air and ground bombardment. The Rif warriors moved carefully, dug shelters, and were fairly immune from the small weight of bombs that could be dropped by the Bréguet-14 bombers, the primary French bomber.

However, the aircraft were still very important in the reconnaissance role and as psychological support for the French troops. Even if airplanes did not inflict much damage on Rif warriors, it was a great morale boost for French ground troops to see air cover overhead. Indeed, the French army became very dependent upon airpower, and units were reluctant to move and maneuver unless supported by aircraft. Still, the French tactics were not as effective as they could have been. The French army continued to fight a highly mobile guerrilla force adept in hit-and-run tactics with the clumsy formations and doctrine of a large-scale European war.[100]

In several aspects, the French air service performed poorly. Although the French had a strong artillery force, it was not used very effectively during the 1926 campaign because the reconnaissance airplanes were poor at aerial artillery spotting — an art that requires extensive training and good communications. The French air service procured only a few radios for its planes, and the radios it did have could only communicate with the rear headquarters and not with the frontline units.[101]

In April 1926, Marshal Pétain unleashed his grand offensive of over fifty battalions supported by tanks, artillery, and airpower. Abd el Krim, with fewer than thirty thousand effective troops, found himself boxed in by overwhelming firepower and the Spanish to the north and the French to the south. On 27 May he ended the Rif War and capitulated to the French. Airpower had played an important, but not decisive, part in the downfall of the Rif Republic. What is impressive is that Abd el Krim and his army held off two large European armies for years and succumbed only to overwhelming numbers and firepower. In many respects, Abd el Krim and his force of warriors proved that airpower, and even Western firepower in general, could not easily overcome colonial rebels who were highly motivated, well armed, and well led. All of the contemporary observers noted with awe the ability of the Rif population to accept bombing attacks without a breakdown in morale.

French Airpower in Syria

Immediately following World War I, France found herself in a political/military situation even more bewildering than the British found in Mesopotamia. Under agreements made during the war, France was to have control of Syria and Lebanon in the postwar period. However, planning for postwar occupation during the war had been sketchy in the extreme, and in 1919 France found itself landing a large army and trying to establish control in a region filled with warring interests with little clear idea of the factions and politics at work behind the disorder.[102] With the collapse of the Ottoman Empire, plenty of modern arms had fallen into the hands of various factions in the region, and the French would not be facing the kind of poorly armed tribesmen that they had been used to fighting before World War I. Other factors led to violence in the region. Turkish troops were fighting Greeks for control of the coast of Asia Minor and Cilicia, and Armenian battalions under nominal French control were seeking to carve out a national homeland in the Mideast. An Arab government had taken control in Damascus and was ready to resist the French. Finally no clear boundaries or zones of national interest had been defined by the major powers. Between 1919 and 1921, when the League of Nations gave France a mandate to govern Lebanon and Syria and established some borderlines, France was compelled to move cautiously and methodically to exert control over the region.[103]

By 1922, the fighting and disorder had died down in the region, and the French were sending troops home and developing a program for a long-term administration of her mandates. Like the British mandate of Iraq, Syria and Lebanon contained several large ethnic factions vying for independence or at least autonomy. Warlike Arab tribes in Syria behaved much like tribes in Iraq and carried on tribal warfare, caravan raiding, and general banditry. Like Britain, France was faced with the need to reduce her expensive colonial garrisons while simultaneously keeping the peace among fractious and violent peoples. Like Britain, the French military stationed in Syria/Lebanon soon developed their own version of air control.[104]

By the end of 1919 the French had built up a force of four Bréguet-14 bomber squadrons in Syria, and General Weygand, the French commander, wanted to use his light bomber units much the way the RAF used their DH-9s. Weygand told Paris that airpower was "indispensable" and requested more air units so he could withdraw ground troops.[105] The British air control model in Iraq was looked on very favorably by the French and, to a large degree, copied in Syria. In 1924 Weygand issued directives for his air units that looked very much like the British air control doctrine. Aircraft would be used to bomb tribal groups when incidents occurred as a means of intimidating tribes into compliance with the French regime.[106] While reducing the ground forces, the French increased their air presence so that by the end of 1923, the French had several squadrons in Syria organized into the Thirty-ninth Air Regiment. By this time the French forces in Syria started looking very much like the British forces in Iraq. The French continued to reduce their ground forces. In 1924 they sent home six infantry battalions and three artillery batteries. By 1925 the ground forces consisted of a modest eleven infantry battalions and two cavalry regiments, four artillery batteries, and three armored car squadrons (this force included fifty-five hundred Syrian Arab soldiers that the French raised to garrison the colony). The air force had increased to eight squadrons.[107]

Syria, like Iraq, was a very volatile region seething with discontented nationalist movements. Heavy-handed French actions along with the arrest of several leaders of the Druze minority by the French government in July 1925 triggered a nationalist revolt by the Druzes. In short order, forty thousand tough Druze warriors put French garrisons under siege and posed a serious threat to France's hold on Syria. Many of the Druze warriors had served in the Ottoman or Arab armies during World War I and were not inclined to be overawed by airplanes and modern European weapons. Indeed, the Druze were well armed. There were plenty of modern arms to include rifles, machine guns, and artillery throughout the region available after the collapse of the Ottoman regime, and it was relatively easy to run guns in from Turkey to Syria. In short, the Druze rebellion was much more like a conventional war than a small tribal outbreak which the French had anticipated. In short order the French government was forced to send a large number of reinforcements to Syria.

In the meantime, the French air service did sterling service in staving off defeat until reinforcements could arrive. French aircraft kept the seven-hundred-man army garrison under siege at Soueida supplied by airdrops from July to September 1925 until relieving forces could fight their way in and extricate them.[108] As French troops arrived, the French air units were constantly engaged in reconnaissance, artillery spotting, and close air support. As in Morocco, the French also carried out numerous bombing missions against the Druze villages.[109] Again, as in Morocco, the bombing also seemed to have little effect upon the Druze morale. The rebels quickly learned to dig deep shelters for protection and enthusiastically fired at French bombers with their rifles and machine guns. Ground fire succeeded in bringing down several French aircraft during the campaign.[110]

The French built up an army of thirty thousand men in Syria to suppress the Druze rebels in a campaign lasting until 1927. The French applied a strategy of bombing rebel towns and villages throughout the campaign, and by the end of the war, many villages throughout Syria lay in ruins. The French even bombed their own capital of Damascus in October 1925. When a few hundred rebels infiltrated into the southern part of the city, the French, fearing a general revolt, apparently panicked and bombed Muslim sections of the city without warning, causing an estimated fourteen hundred civilian dead.[111] As in Morocco, the French were finally able to conclude the war by massive use of conventional forces and firepower.

After the Druze rebellion, the French in Syria pulled out most of their troops and returned to their original strategy of using airpower more judiciously, in the British manner of air control. Intertribal warfare and banditry was kept to a low level by occasional bombing raids and airpower demonstrations.[112]

Italian Airpower in Libya

After World War I, the Italians, like the other European powers, proceeded to suppress various native rebellions in their colonial realms that had been ignored during the grand European bloodletting. Italy's major field of colonial endeavor was in Libya, where the Italian regime faced resistance from several of the nomadic Saharan tribes. The Italian presence in Libya was fairly recent and had only been established after the 1911 to 1913 war with the Ottoman Empire in which Libya had been ceded to Italy. During the 1920s Italy waged a fairly constant campaign to bring the tribes under Italian control.

By 1925 Italy had over twenty-three thousand troops stationed in the province of Tripolitania, fourteen thousand of whom were Libyan and Eritrean soldiers in Italian service, and thirty-seven hundred native irregulars. The Italian forces were well equipped and included a tank company, armored car squadron, and several artillery batteries to provide mobile firepower.[113] The Regia Aeronautica contributed to the military effort in Libya by sending a force of eighty-three aircraft along with the supporting elements.[114]

Libya was of little worth to Italy. Indeed, maintaining the colony cost Italy a lot of money and resources it could not afford. However, establishing Italian control of Tripolitania and Cyrenica, the two provinces of Libya, was seen as important in maintaining the position of Italy as the leading power in the Mediterranean. In short, the colonial effort in Africa was purely a prestige matter for a regime that was based more on bluster and propaganda than on any reasonable measure of power. Indeed, having acquired colonies, the Italians had little concept of how to control or administer them. For example, foreign observers noted that the Italians showed little understanding of Muslim sensibilities in Libya. The preferred Italian method was to show the Arabs a strong hand by "putting down opposition with great severity."[115] As to the latter policy, the air force became an important weapon.

From 1928 to 1931, Marshal Badoglio, governor of the two Libyan colonies, and forces under General Graziani waged a ruthless campaign to force the surrender of the Saharan nomadic tribes. Almost forty thousand Italian troops took part in a campaign supported by about forty aircraft based in Cyrenica and another thirty-three based in Tripolitania. Most of the aircraft employed were two-seat Ro-1 biplanes — designed as observation planes and light bombers. A number of twin-engine Caproni bombers were also employed.[116]

The total force opposing the Italians were a few thousand tribesmen, only a couple of thousand of whom had modern rifles. Air units were effective in providing reconnaissance in a desert terrain that provided little cover for the rebel tribesmen. Mobile columns, supported by aircraft, were able to continuously harass the camel- and horse-mounted rebels. Italian air force detachments conducted a relentless bombing campaign against the tribesmen. Any time the tribesmen assembled, six or more Italian planes, usually armed with machine guns and bombs, would target them. Under constant air attack, the tribesmen soon split into ever-smaller bands.[117]

The Italians, like the Spanish, resorted to indiscriminate bombing of rebel encampments with poison gas. Tribal cattle and goat herds were also attacked from the air. The tribesmen, in turn, made a point of impaling and cutting to pieces any Italian airman forced down by ground fire.[118] By January 1931 the aerial terror campaign had succeeded and the last pitiful remnants of the nomadic tribes surrendered to the Italian authorities. It was one of the cruelest military campaigns in modern colonial history as large numbers of tribesmen, as many as three-quarters, died during the 1920s. Military action killed many, but most died of hunger and disease — due to being chased away from their water sources and grazing grounds by the Italian air force.[119]

Assessment

The colonial wars proved that aviation was tremendously effective as a force enhancer in military operations. A few airplanes in the reconnaissance role proved more effective than traditional cavalry. Aircraft, while not very accurate as bombers in this era, could still bring an impressive amount of firepower to bear on an enemy. Moreover, aircraft were highly mobile and responsive. Colonial air forces could respond in days or hours, where before a military expedition might take weeks to respond. Aircraft could attack deep inside the rebel territory and could be quickly shifted from one threatened front to another. Moreover, aircraft served capably in liaison duties and in evacuating wounded and sick soldiers. In many ways, the airplane made the job of keeping order in the colonies much easier for the European powers.

However, the RAF's hope of policing colonies solely through airpower was never realized. A purely air option in colonial policing worked only in the minor cases of suppressing low-level instances of tribal banditry. The British were never able to do away with the need to keep significant ground forces in the colonies. On the other hand, the deployment of air units made it possible to considerably reduce the size of the colonial garrisons and made the ground troops in places like Iraq much more efficient. By the end of the era, the British in India, where the greater part of British interwar military operations took place, had learned a great many lessons about the employment of airpower in suppressing rebellions and banditry. In 1939 the British forces in India published a manual called *Frontier Warfare* (a publication of the Indian army and Royal Air Force), which provided a comprehensive doctrine for the employment of military force and airpower in the colonial policing. In its scope *Frontier Warfare* was much like the famed Marine Corps' *Small Wars Manual* in recognizing the political aspects of colonial policing and conflict. In India, where the British military had a pretty sophisticated understanding of the tribes that they were dealing with, there was an understanding that force had to be carefully applied and that indiscriminate bombing or a heavy-handed use of force could be counterproductive.[120]

Outside of India, however, the British military leaders seem to have had little understanding of the political implications of the use of military power. In Iraq the British seemed especially clueless about the nature of their large rebellions that they faced. General Haldane, British commander in Iraq during the 1920 national rising, believed that the rebellion had occurred because the British occupiers had been too soft on the Arabs and that the Arabs had naturally taken advantage of British slackness. Haldane declared that "Arabs, like other Eastern peoples, are accustomed to be ruled by a strong hand."[121] An RAF officer explained the fighting in Iraq in another way. "A large percentage of the tribes fight for the mere pleasure of fighting. . . . We oppose the tribes with infantry, the arm that supplies them with the fight. Substitute aircraft and they are dealing with a weapon that they cannot counter."[122] There appears to be no suspicion among the British officers in Iraq that the major rebellions in Kurdistan had anything to do with a political objective — such as the desire for self-government by the Kurds. The British military apparently could not grasp that the "natives" might have strong nationalist sentiments and were fighting for a specific political objective, even though such sentiments had been encouraged by the British during the First World War. Once the war was over, the Colonial Office and Foreign Ministry quickly and conveniently forgot promises of self-government to the Kurds and Arabs. In

Iraq, during the four major rebellions in the fourteen years of the British mandate, the British applied air control and military force to deal with the symptoms of the problem. By treating the symptoms (rebellion), the British failed to seriously look at the primary cause of the conflicts — the politically unsatisfactory arrangement of the Kurds under the Iraqi government.

The French took an approach to airpower and colonial operations that was different from that of the British. British historian David Omissi notes the French were more ruthless in their air operations and normally bombed rebel villages with no warning and with the intent of inflicting heavy civilian casualties.[123] Yet it should also be noted that the French faced conflicts in Morocco and Syria that were basically conventional wars and used their airpower accordingly. The Italian and Spanish use of airpower in colonial conflict was notable only for their utterly ruthless approach in bombing rebel civilians and using poison gas.

Lessons Learned and Not Learned

The colonial wars gave the British and French extensive experience in using air forces in combat operations. The British became fairly adept in coordinating air and ground forces while fighting rebels. French airmen in Morocco showed a good deal of innovation in creating the first specialized medevac units, which saved the lives of many French soldiers. On the other hand, while the French air doctrine stressed the supporting role of aviation for the ground forces in conventional war, it is surprising that the French air/ground coordination was less effective than the British and that little was done to learn some basic lessons and improve this deficiency.

There seems to have been little carryover from the colonial experience into the conventional war doctrines of the British and French air forces. While the British air/ground coordination was effective in the colonies, the RAF notably failed to apply this experience to conventional war doctrine. In the early years of World War II, the RAF did not possess an effective doctrine for close support of the ground troops and, prior to 1942, performed very poorly in this mission. It was much the same in the case of bombing techniques. RAF bombing accuracy in colonial operations was generally poor. Yet this very obvious deficiency illustrated by the colonial operations gained little attention from the RAF leaders. Little was done to improve bombing accuracy prior to World War II, and the inability to accurately bomb German targets plagued the RAF from 1939 to 1942.[124] The colonial operations also illustrated the importance of aerial transport. In colonial operations the European air forces repeatedly improvised air transport forces to rapidly deploy troops, supplies, and air units and provide logistics across great distances. The application of military transport to conventional war ought to have been clear. However, at the outbreak of World War II, neither the French air force nor the RAF possessed a specialized air transport force. In short, while air control was very effective in protecting the RAF's force structure and budget in the interwar period, there was no real interest in learning any lessons that might apply to a serious conventional war.

One of the lessons that might have been learned in the colonial operations is that populations adjust to aerial bombardment. The very first cases of air control such as Somaliland in 1920 seemed to work very well. Aerial bombardment was a novelty and the effect was impressive. However, as the British continued to use air control methods on the frontiers of the empire, the psychological effect largely wore off. Many of the hostile tribes in Aden, on India's Northwest Frontier, and in Kurdistan learned to camouflage their camps and dig air raid shelters for their villages. Tribes in Kurdistan set up a primitive warning system with observers and smoke signals to warn the most likely targets of the approach of British aircraft.[125] In the later campaigns against the Kurdish leader Sheik Mahmud, the rebel capital and center of operations was heavily bombed for months. Yet the rebels still fought on. The Arabs fighting the British in Palestine in the 1930s were not overawed by the RAF's airpower capability. Indeed, the revolt in Palestine was ended not through military force but through a political deal and British compromise that limited Jewish immigration.

The French and Spanish might have learned in the Rif War that the will of the rebel civilians did not break, even under heavy and sustained bombardment of their towns and villages. Indeed, against a determined enemy fighting for a national cause, airpower seems to have had the effect of often strengthening the enemy's will to resist. However, such conclusions drawn from combat experience were not likely to go over well with European air force leaders who were often enamored of the theories of the Italian air war theorist General Giulio Douhet, who argued that aerial bombing would easily break the will of an enemy nation.

Misusing History

The idea of occupying and pacifying a country by airpower alone, or with the air force as the primary force employed, is attractive to airmen. In America, the concept of air control supports the idea that the U.S. Air Force (USAF) ought to be the primary military service of the United States. During the last fifteen years when the United States has found itself involved in various peace-keeping and peace enforcement operations as well as a variety of small wars, American air force officers and airpower theorists have looked at the RAF model of air control as a useful doctrinal guide for current operations.[126] Indeed, the idea of controlling a country by airpower, with few or no ground troops involved, has excited the interest of the USAF among such influential airpower theorists as Carl Builder.[127] The low cost of the air control is an especially attractive feature of the operation. Another positive feature is that aerial policing does not put U.S. soldiers at risk. It is a good doctrine for casualty avoidance.

However, the air control model held up by some American airmen as a doctrinal model is not grounded in solid history but in a romanticized, and false, picture of the reality of colonial air control.[128] First, as already noted, airpower alone worked effectively only in the most minor kinds of tribal police operations. For all but the smallest operations a considerable number of ground troops were used in keeping peace in the colonies. In their enthusiasm for an "airpower alone" solution, some airpower theorists have failed to mention the contribution of ground forces. For example, American airpower theorist Robert Pape uses the example of the RAF deployment to northern Iraq in 1924 as an example of how air forces can successfully coerce a nation. Pape points out that the Turks had made incursions into Kurdistan and had large ground forces on the border in an attempt to exert control in the Mosul region. The incursions were met with a forward deployment of RAF squadrons and a few bombing raids to demonstrate British will, and the British made it clear that if the Turks tried to cross the border in force, RAF attacks could have seriously hindered Turkish operations. Pape argues that airpower coercion worked and the Turks withdrew all forces from the border in October 1924.[129] What Pape does not mention is that the army also deployed two brigade task forces (six battalions, two artillery batteries, one engineer company, and one machine-gun company) north of Mosul at the same time.[130] Although airpower proved to be an effective force multiplier in the colonial operations of Britain and other nations, all the major operations of the era can be best described as joint operations rather than airpower operations. In short, the history of air control in the interwar period offers little support to the idea of conducting police/peacekeeping operations with airpower as the single or predominant force.

RAF planes bombing Chabaish Village, northern Iraq, December 1924. The RAF regularly bombed Kurdish strongholds during the rebellions of the 1920s. (RAF Historical Branch, Crown copyright)

RAF DH-9 modified for medical evacuation in Somaliland campaign. The effectiveness of the RAF "Z Force" operations of 1919 convinced the British government that air control could work in the colonies. (RAF Historical Branch, Crown copyright)

RAF DH-9s in Waziristan, Northwest Frontier of India, 1925. RAF squadrons posted to the Northwest Frontier saw almost constant action against bandits, tribal rebellions, and Afghan raiders from 1919 to 1939. (RAF Historical Branch, Crown copyright)

Bristol Fighter of the RAF's No. 20 Squadron over the Northwest Frontier, 1925. (RAF Historical Branch, Crown copyright)

RAF "Z Force" DH-9 light bomber modified for medical evacuation. Somaliland, 1919. (RAF Historical Branch, Crown copyright)

Tuareg chiefs visiting an Italian air force Caproni heavy bomber squadron in Tripoli, Libya, 1922. Bombers such as these were used with devastating effectiveness in the Italian colonial campaigns. (Italian air force archives)

Eritrean infantry Askaris (Italian colonial troops) with a Caproni bomber and crew. Tripoli, Libya, 1922. (Italian air force archives)

Italian light reconnaissance plane loaded with food supplies for the besieged town of Azizia, 1921. Aircraft transporting food and ammunition kept the garrison from being overrun during one of the colonial rebellions. This was one of the first air supply operations in history. (Italian air force archives)

Italian pilots and an RO-1 aircraft, ready to take off, North Africa, 1924. The sturdy two-seat RO-1 reconnaissance/light bomber aircraft was the workhorse of the Italian colonial air campaigns of the 1920s — much like the British DH-9. (Italian air force archives)

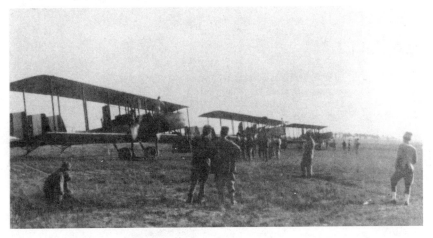

Italian air force Caproni bomber squadron waiting to take off for a bombing mission, Libya, 1925. (Italian air force archives)

RAF Vickers Victoria bomber over Egypt, circa early 1930s. (RAF Historical Branch, Crown copyright)

RAF Vimy bombers over Egypt, late 1920s. (RAF Historical Branch, Crown copyright)

3

The Greek Civil War and
the Philippine Anti-Huk Campaign

In the immediate aftermath of World War II, revolutionary armed struggle thrust itself onto center stage. Two of the earliest postwar conflicts involving the use of airpower in combating communist insurgents occurred in Greece and the Philippines. In both cases the counterinsurgency campaigns were mostly land operations, but airpower played an important role in each. In Greece, for example, Greek ground forces bore the brunt of the fight for almost two years before the Royal Hellenic Air Force even played a role. But after 1948, particularly following the advent of American advice and assistance, airpower was instrumental if not decisive in bringing an end to the conflict. The Philippine air force supported the government's counterinsurgency effort against the Huks almost from the very beginning, but the extent to which it proved instrumental in defeating the Huks remains open to question. For one thing very little has been written about the contribution of airpower in defeating the Huks. But what little has been written would indicate that the role of airpower in the Philippines between 1946 and 1956 was significant if largely unheralded.

The Greek Civil War, 1943–1949

ORIGINS OF THE CIVIL WAR

Roughly the size of Alabama, Greece has been subjected to foreign penetration of its internal affairs for centuries, providing part of the backdrop for the emergence of the Greek Civil War following World War II. At the end of the war, the mainland neighbors of Greece included Albania in the west, Yugoslavia and Bulgaria in the north, and Turkey in the east. Three of these

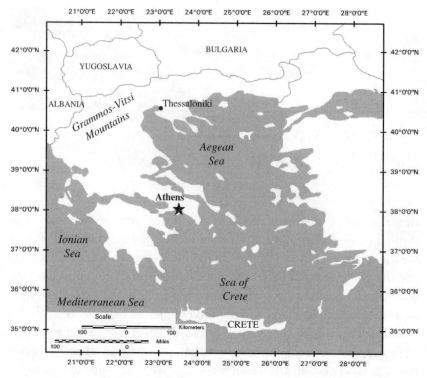

The Greek Civil War, 1943–1949

states were communist when open civil war erupted in Greece in 1947, two of which provided direct support to the communist insurgents. But Greece has had a history of irregular warfare since at least the suzerainty of the Ottoman Turks, when the rugged countryside proved ideal for the mostly criminally inspired guerrillas known as Klefts. Interestingly, intervention by outside powers during Ottoman rule was often welcomed by the Greeks so long as it served local interests or Greek irredentist sentiments. But overt intervention and occupation, such as the Axis occupation from 1941 to 1944, and the subsequent British occupation, invariably provoked armed resistance rooted in the countryside. The task of suppressing such resistance was formidable. At the outbreak of World War II, 40 percent of the population of Greece lived in the mountains that cover two-thirds of mainland Greece. The remainder of the population was concentrated in the cities, with about one-fifth of the population living in the Athens-Piraneus area alone. Aside from the topography, the internal strife that has characterized Greek politics since before World War II made intervention risky to say the least.

Beginning in the nineteenth century, Greek politics have been volatile and dominated by individuals as much as ideologies. Shortly after gaining its independence from the Ottoman Empire in 1832, Greece adopted a constitutional monarchy with an elected chamber, or *voule*. But various factions consistently vied for political ascendancy. A military revolt in 1909 led to a prolonged period of strife dominated by Eleutherios Venizelos, who founded the Liberal Party in 1912. Until Venizelos's death in 1936, Greek politics were polarized in a "national schism" between anti-Royalist *Venizelism,* otherwise known as republicanism or liberalism, and *anti-Venizelism,* or royalism. During World War I the Republicans supported Great Britain, but King Constantine and the Royalists backed Germany. With German fortunes in decline, the king abdicated the throne in 1917. But three years later, Royalist officers engineered a plebiscite that reinstated the king. In 1922 a Liberal coup d'état forced Constantine's son, George II, to abdicate, whereupon the Royalist officers who had brought about his father's return were tried and executed, bringing about a republic in 1924. The republic lasted only a year before another Royalist coup installed the prime minister as president. The Liberals attempted yet another coup, but this one was equally short-lived and the Royalists returned George II to the throne. Shortly afterward, General Ioannes Metaxas, a former chief of staff of the army, rose to become prime minister. Convinced that the Greek Communist Party (KKE) posed the principal threat, Metaxas persuaded the king to suspend the constitution, dissolve the chamber, and impose martial law.[1] Thereafter, Metaxas assumed dictatorial powers and exercised an iron-fisted rule shaped by his training at the Kriegsakademie in Berlin.

Although sympathetic to the anticommunism of Hitler and Mussolini, Metaxas was nonetheless an ardent nationalist, and he led a spirited defense against the surprise Italian invasion of Greece in October 1940. But Metaxas died in January 1941, and despite British military assistance, his regime collapsed when Hitler attacked Greece on 6 April 1941 to rescue Mussolini's failed invasion. With the defeat and expulsion of the British, the Germans and Italians occupied Greece. A Royalist Greek government in exile was established in Cairo. But the Royalists were less concerned with resistance to the Germans than with preparing to suppress communist and other leftist elements upon the anticipated liberation of Greece. In fact the major Royalist resistance organization, the National Republican Greek League (EDES), collaborated with Greek "security battalions" raised by the Germans to hunt down members of the principal leftist resistance movement, the National Liberation Front (EAM), and its armed component, the National Popular Liberation Army (ELAS).

The brutal Axis occupation of Greece, which included a major famine between 1941 and 1942, spurred the KKE to establish the EAM and the ELAS.[2] Immensely popular, the EAM was a coalition of various patriotic and socialist parties and organizations, but excluded Royalists and "Metaxists." By late 1944, the EAM comprised over 1 million of Greece's 7.5 million inhabitants and fielded armed "bands" totaling some 50,000 guerrillas.[3] The communist-led ELAS operated outside Athens in three principal areas: the mountainous regions of Thessaly, Roumeli, and Macedonia. Early in the war, ELAS guerrillas used arms abandoned by the Greek army, but having proved to be the most effective organization fighting against the Germans, they also received arms and ammunition from the Allies. The anticommunist EDES operated primarily in Epirus, in northwest Greece. In 1942 the British took an active interest in supporting the resistance movement in Greece, and in October the first British commandos were parachuted into the country near Stromni in ELAS territory. More British operatives arrived and were organized as the British Military Mission, later the Allied Military Mission when Americans were added. The British had little success gaining the cooperation of ELAS bands but did succeed in persuading EDES units to cooperate. Thus, despite a common enemy, the prewar factional strife that had characterized Greek politics before the war continued under Axis occupation.

In retrospect, the Axis occupation created a political dynamic in Greece in which resistance to the Germans and Italians mixed with internal political competition and strife:

The German invasion and the occupation had discredited completely the traditional political forces. . . . The resistance against the occupiers became an outlet for other political forces, the natural and peaceful development of which had been checked by the Metaxas regime. . . . Meanwhile broad strata of the population . . . were now becoming active and politically aware in the absence of a legitimate central authority. The resistance movement offered itself as a natural outlet for the spontaneous attempts to fill the vacuum created by the break-down of the organized state. . . . The dual nature of the resistance was publicly expressed in demands by the National Liberation Front both for liberation and for free decision about the future constitution of Greece.[4]

In that regard, the communists were far better organized than their competitors in this dynamic arena. With Allied liberation within view, the communists began to make more strenuous bids to assume absolute power in Greece, thus precipitating civil war.

The Greek Civil War is commonly divided into three phases, the first beginning in 1943 and lasting until 1944, when the various guerrilla movements fought one another as much as they fought against the Germans. The second phase occurred in Athens in 1944 following the German withdrawal, when an uprising by the communists was put down by British troops. The third phase began in 1946, when open fighting erupted between communist forces and the postwar Greek government, and lasted until communist forces were defeated by the Greek National Army in 1949.

The first phase of the civil war began about the same time that the Italians surrendered in 1943. Believing they held the initiative, the communist ELAS reorganized itself. Territorial commands became "divisions," and guerrilla "bands" became battalions, which were then grouped into regiments that made up the divisions. As ELAS units disarmed the Italians, they immediately attacked EDES strongholds. The Germans initially declined to intervene in the hopes that the two principal resistance movements might destroy one another. For their part, the British supported the EDES, wishing to forestall communist ascendancy following the war.[5] But having lulled the two guerrilla movements into a false sense of security, the Germans mounted a surprise counterguerrilla offensive in which the ELAS and EDES were both severely damaged. Having recovered somewhat in January 1944, however, the ELAS resumed its attacks on the EDES. But neither side could overcome the other, and an armistice was agreed upon in anticipation of Allied victory in Europe. By the end of German occupation, the ELAS was clearly dominant, fielding some thirty thousand guerrillas to less than six thousand in the EDES.[6]

In May 1944 a Greek coalition government, including the communists, was formed in Beirut, Lebanon, to facilitate the restoration of Greek authority upon the departure of the Germans. The Germans began their evacuation of Greece the following September and by 12 October had abandoned Athens. Fearing a Soviet advance into Greece, British troops diverted from the Italian campaign occupied the Peloponnese and then Athens on 14 October. By early November the Germans had withdrawn north of Salonika and Florina and by the end of the month had left the Greek mainland altogether. During the German withdrawal, fighting between ELAS units and the collaborationist Security Battalions was fierce, with the ELAS gaining almost complete control of the Greek countryside by the end of the war. As a result, the fragile agreement between the communists and the other Greek factions that had been crafted in May survived only a few weeks after the German occupation ended.

The Republican leader of the coalition government, George Papandreou, wanted to form a new Greek army around two units that had served under the British during World War II, the Mountain Brigade and the Sacred Battalion — both of which were staunchly anticommunist. Not surprisingly, the communists wanted these units demobilized.[7] EAM ministers of the Papandreou government then proposed that the two units be merged with ELAS and EDES units of equivalent strength. But attempts at compromise failed and the EAM ministers resigned in protest. The EAM called for a general strike and violence broke out when police fired on the demonstrators. Subsequent ELAS attacks on police stations and the massing of ELAS main forces outside Athens prompted the British to intervene directly.

At the outset of armed hostilities, British and Greek government forces were greatly outnumbered and found themselves besieged in the center of Athens. But the British forces held out, and with the arrival of overwhelming British reinforcements, the ELAS withdrew into the countryside, leaving behind small cells of agitators and terror squads. By December 1944 the British had rushed two divisions, a brigade, and several battalions to Athens, and by January 1945 there were over seventy-five thousand British troops in Greece.[8] In control of the countryside but losing the battle of Athens, and facing overwhelming British superiority, the communists agreed to disband and signed the Varkiza agreement in February 1945. But the Greek government reneged on many of the promises made in the Varkiza agreement. Soon afterward, the EAM went underground, and ELAS forces retreated to the mountains in northern Greece where they renamed themselves the Greek Democratic Army (GDA). The GDA immediately declared war on the central government and were soon assisted in the ensuing military struggle by the new communist regimes in Albania, Bulgaria, and Yugoslavia.

OPEN CIVIL WAR

The third phase, which is generally regarded as the civil war proper, had no clear beginning but can be thought of as having commenced on 30 March

1946 when communist guerrillas attacked a Greek military and police garrison at Litokhoro, on the eastern slope of Mount Olympus.[9] In the months that followed, the guerrillas stepped up their attacks on isolated villages throughout the countryside. "The guerrilla tactics were simple but effective: concentration of forces against an exposed village; attack; destruction of the [police] station; forcible recruitment of young villagers; pillaging of foodstuffs and then retreat to the mountain hideouts."[10] In the beginning, the Greek government and its British advisers considered the guerrilla activity to be primarily a police matter, but as village police posts began to fall with alarming regularity, the Greek National Army (GNA) took on the principal role of pacifying the countryside. Although the British Military Mission was initially instructed to avoid direct involvement in field operations, by July 1946 they were authorized to actively assist Greek security forces if these units faced likely defeat at the hands of the GDA, or if British citizens were threatened. But even then British officers were instructed to use only the minimum force necessary.

Throughout the summer of 1946, the British trained GNA forces for internal security. One of the more important innovations developed by the British linked "commando" operations with airpower. Undoubtedly inspired by British experience in World War II, especially in Southeast Asia, commando companies were raised to conduct long-range and long-duration deep-penetration patrols, "with the object of locating [a guerrilla band] . . . keeping it under observation, and containing it until the nearest army formation [could] be called upon to attack it."[11] These commando operations were to be resupplied by air and, using their enhanced mobility, would act as the eyes of the larger regular army formations. By December 1946 the British Military Mission recommended "major intelligence-based, air-supported offensives by 'highly mobile infantry . . . mountain artillery and recce units,' including Commandos."[12] But until the commando units could be raised, the British concentrated on training and organization of regular GNA formations, and static defense of villages and garrisons remained the principal GNA strategy for countering the ELA.

The decidedly conventional and defensive mentality of Greek military officers in general came in for severe criticism by the British:

When attacked a commander is usually satisfied if the bandits are repulsed. It does not seem to be realised that a band which attacks or merely opens fire on a defended locality provides the GNA with a valuable chance of destroying it. One defensive lay-out which was inspected bore a marked similarity to dispositions common in 1915–1917. Troops were entrenched in a long continuous line behind barbed wire. There was no mobile reserve and little patrolling beyond the wire. A feature within sight of the position was said to be held by the bandits but it was admitted that no patrol had been there. This form of defense bears no relation to the requirements of anti-bandit warfare and merely tends to crush the natural vigor and offensive spirit of the Greek soldier.[13]

Thus, while the GNA remained tied down in static defense, the communist guerrillas capitalized on their ability to move quickly and concentrate their forces to achieve local superiority over the garrisons.

In August 1946, the KKE under the leadership of Nikos Zachariades instructed Markos Vapheiades, the top military commander in the ELAS, to set up a headquarters in the mountains to coordinate the insurgency. In September the guerrillas declared "Free Greece" in large areas of northern Thessaly and western Macedonia. Guerrilla forces continued to grow in strength, and in October Vapheiades established a military command for all of mainland Greece. In early 1946, insurgent strength was approximately twenty-five hundred. By the end of the year, the number had risen to eight thousand active fighters. By the end of 1947, the GDA fielded over eighteen thousand guerrillas. At its peak, the GDA boasted some twenty-five thousand guerrillas in the field.[14] Early in the civil war the GDA was ill-equipped, with weapons left over from the prewar Greek army and those seized from government forces after the war. However, beginning in 1947, Yugoslavia, Albania, and Bulgaria began to ship large quantities of arms and equipment to the Greek communists, much of it captured from the Germans. Antiaircraft weapons were included in these shipments and reportedly accounted for fifty-four government aircraft shot down.[15]

The GNA pacification effort involved a three-stage clear-and-hold strategy. In the first stage, army units would be reorganized and trained for internal security duties. The second phase would involve huge encirclement and clearing actions involving armor and artillery, as well as the relocation of civilian populations. A consolidation phase would follow when a corps area was considered "clear," and civil control would be reinstated. The army's first major effort employing this strategy was launched in April 1947. The objective was to clear the guerrillas from central Greece, then sweep gradually northward to the frontier. Guerrilla units would be surrounded, isolated, and destroyed. But the GNA was incapable of fulfilling such an ambitious plan and the initial thrust failed. Another attempt was made in April 1948, but the guerrillas consistently escaped. The 1948 campaign culminated in a battle for the Grammos Mountains in June. During that battle, some fifteen thousand guerrillas held off over fifty thousand government troops for over two months. The guerrillas withdrew to Albania but later reappeared in the Vitsi area to the northeast. An attack on the guerrillas there failed, and by midwinter the guerrillas had reestablished themselves in the Grammos area as well.

The failure of the GNA to destroy the guerrillas can be attributed to systemic problems within the GNA itself. The army had effectively ceased to exist with Axis occupation, and reconstruction after the war was fitful. The professional officer corps had dissipated during the war, and the GNA was also desperately short of experienced noncommissioned officers. To make matters worse, the soldiers were mostly prewar reservists recalled to active service. Many of the soldiers were communist sympathizers, and morale in the GNA was very low. Training suffered due to lack of equipment and qualified instructors. For two years beginning in 1946, recruits were given instruction in only the most basic of skills. Tactical training, when it occurred at all, concentrated on conventional war fighting and not on the unique requirements of a counterguerrilla campaign. Political interference also weakened the army, as promotions of officers were due more to political favoritism than competence in the field. All of these deficiencies became painfully evident in the clear-and-hold campaigns of 1947 and 1948. GNA units often refused to fight at night and avoided close combat when possible, preferring to rely on artillery and close air support provided by the Greek air force.

But the Royal Hellenic Air Force (RHAF) was equally ill-prepared for its role in combating the communist guerrillas. According to one British memorandum:

[The] RHAF is the Cinderella of the Greek Fighting Services, neither the Government nor general public being greatly interested in it. In particular, the senior officers of the GNA and [Royal Hellenic Navy] greatly out-rank their opposite numbers in the RHAF. As the Greeks are a very rank-conscious nation, this does not make for good inter-service co-operation and the operations of the RHAF suffer accordingly. Despite the successes of the RHAF, the GNA does not treat it as an equal partner, and tends to plan operations without air advice. . . . Similarly, the RHAF gets little or no public credit for the part it played in anti-bandit operations, which are reported as almost entirely an affair of the GNA.[16]

The RHAF suffered from equipment shortages, inexperienced crews, and aircraft inappropriate to the task of counterinsurgency warfare. For example, Supermarine Spitfires, originally designed as interceptors, were used in the ground attack role. Nevertheless, the RHAF used these aircraft extensively, beginning in March 1947. By October 1948, the RHAF was able to field only twenty-one Harvard trainers used for reconnaissance, the Spitfires, and sixteen C-47 Dakota transports.[17]

In January 1947, for reasons that are not entirely clear, the British Military Mission returned to its original policy prohibiting British soldiers from active participation in GNA field operations. "Thereafter, the Mission . . . gradually 'lost touch with the operational situation.'"[18] Fortunately for the Greek government, however, the United States began to take an active interest in the communist threat in Greece. With the promulgation of the Truman Doctrine in March 1947, American aid and advisers began to flow into the country. Gradually, the American Military Aid Group took on the greater share of advising and assisting the Greek military, although the British Mission remained influential to the end of the conflict.

Interestingly, as the British role began to wane, they began to stress airpower in countering the insurgency. Specifically, the British chiefs of staff in London assessed the Greek counterinsurgency effort and concluded that, were the United Kingdom faced with the same problem, Britain would "base ops on the maximum use of airpower" in support of the army. As British counterinsurgency efforts stressing the contribution of airpower would later prove in Malaya, this represented "a significant shift in high-level British thinking about counter-guerrilla warfare. . . . Notwithstanding the fact that it would take several years for this to filter through the Army as a whole . . . the Greek experience helped lay the foundation for a new British approach to counter-guerrilla war."[19]

Regardless, American advisers now had the lead role and moved quickly to improve the effectiveness of the GNA as a fighting force. In a relatively short period of time the GNA was retrained and its strategy and tactics reworked. The arrival of American advisers and American money had several salutary effects. One early effect was a heightened sense of optimism.

Whereas the British Mission had resigned itself largely to training, organization, and logistics in garrison, the Americans planned and participated in operations at the division level. Moreover, owing to American insistence, political influence regarding field operations and the promotion of Greek officers was dramatically reduced. The GNA also doubled in size, reaching 148,000 soldiers in 1948. The special commando units promoted by the British and known by the Greek acronym LOK came into their own during this period and often shouldered the burden of the fighting. As American money built up the army, the Greek government used the savings accrued to the national treasury to pursue developmental initiatives that undercut popular support for the KKE.

As Greek officers and soldiers gained experience and confidence, Marshal Alexander Papagos was named supreme commander of the Greek armed forces. Papagos had been chief of staff under Metaxis. He demonstrated unswerving loyalty to the monarchy and was instrumental in the restoration of the monarchy in 1935. Arrested by the Germans during World War II, he had spent the war years in a prisoner of war camp. Papagos owed his appointment as supreme commander after the war in large part to American secretary of state George Marshall who, after visiting Athens in October 1948, came away with the distinct impression that no amount of American counterinsurgency aid could defeat the guerrillas without effective indigenous leadership. For Marshall, Papagos was the clear choice, and he was named commander in chief in January 1949.

A major change in strategy evolved under Papagos, a "strategy of staggered expansion of control."[20] Unproductive sweeps were discontinued as well as "spasmodic" countermeasures to communist initiatives. Instead, the GNA worked to systematically dominate the terrain in well-defined areas. A target area would be selected, and regular and special counterguerrilla forces would apply relentless pressure on the underground political and logistical apparatus in that sector. When complete, another area would be selected and the process repeated. These areas would then be linked as the progressive plan unfolded. Population relocation played a pivotal role in this strategy in order to eliminate support for the guerrillas. Whole populations were uprooted as a result. It was an enormously expensive effort, with over eight hundred thousand villagers removed from their homes, but it proved useful in drying up intelligence as well as logistical and moral support for the guerrillas.[21]

Under Papagos, the combat forces of the GNA comprised infantry, artillery, armored reconnaissance, tanks, and engineers. Six distinct types of infantry were used: mountain, field, commando, National Defense Corps, gendarmerie, and armed civilian self-defense forces. Mountain divisions were generally reinforced with a squadron of cavalry, additional machine guns, engineers, and mountain artillery. Mountain, field, and commando forces conducted the majority of maneuver operations in the field. National Defense Corps troops, raised locally and under GNA control, were used in static defense of towns and villages. The gendarmerie was an armed force under the control of the Ministry of Justice and operated outside the limits of towns having their own municipal police forces. Finally, local self-defense units were raised in the towns and villages with arms provided by the government.

By mid-1949, there were some 150,000 troops in the regular army; 50,000 in the National Defense Corps; 25,000 in the gendarmerie; 7,500 in the civil police; and approximately 50,000 in village self-defense units.[22] At its peak, the GNA boasted over 170,000 soldiers.[23] With police and self-defense forces shouldering the burden of static defense, the regular army was free to pursue the guerrillas.

While government forces were growing in strength and improving in quality, the guerrilla forces began to suffer in both categories. Population relocation and government pressure effectively depleted the recruit base and began to exhaust the guerrillas' stocks of war material. Throughout the war the GDA consisted almost exclusively of light infantry. These troops were armed mostly with light weapons of a variety of types. Ammunition and food became key logistical requirements and the greatest logistical weakness of the GDA. Ill-equipped and heavily dependent upon long lines of communications to supply depots in northern Greece, the GDA could not sustain prolonged combat operations. Nevertheless, despite these grave deficiencies, the GDA attempted to hold ground in 1948.

By the late summer of 1948, the communists had split into two factions. This fracture was the culmination of a long dispute over the strategic character of the insurgency. On the one hand were those who insisted that protracted guerrilla war could weaken the government, but only direct military intervention by a neighboring communist state could bring the revolution to a successful conclusion. In opposition were those who believed that the guerrilla forces themselves could be "regularized," as Mao had done in China, and the government overthrown by conventional defeat of the Greek armed forces. Markos Vapheiades sided with the former view, but Zachariades believed that foreign communist intervention was unrealistic and therefore supported the idea that the guerrillas could be converted to a conventional fighting force. In the end, Zachariades prevailed over Markos, who was relieved of command. Shortly afterward, the GDA shifted its strategy to positional warfare, intending to defeat the Greek army in battle.

The decision to transform the guerrilla bands into a conventional force was a major strategic error. Nevertheless, by the end of 1948 the GDA had formed eight divisions, controlling some twenty-three brigades, forty-two battalions, and over forty company-sized formations. But as one observer later pointed out, "The gathering of light infantry into nominal 'divisions' did not make them divisions in the sense of a force of combined arms. No supporting arms were added. The available forces were simply gathered into larger formations."[24] In other words the GDA was a regular army in name only.

Problems of manpower and logistics for the communists became magnified by positional warfare. Attempting to seize and hold ground, the GDA took heavy losses in men and material. Moreover, whereas in previous years the guerrillas had used the winter months to withdraw to their northern sanctuaries to rest and refit, in the early winter of 1949 the GDA stood its ground and heavy casualties were the result. Within a short time, casualties began to exceed recruits and mounting losses reduced manpower levels to their lowest level since October 1947. And whereas early in the war the guerrillas were able to replenish their losses, sometimes effectively replacing the entire force, this was no longer the case. The GDA thus found itself in a perilous position, exemplified by the fact that the proportion of female guerrillas rose from 30 percent in some units to over 50 percent.[25]

The summer of 1948 marked another development that spelled the beginning of the end for the GDA: the communist Yugoslavian government closed the Yugoslav-Greek frontier and discontinued assistance to the Greek communists. In addition to favoring protracted guerrilla warfare, the faction to which Markos Vapheiades had belonged was also pro-Tito in its revolutionary outlook. These "Titoists" were regarded as "reactionary" and "deviationist" by the dominant Stalinist element, Zachariades among them. Consequently, with the ascendancy of Zachariades as head of the party and the GDA, the Greek communists effectively signaled an anti-Tito posture.

It was only a matter of time before Tito perceived the danger to his own regime in continuing to assist the Greek communists in their bid to seize power. Thus, following his own break with the Cominform in July 1948, and in keeping with his more accommodationist posture toward the West, Tito closed the frontier and cut off aid to the GDA. By January 1949 supplies from Yugoslavia were reduced to a trickle. The Cominform attempted to recoup this loss by stepping up assistance through Albania and Bulgaria, but Yugoslavia was the linchpin to insurgent success, and with the loss of Tito's support the logistical base for the GDA became untenable. With mounting losses, the GDA withdrew its forces from the southern mainland and the Peloponnese until guerrilla activity in the latter area collapsed altogether. Central Greece was cleared by government forces during the spring and early summer of 1949. By July 1949 the GNA was ready to undertake "Operation Torch," intended to destroy the fortified northern strongholds of the GDA in the Vitsi and Grammos regions.

The Vitsi is a mountainous area of 375 square miles bounded on the north by Yugoslavia and on the west by Albania. It is marked by two main mountain ranges separated by the Livadhopotamos River. With no threat to their north and west, the GDA strongly fortified the south and east with approximately seventy-five hundred troops. Avenues of approach were mined and covered by machine guns, mortars, and artillery. The government assault got under way with air attacks, artillery bombardment, and small-scale probes by ground forces. By 9 August the Ninth Division of "B" Corps had concentrated in the Oinóï area in southwest Vitsi. The Third Commando Division and the Tenth Division were concentrated around Bikovik. The Second and Eleventh Divisions were concentrated in the Florina area. A separate task force, including elements of the Twenty-second Brigade of the Second Division, attacked communist positions on the morning of 10 August. Resistance was heavy, but government forces made good headway and, spearheaded by the Third Commando Division, struck at the center of GDA defenses in a night attack that took them completely by surprise. A gap of some six miles was created in the GDA lines, and the communists quit the field and withdrew to the west. Government forces pursued the retreating communist forces, and by 13 August withdrawal had turned into a rout. In their hasty retreat from Vitsi, GDA forces abandoned all of their heavy equipment and supplies. Of the six guerrilla brigades originally defending the area, only one was able to withdraw completely into Albania. Two brigades were completely wiped out, and the remainder was badly mauled.[26]

Government forces immediately shifted to the Grammos area. Remnants of four GDA brigades had entered the area on 15 August after having withdrawn from Vitsi. Their strength amounted to only about one thousand fighters, and two of the brigades were merged to form a single battalion. These forces joined some five thousand guerrillas already entrenched in a strong defensive position over a two-hundred-square-mile area of the Grammos mountain range. On 24 August government forces opened the battle with intense artillery fire and air attacks by eighteen American-supplied Helldiver dive-bombers and twelve Spitfires. The GNA "A" Corps attacked in two phases. The first phase was conducted by elements of the First, Ninth, and Fifteenth Divisions, plus the Third Commando Division, intended to clear the northern Grammos. At the same time, the Eighth Division and the Seventy-seventh Brigade exerted pressure all along the remainder of the front. During the second phase, the Eighth Division and Seventy-seventh Brigade closed on the Grammos while elements of the Third Commando Division struck at the principal corps objective: the Grammos-Skertsa-Kiafa mountain range to the southwest. Once again the communists put up stiff resistance and progress was slow. Nevertheless, the GNA advance secured its first objective — the Tsarno Ridge — by 26 August. The GDA counterattacked but was repulsed and began a general withdrawal. On the night of 27 August, GDA resistance collapsed and communist forces withdrew in disorder. By 29 August, government forces occupied most of the Grammos, and GDA units quit the field altogether by 30 August.[27] The Grammos area was completely secured, and for all intents and purposes the Greek Civil War had come to an end.

THE ROLE OF AIRPOWER IN DEFEATING THE COMMUNIST GDA

The Greek Civil War was primarily a ground war, but at least one observer has described the RHAF contribution as having been of "decisive importance."[28] Whether and to what extent this is true is open to debate. However, one American participant reported that the RHAF inflicted over half of guerrilla casualties between 1947 and 1948 alone.[29] During the major campaigns in Vitsi and Grammos in 1949, air attacks invariably preceded the ground assault, and GNA troops were aided throughout each campaign by ground attack aircraft in close support. On 10 August 1949, the first day of Operation

Torch, the RHAF flew 169 sorties, more than at any previous time. The average daily sortie rate during the Vitsi operation was 126 missions. During the Grammos campaign, from 24 to 29 August, the RHAF flew 826 attack sorties.[30] Communist casualties during the course of the war might have been even greater had the RHAF not been neglected early in the conflict. Moreover, as the British themselves concluded in 1948, had the RHAF been properly equipped and employed earlier, the insurgency might itself have been defeated sooner.

The GNA received little assistance from the RHAF at the outset of the civil war because the RHAF was unable to provide any. Following the German invasion in 1941, the RHAF collapsed. Only a handful of Greek airmen made their way to Egypt to form the Hellenic Bomber Squadron, employed by the British Royal Air Force (RAF) in long-range patrols over the Mediterranean. At the end of the war, Greek airmen remained under the operational control of the RAF until 1946, when the few available air units were handed over to the Greek government. At the time, the RHAF possessed only 58 obsolete aircraft and just under three hundred experienced pilots. Facing a burgeoning insurgency, the Greek government requested 250 war-surplus aircraft from Great Britain. These aircraft were delivered in the summer of 1947 and included Wellington bombers, Spitfires, C-47 Dakota transports, Anson transports, and light liaison aircraft.[31] The Wellingtons proved to be wholly unsuitable to operations against the insurgents and were grounded not long after their arrival. In their stead, C-47 transports were converted into makeshift bombers and used extensively for that purpose.[32] By the middle of 1947 the RHAF comprised some five thousand officers and men, of which four hundred were flying personnel, and included two Spitfire squadrons, one liaison squadron flying Harvard trainers, Austers, and L-5 Sentinels, one transport squadron of Dakotas and Ansons, a refresher flight of Spitfires, and other assorted types. Training of crews was conducted by the RAF delegation of the British Military Mission, consisting of 15 officers and 130 men.[33]

The potential contribution of airpower was underestimated in the beginning. Moreover, the few experienced crews that existed had performed mostly reconnaissance missions against a conventional opponent during World War II. But during the guerrilla phase of the Greek Civil War, these "pilots were not looking for tanks, artillery or vehicles, or for fairly large bodies of infantry, but for small parties of men, occasionally accompanied by a few mules."[34] The guerrillas operated mostly in mountainous terrain long distances from the nearest RHAF airfields. As a result, RHAF aircraft often reached the scene of fighting too late. As a result, the RHAF remained at best a junior partner in the conflict. The RHAF was not permitted to act independently, and offensive air action was used only to support GNA forces in actual contact with guerrilla formations. "Thus, the activity of the RHAF was tied to that of the GNA, and in areas where the latter was not operating offensively, air operations [came] practically to a standstill."[35] In short, Greek army commanders squandered what little airpower they had at their disposal. As one RHAF report noted:

The Commands often reported that they were in close contact with the enemy and up against strong resistance — whereas this was not the case. The result was that Airforce [sic] support took off prematurely and was over the positions of the ground troops before the attack commenced. . . . Many times we also had to utilize our means in preparation for the attack although the unit possessed artillery. Every effort was made to convince the Commands of the waste in means by using the Airforce and artillery in the same zone.[36]

But with the arrival of American advisers, the RHAF shook off its persona as the Cinderella of the Greek armed services. As one observer put it: "[It] was inevitable that the Americans would see to it that the Greek air force would develop into a decisive factor in the battle against the guerrillas. . . . The RHAF became, in fact, the spearhead of offensive tactics against the guerrillas."[37] Moreover, once the GDA attempted to secure victory through positional warfare, the RHAF found the job of locating and destroying communist formations much easier.

Following the arrival of American advisers, air operations were categorized in three ways: direct support of troops on the ground; isolation of the battlefield; and independent air operations. Direct support took many forms, including command liaison, tactical reconnaissance under the direction of ground forces, air observation, artillery spotting, aerial resupply, psychological operations, and close air support of troops in contact with the enemy. In terms of isolating the battlefield, three mission profiles were the norm. The first involved preplanned air strikes on targets located in advance by aerial reconnaissance or ground intelligence. Armed reconnaissance sorties sought out enemy formations on the move and attacked them. Finally, routine reconnaissance missions located enemy forces and vectored strike aircraft against them. Independent air operations attacked enemy forces on the move, in garrisoned villages, headquarters elements, supply depots and lines of supply, and static defensive positions. Independent operations forced the guerrillas to move almost exclusively at night. All of these operations were limited by a shortage of pilots and suitable aircraft and the difficulty of identifying elusive guerrilla units on the ground.

Despite the fact that the RHAF was seriously handicapped in many respects, the contribution of the RHAF to the counterinsurgency campaign was significant. As one American officer reported after the conflict, "[The] return from the air effort immeasurably exceeded the return from any comparable effort on the ground. Its manpower ranged from a minimum of 5,000 to a maximum of 7,500, as compared to a minimum of 120,000 and a maximum of 150,000 in the regular Army units alone. Moreover, casualties sustained in the air were infinitesimal as compared with those sustained on the ground."[38]

Nevertheless, shortages in crews, maintenance personnel, parts, equipment, and facilities continued to limit the impact of airpower until late in the war. The most serious material deficiency remained the availability of suitable aircraft. Except for the converted C-47 bombers, Spitfire fighters were the primary aircraft available for ground attack missions until the Grammos battle in 1949. It was then that a squadron of American-supplied SB2C Helldivers made their debut, flying over 1,450 sorties using bombs, rockets, and napalm. Thus, it was only at the end of the war that the potential of airpower was fully realized and only when the enemy had transitioned to a more conventional style of warfare. Ironically, much the same thing would occur during the counterinsurgency campaign against the Huks in the Philippines.

The Hukbalahap Insurgency, 1946–1956

ORIGINS OF THE HUK REBELLION

With a total area of over 115,000 square miles, the Philippines comprise over seven thousand islands, fewer than five hundred of which are more than a square mile in size. Over 90 percent of the land area is concentrated in eleven islands — Luzon in the north (over 40,000 square miles) and Mindanao in the south (over 36,000 square miles) being the most prominent.[39] The Philippines has a tropical climate with a dry season extending from November to June and a rainy season from July to October. Rainfall can be prodigious and is affected by the terrain, prevailing winds, and the seasonal monsoons.

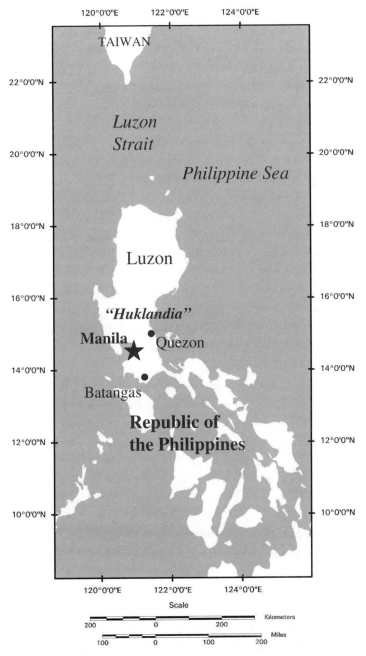

The Hukbalahap Insurgency, the Philippines, 1946–1956

The Huks operated primarily in central Luzon, dominated by flat irrigated rice paddies, rolling grassy uplands that rise to the foothills of the Sierra Madres, which are covered by dense tropical rainforests. The most prominent terrain features include Mount Arayat, rising to over thirty-four hundred feet in the middle of the central plain and the Candaba Swamp, which extends from Mount Arayat to the mouth of the Pampanga River in Manila Bay.[40]

When the Hukbalahap insurgency came into full bloom in 1946, the population of the Philippines was just over eighteen million. Fewer than one-fifth lived in cities, and half of these lived in the capital city of Manila. Almost half of the total population lived on Luzon. Most Filipinos are of Indonesian and Malayan stock, with Caucasians, Chinese, Negritos, and other aboriginal peoples making up only 13 percent of the total population. Tagalog was the nominal national language, but most spoke some seventy distinct dialects. English was also common, even in the most remote parts of Luzon, and a very small minority spoke Spanish.[41]

The Huks did not suddenly emerge full-blown in the aftermath of World War II. Rather, the rebellion evolved as a consequence of social, economic, and political conditions that had existed long before the war. The insurgency itself may be divided into three phases. The first phase began in 1946 and lasted until mid-1950, during which the Huks gained in strength. The second phase began in 1950 and lasted until 1953. At the beginning of this phase the insurgency reached its peak military strength and the zenith of its popular support. But it was also during this period that Ramon Magsaysay was appointed secretary of defense, which led to a dramatic change in counterinsurgency strategy that enabled the government to turn the tables on the insurgents. The third phase began with the surrender of the principal military commander of the Hukbalahap, Luis Taruc, in 1954, and lasted until 1956 when the insurgency effectively ended.[42]

The necessity to turn to a period prior to the postwar rebellion when discerning the true nature of the Huks is evident in the term "Huk" itself. Short for "Hukbalahap," the abbreviation is derived from the first syllables of the Tagalog phrase *Hukbong ng Bayan laban sa Hapon,* or "People's Army to Fight the Japanese." Referring to the postwar revolutionary movement as the Huks is not altogether inaccurate, however, as the Huks were not simply descendants of the wartime resistance — they were actual veterans. To the government soldiers who opposed them and to the peasants of central Luzon who formed the basis of their popular support, as well as to the rank-and-file members of the insurgency itself, the Huks of the late 1940s were the same men who had formed the resistance movement in 1942 to fight the Japanese occupation. Yet focusing on the wartime Huks, which is the norm, also fails to suffice — for the Huks' actual roots can be traced to the peasant unrest that preceded the war. A remarkable consistency is found among those who participated in the postwar insurrection, wartime resistance, and the prewar peasant movements. Wartime Filipinos were just as likely to refer to the Huks as KPMP (*Kalipunang Pambansa ng mga Magsasaka sa Pilipinas,* or "National Society of Peasants in the Philippines"), a peasant organization formed in the 1930s, as those after the war were to refer to the movement as Hukbalahap.[43] Therefore, at its root, the Huk rebellion was a peasant movement.

Scholars and government analysts agree almost unanimously on the proximate cause of peasant upheaval: the breakdown of the traditional agrarian relationship between the *datu* (landlord) and *tau* (peasant). Deterioration began during the Spanish imperial era (1565–1898), but the breakdown reached crisis proportions following American annexation in February 1899. The traditional relationship, often referred to as *datuk,* had at its core a special, almost familial bond between the *datu* and *tau.*[44] The *datu's* claim to land was not legitimate because of purchase and written deed, but rather by tradition — usually through inheritance. Moreover, the *tau* was not bound to the land per his counterpart in feudal Europe; he was free to plow the land of any *datu* who would have him. Moreover, a *datu's* status was not determined by the productive capacity of his land but by the number of *tau* who were sustained by the land and loyally supported the *datu.*

In spite of the durability of the *datuk,* it became apparent in the 1930s that something was amiss with the traditional pattern in central Luzon — the breadbasket of the Philippines. Incidents of peasant unrest increased substantially. Albeit at the time the Philippines boasted the highest average standard of living in Asia, the statistic was misleading. The poorer classes, representing 90 percent of the population, lived in abject poverty, while only 5 percent comprised the middle class, and the remaining 5 percent were fabulously wealthy. Occurring late relative to the remainder of Southeast and Northeast Asia, Philippine society was enduring the shock of transforming from an economy based on internal consumption to an export-led capitalistic economy. With emphasis on the product and associated profit instead of the producer and his loyalty, the landlord (*datu* becoming archaic at this point) had little concern for the welfare of his tenants (*tau* also became inappropriate). Whereas before the landlords had provided start-up loans, funded weddings and other ceremonies, and were generally concerned about the well-being of their *tau*, by the 1930s the landlords no longer felt the need to provide for their tenants anything more than the use of the land. This shift from traditional paternalism to a relationship shaped by agribusiness and export capitalism produced major socioeconomic change, and significant social turbulence was the consequence. The net result was the alienation of the peasants, and the peasants' pursuit of a better life dictated the nature of popular support for the Huks.

Communist Party (Partido Komunista ng Pilapinas, or PKP) control of the Huk movement has been almost axiomatic among scholars and government analysts. Interviews with captured Huks and PKP leaders, however, cast some doubt on the validity of this assertion. That the hierarchy of the Huk movement (field commanders) at least claimed to be communist is a given; but the degree to which the hierarchy was actually controlled by the PKP and expressed the will of the rank and file is questionable. This conclusion is justified for two reasons. First, the ideology of the PKP was incompatible with the normative worldview of the Filipino peasant; and second, the PKP could not put into effect its policies when they conflicted with the movement's innate momentum. Unlike the Chinese peasant, whose normative and secular worldview (a syncretism of Confucianism, Taoism, and Buddhism) did not pose a serious obstacle to communist ideology, the Christian foundation of Philippine society in general, and the majority of central Luzon inhabitants in particular, most certainly did. Moreover, the PKP's revolutionary outlook was in consonance with the Soviet model emphasizing the urban proletariat, not the peasant. The failure of PKP leadership to bridge the distance between themselves and the peasants was evident in the fact that even supporters of the Huks by and large were loath to describe themselves as communists.[45]

There are many examples of PKP leaders being deliberately disobeyed or simply ignored during the rebellion. Two of the most noteworthy deal with the very decisions to begin and cease hostilities. The PKP did not start the rebellion and did not endorse it until mid-1948, and then only after the ouster of top party officials. Prior to PKP endorsement, members of the uprising actually fought in spite of party admonishments to refrain. Only in 1948, after those leaders who had opposed the uprising had been removed, can it be said that the PKP actually "led" the movement. But in 1953, after several years of confronting an effective American-supported counterinsurgency campaign, the PKP leadership, those who had supported the rebellion in 1948, now found themselves, like their predecessors, deviating from the movement's inertia. In 1954, when Luis Taruc, the Huk's top military field commander, surrendered to government officials, the PKP could do nothing more than denounce him for abandoning the revolution. Thereafter, those Huks who continued to fight became little more than criminals and roving bandits, while communism would all but cease to exist in the Philippines until 1968 when it reemerged as the CPP (Communist Party of the Philippines). Nevertheless, prior to and during the Huk rebellion, the communists were a significant social and political force in the Philippines, and their association with the Hukbalahap largely shaped its strategy and by that fact the government's response.

The PKP was overtly organized on 7 November 1930. In October 1932, the Supreme Court of the Philippines declared the PKP illegal and communist leaders went underground. Thereafter, the Socialist Party of the Philippines carried the banner of revolution. In 1938 the two parties merged and declared their affiliation with the Communist International. The communists again went underground during the Japanese occupation and gradually came to control the anti-Japanese Hukbalahap. As the war's end neared, the secretariat of the PKP laid out its plans for revolution in a memorandum to the Central Committee: to establish a "People's Democratic Republic." The strategy comprised two phases. The first would be a period of preparation, or strategic defense. At the proper moment, however, the revolution would go over to the strategic offense, seize national power, and overthrow "American imperialism."[46]

When General Douglas MacArthur returned to the Philippines in October 1944, American regional security interests had been supplanted by more pressing security concerns in Europe. But this did not change the qualitative value of the Philippines to the United States nor the clear-cut pragmatic fashion in which American interests were pursued. Unfortunately, to ensure a pro-American government after the war, the United States dropped its initial efforts to punish wartime collaborators in order to reclaim the *status quo ante bellum*. Thus, although the United States did not actively become involved in suppressing the Huk insurgency until 1950, an inevitable confrontation ensued. During the Japanese occupation, American-led guerrillas operated in the Philippines as part of the United States Armed Forces Far East (USAFFE). The USAFFE also included members of the ancien régime, a fact that by itself serves to explain the initial tensions between the USAFFE and the Huks — especially given the Huk's prewar peasant origins. Tensions flared between the USAFFE and the Huks, and armed clashes between American-led guerrillas and the Huks gained in frequency when the USAFFE declared that any guerrillas not members of the USAFFE (that is, the Huks) were regarded as enemies of the U.S. government. Any chance of settling this dispute evaporated on the eve of MacArthur's return when the USAFFE accepted the collaborationist Philippine Constabulary into its ranks.[47]

The Philippines became independent on 4 July 1946 per the Tydings-McDuffie Act of 1934. The first national elections were held in November. The Huks participated in these elections as part of a collection of leftist organizations known as the Democratic Alliance. Alliance candidates won six seats in the Philippine Congress, including Luis Taruc, the wartime Huk leader. But the newly elected president, Manuel Roxas, and his majority Liberal Party refused to seat them. This blatant political act provided the *causa belli* for many Filipino peasants, and the ranks of the Hukbalahap swelled as a result. When Luis Taruc and the Huks returned to the countryside to take up arms against the new government, they became the principal target of Roxas' "anti-bandit" campaign.

THE COUNTERINSURGENCY RESPONSE

While the Huks clandestinely prepared for armed insurgency, the armed forces of the Philippines became progressively less capable of dealing with the same. Shortly after independence, the army was reduced from 132,000 to only 37,000 men.[48] Of these, roughly 24,000 were in the Military Police Command (MPC), which by default (given the criminal characterization of the Huks) was given the task of putting down the Huk rebellion. American forces were in the Philippines to defend the country against external aggression and therefore could not be used to suppress the Huks.[49] Regardless, the MPC operated under the control of the Philippine Department of the Interior as a national constabulary. But the quasi-police characterization of the effort paid little attention to the socioeconomic, political, and psychological aspects of the insurrection. Worse, the MPC was ill-equipped and badly led, and from 1946 to 1948 did little more than further alienate the people of the barrios.

During the government's "iron fist" campaign of 1946, MPC units sealed off and entered suspect villages in an effort to clear the area of Huk guerrillas. The modus operandi was counterproductive to say the least:

When the soldiers rounded up the barrio people, they would drive them at gunpoint to the nearest town. Meanwhile, the raiders would be busy looting and burning. For a day or two, the troops would live well off the barrio people's poultry and domestic pets. . . . To cover their misdeeds, the soldiers would report that the vandalism was the work of the Huks who had "offered stiff resistance before finally running away."[50]

In an attempt to improve their performance, President Roxas reorganized the MPC as the Philippine Constabulary (PC) in 1948 and appointed Alberto Ramos, who had served in the wartime constabulary controlled by the Japanese, as its chief.[51] With a "collaborationist" at the helm and with PC units deployed primarily to protect the property and other interests of politically influential Filipinos, the PC proved equally inept and brutal in its methods. In fact there is every indication that many peasants who were otherwise innocent of Huk connections or sympathies were brutalized nonetheless for their alleged support to the guerrillas.[52] As a result, the average Filipino peasant feared the PC more than the Huks and had nowhere else to turn other than the Huks for protection from the government.

The Huks themselves were seasoned fighters. With a fighting force of some five thousand active guerrillas, ten thousand lightly armed reserves, and thirty-five thousand other supporters, the Huks had fought over twelve hundred engagements and killed over twenty-five thousand Japanese and collaborationists during the war.[53] Huk tactics during the early part of the insurgency were an extension of their wartime guerrilla tactics. The Huks confined their operations to small hit-and-run raids and ambushes and avoided contact with large government formations. As was the case during World War II, the Huks' basic military organization was a "squadron" of approximately one hundred men, divided into platoons and squads. Two squadrons would form a battalion, two battalions a regiment, and regiments formed military districts. The communist influence was unmistakable in that each squadron included a "political instructor." When possible, political cadres were also included at the platoon and squad levels.[54] During the war the Huks had formed Barrio United Defense Corps (BUDC) units, which were loosely knit and locally recruited villagers that provided intelligence, food, and other support to the

Huks. These units were revived during the insurgency as Sandatahang T anod ng Bayan, or "People's Home Defense Guard," which anchored a massive support base for the Huk insurgency.[55]

In March 1947 the government launched a major offensive through the central plains of Luzon, culminating in an assault on the Hukbalahap stronghold of Mount Arayat. The offensive stalled, however, and at best achieved a tactical draw against the Huks. Over the next year government forces continued their attempt to pacify the area as part of a large-scale crime eradication effort, but as the popular base was solidified and the military wing enlarged, the Huks established military and political training schools and prepared for their transition to the strategic offensive. Anticipating revolutionary success, the Hukbalahap was renamed Hukbong Mapagpalaya ng Balayan, or "People's Liberation Army." Nevertheless, the term "Huk" continued to be applied to the guerrillas, and the area they dominated in central Luzon (Bulacan, Nueva Ecija, Pampanga, and Tarlac) was referred to as "Huklandia." In that regard, by 1950 the Huks reached their peak strength of somewhere between twelve thousand and fifteen thousand armed guerrillas, some one hundred thousand active supporters, with additional passive supporters numbering five hundred thousand or more.[56]

President Roxas died suddenly in April 1948 and was succeeded by the vice president, Elpido Quirino. Unlike Roxas, Quirino attempted to undermine the Huk movement through conciliation and amnesty, including promises of land reform. For a short time the Huk movement lost momentum, but by August it was clear that negotiations had failed, and soon afterward government forces launched a series of major raids throughout central Luzon. Quirino understood that the Huk movement was more than a criminal problem, and he ordered the armed forces to assume responsibility for suppressing the insurgency. To that end, he transferred the five-thousand-man PC to the army's control. Nevertheless, by late fall of 1948 Quirino was losing control of the country, and with chaos at the upper echelons of government, security forces once again resorted to tactics marked mostly by their brutality. Putting small villages to the torch was not uncommon, and the army often attacked defenseless villages with artillery and mortar fire.[57] By 1949 the country was all but paralyzed. The chaotic situation climaxed with the elections of 1949 when Quirino faced José Laurel, the former puppet president during the Japanese occupation. Quirino won the election, but his victory was marked by violence, intimidation, and corruption on both sides. Alarmed by the deteriorating state of affairs, however, Quirino approved a new counterinsurgency strategy, one brought to fruition by the growing involvement of American advisers and the appointment of Ramon Magsaysay as secretary of defense.

AMERICAN ASSISTANCE AND THE RISE OF MAGSAYSAY

While there were sore points between the two governments after World War II, relations between the Philippines and the United States were generally very good. The major postwar irritation concerned the continued U.S. military presence in the Philippines, the Philippine Trade Act of 1946 — which provided for eight years of free trade followed by twenty years of tapering duties — and an amendment to the Philippine Constitution that gave Americans equal citizenship status in the commercial arena. In 1947 a Joint United States Military Advisory Group (JUSMAG) was established in the Philippines. Before 1949, the JUSMAG concerned itself primarily with the threat of external invasion, but with the fall of China to the communists and the avowed communist orientation of the Hukbalahap, the JUSMAG turned its attention to counterinsurgency. Two officers, U.S. Air Force Lieutenant Colonel Edward Lansdale and U.S. Army Major Charles "Bo" Bohannan, would prove instrumental in defeating the Huks.[58] Lansdale had worked in the advertising business before World War II and specialized in psychological warfare.[59] Bohannan was an authority on unconventional warfare.[60] Lansdale in particular developed a very close relationship with the new secretary of defense, Ramon Magsaysay. Lansdale believed that popular support was at once the strength and the Achilles' heel of the insurgency. "The most urgent need," he wrote, "was to construct a political base for supporting the fight" against the insurgents. This meant detaching popular support for the Huks and reattaching it to the central government. The key was to target the underlying cause of popular support for the insurgency.

To that end, a State Department intelligence report written in September 1950, *The Hukbalahap*, clearly indicated that "longstanding and legitimate grievances" were at the root of popular support for the Hukbalahap. The report detailed the breakdown of the traditional agrarian pattern of the *datuk* as the proximate cause of peasant unrest and did not hesitate to identify pro-American elites and government policies as the target of legitimate peasant resistance activities.[61] As the report laid bare, the peasants' comparative disadvantage was virtually insurmountable. Even if the large landowners who served in the national legislature were excluded from the political process, the vast majority of civil servants and elected officials were either family members or financially dependent upon the rural landlords. Therefore, the common peasant could not expect to compete successfully against the landed elites in court or even take advantage of government land policies. The net result was the continued alienation of the peasant with no opportunity to redress his grievances through the government. The Huks, not surprisingly, exploited this situation.

The document defining American policy and initiating U.S. assistance in suppressing the Huk rebellion was NSC (National Security Council) 84/C, approved by President Harry Truman on 10 November 1950. The memorandum capitalized on the State Department intelligence research report, and although it referred more to the Huk movement's communist leadership than its peasant roots, the recommendations clearly targeted the latter as the key to demobilizing popular support for the Huks. This was especially apparent in the document's emphasis on political and economic reform rather than military solutions.[62] The futility of relying solely on the military instrument to suppress what was essentially a peasant revolt had been thoroughly demonstrated: President Manuel Quezon's "mailed fist" policy in 1939 against "agrarian disorder," Japanese "zona" raids during the occupation, and President Roxas' "iron fist" campaign of 1946 all not only failed to suppress the rebellion but materially contributed to it. Therefore, NSC 84/C outlined U.S. objectives consistent with the pragmatic pursuit of American interests. The emphasis on political and economic reform was self-evident: "To accomplish [these] objectives, the United States should . . . persuade the Philippine Government to effect political, financial, economic, and agricultural reforms in order to improve the stability of the country."[63]

Operating from a precise assessment of the fundamental cause of the insurgency, and with a strategy designed specifically to address the legitimate grievances of the peasants, the United States assisted the Philippines in implementing what has since been widely described as a model counterinsurgency effort. The hallmark of the pacification campaign was psychological in keeping with Lansdale's emphasis on detaching popular support from the Huks, especially the flagship program known as the Economic Development Corps (EDCOR), which offered land to surrendered Huks.[64] Broadly speaking, the

Philippine army cleared unsettled land far removed from the center of the insurgency, constructed roads, built houses, and laid out the basic infrastructure of a self-sufficient agricultural community. Settlers, preferably former Huks but also other Filipinos, were provided a loan as start-up capital, the repayment of which was according to very liberal terms. As psychological operations eroded popular support for the insurgency, Philippine army units, spearheaded by elite commandos and "scout ranger" teams, hunted the guerrillas in the countryside. But American advice and assistance would have little mattered without the leadership and personal dynamism demonstrated by Ramon Magsaysay.

Magsaysay was of middle-class origins from the central Luzon province of Zambales. His education was minimal, and for a time he worked as a mechanic in a large bus company. He was not politically active before the war but rather gained prominence during the war as a guerrilla leader. His American commander recognized Magsaysay's energy, integrity, and personal magnetism and placed him in positions of increasing importance. During the war, Magsaysay's association with American guerrilla leaders left a lasting impression and a deep commitment to democratic principles. General MacArthur promoted Magsaysay to the rank of major after the war and appointed him as military governor of the Zambales province. Magsaysay then ran for the Philippine Congress where he won a seat and chaired the House Committee on National Defense. He ran again in 1949 as a member of Quirino's Liberal Party and was reelected by a wide margin. Soon afterward he was appointed by Quirino to become secretary of defense, replacing the incompetent Ruperto Kangleon.[65]

When Magsaysay was named secretary of defense, the PC had already been merged with the armed forces and placed under the secretary's authority. However, once in charge, Magsaysay swiftly instituted sweeping reforms. He was given authority by the president to relieve officers, order courts-martial, and promote officers in the field. Magsaysay's first official act was to relieve Albert Ramos as chief of the PC. He then cashiered Major General Mariano Castaneda as commanding general of the armed forces. Over the next two years, Magsaysay reshaped the armed forces into an efficient and effective fighting force, replacing most of the officers in key billets with hand-picked officers with demonstrated performance in field operations against the Huks. He ruthlessly suppressed the brutal tactics perpetrated by government troops in the past and stopped the petty graft indulged in by many soldiers. But

Magsaysay also increased the pay of enlisted men, which proved especially helpful in that the additional income eliminated the soldiers' previous incentive to loot from the local people. The effect of these reforms was immediate and positive, generating increased morale among the troops and a renewed vigor in field operations. Magsaysay reinforced these trends by making frequent and often unannounced visits to field units, where he relieved those who demonstrated poor discipline or insufficient élan and rewarded those he found to be the opposite.

Having reformed the organization and attitude of the armed forces, Magsaysay set about to reform the counterinsurgency strategy itself. Encouraged by Lansdale, Magsaysay established a Civil Affairs Office, and military units became more involved in civic action programs such as building roads, schools, and clinics. Orders were given to troops in the field to become friends of the people. Magsaysay made military lawyers available, free of charge, to peasants bringing cases before the courts.[66] Perhaps most important, Magsaysay insisted that the army play an active role in the EDCOR initiative. With the army in control of these and other programs, corruption was dramatically reduced at the local level and Magsaysay turned to the corrupt influences surrounding national politics. He posted soldiers and cadets at polling stations to ensure free and fair elections. Two clean and orderly national elections, combined with positive and legitimate reforms, restored the confidence of the general populace in the government — an achievement that ultimately broke the back of the Huk movement.

American economic and military assistance increased after Magsaysay became secretary of defense. The military assistance agreement that had been reached in 1947 was extended and supplemented in 1950, with American aid reaching a cumulative total of $20 million by June 1952. From 1952 to 1953, U.S. aid amounted to $34 million, and another $13 million was added between 1953 and 1954. Thus, although Philippine spending on national defense rose from $55 million in 1949 to $93 million in 1952, American funding accounted for most of the increase and civilian programs did not suffer as a result.[67] With increased funding, Magsaysay was able to enlarge the size of the armed forces and add more and better equipment provided by the United States. In 1949 the army had been able to field only 11,000 combat soldiers, whereas the Huks fielded an estimated 15,000 guerrillas.[68] Only when the PC was merged with the army was the army able to field ten Battalion Combat Teams (BCT) with approximately 1,047 men each.[69] But by 1951 the armed forces had grown to a combined total of over 53,000 troops and Magsaysay was able to add sixteen BCTs, bringing the total to twenty-six.[70]

As Magsaysay labored to transform the Philippine army into an effective fighting force, the Huks made a serious error in judgment regarding their own prospects. From 1945 to 1950 the Huks had pursued a classic revolutionary guerrilla war, building up their popular base while chipping away at government authority in the countryside. But by early 1950 the Central Committee of the PKP was convinced that the existing guerrilla force could be expanded to as many as 150,000 men. Such growth would permit the guerrillas to be "regularized" as a conventional army capable of defeating government forces in positional warfare.[71] To facilitate this expansion, the Huks sent successive waves of "expansionist" units into neighboring provinces to recruit additional troops and prepare for a direct assault on Manila as the opening gambit of the long-awaited strategic offensive.

It is not wholly surprising that the communist leadership could have concluded that the time was ripe for positional warfare. Up to this point in the conflict, the government's performance in the field had been very poor. Although President Roxas had built up the army, commanders in the field were neither trained nor disposed to fighting an unconventional kind of war. The use of *zona* raids, a brutal tactic learned from the Japanese during the occupation, is a case in point. These brutal raids rarely had any effect on the guerrillas themselves and instead exacerbated poor relations with the peasants. Large-scale search-and-destroy operations similarly failed. The army would spend weeks preparing a surprise attack against a known guerrilla formation. Several battalions backed by air support and artillery would create a "ring of steel" around the target area. Sometimes the Huks would simply escape during the night, abandoning the area altogether. Other times the Huks would attack the soldiers before their own operation got under way, throwing government forces into confusion. According to Taruc, the Huks were generally successful at this tactic, escaping from the heavier government forces and then reforming later in another area. If the Huks escaped the area undetected, Taruc described the ensuing operation as both "amusing and saddening to watch." The Philippine air force would bomb and strafe the target area, and then the army would launch its attack, only to find that their prey had escaped. Manifesting their own sense of impending defeat, government forces adopted the practice of entering towns and villages "in an exaggerated combat posture." As one Filipino army officer wrote, "From their demeanor, it was to be assumed that they felt that they were among enemies, that they anticipated momentary attack. The psychological effect of this was deplorable."[72] Thus, by 1949 when the communist leadership determined to regularize the movement, Philippine army units were clearly losing the war in the countryside. With this in mind, it seemed reasonable to conclude that the revolution was ready for the next phase.

But the conventional aspirations of the PKP were in fact premature. The Huks were neither sufficiently well equipped nor experienced in the ways of conventional war. Moreover, neither the PKP nor the Huk military command structure could overcome the systemic administrative and logistical challenge of converting disparate guerrilla formations into a regular army. As had occurred in the Greek Civil War, the Huks became a regular force in name only. They lacked heavy weapons, other supporting arms, and the logistical infrastructure necessary to conduct sustained combat operations. In addition, despite their reputed study of Chinese communist people's warfare, they also lacked adequate safe havens from which to launch conventional thrusts. Moreover, the Philippine army had not been sufficiently debilitated by its earlier setbacks, and with the appointment of Magsaysay the armed forces quickly recovered and became stronger than ever before. In retrospect, the decision to reorganize the Huks as a regular force gave the Philippine army precisely the opportunity it needed to destroy the Huks as a military threat.

As the insurgency began to overreach, the Philippine army began to correct its previous mistakes. Rather than conducting large-scale sweeps, the army was directed by Magsaysay to implement small unit saturation patrolling. Ranging in size from squad level to platoons, these patrols extended the government's presence to remote areas, harassed the guerrillas, and disrupted their movements and communications. As a result, patrolling of this sort by multiple units kept the Huks off balance. In addition, elite scout ranger teams disguised as guerrillas conducted long-duration, deep-penetration patrols that identified Huk formations, thus enabling the BCTs and the Philippine air force to bring overwhelming combat power to bear against them.

Just how much of Magsaysay's own guerrilla experience influenced his thinking in this regard is subject to some debate, but it is certain that once the decision was made to use guerrilla tactics to beat the guerrillas, the army implemented the operational plan with enthusiasm. The BCTs were well suited to this end, being a nominally self-sufficient combination of rifle companies, heavy weapons, reconnaissance, support units, artillery, and transportation. Properly led, the BCTs were effective against not only small bands of guerrillas but larger formations as well. Flexibility and mobility were key to the success of the BCTs. Consequently, during the first few months after the army adopted the new tactics, Huk casualties increased by 12 percent while army casualties fell by 25 percent. The impression made on the average Filipino peasant was equally significant. Noting how army units were besting the Huks at their own game and behaving themselves at the same time, Filipino peasants began to support the army and began to provide valuable intelligence on Huk whereabouts and movements.[73]

In October 1951 Huk military leaders realized their mistake and attempted to return to guerrilla warfare. According to Taruc, "We had to avoid all encounters in which the enemy would take the initiative. When fighting could not be avoided, we resolved to put up a good defensive resistance to sustain morale — but to break contact as quickly as possible."[74] But the Magsaysay reforms had considerably improved the performance and confidence of the Philippine army, and the new small unit tactics were ideally suited for counterinsurgency warfare. Ably supported by the Philippine air force, the army succeeded in suppressing the insurgency to the extent that Luis Taruc surrendered in 1954. Afterward, government forces relentlessly pursued the remaining bands of Huks until the insurgency effectively came to an end in 1956.

THE ROLE OF AIRPOWER

The first Filipinos to undergo flight training attended the Curtiss School of Aviation facility at Camp Claudio in Parañaque in the early 1900s. In July 1920 the Philippine air service was established to ferry mail and passengers between Manila and the ports of Cebu, Iloilo, and Zamboanga. However, the air service was disbanded a year later due to lack of funding. For the next fourteen years there was no indigenous air service in the Philippines, although foreign aviators were numerous. But with war clouds on the horizon, the United States assisted in reviving Philippine aviation on 2 January 1935 with the creation of the Philippine Constabulary Air Corps (PCAC). Less than a year later, on 23 December, the Philippine army was created and the PCAC became the Philippine Army Air Corps (PAAC). The PAAC was folded into the USAFFE on the eve of World War II and at the outbreak of the war comprised over 140 pilots and 1,700 men at four airfields — three in Luzon (Zablan Field in Quezon City; Maniquis Field in Cabantuan, Nueva Ecija; and Batangas Field in Batango) and the other at Cebu City in the Visayas (Lahug Field).

At the outbreak of World War II the majority of PAAC aircraft resided at Maniquis Field (over a dozen 0–1 observation aircraft and B-10 bombers) and at Batangas (six Boeing P-26 fighters of the Sixth Pursuit Squadron). There were also U.S. Army Air Corps B-17 bombers and a P-40 pursuit squadron at Clark Air Field near Manila. When the Japanese attacked the American and PAAC airfields, most of the American and Filipino aircraft were destroyed on the ground, but the Sixth Pursuit Squadron managed to survive the initial attack and put up a furious resistance until overwhelmed by superior Japanese air forces. With all of their aircraft destroyed, PAAC officers and men became "flying infantry" — that is, they were seeded throughout the Philippine army as ground troops. With the fall of the Philippines, many of these airmen became guerrillas and fought against Japanese occupation until the end of the war.

With MacArthur's return, the PAAC was revived and many of the pilots and crews who had survived the war were sent to the United States to receive refresher training. The PAAC regained flying status with the arrival of American-supplied C-47s forming the First Troop Carrier Squadron in September 1945 at Lipa Army Air Base in Batangas. Almost one year to the day after independence, on 1 July 1947, the Philippine Air Force (PAF) became operationally and administratively independent of the army. During this period of build-up, many PAF pilots also flew for the Philippines Airlines, Asia's first commercial passenger service.

When the Huk insurgency erupted in 1946, the PAAC was incapable of providing close support of ground forces owing to a lack of suitable aircraft and properly trained crews. But with the advent of American military aid administered through the JUSMAG, the PAF received a variety of aircraft and other equipment, including the North American T-6 and the Vultee BT-13. The PAF also received North American P-51D Mustangs, an interceptor originally intended for air defense but which became the principal ground attack aircraft for the duration of the insurgency. The pace of American aid was overwhelming: at one point there were more Mustangs than pilots to fly them. Nevertheless, by 1948 the PAF had grown to around four thousand officers, and men and PAF detachments were assigned to each Philippine army military district to support the troops on the ground. These detachments were semiautonomous and equipped to be self-sufficient in forward-deployed locations. While the limited number of C-47s provided a degree of mobility for the army and liaison aircraft improved reconnaissance and intelligence operations, the fighters conducted close air support and independent bombardment missions. At its peak of activity, the PAF flew some 2,600 strike missions against the Huks.[75]

Not unlike the Greek Civil War, the Hukbalahap insurgency was mostly a ground war, and at least one PAF officer conceded afterward that it was "the ground forces [that] made the decisive effort in the armed struggle." But he did aver, however, that without the PAF contribution, "the ground forces would have had a much more difficult task."[76] The value of PAF air strikes remains questionable. According to his autobiographical account of the rebellion, Luis Taruc claimed that in six years of PAF air strikes, only twelve guerrillas were killed.[77] On the other hand, Filipino officers claimed that PAF air strikes inflicted numerous casualties on the Huks.[78] At a symposium in 1963 it was acknowledged that Taruc had discounted the value of air strikes, but one Filipino officer countered that whenever the PAF struck the Huks in any particular locale, they tended to avoid that same area thereafter.[79]

During the early stages of the insurgency, air support came about mostly due to personal connections between army and air force officers who had graduated together from the Philippine Military Academy or from reserve officers training at the University of the Philippines. In short, air support was provided to ground forces whenever possible as a result of personal connections — often despite an absence of official direction to do so.[80] But in addition to command and control problems, political problems slowed the involvement of the PAF in fighting the Huks. The Philippines had just emerged from the destruction of World War II, and public officials were sensitive to the use of aviation against the Huks given the Japanese use of airpower in the Philippines and the alleged "devastating performance of the American Air Forces during the liberation campaign."[81] Consequently, "stringent restrictions were imposed by the Secretary of the Interior [on air operations] without opposition from the Secretary of Defense." When air strikes did occur, the military was reluctant to divulge details, and on two occasions Ruperto Kangleon, then secretary of defense, ordered references to air action and the number of Huks killed as a result to be deleted from after-action reports.[82]

Part of the problem was the poor performance of the PAF, brought about by inadequate air-to-ground communications and the unspecified nature of command relationships. According to one senior Philippine army officer:

We achieved communications by way of light aircraft, such as were unofficially attached to my battalion. My roommate at the academy, then commanding the fighter base, wanted to help in any possible form or manner. He allowed these L-5s to be based on the air strip in front of my command post. In the absence of telephone or radio communications, these L-5s were my link to the Air Force Commander at Basa Air Base. When we got information from the field, we briefed the pilot, who flew to Basa and briefed the commander. Naturally, there was a relatively long reaction time. Often the air strikes would arrive too late.[83]

After Ramon Magsaysay became secretary of defense, command and control was spelled out more clearly, and cooperation between the army and the PAF improved greatly. Considerable strides were also made in air-ground communications. PAF liaison personnel were equipped with radios and vehicles and assigned to army field units. As the army and air force worked together more closely, coordination steadily improved and air-ground operations evolved into a relatively sophisticated framework. Military districts were divided into sectors with three or more BCTs assigned to each. Principal airfields might support several of these sectors, and PAF units often conducted simultaneous operations in concert with surface task forces comprising army and Philippine navy forces. A mobile tactical air control group was co-located with the sector task force headquarters during the operation, and tactical air control parties, many of which performed as airborne forward air controllers, were attached to the BCTs. The sectors would be saturated with fast mobile forces supported by strong reserves, while PAF aircraft would search for, locate, and track the guerrillas, direct ground forces to contact, and then provide close air support.[84] Peak air-ground efficiency and activity was reached in 1952 when the Sixth and Seventh Fighter Squadrons provided continuous air coverage for five BCTs conducting simultaneous operations.[85]

Tactical air missions during the Huk rebellion were of three broad types: close support; intelligence collection and reconnaissance; and transportation and aerial supply. There was no need for "counterair" missions during the insurgency, and although the aircraft used to support the army were not ideally suited to the task, antiaircraft fire from the guerrillas was negligible.[86] Beyond these principal missions, the PAF also conducted psychological operations missions and "possibly most important of all, made it possible for Magsaysay to pay those lightning inspection visits to frontline units."[87]

Close support missions were not a part of the PAF repertoire in 1946 because the only aircraft available at that time were C-47 transports and a squadron of Piper L-4 Grasshoppers (the venerable Piper Cub) and Stinson L-5s (the military version of the three-seat Voyager). The C-47s had the highest priority, and their use was closely controlled. The light aircraft were used primarily for liaison duties and occasional reconnaissance missions. The arrival of the Mustangs gave the PAF its first close support capability. Two fighter squadrons were activated, one at Basa Field, some sixty miles north-northwest of Manila, and the other at Lipa Field, Batangas, roughly sixty miles to the south of Manila.

Early in the insurgency the Huks operated from developed areas in central and southern Luzon. As a consequence of the government's desire to keep air operations to a minimum and avoid civilian casualties, PAF operations during this period were quite limited. However, as the ground forces began to gain the upper hand in 1950, the Huks were forced to withdraw to the less developed areas of north-central Luzon. This gave the PAF freer rein to conduct independent air strikes without fear of collateral damage. As one Filipino officer recalled, "The enemy was then in fairly open areas in the grasslands, in the foothills, and the Candaba Swamp. You could see a grouping of anywhere from ten to several hundred Huks, and that presented a target."[88] From that point forward, the PAF became more active in close support and independent strike missions. Nevertheless, PAF strike operations remained limited by the number of available aircraft, trained crews, and suitable munitions. Requests were frequently made for more weapons, including napalm, but the war in Korea was a higher priority for the United States at this time and these requests went largely unfulfilled.[89] Accordingly, PAF crews improvised, with one innovative enlisted L-5 pilot rigging his airplane to drop 50 mm mortar rounds. It was reported afterward that "captured Hukbalahaps were unanimous in stating that every time they saw an L-5, they could not be sure whether it presaged a large scale ground attack or the L-5 was simply going to harass [them] until it ran out of 50 mm mortar shells."[90]

The L-5 proved to be the workhorse of the PAF during the insurgency. In addition to the improvised bomber related above, the L-5 did yeoman work in intelligence and reconnaissance. Early in the campaign the Huks roamed about with relative impunity. But rather than pursue the guerrillas overland in the forests and swamps, the Philippine army used L-5s to locate and track the Huk bands, thus enabling commanders to more efficiently maneuver BCTs into position. Surrendered Huks or local informants were often carried aloft in L-5s to pinpoint Huk positions. The routine nature of L-5 flights lulled the Huks into a false sense of security, whereupon the Huks would concentrate for training, refitting, or political instruction. Finding where these guerrilla formations were located and keeping tabs on them became a key intelligence function for L-5 crews.

Lacking adequate radios for air-to-ground communications, Philippine army intelligence personnel devised a unique manner for civilian informants on the ground to signal the L-5 pilots regarding Huk activities. During multiple daily flights, the L-5 pilots would observe specific features on the ground, such as an open gate near a farmhouse, an animal tied to the southeast corner of the farmyard, open windows in the farmhouse itself, or haystacks arranged in a particular pattern. These signals communicated essential elements of tactical information, such as the size of a guerrilla force in the area, its direction away from the farm, and whether the guerrillas appeared to be settled in or on the move. With information provided by multiple sources, the Huk concentration could be pinpointed with considerable accuracy. In turn, ground forces could be maneuvered to attack the guerrillas or set up an ambush. If the guerrilla force was small and unworthy of ground action, multiple companies from a BCT could be transferred to another sector to support a major operation while a single company or platoon was left behind.[91] On occasion an L-5 would lead attack aircraft to conduct independent strikes against these Huk concentrations. In one instance, twenty-seven guerrillas were reportedly killed by ground attack aircraft led to the target by an L-5.[92]

In addition to intelligence, tracking, and performing as an aerial controller, the L-5 was used in more traditional reconnaissance roles. A serious logistical weakness of the Huks was food. The Huks were utterly dependent on their mass base of support in the rich agricultural areas for food supplies. Normally, food supplies were provided voluntarily and carried into the mountains by Huk military units or active supporters. But the Huks were not averse to commandeering food supplies when necessary, and as Huk dominance of the agricultural areas began to wane, the bulk of their food stocks was obtained by theft and by growing their own food where possible.[93] As the Huks cleared small plots of land to grow their own food, L-5 and other aircraft were used to locate these "production bases." The PAF did not spray chemicals on these plots, just before the crops were harvested, as the British often did in Malaya. The PAF believed that ground action was preferable. However, on occasion, PAF strike aircraft were led to these areas by L-5s and dropped incendiaries on Huk agricultural plots.[94]

Transportation and aerial resupply proved vital to the counterinsurgency effort, but there were only a handful of C-47s and helicopters were even in shorter supply, with but one helicopter operating in southern Luzon and the other routinely "deadlined."[95] Consequently the L-5 was pressed into service as a transport. As the BCTs pushed the Huks farther into the countryside and scout rangers and other commando units pursued them deep into the tropical forests, L-5s performed numerous resupply missions. Lansdale recalled after the conflict: "Some of the long-range patrol activities could not have taken place without regular air re-supply," and the L-5 was a mainstay in supporting ground forces in this regard.[96] In a major operation to reduce a Huk redoubt in the lowlands, two BCTs marched into an area devoid of roads and marked by rugged terrain overlaid with jungle growth. The mission required over seventy days to complete and covered terrain never before penetrated by such a large formation. The BCTs were supplied by two L-5s, initially by airdrop and later by way of a small airstrip near the village of Boso-Boso. Each L-5 supplied provisions for five companies, conducting five missions per BCT per day, and delivering roughly five hundred pounds of supplies per sortie. As the commander of the operation later recounted, "In this period of 72 days none of my troops — squad or platoon — missed a meal."[97]

Aircraft were also used for psychological operations, including the ubiquitous L-5. These aircraft dropped leaflets and broadcast psychological messages using megaphones and loudspeakers. Military intelligence often knew the identities of Huk leaders and this was used to advantage. During a firefight, the crew of an L-5 would call out the names of individual Huks and ask them to stop fighting, or would tell the Huks that they were surrounded by superior government forces. On one occasion an L-5 crew improvised and thanked an anonymous member of the Huk unit for supplying information that had enabled the army to find them, thus leaving the guerrillas with the suspicion that one among them was a government spy or informant. This practice subsequently became routine. Although there is little quantifiable evidence regarding the success of psychological operations efforts, the general conclusion was that leaflet and broadcast operations demoralized the Huks significantly.[98]

One of the more celebrated capabilities that PAF L-5s and other light airplanes brought to the pacification effort was the ability to extend government presence into rural areas, and in particular facilitate the frequent visits by Ramon Magsaysay to the barrios and frontline military units. By his mere presence, villagers and soldiers were often persuaded that the government cared about them. Magsaysay normally arrived in a light short field aircraft such as the L-4, one "that could be put into a cornfield or land on a dirt road up in the provinces." According to Lansdale, the effects of Magsaysay's visits were "electrifying."

The armed forces never knew when the boss was going to show up and catch them loafing, rather than out patrolling. The civilian population felt that here was a cabinet member who had the ear of the President. A mayor, a councilman, or a political officer out in the locality who was doing the wrong thing felt that someone was looking over his shoulder and would jump him hard. . . . A post office clerk once told me that he was afraid to steal stamps out of the drawer any more because this guy in Defense — mind you, Magsaysay had nothing to do with the postal system — might suddenly show up behind him. He thought this was great. This was the little man's view of the big man.[99]

Aside from dropping leaflets, voice broadcasts, and delivering Magsaysay and other government officials to remote areas of the country, PAF aircraft were also used to support civic action initiatives. Former Huks would often be airlifted to progovernment rallies to speak about why they had surrendered. Often, ex-Huks would be taken by light plane or helicopter "to one meeting, and then within an hour would be flown to participate in another mass rally."[100] The PAF also airlifted surrendered Huks from Luzon to other parts of the country to be resettled as a part of the EDCOR initiative. According to one officer, "The psychological value of . . . the movement of families was high."[101]

In the final analysis, airpower in the Philippines played primarily a supporting role. The small size of the PAF, types and numbers of useful aircraft, the nature of the counterinsurgency strategy, and even the topography of the Philippines defined the role of the PAF. Transportation, reconnaissance, and aerial supply made the greatest contributions to the effort, but close air support, bombardment, psychological operations, and civic action missions played important roles as well. Air support provided the Philippine army with the means to move about the countryside to interdict avenues of escape during major ground operations. Scout ranger and other hunter-killer teams were inserted deep into Huk territory by air. Aerial resupply enabled these units and others as large as battalion-strength to operate in the field without being tied to their home base. Airpower also proved vital in providing tactical intelligence. Moreover, armed reconnaissance missions limited Huk movements, prevented the construction of large guerrilla cantonments, and inflicted casualties on the Huks whenever they were careless. In short, independent air strikes against bivouacs and communications caused the Huks to avoid concentration, and psychological operations undermined Huk morale.

Over time, air-ground operations became highly coordinated, and a sophisticated mechanism of control was established to provide optimal support for the ground forces. Nevertheless, shortages of every sort greatly limited what the PAF could do during the anti-Huk campaign. Regardless, as one Philippine army officer recalled afterward: "I have seen the effect of the right use of airpower, and have always contended that it is not solely a matter of inflicting casualties." The psychological dimension of airpower was very important, to government forces and guerrillas alike. Despite its potential, airpower in the Philippines was never regarded as decisive in and of itself. Success against the Huks came about as a consequence of the integration of civilian and military initiatives that proved instrumental in detaching popular support from the insurgents. Yet airpower played a significant role, and given the very limited number of L-5s, C-47s, and Mustangs at their disposal, the achievements of the PAF were all the more remarkable.

Conclusion

An examination of the insurgencies in Greece and the Philippines reveals some significant differences, the most important being the absence of external support or sponsorship for the Huk insurgency. But there were many similarities as well. In both cases, the insurgencies grew out of wartime resistance movements. Early pacification efforts were regarded as primarily police matters. Both governments proved largely inept in the beginning at suppressing their respective rebellions. In each case the army performed badly at the outset, and the respective air forces were forced to undergo a rebuilding process before they could even become engaged. External advice as well as economic and military aid to the government proved crucial to the successful outcome in each conflict. Inspiring and effective leadership was also crucial to restoring confidence in the government and improving military performance. Also, in each instance, elite forces comprising specially tailored hunter-killer teams were used by the government. Most important, in each case the insurgents attempted to convert their respective guerrilla armies into conventional forces prematurely — a strategic error that sealed their own doom.

Regarding the contribution of airpower specifically, the Greek and Philippine air forces both ceased to exist during World War II and played fairly insignificant roles at the start of each insurgent conflict following the war. External assistance provided the means by which the two air forces were restored, provided by the British and Americans in Greece, and solely by the United States in the Philippines. As each air force grew and improved its capabilities, the contribution of each to the counterinsurgency effort grew as well. Both air forces were imaginative in their use of airpower and often used aircraft designed for a specific purpose in altogether different and innovative ways. In Greece, for example, the C-47 was used as a bomber; in the Philippines the L-5 light liaison aircraft was used in just about every possible way imaginable. Perhaps the most striking similarity was how airpower was employed as the character of the insurgency evolved.

In Greece, the communist resistance organization formed during the Axis occupation at first continued to employ guerrilla tactics against the postwar government. During the early part of the conflict the communists conducted classic hit-and-run guerrilla raids and ambushes. At the same time the GDA built up fairly secure bases in the northern mountain ranges of Grammos and Vitsi. Within these relatively secure areas, the communist forces built a reasonably strong support organization and logistical infrastructure to support military operations. During this period, the utility of airpower in fighting the guerrillas was greatly limited — by the undeveloped nature of the RHAF but more importantly by the inherent difficulty of fighting guerrillas in general.

The most striking mistake made by the communist leadership other than failing to secure a popular base among the rural inhabitants came with the decision to discontinue guerrilla operations and seek victory in positional warfare. Once the guerrilla units were converted to "regular" formations, the GDA became especially vulnerable to airpower. GDA formations operated in the open and attempted to take and hold ground. They built fortifications and aspired to fight government forces in set-piece battles. But they lacked heavy weapons and an adequate logistical infrastructure to sustain such operations. By the end of the civil war, RHAF aircraft were pounding communist-fixed positions, interdicted GDA lines of communication, and provided effective close air support of government forces as they launched a series of offensives that ultimately destroyed the GDA.

The evolution of the Hukbalahap insurgency and the role played by airpower in the Philippines was very similar to that of the Greek Civil War. Having fought the Japanese using classic guerrilla warfare techniques, the Huks continued their guerrilla ways at the outset of the postwar rebellion. Unlike the Greek communists, however, the Huks were quite successful in establishing a popular base of support (which was as much a consequence of government ineptitude and brutality as Huk organizational aptitude). During the guerrilla phase of the struggle, the PC, the army, and the PAF were incapable of suppressing the rebellion. But beginning in 1950, when Ramon Magsaysay was named defense secretary, the armed forces, including the air force, improved dramatically in quality and capability. When the communist leadership made the fatal decision to launch its long-awaited strategic offensive by converting the Huks into a regular army, the much-improved Philippine army forced the Huks to withdraw to the grasslands and mountains of the northern central Luzon where they were exposed to repeated air attacks. In the latter stages of the war, the PAF provided aircraft for intelligence collection, reconnaissance, transportation, civic action, psychological operations, and close air support and bombardment.

The lessons to be learned from the Greek Civil War and the Hukbalahap insurgency are plentiful. Of greatest importance was the need to integrate all of the instruments of national power, civilian and military, in the pacification effort. Second in importance was the need for inspired leadership, as typified by Ramon Magsaysay and Marshal Alexander Papagos. As one Greek analyst put it, "It follows that to fight successfully a guerrilla-type aggression, the target country must wage the struggle under a leadership which can command the loyalty of the armed forces and the genuine support of the majority of the people."[102] Third, within the political strategy for countering insurgency, the military effort was most successful when it was subordinated to the political goals. When the insurgent military strategy was essentially guerrilla warfare, the contribution of airpower was generally one of support, with transportation and reconnaissance taking on prime importance. But when the guerrillas sought to achieve a military victory through positional warfare, the role of air strikes gained in importance.

As the Greek and Philippine examples illustrate, airpower can deny security to the guerrilla, can degrade his logistical infrastructure, and can greatly contribute to his demoralization. An air force can observe, track, and attack the guerrilla alone or in conjunction with surface forces. Airpower provides flexibility and initiative in the movement of ground forces. Should the guerrilla aspire to conduct conventional operations, he exposes himself to concerted strikes from the air. Small air forces can support ground forces by ingenious improvisations, even under the most difficult conditions. In the Philippines, for example, aircraft were used to scour guerrilla territory, collect intelligence, and harass the guerrillas. Aircraft were also used to pin down the Huks so that they could be boxed in with mobile ground forces in a coordinated air-ground operation. Independently, airpower was used to reduce the Huks' ability to take the offensive and to compound their logistical plight.[103] Great Britain and the United States, however, learned differently from their respective experiences.

As discussed earlier, the British promoted innovative ideas such as long-range hunter-killer teams and commandos inserted into enemy territory, wholly supported by airpower. In fact the British Military Mission created an "Air Dropping Supply Course" for the Greek National Army for this very purpose and encouraged the development of Greek commando companies to infiltrate deep into GDA territory. Their mission largely presaged that of Royal Marine commandos and the Special Air Service in Malaya. Field Marshal Montgomery was an avid supporter of the commando concept and urged that greater use be made of airpower to facilitate these unconventional units.[104] As the communist strategy shifted to conventional warfare in Greece, the British responded appropriately — but they did not shelve their original thinking regarding the role of commando operations and airpower in counterguerrilla warfare. In fact Major General E. "Eric" Down, who assumed command of the British Military Mission in March 1948, took note of the special complications of anticommunist and counterguerrilla warfare and advocated a clear-and-hold strategy for future conflicts of a like nature, one employing large numbers of ground troops with air support.[105]

For the United States, the lessons of Greece and the Philippines were not inculcated to the degree of sophistication warranted. The United States became militarily involved in both conflicts only when each had taken on a distinctly conventional flavor. This convinced many American analysts that conventional military principles and doctrine could be employed successfully against guerrillas without modification. They failed to recognize the unique circumstances of the Greek Civil War, concluding that guerrillas could be defeated simply by severing their ties to an external patron and crushing the guerrilla army with more and larger maneuver battalions. The fact that the communist guerrillas had abandoned classic guerrilla tactics in favor of positional warfare, thus ensuring their own defeat, was lost on American military analysts. Consequently, the Greek Civil War only reinforced the conventional predisposition of the U.S. armed forces emerging from World War II. The Philippines, however, should have been a different matter altogether.

During World War II, U.S. troops remaining in the Philippines during Japanese occupation conducted their own guerrilla war against the Japanese army. Ironically, airpower played a prominent role in the guerrilla campaign, and the experience should have alerted the Americans to the peculiar nature of guerrilla warfare in general and the relative value of airpower in unconventional warfare. In early 1945 the U.S. Thirteenth Air Force established liaison detachments to support American-led guerrilla units on Luzon. By March there were five such teams. Most of their efforts were directed against Japanese targets on Cebu, but guerrilla air support teams also assisted guerrilla units fighting on Negros, Bohol, and Mindanao. On Cebu and the Zamboango Peninsula of Mindanao the guerrillas even operated their own airfields. With air support, these guerrilla forces waged a ruthless unconventional air-ground campaign against the Japanese.[106] In hindsight, the guerrilla campaign against the Japanese should have made a lasting impression on the U.S. military in terms of the unique demands of counterguerrilla warfare. Moreover, air support of these guerrilla operations should have made a similar impression with respect to the role of airpower in unconventional operations against guerrillas. But these lessons apparently were lost once conventional operations came to the fore with MacArthur's return.

The American experience with the Hukbalahap would seem to indicate that U.S. officials had learned that an accurate assessment of the roots of insurgency can lead to an appropriate response. Despite the inclination of

American policymakers at the time to focus on the communist leadership of the Hukbalahap, clearer heads insisted on the peasant origins of the unrest and pursued systemic reform as the principal means to undercut popular support for the insurgency. But the favorable outcome of the counterinsurgency effort in the Philippines apparently had little impact on the U.S. military as an institution except for the handful of officers (such as Lansdale and Bohannan) who recognized its import. In hindsight, officers like Lansdale have always been on the margins of American military thought, and with the main U.S. combat effort committed to the conventional war in Korea, unconventional officers such as Lansdale could be dispatched to the sideshow that was the Philippines. It is no small irony that Lansdale was a U.S. Air Force officer.

The dearth of analysis regarding the contribution of airpower to counterinsurgency success in Greece and the Philippines speaks volumes about the marginal view of small wars evident in American military thinking — especially in terms of the role of airpower in small wars. But the contribution of airpower was regarded by Greek and Filipino officials alike as significant, if not decisive in its own fashion. The British apparently capitalized on their own experience in Greece and applied the lessons learned in Malaya. But American analysts drew mostly the wrong conclusions. Stated simply, no changes were required in U.S. military doctrine in general or in the way that airpower in particular was to be used to fight against guerrillas. Regarding the Philippines, American success was probably more the product of greater commitments elsewhere (i.e., Korea) than the consequence of deliberate planning and implementation of NSC 84/C. As a result, the U.S. military considered the pacification effort in the Philippines to be of little consequence and failed to learn from that experience any more than the Greek Civil War. The fatal nature of this error in judgment would be revealed less than a decade later in South Vietnam.

4

The French Colonial Wars, 1946–1962
Indochina and Algeria

Indochina, 1946–1954

At the end of World War II, the French faced a new kind of colonial war, one for which the French government and armed forces were singularly unprepared. In Indochina the French confronted a politically well-organized national movement that demanded nothing less than full independence from France. The postwar French government, suffering from the effects of World War II and a weak economy, at first refused to take the Vietnamese nationalists seriously. When open warfare broke out, France found herself fighting a capable and determined opponent. The French armed forces, it must be said, fought well in Indochina. However, from the beginning, for the French armed forces it was always a matter of too few troops and too little equipment for a huge area. For l'Armée de l'air, it was a war fought on a shoestring. France had far too few resources to spare for Indochina, so the air force made do with a handful of aircraft. Given that the odds for a French victory were virtually nonexistent from the start, the French air force actually performed remarkably well. Without the support of the air force, the French ground forces would not have held on as long as they did.

France had established colonial enclaves in Indochina in the 1840s and by the 1880s had established full control over the whole region of what are now Vietnam, Cambodia, and Laos. Compared with her other colonies, France had relatively little trouble from the local inhabitants. In the 1920s and 1930s the small colonial forces garrisoning Indochina put down a few small rebellions, but these operations were minor police actions compared with the fighting the French saw in Morocco and Syria.

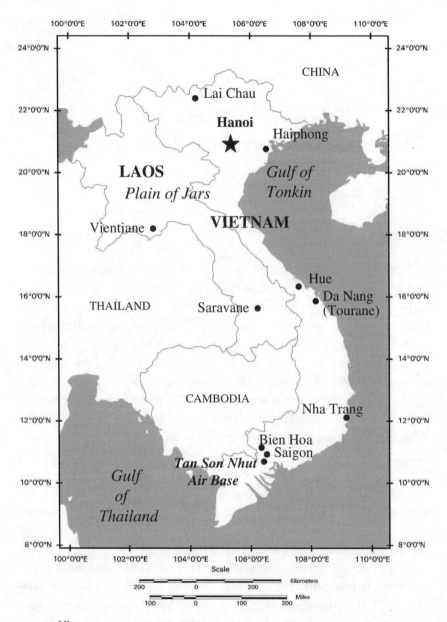

Vietnam, ca. 1954

Generally, the attitude of the French toward the Vietnamese paralleled that of the British toward native populations in their empire. The British believed that certain races and ethic groups in India were "martial races" and naturally made far better soldiers than soldiers recruited from the "unmartial races." The French saw some of their colonial peoples as natural warriors and, as soon as the natives were defeated by French forces, these "martial" peoples were avidly recruited into the French army. In World War I, the French employed over 150,000 Algerians, Moroccans, and Senegalese in combat units at the front and praised their performance in battle. The Vietnamese provided 43,000 soldiers to serve in France.[1] However, the Vietnamese were not considered to be a "military race" and were generally relegated to duty as labor troops.

Before World War II, France kept a small garrison of mostly French-officered native troops in Indochina. The colonial forces were not considered to be especially capable, so were armed only with light weapons and seen as more of a constabulary than an army force. The French air force maintained a small force of six squadrons of obsolete aircraft in Indochina at the outbreak of World War II.[2] The colony was virtually defenseless when the Japanese marched in and occupied bases in Indochina in 1941. In March 1945 the Japanese, fearing an Allied advance into Indochina, reinforced their forces and demanded the total surrender of all vestiges of French authority in Indochina. When the French colonial authorities and military units refused, the Japanese quickly attacked and destroyed them and seized full control of the region.[3]

The Vietnamese Communist Party, formed under the leadership of Ho Chi Minh just after World War I, was a small underground force up to World War II. A small military arm of the party was formed during 1930 to 1931 but was an utterly insignificant force. With the disruption of French authority during World War II, the Vietnamese Communist Party took the lead in organizing the nationalist elements, later called the Viet Minh, as a coalition against both the French and the Japanese. The Viet Minh's military and political opportunities came with the collapse of French power and the Japanese occupation. The Vietnam Liberation Army (later called the People's Army of Vietnam) was formed from a collection of guerrilla and militia units in May 1945 and placed under command of Vo Nguyen Giap.[4] At first, the Viet Minh organized small guerrilla forces, conducted a few small skirmishes with the Japanese, and cooperated with the American office responsible for supporting anti-Japanese guerrillas — the Office of Strategic Services

(OSS) — in rescuing downed Allied fliers. The Viet Minh forces, like other guerrilla forces in Asia, received weapons, supplies, and military advisers from the Allied forces. During the war, the Viet Minh worked hard to organize a political network throughout the whole of Vietnam and built up a small military force of guerrilla units. When World War II ended, General Giap's Viet Minh army had about one thousand regular troops supported by militia forces. By the end of 1945 the Viet Minh could count forty thousand in its regular and militia forces.[5] When the Japanese empire collapsed in August 1945, the Viet Minh were in a good position to take advantage of the power vacuum. On 19 August, the Viet Minh seized power in Hanoi. On 23 August, the Viet Minh–dominated committee seized power in Saigon. On 2 September a "Democratic Republic of Vietnam" was proclaimed and had effectively wrested control from the Japanese. The first Allied troops to arrive in Vietnam, a detachment of the British army, which landed in Saigon on 13 September, was presented with a fait accompli.[6]

Prior to 1945 de Gaulle's Free French government drew up a series of plans to rebuild the French armed forces and reestablish the empire. In March 1945 the Indochinese were promised a new form of postwar government, with some degree of self-government in a "French Union," a kind of imperial citizenship.[7] The French planned for a relatively small force of two colonial infantry divisions and a few air force squadrons to garrison Indochina.[8] France could count on political and military support from the British, who also intended to restore their colonial possessions in Asia after World War II. The U.S. government, however, was openly opposed to French and British imperial plans and promised no support to such endeavors — a major factor for countries heavily dependent upon the United States for financial and military aid. In planning to reassert colonial control, the French had to plan for the prospect of no support from the United States. Thus, the French air force could not expect to employ its squadrons equipped with first-rate American aircraft such as the B-26 or P-47 in Indochina, as the Americans would be able to cut off spare aircraft and parts.[9] The initial French air force contingent in Indochina would have to be equipped with aircraft from Britain or manufactured in France, such as the "Toucan" transport (the German Ju 52) or the Morane Saulnier MS 500 "Criquett" light liaison plane (the German Fiesler Fi 156 "Storch").

THE FRENCH RETURN — NEGOTIATIONS WITH THE VIET MINH

In the immediate aftermath of the Japanese surrender, the northern half of Vietnam was occupied by two hundred thousand nationalist Chinese troops and the southern half of the country by a small British force. Admiral d'Argenlieu, appointed as French commander in chief for Indochina, arrived and the first small contingents of French troops were landed in October 1945. With the Viet Minh in effective control of the local government, d'Argenlieu opted to negotiate a settlement with the Vietnamese nationalists. In the meantime, the Viet Minh used the time well to organize a mass nationalist party and to raise and train a sizable army. By 1946 the Viet Minh had several thousand men under arms and was rapidly growing. They were trained by a group of fifteen hundred to four thousand Japanese soldiers led by Lieutenant Colonel Mukayama (later killed fighting the French), who had surrendered in 1945 and joined the Viet Minh. These provided a cadre of experienced trainers and technicians for the Viet Minh.[10] By the end of the first year of the war in 1947, the PAVN (People's Army of Vietnam) had approximately sixty thousand soldiers.[11] Viet Minh troops were equipped with an assortment of weapons seized from the Japanese, taken from old French stocks, and supplied by the OSS during the Second World War.[12] Nationalist Chinese officers occupying the north obligingly sold the Viet Minh arms and ammunition from their lend-lease supplies.

Ho Chi Minh agreed to allow the French to land troops to occupy North Vietnam upon the condition of Chinese withdrawal. Ho and most of the Viet Minh were eager to replace the Chinese with the French, as they viewed the Chinese as the far greater long-term menace to the Vietnamese. France was seen as a weak power in decline and could be dealt with more easily.

The French, for their part, had no clear strategy for dealing with Indochina beyond offering some sort of membership in the French empire to be called the "French Union." The French moved to support pro-French monarchies in Cambodia and Laos and looked at options such as reestablishing a Vietnamese monarchy to rule under a French protectorate. Neither the French government nor the military were eager to become involved in a major colonial war. General Leclerc, on a fact-finding mission to Indochina, told the government to seek a negotiated solution, as "in 1947 France can no longer put down by force a grouping of people which is assuming unity and in which there exists a xenophobic and perhaps national ideal."[13] A February 1947 poll of the French public showed that 42 percent of Frenchmen supported a nego-tiated solution in Indochina, with only 36 percent favoring a forceful solution.[14]

Nor was Indochina a top priority for the French armed forces. In the after-math of World War II the French high command set about to rebuild and modernize the French armed forces to serve as a large conventional force to protect France and Western Europe from the Soviet threat. General Charles Léchères, air force chief of staff from February 1948 to 1953, saw the buildup of NATO (North Atlantic Treaty Organization) as his top priority. Rearmament and modernization were his primary interests.[15] While the army was working to build up a force of modern mechanized infantry and armored divisions, the French air force moved to equip its force with modern aircraft. Immediately after the war, the French air force equipped its premier squadrons with the British DeHavilland Vampires and Gloster Meteor jet fighters. While the re-organized aircraft industry still kept some German aircraft such as the Ju 52 transport and Fiesler Storch light reconnaissance plane in production, it also succeeded in developing first-rate aircraft equal to any produced by the Brit-ish, Americans, or Russians.[16] In 1947 Dassault began production of the Ouragan jet fighter, a capable fighter-bomber for the period. In 1947 the prototype Dassault 311 twin-engine transport first flew, and in 1949 the Bréguet 765 heavy transport was developed. The latter four-engine plane could carry an impres-sive seventeen-ton cargo load with a range of four thousand kilometers.[17]

From 1947 through the end of the Indochina War, France's primary de-fense interest was in building up the NATO alliance and developing a cred-ible conventional force for the defense of Europe. Indeed, the air force chief of staff saw the conflict in Indochina as a drain on the primary mission of the air force.[18] The first postwar French air doctrine, published in 1947 *(Instruc-tion Provisoire sur L'Emploi Des Forces Aériennes)*, placed the air superiority battle and defense of the national airspace as the primary mission of the air force, and this meant a modern air force capable of taking on the Soviets.[19] After World War II, there was even strong support among the top officers of the air force to establish a heavy bomber force on the British and American wartime model in order to deter the Russians.[20] Although the French air doctrine of 1947 focused on a major European conventional war, support of the "French Union" was also named as a major mission of l'Armée de l'air. In some cases, the French air doctrine of 1947 was quite innovative. The air force intended to build up a significant air transport force so troops could be quickly transported to trouble spots in the empire.[21] However, the strategic mission of the transport force was not only to transport French troops from France to subdue colonial problems but, more important, to be able to transport French colonial troops from North Africa to France in case of conflict with the Soviet Union.[22] The emphasis of French doctrine on large-scale conventional air war was clear. There was little in French air doctrine that could be applied to dealing with a guerrilla war — such as the French were about to fight in Indochina. The French air force would have to improvise a doctrine for that war and fight the war with minimal resources, as U.S. aid would not be available for imperial conflict and the priority of defense effort had to go to Europe.

THE WAR BEGINS: 1946 TO EARLY 1947

French ground, naval, and air forces for the reoccupation of Indochina trickled into the region in late 1945 and early 1946. In November 1945 the First Fighter Squadron landed in Saigon. As their Spitfire Mark IXs had not yet arrived from France, the RAF unit occupying Tan Son Nhut Airfield at Saigon turned over eight Spitfire Mark VIIIs to the French before departing.[23] Another fighter squadron was set up and equipped with obsolete Japanese air force Ki 43 (Oscar) fighters found at the former Japanese airfields.[24] Two transport squadrons arrived in late 1945, GT 1/34 "Béarn," which flew Ju 52s from Bien Hoa Airfield, and GT 2/15 "Anjou," which was equipped with C-47s and based at Tan Son Nhut.[25] A naval air squadron equipped with a motley collection of aircraft, including old Catalina flying boats and captured Japanese Aichi E 13 seaplanes, rounded out the French airpower in Indochina by 1946.[26] The transport groups saw a great deal of service in reestablishing French authority throughout the region. Between September 1945 and April 1946, transport squadrons flew eleven hundred tons of freight and eight thousand passengers.[27]

Some minor fighting occurred in March 1946 as the French moved to reestablish their authority in North Vietnam, Cambodia, and Laos. The Spitfires and Ki 43 "Oscars" of the fighter squadrons flew close air support. The French had no bomber units in Indochina, so the Ju 52s and C-47s of the transport units had bomb racks fitted to their planes and used them as improvised bombers.[28] Ho Chi Minh traveled to Paris in the summer of 1945 to negotiate with the French. Negotiations broke down when President Charles de

Gaulle and leading French politicians acknowledged that granting full independence to colonies such as Vietnam would sound the death knell for the
status of France as a world power.[29] Relations between the French and Vietnamese continued downhill. On 20 November 1946, severe fighting between
the French and Viet Minh broke out in Haiphong. In December, the fighting
spread to Hanoi where the Viet Minh attempted to drive the French garrison
out. The small French air force in Indochina was thrown into battle to provide
heavy firepower for the French forces. The Spitfires and Ki 43 Oscars flew
ground support missions for ground forces in Hanoi and Haiphong, and the
transports were again used as bombers. At this point in the war, the Viet Minh
were not in any position to face French firepower, which included not only
the air units but also the French fleet at Haiphong and French artillery. The
Viet Minh total military force at this time amounted to approximately fifty
thousand men armed only with light weapons. Ho Chi Minh, his government,
and his military forces retreated from Hanoi in January 1947 and set up headquarters in the countryside. The Indochina War gained its defining characteristic as a guerrilla war. The French would hold the major cities and enclaves
around them while the Viet Minh would control the countryside. Ho Chi
Minh and General Giap wisely reckoned that the French did not have the
resources to hold more than a small part of the country.

For the next eight years the primary theater of war would be in North
Vietnam, although the central highlands of South Vietnam would also see
some heavy fighting. The French had set up pro-French governments in Laos
and Cambodia and had little trouble in reoccupying South Vietnam. Most
of the North, however, was solidly in the hands of the Viet Minh.

The French, now involved in open conflict, moved quickly to reinforce
their forces. As Indochina was a colony, France could not, by law, employ
conscript forces there. All troops in the theater had to be regular army volunteers, Foreign Legion, or other colonial troops (North African units would
make up a high percentage of the forces engaged in Indochina). Naturally,
locally recruited forces would also play a central role in serving the French
cause. While Ho Chi Minh and the Viet Minh could rightly claim to be the
leaders of a truly national movement representing most Vietnamese, there
were many Vietnamese, such as the Catholics, who strongly opposed the Viet
Minh and willingly provided many troops to the French-led army or to the
French police and militia units.

With the outbreak of open war, the French forces in Indochina were more than doubled to more than one hundred thousand men by mid-1947. Most of the South remained in French hands, while in the North the French held the enclaves of Haiphong and Hanoi and the rich agricultural lands of the Red River delta. The rest of the North was in the hands of the Viet Minh, who continued to build up and train their forces.

The French air force sent a few reinforcements to Indochina. However, in the early days of the war, the French were forced to fight the war on a shoe-string budget. The third transport squadron of Ju 52s was formed in Vietnam in October 1947.[30] In January 1947 a squadron of DeHavilland Mosquito light bombers (GC I/3) arrived.[31] By this time the French urgently needed an effective bomber for close air support. The Spitfires of the fighter squadrons were modified as fighter-bombers for the support role with an armament of four 20 mm cannons and two 500-pound bombs. The aircraft were easy to handle, could take off and land on short dirt airstrips, and were loved by pilots. However, the Spitfire had several drawbacks in the close air support role. It was a short-ranged aircraft, with only one and a half hours of flying time, and it was very vulnerable to ground fire. Its liquid-cooled engine could be put out of action by one lucky bullet. L'Armée de l'air was fortunate that the Viet Minh possessed no real antiaircraft capability at this stage of the war. The French air force wanted to send squadrons of P-47 Thunderbolts to Vietnam. The rugged and heavily armed P-47 was arguably the best fighter-bomber of World War II and ideally suited to the close air support role, the primary mission of the French air force in Indochina. However, fear that the Americans would embargo spare parts in opposition to France's colonial policy killed the P-47 deployment.[32] France had to continue to rely primarily on British aircraft or aircraft of her own manufacture, no matter how unsuitable they were.

The Mosquito bomber squadron conducted operations for only five months before being withdrawn from service. It had features that the Spitfire lacked, such as range and larger bomb load. However, it also needed long runways and posed more maintenance problems. While the Mosquito had been an outstanding light bomber in the Second World War and performed well in the temperate climate of northern Europe, the tropical climate and high humidity of Vietnam quickly degraded the plywood body of the Mosquitoes, making them literally fall apart.[33] Thus, the small fighter-bomber force carried the full burden of the air war in late 1947 to early 1948, and combat attrition and maintenance problems plagued the force. Of twenty-eight Spitfires available in theater in October 1947, only eighteen were operational to support the major French ground offensives that month. Two new Spitfire fighter squadrons arrived and one squadron rotated out, so that the burden of air support for operations in late 1948 was borne by one squadron.[34] Some additional support was provided by the French navy air arm, which contributed patrol aircraft and a unit of Douglas Dauntless dive-bombers to support operations.

One of the effects of using primarily British or French aircraft was the additional burden for French maintenance capabilities. The French-built Ju 52s needed more maintenance than American C-47 transports. For example, the Ju 52's BMW engines needed a major overhaul every 450 flight hours. The C-47's Pratt and Whitney engines needed a major overhaul only every 1,500 flying hours.[35] Problems such as these, combined with a too-small maintenance and support force, meant that operational rates of the French air force were fairly low during the conflict, often with no more than 50 percent of the aircraft available for operations.

General Bodet arrived as air force commander in April 1947 and proceeded to reorganize the air force in Indochina. Two tactical air groups were formed: Tactical Group North (TFIN) was attached to the northern Indochina command and initially had one fighter squadron, a transport squadron, a section of liaison aircraft, and some artillery spotting aircraft. Tactical Group South (TFIS) was personally commanded by the air commander for the Far East and had a fighter squadron, one transport squadron, and part of another transport squadron, a liaison unit, and two artillery spotting aircraft sections. The Tactical Group South, because of the large amount of territory it had to cover, was further divided into two subgroups: Cochin China (southern Indochina) and Annam (central Indochina).[36] This decentralized approach to employing airpower worked fairly effectively. The French air units in Indochina had no strategic or air defense missions requiring centralized control. The whole focus of the air force was support of the ground troops, and the air force sensibly mirrored the organization of the ground forces (northern and southern commands) to make direct coordination simple.

THE FIRST MAJOR AIR OPERATION

With the arrival of army units in the theater, the French decided upon an operation to end the war in one grand stroke. Intelligence reported that

Ho Chi Minh had his headquarters in the town of Bac-Kan, about sixty miles from Hanoi. The Viet Minh had established a large base area in the hill region northwest of Hanoi. If the French could capture Ho Chi Minh and surround his main army with their mobile forces, the war could be brought to an end.

On 7 October 1947 the French initiated "Operation Lea" with a paratroop drop of a half brigade of paratroops on Bac-Kan and other paratroop drops in the Viet Minh rear at Cho Moi and Cho On. The paratroops would capture Ho Chi Minh's government while motorized and mechanized units would move rapidly to envelop the whole area in a huge pincers. The French would use twenty armor, infantry, and artillery battalions in three columns. One column would sweep north and then west, sealing off the Chinese border. One column would envelop the Viet Minh base area from the south, and three battalions would sweep up the Red River on landing craft and amphibious vehicles.[37] The columns would act as pincers and meet beyond Bac-Kan, enclosing the main Viet Minh force.

The paratroop operation and the motorized offensive worked fairly well and won some tactical successes for the French. However, the goal of capturing the Viet Minh government was not realized. The 950 paratroops who landed at Bac-Kan had to be dropped by the Transport Squadron's Ju 52s in three lifts, as the handful of French transports could carry only a couple of companies at a time. Ho Chi Minh and his senior staff escaped in the nick of time; Ho's unopened mail was found on his desk in the headquarters. French army troops, supported by all of the Spitfire fighter-bombers in the theater, overran Viet Minh depots and camps and engaged several Viet Minh units and cut them up badly. Operation Lea was concluded on 8 November and was quickly followed by another large mobile operation against Viet Minh forces northwest of Hanoi at Thai Nguyen and Tuyên Quang. The eighteen French battalions again severely damaged some Viet Minh units. The two operations cost the Viet Minh ninety-five hundred casualties.[38] However, in neither operation did the French have enough troops to effectively surround large jungle areas. Most of the lightly armed and equipped Viet Minh forces were able to slip through the French lines and retreat to the west — in the fashion of true guerrilla fighters, to escape and fight another day.

For their part, the French were very impressed at the effectiveness of their paratroops. A fairly large paratroop force was soon formed, and one of the characteristics of the war in Indochina was the extensive use of paratroop operations by the French. In many cases the paratroop operations were tactically successful. The primary use of paratroops was as mobile fire brigades to reinforce isolated garrisons under attack by the Viet Minh. Later in the war, they were used to raid the enemy rear and provoke the Viet Minh to attack — and thus become open targets for concentrated French air and ground firepower. When used in support of mobile operations, paratroop drops in the enemy rear were unable to cut off avenues of retreat and were never able to surround and destroy the Viet Minh units as planned. The dense terrain of Vietnam and the French tendency to be bound to the roads by their heavy equipment made it easy for the Viet Minh to evade the French offensives.

The tactical air command organization of the French air force in Vietnam proved effective. Coordination of the ground forces and the tactical air commands was considered good. Air force officers served with the army's mobile combat groups, and the air force set up training courses for the ground officers to educate them in coordinating air support and in the capabilities of air power.[39]

From the start of the war, one of the primary missions of the air force was reconnaissance. In the early stages of the war, the French reconnaissance units were equipped with light Morane Saulnier 500 airplanes, which carried out constant patrols to spot Viet Minh activity. In this, the French air reconnaissance units were singularly ineffective. Knowing that the French controlled the skies, the Viet Minh became masters of camouflage. Base camps and depots were painstakingly camouflaged, and the Viet Minh learned to hide troops and supplies in underground tunnel complexes, impossible to spot from the air and almost impossible to find on the ground. Viet Minh forces usually moved at night or, if they moved by day, hiked wearing camouflage netting and regularly changed their camouflage as they encountered different foliage. In a heavily forested and largely jungle country like Vietnam, aerial reconnaissance was already at a great disadvantage. Later in the war, as the French air reconnaissance force was enlarged to a full group and equipped with the reconnaissance version of the F-8 Bearcat and B-26 bomber, the French had no more success in spotting even large Viet Minh troop movements.[40]

When the Viet Minh assembled forces and struck at French outposts or ambushed a French column or river convoy, the MS 500s served very capably spotting for the artillery or bringing fighter-bombers on to the targets. Because of the professional efforts of the air reconnaissance units, the French fighter-bombers and artillery were able to put firepower on the targets with great accuracy. The Viet Minh, faced with the French firepower advantage, learned to counter French air and artillery support by engaging the French units at close range, so that the aircraft couldn't bomb without fear of hitting French troops.

After the major operations of 1947, the war settled into a stalemate for the next two years with the French holding a large enclave of territory from Hanoi and Haiphong including the Red River delta as well as a string of forts along the Chinese border. The Viet Minh would assemble forces to attack isolated French outposts or set up ambushes for French columns along the main roads or boat traffic on the Red River. This phase of the war was characterized by numerous small battles in a war of attrition. The French, for their part, mounted a series of large sweep operations to engage and destroy Viet Minh units using gunboats, armor, and motorized troops with air support from the fighter-bombers. From 1947 to 1949, both sides built up their forces and there were few large engagements. The French air force situation improved in 1949 when four squadrons of American P-63 Kingcobra fighters arrived (with the Cold War now at a high pitch, the United States was not likely to confront France on issues related to use of U.S. equipment in the colonies). Most of the Spitfires, fairly worn out by this time, were taken out of service, but one squadron remained in central Indochina.[41] The P-63 was a better close air support machine with more armor than the Spitfire, much better range, and better firepower with a 37 mm cannon in the nose.[42]

THE AMERICANS AND CHINESE POUR IN AID, 1950–1951

The nature of the war changed dramatically when China fell to the communist forces of Mao Tse Tung in October 1949. The Red Chinese regime quickly agreed to supply the Viet Minh, a large part of the supplies coming from the vast quantities of American weapons and equipment captured from the Chinese nationalist forces. In 1950, the Chinese also agreed to set up training camps for the Viet Minh forces in southern China so that the Viet Minh would be able to train and equip large forces in a sanctuary. Up to this time, the Viet Minh army, which had grown to three hundred thousand men by 1949, was normally organized into battalions, with sometimes three to four battalions grouped together as a regiment.[43] In August 1949 the PAVN started forming its first division. Later, the PAVN was able to form heavy divisions of two artillery regiments and an engineer regiment equipped with guns and ammunition supplied by the Red Chinese. Along with the Chinese aid came some light antiaircraft guns that would make life much worse for the French pilots who, up to this time, only had to face ground fire from light weapons.

The U.S. political opposition to French imperialism in Indochina changed with the fall of China to the communists. The United States began to see the French in Indochina as a force containing communist expansion. The anti-imperialist arguments also fell when the French proclaimed a Vietnamese republic in the south with the former emperor of Annam, Bao Dai, as president in March 1949. The Republic of Vietnam was largely a fiction as the French retained control of foreign, military, and economic policy. Officially, France was no longer fighting a colonial war but as a part of the French Union. As soon as the French-sponsored Vietnamese Republic was proclaimed, it applied for military aid from the United States. The French Far East air commander from March 1950 to April 1951, General Hartemann, predicted the reaction that the United States would have to the growth of communism in Asia. In 1950 he proposed that the United States support the French by providing aircraft for four fighter groups, two bomber groups, and four transport groups.[44] In early 1950 U.S. support started to trickle in. When the war in Korea broke out in June 1950, the United States saw the need to contain communism as much more urgent, so large amounts of equipment began to flow to the French armed forces in Indochina. The United States agreed to supply several squadrons of material to the French air force in Indochina to include F6F Hellcats and F8F Bearcats (former U.S. Navy fighters) as well as enough B-26 bombers to equip two squadrons and additional transport aircraft. The first Hellcats arrived in October 1950, and the first B-26 bomber squadron (GBI/19) was formed in early 1951. The Bearcats began arriving in February 1951, and eventually 120 of these superb fighter aircraft would be supplied and equip seven squadrons of the French air force in Indochina.[45]

An important part of the air reinforcements after 1950 was the air arm of the French navy. From 1951 to the end of the war, the French navy kept at least one aircraft carrier, namely the ex-U.S. Navy escort carriers *La Fayette* and *Bois Belleau* and ex-British carrier *Arromanches*, on station in the Gulf of Tonkin. The carriers usually carried a complement of twelve Hellcats or Bearcats and nine Helldiver dive-bombers. The French naval aircraft operated under air force command and flew hundreds of ground support missions. A detachment of seven navy Grumman "Goose" flying boats provided reconnaissance support, and a squadron of six ex–U.S. Navy

"Privateer" four-engine patrol planes provided heavy bomber support for long-range missions.[46]

With American aid arriving, the availability of high-quality aircraft was no longer an issue for the French as it was in the first four years of the war. The problem was the lack of air force personnel and infrastructure. In April 1951 General Hartemann was killed in an aircraft accident and replaced by General Chassin. The new commander pointed out that the ten thousand air force personnel assigned to his theater were barely enough to operate and maintain the four fighter groups, two bomber groups, and three transport groups at his disposal. Furthermore, the combat experience of 1950 showed that the three hundred planes available to the Far East air force was insufficient to deal with Viet Minh attacks and support the ground operations. The French air force high command was sympathetic, but with economic problems at home and French defense commitments around the world, the government in France was unable to increase the air force personnel in Indochina.[47]

With a new Vietnamese government set up in the south, the French worked to build up a large Vietnamese army to counter the Viet Minh. There were far too few French troops in Indochina to counter a Viet Minh force that was rapidly growing and receiving modern weapons from China. An increased and reorganized Vietnamese force could take over the regional and local security duties and free up the French regulars from static defense. The Vietnamese National Army (AVN) grew quickly and, by 1953, had a strength of more than 155,000 men with another 53,000 serving under direct French command, often in mixed French/Vietnamese units.[48] The French regular forces were reorganized into "mobile groups," a task force containing one to two infantry battalions, a light armored squadron, and an artillery battalion — a force capable of moving rapidly and engaging the Viet Minh with heavy firepower. However, the new French approach was problematic. The mobile groups relied on road movement and were highly vulnerable to the well-laid ambushes of the Viet Minh. Nor were the French able to free up their forces from securing the rear areas. Since the start of the war, the Viet Minh managed to maintain a strong force of regional and local guerrilla units inside the French enclave in the north — soldiers who farmed by day and laid mines and ambushes by night. Small outposts deep within the French lines were constantly raided.

While the guerrilla units of the Viet Minh tied down huge numbers of Vietnamese troops in outpost lines, fortifications, and rear security, the regular units of the Viet Minh were being reorganized and retrained in China as full divisions complete with artillery and antiaircraft guns and capable of taking on the French forces in major conventional battles.

The Viet Minh took the initiative in September 1950 with an attack on Dong Khe, one of several major French outposts set up along the Chinese border and dependent upon supply by Route 4, an easily cut main road. The Viet Minh attack on Dong Khe succeeded, but the town was retaken two days later by a paratroop assault that caught the elite Viet Minh regular 308th Brigade by surprise and inflicted heavy casualties on the Vietnamese. In October, a series of carefully planned assaults overran Cao Bang and pushed the French out of the whole line of border forts. The French attempted to replay the paratroop drop of the September battle and dropped three battalions to try to save the garrison retreating from Long Son, the largest French outpost. All of the paratroop units, as well as road-bound relief columns, were cut to pieces by Viet Minh regular forces that drew them into grand ambushes. By the middle of the month, the French had seen one of their worst defeats of the war. All of the border forts in northern Tonkin were lost. The French suffered 6,000 casualties, and the Viet Minh captured 13 artillery pieces, 125 mortars, 940 machine guns, 1,200 submachine guns, 8,000 rifles, and 1,300 tons of ammunition. This was enough to equip a whole new division.[49]

MAJOR BATTLES OF 1951–1952

In December 1950 Marshal de Lattre de Tassigny took command as both head of the civilian government and military commander in chief in Indochina. He instituted several changes in strategy and tactics for the French. Now that the Chinese border was almost completely in Viet Minh hands and the Viet Minh could receive supplies and heavy equipment by truck from China, de Lattre directed that his newly constituted force of B-26 bombers carry out interdiction missions against the major Viet Minh supply routes. The bombers were also to attack Viet Minh depots and headquarters located in towns and villages.[50] The new air strategy was unsuccessful. In contrast to the Viet Minh, whose agents could observe the French at close range, the French never had adequate intelligence to make an interdiction or strategic campaign work. Even at the height of the Dien Bien Phu battle in 1954, when the Viet Minh moved large quantities of supplies by truck, a maximum French effort failed to cut Viet Minh supply lines by air. As far as strategic bombing of depots and bases, the French bombed numerous villages but apparently did no serious harm to the Viet Minh.

Confident after the success of the border outpost battles, General Giap initiated a major offensive against the French belt of fortifications protecting Hanoi and the Red River delta in order to actually drive the French into the sea. The offensive began on 13 January, and the Viet Minh 308th Division overran some French outposts west of Hanoi and shattered a mobile group sent to relieve the defenders. The Viet Minh overran more French units, and it appeared that they would break the main French defense line when de Lattre ordered reserve battalions airlifted to the north. In the meantime, on 17 January every French fighter-bomber in Indochina, as well as transport aircraft able to drop bombs, was mustered to support the hard-pressed French defenders. In the heaviest air attacks of the war, the Viet Minh were defeated with heavy losses at Vihn-Yen. The French used napalm liberally during the battle and the massive air attacks broke the will of the Viet Minh attackers, who lost six thousand dead and five hundred prisoners in the battle.[51] Giap realized that the Viet Minh were not yet ready for a general offensive. Instead, he would try to maintain the initiative by constant smaller offensives against French outposts. By this time, the war became one of attrition. Neither side had the forces to decisively defeat the other. When one side lost the will to fight and take heavy casualties, then the other side would win.

GUERRILLA SUPPORT AND MEDEVAC

One of the most innovative and successful of the French strategies was the formation of a large anti–Viet Minh guerrilla force to operate in Viet Minh territory. Starting in 1950, the French sent small teams, usually one officer and four to five noncommissioned officers (NCOs), to organize and train groups of the hill tribesmen of northern Vietnam to defend their territory against the Viet Minh. The T'ai, Meo, and Moi tribesmen of the Vietnamese highlands were ethnically different from the Vietnamese and spoke their own languages. They had no desire to live under Viet Minh rule and welcomed French assistance and support. Weapons and supplies were airdropped or brought in by MS 500 liaison planes to small airstrips hacked out of the jungle. Each French commando team organized the hillmen into groups of four hundred men and carried on a guerrilla war against the Viet Minh, ambushing supply columns and attacking small outposts. By 1953 approximately fifteen thousand to twenty thousand French-led guerrillas were fighting for the French and causing the Viet Minh serious trouble. For example, in 1954 four-teen Viet Minh battalions were engaged in countering the French-led guer-rillas.[52] The whole operation was supported by three hundred tons of airdrop and airlift per month.[53] It was a small effort that paid good dividends in terms of tying down Viet Minh troops. However, it was yet another burden on the already overburdened French transport force.

From 1950 on, the French also employed a small force of helicopters in the medevac role in Indochina. A small unit flying American Hiller 360s arrived in 1950 and served under the Tactical Air Command. A second unit equipped with the more powerful H-23 helicopters arrived in 1952, and in 1953 the S-5, which could handle six wounded in one lift, arrived in the theater. A total of forty-two helicopters were sent to Indochina, of which eleven were lost to enemy action. Thousands of soldiers were evacuated to safety, and although the helicopters showed themselves to be highly vulnerable to ground fire, the army was impressed enough to form its own light aviation branch in 1954 to operate helicopters.[54]

THE LATER BATTLES, 1952–1954

During the second half of the war, the French turned to large paratroop opera-tions as a means of bringing the enemy to battle or to reinforce threatened outposts. In November 1951 the French dropped three paratroop battalions in a surprise attack on Hoa-Binh, a Viet Minh base area fifty kilometers west of Hanoi. The attack quickly overran the Viet Minh base area and was supported by a force of fifteen infantry and two armor battalions and a large artillery force that rushed up the Black River Valley to link up with the paratroops. While the early stages of the operation were successful in disrupting the Viet Minh and inflicting heavy casualties, the Viet Minh responded by attacking the French supply columns vulnerable to ambush along the narrow roads. Eventually, the French found the effort to maintain a garrison at Hoa-Binh too costly and with-drew back to their defense lines around Hanoi in February.[55]

One of the most successful paratroop operations of the war was the cam-paign at Na-San, a French outpost deep in the western highlands of North Vietnam. In October 1952, General Giap launched a major offensive to clear the highlands and attacked Na-San, hoping to quickly overrun the two-battalion garrison. The French moved quickly to reinforce Na-San with paratroop battalions and air landed artillery. A strong force was built up and supplied solely by aircraft, as Na-San was too deep in the highlands to receive reinforcement by ground transport. Giap threw two divisions into a series of frontal assaults against Na-San and his forces were cut to pieces. The French learned the lesson that one could establish an "air-land" base deep in enemy territory, maintain it by airlift, and compel the Viet Minh into a set-piece battle in which French firepower would decimate the Viet Minh.[56]

Marshal de Lattre, probably the best French commander of the war, became ill with cancer and returned home to France in late 1951 to die in January 1952. His replacements were officers of lesser ability. De Lattre's deputy, General Salan, assumed command in late 1951 and led the French Union forces until May 1953 when Lieutenant General Henri Navarre assumed command.

DIEN BIEN PHU

At this point in the war, the best the French could hope for was a negotiated peace with the Viet Minh. However, before sitting down to negotiate, Navarre wanted to improve the French position by inflicting some severe defeats on the enemy. With the example of Na-San in mind, Navarre came up with a plan to establish an "air-land" base deep in enemy territory to force the Viet Minh into a set-piece battle. For the major operation he selected the old French airfield at Dien Bien Phu, located in a large valley on the Black River near the Laotian border. A strong French force at Dien Bien Phu would support the rapidly eroding French position in Laos and would block any Viet Minh movement to support communist forces in Laos. Navarre trusted the air force to supply and support the force at Dien Bien Phu, as the post was 150 miles west of Hanoi and would be impossible to supply over land. As Dien Bien Phu was at extreme range for air support from the airfields at Hanoi, the air force would base a force of fighter-bombers there for close air support of the ground troops.

The story of Dien Bien Phu is well known and will not be recounted in detail here. Bernard Fall's *Hell in a Very Small Place* (written 1968) remains the best history of that famous French disaster.[57] However, the story of Dien Bien Phu as a dramatic failure of airpower needs to be noted. On 20 November 1953, General Navarre initiated "Operation Castor," a mass paratroop drop of two battalions to establish an airhead at Dien Bien Phu. The French should have had doubts about the viability of the operation when Colonel Nicot, the air transport commander, had to frantically scrounge up every rated transport pilot in the theater, including himself and all of his staff, to pilot the sixty-five transport aircraft required for the airborne drop. The Americans had begun providing the French with the C-119 transports, which carried seven tons of cargo as opposed to the three tons of the C-47s, which composed most of the French transport force. However, the French ability to use the new transports was limited by the failure of the air force to send enough trained aircrew to Indochina to fly the planes.[58]

Yet the initial airdrop went well, and the French soon built Dien Bien Phu into a sizable "air-land" base. A main airfield was constructed on the valley floor along with several small auxiliary landing strips. By early 1954 Dien Bien Phu had become the largest French troop concentration in Indochina with almost eleven thousand troops stationed in the valley, dug into eight fortified positions. To support operations the French flew in twenty-four 105 mm and four 155 mm artillery pieces. The air force stationed Bearcat fighter-bombers at the base as well as MS 500 liaison planes for artillery spotting. Some helicopters were also flown in.[59] The French were ready to destroy the frontal attacks that they expected that Giap would send against them — as he had done with disastrous losses during other French airborne offensives. However, this time, Giap was not so obliging and the French faced little resistance during their first few weeks at Dien Bien Phu.

Giap left the French alone for awhile and mobilized one hundred thousand people to disassemble and haul one hundred 75 mm and 105 mm guns and one hundred heavy mortars along with large ammunition stocks down jungle trails and up steep hills to positions along the long ridgeline overlooking the French outposts. The Viet Minh then built a series of painstakingly camouflaged bunkers and gun positions that looked down on the French fortifications only two to four kilometers away. French air force reconnaissance spotted the movement of guns and evidence that heavy equipment was being moved into the Dien Bien Phu area as early as December. An overconfident French high command dismissed numerous warning signs, as the French did not believe that guns could be brought into the mountainous terrain and, if any were, the Viet Minh would not be able to bring up a significant supply of ammunition.[60] To deal with the French airlift capability, Giap deployed twenty-four 37 mm antiaircraft guns and hundreds of heavy machine guns and 20 mm antiaircraft guns in the hills overlooking the French airfield. Any French aerial reinforcements would fly into a wall of antiaircraft fire.[61] Giap concentrated forty thousand infantry around Dien Bien Phu to take the French positions by storm. For the first time in the war, the Viet Minh would have the firepower advantage.

The Viet Minh began the siege of Dien Bien Phu on 13 March 1954 with a massive artillery barrage that destroyed several aircraft on the airfield. One of the French fortified positions was overrun the same day. Viet Minh artillery fire was so heavy and accurate that the airfield was shut down within a few days. Further resupply or reinforcement would have to be by airdrop. However, the antiaircraft fire was so heavy that the transports could fly safely only at high altitude, eighty-five hundred feet, to carry out supply drops. At this altitude, the drop accuracy was minimal, and much of the vital ammunition and food supplies for the defenders fell inside Viet Minh lines. Another problem was the lack of capacity of the French air force transport units. Even with the help of a dozen C-119 transports rushed to Indochina by the Americans, the French simply did not have enough airplanes and aircrew to support the besieged force. The fifteen thousand troops at Dien Bien Phu (four thousand men were airdropped in to reinforce the garrison) needed 200 tons of supplies a day to maintain combat effectiveness. Even with maximum effort, the French were unable to drop more than 120 tons a day into Dien Bien Phu during the siege.[62]

The French air force fighter-bombers, operating from Hanoi at the limit of their range, were unable to provide effective air support to the besieged garrison at Dien Bien Phu. The Viet Minh guns were so well camouflaged that few, if any, of the two hundred guns and heavy mortars were hit by French bombing. Antiaircraft fire was fierce, and the French lost several aircraft over Dien Bien Phu.[63]

By means of fierce and costly frontal assaults, Giap's forces slowly overran the outlying French positions. On 8 May, the surviving French troops at Dien Bien Phu, hungry, their artillery destroyed, and low on ammunition, surrendered to General Giap. This effectively ended the Indochina War as the French quickly agreed to armistice talks and a political settlement in which the French would pull out of the north completely and allow national elections for all of Vietnam.

ASSESSMENT

The Indochina War was one the French had little hope of winning from the start. France had to try to reestablish a colonial regime in the worst of circumstances. France was bankrupt and weak and had few resources to fight a major war. Moreover, Ho Chi Minh, General Giap, and the Viet Minh leadership proved to be adept political organizers and capable military strategists. When the French finally did get significant military aid to fight the war during 1950 to 1951, the Viet Minh position in most of northern Vietnam was so strong that any hope for a military victory was pure illusion. Still, the French soldiers and airmen fought very capably and inflicted massive losses on the Viet Minh forces.

For the French air force it was a war with too many missions, too much territory to cover, and far too few airplanes and personnel to carry out the mission. All these aspects considered, the French air force and naval air arm fought a very good war indeed. From the start of the war, the shortage of French aircraft was chronic. Until March 1954 and the emergency at Dien Bien Phu when the Americans poured in extra transport, bomber, and fighter aircraft, the French never had more than 275 aircraft in the whole Indochina theater. The worst shortage was of transport aircraft. Considering the extensive use of paratroops and aerial supply missions throughout the war, the transport force was probably less than half the size it should have been. The bravery of the force can be seen in the high casualties the airmen suffered. During the course of the war the French air force and naval air arm lost 146 officers killed and missing, 403 NCOs, and 101 enlisted soldiers for a total of 650 killed. In addition, 70 civilian airmen working for the French also lost their lives in combat operations.[64]

Airpower was certainly an important part of the French firepower doctrine of the war. A large number of the casualties inflicted upon the Viet Minh during the large battles of the war were caused by French fighter-bombers and bombers in close air support. In numerous actions, timely close air support was the only thing that enabled French units to hold out against Viet Minh attacks or survive Viet Minh ambushes. In many small battles the arrival of Bearcats or Hellcats with a load of napalm was the turning point. Without the close air support provided by the handful of fighter-bombers in the theater, French losses would have been much higher, and it is unlikely that the French army could have staved off defeat in 1950. However, even the extensive use of airpower could not prevent a determined and capable enemy from winning major battles on the ground. In the last days of the war, after the surrender of Dien Bien Phu, French Mobile Group 100, well equipped with armor and artillery and built around an elite regiment that had fought in Korea, was cut to pieces by the Viet Minh in the central highlands of South Vietnam. Despite heavy air support by every bomber and fighter available, Mobile Group 100 lost most of its men and vehicles to a series of well-staged ambushes by the Viet Minh. The Viet Minh had learned how to deal with airpower by camouflage and by engaging the French at close range so that the aircraft could not attack without hitting French troops as well.[65]

In short, even if the French had possessed all the aerial forces that they needed in Indochina, they still would not have gotten a much better result from the war. In the final analysis, the Viet Minh were willing to take horrendous casualties to reestablish their national independence, and the French were not willing to accept even a fraction of those casualties to maintain the hollow sham of the French Union.

The Algerian War

Algeria was the crown jewel of the French colonial empire. Of course, legally speaking Algeria was not a colony but rather a part of metropolitan France, and Algerian delegates sat in the National Assembly. Ever since French troops had begun the conquest of Algeria in 1830, France had developed deep emotional ties to that land. One of the decisive factors in the French relationship with Algeria was the presence of one million French settlers, most of whose ancestors had come from Italy and Spain to settle in Algeria in the 1800s. The million French *colons,* or *pieds noirs* (black feet) as they were nicknamed, constituted a group of large landowners in the rural areas, and the middle class and civil service of the major cities of Algiers, Oran, and Constantine. The *pieds noirs* dominated the politics and business of Algeria, and prior to World War II, the nine million Arab residents of Algeria had little say in the affairs of their country.

By the end of World War II, unrest among the Arab community of Algeria had been seething under the surface for decades. The Arab and Berber peoples of Algeria had more than proven their loyalty to France by sending a large number of troops to fight for France in both world wars. Indeed, many Algerians fought for France in the colonial campaigns in Morocco and Syria in the 1920s and in Indochina from 1946 to 1954. Before and during World War II, the French government made promises to reform the government of Algeria, extend the franchise, allow Arabs to vote, and allow an Arab role in

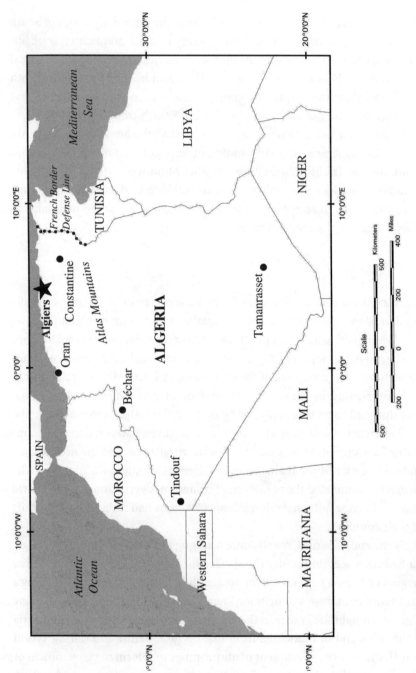

The War in Algeria, 1954–1962

local government. However, the intransigence of the *colons* in Algeria and the volatile and unstable nature of the governments in the Third and Fourth Republics ensured that any real hope for reform in Algeria was blocked. By 1945, while the French *colons* enjoyed a high standard of living, good schools, and government services, the Algerians were mostly dirt poor, illiterate, and barely eking out a living working for French landowners and businesses.

Decades of broken promises of reform and poverty finally exploded on 8 May 1945, when the VE Day celebrations in the market town of Sétif, eighty miles from Constantine, turned into spontaneous anti-French riots. The riots by the Algerians turned into a brutal massacre of over one hundred *colons,* complete with mutilation of bodies, rapes, looting, and burning of homes and businesses. The French military and police quickly retaliated with the utmost violence. American lend-lease-supplied Douglas Daunt-less dive-bombers bombed more than forty of the villages in the area. French ships shelled some villages. *Colon* vigilantes lynched Arabs suspected of participating in the revolt, while French troops and police pacified the Arab community in a manner reminiscent of German SS antipartisan operations. Estimates of Arab dead range from the official French figure of 1,020 to 1,300, to 45,000 given by the Algerians. A figure of 6,000 Arab dead is considered a fair estimate.[66]

The Sétif massacre had, at first, alarmed the French government and the *colons*, and some reforms were introduced into the Algerian political system. In 1947 a few minor reforms were instituted. The direct rule of Algeria by Paris was abolished and an elected Algerian Assembly was created, which allowed Algerians to modify French metropolitan laws for Algeria and to vote on a budget and financial issues. However, the Algerian Assembly was organized into two colleges of sixty delegates each, one college elected by the one million French *colons,* and the other elected by the nine million Arabs. Other reforms demanded by the Algerians, such as the recognition of Arabic as an official language, the franchise for women, ending military government in the Sahara, were all tabled by the French National Assembly, which was afraid of offending the *pied noir* delegates. The reforms of 1947, and especially the widespread election fraud by the *pieds noirs* in the municipal elections, did little to satisfy the Algerians.[67] When the French moved to suppress any Algerian political group or movement that appeared subversive, such groups simply went underground.

THE REVOLUTIONARIES

In early 1954 a group of nine young (average age thirty-two) Algerian nationalists met to organize a party to fight the French and work for the full independence of Algeria. Many of the original organizers of the party, the Front de
Libération Nationale (FLN), had a long history of nationalist political agitation and some had served time in French prisons. There was no interest in any
compromise with France on terms of anything less than full independence for
Algerians. The ideology was a mixture of nationalism and Islamic fundamen-
talism with a bit of Marxism thrown in. The long-term program of the FLN
was to build up an organization throughout the country and organize guerrilla
forces to conduct an offensive war to drive the French out. The FLN put considerable hope in receiving both political support and military support, in the
forms of arms and equipment, from the Arab nations — most importantly the
anti-Western regime of Nassar in Egypt. When first approached, Egypt and
other Arab nations expressed encouragement but provided no arms. The FLN
had to start the war first, then arms would be forthcoming.[68]

The FLN organized their military forces into six regional commands, called
Wilayas, and units would be based upon an 11-man section *(faoudj)*, 110-man
company *(katiba)*, and 350-man battalion *(failek)*. In the course of the war, the
shortage of arms and lack of trained guerrillas meant that the largest force normally employed by the FLN inside Algeria would be the *faoudj* or *katiba*. With
the French loss of Indochina also came the French government's decision to
quickly grant the protectorates of Morocco and Tunisia full independence. The
Algerian nationalists could therefore count on the sympathetic Arab governments of Morocco and Tunisia to provide support to guerrilla forces and to
allow their countries to be used as a base to build up an Algerian guerrilla army.

The FLN initiated a national military offensive on 1 November 1954 with
no more than seventeen hundred guerrillas and auxiliaries armed with a few
hundred small arms to include old shotguns and hunting rifles. The initial
attacks were carried out as more of a series of disjointed terrorist attacks with
a few police stations attacked, bridges blown, pro-French Algerian leaders
assassinated, and some arson attacks against French industries. The FLN
offensive, meant to have a decisive and dramatic impact, inflicted few casualties. Instead of inspiring French panic, the weakness of the initial onslaught
gave the French the impression that they were dealing with a minor rebellion instead of the beginning of a people's war. At this point, the French had

only a small military presence in Algeria. There were fewer than fifty thousand troops in the country in 1954 and little in the way of airpower. Indeed, by the end of the year the total French helicopter force in Algeria was one helicopter rented from a civilian company.[69] However, a few reinforcements arrived, notably the Twenty-fifth Paratroop Division, and the French began an aggressive campaign in the Aurès Mountains (Wilaya 1), the most active military region of the FLN. In the winter of 1954 to 1955 the French managed to track down and kill the top leaders in the Wilaya and disperse the guerrilla bands that had formed.[70]

In 1955 the FLN, recognizing its military weakness, carried out its war by means of a large-scale terrorist campaign that first targeted the French *colons* in order to drive them out. Isolated French farms were attacked and French civilians killed, French businesses were bombed and torched. The second part of the campaign was much more extensive. Pro-French Algerians, such as French-appointed village leaders and their families, were specifically targeted for assassination. Indeed, a great part of the casualties of the war were Algerians killed by the FLN. By means of terror, the FLN ensured that there were no neutrals in the war. Algerians would decide to support Algerian independence and the FLN or the continued French rule of the country. There was to be no middle ground.

The French strategy against the FLN played into the hands of the FLN propagandists. As expected, the French responded to terror attacks upon their civilians by reprisals against nearby Algerians — often the innocent, as the perpetrators of terror attacks were usually far away by the time military and police forces arrived at the scene. The French used the doctrine of "collective responsibility" in fighting guerrillas in the same manner as the Germans in fighting partisans in World War II. If sabotage occurred, then all of the males of the nearest village would be held accountable and rounded up and shipped to internment camps. In other cases, the French reprisals for especially egregious terror attacks by the FLN became especially violent. When thirty-seven French civilians were brutally massacred by Algerians in the mining town of Philippeville in August 1955, French troops went berserk and slaughtered more than one thousand local Algerian villagers and gave no quarter to women or children.[71] Most of the Arabs killed were innocent of any wrongdoing. The FLN were pleased when the French were provoked to respond with extreme brutality because "the people will now hate the French more."

THE FRENCH BUILDUP

The French rapidly reinforced their forces in Algeria. Since Algeria was part of metropolitan France, there were no restrictions on the use of conscripts to fight the rebellion. Unlike Indochina, France was prepared to send whatever forces were required to keep Algeria under French rule. By July 1955 the forces in Algeria had grown to 105,000. By the end of 1956 there were about 400,000 French troops in Algeria, a strength that was maintained until the end of the war in 1962.[72] In 1957 the French defense minister, André Morice, declared that the French forces in Algeria had "an absolute priority" for equipment and personnel over NATO and other French commitments. In Algeria, he declared, France was developing the equipment and tactics to fight communist subversion."[73] In addition to more than twenty thousand Algerians serving in the regular army, France was also able to raise a sizable Algerian militia willing to defend their villages from the FLN guerrillas. The *harkis,* armed with an assortment of shotguns and old rifles, served under the direction of a corps of Arabic-speaking French specialists in civil affairs (SAS — Sections Administratives Specialisées) and were very effective in limiting the support of the FLN in the countryside. By 1960, sixty thousand *harkis* were under arms.[74] It should be noted that throughout the Algerian War, as many Algerians fought for France as for the FLN nationalists. Unlike Indochina, the French instituted some political reforms and carried out an extensive civic action program in the countryside, the areas where the FLN needed a sympathetic population to thrive.

The French air force presence in Algeria grew rapidly. At the start of the war there were slightly over 8,000 air force personnel in North Africa.[75] By June 1955 this force had grown to 12,500 men and would increase to 30,000 men by 1960 (32,000 by early 1961).[76] With the experience of Indochina behind them, the French high command saw the role of aviation as especially important in this type of war, and the aviation infrastructure was dramatically increased as dozens of new landing strips were built around the country and major improvements made to the larger air bases. Aircraft available to the air force and army increased from 197 aircraft at the start of 1955 to 686 airplanes and 82 helicopters by November 1957.[77] While the number of airplanes leveled off in 1957, the number of helicopters used in operations was increased dramatically. By 1960 the French armed forces had 400 helicopters in service, ranging from the French-made Alouette light reconnaissance helicopters to the heavy U.S.-built Sikorsky H-19s and H-34s, which could carry twelve or more soldiers into battle. The Vertol H-21 two-rotor helicopter, nicknamed "the banana," could carry an impressive load of twenty soldiers.[78] Although helicopters had seen service in the medevac role in Burma in 1945 and throughout the Korean conflict and had been used as tactical troop-lift by the British in Malaya, Algeria was the first war to see the helicopter used extensively as a gunship. By 1958 the French had become proficient in using the helicopter in battle. Most helicopters were for troop-lift, but the French had a policy of arming one in every six helicopters. Helicopters such as the H-21 were commonly armed with two .30-caliber machine guns and two rocket pods, each with thirty-six 37 mm rockets on each side. The 37 mm rockets gave a wide dispersal of fire, which was useful for covering combat insertions. The French navy H-21 helicopters had a 20 mm cannon mounted in the doorway.[79]

Although the French air force had been reequipped with first-rate modern aircraft following World War II (with few of the modern planes going to Indochina), the new high-performance Dassault fighters and F-86 Sabrejets were unsuitable for the conditions of counterinsurgency warfare. Although a few jets would serve in Algeria in the fighter-bomber role, the French air force found the ideal aircraft for the conditions of the Algeria war was the American World War II T-6 trainer. The T-6 was slow (top speed barely over 200 km) but cheap (thousands were available after World War II), sturdy, and easy to maintain. It could operate from small tactical landing strips (something jet fighter-bombers couldn't do) and loiter far longer than a jet. Its slow speed meant that the pilot and observer could fly low and observe the terrain closely. Moreover, the T-6s could be adapted to carry a moderate ordnance load of two 7.5 mm machine guns, a 100-liter napalm tank, four 10 kg bombs, and six rockets.[80] France would maintain over three hundred T-6s as reconnaissance and attack aircraft in Algeria. It was the primary aircraft of the war, and between 1957 and 1959, twenty-three squadrons were equipped with it. In 1960 the T-6s began to be replaced with more modern T-28s, which carried more armament.[81]

The French air force also employed three P-47 squadrons in Algeria. In the final stages of the war, some of these World War II planes were replaced with U.S.-built A-1 Douglas Skyraiders, one of the best ground attack aircraft ever built. The bomber force consisted of three squadrons of B-26s. To round out the French airpower, there were three squadrons of MS 500 light planes for artillery spotting (used from 1956 to 1958), and a transport force of several squadrons that included the old reliable C-47s as well as the new Noratlas. Additional support was provided by the naval air arm, which provided three squadrons of F4U Corsairs and one squadron of F6F Hellcats as fighter-bomber support throughout most of the war.[82] The navy also committed several detachments of heavy helicopters to make the French Marine Commandos a highly mobile and deadly force against the FLN guerrillas.[83]

ORGANIZATION AND TACTICS

In contrast to Indochina, the French government provided enough troops and resources for the war so the military was able to saturate Algeria, both the cities and the countryside, with a large number of troops. For most of the French soldiers in Algeria, the war was one of guard duty, manning small garrisons and patrolling the local areas. Occasionally French troops were the target of a terrorist attack or would engage in a firefight with a small FLN element. However, the French were able to assemble a large and highly mobile force of three elite divisions, the Tenth and Twenty-fifth Paratroop Divisions (all volunteers) and the Eleventh Infantry Division, which included a Foreign Legion regiment. Various other elite units such as the French air force commando companies, trained to operate as paratroops and airmobile infantry, and French navy marines supplemented the mobile force.[84] These elite troops, supported by the T-6 aircraft and fighter-bombers and with helicopter-provided mobility, were able to carry the battle to the enemy deep in the mountainous regions of Algeria and engage in large-scale sweeps for the insurgents. When local army units ran into any significant guerrilla forces, the elite mobile units stationed around the country could quickly respond by helicopter and move to envelop and destroy the FLN units.[85]

The Algerian War featured few large actions. Rarely did the FLN manage to assemble more than a *katiba* (company) and stage a large operation. The Algerians stuck to a hit-and-run kind of warfare, ambushing small French patrols and carrying out small-scale attacks. Rarely did the FLN try to fight any major defensive battles — unless they were cornered and had little choice. In such cases, French firepower usually won the day.

Airpower played a central role in the war by its constant presence. T-6s flew armed reconnaissance patrols to spot movement by FLN forces in the countryside. If a French patrol made contact with the FLN or was ambushed,

T-6s on patrol could respond in minutes and keep the FLN under aerial observation and use their machine guns and bombs to hold off the FLN until other T-6s could take their place. In the meantime, helicopter-borne infantry could respond to support and cut off the FLN force.

All of this required a lavish communications network, far better than the French had in Indochina. Indeed, the French forces in Algeria were well equipped with radios and a thorough communications network, complete with radio relay stations, was established throughout the whole country, and the air and ground forces were efficiently tied together. The French also set up an elaborate system of radio monitoring and direction finders to monitor and locate rebel radio transmissions.[86]

The French approach to airpower was to decentralize the air command system in a manner similar to Indochina. The Fifth Air Region was the headquarters for all French air force assets in Algeria. By early 1956, the air force in Algeria was organized into three tactical air commands (GATACs) with headquarters in Oran (west), Algiers (central Algeria), and Constantine (east) that corresponded to the three army corps commands in Algeria. There was a separate air zone for the Sahara region.[87] Each of the GATACs was further organized into four geographical zones (divisional zones) with a headquarters and commander for each. The corps/GATACs and divisional zones controlled army and air forces through a joint operations center. The air assets of the air force and army, augmented in the coastal areas by the considerable air units of the French navy, were generally distributed throughout the zones with a reserve of airplanes and helicopters held by the GATAC. The mission of the air forces was support of the ground forces, and the air units operated normally under overall command of the army corps area commanders. However, the divisional zone commanders and the regimental sector commanders had considerable autonomy to fight the war in their own areas. The reserve of helicopters and aircraft held by the GATAC served to support large sweep and combat operations and would be shifted around the country as the operational need arose.[88]

Distributing aircraft in small packets around Algeria made great sense for that kind of guerrilla war. Unlike Indochina, the small scale of the fighting meant that there were few instances where it was necessary to mass a large number of aircraft. Having a few aircraft respond quickly was more important than a large force that responded slowly. The ubiquity of the T-6s and light aircraft over the countryside also served as an important psychological factor in the war.

French troops on the ground knew that they could rely on rapid air support, and the FLN were hampered in any attempt to assemble a large force by the knowledge that French aerial reconnaissance was ever present. Moreover, the FLN possessed no antiaircraft weapons, and so the only threat to French aviation was small arms fire. While many of the French airplanes and helicopters were damaged by FLN fire, aircraft were rarely brought down. The French in Algeria enjoyed a far lower loss rate than they did in Indochina.

In addition to distributing air units around the country, the French set up several joint operations centers to coordinate air-ground operations. In December 1958, after de Gaulle became president of France, he appointed General Maurice Challe, an air force officer, as commander in chief of all forces in Algeria. Challe, considered to be the most capable of the French military commanders in Algeria during the war, instituted numerous reforms in doctrine and tactics and brought a new vision for fighting the war. One of his first steps was to refine the command and control system. GATACs were given complete control of all light aviation flights in their area, and each GATAC was provided with an aerial support brigade to provide for logistics, aircraft maintenance, and base support.[89]

BATTLE OF THE FRONTIERS

The FLN took heavy losses in early 1955 but managed to survive the French counteroffensive and grow steadily in influence. In early 1957 the focus of the war became urban when the FLN began a terror campaign in Algiers and organized a series of strikes. The French reacted by imposing martial law and by sending in a paratroop division that broke the FLN organization by the most ruthless means, including torture. In the meantime, Tunisia and Morocco had become independent, and the FLN had two secure bases in which to form and train an army with the aid and weapons now flowing in large quantities from Arab nations. Using Tunisia and Morocco as sanctuaries, the FLN planned to move trained units, weapons, and supplies into the interior of the country, especially to the Aurès and Kabylia Mountains where there was already a strong FLN presence. At this time, the FLN rebels in the countryside were very poorly armed and scattered about in small bands, scarcely a real threat to French control. The FLN hoped to change the dynamics of the war with the thousands of men being trained in the Tunisian and Moroccan sanctuaries.

The French responded by building an elaborate defense line on the Moroccan and Tunisian borders complete with minefields, an electrified fence, and numerous observation posts. The civilian population was cleared out of the border regions so that the FLN troops could not get local support or find cover with the population. The whole area was made a free-fire zone. The key to holding the defense lines and preventing the infiltration of large numbers of FLN troops or large quantities of supplies was a highly mobile force stationed at key intervals to respond quickly to any attempt of the FLN to rush through the barrier lines. The most elaborate of the defense zones was the one along the Tunisian border, which ran south from the Mediterranean for two hundred miles and ended with the dunes of the Sahara. South of the line was covered by air patrols, which would be able to easily spot infiltrators in the barren country. The Moroccan and Tunisian border lines were completed in September 1957.

France put eighty thousand of her best troops, such as the Foreign Legion, on the borders, and these troops received the priority of helicopter support. From January to May 1958, the two borders were the scenes of the largest battles of the war as FLN units as large as eight hundred men tried to push their way through the border region to the mountainous interior of Algeria. It was a disaster for the FLN. An estimated six thousand FLN rebels were killed trying to break through the frontier barrier before the FLN called off the attempts to infiltrate.[90]

LATER ACTIONS, 1958–1961

After the success on the borders, Challe was able to put together a large "general reserve" of more than three divisions to carry out large-scale operations to destroy the FLN forces in the mountainous hinterland. The "Challe Plan" began with a major operation of over twenty thousand troops from February through March 1959 to surround and destroy the FLN forces of Wilaya 5 in western Algeria ("Operation Couronne"). Again, helicopters were central to using mobile troops to block and surround FLN detachments, and four hundred helicopters were available in Algeria by 1959. The helicopter groups were usually organized into detachments ("combat cells") of seven heavy H-21s and one light Alouette helicopter for command and reconnaissance. These units could rapidly move companies in two shifts.[91] Operation Couronne proved very successful and most of the FLN forces in the Oran region were tracked down and destroyed. After the FLN forces were destroyed or dispersed, the SAS would move in and conduct civic action and establish protected villages to prevent a resurgence of the FLN.

The grand sweep and envelopment operations continued throughout 1959. "Operation Étincelles" struck the FLN in the Atlas Mountains from April to June. In July "Operation Jumelles" targeted the FLN in Wilaya 3 in the mountains south of Algiers. "Operation Pierres Precieuses" was carried out in the Kabylia Mountains near Constantine from September to November 1959.[92] By late October the French could claim that 3,746 insurgents had been killed, captured, or wounded. Throughout the mountains of Algeria the FLN groups were being broken up and hunted down. By early 1960 FLN morale had hit rock bottom, as the guerrillas were losing weapons to the French far faster than they could be replaced. General Challe's innovative and aggressive strategy had basically broken the FLN as a military force by early 1960.[93] By the time Challe returned to France in April 1960, he could look to an impressive record of military success.

OTHER AIR ACTIONS

As in Indochina, the French bombed villages known to be FLN strongholds in retaliation for FLN attacks on French troops in the vicinity. Such bombing did not seem to have much effect on diminishing support for the FLN. In one case, a French bombing raid provoked a major international protest and seriously damaged the French position in world opinion. The French had long known that the village of Sakiet, just inside the Tunisian border, was a base for the FLN forces trying to infiltrate Algeria. After some French troops patrolling the border were killed in a FLN ambush, on 8 February 1958 the French decided to take stern action to go after the FLN camp. A squadron of B-26s flattened the village in a matter of minutes. Although Sakiet was an FLN base, it also contained many Tunisian civilians. The French bombing occurred on market day, so there were more civilians in town than usual, and at least eighty civilians were killed; one of the buildings leveled was a school. The resulting press coverage and photos of the wrecked school and injured children caught the attention of the world and the United Nations (UN). There were numerous protests against the French action, and the Arab world was outraged and further inspired to support the FLN. At Sakiet, the French handed the FLN their most important propaganda victory of the war.[94]

The French also used airpower to support a psychological warfare campaign. Leaflet drops over the isolated villages encouraged FLN members to surrender. Other leaflets promoted the civic action programs of the French administration.[95] One leaflet dropped over the Sahara stressed the effectiveness of French airpower in destroying the rebels. The pamphlet, printed in French and Arabic, starts with a crude picture of desert rebels killing a detachment of French soldiers. In the next panels a French reconnaissance aircraft spots the camel-mounted tribesmen. In the last panel, French soldiers, led to the rebels by aircraft, kill them all. The final message in large print says "Crime Does Not Pay."[96]

MILITARY VICTORY — POLITICAL DEFEAT

By 1960 the French had won the war on the battlefield in the cities and in the countryside. The FLN had been broken after a bloody campaign in Algiers. The major operations on the Aurès and Kabylia initiated by General Challe had broken the back of the major FLN forces. The military forces of the FLN were broken into demoralized, poorly armed small bands. Hunger was a major problem for the FLN fighters as the *harkis* were able to drive them away from villages where they might obtain food and support.

Yet, on the political side, the FLN was winning the war. The French carried out a few halfhearted reforms for the Algerians after the start of the rebellion, but it was much too little and too late. The *pieds noirs* violently opposed any concessions to the Algerians that would give them real political power. France took a beating on the world stage as the newly independent Third World countries took the side of the FLN. It was politically embarrassing for the French to have the Algeria issue repeatedly brought up in the UN, and Algeria became a millstone for the French public. Reservists and conscripts brought back tales of brutality and torture by the French and the Algerians, and the war was costing France a vast sum of money. The Algerian crisis brought Charles de Gaulle back to power in 1958, and although initially inclined to win the war and keep Algeria a French possession, de Gaulle came to see Algeria as a cause that was hurting the French economy and tearing the political fabric of the nation apart.

If the French had negotiated a new political order with the Algerians and given them a genuine program of home rule in the early stages of the rebellion, France and Algeria might have come to an amicable agreement with home rule for Algeria and French direction of foreign, defense, and economic policy. However, the longer the war dragged on, the more the Algerian opinion polarized toward independence as the only possible solution. By 1960 de Gaulle's reform proposals had not been warmly received by the Algerians, and the Algerian public opinion shifted increasingly to support the concept of full independence. Through 1961 de Gaulle negotiated with the FLN on terms of independence, despite a rebellion by the *pieds noirs* and a mutiny by part of the army opposing an independent Algeria. De Gaulle, convinced more than ever that Algeria was a drag on France, agreed to independence for Algeria in 1962.

ASSESSMENT

Algeria is a classic case of winning the battles and losing the war. The French armed forces performed admirably in the Algerian War. The French proved to be tactically and operationally adept against a very tough and determined enemy. The French conducted a very effective civic action campaign that kept many Algerians firmly on the side of France in the war. The French interdiction campaign on the borders was a great success, with as much as 70 percent of supplies for the FLN interdicted by the French forces. The French conducted joint air-ground operations very successfully. The aviation side of operations was especially successful. The tactics of using the T-6 in armed reconnaissance and close air support were quite effective as was the French use of helicopters as battle aircraft in the world's first large-scale helicopter operations.

Considering the large number of troops engaged in Algeria, French military and civilian losses in the seven and one-half years of war were fairly light. The French forces lost 17,456 dead, 1,000 missing, and 64,985 wounded. There were over 10,000 casualties among the French civilians in Algeria with 2,788 killed. In contrast, the Algerian losses had been very high. An estimated 141,000 Algerian male combatants were killed. As many as 12,000 FLN members were killed in the internal purges that plagued the FLN, and an estimated 66,000 Muslim civilians were killed by FLN assassination and terrorism. The number of wounded is only to be guessed at.[97] The casualty figures from Algeria are another example of a common twentieth-century phenomenon — that a determined people motivated by nationalism and armed with little more than patience and a willingness to die in large numbers can win against a well-led and armed modern military force supported by the latest technology and plenty of airpower.

A squadron of F-8 Bearcats at Dien Bien Phu airfield, late 1953. The F-8 was designed as an air-to-air interceptor for the U.S. Navy and was deployed at the end of World War II, but failed to see action in that war. After 1951 the Bearcats became the main fighter-bomber of the French air force. The rugged, radial-engined fighter performed quite well in a role for which it was never designed. (USAF)

French B-26 bombers being readied for a mission. The B-26 was employed extensively in interdiction missions to try to cut the flow of supplies from China into Indochina from 1950 to 1954. The B-26 was a fine bomber, but there were not enough of them and the attempt at aerial interdiction failed. (USAF)

French C-47 transport squadron at Do Son airfield, 1954. American-supplied C-47s replaced the Ju 52s as the primary air transport plane of l'Armeé de l'air in Indochina after 1950. The French transport force performed extremely well throughout the war. However, as with all the other forms of French airpower, there were far too few to accomplish the mission. (USAF)

Ms 500 "Criquet" light reconnaissance planes of the First South Vietnamese Air Force Squadron, flying in support of the French army, 1954. Late in the war the French began forming an air force for the South Vietnamese. The first aircraft for the South Vietnamese were light reconnaissance planes and C-47 transports. These aircraft bear South Vietnamese markings. (USAF)

French airborne operation, North Vietnam, 1953. The French conducted numerous large-scale airborne operations in Indochina. (USAF)

French paratroops in Algeria. The French used their paratroop force extensively in the Algerian War, but most of the airborne operations were small-scale missions when compared with Indochina. (USAF)

5

The British Colonial Wars, 1945–1975

Malaya, South Arabia, and Oman

Before the outbreak of World War II, Great Britain was a major power with vast imperial holdings around the globe. When the war ended, Britain still held its colonial possessions and gained additional territory resulting from the defeat of the Axis powers. Not only were British troops still garrisoned throughout the empire, they also occupied portions of Austria and Germany and took control of former Italian possessions in North Africa. At the same time, Britain assumed administrative control of the Dutch East Indies, and British troops were necessary to fill the vacuum left by the Japanese surrender in French Indochina. Yet in little more than a decade after the war, Britain retained little of its former empire. India and Ceylon gained their independence in 1947. Palestine was lost in 1948. In 1951 the Egyptians denounced the Anglo-Egyptian treaty of 1936, and the British subsequently agreed to leave in 1954. Malta and Cyprus followed suit in the early 1960s. Within twenty-five years, Britain found itself a middle power with a struggling economy and only a small fraction of its empire intact.

Against this backdrop, the British army following World War II was dramatically reduced, from around three million men under arms to less than four hundred thousand.[1] In the Royal Air Force (RAF) the reductions were even more striking. For example, when the communist insurgency in Malaya came into full bloom in 1948, RAF personnel had sunk from nearly 125,000 in Air Command Southeast Asia alone to less than nine thousand in the whole of Air Command Far East. Frontline strength had also been reduced, from 1,324 operational aircraft in more than seventy squadrons in 1945 to just over ten squadrons comprising little more than one hundred aircraft.[2] In retrospect, the British military faced a challenge in policing the empire after World

War II not unlike that posed after World War I. In the aftermath of a major world war, when the British economy was floundering and the empire was faced with serious disorders at the far reaches, the armed forces were demobilizing at a dramatic pace and yet at the same time reassuming the burdensome duty of imperial security. Not surprisingly, the RAF would be called upon to play a vital role in securing imperial objectives.[3]

Imperial Policing: Setting the Stage

As evidenced in Major General C. E. Callwell's seminal work, *Small Wars: Their Principles and Practice,* first published in 1896, the characteristic British approach to small wars has been to stress practicality rather than theory.[4] But if British practicality is anything, it is rooted in Clausewitzian theory: determine the nature of the war, assess the capabilities of the enemy, establish clear objectives, and devise operational and tactical solutions to realize the stated objectives.[5] Irrespective of the Clausewitzian dimension, however, British imperialism up to the outbreak of World War II dealt with colonial disorders as essentially a military problem, with little regard for the social, economic, or political aspirations of native peoples under British dominion. Callwell identified three classes of campaigns: conquest and annexation; putting down insurrection; and responding to insult — the latter generally described as "punitive expeditions." In each instance, the military objective was to engage the enemy and decisively beat him. In terms of any role that popular support for the rebels might play, Callwell posited that the "rifle and sword" and "a vigorous offense" would have the intended effect of "keeping at home those who hesitate to take up arms . . . thereby diminishing the fighting strength of the enemy."[6]

With the introduction of airpower into the colonial milieu after World War I, little changed in terms of context — RAF airplanes bombed known or suspected enemy formations as an extension of the military character of small wars. In fact Callwell's work was included in the curriculum at the RAF Staff College at Andover.[7] It is reasonable to assume, then, that RAF officers generally inculcated the idea that airpower was simply an extension of traditional military coercion, albeit they made claims at the same time that airpower was a more humane instrument in that regard.[8]

British colonial governors before World War II held the prevailing view that civil disorders were the product of man's "inherent and compulsively irratio-

nal urge to violence and mischief."[9] Primitive societies were especially suscep-
tible to rebellion and insurrection and responsive only to force. General Gar-
net Wolseley, who razed the Ashanti capital of Kumasi during the Second
Ashanti War in 1874, was quoted by Callwell to this end: "In planning a war
against an uncivilized nation . . . your first object should be the capture of
whatever they prize most . . . the destruction or deprivation of which will probably bring the war most rapidly to a conclusion."[10] The "burn and scuttle" strategy that characterized British punitive expeditions was largely successful because
native peoples lacked a unifying ideology or national consciousness with which
to focus their resistance. But as Douglas Porch has pointed out,

This would change as imperialism produced from within its own ranks a leadership capable of articulating a coherent vision for resistance. Nationalism, Marxism,
or Islam supplied ideologies that rationalized and focused discontent. Theorists of
revolution, Mao Tse-tung prominent among them, supplied blueprints that showed
indigenous societies how to anchor their resistance in a social organization able to
resist the pressures of European operational methods of the sort laid out by Callwell.[11]

Within this modality, anticolonial sentiment reached a critical mass during the early part of the Cold War, precipitating independence movements
on a global scale. Given the ideological *allentours* of revolutionary warfare
after World War II, it is not surprising that the former colonial military strategy, whether conducted on the ground or by air, would be, if anything, counterproductive. As one astute RAF officer noted in 1954:

In the period between the wars the tribal insurgent was often a strictly part-time
combatant. One of several motives could inspire him to revolt: religious enthusiasm, hunger, nationalism, or frequently just sheer *joie-de-vivre* and enjoyment of a
good fight. The seeds of his rebellion were thus sown in pretty shallow ground. . . .
In [such] circumstances, quick retaliatory action firm enough to show him that the
game was not worth the candle usually sufficed to put an end to the matter. . . .
Today our opponent is a different man. . . . He is no longer a part-time, self-
supporting, amateur enemy, who can be discouraged by a sharp lesson on the error
of his ways. He is engaged in a full-time, fully organized military and terrorist campaign for as long as his masters decide to commit and support him. Therefore,
counter-measures must now be strong enough to eliminate him completely or
override the powerful influences that control both him and his master.[12]

Despite his emphasis on operational solutions, Callwell did articulate certain principles that would remain valid during the Cold War. As Ian Beckett

has proposed, "It is arguable that the essential flexibility of the traditional British approach ensured that what were by now accepted principles of military subordination [to civil authority] . . . and a recognition of the need to split active insurgents from their local supporters were ideally adaptable to specific conditions."[13] Imperial policing presupposed civil authority as superior to military in the colonies, and British soldiers understood their role in that regard. British army units therefore adapted to local conditions and trained accordingly. Indeed, the only manual produced by the War Office during the interwar period specifically for imperial policing emphasized "duties in aid of the civil power under circumstances hitherto neglected in training literature."[14] Like Callwell, the manual pointed out that fighting against an irregular enemy required operational and tactical methods outside of traditional warfare: "The enemy, although possibly well-armed . . . acts largely by subterranean methods, offering no opportunity of locating or defeating his forces by the ordinary methods of war."[15]

The same year that this manual appeared, Major General Sir Charles Gwynn, commandant of the British Army Staff College from 1926 to 1930, published a lengthy study entitled *Imperial Policing*, which drew upon a wide range of case studies that similarly emphasized civilian control and coordination of civil-military efforts.[16] These principles were therefore at the core of British military thinking, including that of the RAF. Thus, establishing a link between the political objectives of the civil power and airpower in colonial campaigns, one RAF officer asserted in 1928: "Authorise air action, and leave the airman, in conjunction with the political authorities, to carry it out in the way he understands."[17]

The theme of practicality and subordination to civil authority in the British military tradition would prove pivotal after World War II. Prior to the Malayan Emergency, the British attempted to continue their previous colonial military strategy, to include emphasizing air control in some areas. But as stated earlier, the emergence of revolutionary insurgency presented the British with a social and political context not faced during the interwar years. Consequently, the ability of the RAF to unilaterally prevail in such conflicts was substantially if not wholly undermined. The entire concept of air control presupposed that airpower could not only provide support to imperial troops on the ground but could in fact be substituted for these forces in some areas. But punitive expeditions before World War II were little concerned with winning the political allegiance of recalcitrant natives, and despite claims to the contrary, RAF operations were often quite brutal as a result.

Given the necessity to "win the hearts and minds" of the people in revolutionary war, the role of offensive airpower was greatly diminished. For one thing, the underlying theory of modern counterinsurgency as it emerged in Malaya eschewed the indiscriminate use of firepower, aerial or otherwise. As one authority on revolutionary insurgency noted afterward, "In a form of warfare in which political considerations regularly outweigh the military, air attacks against 'suspected enemy groups' are all too likely to be self-defeating. The loss of support brought on by each innocent man or woman killed is likely to far outweigh the possible gain of hard-core rebels killed."[18] The late Bernard Fall similarly asserted, "In revolutionary war where ideology plays the key role, the air element is unlikely to play a decisive part."[19] Yet airpower would play an important role in countering insurgency throughout the empire after World War II and proved decisive in its own fashion — but not in the same sense as promoted before the war.

The RAF Following World War II

The 1950s and 1960s were watershed years for the RAF. In addition to playing a supporting role in countering insurgency throughout a dwindling empire, difficult relations with the United States and the perceived need to acquire a nuclear retaliatory capability set the azimuth for much of what occurred to the RAF following World War II. President Truman's decision to forego the 1943 Quebec agreement and the 1944 Hyde Park agreement, which together had, inter alia, promised full cooperation for military purposes, clearly signaled that the United States sought to retain a nuclear monopoly. This was underscored in 1946 when the U.S. Congress passed the MacMahon Act, which prohibited sharing nuclear information.[20] The British government therefore embarked on its own nuclear policy, one that was initially vested wholly in the RAF — the "V Bomber."[21]

Beginning in the early 1950s, the Air Staff accorded the V-Force a special priority, and it quickly consumed a major portion of the RAF budget at a time when Great Britain was making dramatic cuts in overall defense spending. The consequent diminishing resources became a dominant theme in RAF deliberations regarding strategy, acquisition, and force structure. The 1960s were in some respects an even more difficult period for defense budget decisions: that decade was dominated by debilitating economic crises, including a major devaluation of British currency. Disputes with the army and navy over such issues as ownership of helicopters and the relative superiority of land-based airpower versus sea-based airpower were accentuated. This opened a much wider debate regarding Britain's role in the international arena and how airpower could fulfill British global commitments.

Unlike during the interwar period, when many RAF officers promoted airpower as an effective substitute for forces on the ground in policing the empire, few airmen made such claims following World War II. Indeed, one RAF group captain in 1946 reflected on the role of airpower in small wars, arguing in distinctly prophetic terms that

since the essence of occupation is the presence of troops in the territory, it is probable that the greatest contribution which the air force can make is to carry the Army around the country. In this way, it will be possible to combine the speed and penetration of the air force with the discriminatory action of troops on the ground. If, in addition to being carried by air, the ground forces can also be maintained by air, the whole problem of control is greatly simplified.[22]

In 1954, Marshal of the RAF Sir John Slessor reflected this sentiment in a lecture to the Royal United Service Institution, going so far as to say that the British army would be "the primary arm in . . . small wars."[23] Although speaking mostly in terms of small wars on the level of the Korean conflict, Slessor was quick to point out to a questioner that the same principle applied to "minor wars" of the sort flaring up in French Indochina and within the British Empire.[24] In that regard, Air Marshal Sir Robert Saundby similarly asserted that the role of the RAF would be "to support the Army acting in aid of the civil power."[25] Air control in the form of "air substitution" was never seriously proffered after World War II, although its legacy was invoked on more than one occasion.[26] Nevertheless, the contributions of the RAF in the various colonial campaigns that followed were described by army and RAF officers alike as vital to British success in policing the empire. As one Australian army brigadier general would later note, without the essential, "day-to-day" support provided by the RAF, the army could have achieved little.[27]

Malaya, 1948–1960

The insurgency in Malaya officially lasted twelve years, but its origins can be traced as far back as the early nineteenth century. Great Britain first seized control of a portion of the Malay Peninsula in the latter half of the eighteenth century in order to secure its commercial interests in the region as well as safeguard the strategically vital Straits of Malacca. In 1824 the Dutch ceded the peninsula to Britain, but in 1826 the British negotiated a treaty with the dominant regional power, Siam, agreeing to permit the various Malay states to remain autonomous. But when substantial tin deposits were discovered, the British East India Company established a trading post at the mouth of the Kedah River and Britain's interest in the whole of the peninsula became acute. Consequently, through diplomatic and economic incentives, Britain persuaded several of the various governments of the region to form the Federated Malay States in 1896. By 1909 the British had extended their control to the boundaries of the Malay Peninsula.[28] Following World War I, the federation experienced pronounced economic growth, and with Singapore emerging as the cornerstone of British defense strategy in the Far East, a pros-

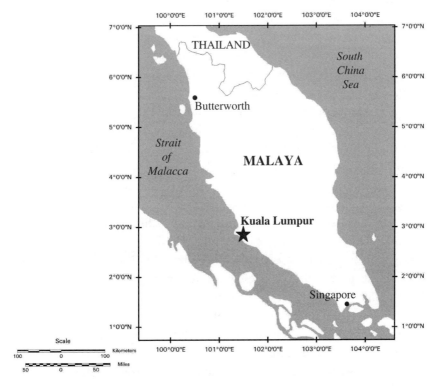

The Malayan Emergency, 1948–1960

perous and enduring relationship with Britain seemed secure. That is, until communist agitation and insurgency threatened to overturn British authority in Malaya following World War II.

Communism in Malaya was not an indigenous movement. The need for labor to work the tin mines prompted large numbers of Chinese to immigrate to Malaya in the 1850s; another surge occurred in the early 1900s. By 1921, Malaya's Chinese population had grown to 1.17 million; in 1952 the population was just over 2 million; and by 1960 the Chinese community exceeded 3 million.[29] When the Emergency was declared in 1948, there was a total of 4.9 million people, of whom over 2.5 million were native Malays and just under 2 million were Chinese. The remainder were mainly of Indian origin.[30] Native Malays regarded the Chinese immigrants as interlopers, and their alien status relegated the Chinese to segregated communities and to the margins of Malay society and politics.

With the emergence of Chiang Kai-shek's Kuomintang as a political force in China, nationalist sentiments among the Malay Chinese began to take shape in the 1920s. In 1924, infiltrators from Shanghai sought to organize the Malay Chinese and succeeded in penetrating labor organizations throughout the federation. Drawing its membership almost exclusively from the Chinese minority, the Malayan Communist Party (MCP) emerged in 1930 and subsequently fomented a series of labor strikes that almost crippled the country.[31]

Following the Japanese occupation of Singapore and Malaya during World War II, the British reluctantly enlisted the aid of the MCP in establishing a network of resistance. At the time, the MCP was the only indigenous organization capable of mounting any kind of armed resistance to the Japanese, and 165 MCP members were selected to receive special guerrilla warfare training.[32] These key members of the MCP formed the core of the Malayan People's Anti-Japanese Army (MPAJA). The MPAJA garnered some initial military successes against the Japanese, but by the end of 1942 it was on the verge of collapse due to relentless Japanese pressure. Therefore in February 1943 the British infiltrated specially trained operatives known as Force 136 to lead the MPAJA in preparation for Allied liberation. In addition to providing training and leading MPAJA forces in the field, the British also provided considerable quantities of arms and munitions. Reinvigorated, by the end of the war the MPAJA was a well-armed and highly organized guerrilla organization with some four thousand active fighters and around six thousand support personnel.[33]

During the occupation, the Japanese authorities forced over a million Chinese "squatters" into the countryside to grow food for the Japanese army. Others fled from the Japanese, and still others continued to arrive illegally from mainland China, all of whom settled in the squatter communities. The abrupt Japanese surrender on 14 August 1945 took Allied authorities in the region by surprise, and during a three-week interregnum the MPAJA attempted to take control of the country, establishing so-called people's committees throughout the squatter communities. Internal divisions within the MPAJA prevented a successful coup d'état, and Lord Mountbatten, supreme Allied commander Southeast Asia, moved swiftly in late August to retake Malaya and Singapore. The latter was secured by a naval task force before the end of the month. Soon afterward, British troops retook the peninsula, and a military administration was established by the end of September. Commonwealth troops moved into the countryside to restore order.[34]

With British authority reestablished, many guerrillas surrendered their arms when the MPAJA was officially disbanded in December 1945, but a substantial number of guerrillas remained armed and retreated to the jungle as the communist leadership went underground. Largely ineffectual during the war, the MPAJA had nevertheless acquired an aura of respectability among the Chinese minority, and after the war the MCP became the undisputed leader of Chinese nationalism in Malaya.[35] Thus, when the majority Malay population rejected a British proposal for an independent unitary state in 1948 in favor of a federation under British protection, the MCP declared a guerrilla war with the intent of overthrowing the central government and British rule.[36] The Chinese squatter communities provided the basis of popular support for the communist insurgency.

Antigovernment violence immediately erupted, and on 18 June 1948 the government instituted a state of emergency. One month later, the MCP was declared illegal. But the MCP was well organized with a central committee governing the political activities of regional bureaus, as well as state, district, and branch committees. In addition, a military wing of the MCP was formed from the remains of the MPAJA. The insurgent organization comprised two wings. The first was called the Malayan Races Liberation Army (MRLA), comprising eight and later ten regiments spread throughout the peninsula. The MRLA was a full-time military organization armed with the weapons and ammunition left over from World War II that had not been handed over to government forces. The larger clandestine organization, the Min Yuen, or "People's Movement," provided moral support for the MRLA, collected intelligence, disseminated propaganda, and, most important, provided food, medicine, and other logistical support to the fighting elements. Communism had little appeal, however, for ethnic Malays, Indians, and other ethnic groups in Malaya; consequently, the MCP, MRLA, and Min Yuen were composed almost entirely of Chinese.

Restoring law and order and separating the MRLA from its popular Chinese base were the principal immediate aims of the government. With this end in mind, the high commissioner, Sir Henry Gurney, assumed extraordinary powers and called out the armed forces "in aid of the civil power."[37] Eleven battalions — three Malay, six Gurkha, and two British — were placed under civil control and integrated with the federation of Malay police at all levels. But the MRLA took the initiative at the outset of the Emergency, and government forces were on the defensive. Soldiers were therefore used primarily to guard vital installations and secure the tin mines, rubber plantations, and other commercially important activities around the country. When military units did conduct operations in the field intending to seek out and destroy guerrilla formations, they proved ineffective. For example, at the battle of Tasek, some eight hundred troops cordoned off an area believed to contain fifty guerrillas. But after two days of fighting, the operation yielded only six guerrillas killed and none were leaders.[38]

As government forces struggled and the MRLA expanded its offensive, Lieutenant General Sir Harold Briggs arrived in April 1950 to direct the counterinsurgency effort. Briggs was a veteran of the jungle war in Burma during World War II and had a clear appreciation of the military challenge before him.[39] Malaya was roughly the size of Florida, and two-thirds of it was covered with almost impenetrable jungle. Running the length of the peninsula down the center were jungle-covered hills rising to a height of over seven thousand feet in some places. West of these hills, roads and railways were in reasonably good shape, but on the eastern side communications were very poor and in some places nonexistent. Airfields capable of supporting anything other than light aircraft were in extremely short supply. The main RAF headquarters and the principal airfields were located on Singapore Island, with only two "all-purpose" airfields available on mainland Malaya — one at Butterworth in the north and the other at Kuala Lumpur.

The latter airfield became the principal base for air operations against the guerrillas, code-named Operation "Firedog." There were a few smaller airfields that could accommodate medium transport aircraft on the west coast, but the east coast was almost devoid of suitable airfields between Singapore and Kota Bharu. Since the principal mission of the RAF in the Far East theater after World War II was air defense, primarily aimed at the growing Chinese threat, the available airfields and aircraft were regarded as sufficient to the task: two Beaufighter light bomber squadrons, two Spitfire squadrons, three Dakota (DC-3) squadrons, one Mosquito photoreconnaissance squadron, three squadrons of Sunderland flying boats, and one flight of Auster light liaison/observation aircraft.[40]

With the limited air and ground forces at his disposal, General Briggs set about to suppress the insurgency. The "Briggs Plan" focused on the operational task of finding and killing guerrillas but also on organizing the civil bureaucracy to manage the effort. The general military aims of the Briggs Plan were to "lower the insurgent potential, both directly by ground and air operations, and indirectly by denying them their sources of supply and support."[41] Regarding the latter aim, the centerpiece of the Briggs Plan was to isolate the rural Chinese population from the guerrillas by collecting Chinese squatters into protected enclaves. The plan for resettlement of Chinese squatters was dubbed "New Villages."[42] Regarding the former aim, Briggs reduced the military forces dedicated to holding key positions to a minimum so that the surplus could be used to "launch a progressive programme of cleaning-up operations, starting in Johore in the South, and working steadily up country towards the Northern frontier."[43]

As the Briggs Plan unfolded, Sir Henry Gurney was killed in an ambush on 6 October 1951, and one month later Briggs was forced to resign due to failing health. At this point Prime Minister Winston Churchill appointed General Sir Gerald Templer as high commissioner to replace Gurney. At the same time, Arthur Young of the London Police Department was appointed to head the Malayan police forces. Templer and Young continued the basic thrust of the Briggs Plan and worked closely to cement civil-military relations. One of the more successful measures was "food denial." In short, the government controlled all food stocks and distribution so that no one possessed an amount in excess of "need."[44] Since the MRLA was wholly dependent upon the Min Yuen for food and other supplies, the need to make contact with the villages made the guerrillas vulnerable to military and police patrols. In addition to the food denial program, Templer emphasized "the vital importance . . . of an honest and competent civil service functioning under the law."[45] The police rather than the military enforced the emergency regulations, the food denial program, and other measures. The central role of the police gave the overall counterinsurgency campaign the air of a large-scale crime eradication effort.

Templer and Young's efforts began to pay immediate dividends. In 1952 over fifteen hundred guerrillas were killed, captured, or surrendered. Several key guerrilla leaders were also eliminated, including one central committee member who was murdered by his own bodyguards in order to collect the reward offered by the government.[46] The MRLA offensive was blunted and the MCP was in disarray. In mid-September Templer declared the first "white area," within which emergency restrictive regulations were terminated. In January the white area was enlarged and other white areas declared. In mid-1955, the Malayan people adopted a new constitution, which was followed by national elections and significant autonomy for Malaya. Guerrilla activity continued to fall off, and the rump was constantly pressured by deep-penetration "hunter-killer" teams. By July 1957, of Malaya's fifty-one thousand square miles, thirty thousand had been declared white. Two months later Malaya became independent, and a little over two years later the Emergency officially ended.[47]

GROUND POWER AND AIRPOWER

Deployed against the MRLA was a composite force drawn from the various branches of the civilian police and the armed services. The Royal Navy performed coastal and riverine patrols and on occasion coastal bombardment in support of the ground forces. The eleven original understrength infantry battalions and nine thousand police grew rapidly to twenty-three full-strength battalions, sixty-seven thousand police, and three hundred thousand Home Guards.[48] The Home Guard was essentially civilian paramilitary units assigned to Chinese villages and Malay *kampongs*. The police were organized into three main elements: the Regular Police, the Special Constabulary, and the Police Field Force. The Regular Police performed routine police work and community relations. The Special Constabulary was geographically raised and assigned to static defense positions such as plantations and industry. The Police Field Force was essentially a gendarmerie and performed in a manner similar to the infantry battalions.[49] At one point the police outnumbered soldiers and at their peak almost doubled the military figures.[50] Army units were also geographically situated in order to establish a permanent presence as well as accustom themselves to the terrain, the local police, and the population. Of crucial importance to the counterinsurgency effort was intelligence and counterintelligence, and a Special Branch was created within the Federal Police to orchestrate intelligence operations.[51]

The Malayan Emergency passed through four phases. The first phase lasted from June 1948 to October 1949, when the guerrilla war was contained by military and police action. The second phase lasted from October 1949 to August 1951, when the MRLA attempted to renew its offensive and regain the initiative. The third phase began in August 1951 and lasted until the middle of 1954, when the security forces pursued an integrated civil-military strategy that drove the MRLA deep into the jungle. The final phase began in July 1954 when the MRLA was clearly on its heels and was pursued relentlessly until the Emergency officially ended on 31 July 1960.[52]

Small unit tactics were the key to the ground war, and only when firm intelligence indicated that large formations of the MRLA were present did the army conduct battalion-sized operations or larger.[53] At first, small elite units composed of British, Gurkha, and Malay soldiers known collectively as the "Ferret Force" undertook long-duration patrols intended to locate guerrilla sanctuaries and then direct regular army units to engage and destroy the guerrillas. This force was abandoned, however, and the personnel were dispersed as pathfinders and instructors in the regular army.[54] Nevertheless, deep-penetration patrols, often led by Dyak native trackers from Borneo, and saturation patrolling became the basic military strategy. British Special Air Service (SAS) and Royal Marine commandos also parachuted into the jungle to establish posts throughout the aboriginal areas.[55] Thus, by extending the presence and protection of the government to remote areas, the military quickly made the Malayan countryside an inhospitable place for the MRLA. It was in support of this effort, rather than by direct offensive action, that the RAF proved invaluable.

For largely administrative reasons, the RAF left Malaya after World War II, but when the guerrilla war began in June 1948, RAF Task Force Malaya, consisting of Dakota transports of No. 110 Squadron and Spitfires of No. 28 and 60 Squadrons, arrived at Kuala Lumpur on 4 July. The task force was

commanded by Air Vice Marshal A. C. Sanderson, who set up a joint headquarters with the local British army commander. Soon afterward, a flight of
the RAF Regiment arrived and took over defense of the airfield.[56] On 21 July,
Spitfires conducted the first air strike of the Emergency, attacking a guerrilla
hideout with rockets, cannon, and machine guns, and killing at least ten
rebels.[57] Shortly afterward, MRLA forces overran a police outpost and entrenched themselves. A joint Gurkha and police force successfully dislodged
the guerrillas with close air support from task force Spitfires. The RAF task
force was reinforced in August with a contingent of Beaufighters from No. 45
Squadron from Ceylon, which, along with several Spitfires, made their debut
in Southeast Perak, wreaking havoc on hideouts and killing numerous guerrillas.[58] The Beaufighters also made the first night attack of the campaign on
23 August against a known rebel position near the tin mining center of Ipoh,
using bombs, rockets, and cannon fire.[59]

In May 1949, the Spitfires of No. 28 Squadron were removed to Hong Kong,
but the Hawker Tempest–equipped No. 33 Squadron arrived to replace them.
In September, Sunderlands of No. 205 Squadron arrived from Ceylon bringing RAF airpower in Malaya to seventeen Spitfires, sixteen Tempests, eight
Beaufighters, and ten Sunderlands.[60] In October, No. 45 Squadron began replacing its Beaufighters with Bristol Brigand light bombers. Although in some
ways superior in performance to the Beaufighter, the Brigand was unreliable,
and the airplane was plagued with problems associated with its guns, undercarriage, and propellers.[61] In the closing months of 1949, the number of air strikes
increased, with the largest strike taking place on 21 October. In March 1950,
eight Avro Lincoln bombers of No. 57 Squadron arrived at Tengah airfield in
Singapore from their home base at RAF Waddington, near Lincoln. This unit
was replaced by No. 100 Squadron in June, and they were joined by Lincolns
of the Royal Australian Air Force (RAAF) No. 1 Squadron that same month.
Early in their employment, Lincoln bombers would follow up their bombardment with low-level attacks in which the gunners strafed the target, but this
practice was discontinued within a few weeks.[62] But with an eleven-hour
endurance and a maximum bomb load of fourteen thousand pounds, the
Lincoln was used extensively, primarily in area bombing of known or suspected guerrilla concentrations and to interdict escape routes. Bomber Command detachments made routine deployments to Malaya for the remainder
of the campaign, and in February 1955 the first Canberra jet bombers of

No. 101 Squadron deployed to Tengah. From 1955 to 1956 eight Canberra squadrons comprising Operation "Mileage" operated in Malaya out of Butterworth.[63]

Jets other than the Canberra arrived in Malaya in December 1950 with the introduction of de Havilland Vampires into No. 60 Squadron and later No. 45 Squadron. The first strike sorties conducted by Vampires occurred in April 1951. The Vampires performed well but were nevertheless replaced by de Havilland Venoms in 1955.[64] The most successful strike aircraft of the Emergency, however, was the twin-engine de Havilland Hornet. Derived from the highly successful Mosquito of World War II, the Hornet was the last and the fastest of the RAF's piston-engined fighters. The Hornet replaced the Tempests of No. 33 Squadron in March 1951 and flew alongside No. 45 Squadron's Vampires as a mainstay of counterguerrilla air operations until the squadron was withdrawn in 1955. After 1955, with the insurgency in decline, the RAF withdrew several squadrons. By 1960, RAF operations were minimal, with strike missions performed primarily by Canberras of No. 2 Squadron of the RAAF and No. 75 Squadron of the Royal New Zealand Air Force (RNZAF), as well as Sabres of No. 3 and No. 77 RAAF Squadrons operating out of Butterworth.[65]

Despite the confusing number of different types used throughout the Emergency, there were never more than fifteen squadrons in Malaya.[66] In general, RAF air strength gained between 1948 and 1955 and began to decrease when the MRLA was itself in decline. In the offensive role, two RAF fighter squadrons, one light bomber squadron, and a flying boat squadron were dedicated to Malayan operations at the beginning of the campaign. These were increased to two medium bomber, two light bomber, two fighter, and two flying boat squadrons in 1950. By 1953 there were two medium bomber, three fighter, and two flying boat squadrons. By 1956, frontline strength was reduced to one medium bomber, one light bomber, and three fighter squadrons. By the end of the campaign there were only three light bomber and three fighter squadrons, and in the last eighteen months of the Emergency these few remaining forces were assigned to the Commonwealth Strategic Reserve, and RAAF and RNZAF squadrons assumed the bulk of offensive aerial operations.[67] Transport operations during the Emergency were conducted almost entirely by four RAF squadrons.[68] In addition to RAF, RAAF, and RNZAF fixed-wing strike and transport aircraft, three helicopter squadrons (two RAF and one Royal Navy) along with light aircraft of various types were attached to the British army in Malaya. Royal Navy fixed-wing aircraft also supported the counterinsurgency effort. Fleet Air Arm fighters en route to Korea joined the air strikes, and six Lancaster bombers of Coastal Command were deployed to Malaya in 1950.[69] Thus, in the early stages of the campaign, World War II vintage aircraft were used exclusively, with the addition of helicopters in 1953; but by the end of the Emergency, jet aircraft were clearly dominant.

Airpower in its more orthodox role of air superiority and strategic attack was not required in Malaya. Consequently, air action during the Emergency fell into two broad categories: "direct action" and "indirect action." Direct action, or offensive strikes, was intended to "harass the bandits, to keep them on the move, to destroy their camps and food sites, and, of course, to kill as many as possible."[70] Indirect action entailed primarily the use of transport aircraft for dropping supplies to patrols and far-flung outposts, dropping parachutists, psychological operations, aerial spraying of areas cultivated by the guerrillas, and communications. During the early part of the Emergency, these indirect operations were performed by No. 48, 52, and 111 Squadrons and the Far East Communications Squadron, all flying Dakotas.[71] Indirect operations also included reinforcement and rescue by helicopter, as well as reconnaissance missions, both visual and photographic.[72]

The impact of offensive strikes was greatly limited by the terrain and the elusive nature of the enemy. The dense, unbroken triple-canopy jungle was 150 feet high in some places, obscuring acquisition of the target even by slow-moving propeller-driven aircraft. In addition to affording protection from observation, the jungle also lessened the effect of the weapons themselves, as rockets, cannon and machine-gun fire, and even the effects of high explosive bombs were absorbed by the foliage. The guerrillas, of course, presented a fleeting target — when they could be found at all — and aerial reconnaissance often alerted the guerrillas to impending air attack. By the time strike aircraft arrived, the guerrillas often had evacuated the target area. Outside of area bombing of predetermined targets, most air strikes were in support of friendly forces in actual contact with the enemy. But the jungle was "particularly obstructive to direct air action," and even these strikes were only marginally successful at best.[73]

Most participants and later observers agree that the limited effectiveness of offensive air action was more than offset, however, by the contribution of indirect air action. Thus, the order of importance of RAF operations overall was generally assessed to be air supply and transport, photoreconnaissance, close air support, long-range strikes against targets beyond the reach of units on the ground, and communications.[74] Airborne insertion of troops and aerial resupply were described almost universally as the most effective counter-insurgency use of airpower in Malaya. According to one RAF officer, "Supply dropping . . . coupled with troop-lifting and casualty evacuation by helicopters . . . combined to multiply the number of troops and police deployed on productive jungle patrols by a factor of not less than four."[75]

Air operations against the MRLA during the Emergency comprised essentially two phases. The first phase extended from the beginning of the Emergency in 1948 to early 1953, when the guerrillas operated fairly openly on the margins of the jungle and attempted to take and hold ground on occasion. The second phase occurred from roughly March 1953 until the end of the insurgency, when the guerrillas retreated to the deep jungle, pursued by security forces.[76] Throughout the campaign, the MRLA, like all guerrillas, held two distinct advantages over the government forces: flexibility and the ability to maintain the initiative by surprise. The British sought to offset these advantages in part through airpower. Capitalizing on the inherent flexibility of airpower to achieve its own measure of surprise through rapid insertion of ground forces into known or suspected guerrilla territory, the British forced the guerrillas onto the defensive in a very short period of time and maintained the initiative by providing air support to long-duration, deep-penetration patrols and jungle outposts. The helicopter proved especially adept in this role and, according to at least one senior officer, "almost revolutionized the jungle war."[77]

The vertical takeoff and landing capability of the helicopter was ideally suited to the jungle environment of Malaya, and its casualty evacuation potential was exploited with the establishment of an RAF Casualty Evacuation Flight in May 1950 at Kuala Lumpur. Suitable machines were unavailable to the RAF at the time, so three Royal Navy Dragonfly helicopters were diverted from the fleet to the RAF. Once they arrived, these helicopters were an instant success.[78] As the usefulness of the helicopter became fully appreciated over the next several years, the three original machines became overtasked and additional helicopters were requested. As a result, the Casualty Evacuation Flight was built up and eventually became RAF No. 194 Squadron.

At roughly the same time, the Royal Navy stood up the No. 848 Squadron with American-built Sikorsky S-55 helicopters and transferred them to Malaya by aircraft carrier. No. 848 Squadron arrived on 8 January 1952 and immediately began operations out of Singapore. Between its arrival in January and 1 June 1952, No. 848 Squadron "carried more than 4,000 troops on operational lifts, and moved 100,000 pounds of freight in 1,500 flying hours."[79] Shortly afterward, the Dragonflies of No. 194 Squadron were replaced by the Sycamore, which had better performance. These two squadrons, along with No. 155 Squadron operating the Westland Whirlwind helicopter (a less capable version of the navy's Sikorsky S-55), formed No. 303 Wing in 1953.[80] Together, these three squadrons comprised twenty-six medium-lift and fourteen light-lift helicopters.[81] By the end of 1953, these helicopters were fully exploited to counter the guerrillas' natural advantages of flexibility and initiative. This was accomplished in three ways: by troop deployment and redeployment in support of offensive operations; by aerial spraying; and by establishing and supplying jungle outposts.[82]

Siting and aerial resupply of jungle outposts was a key feature of British success against the MRLA. When an SAS unit composed of British and Malay volunteers was organized under General Briggs, these soldiers parachuted into the jungle where known or suspected MRLA food dumps were located. Once inserted, a base was established from which patrols radiated outward seeking guerrilla encampments. Often the patrols would remain in the jungle for thirty days or longer, supplied exclusively by fixed-wing aircraft, primarily Dakotas.[83] Later, helicopters were used for this purpose in addition to moving troops to ambush sites and for evacuating wounded and sick soldiers. By 1954 these deep-penetration patrols were forcing the guerrillas to move ever deeper into the jungle, away from populated areas and their principal means of logistical and moral support. When the MRLA subsequently impressed jungle-dwelling aborigines into providing food, SAS and Royal Marine commandos constructed "forts" in aboriginal areas. These forts were also supplied by air.[84] The tribesmen moved into either these enclosures or very close by for protection. Not long afterward the tribesmen began to actively assist British forces, and guerrilla formations gave the forts a wide berth. The guerrillas were therefore compelled to grow food for themselves, which required clearing the jungle to allow sunlight to penetrate to the ground, which in turn was visible to observation aircraft.

The success of these deep-penetration patrols and forts supplied by air cannot be overstated. As one enthusiastic Canadian army officer observed, the use of airpower in this fashion was "unorthodox," but the net effect realized the traditional role of airpower in achieving "isolation of the battlefield."[85] A Royal Navy officer also assessed this method to have been of "greater importance than the slow, difficult campaign of extermination."[86] And an Australian army brigadier wrote: "Indeed, the complete dependence on air supply [was] the finest, if silent, tribute to the Air Forces."[87]

As the counterinsurgency effort in Malaya unfolded, the air and ground efforts became integrated in a fashion previously unheard of and served to neutralize the guerrillas' own advantages. As another officer wrote during the Emergency, "In this type of warfare, the initiative tends to remain with the enemy. . . . [But] the initiative is being wrested from the terrorists by relentless hunting, by improved security, and by increased mobility. In the last, the advent of the helicopter has considerably strengthened our hand."[88] What little controversy emerged with respect to the employment of airpower in Malaya regarded the type of aircraft best suited to the counterinsurgency environment.

Helicopters had proven enormously useful but also enormously expensive and temperamental. The two principal helicopters used in Malaya were the Whirlwind medium helicopter and the Sycamore light helicopter. The two aircraft cost at the time, respectively, £78 and £58 per hour to operate, whereas the fixed-wing Pioneer and Auster light aircraft cost £35 and £13 to operate respectively. Maintenance of helicopters was very complex and demanding, and the skill level of the pilots was necessarily high, especially in Malaya where helicopters were often flown at the limits of their performance. "As a result of the high operating cost, coupled with the high capital cost of helicopters, it [therefore became] necessary to exercise the utmost economy in their use."[89] Beyond the relative utility of helicopters versus fixed-wing aircraft, there was also the question of propeller-driven aircraft versus modern jets.

Many RAF officers were convinced that otherwise obsolescent World War II vintage aircraft had many advantages over jets in counterinsurgency. These officers pointed to the need for slow speed, long loiter time, and pinpoint accuracy in counterguerrilla operations. Jets could not loiter for any useful length of time, their cruising speeds were high, and their accuracy in delivering World War II high explosive "dumb bombs" was poor. As one officer complained, "They [were] designed for full-scale modern warfare, and design features suitable for it are often quite the reverse for anti-guerrilla action."[90] Jets were also described as highly uneconomical. As a result, when

Hornets were replaced by Vampires and Venoms, and Lincolns were replaced by Canberras, it was done with considerable misgivings. Nevertheless, the RAF could not afford two air forces, one operating piston-engined aircraft intended solely for internal security operations and another jet-equipped air force to counter first-rate adversaries such as the Chinese and Soviets, fielding modern high-performance combat aircraft of their own. Moreover, "trials using jet aircraft in the strike role had proved entirely successful, and from 1954 onwards jets [were] employed on hundreds of strike operations in Malaya with the result that the feasibility of employing . . . high-performance fighter and bomber aircraft in this role [was] demonstrated beyond doubt."[91] In the end, the decision to equip the RAF with jets was a foregone conclusion, and as propeller aircraft left the inventory, jets replaced them — including in Malaya. Ironically, the U.S. Air Force had faced a similar controversy during the Korean War and would repeat the controversy during the Vietnam War.[92]

DENOUEMENT

The MRLA never officially surrendered. When the last of the emergency regulations were lifted in July 1960, there remained approximately five hundred active guerrillas between Kedah and Northern Perak.[93] But the cost of the Emergency had been considerable.

From 1948 until Malayan independence in 1957 it has been estimated that the total cost exceeded £700,000,000, of which £525,000,000 was provided by the United Kingdom. At the end of 12 years nearly 7,000 communists had been killed and 4,000 surrendered or been captured. But also more than 2,000 civilians had lost their lives as had over 1,000 Malayan police and 500 British, Malayan, Gurkha, Australian, New Zealand, Fijian and East African Servicemen. The advance of communism in South-East Asia had been halted — but at a great price.[94]

Nonetheless, the insurgency was officially at an end, and the British had pioneered modern counterinsurgency concepts that others would seek to emulate elsewhere. The most important lesson advanced by the British regarding counterrevolutionary warfare in the aftermath of World War II was the fact that the "military effort is inextricably entangled with the political and psychological."[95] Certain principles were derived from this fundamental proposition. First, the guerrillas had to be isolated from the population and every effort made to win public confidence. Good intelligence is crucial to successful counterinsurgency. An efficient chain of command, one that

integrated civil and military activities, was equally important. Military operations, particularly offensive operations, had to be understood within the
context of the larger political dimension. Finally, mobility and flexibility were
key to maintaining the initiative against a foe who generally holds the advantage in that regard.[96]

RAF officers came away from the Malayan Emergency with lessons learned
of their own. Although hotly disputed by some, the utility of high-performance
jet aircraft in counterguerrilla operations was generally assessed to be sound.
Helicopters were clearly a useful tool, but not surprisingly some RAF officers
believed they should be controlled by the RAF rather than the army in order
to better integrate their use with fixed-wing aircraft. In a similar vein, RAF
officers continued to regard airpower as indivisible and coequal to the army.
But RAF officers also understood that airpower was used primarily to support ground power in counterinsurgency. In this sense, the RAF experience
in Malaya convinced one officer of the wisdom of Field Marshal Montgomery, who wrote: "Army plus Air must be so knitted that the two together form
one entity — if you do this, then the resultant military effort will be so great
that nothing will be able to stand against it."[97] Whether the RAF would continue to embrace this axiom would be revealed as Great Britain faced additional insurgent challenges in the 1960s and early 1970s.

South Arabia, 1964–1967

According to the RAF, a convincing illustration of the value of air control
occurred in South Arabia in the 1920s. A 1954 American study entitled "Project
Control" revealed that the British use of airpower in Aden to control the native
population was an outstanding example of economy of force in imperial
policing.[98] The study reported that the British had garrisoned twenty-five
thousand troops in Aden in 1925, but in 1926 a mere two thousand RAF personnel had replaced them. The cost to the British treasury for ground forces
in Aden in 1925 was some twenty-five million dollars, whereas the cost to
employ the RAF in Aden was around two million dollars. In 1925, the British suffered one thousand casualties on the ground, but in 1926 the RAF
experienced a single casualty.[99] The study was subsequently used as the basis
for recommendations that the U.S. Air Force employ air control principles
to "control the behavior of hostile or potentially hostile nations."[100] But by

the end of the 1960s, the British had themselves concluded that air control could no longer be used exclusively to meet imperial objectives, even in South Arabia.

IMPERIAL STRATEGY AND SOUTH ARABIA

The earliest concerns of Great Britain regarding the "comparatively unknown Arabian Peninsula" stemmed from strategic considerations related to the eastern Mediterranean and India. Struggles between Britain and France in

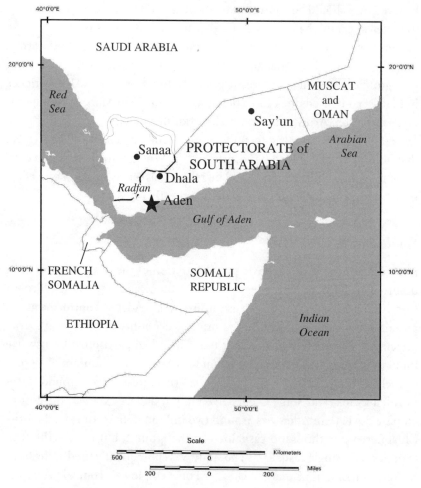

Aden and Protectorate of South Arabia, ca. 1964

North Africa and the Middle East at the end of the eighteenth century made the defense of overland routes to India crucial, particularly after Napoleon invaded Egypt in 1798. This struggle with France continued throughout the nineteenth century, but it was the emergence of the Russian threat in the region that prompted the British to acquire Cyprus and then establish a protectorate over all the "coastal Sheikhs" in South Arabia. Once the Suez Canal was completed in 1869, South Arabia became even more important as it lay astride the Red Sea. Thus, as the nineteenth century concluded and the twentieth century emerged, Britain extended its influence in the region in order to protect "the vital sea communications of the Empire" as well as "prevent any extension of other European influence."[101]

World War I unleashed latent nationalist sentiments in the Arab world that gave rise to the Pan-Arab movement after the war. Various Arab states were created during and after the war with the promise of full independence, and the Nejd and Yemen were given immediate independence following the end of hostilities. Cooperation between these states was encouraged by two principal factors — the need for self-defense against the European powers and the common Muslim identity of the Arab peoples. Arab nationalism was given expression by the Arab Covenant of 1931, which clearly articulated Arab aspirations for full independence and unification by a federation.

But unification was an ideal that could not find purchase against the parochial self-interests of each Arab state. Competition between these states diminished their ardor for Pan-Arabism, which remained dormant until the end of World War II. Nevertheless, Egypt, Syria and Lebanon, Transjordan, Iraq, Yemen, and Saudi Arabia were able to form the Arab League during World War II. Moreover, during and after World War II, the British attitude toward autonomy in the Arab world was more positive, and only Palestine remained "under mandatory control — a running sore in an otherwise healthy Anglo-Arab understanding."[102] Aden, however, was another matter.

The British East India Company seized the coastal town of Aden in 1839 as a coaling station. Aden had been a major commercial trading center in the region since antiquity, but its principal strategic value to the British lay in its location relative to India. Britain therefore held a "longstanding jealousy" regarding the potential influence of any powerful European state in the region, thus precipitating the seizure of Aden.[103] The interior was dominated by the sultanate of Lahej and a collection of other smaller potentates. Following British assistance in fending off Turkish incursions, particularly in the Yemen, the various emirates and sheikhdoms in the region acquiesced to British "protection." The Aden Protectorate thus emerged in the late 1800s: a Western Aden Protectorate comprising eighteen tribal territories adjacent to and northeast of Aden; and a larger Eastern Aden Protectorate. Although Britain was responsible for defense of the protectorate, internal administration remained primarily in the hands of indigenous tribal rulers. The port of Aden itself, however, gained the status of a crown colony in 1937, and British colonial governors ruled there as an adjunct to India.

As a "free port," Aden prospered. During the interwar years, the Aden Protectorate, "like so many parts of Arabia under British control . . . was a bureaucrat's empire, planned by experts and administered by officials working here and there in co-operation with the semi-bureaucratic servants of large concessionary companies, which themselves were linked in one way or another with Government."[104] It is therefore not surprising that anything offering economies of rule that would little interfere with the political and commercial status quo would find a receptive audience. Thus, when the Air Ministry suggested that internal security and external defense of Aden could be achieved with only one squadron of twelve bombers, an armored car unit, and local native levies, this was very well received by the British Treasury and the civil servants in the protectorate itself.[105] The RAF therefore took the lead in policing the indigenous tribes of South Arabia.

Fortunately for Britain during World War II, there was little unrest in South Arabia. Consequently, RAF air control operations continued. But with the end of the war in 1945, nationalist unrest reemerged as a more serious threat to British authority in the protectorate, and the continued effectiveness of air control was immediately brought into question.

Advancing technology, which had carried the British forward in the inter-war period, now reversed its role. Where aircraft had enabled centralised military power to penetrate the furthest fastness, radio now strode out to catch at the thoughts of men in inaccessible towns and hamlets and bring them into contact with broader movements beyond their parochial world. . . . Cairo Radio began to speak in the tones of revolutionary Arab nationalism, the development of cheap, transportable transistor radios created a mass audience among the poor and the remote. Men who had long lived in isolation now found a common political language and a breathtaking, liberating community of sentiment with multitudes in their own land and across the Arab world.[106]

In 1950, the Adeni Association was formed, a political organization calling for full independence for Aden. In 1952 the more radical Renaissance Movement emerged, calling for a unitary state that included Aden and the inland sultanates. These nationalist organizations received moral and material support from the trade union movement, which, by December 1956, included over twenty registered unions. Labor strikes erupted in the port of Aden in 1954 and again in 1956, the latter of which involved serious clashes between strikers and the police. Also, between 1954 and 1957 the tribal levies raised by the British during the interwar years mutinied and collapsed. The first serious violence directed specifically against the British occurred in 1955, when two RAF officers and several local policemen were killed in an ambush. In 1957, rebellious tribesmen also attacked the British in Beihan and Yafai. In 1958 a state of emergency was declared following a series of bomb explosions that accompanied another spate of labor unrest. Successful revolution in neighboring North Yemen in 1962 emboldened the nationalists in Aden as they sought to extend their influence inland. In October 1962 militants in Yemen formed the National Liberation Front (NLF), which immediately set about to export revolution to Aden. Fighting between NLF guerrillas and security forces belonging to the British-promulgated federation, particularly in the Radfan, evolved into a general anti-British guerrilla campaign by 1963.[107]

As Arab nationalism gained a foothold in the protectorate, the strategic value of the region would seem to have been reduced markedly following Indian independence in 1947. But the strategic value of the Middle East after World War II lay primarily with its oil reserves and certain Cold War imperatives. Britain and other Western powers were greatly concerned that the political vacuum that would result from complete British withdrawal from the region would be filled by nationalist elements of a decidedly communist persuasion.[108] Were the oil fields of the Gulf states to fall into radical hands, the economies of the West would be seriously threatened. Moreover, the issue of lines of communication, particularly the Suez and the Red Sea, remained of considerable concern to Great Britain. It was therefore deemed a "vital necessity" to retain a permanent presence in Aden in order to secure imperial objectives and deter an attack on empire communications.[109] Consequently, Aden became a major British military base after World War II, and from 1960 to 1964 Britain spent approximately eleven million pounds a year on the construction of permanent facilities.[110] When nationalist elements turned increasingly to armed resistance, the British launched a counter-insurgency campaign to suppress the rebels. Not surprisingly, the RAF would play a vital role in the effort.

INSURGENCY AND RESPONSE

The insurgency was divided between a rural guerrilla war in the interior and an urban campaign of terrorism in the Port of Aden itself. The "Red Wolves of the Radfan" were natural guerrillas, having warred against neighboring tribesmen for centuries. The most reliable estimates of tribesmen in revolt totaled some forty thousand, with less than eight thousand being active fighters.[111] Following an unsuccessful assassination attempt against the high commissioner in December 1963, three battalions of the federal army, raised and officered by the British, moved into the interior as part of Operation "Nutcracker." Emergency regulations were also imposed in Aden, which initially succeeded in stifling insurgent activities. In the Radfan, the mountainous interior of South Arabia, the military effort faltered, and in March 1964 the federal troops were withdrawn. The following month a renewed and larger effort, called "Radforce," aimed at seizing two key positions (code-named "Cap Badge" and "Ricebowl"), was made with mainly British troops flown in to reinforce federation and British troops in Aden. These reinforcements included infantry, Royal Marines, SAS, paratroopers, artillery, and tanks. But this operation also bogged down at first, and British forces skirmished with troops of the Yemen Arab Republic (North Yemen).

In Great Britain a Labour government was elected in 1964 and with it came "a more studied regard for underlying British interests" in South Arabia. The military base at Aden "was to be retained, but only if it did not involve tying down British forces in support of an unpopular local regime."[112] As British diplomats worked to bring about a more acceptable polity in South Arabia, the NLF launched a major terrorist campaign in the city of Aden. Violent demonstrations coincided with terrorist attacks on British servicemen, and general order broke down. The British government soon concluded that the situation in Aden had become untenable, and in February 1966 London announced that Britain would abandon its base in Aden by 1968. Between April and June 1967, British troops were withdrawn from the interior, and by August the interior was fully in the hands of rebel forces.[113] Aden itself was progressively abandoned by the British until only a small perimeter protecting the airfield and British military barracks remained. On 29 November 1967, the last British soldiers departed Aden by helicopter and Aden was handed over unconditionally to the NLF, ending 128 years of British rule.[114] Shortly afterward, the People's Democratic Republic of Yemen (South Yemen) was created.

AIRPOWER IN SOUTH ARABIA

As had occurred in the Far East, the RAF presence in the Middle East was greatly reduced following World War II. Only No. 8 Squadron flying Brigands resided permanently at Aden. In 1952 the squadron replaced its Brigands with Vampire jets and in 1955 received Venoms and a flight of Gloster Meteors. In 1959, the squadron was again reequipped, this time with the superb Hawker Hunter. As events unfolded, No. 8 Squadron rotated with No. 208 Squadron, also flying Hunters, between Khormaksar airfield in Aden and Bahrain, forming the nucleus of the Khormaksar Strike Wing. When the guerrilla war broke out in the protectorate in 1963, No. 43 Squadron Hunters from Cyprus joined No. 8 and 208 Squadrons in Aden. In addition to these strike aircraft, there were Avro Shackletons, Twin Pioneers, Beverleys, Argosies, and Valettas providing transport services, as well as Belvedere and Sycamore helicopters, complemented by Royal Navy helicopters and British army DHC-2 Beavers.[115]

When the NLF launched the guerrilla campaign in the interior, the high commissioner, Sir Kennedy Trevakis, wished to continue the previously successful strategy of air control. Trevakis feared that the use of ground forces would provoke otherwise cooperative tribesmen in the area to join the NLF and thereby escalate the conflict. However, the British Middle East Command, headquartered in Aden, opposed the idea. They argued that aerial operations would be largely ineffective in securing the border between the Western Aden Protectorate and North Yemen, and airpower alone would be wholly ineffective in suppressing the insurgency in Aden itself. In the aftermath of Malaya, most British military authorities had concluded that "the traditional method of disciplining restive natives [punitive expeditions, either by ground or air] had become not only politically unacceptable, but also an international embarrassment."[116] Bombing obstreperous tribesmen from the air offended modern sensibilities and was ineffective in the face of ideologically inspired rebellion. Air control was therefore ruled out as a viable and exclusive means to manage the insurgency.[117] As was the case in Malaya, however, military force would be subordinated to civil authority, and airpower would be used in support of the ground forces. Moreover, operational control of air assets would fall under the purview of the general officer commanding, a British army officer.

Operation Nutcracker was launched on 4 January 1964, commanded by Brigadier General J. D. Lunt. Federation forces possessed no aircraft of their own, so RAF aircraft provided air cover and ground support. Air cover was necessary in that Yemeni helicopters and Soviet-built MIG aircraft had attacked frontier villages and forts.[118] The RAF retaliated by attacking the Yemeni frontier fort at Harib with Hawker Hunters.[119] The fort at Harib was a strictly military target two miles from the village of the same name, but RAF aircraft dropped warning leaflets fifteen minutes prior to the strike to avoid unnecessary civilian casualties. Afterward, the RAF claimed the attack was a complete success and that no civilian casualties were incurred.[120] But the Yemenis immediately charged Great Britain with a "barbaric air attack" in which twenty-five civilian casualties were the result.[121] Nevertheless, the air attack had achieved the intended object: the Yemenis stopped their own cross-border air attacks. In addition to the attack on Harib and providing air cover, RAF Hunters also performed close air support missions directed by forward air controllers.

During the second push in February, commanded by Brigadier General Louis Hargroves, two squadrons of Hunters, a Shackleton squadron, a Twin Pioneer squadron, helicopters, and Beavers of the army's No. 653 Squadron supported the effort.[122] Again, RAF Hunters performed combat air patrol missions and supported the forces on the ground. In one notable battle, Hunters from No. 43 and 208 Squadrons were instrumental in the rescue of forty SAS soldiers who had been discovered and pinned deep within guerrilla territory. On 29 April 1964, Hunters flew eighteen sorties firing over 125 rockets and over seven thousand rounds of ammunition, killing some twenty to thirty guerrillas. The SAS soldiers broke out that night, reaching safety on 1 May. Several days later, Hunters provided close air support for two companies of 45 Royal Marine Commando. The Hunters strafed rebel positions in such close proximity to the marines that one was injured by a spent 20 mm shell casing. Beavers from No. 653 Squadron also flew "daring resupply sorties dropping ammunition and water" to the troops on the ground. With the two key pieces of terrain secured, British forces launched an attack in force on the guerrilla stronghold in the Jebel Huriyah. This time the guerrillas tried to hold their position, and the British ground assault was preceded by Hunters firing rockets and cannons. The air strikes were so severe that the guerrillas "were unable to defend the peak of the Jebel, which was occupied on 11 June."[123]

The Radfan was, at least for the moment, under British control; however, the insurgency in the Port of Aden was only beginning to reach its peak following the battle of Jebel Huriyah. As discussed earlier, the British attempted to duplicate in Aden their success in Malaya by stressing political reform, minimum force, and improvements in civil administration — but without success. The initiative had already passed to the rebels. The situation deteriorated rapidly, and No. 8 and 208 Squadrons were removed from Aden, leaving only No. 43 Squadron to cover the British troop withdrawal from the Radfan and Aden. No. 43 Squadron Hunters flew over three hundred sorties in September and October 1967 before these aircraft were also removed and the mission of air support fell to strike aircraft of the Royal Navy. The last Hunter strikes were conducted on 7 November 1967, three weeks after the squadron had officially been disbanded.

In addition to strike aircraft such as the Hunter, transport aircraft were used from the beginning of the insurgency to evacuation of British forces. These aircraft consisted of Twin Pioneers of No. 21 Squadron, Argosies of No. 105 Squadron, a small number of Andovers and Blackburn Beverleys, and a single Dakota. The Argosies were used mainly for communications, whereas the Twin Pioneers and Beverleys were dedicated to support of the ground forces. The Andovers arrived too late to have much of an impact. The Beverley was the workhorse of the counterguerrilla campaign, its short field performance and ruggedness being well suited for South Arabia. Although aerial resupply played a vital role in Malaya, it played a far smaller role in Aden and, though important, did not have the decisive impact that it had in Malaya. The last Beverley departed on 6 November 1967, and only the Argosies remained to move personnel and equipment to Bahrain at the very end.[124]

The helicopter, which had proven invaluable in Malaya, proved equally useful in Aden but did not garner quite the same acclaim. Before the guerrilla war broke out in 1963, what few helicopters existed at Aden were dedicated to search and rescue as a part of the Aden Communications Squadron. But as the counterinsurgency campaign unfolded, the tactical value of the helicopter was quickly recognized and British army Sioux and Scout helicopters began reconnaissance, liaison, patrol insertions, and resupply missions.[125] The RAF No. 26 Squadron flying Belvederes was also posted to Khormaksar airfield in Aden to support field operations by the ground forces. In addition, a flight of Sycamores continued to perform search-and-rescue missions, and Royal Navy helicopters were employed for airlift, security patrols, and other internal security operations. The Belvederes performed yeoman service in 1964, inserting patrols, performing resupply sorties, and moving troops and heavy equipment. Belvederes, Wessex, and Sycamore helicopters played a vital role in Operation Nutcracker and proved equally important to the Radfan operations, but there were never enough.[126] Moreover, the Belvederes were plagued by mechanical problems and, owing to constant use and the harsh climate, were largely unserviceable by the end of 1964.[127] The squadron was effectively grounded and was disbanded in November 1965. Wessex helicopters assigned to No. 78 Squadron, however, continued to support the campaign up to the end and in the final months provided valuable support. In November 1967, No. 848 Squadron of the Royal Navy, which had served in Malaya, together with No. 78 Squadron, ferried men and equipment to Royal Navy ships as Aden was evacuated. The final sortie was flown by a Wessex from No. 78 Squadron to HMS *Intrepid* on 29 November. The final departure of No. 78 Squadron Wessex helicopters marked the end of forty-eight years of continual RAF presence in Aden.[128]

Thus, by the end of the 1960s Great Britain had accumulated considerable experience in countering insurgency in its crumbling empire. Malaya had been a success, but Aden was an unmitigated disaster. It remained to be seen whether and to what extent the British had learned from their mistakes in South Arabia. But in coming to the aid of Oman, Britain recovered its successful counterinsurgency strategy and airpower would again play a major role.

Oman, 1970–1975

Oman is a small state on the eastern flank of the Arabian Peninsula. In 1798, the sultan of Muscat and Oman (later referred to simply as Oman) entered into a treaty of protection with Great Britain, but British interests in the small state were peripheral until 1939 when a British oil company was granted prospecting concessions.[129] The reign of Sultan Said ibn Taimur, beginning in 1932, was particularly repressive, and a series of insurgencies troubled Oman for decades. In 1954, the various sheikhs in the region elected Ghalib ibn Ali as

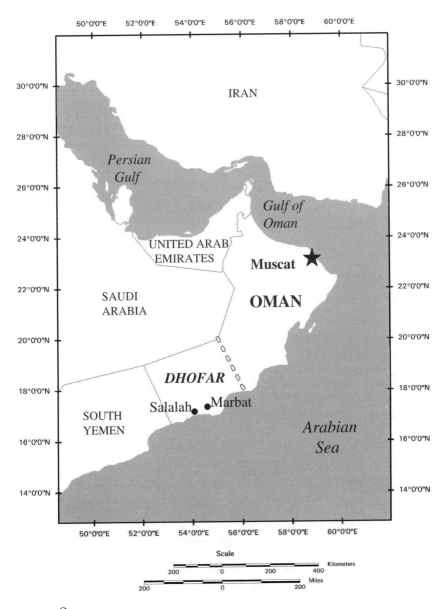

Oman, ca. 1970

Imam and Omani progressives flocked to the Imam in opposition to the sultan. In 1955, when the sultan moved against Ghalib's followers, his security forces comprised the Muscat Regiment, the two-hundred-man Battinah Force, and the three-hundred-man Muscat and Oman Field Force, the latter raised to protect the oil company. The campaign fared badly, and the sultan invoked his treaty with Great Britain for assistance.

Opposition withered upon the arrival of British troops, and they were withdrawn almost as quickly as they arrived. But opposition forces had not surrendered, merely relented. In 1957 the Oman Liberation Army was formed in Saudi Arabia and prepared for guerrilla war. The following year, the British agreed to assist the sultan in the reorganization and training of his troops. The British commanding officer arrived in April and was named chief of staff of the sultan's armed forces. The disposition of forces in 1958 were the former Muscat Regiment consisting of 250 men, a Northern Frontier Regiment of 450 men, an artillery troop, attached British soldiers and Royal Marines, and a small number of RAF personnel and five Pioneer aircraft. In November, additional SAS troops arrived from Malaya.[130] With these forces seconded to the sultan, Said was able to suppress rebel activity for several years.

But in 1963 the rising tide of nationalism throughout the Arab world and especially in the nearby Aden Protectorate encouraged militants in the sultanate. That same year, mountain tribesmen in the Dhofar rose up in revolt. Although the proximate cause of the rebellion was traditional resistance to the incumbent regime, the conflict quickly became ideological in nature. In 1965, the Dhofar Liberation Front was formed, controlled by tribally oriented separatists. The front was reorganized in 1968 as the People's Front for the Liberation of the Occupied Arabian Gulf (PFLOAG). The PFLOAG was thoroughly Marxist and took control of the rebellion, receiving material and moral support from the Soviet Union, China, Iraq, and South Yemen.

INSURGENCY AND COUNTERINSURGENCY IN THE DHOFAR

The insurgency unfolded in three stages. The first stage lasted from its inception to 1967 when the fighting was confined primarily to the central region of the Dhofar. The second stage ran from 1967 to 1970, when the guerrillas gained the upper hand. But in 1970 a coup installed the sultan's son, Qaboos, as the new sultan, and the insurgency foundered. The third and final stage followed the coup and lasted until the guerrillas were defeated in 1975.[131]

Like the Radfan, the Dhofar was ideal ground for guerrillas, being mostly mountainous apart from a narrow coastal plain. The people of the Dhofar were a polyglot admixture of nomadic tribes. Almost all of the government soldiers were recruited from outside the Dhofar and therefore regarded the Dhofar as "foreign" soil. Throughout the 1960s, government forces, advised and led by the British, had conducted search-and-destroy missions with little success. But with the assumption of power by Sultan Qaboos in 1970, the tide turned.

Before the assumption of power by Sultan Qaboos, the military situation in Oman had been serious. Said's forces were unable to contain the rebellion, and rebel forces came perilously close to seizing control of the country. During this period the PFLOAG established political control in "liberated" areas and set up agricultural collectives and built schools in order to indoctrinate the people in Marxist doctrines — to include the repudiation of Islam. Those who opposed these initiatives were sometimes killed and at a minimum had their lands and cattle confiscated and their children removed for training in South Yemen and the Soviet Union. The Dhofari tribes soon found that they had merely exchanged the harsh rule of Said for the tyranny of PFLOAG.

Consequently, communist efforts aimed at gaining the popular support of the tribes failed, and this key vulnerability was exploited by Sultan Qaboos. More enlightened than his father, Qaboos embarked on an ambitious program of political and economic modernization aimed at bringing about general reform. Had the rebellion not been communist inspired and backed by external actors, there is some indication that it would have ended in 1970. In the first month following the coup, some two hundred guerrillas surrendered and swore allegiance to the sultan.[132] In addition to civil development, Qaboos also set about to strengthen the armed forces. From 1970 to 1973, the size of the military quintupled. Moreover, 250 British army officers and RAF pilots were seconded to the sultan's army and air force, along with several hundred RAF technicians and ground defense personnel, as well as 100 soldiers in British military advisory training teams.[133] The bulk of the counterinsurgency effort was shouldered by the British-led Dhofar Brigade.

The Dhofar Brigade, headquartered at Salalah airfield, was commanded first by Brigadier General Jack Fletcher, from 1972 to 1974, and later by Brigadier General John Akehurst, from 1974 to 1976. As in Malaya, military and civilian activities were integrated under the direction of the Dhofar Development Committee. According to General Akehurst, this committee "epitomized the essential ingredient of anti-terrorist operations — that the military is in support of the civil power, never the other way around."[134] The ground forces were spearheaded by two Omani infantry battalions, two Baluch infantry battalions recruited in Pakistan, an armored car squadron, three independent companies, and supporting artillery. All of the battalions were commanded by British loan service or contract officers. In addition, an SAS squadron known as the British Army Training Team served under the Brigade headquarters. The SAS trained and led former guerrillas known as *firqats*. Although temperamental and difficult at times to control, the *firqats* were in many respects the key to the military counterinsurgency effort.[135] In addition, King Hussein of Jordan dispatched an infantry detachment to Dhofar in 1972, and from December 1973 to November 1974 an Iranian-reinforced infantry battalion served in Dhofar.[136] Finally, three British army engineer squadrons spearheaded the civil development program, and air assets were provided by the Sultan of Oman Air Force (SOAF).

Prior to the coup, the SOAF comprised "a handful of DC-3s and a couple of Provost piston engined fighters. . . . [But] by 1975 the SOAF had about 75 aircraft . . . a fifteenfold increase."[137] These aircraft included BAC-167 Strikemasters (a converted jet trainer), Short Skyvan transports, AB 205 "Huey" helicopters, several Viscounts and BAC 111s, and an assortment of light fixed-wing and rotary-wing aircraft. In 1975, King Hussein also provided twelve Hawker Hunters to the sultan, which were used late in the campaign to strike at South Yemen for supporting the insurgents. The SOAF contingent assigned to the Dhofar Brigade was commanded by an RAF officer who served directly under the brigade commander. "It defied a time-honoured Royal Air Force principle in that it came under the command of the Army brigadier, but as all its work was in close support of the Army the circumstances were unusual and few disapproved of the arrangement."[138] The SOAF allocation to the Dhofar Brigade included eight Strikemasters, four Agusta-Bell AB 205 helicopters, four Skyvan transports, two Agusta-Bell AB 206 Jet Ranger helicopters, and two Britten Norman Defender light liaison aircraft. "The aircraft were all flown by a mixture of loan service and contract pilots and serviced under contract by the appropriately named Airwork Services Limited."[139] The Iranian forces included Chinook helicopters and were supported by Iranian C-130s flying directly from Teheran.

Not unlike Malaya, airpower offset the inherent advantages possessed by the guerrillas by providing the Dhofar Brigade with flexibility and mobility. Helicopters again proved especially useful in this regard, and General Akehurst opined in 1982 that "without the helicopters the war might still be going on yet."[140] The brigade carried out surprise heliborne operations and moved reinforcements quickly to wherever needed. Prompt medical evacuation also helped maintain high morale among the oftentimes isolated ground forces. The Strikemasters operated in pairs and were never more than fifteen minutes flight time away. The Skyvans delivered personnel and supplies to even the most rugged airstrips. Cooperation between the air and ground elements was described as excellent and, as the counterinsurgency campaign developed, the elements were woven together to provide a powerful strike force.

By February [1975] Akehurst realized he had enough helicopters to launch heliborne operations into areas the enemy had considered safe. He launched Operation Broomstick against a ridge on which the enemy had placed Katyusha rockets. The operation was preceded by an attack by Strikemasters, which, in fact, was so successful that the troops arrived on the ridge unopposed, as the enemy had already fled. In Operation Himaar, quite similar to Broomstick, the guerrillas did not flee after the air attack, but the troops landed, were given close air support, and gained the initiative.[141]

On other occasions, SOAF Strikemasters and heliborne forces turned the tables on guerrillas that had invested government garrisons, such as at the Battle of Marbat on 19 July 1972.[142] But air operations also became more dangerous in 1975 when Soviet-supplied surface-to-air missiles were introduced by the guerrillas. In August of that year a Strikemaster was shot down by a SAM-7 near the border with South Yemen. In all, twenty-three SAM-7s were fired before the campaign ended, downing a helicopter in addition to the Strikemaster.[143]

By December 1975 the Dhofar was secure. Teams of engineers set about to build schools, sink wells for drinking water, and repair mosques, and civil action teams worked to deliver such services as education and medical treatment for the local tribesmen and their families. The process was very similar to what had been done in Malaya. As an area was declared "white," the civil development agencies would move in under the protection of security forces, including paramilitary *firqats*. It was an expensive campaign, costing the sultan three hundred million pounds in 1974 alone — a third of which was spent on defense.[144] Nevertheless, the impact of the civil development program and relentless military pressure caused the guerrillas to lose large numbers of fighting men by December 1974. Mopping up continued through 1975 and into early 1976, but by then the rebels no longer represented any real threat to Oman.

Conclusion: The Limits of Air Control

Of the three counterinsurgency campaigns described in this chapter, two ended with British victories and one in defeat. The varied results depended in large measure on the ability of British authorities to implement a coordinated civil-military strategy that undermined the insurgent popular base and at the same time wrested the initiative away from the guerrillas in the field. Regarding the latter aim, airpower proved to be pivotal. But as the defeat in Aden proved, military success in the field facilitated by airpower is no guarantee of victory in counterrevolutionary warfare. But one thing seems clear — without airpower, the counterinsurgent is at a severe disadvantage against an opponent with natural advantages of initiative, surprise, flexibility, and mobility. Thus, when General Akehurst reflected on the successful campaign in Oman, he regarded airpower to be crucial. The same was true in Malaya and Aden, where Air Vice Marshal Mellersh and Air Marshal John Kemball described airpower as "essential" respectively.[145] And despite the unhappy outcome in Aden, had British airpower not been present, the end would no doubt have come sooner and at much greater cost.

In Malaya, the British correctly understood that political considerations must be elevated above military ones in counterinsurgency. The chief tenet of the Briggs Plan was to deny the communists political legitimacy, which Templer carried through to conclusion. The central role of the police effectively branded the guerrillas as brigands; intelligence operations enabled the government to bring military power to bear where it would prove most effective; and restrained military operations and the New Villages served to separate the general population from the guerrillas without alienating the former to too great a degree. The food denial program targeted the Achilles' heel of the insurgency. Finally, through constant harassment by small unit operations, the British army, other Commonwealth forces, and indigenous troops wore down the guerrillas. Airpower was deemed most useful in this effort by providing indirect support through movement of troops, aerial resupply, reconnaissance, and psychological operations. Direct support in the form of air strikes, although important, was consistently relegated to a secondary role by British army and RAF officers alike.

In Oman the civil-military dimension was again pivotal. Until the 1970 coup, Omani counterguerrilla operations were ineffective, despite significant British support. Only when Sultan Qaboos targeted the vitals of the insurgency by initiating systemic political, economic, and social reforms did the counterinsurgency effort bear fruit. As the PFLOAG lost the war for the hearts and minds of the Dhofari tribesmen, airpower provided the same flexibility and mobility to the Dhofar Brigade that had proved decisive in beating the guerrillas in Malaya. In Oman, as in Malaya, indirect operations were more important than direct operations, but owing mostly to the terrain and the operations of the guerrillas, offensive air strikes played a greater role in Oman. In both conflicts, the helicopter proved an especially valuable tool.

The military elements that proved successful in Malaya and Oman were similarly present in Aden. What was missing was a coordinated civil-military strategy aimed at undermining the popular base of the guerrillas. Despite the nominal success of Radforce in expelling the guerrillas from the Jebel, the collapse of British and native authority in Aden forced the withdrawal of the British from the protectorate. Nevertheless, as Julian Paget noted in his own analysis of British military operations in Aden, the successful Radfan campaign "hinged on the correct use of air."[146] Given the lack of adequate communications, the topography, and the logistical requirements for modern counterinsurgency warfare, only airpower could provide the necessary means to meet Radforce mobility and firepower requirements. Airpower proved crucial to successful military field operations, but the loss in Aden was, in the end, a political defeat.

A successful counterinsurgency campaign is a complex effort. Generally speaking, no single element can be pointed to as having won or lost the war. Rather, it is the dynamic and integrated combination of many elements that determines success or failure in counterinsurgency — including the use of airpower. However, if one element must be singled out as the key, it is the integration of the civil and military dimensions into a unitary counterinsurgency whole. In Malaya and Oman, the overall strategy was devised and implemented from the top down. This was particularly true of General

Templer's efforts in Malaya. Civil and military authorities in both conflicts showed a high degree of initiative and a willingness to employ unorthodox methods with the central objective of getting the job done — the hallmark of the British military tradition of practicality and adaptation in small wars. The willingness of the RAF to similarly adapt, despite the legacy of air control, is noteworthy. In Oman, the British not only subordinated the military dimension to the civil, but also seconded British military authority to the host nation. Moreover, the Dhofar Brigade commander was seconded to the Omani chief of staff. And the RAF commanding officer reported directly to the Dhofar Brigade commander. All of whom carried out their duties with the understanding that their role was in aid to the civil power.

In the final analysis, airpower was not regarded as subordinate or superior; rather, it was regarded as a partner or colleague. With the conclusion of the campaign in Oman, General Akehurst noted, "Indeed the confidence, respect and friendship that developed between the pilots and soldiers, forged by their total reliance on each other, became a shining example of how good interservice cooperation can be, given the right circumstances."[147] In Malaya, RAF officers retained the airman's emphasis on the indivisibility of airpower but appreciated the support role as being the dominant role for airpower in counterinsurgency warfare. Indeed, Emergency Directive No. 2, paragraph 23, clearly defined the role of airpower in Malaya: "The RAF is also operating in support of the Civil Power. The primary task of the RAF is to operate in conjunction with and in support of the ground forces."[148] The RAF retained its coequal identity in Aden, but operational control of RAF strike aircraft and helicopters was exercised by the brigade headquarters located at Thumeir in the Radfan, some sixty miles from Khormaksar airfield in Aden. Nevertheless, only in Oman did air assets fall directly under the command of an army officer, but these were only a fraction of the overall SOAF forces. Moreover, as the brigade commander noted, these aircraft existed solely to support the ground forces operating in the Dhofar, and it seemed only reasonable that they be under the direct control of the ground commander. In that regard, as one RAF wing commander noted in 1965, "In the final analysis guerrilla organizations are only eliminated by men on the ground, be they government officials or soldiers."[149]

In each conflict, airpower played an important if not a decisive role in the success of counterguerrilla operations. Airpower provided heavy firepower when and where needed, as well as logistical support and mobility; and it gave the government forces the initiative when used properly. It was not air control in the sense that it was understood during the interwar years, but there was general agreement among airmen and soldiers alike that success in modern counterinsurgency relied heavily on airpower.

The legacy of air control, however, still held a grip on many British authorities — both civilian and military. When the guerrilla campaign in the Radfan Mountains began, the high commissioner wanted to employ air control as had been done before World War II. Sir Trevakis claimed that ground operations "would be less effective, more wasteful, and probably more dangerous than air action, that the presence of British troops in the Radfan could well excite far greater opposition than would otherwise be the case, that casualties which they would most certainly incur would delight our enemies, and cause doubt and dismay in Britain."[150] Military authorities convinced Sir Trevakis that air control was no longer a viable strategy and yet, once the guerrillas were beaten in 1964, the British army commanding general handed back the Jebel to the RAF that they might reimpose "the traditional methods of 'air control.'"[151]

Thus, in retrospect, one can make a reasonable argument that Sir Trevakis was right from the very beginning. The hinterland was not the primary object of British policy and strategy in South Arabia — Aden itself was the object. Had the RAF been permitted to exercise air control in the Radfan, there would have been no need to take the Radfan and garrison troops there. British authorities could have concentrated on the insurgency in Aden. SAS and other commando operations could have been conducted to keep the guerrillas off balance in the Radfan, and RAF aircraft operating from the relative safety of Khormaksar airfield could have struck at known guerrilla concentrations. True, the nature of the conflict was radically different in 1964 from what it had been before World War II, but given the results of Radforce, the same results could arguably have been achieved through airpower alone. On the other hand, successful air control in the Radfan would have made little difference to the outcome of the war in the absence of success in suppressing the insurgency in Aden.

The key difference between air control as it was exercised between the world wars and the use of airpower in countering insurgency following World War II was the motivation of the insurgents. Before 1939 rebels fought for economic gain and other more traditional motivations. In Aden, for example, tribesmen in the 1920s were simply eager to plunder caravans along the Dhala Road. Air control worked because the tribesmen were not committed to any particular cause and submitted to British justice through air control. But in the 1960s the tribesmen fought for nationalistic ideals grounded in independence. Simple retribution in the form of air bombardment was insufficient to persuade the guerrillas to abandon their goals. This key feature was not limited to Aden, but British authorities in Malaya and later Oman seemed better able to grasp the fundamental political and social nature of modern revolutionary war. In addition to the role played by dissident motivation, modern sensitivities regarding human rights and other concerns stigmatized the unrestrained use of airpower to control native peoples. Thus, during the colonial wars following World War II, the British were forced to adapt — including the use of airpower. In this regard, the traditional British military emphasis on practicality placed the RAF in good stead. As one British air marshal opined in 1998:

My belief is that doctrine mainly serves to constrain the imaginative use of the flexibility of air power. In every situation there are different circumstances and parameters. On one hand you have the aircraft that you bought and the air power characteristics that it possesses. On the other, you have a military situation in which you wish to use the aircraft which reflects both geography and politics. How you use a weapon system should be a result of analysis of the situation that prevails at the time, and should not be dependent on a general doctrine that was developed without relation to specific situations.[152]

Thus, in the end, one can argue that the traditional British military emphasis on practicality over theory, as colored by the insight gained from the RAF experience in Malaya, Aden, and Oman, continues to inform RAF thinking with respect to the role of airpower in small wars.

Royal Air Force Squadron No. 84 Brigand in Malaya. The first Brigands arrived in October 1959, replacing the Beaufighters of No. 45 Squadron. Although in some ways superior in performance to the Beaufighter, the Brigand was unreliable, and the airplane was plagued with problems associated with its guns, undercarriage, and propellers. (RAF Historical Branch, Crown copyright)

No. 1 Squadron Lincoln bombers of the Royal Australian Air Force at Tengah airfield, Singapore. With an eleven-hour endurance and able to drop seventy one-thousand-pound bombs anywhere on the Malayan Peninsula, the Lincoln was used extensively, primarily in area bombing of known or suspected guerrilla concentrations and to interdict escape routes. (RAF Historical Branch, Crown copyright)

Royal Air Force Venom fighters of No. 8 Squadron, Khormaksar airfield, Aden. The Venoms replaced Vampire jets in 1955, which had replaced Brigands in 1952. In 1959, the squadron was again reequipped, this time with the superb Hawker Hunter fighter-bomber. As events unfolded, No. 8 Squadron rotated with No. 208 Squadron, also flying Hunters, between Khormaksar airfield in Aden and Bahrain, forming the nucleus of the Khormaksar Strike Wing. (RAF Historical Branch, Crown copyright)

Royal Air Force Whirlwind helicopter over Malaya. Capitalizing on the inherent flexibility of airpower to achieve its own measure of surprise, the British forced the guerrillas onto the defensive and maintained the initiative by providing air support to long-duration, deep-penetration patrols and jungle outposts. The helicopter proved especially adept in this role and, according to at least one senior officer, "almost revolutionized the jungle war." (RAF Historical Branch, Crown copyright)

British army Gurkha soldiers disembarking from a Royal Air Force Westland Whirlwind helicopter of No. 155 Squadron in Malaya. Helicopters proved enormously useful but also enormously expensive and temperamental, and as a result were centrally managed to ensure their most cost-effective use. The helicopter proved equally useful in Aden and Oman, but did not garner the same acclaim as it had in Malaya. (RAF Historical Branch, Crown copyright)

Royal Air Force "Valetta" transport over Malaya. Transport aircraft performed in a variety of roles, including aerial resupply and insertion of troops as well as psychological operations and communications. For the duration of the Emergency, transport functions were conducted almost entirely by four RAF squadrons. During and after the Emergency, the transport mission was hailed as a decisive airpower mission. (RAF Historical Branch, Crown copyright)

Above and facing page: Royal Air Force Dakota dropping supplies
to government forces in Malaya. Before the arrival of more
modern aircraft, No. 48, 52, and 111 Squadrons and the Far East
Communications Squadron all flew Dakotas, performing such
"indirect" missions as dropping supplies to patrols and far-flung
outposts, dropping parachutists, psychological operations, aerial
spraying of areas cultivated by the guerrillas, and communications.
(RAF Historical Branch, Crown copyright)

As the Emergency in Malaya climaxed, Prime Minister Winston Churchill appointed General Sir Gerald Templer as high commissioner. Templer emphasized restrained military operations in the context of civil development. The chief tenet of the British effort in Malaya was to deny the communists political legitimacy, which Templer carried through to conclusion. (RAF Historical Branch, Crown copyright)

Royal Air Force Bristol Airfreighter, one of the more modern transport aircraft that augmented C-47 Dakotas late in the Malayan Emergency. (RAF Historical Branch, Crown copyright)

Airpower in South Vietnam, 1954–1965

The amount of material on the Vietnam Wars (that is, French and American) is enormous. Much has also been written about the role of airpower in Vietnam, but most of these works focus on the period following the introduction of American ground forces in 1965, and even these works tend to focus on the air war over North Vietnam. What little has been written about airpower in Vietnam before 1965 tends to concentrate on U.S. Air Force special operations activities, with distressing lacunae regarding the efforts of the French and later the South Vietnamese air forces. The French experience, and that of the French air force in particular before 1954, is detailed in another chapter of this book, but briefly reexamining that period is necessary in order to establish continuity in terms of the impact on the South Vietnamese air force and the U.S. Air Force in South Vietnam before 1965.

The French experience in Vietnam was studied and described by a number of American analysts following the French defeat by the communists, but the U.S. military at the time apparently concluded that the French had bungled the effort, and any lessons to be learned were cautionary at best. In short, France sought to reassert its one-hundred-year-old colonial rule following World War II, which required suppressing an internal independence movement led by the communist Viet Minh under Ho Chi Minh. Following their disastrous defeat at Dien Bien Phu, the French agreed to withdraw from northern Vietnam and to the terms of the Geneva Accords of 1954, which divided the country at the seventeenth parallel.[1]

Between 1945 and 1954, the French air force played an important if not pivotal role in fighting against the Viet Minh, described in a three-volume analysis of the conflict written by the French high command. Albeit weighted

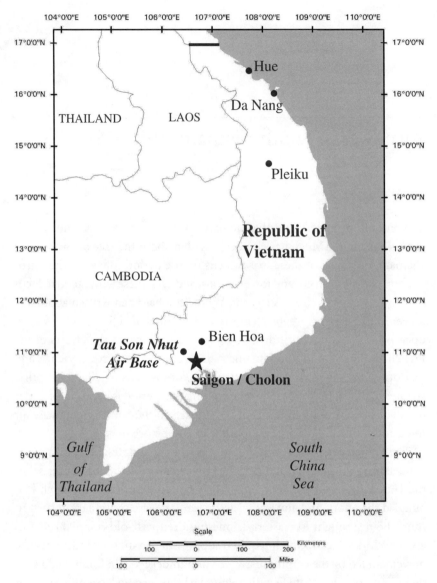

Republic of Vietnam, ca. 1961

heavily toward the ground war, the report emphasized the inherent complexities of using airpower to defeat guerrillas. Moreover, it specifically called into question the central tenets of airpower theory as articulated by the U.S. Air Force — what the French referred to as "the extremist thesis of Douhetism."[2] It appears, however, that the U.S. Air Force did not receive translations of the French report until the late 1960s, and there is little indication that the material had any impact on American thinking about the nature of the conflict in Vietnam, nor the utility of airpower in combating the communist insurgency. Yet the first volume included captured Viet Minh documents describing how guerillas could thwart airpower.[3]

Nevertheless, having successfully defeated communist insurgencies in Greece and the Philippines, American analysts had little regard for the French experience in Vietnam and paid little attention to airpower in small wars in any case. Moreover, for its own part, the U.S. Air Force was not inclined to alter its fundamental beliefs regarding airpower, as evidenced by views expressed by official air force sources in the early 1960s. In a statement to the House Armed Services Committee in 1962, vice chief of staff of the air force, Frederic Smith, asserted, "It is our conviction . . . that the core of our security planning lies in the maintenance of an effective capability to prosecute successfully a general war. . . . In the broad spectrum of conflict called limited war, a variety of responses may be desirable, ranging all the way from a show of force through the delivery of nuclear weapons."[4] Indeed, while commanding U.S. Air Forces in Europe in 1960, General Smith went so far as to extol the use of nuclear weapons in "any war short of direct combat between the great powers." "It is clear," he wrote, "that nuclear weapons cannot be used haphazardly if we are to keep the war limited and avoid undue destruction to the friendly countries we are defending"; nevertheless, "The commander on the spot must have the option of expending [nuclear] weapons in the zone of conflict within his allocated stockpile in accordance with his judgement of the situation."[5] In short, nuclear weapons were as useful in counterinsurgency as in major war.

In retrospect, the U.S. Air Force disregarded history and the lessons of the recent past when, in 1965, the chief of staff of the air force described the use of airpower in South Vietnam as "truly unique in the annals of aerial warfare."[6] Thus, despite having operational models available from the Greek Civil War and the Hukbalahap insurgency in the Philippines, the British experience in Malaya, and even as far back as the Marine Corps' successful use of aviation in Nicaragua from 1927 to 1933, the U.S. Air Force entered into the Vietnam imbroglio with almost no idea of what role airpower should play in counterinsurgency.

Vietnam, Guerrilla Warfare, and the French

Vietnam spans over 1,200 miles from the ninth parallel to the twenty-sixth parallel and covers over 127,000 square miles. About 80 percent of the countryside is covered by vegetation, with 49 percent being jungle. The remainder consists of open plains and deltas, the Mekong in the south and the Red River in the north being the most important. Smaller deltas are found along the coastline of central Vietnam. A series of mountain chains, the Annamite Cordillera, runs the length of the border with Laos and Cambodia and forms the watershed for the many rivers that run to the sea. The mountains range in altitude from four thousand feet to over ten thousand feet and are generally covered with lush tropical forest. In 1962, when American assistance to the South Vietnamese government began to accelerate, the country contained over 30.5 million people, over half of whom lived north of the seventeenth parallel. Some 29 million inhabitants lived on only 20 percent of the land, the remainder being largely seminomadic. The people themselves were, for the most part, ethnically and culturally homogenous, despite diverse origins and histories. The major minority groups were the Chinese and Khmers (Cambodians) along with various aboriginal "hill people" such as the Meo and Muong, all of whom comprised some 15 percent of the total population. Vietnamese was the dominant language with an eclectic admixture of minority tongues.[7]

By virtue of its geography, Vietnam has been the victim of incessant invasions and occupations by foreign peoples. The earliest indigenous tribes were colonized by the Chinese so that by the time a distinctive "Viet" national identity emerged in the area of northern Vietnam known as Tonkin (Nam Viet), Vietnamese culture was the product of over 150 years of Sinicization. During the period of absolute Chinese rule, the Vietnamese were known as "Annamese," derived from An Nam, or "pacified south." The Annamese absorbed much from Chinese culture: Confucianism, Taoism, language forms, political theory, and no doubt military theory. Consequently, as Douglas Pike, Bernard Fall, P. J. Honey, George Tanham, and others have pointed out, modern Vietnamese military strategy is an interesting product of Chinese and indigenous military influences.

In A.D. 939, the Vietnamese were successful in throwing off the Chinese yoke. Thereafter, Vietnamese settlers ventured south into the largely unoccupied peninsula encompassing the Mekong Delta between Saigon and the Bassac River. Over the ensuing centuries, southern Vietnam evolved a distinct culture of its own. In fact, during the sixteenth century, Vietnam was beset by a series of fratricidal civil wars between the Nguyen oligarchies in the south and the Le Loi dynasty in the north. The result was a cultural partition of Vietnam along the seventeenth parallel, the same line of demarcation agreed upon in the Geneva Accords of 1954.

The Vietnamese military tradition of guerrilla warfare emerged in the tenth century when the Vietnamese resisted a Tang Chinese invasion. In 1284, defending against another Mongol-Chinese invasion, the Vietnamese, led by Tran Hung Dao, perfected their guerrilla technique, "abandoning the cities, avoiding frontal attacks, and harassing [their] enemies."[8] After a disastrous defeat at the hands of the Vietnamese in 1287, the Mongol (Yuan) dynasty abandoned ambitions in Vietnam. Subsequent Vietnamese imperial designs on neighboring Thais and Khmers, however, were cut short by the Chinese Ming dynasty, which invaded and temporarily reimposed Chinese suzerainty in the north. But once again resorting to guerrilla warfare, the Vietnamese successfully extirpated the Chinese in 1418 — only to face French colonization in the middle of the nineteenth century.

The French first arrived in Vietnam in 1626. Over the ensuing decades, France made considerable inroads to promote its commercial interests in the region. On 6 June 1884, indigenous Vietnamese rulers accepted a French protectorate, but only after a prolonged period of armed resistance on the part of the Vietnamese manifested in the same guerrilla warfare formerly employed against the Chinese.[9] To that end, the Vietnamese established strong base camps from which mobile guerrilla forces attacked the French, leading one French commander in 1862 to complain: "They appear from nowhere . . . destroy everything and then disappear into nowhere."[10] Nevertheless, beginning in 1885, the French dominated Vietnam and the whole of Indochina until 1940, when the Japanese invaded the region and French colonial authorities were instructed by the Vichy government in Paris to administer the protectorate on behalf of the Japanese. But in early 1945, the Japanese discarded the collaborationist French authorities in Vietnam and installed a local aristocrat, Bao Dai, as "emperor."

During World War II, Vietnamese nationalists united under the leadership of Ho Chi Minh and the communist Viet Minh to resist Japanese occupation. Interestingly, Ho Chi Minh and his top military commander, Vo Nguyen Giap, cooperated with American operatives and the anti-Vichy French in Vietnam during the war. Thus, when the Japanese surrendered in August 1945, the Viet Minh assumed that independence from France would be granted, but the French instead moved to reassert their colonial control of the region. Consequently, the Viet Minh reactivated the wartime resistance organization and Giap was placed in command of the military wing. The Viet Minh then successfully appealed to Bao Dai to abdicate the throne, whereupon the Indochina Communist Party seized control in Hanoi in northern Vietnam. On 2 September 1945, Ho Chi Minh declared independence and the creation of the Democratic Republic of Vietnam. The United States urged the French to accept Ho Chi Minh as head of state, and in 1948 the French agreed to recognize the northern Democratic Republic (a "Free State within the French Union") as well as the southern State of Vietnam. But the French were unwilling to wholly relinquish colonial control, and Giap responded by launching a conventional offensive against French forces. But with only sixty thousand poorly equipped troops, the Viet Minh offensive failed, and as French forces drove them into the hills of northern Vietnam, the communists reverted to traditional guerrilla tactics.

The French military strategy was doomed from the outset. In northern Vietnam, the French built a series of forts to control and pacify the countryside, but the communist guerrillas ignored these fixed positions and infiltrated the countryside to proselytize the peasants as part of a larger, protracted revolutionary guerrilla war. By the end of 1953, some five thousand of seven thousand villages and hamlets were under Viet Minh control, with perhaps as many as 60 percent under their control in southern Vietnam.[11] But instead of providing for a measure of self-rule to undercut the appeal of the insurgents, the French placed their faith in a military strategy wherein the Viet Minh would be lured into a decisive battle in which French airpower and artillery would decide the issue. The remote village of Dien Bien Phu in northeastern Vietnam, 170 miles west of Hanoi, was chosen as the site of this decisive pitched battle. Dien Bien Phu was situated in a basin about twelve miles long and ten miles wide, encompassed by wooded hills. In November 1953, French paratroopers occupied the site and reopened an old French camp. A dozen French battalions, backed by 75 mm and 105 mm howitzers, M-24 Chaffee light tanks, and six Grumman F8F "Bearcat" fighters, awaited Giap's forces. But by March 1954, the sixteen thousand French troops defending the camp had been surrounded by some forty thousand communist troops.[12]

The communist military strategy between 1946 and 1954 has generally been credited to Giap, but the underlying theory was first advanced by Truong Chinh, a principal Communist Party theoretician.[13] Truong Chinh was heavily influenced by Mao Tse-tung's military theory, but he adapted it to the Vietnamese military tradition and Vietnamese culture. He acknowledged that protracted war was the key to wearing down the French but broke with Mao on the issue of regularization of guerrilla forces. Mao had insisted that guerrilla warfare merely created the conditions leading to "mobile" or positional warfare and maintained that the guerrilla army must be regularized to that end.[14] Truong Chinh evolved a peculiarly Vietnamese strategy. In short, it would be a "war of interlocking" (an awkward English transliteration of the French *guerre en dents de peigne*), by which he meant the concomitant and interconnected operations of regular forces and guerrillas.

Truong Chinh believed that guerrilla warfare and conventional warfare should dovetail in the Taoist sense of yin and yang, which considers two forces of complementary and contrasting principles to be a unitary "whole," one making up for what the other lacks. Although Truong Chinh also subscribed to the Maoist idea of a three-phased approach, he advocated concurrent operations by regular formations and guerrillas in each phase, with guerrilla forces predominant in the first, or strategic defensive phase, and regular forces dominating the third, or strategic offensive phase. Throughout all of the phases, when regular forces could win, they were to attack; but when regular forces were overmatched, they were to avoid set-piece battle, and the guerrillas moved to the forefront to harass and weaken the enemy. American intelligence analysts were well aware of Truong Chinh's influence on Vietnamese communist military strategy. In 1969, the Strategic Research and Analysis Division of the Directorate of Intelligence Production, J-2, Headquarters U.S. Military Assistance Command Vietnam, produced a report stating that Truong Chinh had "set forth a strategy . . . that described with amazing accuracy the developments that [led] to the defeat of the French by the Viet Minh" in 1954.[15] Ironically, the report also stated that the communists were using the same strategy against U.S. and South Vietnamese forces with the same success.

Between December 1952 and March 1953, there were no large-scale encounters between the French and communist forces, but Giap used his guerrilla formations to screen the main force units as they massed for an invasion of Laos. Hoping to interdict Viet Minh lines of communications and force a set-piece battle, the French garrisoned Dien Bien Phu, which lay astride Giap's main logistical artery. But to the astonishment of the French commander, the Viet Minh dragged artillery through the northern highlands to the hills surrounding Dien Bien Phu. Communist artillery subsequently pounded the French positions, and Viet Minh antiaircraft fire dominated the valley. Overland resupply to the garrison was cut, and although the French dedicated their entire C-47 fleet (along with numerous C-119s) to aerial resupply of Dien Bien Phu and a handful of other encampments, they were unable to adequately resupply French forces. Following a blunted attack in late March 1954, Giap launched a concerted assault on 1 May 1954. On 7 May, the Viet Minh 308th Division broke through French defenses and by the evening of the same day the French had surrendered.

Following their humiliating defeat at Dien Bien Phu, the French agreed to the partition of Vietnam at the seventeenth parallel, with the Viet Minh controlling the north while the French withdrew to the south. On 9 October 1954, the last French troops left Hanoi, which became the capital of North Vietnam.

By agreement and under the supervision of an International Control Commission, no further military forces were to be introduced into Vietnam, and a general election was scheduled for July 1956 to reunify the two parts. Bao Dai was reinstated as ruler of South Vietnam, and in July 1954 he chose a strong anticommunist as premier, Ngo Dinh Diem. With American and French assistance, Diem managed to overcome his rivals and the various armed "sects" that held sway in South Vietnam and later succeeded in ousting the emperor himself. He refused to participate in reunification efforts, claiming that the communists intended to perpetrate election fraud in order to secure victory in the elections. Instead, he declared South Vietnamese independence. Following a referendum, Diem was named president of South Vietnam on 26 October 1955. That same year, South Vietnam adopted a new constitution, which allowed Diem to rule the country in an autocratic fashion. The following year, Le Duan, the principal Viet Minh leader remaining in the south after the Geneva Accords, launched an insurgency to overthrow Diem.

Shortly after Diem seized power, the Viet Minh cadre remaining in South Vietnam retrieved weapons left over from World War II and prepared for a guerrilla war against the government. These Viet Minh veterans formed the nucleus of the guerrilla organization that later became known as the Viet Cong. The Viet Cong recruited from various dissident groups that had been crushed by Diem during his seizure of power as well as disaffected peasants in the countryside. The mountain tribes, thoroughly alienated by Diem's auto-cratic policies, were also a major source of support. The Viet Cong created a shadow government and conducted raids, sabotage, and acts of terrorism to weaken the control of the central government over the rural population.[16] The tempo of fighting between the Viet Cong and government troops increased between 1957 and 1960 when Ho Chi Minh vowed at a Party Congress to "lib-erate" South Vietnam. In December 1960, the National Liberation Front for the Liberation of South Vietnam was formed. Over the next decade, the tiny South Vietnamese armed forces would be expanded to deal with the insur-gency, and the air force in particular experienced explosive growth.

L'Armée de l'air and the South Vietnamese Air Force

The South Vietnamese air force came into existence following World War II and was given birth by the French. As discussed in another chapter of this book, the French had followed a long-standing policy of incorporating in-digenous troops into its colonial forces. In 1948, when the French agreed to recognize the two states of Vietnam, they concluded it would be advantageous to create a national Vietnamese army in the south. These units would be used to augment French forces, effectively doubling the number of forces avail-able to fight the Viet Minh. The resultant Vietnamese National Army was placed under the command of French officers and grew slowly at first, but by 1951 was able to field some thirty-five thousand regular forces supported by approximately the same number of auxiliaries. That same year, the French took steps to create an indigenous Vietnamese air force, opening a training center at the French air base at Nha Trang. Vietnamese pilots were trained in observation techniques in the Morane Saulnier MS 500 Criquet, a light liai-son and observation aircraft derived from the German Fiesler Storch. Shortly afterward, the First Air Observation Squadron was established at Nha Trang and a headquarters was created in downtown Saigon, known as the "Air Force Office."[17] The First Squadron was often used to provide replacement crews for French units, which offered a measure of combat experience for the fledgling air force, but the French exercised tight control over the Vietnamese squadron and its contributions to the war effort were not significant.[18] Nevertheless, in August 1951, the French transferred a small number of Dassault MD 312 Flamant light twin-engine transport aircraft to the South Vietnamese, and the 312th Special Missions Squadron was formed at Tan Son Nhut airfield near Saigon.[19]

Vietnamese pilots received their basic flight training in French flying schools at Avord in France, Blida airfield in Algeria, and in Morocco. Nguyen Cao Ky, who rose to air vice marshal and commanded the South Vietnamese air force, trained in Algeria and France. The first pilot training to take place in South Vietnam began at Nha Trang in 1952, including Nguyen Ngoc Oanh, who later commanded the training center. Maintenance courses were established at the training center in 1952 as well as recruit and aviation cadet training. On 15 December 1952, the facility was designated the "Air Instruction Center."[20]

Expansion of the South Vietnamese air force was slow at first, but as pilots and crews graduated they were assigned to the two Vietnamese squadrons to replace losses, and in 1953 two additional observation squadrons were raised. During this period, the Criquets remained a mainstay of Vietnamese air operations, but the French also transferred American-supplied Cessna L-19 "Bird Dog" light liaison aircraft to the South Vietnamese. Later, the MD 312 Flamants were replaced by ten Beech 45 "Expediter" light transports, sixteen C-47 "Dakotas," and a lone Republic RC-3 "Seabee" amphibian. The 312th Squadron was then redesignated as the First Liaison Squadron and given the mission of carrying passengers and freight along the coast between Saigon and the former imperial capital of Hue. But despite the additional aircraft and new squadrons, the South Vietnamese air force remained an auxiliary arm of l'Armeé de l'air.[21]

The Geneva agreements signed in 1954 deprived France of its Southeast Asian colonies, and the French agreed to withdraw their military forces from Vietnam. The official transfer of aircraft from French to South Vietnamese control took place on 1 July 1955 — a date considered to be the birthday of an independent South Vietnamese air force.[22] At the time, the South Vietnamese fielded two transport squadrons, one "combined liaison-tactical squadron," and two "straight liaison squadrons." Frontline strength amounted to fifty-eight aircraft of various types, the majority being light liaison aircraft based at Da Nang, Nha Trang, Bien Hoa, and Tan Son Nhut airfields. Between 1956 and 1958, all of the French aircraft were replaced with American aircraft as part of American military aid programs, and fifty-five North American T-6 "Texan" trainers, along with additional L-19s, T-28 "Trojan" trainers, and Cessna U-17 "Skywagons" were received at Nha Trang. The Air Instruction Center was then redesignated Tactical Base Number 1 in July 1955, but was generally referred to as the "Air Training Base." Owing to this substantial growth, the headquarters was moved from downtown Saigon to Tan Son Nhut in early 1956 and was officially named Headquarters Vietnamese Air Force on 3 October 1956.[23]

With American aid administered through the French, the South Vietnamese air force continued to grow, adding twenty-five F8F Bearcat fighters in June 1956 and forming the First Fighter Squadron — the first South Vietnamese combat squadron.[24] The Second Fighter Squadron was formed at Da Nang later that same year. At first both squadrons flew the F8F, but these aircraft were soon replaced by ground attack versions of the T-28, and in 1960 the first A-1 "Skyraiders" were received. By the end of 1965, the South Vietnamese air force boasted 6 operational fighter squadrons with 146 Skyraiders.[25]

In April 1956, the First Helicopter Squadron was formed at Tan Son Nhut. This small squadron comprised only four pilots, twenty-five enlisted men, and a handful of obsolete Bell H-13 "Sioux" light utility helicopters. A second helicopter squadron was created at Da Nang in October 1961. Over time, the H-13s were converted to the general purpose Sikorsky H-19 "Chickasaw," but the H-19 proved inadequate, and Sikorsky H-34 "Choctaws" were secured from the United States as a replacement. But the H-34 was plagued with maintenance problems and was rarely employed in field operations.[26] It was not until the arrival of U.S. Army helicopter units that the South Vietnamese army obtained the air mobility deemed necessary to fight against the Viet Cong.

Despite its growth and independent status, the South Vietnamese air force remained a supporting arm of the South Vietnamese army in the 1950s. In its counterinsurgency role, the South Vietnamese air force was always intended to support the South Vietnamese army and was equipped mainly to provide liaison, observation, and limited transportation capability. In short, the South

Vietnamese air force was not conceived with a close support capability and certainly not with an offensive "strategic" capability. But the French hand-over to the Americans ushered in a period of major transition for the fledgling air force, and as the conflict in South Vietnam deepened, the South Vietnamese air force took on a greater combat role.

The Arrival of the Americans

As early as the closing months of World War II, the U.S. government had become concerned about Soviet expansionism. In April 1945, an Office of Strategic Services policy paper stated that the Soviets seemed intent upon world domination and the United States should take steps to block Soviet aggression.[27] Spurred by this report and others, U.S. policymakers shifted from a perspective of the Soviets as wartime ally to one opposing Soviet imperialism.

As the so-called Cold War deepened, the Truman Doctrine was at the heart of public policy that ultimately led the United States to intervene directly in Vietnam. After Mao's victory in China in 1949, the United States took a more general anticommunist stance, "universalizing" the doctrine.[28] Indeed, the specific threat to Indochina that precipitated U.S. commitment to defend the region was the "loss" of China and China's subsequent role in the Korean War. Yet U.S. concern regarding the "Associated States of Indochina" (Vietnam, Cambodia, and Laos) preceded the Korean War. On 7 March 1950, Undersecretary of State Dean Rusk sent a memorandum to the Defense Department stating, "The resources of the [United States] should be deployed to reserve Indochina and Southeast Asia from further communist encroachment."[29] On 24 April 1950, President Truman approved NSC (National Security Council) 64, ordering "all practicable measures be taken to prevent further communist expansion in Southeast Asia."[30] In May of that same year, Secretary of State Dean Acheson announced that the United States would provide direct assistance to the French in support of their efforts to defeat communist insurgency in Vietnam.[31] Moreover, as the French withdrew, direct assistance would be made available to the South Vietnamese government.

Thus, as early as 1950, the United States became increasingly committed to the defense of South Vietnam, and when President Eisenhower became alarmed about "falling dominos," U.S. analysts pressed for direct American military intervention. By January 1954, Secretary of State John Foster Dulles and his brother, Allen Dulles, director of the Central Intelligence Agency, had developed plans for covert operations in northern Vietnam to be headed by Colonel Edward G. Lansdale, who had been instrumental in the defeat of the Huks in the Philippines. Lansdale was given broad authority to initiate psychological operations in Vietnam similar to those he had conducted in the Philippines. As Colonel Lansdale embarked on his covert mission, a citizens' lobby — "American Friends of Vietnam" — was formed to promote public support for anticommunist efforts in Vietnam. In June 1956, Senator John F. Kennedy spoke at a symposium sponsored by the lobby, the theme of which was "America's Stake in Vietnam."

Kennedy argued that Vietnam represented "the cornerstone of the Free World in Southeast Asia." Burma, Thailand, India, Japan, the Philippines, and obviously Laos and Cambodia would also succumb to aggression if "the red tide of communism overflowed into Vietnam." In that light, Vietnam represented "a proving ground of democracy in Asia." With this in mind, Kennedy claimed that the United States was "directly responsible" for what happened to Vietnam and therefore could not afford to fail in its defense.[32] Thus, when Kennedy took office as president, he was publicly committed to defending Vietnam against communist subversion and aggression.

A speech given by Soviet premier Nikita Khrushchev in Moscow on 6 January 1961 in which he outlined a comprehensive strategy for "world conquest" provided the impetus for Kennedy's sense of urgency. According to Khrushchev, war could be divided into three categories: general war, which he rejected as too dangerous; local, or limited wars, which he feared because of their potential to develop into general war; and "wars of national liberation," which he endorsed as "inevitable and desirable."[33] President Kennedy interpreted "wars of national liberation" to mean Soviet-inspired subversion and aggression. In the developing world, instability and anticolonial resentment would be exploited through a strategy of promoting revolutionary insurgency.[34] Inasmuch as a national liberation front had been formed in South Vietnam with North Vietnamese backing, Kennedy directed Secretary of Defense Robert McNamara to place greater emphasis on counterinsurgency as a countervailing strategy to wars of national liberation, and in 1961 he signed National Security Action Memorandum 2, instructing the armed services to develop a counterinsurgency capability.[35]

Early U.S. Military Machinations

In the first half of 1961, none of the armed services had forces specifically trained to fight against insurgents. The U.S. Army had three special forces groups, but these had been raised and trained to conduct unconventional warfare behind Soviet lines in Europe should conventional war break out. Neither the navy nor the Marines had specially tailored forces, and although the U.S. Air Force had fielded three wings dedicated to "unconventional operations" during the Korean War, these wings were reduced to two squadrons by 1956 and were deactivated in 1957.[36]

From the outset of President Kennedy's calls for a reorientation of U.S. forces to counter revolutionary guerrilla warfare, the armed services resisted. Collectively, the armed services were determined to "dismiss the contrast between conventional and counterinsurgency combat as an exaggerated premise." Thus, on one occasion, Army Chief of Staff General George Decker "stoutly stood up to the President with the assurance that 'any good soldier can handle guerrillas.'"[37] Nevertheless, counterinsurgency was at the heart of the Kennedy administration's new "Flexible Response" strategy, and at the urging of General Maxwell Taylor, Kennedy's principal military adviser, a new cabinet-level body, the "Special Group for Counterinsurgency," was formed to ensure that the military departments complied with the president's wishes in the matter. Interestingly, before Kennedy's election in 1960, a number of U.S. Air Force leaders had foreseen the growing emphasis on counterinsurgency. As a result, the Air Staff prepared a study on "cold war problems" and presented it to the new president on 28 March 1961. Liking its analysis, Kennedy sent the study to McGeorge Bundy, special assistant to the president for national security matters, and many of the study's recommendations were incorporated into the president's program.[38] But, as will be examined in detail later, the motivation for U.S. Air Force interest in counterinsurgency was more one of self-interest than anything else.

Nevertheless, the U.S. Air Force acted to comply with the president's demands that structural changes be made regarding counterinsurgency, and on 14 April 1961, the 4400th Combat Crew Training Squadron was activated at Eglin Air Force Base in northwest Florida. The concept of operations for the new squadron was to train U.S. Air Force crews in aircraft suitable for counterinsurgency; prepare these aircraft for transfer to friendly foreign air forces; provide training to foreign personnel on operations and maintenance of these aircraft; and finally to develop tactics for employment of these aircraft in countering insurgency. The Air Staff believed that creating a special unit for counterinsurgency was "adequate to meet the needs" of the president's requirements, "particularly since it was flexible and subject to quick modification."[39]

As the U.S. Air Force took its first faltering steps to develop a counter-insurgency capability, American aid and personnel began to flow into South Vietnam. But U.S. aid had begun long before 1961, starting with the creation of the Military Assistance Advisory Group in 1950. From 1950 to 1954, over one billion dollars in aid was provided to France and South Vietnam to combat the insurgency. At first, the American military mission was primarily a logistical support element, but after the Geneva Accords U.S. troops began actively advising the government of South Vietnam. On 22 October 1954, the advisory group was authorized to set in motion a "crash program" to improve the combat effectiveness of "Free Vietnamese forces," and on 1 January 1955, a formal agreement was reached whereby the United States would provide direct aid to the South Vietnamese government under the auspices of the U.S. Military Assistance Program.[40] Shortly afterward, at the request of the South Vietnamese government, the French withdrew their advisers.

The American military mission was headed by a U.S. Army brigadier general and was staffed mostly by U.S. Army officers. According to the commanding general's later reflections, the advisory group had two principal objectives: first, to create a conventional army of divisional-sized units and supporting elements to meet any North Vietnamese invasion; and second, to establish "follow-through programs" to sustain these conventional forces. The infantry divisions would, as an aside, perform internal security duties. The decision to prepare the South Vietnamese for conventional warfare stemmed from the American view that the guerrilla activities of the Viet Cong were a precursor to conventional invasion of South Vietnam by North Vietnam. Admiral Ulysses S. Grant Sharp, commander in chief of U.S. Pacific Command during the latter stages of the American war in Vietnam, admitted to this outlook in his 1968 report entitled *Report on the Vietnam War*. "Originally," he wrote, "and in light of our recent experience in Korea, the emphasis was placed on developing South Vietnamese forces capable of meeting an overt thrust across the Demilitarized Zone."[41]

Thus, at the strategic level, the United States misunderstood the nature of the conflict in South Vietnam, in which a large proportion of the population held legitimate grievances against the Diem government. As a result, the United States military mission misconstrued Viet Cong activities as simply preparatory to conventional invasion by communist North Vietnam.[42] Therefore, at the operational and tactical levels, the U.S. advisory group concentrated on increasing the military capacity of the South Vietnamese to resist an invasion rather than stress counterinsurgency initiatives such as systemic reforms and other measures that had proven instrumental in breaking the back of communist insurgencies elsewhere. Nevertheless, irrespective of the genuine insurgent *allentours* of the conflict in South Vietnam before 1965, the South Vietnamese army was organized, trained, and equipped by the United States for conventional warfare.

Ironically, when large numbers of U.S. ground combat forces were introduced in 1965, the South Vietnamese army was relegated to internal security duties, for which they had not been trained. The North Vietnamese had infiltrated large numbers of regular troops into South Vietnam, and the U.S. commander, General Westmoreland, decided to use U.S. forces to seek out and destroy communist main force units. But the regular North Vietnamese troops fought alongside the Viet Cong in the very war of interlocking that had proved successful against the French. In his 1968 report, Admiral Sharp acknowledged this unique disposition of communist forces and the challenge it posed:

The communists avoided major contact . . . fighting defensively when forced to do so, and attempting to rebuild and reinforce for operations at an opportune time. Tactical guerrilla warfare was intensified without fragmenting Main Force units or discarding plans for their buildup and use. . . . Enemy strategy hinged on continuing the war in the hope of outlasting our determination.[43]

In truth, South Vietnam's political and military leaders had supported the idea of conventional configuration of the armed forces (themselves fearing a North Vietnamese invasion), but they also emphasized the development of territorial forces to fight the Viet Cong.[44] Unfortunately, American aid had been structured to raise a conventional army and at first "no provisions were made to provide . . . funding for the paramilitary territorial forces, the Civil Guard, and the Self-Defense Corps militia" useful in counterrevolutionary warfare. Funding for these forces was eventually made available but even then only in small amounts.[45] Thus, the conventional mind-set of the South Vietnamese army defined their "pacification" efforts in South Vietnam, and South Vietnamese commanders maintained this predilection to the end. "In fact, the pacification support mission was not popular with [South Vietnamese army] commanders who, naturally, derived their values from their American mentors."[46] The net effect was wholly counterproductive from a counterinsurgency standpoint. As one British expert pointed out at the time, "What in effect was happening was that the [South Vietnamese] army, organized on conventional lines to defeat a foreign invader . . . created a completely wrong attitude [which led] to operations and actions which might have been excusable as acts of war if carried out in enemy territory."[47]

By September 1959 the South Vietnamese army had been organized into seven conventional infantry divisions with over ten thousand soldiers in each. Three corps headquarters were established (I Corps at Da Nang in the north; II Corps at Pleiku in the Central Highlands; and III Corps at Saigon in the south), which were further subdivided into nine tactical zones (a fourth corps would be added by 1965). The corps commanders were virtually autonomous, reporting not to a supreme military commander but directly to President Diem.[48] Each division consisted of three infantry regiments; artillery, mortar, and engineer battalions; and company-sized support units. Four armored cavalry regiments were also raised, each with a squadron of American-supplied M-24 light tanks and two squadrons of M-8 self-propelled 75 mm howitzers. There were also eight independent artillery battalions, equipped with heavy artillery.[49]

In October 1961, President Kennedy authorized American advisers to more actively advise South Vietnamese units and to participate in counterguerrilla combat operations. He also dispatched General Maxwell Taylor to Saigon to investigate the political and military situation. Composed of White House, Department of State, and Defense Department officials, the "Taylor mission" warned the president that the situation in South Vietnam had reached crisis proportions and recommended strong actions to arrest the growing strength of the Viet Cong. The report pointed to a corrupt and disintegrating government; an army oriented to fight the wrong war, yet committed to the status quo; and the conditions that had fostered discontent and given rise to the Viet Cong still extant. Yet the report recommended propping up the Diem regime (since no alternative seemed available) as well as accelerating military assistance and deploying U.S. ground combat forces to provide a screen against northern invasion while the South Vietnamese army concentrated on defeating the Viet Cong. Kennedy accepted the first two recommendations, resisted the urge to deploy ground forces, but authorized a buildup of the advisory contingent.[50] To provide more air support, the Taylor mission also recommended the deployment of U.S. Air Force advisers and aircraft to train the South Vietnamese air force in counterguerrilla tactics.[51]

The subsequent dramatic expansion of the South Vietnamese armed forces was accompanied by similar expansion of the American military mission. On 8 February 1962, President Kennedy authorized the creation of a subordinate unified command under the Commander in Chief, U.S. Pacific Command, Admiral Harry Felt, to manage the training of South Vietnamese forces. U.S. Army Lieutenant General Paul Harkins was selected as commander. General Harkins reported to the secretary of defense through Admiral Felt and the Joint Chiefs and was coequal to the U.S. ambassador to South Vietnam, Frederick Nolting, whom he would consult on policy matters. General Harkins also commanded the Military Assistance Advisory Group, which continued to manage military aid to South Vietnam. Though broader in scope and larger than its predecessor, the U.S. Military Assistance Command, Vietnam, retained the former organization's ground orientation "and this quickly engendered a heated interservice conflict over the conduct of the war and especially over the use and control of airpower."[52] Of the five general officers assigned to key positions in the new organization, only one air force officer was of flag rank. Of the 105 officer billets authorized throughout the staff, 54 were army officers, another 29 officers were from the navy or Marine Corps, and only 22 were air force officers. Consequently, as before, the U.S. Air Force contingent believed it had little to say in how airpower was to be employed in South Vietnam.[53]

The debate regarding the proper role of airpower in South Vietnam did not originate, however, in the American military mission's office in Saigon. Headquarters U.S. Army had maintained all along that organic army aviation — that is, helicopters — was better suited to counterguerrilla warfare and counterinsurgency. Thus, on 16 January 1962, before President Kennedy authorized an expanded military mission in South Vietnam, the U.S. Army submitted a memorandum to Defense Secretary McNamara claiming that the U.S. Army should control counterinsurgency operations on foreign soil. The argument had two parts. First, inasmuch as the U.S. Air Force was accorded primary responsibility for strategic warfare, it made sense for the U.S. Army to be accorded responsibility for the lower end of the conflict spectrum. Second, in that the indigenous army would undoubtedly assume the primary role in combating an insurgency, it seemed only appropriate that the U.S. Army should take the lead in American assistance as well. U.S. Air Force leaders countered that this perspective was too limited and an oversimplification of the problem and officially objected to the army's proposal in February 1962.[54] This, despite the fact that the U.S. Air Force Current Operations Plan 11–62, which articulated the service's general Cold War perspective, "had taken no formal notice of counterinsurgency" in 1961.[55]

Regardless of the lack of any official concern for the insurgent threat before the U.S. Army proposal, General Curtis LeMay, chief of staff of the air force, argued that counterinsurgency required the integration of "all parts of a nation's social, economic, and governmental structure, not one segment alone." To that end, counterinsurgency "required the total application of the nation's resources and not just that of the national army." Not surprisingly, General LeMay claimed that airpower should play a major role. The Joint Staff concurred with LeMay's argument and recommended to Secretary McNamara that a "joint" plan for South Vietnam be developed.[56] But having preserved an airpower role in counterinsurgency (and in South Vietnam), LeMay did not order any major modifications to doctrine or force structure.

In 1962, the South Vietnamese Army grew to 219,000 soldiers. The Civil Guard expanded to 77,000 and the Self-Defense Corps to just under 100,000. A new paramilitary force was also created at this time, the Civilian Irregular Defense Group, and by the end of 1962 totaled some 15,000 militiamen.[57] As the ground component expanded, Defense Secretary McNamara concluded that the South Vietnamese air force should also expand to support the South Vietnamese army.[58] The result was a period of explosive growth of the South Vietnamese air force between 1962 and 1965. In these three years, the South Vietnamese air force grew from 4,000 personnel to over 15,000, and frontline strength grew from six to sixteen squadrons, and from 96 to over 460 aircraft.[59]

The transformation of the South Vietnamese armed forces was accompanied by the creation of an American combat development test center, placed under the control of the South Vietnamese Joint General Staff in Saigon. In

September 1961, Defense Secretary McNamara had informed the Joint Chiefs that he viewed South Vietnam as a "laboratory for the development of improved organizational and operational procedures for conducting sublimited war."[60] The test center was to be the centerpiece of experimentation in counterinsurgency concepts. But the activities of the center soon "engendered heated controversy over the use of tactical airpower."[61] To U.S. Air Force leaders, the U.S. Army intended to use the center to verify its predilections regarding organic rotary-wing tactical aviation in an attempt to wrest away certain traditional U.S. Air Force roles and missions. To preempt this, General LeMay proposed a "joint" operational evaluation group with U.S. Air Force representation in order to "restrain the Army from introducing air units and equipment into Southeast Asia under the guise of testing."[62] The Joint Chiefs agreed to the proposal, but the U.S. Army created its own test unit nonetheless. In response, a special U.S. Air Force unit was also created as a special staff section under Brigadier General Rollen Anthis, who was the air force section chief of the Military Assistance Advisory Group. The U.S. Army test unit began unilateral testing in late 1962, evaluating such weapon systems as armed helicopters, and the U.S. Air Force test unit began operations in early 1963.[63]

Not surprisingly, the divergent test units reached different conclusions about similar concepts. The U.S. Air Force claimed that the army's tests were intended to validate foregone conclusions regarding the use of helicopters and other cherished initiatives. For example, the U.S. Army test unit concluded that "armed helicopters were the most effective, single, aerial system for counterinsurgency and that they should provide the additional close support that fixed-wing aircraft could not give."[64] In addition, the U.S. Army test unit concluded that the CV-2 "Caribou," the largest fixed-wing aircraft ever operated by the U.S. Army, was preferable to the U.S. Air Force C-123 because the former could operate from a larger number of airfields in South Vietnam. Moreover, being under the control of the army field commander, the CV-2 would be more responsive than those transport aircraft under centralized air force control.[65] Not surprisingly, the U.S. Air Force countered that centralized control was more efficient and offered that an improved version of the C-123 could operate from 88 percent of the airfields in South Vietnam, comparable to the CV-2.

As competition between the U.S. Air Force and U.S. Army increased, and recognizing that "if the Air Force failed to provide adequate air support to the Army, the Army would furnish its own," General LeMay ordered the Air Staff to plan for deployment of forces to South Vietnam. In addition, Defense Secretary McNamara directed the Air Staff to work with the South Vietnamese to improve the latter's tactical air control system, including the creation of an air operations center, air support operations centers, and training of South Vietnamese combat crews and forward air controllers. The first unit to deploy to South Vietnam was a mobile combat reporting center, ordered to Tan Son Nhut from the 507th Tactical Control Group, Shaw Air Force Base, South Carolina, in October 1961.[66] Deeper U.S. Air Force commitment to the widening conflict was assured, however, when a detachment from the 4400th Combat Crew Training Squadron was deployed to South Vietnam that same year.

Jungle Jim and Farm Gate

The unofficial nickname for the 4400th Squadron was "Jungle Jim." Jungle Jim initially comprised only 124 officers and 228 enlisted men, along with sixteen C-47s, eight B-26 "Invaders," and eight T-28s.[67] The mission of Jungle Jim was to train, among others, South Vietnamese air crews in counterguerrilla tactics. The T-28s and C-47s were extensively modified to this end. The T-28 trainers were modified as a ground attack aircraft with the addition of armor plating, racks for bombs and rockets, plus two fixed forward-firing .50-caliber machine guns.[68] The modified SC-47 had twice the normal fuel capacity of the normal C-47, was strengthened for operations from unimproved airstrips, and was equipped for rocket-assisted takeoffs. The B-26 had begun its career in World War II as the A-26, a more rugged and capable version of the A-20 "attack bomber." The "attack" classification was abolished after World War II, and the B-26 saw service in the Korean War where it operated as a close support and reconnaissance platform. Recognizing that the rugged and reliable "Invader" could cope with the unique demands of counterguerrilla warfare, a "revamped and revitalized" B-26 "Counter-Invader" was restored to duty and proved "to be the most versatile aircraft in the Air Force's counterinsurgency inventory" during the early part of American intervention.[69] Aside from training foreign pilots and developing tactics, techniques, and procedures for counterguerrilla air warfare at its base in northwest Florida, Jungle Jim was also charged with "preparing small cadres for conducting — at the scene of insurgency activity — the training of friendly foreign air forces in counterinsurgency operations."[70] In short, Jungle Jim was to deploy small detachments overseas to provide "on-site" counterinsurgency training for friendly foreign air forces. It was in this advisory role that U.S. Air Force aircraft and personnel were sent to South Vietnam to help fight against the communists.

By August 1961, Defense Secretary McNamara had concluded that an aerial interdiction campaign was necessary to sever North Vietnamese support to the Viet Cong.[71] To that end, a small detachment of the 4400th Squadron — code-named "Farm Gate" and later Detachment 2A — deployed to South Vietnam to advise, train, and assist the South Vietnamese air force in conducting interdiction and close support missions.[72] Farm Gate comprised four SC-47s, four RB-26s,[73] eight T-28s (all with South Vietnamese national markings), and 151 personnel. The detachment arrived in an independent status but soon came under the control of the Second Advanced Echelon, a provisional element of the Thirteenth Air Force, commanded by Brigadier General Anthis. Although Farm Gate officially reported to the commander of Pacific Air Forces through General Anthis, unit officers routinely bypassed this chain of command and communicated directly with Jungle Jim back in Florida. The detachment operated from Bien Hoa airfield, roughly thirty miles from Saigon. On 6 December 1961, Farm Gate was authorized to fly combat missions against the Viet Cong, provided a Vietnamese crew member was in each aircraft.[74] The detachment flew its first sorties on 19 December and by 7 January 1962 had flown fifty-nine missions ranging from air strikes to photo-reconnaissance, troop and supply drops, and transportation.[75]

The U.S. Pacific Air Forces counterinsurgency plan called for Farm Gate to train the South Vietnamese in air operations against the Viet Cong and develop tactics for the employment of airpower in counterinsurgency.[76] Farm Gate missions were described as falling into two broad categories: support and tactical. Support missions included transportation, liaison, observation, rescue, and medical evacuation. Tactical missions included "combat training in close support and interdiction as well as combat airlift and reconnaissance missions."[77] But Farm Gate personnel believed that they were really in South Vietnam to support U.S. Army special forces soldiers in unconventional warfare operations such as inserting hunter-killer teams into enemy territory, aerial resupply, and so forth.[78] Not surprisingly, then, although Farm Gate continued to provide training to South Vietnamese air crews, in time the American airmen largely abandoned the training mission, and combat operations became more and more frequent until ultimately Farm Gate bore little resemblance to its original purpose. Reflecting on this evolution, Brigadier General Harry C. "Heinie" Aderholt, an almost legendary figure who commanded the First Air Commando Wing in 1964, spoke bitterly of this fact:

Either because the 2nd Advanced Echelon in Saigon didn't understand or didn't give a damn, the Farm Gate boys started flying close air support for the Vietnamese army. . . . That should have been a job for the [South Vietnamese Air Force] and its A-1s, not the Americans. . . . [General] Anthis . . . didn't know shit from Shinola about [counterinsurgency] warfare. . . . We should never have had our regular Air Force and Army units over there. It should have been dealt with as an insurgency, and it should have been the Vietnamese's fight and not ours.[79]

Nevertheless, at the time it was deployed to South Vietnam, Farm Gate represented over half of the U.S. Air Force counterinsurgency capability, and yet it was becoming clear that American involvement in South Vietnam was going to continue to grow. Consequently, the Air Staff doubled the size of the 4400th Combat Crew Training Squadron to become the First Air Commando Group, with authorizations for over 790 personnel and sixty-four aircraft.[80] This was followed by the creation of the Special Air Warfare Center at Eglin Air Force Base, which would comprise the First Air Commando Group and the newly formed First Combat Applications Group. On 27 April 1962, the Special Air Warfare Center became operational with an authorized strength of 860 personnel and eighty-two aircraft.[81]

As the "special air warfare" mission took on greater importance, the U.S. Air Force formally took notice of counterinsurgency when the Current Operations Plan for 1962 dealt with the topic at great length. "Specifically, the Air Force — through the proper application of airpower — could meet requirements for current reconnaissance, highly accurate firepower delivery to support ground troops, quick reaction and flexibility, rapid transportation and resupply of ground forces, casualty evacuation, and rapid and dependable communications over enemy territory."[82] It is notable that the document described the contribution of airpower to counterinsurgency almost exclusively in terms of the direct role of the U.S. Air Force, not the role of indigenous air forces or training those air forces. Not surprisingly then, in the spring of 1962, Farm Gate was reinforced with five additional T-28s, ten B-26s, and two C-47s to enhance the combat capability of the unit. By the summer of 1963, Farm Gate had grown to twelve B-26s, thirteen T-28s, four Helio U-10 "Couriers," and six SC-47s and was redesignated the First Air Commando Squadron (Composite), assigned to the Thirty-fourth Tactical Group, Second Air Division (formerly the Second Advanced Echelon).

But as Farm Gate grew, so did the South Vietnamese air force with attendant growing pains. The addition of a new fighter squadron placed a strain on pilot training, and as a stopgap until pilot training could catch up, two dozen South Vietnamese pilots were transferred from transport duties to the new fighter squadron. The impact on the First Transportation Group at Tan Son Nhut was considerable and at a time when air mobility was proving to be a vital counterinsurgency function of the South Vietnamese air force. To offset this loss of veteran transport pilots, thirty American pilots (known as the "Dirty Thirty") were assigned temporarily to the South Vietnamese air force to fly C-47s, ultimately logging around twenty thousand flying hours.[83] Thus, the U.S. Air Force commitment continued to expand.

Even with the addition of another fighter squadron in 1962, the South Vietnamese air force remained relatively small. But this situation was soon to change dramatically. By 1965 there would be five operational wings, a support base at Pleiku, the training center at Nha Trang, and a logistics wing and depot at Bien Hoa. Between 1962 and the summer of 1963, the South Vietnamese air force expanded in personnel from 4,000 to 7,711. By January 1965 the total was over 10,000 and by the end of that year just under 13,000. With such explosive growth the training center was overwhelmed and all flying training was moved to the United States. Not surprisingly, the deeper involvement of American airmen affected the organization of the South Vietnamese air force so that it evolved a formal command structure modeled on that of the U.S. Air Force. Leadership, however, remained thin, and what few seasoned commanders were available rose rapidly in rank and influence. Without a doubt the most important South Vietnamese air force figure during this time was Nguyen Cao Ky, who rose rapidly to air vice marshal and was named commander of the service in December 1963 at the age of thirty-three. Air Vice Marshal Ky and the South Vietnamese air force were instrumental in putting down an attempted coup d'état in September 1964, and increasingly thereafter Ky was deeply involved in the political life of South Vietnam until the communists overran the country in 1975.[84]

In addition to personnel growth, the South Vietnamese air force experienced substantial growth in the numbers and types of aircraft. Between December 1961 and December 1965, the total inventory grew from 70 to over 390 aircraft. The size of the fleet doubled in 1962 alone. By the beginning of 1964, the South Vietnamese air force had twenty-nine attack versions of the T-28 and twenty-two A-1s. There were also twenty-four H-34 helicopters, thirty-four C-47s, and forty-eight L-19 and other liaison types. In 1965, the South Vietnamese would begin another expansion and modernization program that would eventually bring modern jets into service, including the Northrop F-5A/B "Freedom Fighter," the Cessna A-37B "Dragonfly" (a trainer converted to the attack role), and even Martin B-57 "Canberras" on loan from the U.S. Eighth Air Force.[85]

The U.S. Air Force had strongly advocated jet aircraft as early as 1961. Indeed, assuming that jets would be authorized for transfer to the South Vietnamese air force, the Air Staff programmed six Lockheed T/RT-33 "Shooting Star" trainers and photoreconnaissance aircraft for transfer in 1961. Training of South Vietnamese pilots began in the summer of 1962. Although the Geneva Accords of 1954 prohibited the introduction of jets into Vietnam, the United States had deployed RF-101 "Voodoos" (Operation "Pipestem") and a photo processing unit in October 1961 under the guise of providing photographic support for flood relief operations in the Mekong Delta. In reality, these aircraft were used for reconnaissance missions, flying a total of sixty-seven sorties over thirty-one days. But their use in South Vietnam elicited little international criticism; ergo, the U.S. Air Force and the Joint Chiefs urged Defense Secretary McNamara to authorize the six T-33s to be released to the South Vietnamese without delay. However, the State Department opposed the transfer, citing the fact that the International Control Commission and other Southeast Asian states would view the introduction of jets into the South Vietnamese air force as "a definite escalation of the war."[86] As a result, McNamara declined to support the initiative, and jets did not enter the South Vietnamese inventory until August 1965 when four B-57 Canberras were "loaned" to the South Vietnamese air force. Two years later, however, McNamara was persuaded to permit the transfer of seventeen F-5Cs and two F-5Bs to the South Vietnamese. But even with the introduction of these jets, the A-1 Skyraider remained the mainstay of the South Vietnamese air force throughout the war, especially after the T-28 was phased out in April 1965.[87]

South Vietnamese air force combat operations increased between 1962 and 1965. Before the arrival of Farm Gate, Vietnamese crews and aircraft had shouldered the air war alone (averaging about 2,200 sorties per month), but with the arrival of the Americans, and as the conflict deepened and intensified, joint missions with U.S. Air Force aircraft increased. Joint combat sorties amounted to 2,500 out of some 7,000 sorties during the first six months of 1962. Reportedly, 38 percent of Viet Cong casualties were attributed to joint operations mounted by Farm Gate and South Vietnamese crews in the first eight months of 1963. As the size and scope of the South Vietnamese air effort continued to expand, so too did the sortie generation rate. In 1964, South Vietnamese air force fighter pilots logged over 24,000 combat hours in over 14,000 sorties, an average of 281 hours and 166 sorties per pilot for the year. In 1965, the figures increased to over 65,000 hours and 3,238 sorties for an average of 231 combat sorties per pilot for the year. This amounted to an average of one mission flown on every two out of three days in 1965. By the end of 1965, South Vietnamese fighter pilots flew a grand total of 118,120 operational sorties.[88]

But sorties do not tell the whole story. As discussed earlier, the phenomenal growth of the South Vietnamese air force was accompanied by serious growing pains. A pressing problem was space: there were too few airfields in South Vietnam, and they all had become quite crowded. Problems associated with ramp space and support facilities were only exacerbated by the arrival of more U.S. aircraft as the American commitment deepened. By the end of 1965 there were over twenty-four thousand military personnel and four hundred aircraft at Tan Son Nhut alone, although the airfield was originally designed for around four thousand personnel and seventy-five aircraft.[89] Aircraft maintenance was also a serious problem. The South Vietnamese people were not generally well educated and the economy had always been agrarian; therefore, recruiting and training of personnel for the specialized maintenance that is required for aviation technology presented an unending challenge to South Vietnamese authorities. Effective leadership also proved to be a continual challenge. The South Vietnamese air force was run at the squadron level and driven by personalities. There was little formal coordination between the squadrons and higher headquarters, and there were no command posts at the wing and headquarters echelons. Finally, pilot proficiency proved to be a constant source of concern, with Vietnamese pilots rated across a broad spectrum from "poor" to "excellent," or as one report put it, "Opinions of [South Vietnamese] effectiveness varied widely — from high praise to scathing condemnation."[90] The greatest problem was poor performance related to instrument and night flying.[91] Many of these problems arose from the extremely difficult challenge of balancing training with operational mission requirements in a developing air force engaged in round-the-clock combat operations.

The missions performed by the South Vietnamese air force were delineated into four general categories: close air support; air cover for troops and convoys; interdiction; and secondary tasks such as air escort, search and rescue, air defense, and training. The first three tasks comprised over 80 percent of the missions flown by the South Vietnamese, mostly by A-1s. According to one report, the South Vietnamese considered close support missions to be any time ordnance was dropped "in close proximity" to friendly forces, but apparently this had no precise meaning. Air cover missions were nominated by a corps commander, and if enough sorties were available, South Vietnamese aircraft flew missions to protect troops on the ground from ambush, often providing continuous air coverage during daylight hours. However, if the covering aircraft attacked any ground targets, the mission was reclassified as close air support. Interdiction missions were the only truly independent air strikes conducted by the South Vietnamese, were generally better planned than other missions, and on occasion were conducted in parts of North Vietnam.[92]

Tactical air control of South Vietnamese aircraft was a perennial problem. In the early period of expansion, aircraft dedicated to providing air cover could not detach and be redirected to alternative targets. Yet on many occasions the mere presence of air cover dissuaded the Viet Cong from attacking surface forces, which, when this occurred, made the air cover superfluous. But these aircraft could not be redirected elsewhere owing to the primitive state of tactical air control in South Vietnam. Consequently, unused ordnance was often jettisoned on bombing ranges or the aircraft returned to base with munitions still onboard — a dangerous prospect that the crews understandably wished to avoid.[93] Improved and centralized control therefore became very important, and in January 1962 an Air Operations Center was established at Tan Son Nhut to serve as a central command post for the South Vietnamese air force and Farm Gate. The center was jointly manned, with a Vietnamese officer as the chief and an American as deputy. The center became the "hub for coordinating the activities of the two air forces." With centralized control established, Farm Gate undertook to train South Vietnamese crews in forward air control, which began in February 1962.[94]

In addition to the problems associated with growth and command and control, the South Vietnamese faced a more fundamental problem in terms of its role in the counterinsurgency effort and in relation to the South Vietnamese army. Much of the tension between the South Vietnamese armed services was a reflection of the continuing animosity between the U.S. Air Force and the U.S. Army. A principal criticism leveled by U.S. Air Force officers in South Vietnam remained that the advisory mission was U.S. Army–dominated and therefore did not understand nor appreciate the role that airpower could play in fighting against the Viet Cong. As one report bitterly noted:

The major obstacle to the enlargement of the Air Force role in South Vietnam . . . was the U.S. Army. Its aviation arm, consisting of Mohawk, Caribou, and liaison aircraft and helicopters grew by December 1962 to about 200 while the Air Force only had 63. In its support role, the Army frequently . . . used its aircraft outside the centralized tactical air control system rather than call upon Farmgate [sic] and [South Vietnamese air force] units. This practice brought the Army into a continuing, abrasive conflict with the Air Force.[95]

U.S. Air Force officers were especially disturbed by the idea of a South Vietnamese army air corps that was being pushed by the U.S. Army. By the time the U.S. Air Force intervened in the matter, the South Vietnamese army had gone so far as to request the transfer of South Vietnamese air force aircraft to create four fixed-wing army aviation units. Defense Secretary McNamara took the matter under advisement.

When McNamara asked the [Joint Chiefs] in October [1961] to review this proposal, that body could not reach an agreement. The proposal contravened long-established Air Force doctrine, and LeMay objected vigorously. He argued that the [South Vietnamese air force's] administration, logistic [sic], and maintenance responsibilities could not be separated from its operational activities. If divided, it could delay massing available airpower against a large opposing force. And, if the forces of Southeast Asia Treaty Organization entered the war, an air component would be needed to control all airpower that might be used.[96]

McNamara decided against the proposal and without Pentagon backing, the South Vietnamese army dropped its own plans despite continued encouragement from U.S. Army advisers in Saigon. Nevertheless, the U.S. Army's complaint pointed up the problem of coordination and cooperation between fixed-wing support and ground forces — a flaw that became all too apparent a little over a year later during the battle of Ap Bac.[97]

On 2 January 1963, the South Vietnamese Seventh Division launched an assault on a well-entrenched Viet Cong battalion near the village of Ap Bac, about thirty miles southwest of Saigon. The South Vietnamese were airlifted to Ap Bac in U.S. Army helicopters. But the U.S. Air Force liaison officer assigned to the division learned of the planned attack only four days before it was to take place, and by that time all available fixed-wing aircraft had been committed to a major airborne assault along the Cambodian border. Nevertheless, the attack went forward as planned with five U.S. Army UH-1B helicopter gunships providing close support. But as the attack got under way, the air assault unraveled quickly as the Viet Cong put up stiff resistance. A reserve force was then airlifted to the battle to reinforce the troops already fighting for their lives. As the helicopters approached the scene of the fighting, the Viet Cong threw up a hail of automatic weapons fire, and a CH-21 "Shawnee" helicopter was shot down immediately. The supporting gunships made repeated strafing passes, but one of these was shot down along with another CH-21 sent to rescue the first. A South Vietnamese air force forward air controller in an L-19 then made an emergency request for fixed-wing air strikes and Farm Gate aircraft, including B-26s, were diverted to Ap Bac. These air strikes forced the guerrillas to abandon the field and saved the beleaguered South Vietnamese soldiers, but in the confusion the guerrillas were able to escape.[98]

During the battle at Ap Bac, three American advisers were killed and another ten were wounded. South Vietnamese forces lost sixty-five killed in action and around one hundred wounded.[99] Of the fifteen U.S. Army helicopters used in the assault, five had been shot down and all but one of the remainder were heavily damaged. U.S. Army advisers claimed that South Vietnamese tactical incompetence was the principal culprit for the disaster. But U.S. Air Force advisers claimed the U.S. Army had deliberately failed to request adequate fixed-wing support in order to carry out a "test" of its armed helicopters. U.S. Air Force advisers subsequently used the disaster at Ap Bac as proof of the need for centralized control of all air operations — including helicopter assaults conducted by ground forces.[100] General Anthis, Second Air Division commander, requested authority over all air units in South Vietnam. But Admiral Felt was unwilling to open that Pandora's box, and General Harkins retained authority over U.S. Army aviation units.[101] Neverthe-less, Admiral Felt ordered that future air-mobile operations conducted by the South Vietnamese army be coordinated with the South Vietnamese air force and Farm Gate, telling General Harkins that "helicopters were no adequate substitute" for fixed-wing close support.

The failure at Ap Bac reverberated in the halls of the Pentagon. As a result, a team of senior U.S. military officers was dispatched to South Vietnam to resolve the dispute over operational control of air units. The delegation was headed by General Earle Wheeler, the U.S. Army chief of staff. Nothing substantial came out of the visit. The team's report merely commented that the relationship between Harkins and Anthis was satisfactory and that there were no systemic weaknesses in joint planning of operations. In a separate report, however, U.S. Air Force Lieutenant General David Burchinal, deputy chief of staff for plans and programs, was less sanguine. Contrary to the majority view, General Burchinal argued that all air units in South Vietnam should be centrally controlled by a qualified airman, and he urged the assignment of a U.S. Air Force lieutenant general to the American military mission in Saigon as an air deputy commander. Despite Burchinal's proposal, at the end of 1963, the composition of the Military Assistance Advisory Command in Saigon remained unchanged. Nor were the command relationships altered in any fashion.[102] Not surprisingly, the "American dispute did little to impress upon the Vietnamese the importance of coordination between their own army and air units."[103] In the end, air operations between 1961 and 1965 reflected the disjointed nature of counterinsurgency as practiced by the Americans in South Vietnam — especially with respect to the contribution of airpower.

Air Operations, 1961–1965

The opening months of 1961 were marked by the arrival of Farm Gate and expanded operations by the South Vietnamese air force.[104] Soon afterward, other U.S. Air Force aircraft began to flow into the region. In October, Admiral Felt ordered the deployment of four RF-101 reconnaissance aircraft from the Forty-fifth Tactical Reconnaissance Squadron in Japan to Don Muang, Thailand, in Operation "Able Mable." These aircraft became operational in November, briefly overlapping with the RF-101s of Pipestem. By the end of the year, Able Mable aircraft had flown 130 sorties over South Vietnam and

Laos. In November, three specially equipped SC-47s were deployed to South Vietnam to provide psychological operations support. During roughly the same time frame, the South Vietnamese First Fighter Squadron, flying A-1s at Bien Hoa, conducted on average one combat sortie per day, while the Second Fighter Squadron was readied for combat operations at Nha Trang. The First, Second, and Third Liaison Squadrons also became fully operational but were short of pilots.

In January 1962, per Defense Secretary McNamara's instructions to accelerate the buildup of the South Vietnamese armed forces, sixteen C-123 "Providers" from Pope Air Force Base, North Carolina, were ordered to South Vietnam in Operation "Mule Train" to provide the nucleus for anticipated expansion of the airlift mission. These aircraft provided transportation, air-dropped supplies, inserted special forces in Viet Cong territory, and provided training in tactical airlift procedures to the South Vietnamese. In addition, six C-123s from Langley Air Force Base in Virginia were deployed to Tan Son Nhut in November 1961 as part of the controversial Operation "Ranch Hand" aerial defoliation program.

Operation Ranch Hand was intended to reduce the incidence of ambushes as well as reduce food production for the Viet Cong. The combat development test center had begun experiments as early as August 1961. The idea was to spray a swath two hundred yards wide on each side of principal roadways as well as border areas where the guerrillas infiltrated from Cambodia. In addition, once friendly Vietnamese civilians had been removed and provided for, areas of cultivation would be sprayed as well. The six C-123s would provide the bulk of aerial spraying capability, but the South Vietnamese would also operate specially equipped helicopters similar to those used by the British in Malaya in the 1950s to destroy communist guerrilla food production centers.

The defoliation effort was controversial from the outset. The State Department wished to deflect criticism of the United States by flying aircraft with South Vietnamese markings, but the Joint Chiefs ordered that the C-123s carry American markings but conceded to allowing a South Vietnamese crew member to participate. On 13 January 1962, aerial spraying missions began along sixteen miles of road between Bien Hoa and Vung Tau. Not surprisingly, the Viet Cong immediately claimed the chemicals used caused numerous ill effects to innocent civilians and caused considerable property damage. The various claims of damage were evaluated and some were deemed valid. Nevertheless, in May 1962, General Harkins reported that of twenty-one areas sprayed, air-to-ground visibility had improved by 70 percent and ground visibility by 60 percent. Moreover, it was claimed that defoliation had prompted the surrender of 112 Viet Cong guerrillas who had been frightened by the chemical spraying.[105] The apparent good results prompted the Joint Chiefs to press for expansion of the defoliation initiative.

But Secretary of State Dean Rusk objected strenuously to continued defoliation operations, particularly the use of chemicals on food crops.

Rusk thought there was insufficient evidence that the crops belonged to the Viet Cong, feared adverse international reaction, and warned that a premature program could prompt the Viet Cong to step up attacks against strategic hamlets. Observing that the way to win a guerrilla war was to win the support of the people, Rusk argued that crop destruction ran counter to this rule. At best, he thought it should be attempted only in the latter stages of an anti-guerrilla campaign.[106]

Continued State Department opposition led to a reduction of Ranch Hand operations. By May 1963, the defoliation program was effectively at an end. Nevertheless, the Joint Staff claimed the initiative had been a success, pointing to reduced and eliminated vegetation along eighty-seven miles of roads and canals and around military installations, as well as the destruction of 756,000 pounds of food on 104 acres of cultivated land in two provinces "without adverse effects on friendly Vietnamese."[107]

As Operation Ranch Hand missions were diminishing, the overall flow of American personnel and equipment into South Vietnam increased, and American advisers were determined to take the offensive against the Viet Cong. In late 1961, Admiral Felt's staff prepared an Outline Campaign Plan for the South Vietnamese intended to strike at the guerrillas in I and II Corps and along the border. Known as Operation "Sunrise," the plan was loosely based on British operations in Malaya. Beforehand, U.S. Air Force advisers had proposed a quick reaction force comprising South Vietnamese airborne troops supported by American and South Vietnamese transport and strike aircraft. But U.S. Army advisers objected that the air force plan conflicted with Operation Sunrise, and Admiral Felt rejected the quick reaction plan. As a result, Farm Gate aircraft were used primarily to support the "clear-and-hold" strategy of Operation Sunrise.

Regardless, when Farm Gate was integrated into the South Vietnamese air force air control system, the Americans confronted the legacy of previous

French insistence on control at the highest level. South Vietnamese army divisions made requests for air support through the corps commander. If approved, the request would be forwarded to the Joint General Staff in Saigon. Staff officers in Saigon — usually South Vietnamese army officers with no experience in air liaison — would determine the validity of the request and the air assets available. If approved by the Joint General Staff, South Vietnamese aircraft would be assigned to conduct the mission. With the deployment of Farm Gate aircraft to South Vietnam and the explosive growth in size and scope of operations of the South Vietnamese air force, it became necessary to impose a more rigorous system of control over air operations. Not surprisingly, there was opposition at first: centralized control by airmen impinged upon the previous prerogative of the South Vietnamese corps commanders to regulate air activity in their own areas of responsibility. Nevertheless, the rudiments of a centralized air control system were established, beginning with the creation of the Air Operations Center in January 1962.[108] The control system was improved upon when U.S. advisers created a Joint Operations Center. But problems persisted, limiting the effectiveness of both centers.

Of considerable concern to American and South Vietnamese civilian officials alike was the potential for air strikes to kill or injure innocent civilians. On 26 May 1962, a Farm Gate aircraft had struck the village of Da Ket, south of Da Nang, resulting in civilian casualties. General Anthis exploited the heightened concern regarding unintended collateral damage to stress the need for centralized control. He briefed President Diem on the tactical air control system, stressing how the system would not only permit a more rapid response to calls for air support, but the use of airborne forward air controllers would mitigate the likelihood of collateral damage. President Diem subsequently ordered the South Vietnamese army to relinquish control over air missions.

The State Department questioned the wisdom of attacking villages altogether and recommended that the British rules of engagement used in Malaya be duplicated in South Vietnam. But despite the civilian deaths at Da Ket, U.S. Air Force officials pointed out that an estimated four hundred Viet Cong had been killed as well. In short, they argued that these air attacks were not failures because "they attained their objective of clearing the area of guerrillas" despite the deaths of several civilians.[109] The commander of Pacific Air Forces therefore expressed his concern that an exaggerated reaction to collateral damage would limit the usefulness of airpower in South Vietnam.

Nonetheless, it was clear that precise targeting was required by the nature of the conflict. Guerrilla warfare blurred the distinctions between insurgents and civilians, and President Diem emphatically insisted that air operations be conducted with extreme caution. As a result, Farm Gate operated under strict rules of engagement intended to emphasize utmost care in the selection and attack of ground targets. By 1962, Diem insisted that neither Farm Gate nor South Vietnamese aircraft be allowed to fire on ground targets unless they were under the positive control of a Vietnamese forward air controller. However, McNamara simply warned U.S. commanders about the counterproductive effect of killing civilians but imposed no new rules of engagement, merely suggesting that pilots weigh "risk against gain" in striking targets that were not clearly Viet Cong.[110]

Despite McNamara's warning about collateral damage, civilian deaths as a consequence of air strikes grew. In effect conceding that certainty in targeting could not be achieved in counterguerrilla warfare, General Anthis therefore proposed the idea of "free areas," where air strikes could be conducted without regard for collateral damage and without positive control. Soon afterward, President Diem approved the proposal but ordered that Farm Gate aircraft were still required to have targets marked by Vietnamese L-19s, whereas South Vietnamese strike aircraft could operate without positive control. The idea of free areas came under review, however, when air strikes came close to the Cambodian border. Earlier in the year, Farm Gate aircraft had been accused of bombing and strafing a village on the Cambodian side of the border, prompting the U.S. State Department to pressure the South Vietnamese government to apologize. General Anthis then ordered Farm Gate to refrain from operations within five miles of the border. As air operations in the free areas neared the border once again, the Cambodian government objected, and the U.S. Joint Staff banned air and ground operations within ten kilometers of the border.[111]

Yet collateral damage continued to occur, and the communists exploited civilian deaths for propaganda purposes.[112] Targets on the ground were often described by South Vietnamese forward air controllers simply as "groups of huts" or "troop concentrations," and the targets themselves were frequently obscured by jungle cover.[113] The problem of precise identification was due in large part to the inexperience of South Vietnamese crews and their use of ineffective tactics. South Vietnamese L-19s routinely flew at an altitude of three thousand feet or higher, far too high to precisely distinguish between a group of Viet Cong guerrillas and a collection of Vietnamese peasants. The observer in the rear of the L-19 marked targets for incoming ground attack aircraft by radio direction or by hand-thrown smoke grenades. Radio communications were especially difficult. In addition to the airplane's radio, the crews carried an army field radio to communicate with troops on the ground. But the L-19 crew could not operate both radios simultaneously. Air-to-ground and air-to-air communications were therefore haphazard at best, and in the confusion that often accompanied such missions, mistakes were made and the wrong targets were struck.

As 1962 closed and 1963 opened, the conflict in South Vietnam seemed to be at a turning point in the opinion of many American officials. In July 1962 McNamara declared that the "crash" program was at an end and that long-range systemic planning for defeating the insurgency was now necessary. Assuming that the Viet Cong would be checked by 1965, McNamara ordered the U.S. armed services to prepare a comprehensive plan for training and equipping the South Vietnamese to shoulder the burden of counterinsurgency themselves as American forces withdrew from South Vietnam.

Harassment and interdiction missions grew in importance during this period, particularly after intelligence reports put the Viet Cong order of battle in April 1962 as 18 battalions, 79 companies, and 137 platoons — or somewhere between 16,000 and 25,000 guerrillas.[114] Admiral Felt urged General Harkins to fight the Viet Cong on their own terms: "It is," he wrote, "basic to our side that the initiative be denied the [Viet Cong]. Our concept is to harass them, push them down and extend them far beyond the capabilities of their logistics support, thus destroying them."[115] To support harassment and interdiction operations, the combined U.S.–South Vietnamese air force staffs established direct air support centers to provide instant response to the fluid nature of counterguerrilla air operations. However, these centers proved ineffective in that they became tied to specified regions within corps boundaries, and the South Vietnamese army proved unable and largely unwilling to attempt the kind of unconventional warfare envisioned by Admiral Felt.

Irrespective of the counterguerrilla strategy employed by the ground forces, stepped-up operations required more air support. In August 1962, four U.S. Air Force U-10 (L-28) aircraft arrived to improve air-to-ground communications and provide additional spotter support. By now Farm Gate was officially designated as the First Air Commando Squadron (Composite), with Detachments 1 and 2 located at Plei Ky and Soc Trang airfields respectively. An additional C-123 squadron (Operation "Sawbuck II") arrived as well. To better manage the growing C-123 fleet in South Vietnam, the Tactical Air Transport Squadron (Provisional 2), 464th Troop Carrier Wing, was created. In addition to U.S. Air Force aircraft, eight U-1 "Otters," sixteen Cessna O-1A light observation aircraft, ten UH-1B helicopters, and a company of CV-2 Caribou transports were dispatched to augment U.S. Army forces in South Vietnam.[116] The army had first deployed CV-2s to Thailand and then South Vietnam in 1961. When the second aviation company arrived in 1963, General Harkins agreed to place all thirty-two CV-2s under the coordinated airlift system, but he directed that these aircraft still be dedicated to U.S. Army advisers attached to the corps to provide immediate support when requested.[117]

The number of sorties by U.S. Air Force aircraft increased steadily in the latter part of 1962 and into 1963. Farm Gate T-28s and B-26s flew over 2,900 missions, and C-47s flew 843 sorties (of which 649 were in support of special forces). The C-123s flew over 11,600 sorties, carrying over 17,000 tons of cargo and transporting some 45,000 South Vietnamese troops. The total sortie rate for the year exceeded 15,800. Farm Gate and the South Vietnamese air force claimed that 28 percent of the 25,000 Viet Cong casualties recorded in 1962 were caused by air action. Of this total, Farm Gate alone claimed to have inflicted 3,200 casualties on the communists. Headquarters Pacific Air Forces credited Farm Gate with more than a third of Viet Cong casualties. And the Defense Intelligence Agency allowed that U.S. aircraft had resulted in 56 percent of communist guerrillas killed and wounded.[118]

Increased combat air operations demanded increased reconnaissance, and two more RF-101s (operation "Patricia Lynn") joined the Able Mable aircraft, which had arrived in November 1961. In March, four reconnaissance versions of the B-26 arrived (Operation "Sweet Sue"), all capable of night operations. By May, these aircraft accounted for roughly 70 percent of all targeting information in South Vietnam.[119] The RF-101s and RB-26s were later joined by two RB-57Es. By mid-1963, these twelve U.S. Air Force aircraft were complemented by six U.S. Army Mohawks.[120] Also, the South Vietnamese received three camera-equipped RC-47s and eighteen RT-28s and activated the 716th Composite Reconnaissance Squadron at Tan Son Nhut. With the arrival of these additional American reconnaissance aircraft, along with the improved strike capability of the South Vietnamese Air Force, air operations reportedly made it exceedingly difficult for the Viet Cong to move and hide their activities, except at night.[121]

In addition to close support, interdiction, and reconnaissance, air cover and air escort were considered vital in 1962. The task of air cover was intimately connected to the idea that the South Vietnamese air force existed to support the ground forces. Moreover, the primitive tactical control system and the relatively slow cruising speed of the T-28 and the A-1 forced the South Vietnamese air force to adopt air cover in order to be immediately responsive to the needs of ground forces commanders. Interestingly, the U.S. Marine Corps had used air cover and air escort extensively in Nicaragua in the 1920s and early 1930s, and the basic concept remained unchanged. Flying overhead, covering aircraft would reconnoiter ahead of ground forces and prevent ambushes as well as provide air-delivered ordnance on short notice. Air cover for convoys was regarded as an especially important role. Following a particularly devastating Viet Cong ambush of a military convoy in June 1962 near Ben Cat, killing twenty-three South Vietnamese soldiers and two U.S. Army advisers, and another ambush in August, President Diem ordered that all "important" convoys receive air escort.[122] To that end, air escort normally consisted of three aircraft: an L-19 and two ground attack aircraft such as the T-28 or A-1. On occasion, a single B-26 could substitute for the two fighter types.[123]

The year 1962 closed with mixed results. Reportedly, somewhere between 25,000 to 33,000 Viet Cong had been killed or wounded,[124] over 11,500 "structures belonging to the insurgents" had been destroyed or damaged, and more than 1,500 boats (also presumably belonging to the guerrillas) had been sunk (Farm Gate alone was credited with 4,000 structures and 275 boats).[125] But there is no small irony in the claim of structures and boats destroyed. As the author of the report related, sinking small vessels might have seemed "inconsequential, but in the Mekong River delta region . . . boats [represented] virtually the only means of transportation in an area that [had] few roads, even fewer bridges, and literally thousands of canals and waterways."[126] One wonders how many of these boats and structures were not Viet Cong at all, the destruction of which further alienated the local people, thereby swelling the ranks of the Viet Cong. As one astute observer noted in 1963:

In a form of warfare in which political considerations regularly outweigh the military, air attacks against "suspected enemy groups" are all too likely to be self-defeating. The loss of support brought on by each innocent man or women killed is likely to far outweigh the possible gain of hard-core rebels eliminated. The speed of even the slowest fixed-wing aircraft is so great that the pilot has little chance of positively identifying an enemy who is not wearing a uniform, unless the latter obligingly waves a rifle or shoots at him.[127]

The notion that boats and huts destroyed from the air was a useful measure of success in counterinsurgency is not surprising, however, given that the U.S. Air Force had paid very little thought to the role that airpower would play outside of the need to develop tactics for bombing and strafing ground targets with vintage aircraft. But the application of airpower in this sense was no different from that in conventional warfare, a fact that would prove significant in the coming years in South Vietnam.

Nevertheless, the pace of aerial operations increased dramatically in 1963. U.S. Air Force nonjet sorties in 1963 exceeded 42,000, a considerable jump from the approximately 16,000 sorties in 1962. With an active inventory hovering around twenty-five aircraft, Farm Gate B-26s and T-28s flew some 8,500 sorties in 1963. South Vietnamese A-1 sorties rose from 4,500 in 1962 to over 10,000 in 1963. U.S. Army sorties rose dramatically as well, from 50,000 in 1962 to over 230,000 in 1963.[128] As the number of American aircraft and missions continued to grow in 1963, and with the concurrence of Admiral Felt, the U.S. Air Force abandoned the idea that personnel sent to South Vietnam required specialized counterinsurgency training. Farm Gate aircraft were conducting otherwise conventional aerial missions that did not require the crews to acquire any unique understanding of the nature of counterrevolutionary warfare. This decision cleared the way for the U.S. Air Force to dramatically increase the rate with which U.S. Air Force personnel could be sent to South Vietnam. Thus, in February 1963, General LeMay ordered that American markings be used on all Farm Gate aircraft, stating: "Current classification restrictions on Farm Gate are considered unnecessary. Actual operation is well known . . . and classification has become an administrative burden."[129] The fiction of American advice and assistance had given way to the fact that the war in South Vietnam was being "Americanized" — including the air war.

Although the Americans were increasingly taking over the war, the South Vietnamese air force continued to grow and, as a result, in early 1963 the South

Vietnamese air force renumbered its squadrons, ostensibly to confuse the Viet Cong. The former single-digit system was replaced with a three-digit system in which the first number identified the type of unit.[130] Four new squadrons were formed in 1963 and early 1964 — the 518th and 520th Fighter Squadrons at Bien Hoa, both flying the A-1; the 217th Helicopter Squadron at Da Nang, flying H-34s; and the 116th Liaison Squadron at Nha Trang, flying L-19s. As the number of squadrons proliferated, they were organized into wings, with each wing assigned to a particular base.[131] To support this growth, the Nha Trang training center was reopened in 1963, training mostly liaison pilots.

But despite massive American assistance and phenomenal growth in each of the South Vietnamese armed services, the overall situation in South Vietnam deteriorated rapidly in 1963. Rioting took place from Hue to Saigon, centered on Diem's arbitrary and repressive rule. An attempted coup failed to materialize early in 1963, but the repercussions resulted in a cutback of American aid by the Kennedy administration. Realizing that the Americans would probably welcome a change in government, senior South Vietnamese officers led by Major General Duong Van Minh staged a successful coup in early November that resulted in the death of President Diem. The following day, the junta formed a military government. But the overthrow of Diem did nothing to arrest the Viet Cong, who gained in strength with each passing month.

Most alarming to the South Vietnamese air force during this period was the rapid growth in Viet Cong antiaircraft capability. The Viet Minh had demonstrated a respectable air defense capability as early as 1953, shooting down 10 French aircraft and damaging another 244.[132] But Viet Cong antiaircraft capability was a whole order of magnitude greater, scoring 89 hits against Farm Gate and other American aircraft in the last four months of 1962 but over 250 hits in the first four months of 1963. Almost two-thirds of these hits were made against aircraft flying below one thousand feet. On 24 November 1963, the Viet Cong hit 24 American and South Vietnamese aircraft, destroying 5 — the highest in the war to that point. During the last three months of 1963, over 124 aircraft were hit, some with heavy caliber weapons. In all, from November 1961 to March 1964, 114 U.S. aircraft were shot down in South Vietnam, of which 34 were U.S. Air Force, 70 were U.S. Army (including 54 helicopters), and 10 belonged to the U.S. Marine Corps (all helicopters).[133] South Vietnamese losses were equally heavy. Unable to operate in this high-threat environment, the T-28 was withdrawn from service. Thereafter, the more survivable A-1 became standard throughout South Vietnamese fighter squadrons.

Even flying the A-1, South Vietnamese pilots were reluctant to fly below two thousand feet, greatly limiting the precision of their strikes. Over time, South Vietnamese reluctance to press their attacks against the Viet Cong was characterized by American advisers as a lack of aggressiveness, and not surprisingly, South Vietnamese air force units were accused of unreliability, prompting a growing sentiment that "Americans must run things."[134] Consequently, the American presence and participation in combat operations continued to expand. In July 1963, the Nineteenth Tactical Air Support Squadron was activated at Bien Hoa with sixteen O-1s (the U.S. Air Force version of the L-19) and six more at Can Tho to provide forward air control for American units as well as South Vietnamese squadrons. By year's end the Nineteenth Squadron had flown over 3,800 sorties.[135]

As the air war expanded, U.S. Air Force advisers pressed for more interdiction missions. Once more the issue of unintended collateral damage came to the fore. Assistant Secretary of State for Far Eastern Affairs W. Averill Harriman questioned these independent interdiction missions on the grounds that these sorties were more likely to strike civilians by mistake.

[Harriman] stressed the political nature of the war, Vietnamese resentment against air strikes that might aid Viet Cong recruitment, the unsuccessful interdiction experience of the French, the political unawareness of provincial and district chiefs who supplied the target information, and the restrictions of the 1954 Geneva agreement. To Harriman, the basic question was the political cost versus the military advantage of interdiction, whether by U.S. or Vietnamese pilots.[136]

But such a position contravened long-held and cherished U.S. Air Force assumptions and the "Air Staff especially disagreed that the war was only political or that occasional harm to innocents created a military problem."[137] McNamara offered no comment, the Joint Staff interposed no objections, and U.S. Air Force and South Vietnamese aircraft stepped up interdiction missions as a result.

Considering the possibility that North Vietnamese aircraft might contest Farm Gate and South Vietnamese interdiction operations, air defense radar centers were constructed at Tan Son Nhut, Da Nang, and Pleiku. In March 1962, surveillance radar at Pleiku and Man Iang had detected unidentified tracks of interest, but Farm Gate aircraft were unable to intercept the unidentified aircraft. Shortly afterward, three U.S. Air Force F-102 and one TF-102 interceptors were ordered to Tan Son Nhut from Clark Air Base in the Philippines in Operation "Water Glass" (redesignated "Candy Machine" in October 1963). These aircraft rotated with U.S. Navy AD-5Q interceptors, but all of these aircraft were later withdrawn in light of the absence of an air threat. Nevertheless, while they were on hand, the interceptors contributed to overcrowding at South Vietnamese airfields, and it was not long before such lucrative targets became irresistible to the Viet Cong. On 1 November 1963, the Viet Cong attacked the air base at Bien Hoa, destroying a large number of South Vietnamese and American aircraft, including thirteen B-57s and six A-1s.[138] Other attacks directed specifically at American forces followed, and in retaliation President Lyndon B. Johnson authorized a series of U.S. air strikes against communist forces in South Vietnam, Laos, and southern North Vietnam. By this act, the war entered a new phase.

Four days after taking the oath of office, President Johnson reaffirmed the American objective of preventing a communist takeover in South Vietnam. He instructed the Department of State to prepare a white paper detailing the involvement of the North Vietnamese in the insurgency in South Vietnam, and on 22 January 1964 the Joint Chiefs responded with a ten-point program of "bolder actions" to arrest the deteriorating political and military state of affairs in South Vietnam. The proposal amounted to taking over the war from the South Vietnamese. In addition to committing large numbers of U.S. ground combat forces to South Vietnam, the proposal also recommended various overt and covert missions in the region and air strikes in North Vietnam.[139] Much of the plan was approved, including clandestine air operations over North Vietnam and reconnaissance missions over the Plain of Jars in Laos. Public officials soon afterward acknowledged that the United States was stockpiling war material to support the possible intervention of ground combat forces and drafted a congressional resolution sanctioning air attacks on North Vietnam.

In March 1964, the restrictive rules governing air strikes were relaxed. But as the pace of air operations accelerated, the World War II vintage aircraft of Farm Gate began to wear out. A serious problem was wing fatigue associated with the B-26s. General Anthis had hoped more cautious tactics would permit their continued use until they could be replaced with eighteen "rebuilt" B-26Ks. But a B-26 lost a wing in flight on 16 August, killing two Americans and one South Vietnamese crew member, and another B-26 crashed due to mechanical problems in September. Thereafter, the B-26s ceased combat operations. The previous April, two T-28s had been lost, both losing their wings in flight.[140] The loss of the B-26s in particular was significant, and the newly arrived commander of the Second Air Division, Major General Joseph Moore, lamented that "the 2nd Air Division [was] practically out of business."[141] Thus, even with the addition of the South Vietnamese 518th Fighter Squadron flying new A-1H fighter-bombers, the South Vietnamese air force and Farm Gate together were barely able to satisfy only about half of the requested air strikes in 1964. Much of the problem lay in the continuing difficulties associated with the air control system, but the biggest problem was a shortage of aircraft. Of 1,546 requests for air support received in the first three months of 1964, over 400 were not fulfilled — 230 of these were not honored due to a lack of available aircraft. But by the end of 1964, this situation would dramatically change, beginning on 2 August when the USS *Maddox* was fired upon by North Vietnamese patrol boats in the Gulf of Tonkin.

As a result of the attack on the USS *Maddox* and another attack on the *Maddox* and the USS *Turner Joy,* U.S. Navy fighter-bombers from the aircraft carriers USS *Ticonderoga* and *Constellation* bombed four naval bases and an oil storage depot in North Vietnam. Two American aircraft were shot down. On 7 August 1964, the U.S. Congress approved a measure that authorized President Johnson to use all measures necessary to repel any further attacks against U.S. forces and to assist the government of South Vietnam. President Johnson subsequently signed the Southeast Asia (Gulf of Tonkin) Resolution and approved emergency measures to move additional U.S. forces into the region, including elements of the U.S. Air Force.

Almost immediately, modern frontline jet aircraft were deployed to South Vietnam, including F-102 interceptors, F-100 and F-105 fighters, B-57 bombers, KB-50 tankers, and RF-101 reconnaissance aircraft.[142] In addition, forty-eight C-130 tactical transports were moved to the Philippines and Okinawa, and forty-eight KC-135 "Stratotankers" were deployed to Hawaii and Guam. An additional task force of KC-135s deployed to the Philippines. At this point the Second Advanced Echelon became the Second Air Division at Tan Son Nhut, and all U.S. Air Force aircraft in South Vietnam were placed under the control of this headquarters separate and apart from the joint American and

South Vietnamese air operations center.[143] By the end of 1964, American units began operating independently and wholly in American markings.

As the U.S. intervention was stepped up in 1964, the North Vietnamese increased their own infiltration of regular forces into South Vietnam. Not surprisingly, South Vietnamese and American aircraft encountered heavy ground fire in areas dominated by North Vietnamese forces, especially in I and II Corps. Late in the year the Viet Cong launched a major offensive, abandoning their traditional hit-and-run tactics in favor of coordinated assaults on government-controlled villages and military outposts. The South Vietnamese army proved reluctant to engage the Viet Cong, and South Vietnamese air force and U.S. Air Force aircraft were increasingly called upon to rescue beleaguered garrisons throughout the country. A major defeat of South Vietnamese forces at Binh Gia, in which fixed-wing air support failed to show in time due to squabbles regarding proper procedures, was followed by another major raid by the Viet Cong on American forces at Pleiku.[144] On 27 January, South Vietnamese generals staged another coup. While the political situation verged on total collapse, heavy fighting continued in the countryside around Saigon, and the Viet Cong appeared to be gaining the upper hand. In response, President Johnson approved the deployment of American ground combat forces to South Vietnam to stave off communist victory, and on 8 March 1965, the Ninth Marine Expeditionary Brigade (later redesignated III Amphibious Force), commanded by Brigadier General Frederick Karch, came ashore at Da Nang. Only a month before, President Johnson authorized Operation "Rolling Thunder," an air campaign intended to coerce North Vietnam to cease its support to the Viet Cong and halt its infiltration of men and material into South Vietnam. Thus, the counterinsurgency effort effectively came to an end and with it the employment of airpower in counterinsurgency in South Vietnam.

Conclusion

From the departure of the French in 1954 through the advisory years to complete Americanization of the war in 1965, airpower in South Vietnam was defined primarily by two themes. The first theme was the American concept of airpower itself. The second theme, derived from the first, was the hostility and competition between the U.S. Army and the U.S. Air Force regarding counterinsurgency warfare and their respective attempts to gain the upper hand in determining how the war in South Vietnam was to be fought and to what extent airpower would contribute to the effort. Aside from the lessons of Greece, the Philippines, and Malaya, the French experience in Vietnam should have been instructive.

In 1966, General André Beaufre, who had served with the French army in Vietnam between 1947 and 1954, reflected on the American counterinsurgency effort up to 1965 and offered several pointed remarks about the American conceptualization of airpower in general and the utility of airpower in counter-guerrilla warfare in particular. He wrote that the American failure to suppress the insurgency between 1961 and 1965, which led to escalation of the air war into North Vietnam, was rooted in the paralogism of "classical" airpower theory, specifically with respect to guerrilla warfare. "First, it has been confirmed once again that air power [sic], when it is armed only with classical bombs, has not the strength that too many theorists grant it. . . . [Moreover], the airplane needs 'paying' objectives, which guerrilla warfare hardly affords."[145]

"Classical" airpower theory, at least as the Americans understood it, could be distilled to three fundamental tenets: that airpower is inherently offensive, manifestly strategic, and by that fact must be independent in order to realize its full potential. In that regard, Beaufre was accusing American airmen of being pseudo-syllogistic insofar as the role of airpower in counterinsurgency was concerned. Insurgents generally do not have strategic assets and infra-structure that can be targeted by airpower. Moreover, guerrillas generally do not have easily identifiable fielded forces and quite often mingle with the ci-vilian population. Inasmuch as the Viet Cong did not present a lucrative tar-get for strategic air attack, it became necessary to take the air war to North Vietnam. But as General Beaufre averred, the graduated air attacks on North Vietnam did not dissuade the Viet Cong. On the contrary, "this pressure set off an escalation of guerrilla warfare" in South Vietnam and prompted the North Vietnamese to retaliate for the air strikes in the north by sending regular divisions into the south in what Beaufre called "big guerrilla warfare."[146]

Aside from the inappropriateness of classical airpower theory in terms of the utility of strategic attack against insurgents, the airpower polemic also caused the American counterinsurgency effort to fractionate, as evidenced by the bickering between U.S. Army and U.S. Air Force officers assigned to the military mission in Saigon. The question of who was in charge of the

American effort and who had control of air assets — rotary-wing as well as fixed-wing — was a continual source of friction. In the end, the vitiating nature of the dual identity of the advisory effort upon the application of airpower in combating the insurgency materially contributed to its ineffectiveness and arguably led to American and South Vietnamese defeat. The existence of two essentially separate and competing advisory bodies within an ostensibly joint (American) and combined (that is, in conjunction with the South Vietnamese) effort exemplified the paralogism of the American counterinsurgency effort. Not surprisingly, the controversy had deleterious effects on the South Vietnamese armed forces and their ability to take the fight to the Viet Cong.

General Beaufre's reference to "theorists" was especially insightful given the understanding of airpower theory on the part of U.S. Air Force officers on the eve of American intervention in South Vietnam. In addition, it is reasonable to assume that by "paying objectives" General Beaufre meant "targets," the destruction of which would produce significant, ostensibly strategic military and political results. In that light, it is necessary to briefly examine the American concept of airpower theory in the context of how it was applied in South Vietnam.

As discussed elsewhere in this book, the American concept of airpower in the late 1950s and early 1960s was born in the years between the world wars. U.S. Air Force officers at home and in Saigon shared a broad consensus and an unswerving devotion to certain truths regarding airpower: the superiority of the offensive; the necessity for air superiority; the dominant role of strategic bombardment; and the need for independence — not merely of air action, but also of command and control of air units and ultimately institutional autonomy itself. In that regard, U.S. Air Force officers in the 1960s were the lineal descendants of airpower thinkers of the interwar period, men like Brigadier General William "Billy" Mitchell, whose ideas were at the root of strategic bombardment theories that emerged from the Air Corps Tactical School before World War II.[147]

Following independence in 1947, U.S. Air Force leaders inculcated what amounted to an absolute model of airpower in warfare. To make matters worse, airpower had always been thought of by its proponents to render historical experience irrelevant. Unlike naval theorists such as Alfred Thayer Mahan, who insisted that his suppositions regarding sea power were drawn from the lessons of history, Giulio Douhet, Billy Mitchell, and other airpower "theorists" regarded the advent of airpower as having superceded old dogmas.[148] But in their new orthodoxy, American airmen resisted any adaptation of the central tenets of airpower theory as they understood it in order to respond to novel demands, such as limited and guerrilla war. Consequently, the failure of airpower to deliver on its promise during the Korean War was explained away afterward by claiming that the conflict in Korea was an anomaly (and in some quarters it was described as a success). And if the dearth of analysis regarding the employment of airpower in the Greek Civil War and in the Philippines is any guide, the U.S. Air Force regarded these conflicts as having no import whatsoever.

U.S. Air Force thinking about airpower outside of strategic attack was decidedly lacking. Much of the answer for this narrow view is attributable to the fact that early American airpower proponents considered the vision of an independent air force to be inextricably tied to its strategic utility. The development of the atomic bomb and its role in the subjugation of imperial Japan, which for some was the ultimate fulfillment of Douhet's prophecies, only reinforced this mind-set. But in their rejection of old dogmas, U.S. Air Force leaders had created a new one. Regardless of the genuineness of their commitment to the vision of strategic airpower, they interpreted airpower theory in a manner that limited its validity and utility in other than general or total war between industrialized states. This limited view of airpower would prove a major handicap in counterinsurgency warfare. As the debacle in South Vietnam attests, such a limited view was, in the end, counterproductive.[149] One observer astutely noted regarding the American role in South Vietnam: "Intervention of U.S. military units also introduces U.S. military doctrine — a fearsome prospect for any country, as Vietnam . . . found out to its cost."[150] Or as one senior British officer wrote following the Malayan Emergency: "Air support . . . can be an actual disadvantage if wrongly used."[151]

When U.S. Air Force leaders responded to President Kennedy's call to emphasize counterinsurgency, the response itself was dramatic evidence of the service's tendency to marginalize conflict other than general war. First, there were no major doctrinal changes made to reflect the new emphasis, and the service saw no need to reassess the validity of closely held precepts regarding airpower in the context of revolutionary warfare. Although numerous articles appeared in a variety of professional military journals during the 1950s and early 1960s regarding insurgency and counterguerrilla warfare, very few dealt with airpower. Moreover, U.S. Air Force basic doctrine published between 1953 and 1960 was "written as if the struggles in Southeast Asia did not exist."[152] Aside from a few published essays of varying quality and a handful of student research projects at the Air University at Maxwell Air Force Base in Alabama, "Air Force airmen seemed either supremely uninterested in the subject, or assumed that in terms of airpower, protracted revolutionary warfare was just conventional warfare writ small."[153]

Upon their arrival in the latter part of the 1950s, U.S. Air Force advisers found a South Vietnamese air force that was struggling to get on its feet, much less wage an independent aerial campaign against the Viet Cong. Massive American aid and the arrival of Farm Gate were intended to correct this problem. But U.S. Air Force advisers faced a challenge in some ways more pressing than enlarging and improving the South Vietnamese Air Force: they also faced their old nemesis, the U.S. Army. The advisory mission in Saigon was headed by a U.S. Army officer and a majority of the choice posts were held by other than U.S. Air Force officers, mostly soldiers. With the arrival of three U.S. Army helicopter units in January 1962, the two themes of airpower theory and interservice animosity merged, creating a dynamic and corrosive environment that arguably had more to do with the divorce between the U.S. Army and the U.S. Air Force than defeating the Viet Cong. By the end of 1962, the U.S. Army had 199 aircraft in South Vietnam compared with only 61 U.S. Air Force aircraft. A year later, the U.S. Army fielded 325 airplanes, or 47 percent of the 681 American aircraft operating in South Vietnam.[154] Clashes between U.S. Army and U.S. Air Force advisers became frequent, and the squabble in Saigon was echoed in the halls of the Pentagon. As the director of plans for Headquarters U.S. Air Force noted: "It may be improper to say we [are] at war with the Army. However, we believe that if the Army efforts are successful, they may have a long term adverse effect in the U.S. military posture that could be more important than the battle presently being waged with the Viet Cong."[155]

Ironically, General Anthis questioned the growth of the U.S. Army helicopter fleet in South Vietnam because such growth was contrary to the U.S. policy of developing an indigenous South Vietnamese capability to fight the Viet Cong. General Harkins defended the deployment of large numbers of American helicopters as a stopgap measure until the South Vietnamese could acquire sufficient numbers of their own helicopters. When General Anthis sought to place all aviation assets under his control in keeping with the precept that airpower is best controlled by an airman, General Harkins denied the request. But as the disaster at Ap Bac showed, helicopter gunships by themselves were unable to deliver the amount of aerial fire support required for ground forces engaged in battle with main force Viet Cong units and later North Vietnamese regulars. In order to provide the necessary fixed-wing support, it became necessary to enlarge the South Vietnamese air force. To support this increase, more U.S. Air Force advisers were needed, so that by the end of 1963 there were over 4,600 U.S. Air Force officers and enlisted personnel in South Vietnam.

The influx of American airmen dramatically altered the role of airpower in South Vietnam. Whereas earlier in the conflict the South Vietnamese air force understood its role to be in support of the South Vietnamese army, U.S. Air Force advisers evangelized the South Vietnamese airmen, promoting an American-style air war, one largely freed of surface tethers. Air strikes could be mounted to destroy Viet Cong strongholds and interdict communist supply lines — an independent effort in the best keeping of the American airpower tradition. Yet, at the same time, American airmen became convinced that the South Vietnamese were incapable of conducting the air war in a conclusive fashion. Consequently, the U.S. Air Force advisory mission expanded far beyond its original mandate to the point that the air war in South Vietnam became an American air war as early as 1964 and certainly by 1965.

The original mandate of Farm Gate was to provide training support to the South Vietnamese in a strategically defensive effort. This in itself was counter to U.S. Air Force philosophy, theory, and tradition. Yet the strategic objective was not to target the vitals of an enemy state, but to assist the South Vietnamese government to defeat an internal threat. As the British had learned in Greece and Malaya, and as the United States should have learned in Greece and the Philippines, unless and until guerrillas begin operating as conventional forces, they are seldom vulnerable to air attack. In that sense the lethal application of airpower takes a back seat to the other uses, such as the rapid insertion and movement of troops, aerial resupply of isolated units, reconnaissance and intelligence collection, and psychological warfare. For one thing, aerial firepower often results in unintended civilian casualties, which is wholly counterproductive in a type of warfare where the popular support of the civilian population is the key to victory. Yet U.S. Air Force officers approached this strategically defensive task with an offensive predisposition, one that inexorably led them to conclude that widening the war to strike at North Vietnam was worth the political and military risks. As General Thomas D. White, air force chief of staff, remarked in 1961: "Our philosophy is based on the fact that offense is the best defense."[156] As the situation in South Vietnam deteriorated and the involvement of North Vietnamese cadres became indisputable, the Johnson administration was persuaded and the first retaliatory air strikes commenced in 1965. Very quickly, the U.S. Air Force role evolved from a handful of air commandos to the application of the full coercive force of American airpower.

A third theme warrants discussion here in terms of the U.S. Air Force role in South Vietnam before 1965. Until air strikes were launched against the north, the U.S. Air Force did not take the role of airpower in the Vietnamese conflict seriously because it gave priority to other, ostensibly more pressing issues. Small wars of the sort going on in Southeast Asia were marginal to the primary concern of strategic nuclear war with the Soviet Union. The best evidence of this perspective is Farm Gate itself. The U.S. Air Force only took note of counterinsurgency when the U.S. Army attempted to secure the dominant position in conflict less than general war. Having thwarted the army's gambit, the U.S. Air Force was forced to respond in some fashion to President Kennedy's direction that "the troop basis of U.S. armed forces" be modified "to insure an adequate capability . . . required in counterguerrilla operations, or in rendering training assistance to other countries." For the U.S. Air Force, the creation of a tiny special unit for counterinsurgency was considered "adequate."[157] Indeed, the first doctrinal response on the part of the U.S. Air Force did not appear until March 1967 with the publication of Air Force Manual 2-5, *Tactical Air Operations, Special Air Warfare*.[158] The title itself is revealing. The role of airpower in counterinsurgency was considered, inter alia, to be "tactical" and "special" and therefore outside the mainstream of air force thinking. The war in Vietnam did not alter this orthodoxy. Within five years after American withdrawal from South Vietnam, U.S. Air Force special air warfare was *caput mortuum*.[159] By 1974, special warfare assets had declined from 19 flying squadrons with 550 aircraft and over five thousand personnel to less than 40 aircraft.[160]

In the final analysis, the American experience in South Vietnam is a stark reminder that in counterinsurgency, airpower is but one variable in a complex equation. Airpower is not an end in and of itself. This is perhaps especially true in counterinsurgency where social, political, economic, juridical, and other issues beyond the military dimension are the key to victory or defeat. Yet the inevitable interplay that occurred between the U.S. Air Force and the U.S. Army in South Vietnam exacerbated the decades-old rivalries between the two services — to the detriment of the counterinsurgency effort in South Vietnam.

The Vietnam War was a conflict the U.S. Air Force had not envisioned and had not adequately prepared for. That airpower could have contributed significantly to defeating the Viet Cong seems without question. Airpower proved instrumental in previous victories against insurgents, from Nicaragua in the 1920s to Malaya in 1960. But without a clear idea of its purpose in South Vietnam, nor a clear conception of what role airpower was to play in combating the insurgency, the U.S. Air Force labored to reshape the South Vietnamese air force into a reflection of itself, albeit writ small. The extent to which airpower could have proven *decisive* had it been more appropriately applied in South Vietnam remains open to question. As one British general officer reflected after the Malayan Emergency, "It can be argued that we could have won the war . . . without any air power at all." Nonetheless, he acknowledged that the intelligent use of airpower shortened the war in Malaya and in that sense was, in its own fashion, decisive in defeating the insurgents.[161]

The American concept of classical airpower theory as it affects conventional war has a pellucid edge that is absent in small wars. U.S. Air Force officers in the 1950s and 1960s thought of airpower in terms of key vulnerabilities in industrialized societies that could be struck in what amounted to a "decisive point." It is difficult enough to ascertain these key vulnerabilities in "big" war; the challenge is magnified in small wars where the unique juxtaposition of political and operational restraints invariably plays a major role in the application of airpower. The problem in South Vietnam was that there was never any agreement on how airpower was to be employed, its relationship to other instruments of counterinsurgency, and what practical steps were necessary for airpower to contribute to ultimate victory. The danger of such confusion, as Clausewitz wrote, is manifest: "So long as no acceptable theory, no intelligent analysis of war exists, routine methods will tend to take over even at the highest level."[162] In that light, without agreement on the nature of the war, how to fight it, and the role that airpower was to play, the U.S. Air Force approached the conflict in South Vietnam in a manner that Marshal Maurice Comte de Saxe described in *Mes Rêveries* over 250 years ago: "In default of knowing how to do what they ought, [they] are very naturally led to do what they know."[163]

South Vietnamese Air Vice Marshal Nguyen Cao Ky (left) and U.S. Air Force Colonel William Bethea, commander of the Thirty-fourth Tactical Group, which helped the South Vietnamese air force transition from the T-28D to the A-1E fighter bomber. In 1963, Ky took command of the South Vietnamese air force and was deeply involved in the political life of South Vietnam, rising to prime minister, until the communists overran the country in 1975. (USAF)

South Vietnamese paratroops boarding U.S. Air Force C-123 transports at Tan Son Nhut airfield. In January 1962, sixteen C-123 "Providers" were ordered to South Vietnam in Operation Mule Train. These aircraft provided transportation, air-dropped supplies, inserted special forces in communist-held areas, and provided training in tactical airlift procedures to the South Vietnamese. (USAF)

U.S. Air Force Sikorsky H-19 helicopter at Tan Son Nhut airfield. In the South Vietnamese Air Force, the H-19 "Chickasaw" replaced the obsolete Bell H-13 "Sioux" light utility helicopter, but the H-19 was later replaced by the Sikorsky H-34 "Choctaw." However, it was not until the arrival of U.S. Army helicopter units that the South Vietnamese army obtained the air mobility believed necessary to fight against the Viet Cong. (USAF)

Former French air force F-8F "Bearcat" in South Vietnamese markings. With American aid administered through the French, the South Vietnamese air force grew rapidly, adding twenty-five F-8F fighters in June 1956, forming the First Fighter Squadron—the first South Vietnamese combat squadron. (USAF)

Farm Gate aircrews and ground personnel in South Vietnam. A detachment of the 4400th Combat Crew Training Squadron at Elgin Air Force Base, Florida, Farm Gate deployed to South Vietnam to advise, train, and assist the South Vietnamese air force in operations against the Viet Cong, as well as conduct missions beyond the capability of the South Vietnamese. (USAF)

U.S. Air Force and South Vietnamese airmen stand before a T28D along with a display of standard combat load of munitions. In the background are other Farm Gate aircraft, including several B-26 bombers, an A-1E fighter bomber, and a C-47 in the distance. By the beginning of 1964, the South Vietnamese air force had twenty-nine attack versions of the T-28. (USAF)

A-1E and T-28D fighter-bombers. The more survivable A-1E replaced the aging T-28 as the mainstay of the South Vietnamese air force, the latter being phased out in April 1965 due to the dramatic improvement in Viet Cong antiaircraft capability. Unable to operate in the higher threat environment, the T-28 was withdrawn from service. (USAF).

U.S. Air Force H-19 helicopter at Tan Son Nhut airfield. (USAF)

7

Airpower and Counterinsurgency in Southern Africa

By 1960, the African independence movements were in full swing and the great colonial powers, Britain and France, were rapidly disposing of their colonial empires. In 1960 Belgium announced that its huge colony of the Congo would be granted independence, and Britain prepared to quickly grant independence to Ghana, Nigeria, Kenya, and Tanzania and planned for independence of northern and southern Rhodesia. France also moved to grant independence to her several African colonies. In most cases, the process was a hasty one, and little was done by the colonial powers to prepare their colonies for full independence as functioning democracies. In several cases, the decolonization process went badly as the Europeans turned over the government of their colonies to parties and factions with little use for democracy and little experience in how to run a modern nation. In some former colonies, the Congo being the prime example, any semblance of order collapsed almost immediately. Despite the messiness of decolonization, the governments at home in Europe had sensibly decided that colonies were no longer an asset but a liability. This was especially true in military terms as the cost of maintaining military garrisons far outweighed any strategic or economic gains to be had.

Portugal, the oldest colonial power in Africa (Portugal had outposts on the African coast as early as the 1400s), was the one European nation to defy the trend toward independence and decided to hold on to its three colonies (Angola, Mozambique, and Guinea-Bissau). South Africa, which administered South West Africa (Namibia) as a mandate granted by the League of Nations after World War I, also defied the trend and insisted on maintaining control with a white-led government. In 1965, the white minority that controlled Rhodesia refused British pressure to go the way of northern Rhodesia and Malawi and become independent with power granted to the black native majority. The Rhodesians defied Britain, declared independence, and formed a white-led republic.

All of these nations faced prolonged insurgencies from nationalist movements demanding independence and black rule. The Portuguese battled large independence movements in their three colonies from 1961 until independence was granted in 1974. South Africa maintained control of Namibia and fought SWAPO (South West African People's Organization), a nationalist movement, until elections and independence came in 1990. Rhodesia fought two major insurgent groups from 1965 to 1980 when a political deal granting majority black rule was cut.

The protracted and bloody wars in southern Africa pitted small professionally led armies, police, and reserve forces against guerrilla forces and "people's movements" often modeled on the "people's war" theory developed by Mao Tse-tung. In the Portuguese colonies and Rhodesia, the fight against the guerrillas was conducted on a shoestring budget. Neither Portugal nor Rhodesia had the wealth, population, or resources to fight the kind of campaign the French had fought in Algeria to saturate the country with soldiers and bring overwhelming military forces into the field. The wars those countries fought were with very limited forces and equipment. The exception was South Africa, a large, wealthy nation that could deploy a large and well-equipped army and air force for its counterinsurgency operations. However, South Africa had an additional security burden when it found itself facing a conventional war in Angola after 1975.

Airpower played a very important part in each of these wars. The independence wars in southern Africa offer numerous lessons in how small nations with limited resources can maximize their combat power by using airpower efficiently. Since the Portuguese, Rhodesians, and South Africans had huge territories to control with relatively few forces, the southern African nations relied extensively on their air arms to provide mobility and firepower for counterinsurgency forces. The Portuguese and Rhodesians fought at a disadvantage as their nations faced arms embargoes and some economic sanctions for their defiance of UN and world opinion. Yet, both of those nations demonstrated considerable ingenuity in maintaining their aviation forces by clandestine operations to obtain aircraft and weapons on the world market. In many cases, civilian aircraft were modified and used in support of the counterinsurgency operations. In order to combat insurgency, the Portuguese, South Africans, and Rhodesians demonstrated a high degree of innovation and tactical competence by developing organizations, doctrine, and tactics that maximized their limited combat power. The South African forces demonstrated a high degree of professional competence as relatively small South African forces repeatedly engaged and destroyed much larger, well-equipped Cuban and Angolan units in operations designed to protect the northern border of Namibia.

The Portuguese Colonies, 1961–1974

The revolt that broke out in Angola in January 1961 took Portugal completely by surprise. Angola was the largest and most important of Portugal's colonies with a settler population of over three hundred thousand and several million blacks. Portugal's African colonies had long suffered from poor administration, and the home government had done little to educate its colonial population or to encourage decent living conditions. Portugal's African population was desperately poor and uneducated, even worse off than the Algerians under France, and was subject to numerous petty tyrannies including a forced labor program to support the white-owned plantations. When the neighboring Congo gained independence in 1960, Angolan nationalists gained a source of supply for weapons and ammunition; several of the Congolese tribes were kin to the Angolans, so rebels could count on clandestine support from factions in the Congo.[1]

There were no large or well-organized political movements in Angola in 1961 advocating independence. The several major revolts that year were basically a spontaneous reaction against Portuguese misgovernment. The first uprising appeared against the planters in central Angola as a protest against the compulsory labor system. Large-scale damage was inflicted to settlers' crops and property before the military could suppress the revolt. In March, a group called the UPA (União das Populações de Angola), with four thousand to five thousand insurgents supplied from the Congo under Holden Roberto (related to President Mobutu of the Congo), initiated a major uprising across the north of Angola. In the first wave of attacks, more than two hundred Portuguese settlers were massacred as well as several thousand Africans, especially of the Ovimbundu tribe, regarded as friendly to Portugal. The attacks aimed to destroy the settlers' plantation economy and were especially shocking in their brutality.[2] Portuguese and African civilians were tortured and mutilated by rebels as the revolt spread.

Of all the colonial powers, Portugal was the least capable of waging a major overseas war. In 1961 Portugal was the poorest and least industrialized country in Western Europe. For three decades it had languished under the heavy hand of the dictator Antonio Salazar and the Portuguese armed forces, which had not seen combat since 1918 (when they performed badly), and were manned with conscripts led by officers usually better known for political loyalty than military competence. Portuguese forces were not trained or equipped to fight a colonial war. The only advantage Portugal had was its membership in NATO. Although the Salazar dictatorship was distasteful to the Americans and Western Europeans, NATO desperately needed Portugal's air bases in the Azores as a refueling point for crossing the Atlantic. By providing vital bases to NATO, Portugal received generous military aid during the 1940s and 1950s in the form of surplus U.S. and European aircraft. As it turned out, many of the obsolete aircraft provided to Portugal, such as the T-6 trainer (so successful in Algeria), were ideal for operating in the kind of low-level counterinsurgency war the Portuguese encountered in Africa.

The Portuguese military forces were mostly taken by surprise when rebellion broke out. The entire garrison of Angola constituted two infantry regiments of African soldiers with Portuguese officers in the capital of Luanda, about three thousand men, and only two battalions were properly trained. The Portuguese air force (FAP) was somewhat better prepared. Portugal recognized the importance of aircraft to maintain its rule in its large African territories. In 1960 the FAP began building two large new airfields in Angola and had a handful of aircraft available when the revolts broke out.[3] The first reinforcements that Portugal could send to Angola were Lockheed PV-2 Harpoon bombers, twin-engine naval patrol bombers that first saw service with the U.S. Navy in 1944. These played a central role in stopping the rebel momentum and defeating the initial rebellion.

Large districts of northern Angola, as well as the towns of Cuimba and Bemebe, were abandoned to the rebels as the settlers organized themselves into militias and tried to hold out. In late April a group of settlers was besieged in the small town of Mucaba, near Bembe, and radioed for help. Three PV-2 bombers (each with a one-ton bomb load and five .50-caliber machine guns in the nose) and two armed T-6s were dispatched to beat off the rebel attacks. Attacking with napalm, fragmentation bombs, and machine guns throughout the day, the air force inflicted heavy casualties on the rebels and drove them away. The defeat of the rebels at Mucaba was one of the turning points in the 1961 revolt.[4]

By May fifty thousand soldiers began to arrive from Portugal along with significant air force reinforcements. In addition to six PV-2 Harpoon bombers, F-84 jet fighter-bombers were deployed. Civilian light aircraft and transports were pressed into service to supply isolated towns and garrisons by air. Some of the FAP's light transports were hastily reconfigured as bombers.[5] In June the army, with strong air support, embarked on a ruthless campaign to retake northern Angola. Aerial bombing and napalm attacks were a common feature of the campaign. The rebels made the mistake of trying to defend the territory they had won by conventional tactics. The insurgents had set up fairly elaborate defense lines around their main strongholds and, buoyed by their early easy successes, grossly underestimated Portuguese military capability and will. Several thousand well-armed rebels were killed in August defending their three main strongholds. The Portuguese were able to employ large ground units, artillery, and bombing with napalm and shrapnel munitions against the rebels. By October, the revolt had been put down and the surviving rebels had retreated to the Congo. An estimated two thousand Europeans and fifty thousand Africans had died during the 1961 Angola revolt.[6]

PORTUGUESE STRATEGY

After the shock of the bloody 1961 Angola revolt and growing unrest by nationalists in the other colonies, the Portuguese government under Salazar made a firm commitment to hold on to the colonies.[7] This strategy would require a massive military buildup in the colonies, money and personnel for civic action programs to gain African support, and some limited reforms of the archaic and abusive colonial government structure.

The first step was the military buildup. In 1961 Portugal's entire armed forces totaled 79,000 men (army 58,000, navy 8,500, air force 12,500). The total force in Africa was a mere 6,500 at the start of the year. By the end of the year, Portugal had committed 40,000 European troops to Africa and began the process of recruiting and training large native forces to fight the insurgency. The commitment of forces by tiny Portugal to the African wars continued without letup. By the end of the war in 1974, Portugal had 217,000 men in her armed forces, 149,000 of them in Africa.[8] At the start of the conflict, the Portuguese army and air force were conventionally oriented NATO forces. However, understanding that Portugal had barely the resources for the African war, the army and air force were retrained and reoriented toward counterinsurgency. The experiences of the French in Algeria and the British in Malaya and Kenya were studied, as was the growing U.S. Army doctrine of unconventional war.[9] A military commander in chief was appointed in each of the African colonies (Guinea, Mozambique, and Angola), and military commanders were given some of the normally civilian responsibilities such as policing, civic action, and intelligence. The usual procedure was to follow the French Algerian War model, which was to divide each combat theater into military zones and give each zone commander considerable leeway to fight the war in his own area of responsibility. Again following the Algerian model, cooperation between the civil and military organizations was emphasized. The Portuguese military came to understand that to win the war, they had to succeed on the social and political side as well as on the battlefield.[10] By the mid-1960s, Portugal was successful in reorienting and reorganizing its army and air force as a counterinsurgency force for the African war.

Because of the small size of the Portuguese forces and the large area of the theaters of war, airplanes and helicopters assumed a central importance in prosecuting the military strategy. The Portuguese initiated a major program of airfield building and expansion throughout their colonies. By 1964 Angola had 403 airfields, most of them small strips suitable for Dornier 27s or T-6s, but 17 of the fields could take large transports. Mozambique had 216 airfields by 1964.[11] In the first stages of the counterinsurgency campaign, the primary air weapon was the battle-tested T-6. The Portuguese had several dozen of these, and more were quickly acquired from France when the French air force declared its T-6s surplus after the Algerian War. Another aircraft used in large numbers throughout the war was the light Dornier Do 27 monoplane (Portugal bought over one hundred). The Do 27 was a high-wing utility aircraft capable of carrying six passengers and landing at rough dirt airstrips or clearings. The Do 27 was used for medevac and light transport and as a liaison craft to get commanders around the battlefield. In combat, it was used extensively as a reconnaissance plane and artillery spotter. The Do 27 could fly slowly at treetop level, and well-trained observers became proficient in spotting guerrilla bands or signs of guerrilla activity from low-level observation. The FAP organized counterinsurgency squadrons containing both T-6s and Do 27s. By 1962 the Portuguese had one T-6/Do 27 squadron operating in Guinea and two in Mozambique.[12] In the early stages of the war, these light aircraft were backed up by the heavy firepower of the PV-2 bombers. Detachments of three to six PV-2 bombers saw service in each of the three colonies.

The Portuguese knew that the old T-6s were a stopgap measure until a more suitable counterinsurgency airplane could be found. In 1965 the air staff made a sound decision to acquire thirty to forty used Fiat G.91R trainers from the German Luftwaffe. The G.91 was a mid-1950s design that had proven very successful as an advanced trainer for the Luftwaffe. It had also served in the tactical reconnaissance and close air support roles. The G.91s (nicknamed "Ginas") could be armed with four .50-caliber machine guns and carry two thousand pounds of bombs on four external points. The Ginas carried enough fuel to give them a couple of hours of loiter time. Moreover, they handled well and could absorb a fair amount of punishment. The FAP began buying Ginas in 1965, and the first G.91 squadrons began to arrive in Africa in 1966.[13] Squadrons of eight to twelve G.91s served in all war theaters, and it largely replaced the T-6 as the primary close support aircraft, although T-6s continued to see service until the very end of the conflict.

The Portuguese air force was dramatically increased during the war. As aerial transport around the war theaters and within Angola and Mozambique was important, the FAP acquired Noratlas transports from France and eight DC-6 transports, capable of carrying fifty thousand pounds of cargo, from the United States. Of course, the ubiquitous C-47 saw plenty of service, and the Portuguese also acquired fourteen surplus Ju 52 transports from the French.[14] Since the small number of PV-2 bombers did not suffice for the requirement to provide heavy firepower for the ground forces, the FAP offered to buy twenty-nine surplus B-26 bombers from the United States in 1965. The United States, however, disapproved of Portugal's colonial policy and supported an international embargo of military equipment to Portugal. The U.S. State Department rejected the purchase request. Working through a front corporation, the Portuguese air force managed to buy seven B-26 bombers and get them to Africa before the U.S. government shut down the operation.[15]

The Portuguese realized early on that helicopters would play an important role in countering insurgency. The Portuguese first considered buying

Agusta-Bell helicopters from Italy, but rejected the idea because of the impact that the U.S. embargo would have upon an Italian-American helicopter. However, France proved far more amenable to selling arms to an ally, and the excellent Sud Aviation Alouette III, a design that had proved its worth in Algeria, was offered for sale. During the course of the war, 143 Alouette IIIs were bought from France, with most going to support operations in African colonies.[16] However, the Alouette's relatively small size and load capacity proved to be a major restriction in combat. The Alouette could carry only four fully loaded soldiers, so that a normal flight of four to five helicopters could put only sixteen to twenty men on the ground. However, the Portuguese also found, as had the French, that the Alouette could be adapted to the gunship role, and the 20 mm automatic cannon was found to be an extremely accurate and deadly main armament.

THE INSURGENT FORCES AND STRATEGY

In Angola, Portugal's largest and most valuable colony, three major revolutionary groups arose from the ashes of the 1961 revolt. The largest of the revolutionary groups was the MPLA, which had its base in Zambia. The MPLA generally followed a Maoist doctrine of insurgency. The FNLA had a Marxist ideology and made its main base in the Congo. The two groups were bitter rivals from the start and spent almost as much effort in fighting each other as they did the Portuguese. A third revolutionary party, UNITA, was formed in southern Angola but was too small to have any major impact on the war. UNITA also fought against the MPLA during the war. All of the groups received fairly generous support from the Soviet bloc, and East German and Cuban advisers were sent to Africa to train the Angolan insurgents. By the late 1960s, the insurgent forces, numbering several thousand, were well supplied with light weapons, mines, light mortars, and rocket launchers.[17]

The Portuguese victory in 1961 halted any serious insurgent activity in Angola until 1965 and 1966. In the meantime the insurgent groups patiently and quietly trained and organized forces in Zambia and the Congo. In the mid-1960s the MPLA, the largest of the revolutionary movements, began sending small bands of guerrillas into Angola and attacking Portuguese outposts, settler farms, and businesses. The small-scale operations also included planting bombs and mining roads. By this time, the Portuguese had built up their forces and were well prepared to conduct a counterinsurgency campaign.

The MPLA, while causing some damage, paid a heavy price in casualties. By 1970 the MPLA turned to employing larger forces, infiltrating groups of twenty men into Angola. In 1971 they mounted a major offensive against both the Portuguese forces and UNITA. The MPLA chose the rainy season for going on the offensive, as low cloud cover restricted the Portuguese ability to conduct reconnaissance in light aircraft. Yet, the MPLA offensive failed to seriously damage either the Portuguese forces or UNITA. Indeed, when the MPLA employed larger groups on operations, it made it much easier for the Portuguese to find the insurgents and to bring heavy firepower down upon them.[18]

In Mozambique there had been no bloody revolt in 1961. However, there was a strong nationalist sentiment among the population and FRELIMO, a nationalist revolutionary party under the very capable leadership of Eduardo Mondlane, was formed in 1962 from a collection of small pro-independence groups. FRELIMO found sanctuary and support in Tanzania and accepted aid from African and nonaligned countries as well as from communist countries. Under Mondlane, FRELIMO was less Marxist and more sympathetic to the West.[19]

The insurgency in Mozambique began in 1964 with small FRELIMO forces infiltrated into northern Mozambique. By the end of 1966, FRELIMO had seventy-five hundred insurgents under arms and was slowly expanding the scale of its operations. In 1969 the character of FRELIMO was changed when Mondlane was assassinated in Tanzania (probably with Portuguese connivance) and was replaced by Samora Machel. The new FRELIMO leader was a dedicated communist and turned to the Soviet Union for support — which was quickly forthcoming. By 1970 FRELIMO was able to put fairly large forces into northern Mozambique, and by 1971 to 1972 FRELIMO had effective control of much of the countryside in the north as the Portuguese were slowly pushed into fortified towns and enclaves. By the end of the war in 1974, FRELIMO effectively controlled about a quarter to a third of the country.[20]

The most successful insurgency against the Portuguese was mounted in Guinea, a small colony on the central African coast about the size of Belgium. The revolutionary party in Guinea (PAIGC) was organized in the late 1950s under the leadership of a Cape Verdean, Amilcar Cabral. Cabral was the most astute and most capable of the revolutionary leaders in the Portuguese colonies. Cabral followed a largely Maoist model of insurgency but was flexible enough to adapt Mao's model to African conditions. Cabral and PAIGC systematically built up a network of trained cadres and carried out a careful program of organizing the population in the countryside. In areas under insurgent control, a formal government apparatus was formed, elections held, and village and town councils set up. By the mid-1960s, PAIGC had established a functioning alternative government throughout much of Guinea. The insurgents in Guinea found a welcome sanctuary in independent Guinea-Conakry and later also had bases in nearby Senegal. PAIGC received arms and financing from the Soviet bloc and began with small-scale military operations against the Portuguese with groups of twenty to one hundred men.[21] By 1971 PAIGC could field a force of six thousand well-armed guerrillas.

Portugal had no significant settler community in Guinea and viewed the colony more as a liability than an asset. The only reason that Portugal mounted a campaign to hold the country was to deny the insurgents in Angola and Mozambique a moral and political victory by acknowledging a successful insurgent campaign for independence. By 1968 Portugal was clearly losing the war in Guinea, and most of the country was in rebel hands. However, in that year, a very energetic and capable Portuguese commander, General Antonio de Spinola, took command in Guinea and turned the situation around. Granted civil as well as military power, Spinola initiated a "Better Guinea" civic action program aimed at improving the lot of the native population. A major road construction program was initiated; numerous schools were built and medical clinics set up. New African army units were created, and Spinola got his troops out of their fortified posts and sent them and the air force out to aggressively find and fight the insurgents. At the same time, Spinola understood that Guinea could not be held in the long term and opened a series of secret negotiations with the rebels. While Spinola did not bring victory to Portugal, he at least stabilized a losing situation. Spinola left Guinea to serve as army vice chief of staff in 1972 and served for a short time as president after the revolution of 1974.

In 1973 a dissident nationalist faction assassinated Amilcar Cabral. This would have been a grave blow to an independence movement in other countries, but PAIGC had been built on solid foundations and did not collapse or stop the struggle. The insurgency proceeded successfully, and by the end of the war in 1974, less than half of Guinea was in Portuguese hands. Indeed, by this time it was clear to the African revolutionaries that the Portuguese presence in Africa was quickly fading and that it was only a matter of time until full independence came.

PORTUGUESE COUNTERINSURGENCY OPERATIONS

After the 1961 revolt in Angola and unrest brewing in the other colonies, Portugal began a major effort to build up the colonial military garrisons. Most of the Portuguese troops sent to the colonies were infantry along with a few artillery and light mechanized units. At the same time the Portuguese began an intensive program to recruit Africans to serve in a variety of military and police commands. A large number of regular army units manned by Africans and officered by Portuguese were created. As with the French in Algeria, the Portuguese had little trouble recruiting large numbers of African subjects to fight for them. In 1965 30 percent of the regular army troops committed to the war were African recruits. This number grew to 40 percent by 1971.[22] Again, as in Algeria, the Africans fighting for Portugal probably outnumbered the insurgents fighting for independence.

A major feature of the war was the formation of a variety of "local troops" in each colony to serve as militia or paramilitary forces. Portugal had very limited personnel resources and could only hope to win a protracted war with large numbers of African recruits. Self-defense units for village and local defense were organized in each colony and thousands of Africans served. Special elite African commando and paratroop units were formed for counterinsurgency operations. Some units were even formed from ex-insurgents. Tens of thousands of Africans served with the Portuguese forces and, by most accounts, served well.[23]

The Portuguese relied heavily upon the French counterinsurgency model developed in Algeria. Command was decentralized and each colony was divided into operational zones, each with its own commander, who maintained a reaction force or reserve of his best troops ready to engage any enemy forces that were located by local forces or air reconnaissance. Air support, however, was normally centralized. Most of the Portuguese strike aircraft were located at a few major bases and deployed as necessary by the commander in chief in each colony. The Portuguese used light infantry companies of 120 men (four platoons) as their primary combat force for routine operations, and for raids against enemy units and bases. All of the services created companies of elite troops to serve as reaction forces. The army deployed companies of specially trained commandos to Africa, the air force built up its paratroop force, and the navy established special marine detachments of seventy to eighty men trained to operate along the coasts and rivers.[24]

Portugal was unable to employ more than a few motorized units in Angola and Mozambique, regions characterized by vast distances, rough terrain, and few roads. Helicopters were expensive, hard to come by, and could not be readily expended in daily reconnaissance operations. Thus, one Portuguese answer was the revival of horse cavalry to track insurgents in the heavy brush country of eastern Angola, a region largely impassable in the rainy season. A force of three hundred cavalrymen was formed and proved effective in covering 250,000 square kilometers of Angola's roughest territory.[25]

There were also numerous sweep operations in Angola and Mozambique involving several battalions supported by artillery and airpower. In Angola there were three fairly large operations between 1970 and 1972 with the aim of eliminating MPLA power in the Moxico region; these met with limited success.[26] The most successful large operation, which made extensive use of paratroops and helicopters, was Operation "Gordion Knot" in northern Mozambique, which began in June 1970. Within seven months the Portuguese mobile forces killed or captured over twenty-five hundred guerrillas.[27] However, some foreign observers were highly critical of the Portuguese way of war in Angola and Mozambique and labeled the tactical and operational performance of the Portuguese army as thoroughly mediocre.[28] While the Portuguese used some of the characteristics of the French doctrine in Algeria as a model, there was a lot the Portuguese had missed. Unlike the French in Algeria, the Portuguese did not have effective joint operations centers to coordinate operations. Intelligence, always a key aspect of fighting guerrillas, was also poorly coordinated. While the Portuguese had plenty of aerial reconnaissance assets, little use was made of aerial photography in planning operations. Portuguese operations in populated areas tended to be heavy-handed and firepower heavy. Only a few of the Portuguese officers and units showed the same tactical competence as the British had demonstrated in Malaya, according to one Rhodesian observer who had fought with the British in Malaya. Thanks to the combination of heavy firepower, which tended to cause civilian casualties and turn the natives against the Portuguese, and clumsy tactics, which allowed guerrillas to evade Portuguese sweep operations, the guerrillas were able to survive and carry on the war.[29]

Most of the counterguerrilla operations in Angola and Mozambique consisted of small unit actions employing platoons and companies. A helicopter force, usually thirty to forty helicopters, was available in both Angola and

Mozambique and was used to carry small local reaction forces to trap rebel bands in the bush. In larger operations the Noratlas transports, acquired from France at the start of the conflict and a mainstay of the Portuguese air transport force in the theater, were used to drop paratroops to box in rebel forces.[30] Generally, the fighter-bomber force was not massed but used in flights of two to four aircraft, which carried out armed reconnaissance and provided close air support to ground troops. In 1969 Portugal began to purchase Sud Aviation Puma helicopters, each capable of carrying twenty soldiers; these were a tremendous improvement over the Alouettes. However, Portugal acquired only twelve of the heavy helicopters, not enough to make a major difference in the ground operations, which were becoming more intense.[31]

One of the major uses of airpower in all of the Portuguese colonies was spraying herbicides to reduce cover, especially along roads, to make ambush difficult and to deny crops to the rebels. Starting in the late 1960s, extensive defoliation programs were initiated.[32] As the colonial wars progressed and fairly large parts of Guinea and Mozambique had fallen under rebel control by the late 1960s, the Portuguese turned to a campaign of bombing villages known to house bases and headquarters. There is no clear record of how many rebels or civilians were killed by Portuguese bombardment. However, bombing rebel areas in Guinea and Mozambique does not seem to have had any appreciable effect in reducing or damaging the insurgent power.

END OF THE WAR IN THE PORTUGUESE COLONIES

By the early 1970s, the Portuguese were holding their own in Angola but were steadily losing ground in Guinea and Mozambique. Relative to its size, Guinea had the largest concentration of airpower during the conflict with a strong squadron of Fiat G.91s and T-6s, a few Harpoon bombers, and twelve Alouette III helicopters.[33] Airpower was important in restricting the ability of the rebels to move large groups or to move in daylight, as any large movement would be immediately spotted and attacked. However, by 1972 PAIGC acquired Soviet SAM-7 shoulder-fired antiaircraft missiles and changed the dynamics of the air war. During 1973 to 1974 three Fiat fighters were lost to SAM missiles. A T-6 and two Do 27s were also lost to SAMs, while another two Fiats were lost to conventional antiaircraft fire.[34] The SAM threat limited Portuguese air operations at medium altitude (one thousand to eight thousand feet). SAMs also made their appearance in Mozambique in 1973.[35]

As the war continued into the 1970s, the morale of the Portuguese forces steadily declined, especially among the conscripts who made up a large part of the regular forces sent out from Portugal. Few young Portuguese felt any special desire to fight to maintain an African empire. The end of the conflict came not from any rebel success on the battlefield but from revolution at home. General Marcelo Caetano had taken over the reins of the Salazar regime when the old dictator had had a stroke in 1969, and was as unwilling as Salazar to relinquish the Portuguese empire. Caetano, much to the disgust of his senior officers who had fought in Africa and knew that the Portuguese African empire was a lost cause, ignored economic problems, international disapproval, and the low morale of his conscript forces as he prosecuted the war. In April 1974 many senior officers had had enough and a military junta overthrew Caetano. Almost immediately, the new regime announced that independence would be granted to all of the African colonies in 1975.

The Rhodesian War

RHODESIA DECLARES INDEPENDENCE

In the early 1960s southern Rhodesia was one of the most prosperous of Britain's African colonies. The country was rich in mineral and agricultural resources. The white settlers, 250,000 in a population of 4.5 million blacks, made a good living in business and in farming, which supplied, among other things, a large proportion of Europe's tobacco. The black population, having been brutally conquered and suppressed in the 1890s, had been fairly docile until the 1950s when independence movements began to attract attention and support. The standard of education, medical care, and economic development of the black Rhodesian population was far higher than that of the blacks in Portuguese or French colonies, and rule by the white settlers was not especially oppressive, in contrast to several other colonies.

Yet the winds of independence were blowing over the continent in the early 1960s, and Britain, France, and Belgium were all eager to negotiate independence with the black African populations. Kenya, Tanzania, and Nigeria all gained independence. In 1964 southern Rhodesia's neighbors, northern Rhodesia and Nyasaland, became independent under the names of Zambia and Malawi respectively. The British government entered into negotiations with the white settler government in Rhodesia and demanded an independence

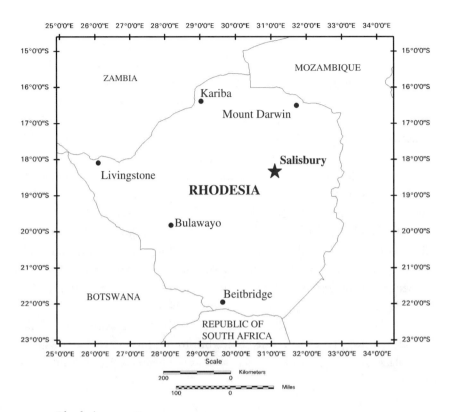

Rhodesia, ca. 1965

timetable and a transition to black majority government. The prosperous white settlers of Rhodesia, seeing the disorder and carnage that had come to much of newly independent African lands, insisted upon maintaining white minority rule. After a series of frustrating negotiations with Britain in November 1965, the white settlers of Rhodesia, led by Ian Smith, rejected British demands and declared Rhodesia to be an independent republic — the first such declaration of independence by a British colony since 1776.

Rhodesia was immediately faced with economic sanctions by Britain and the United Nations. The Rhodesian economy was expected to collapse and the independent republic expected to concede to British demands in a few months. Yet, the British government and the UN greatly underestimated the determination of the white Rhodesians who managed to maintain their independence for fifteen years against international opposition outside and two major insurgent movements inside the country. On the other hand, Rhodesia's position was certainly not hopeless, as they had allies ready to undermine British and UN economic sanctions. The Portuguese quietly maintained solidarity with a kindred regime and provided full rail access for Rhodesian goods through Mozambique. South Africa, a neighbor also facing international sanctions for its apartheid policies, was in a position to provide considerable economic and military support to Rhodesia.

In fact, the Rhodesians became adept at sanctions busting and keeping their economy going. Rhodesian businessmen managed to find other markets for tobacco and mineral exports and other suppliers for needed oil and manufactured goods imports. Surprisingly, after the initial shock of the sanctions, the prosperous Rhodesian economy continued to grow well into the mid-1970s. The two major African nationalist parties, ZANU and ZAPU, had hoped that a combination of international pressure and British intervention would produce an independent, majority black government. Yet, with the Rhodesian whites open and successful in their defiance of Britain and the world, the two parties had little choice but to opt for an armed struggle to win black African rule of Rhodesia — or as the blacks called it, Zimbabwe.

THE INSURGENTS

The blacks belonged to two major tribal groups, the more numerous Shona and the Matabele. The black nationalist political movements that fought the white government were split along tribal lines, and the insurgent campaign was characterized by a lack of cooperation and coordination between the two groups. Indeed, from the beginning, the relationship between the two parties was one of violence and mistrust. Ideologically both parties were Marxist with a blend of African national and tribal traditions thrown in. ZANU's membership was mostly Shona and was led by Ndabanigi Sithole and later by Robert Mugabe. Its political/military strategy generally followed the Chinese Maoist model with an emphasis upon building up a revolutionary cadre and a strong political organization within Rhodesia. Its armed forces, named ZANLA, would wage an aggressive guerrilla war with small units that would wreak so much havoc that the white regime would eventually collapse. ZANU found a welcome sanctuary in Tanzania and would mount operations against Rhodesia through Mozambique.

ZAPU was mostly recruited from the Matabele tribe, and its revolution-ary/military ideology was based on more of a Soviet model. ZAPU's military arm, ZIPRA, was a more conventionally armed and trained force that would wait in its Zambian sanctuaries on Rhodesia's northern border for the right time to invade, liberate at least a part of the country, and defeat the Rhode-sian forces in a conventional battle. Both parties received support from other African nations. Zimbabwean freedom fighters began training in camps in Ghana, Algeria, and Tanzania as well as in the Soviet Union and Red China.[36]

The guerrilla war began in 1966 when small bands of ZAPU troops infil-trated across the Zambesi into northern Rhodesia. The early stages of the war, from 1966 to 1968, were disastrous for the ZAPU forces. After crossing the Zambesi River, the guerrillas had to cross the desolate Zambesi Plain, which had little water or food. The guerrillas were soon exhausted from carrying their weapons and supplies through the inhospitable terrain and were vul-nerable to being spotted by aircraft. Most guerrilla bands were quickly tracked down and destroyed before they could do any harm. Suffering heavy losses, ZAPU's morale and readiness to fight declined rapidly.[37] The defeat of the early guerrilla operations gave the Rhodesian regime a good deal of confi-dence, and Ian Smith boasted that white rule would last "a thousand years." From 1966 until 1972, guerrilla forces killed only two white settlers.[38]

RHODESIAN FORCES AND STRATEGY

At the time of independence, the Rhodesians had a small but well trained and very capable army, air force, and police. In the early 1960s unrest in Africa prompted the Rhodesian government to establish some all-white professional military units, namely the First Battalion of the Rhodesian Light Infantry, C Squadron of the SAS, and an armored car squadron. The reserve force, con-taining both white troops and black units with white officers, was greatly expanded as the Rhodesian Regiment was increased to ten battalions. A police reserve force of thirty thousand men was formed.[39]

For a small country, Rhodesia had a relatively large and modern air force. In 1965 the Rhodesian Air Force (RhAF) consisted of six squadrons with a good balance of ground attack, bomber, reconnaissance, transport, and train-ing assets. The air force had over one thousand professionals stationed at two major air bases (New Sarum near Salisbury and Thornhill near Gwelo). No. 1 Squadron had been recently equipped with twelve Hawker Hunter fighters, a very capable ground attack machine. No. 2 Squadron was equipped with twenty-five Vampire fighters, an old but still effective aircraft. No. 3 Squadron contained the transports assets, seven C-47s. No. 4 Squadron was a training unit equipped with fourteen Provost trainers (which could be modified for the counterinsurgency role). No. 5 Squadron was equipped with twelve Canberra bombers. No. 7 Squadron was the air force's helicopter unit and was equipped with eight Alouette III helicopters, which Rhodesia had begun acquiring in 1962. Another squadron, No. 6, was added as a counterinsurgency air unit in 1967 and was first equipped with modified Aeromacchi AL 60-B2 trainers.[40]

The Rhodesian army was a well-trained conventional force and had the benefit of some officers and NCOs who had seen service with the British in Malaya. For example, Lieutenant Colonel Ron Reid-Daly, commander of the Selous Scouts, formed as a specially trained counterguerrilla force, was a veteran of the British SAS in the Malaya campaign.[41] The RhAF, like the army, was at a high state of efficiency and had acquired experience in counterinsurgency operations under British command. Two Vampire fighter squadrons had served with the RAF in Aden to help suppress rebellious tribesmen in 1958. Rhodesian transports had supported the RAF in the Kuwait crisis of 1961 and had taken part in flood relief operations in Kenya. The Canberra Squadron had served with the RAF on Cyprus between 1959 and 1963. Rhodesian aircraft had also helped put down trouble in Nyasaland in 1959 and supported the airlift of refugees from the Congo.[42]

The international embargo of goods and equipment to Rhodesia was expected to cripple the Rhodesian armed forces by denying them vital aircraft parts. However, the embargo failed, thanks to the Rhodesian ingenuity and considerable help from their South African allies. Local engineers were able to manufacture complex aircraft engine parts that kept the Canberra bombers, and one hundred aircraft of twelve different types, flying.[43] The Rhodesians found that the standard British one-thousand-pound bomb was fine for knocking down German cities in World War II, but was a poor antipersonnel weapon for African conditions. So the Rhodesians developed and locally manufactured two very effective fragmentation bombs with contact fuses on long probes and parachutes to give a steep impact angle.[44] Throughout the long conflict, South African support was an essential part of Rhodesian military capability. After the first guerrilla incursions in the 1960s, South Africa sent a battalion of police to fight as infantry in Rhodesia.[45] However, South

Africa's most important military contribution was its helicopter force. At the height of the war, in the mid-1970s, as many as half of the helicopters and pilots in the RhAF were South Africans. No. 7 Squadron had more than forty helicopters in service in the 1970s, and approximately half of the helicopters and pilots were on attachment from the South African Air Force.[46]

With a small economy and armed forces, Rhodesia did not have the option of saturating the country with soldiers. Nor did Rhodesia have the resources to operate large-scale civic action programs to win over the black population. There was some effort to deny the guerrillas support by resettling some of the population in protected villages, but Rhodesia could not afford this on a grand scale.[47] Thus, the Rhodesians turned to their only realistic military strategy, which was to set up small and highly mobile forces throughout the country and to catch the infiltrating guerrillas as they came over the border. The object was to destroy guerrilla bands before they could reach the heavily populated sections of the country and initiate widespread harassment attacks in the larger towns and urban areas.

COUNTERGUERRILLA OPERATIONS, 1972–1980

In 1968 there were some small incursions by ZAPU and ZANU groups that were quickly dealt with by the Rhodesian forces. Two attempts by African leaders to unite ZAPU and ZANU in 1971 and 1972 failed, and no coordinated offensive could be brought against the white regime. Up to the end of 1972, the Rhodesian forces had the situation well in hand.[48] However, the Portuguese hold on northern Mozambique was cracking by early 1973 and the anti-Portuguese insurgents, FRELIMO, allowed the ZANU forces (ZANLA) to establish bases in northern Mozambique, which threatened the northeastern region of Rhodesia. The guerrilla incursions became more frequent, and white farmsteads came under increasing attack. The Rhodesians responded by setting up a joint command for all army, air force, and police for northeastern Rhodesia and deploying twenty companies of troops to the region during 1972 and 1973.[49]

While the Rhodesians won the first phases of the insurgency, their early tactics were clumsy and their losses fairly high. However, the Rhodesians were quick to apply the lessons of the battlefield and develop highly mobile tactics to engage and defeat the guerrilla bands infiltrating the country. The RhAF was key to applying mobility and firepower to the battle. By 1974 the Rhodesians had modified some of their Alouette IIIs as gunships, armed with a highly accurate and lethal 20 mm Matra automatic cannon. The gunship Alouettes were called "K Cars" (Killer Cars), and the transport Alouettes (most of the helicopter force), which could each carry four soldiers as passengers, were named "G Cars." Small reaction forces, named "fire forces," were set up which could respond to any attacks on white farmsteads or to intervene when reconnaissance spotted guerrilla bands (anywhere from six to thirty men) infiltrating through the brush country. The helicopters and C-47 transports were key to providing mobility to the reaction forces. All of the regular infantry of the army were trained as paratroops, ready to go into battle dropping from the C-47s. The Rhodesians set up nine bases around the country, each with an airfield capable of handling C-47s and helicopters, to serve as fire force bases of operations.

By the mid-1970s a typical reaction force (soon called a "fire force") operation went as follows. When guerrillas were spotted, a K Car would carry the force commander and serve as an aerial command post. A C-47 would be directed to drop a section of sixteen to twenty paratroops, normally on high ground, to serve as a sweeping force. The drops were carried out at low level, often as low as three hundred feet, in order to prevent dispersion of the force and to minimize the vulnerable drop time. Usually four G Cars, each carrying a section leader, a machine gunner, and two riflemen, would be directed by the force commander to landing zones to serve as blocking forces to box in the guerrilla band. When the reaction force located and engaged the guerrillas, the K Car could serve as fire support with its 20 mm cannon. Often, additional air support could be provided by a light counterinsurgency aircraft (Cessna "Lynx"), which could add 63 mm rockets, napalm, and blast bombs and twin .303 machine guns to the fire support. The combination of firepower and good training by the Rhodesians resulted in a more than ten-to-one kill ratio by the fire forces.[50] The Rhodesians constantly made minor modifications to their tactics and weapons and maintained the tactical/operational edge over their enemy. By the last stages of the war, the fire force inflicted horrendous casualties upon guerrillas while taking minimal losses themselves. In the last phase of the insurgency, April 1979 to December 1979, the Rhodesian Light Infantry, which provided the fire force troops, killed 1,680 guerrillas.[51]

The independence of Mozambique in 1975 and the support provided by the FRELIMO government to ZANU changed the dynamics of the war and opened up the whole eastern region of Rhodesia to guerrilla infiltration.

Before the independence of Mozambique, ZANU forces trying to operate in that country could come under Portuguese attack. The Portuguese routinely looked the other way and allowed their Rhodesian friends to cross the border in "hot pursuit" of guerrilla bands. Now Mozambique became a friendly sanctuary for Mugabe's ZANU guerrillas, and the numbers in training camps increased dramatically. ZANU was able to establish large logistics and training bases near the Rhodesian border, and the war became much more intense.

The Rhodesians continued to improve their intelligence collecting throughout the war. Light, elite forces such as the Selous Scouts and the SAS were able to operate in small groups for days in the thick brush country along the Mozambique border. A horse-mounted unit, Grey's Scouts, was formed to patrol the rough country. These small units often acted as reconnaissance forces to spot infiltrating guerrilla bands for the fire forces. Light civilian aircraft also played an important part in the war. Light aircraft and their pilots were commandeered for service in the police air reserve and flew reconnaissance in rural areas looking for sign of guerrillas. Pilots and observers, flying low and slow, became adept at spotting guerrilla tracks and signs in the bush and passing the information to the fire force. By 1978 the Rhodesians had set up a joint military operations center for the whole country where intelligence could be processed. Although infiltration had become much heavier, most of the country was still securely in the hands of the white settlers. Farms outside of the border areas were fairly secure, and there were very few terrorist incidents in the cities. The mining of rural roads and some small attacks by the guerrillas were an irritation, and the guerrilla offensive was failing to undermine white morale. However, the pressure on Rhodesia came mostly from outside the country. High oil prices and the sanctions made life hard, along with the constant demands for military service on the white population. In order to win the military side of the war, white Rhodesians often had to spend six months of the year in uniform. By the late 1970s, many whites began to leave the country, demoralized by the constant stress of war and sanctions. However, the heaviest blow to Rhodesian confidence came in 1976 when South Africa, pressuring Rhodesia to make concessions and accept a black government, withdrew its troops and helicopter pilots. South Africa believed that it could accept a stable, black-governed buffer state to its north and started to push the Rhodesian government to the peace table.

CROSS-BORDER OPERATIONS

With insurgent bases being set up in neighboring countries, the Rhodesian government developed a strategy of carrying the war to the insurgents by striking at the main guerrilla bases. The first major Rhodesian cross-border strike was carried out against a ZANLA base at Pafuri, Mozambique, on 28 February 1976 when Hunter fighters bombed the base. Rhodesian aircraft bombed ZANLA and ZIPRA bases in Mozambique the next month, and in August six hundred Selous Scouts, with full air support, attacked a ZANLA camp in Mozambique and killed six hundred guerrillas.[52] In order to gain a better position at negotiations going on between the warring parties in Geneva, the Rhodesians decided to use their mobile forces for a major strike against the ZANLA forces in Mozambique. In a three-day operation, 31 October to 2 November 1976, the Selous Scouts, SAS, Rhodesian Light Infantry, and Rhodesian African Rifles struck several ZANLA base camps and logistics centers in the Tete province of Mozambique. Most of the troops were in motorized columns, but some were carried by helicopter. Much of the Rhodesian Air Force flew in support of the operation, and the close air support provided by fighters and K Cars kept ZANLA forces from mounting an effective counterattack. Toward the end of the operation, helicopters evacuated 140 Rhodesian troops who were cut off deep in enemy territory. Operation "Mardon" had a decisive effect in the short term. The Rhodesian attack did not kill a large number of guerrillas, but it did force hundreds to flee in disarray. Fifty tons of ZANLA weapons and war supplies were destroyed, and the effect upon ZANLA morale was significant. Mugabe's ZANLA guerrillas now knew that they no longer had a safe sanctuary in Mozambique, and the operation set back ZANLA's plans for an offensive by several months.[53]

While carrying out occasional air strikes against ZANLA bases in Mozambique, in October 1978 the Rhodesians turned on the ZIPRA forces in Zambia. In "Operation Green Leader" the Rhodesians took over Zambian airspace for three days and dropped paratroops at the ZIPRA base at Chikumbi, just twelve miles from the capital at Lusaka. During the operation three major ZIPRA bases were attacked by ground and air forces, and an estimated fifteen hundred guerrilla troops killed with little loss to the Rhodesians.[54] The political situation changed again when, after heavy international pressure, the Smith government allowed elections for the whole country, which put Bishop

Abel Muzorewa's United African National Council in the majority in Parliament and made Muzorewa, a moderate Democrat, the new prime minister. Even though Rhodesia now had a majority black government, ZANU and ZAPU had been banned from the election and carried on the war. While peace talks were in progress, the RhAF crippled the ZAPU forces in Zambia by bombing their camps and destroying three bridges that cut the southern part of the country off from Lusaka.[55] One final, grand operation designed to cripple the estimated fifteen thousand ZANLA troops in Mozambique was mounted in September 1979. It was the most complex operation of the war for the Rhodesian forces. In a seven-day operation from 1–7 September 1979, the ZANLA base at Mapai was repeatedly bombed by Hunters and Canberras. The RhAF cut several important bridges, which cut the logistics lines from Maputo. Heliborne troops of the SAS and Rhodesian Light Infantry attacked camps and set up ambushes to trap fleeing troops. The air strikes on the ZANLA base at Barragem were deadly, and after the Hunter fighters bombed the base, the SAS moved in on the ground. The Rhodesians inflicted heavy casualties and damage upon ZANLA. However, the Rhodesians did not describe Operation "Uric" as a complete success because of the loss of two helicopters and fifteen troops killed by ZANLA RPG rockets. Even though the Rhodesians killed four hundred guerrillas, the loss of fifteen troops dead and two aircraft was considered too high a price.[56]

END OF THE WAR

Militarily, the Rhodesian strategy was sound. The cross-border raids, in which the air force played a central role, were generally very successful. ZANLA and the smaller ZIPRA forces in Zambian and Mozambique sanctuaries were badly damaged and thrown off balance by the deep strikes. Even by the end of the war, the Rhodesians maintained effective control throughout the country. Even though ZANLA had infiltrated over ten thousand guerrillas into Rhodesia by 1979, they were unable to inflict major damage or casualties upon the Rhodesian forces and white settlers. The war was finally decided by the exhaustion of the white government, which saw no end in sight for the war. In December 1979 Britain brokered a negotiated settlement that granted free elections with ZANU and ZAPU participation, with guarantees that the rights and property of the white minority would be protected after a new government came to power. Guerrillas were disarmed and allowed to return to Rhodesia. In 1980, under elections monitored by five nations, Robert Mugabe was elected president and Rhodesia became Zimbabwe.

South Africa's War in Namibia

South West Africa, now called Namibia, is a vast, very sparsely settled region, a total of 825,000 square kilometers. Most of the country consists of desert, but the northern regions can often support agriculture. South West Africa is well known for its mineral riches, including diamond fields and uranium deposits.

South West Africa was originally a German colony that was conquered by the Union of South Africa forces during a brief campaign in World War I. After the war the territory was turned over to South Africa to be administered as a League of Nations mandate. For decades South Africa had little trouble in administering its own colony. The population consisted of a few thousand (mostly German) settlers who farmed, ran the diamond mines, and owned the businesses. The few hundred thousand black inhabitants led a mostly tribal life with subsistence agriculture and worked as laborers for the white-owned businesses, farms, and mining concerns.

As in most colonies, there were occasional outbreaks of trouble from native leaders, and it was natural in a land with a small population, few roads, and vast distances that the South Africans would turn to airpower as a means of keeping order in their colony. The British approach of air control was used in South West African troubles from the earliest years. A force of four hundred settler-militiamen supported by a few South African Air Force (SAAF) aircraft quickly suppressed a minor rebellion by the Bondelswarts tribe in 1922.[57]

Police and militia, supported by three South African Air Force biplanes, put down another small revolt in 1925. Upon the appearance of the aircraft, the rebels quickly surrendered.[58] Problems with the chief of the Ukuambi tribe in 1932 were settled by the deployment of three aircraft and two armored cars from Pretoria.[59] British air control doctrine was followed. As the colonial government's problem was with Chief Iupumbu, leaflets were first dropped on the populace warning them to stay away from Iupumbu's residence. The bombing the next day was more of a demonstration rather than a serious attack, and the chief, impressed by South African firepower, quickly made peace.[60]

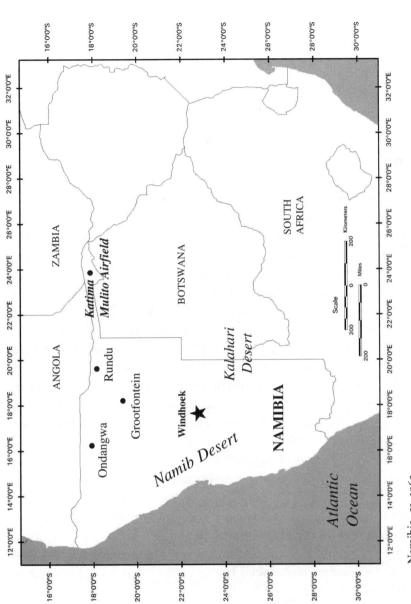

Namibia, ca. 1962

BEGINNING OF NAMIBIAN INDEPENDENCE MOVEMENTS

As in other regions of Africa, the black population of South West Africa yearned for home rule and independence after the Second World War. Although the South African government and the white settlers did not have the record of callousness and indifference to native interests that characterized the Belgians and Portuguese and had never been as heavy-handed as the French in suppressing dissent, the independence cause was still widely supported. The black population was mostly poor and illiterate, and the South African–imposed apartheid laws created hostility to colonial rule.

The Namibian independence movement, SWAPO (South West African People's Organization), was established in the 1950s and in 1962, after violent rebellions had broken out against colonial rule throughout Africa, called for armed resistance with the goal of pushing the South Africans out.[61] SWAPO's military arm, the People's Liberation Army of Namibia (PLAN), was formed in 1962.[62] The South African government, in turn, labeled SWAPO as terrorist and communist, although SWAPO called for democratic elections. At the same time, several other South West African political parties were formed, and these too sought reforms and free elections. SWAPO, composed mainly of Ovambo tribesmen — the largest tribe in South West Africa — had the advantage of numbers and came to dominate the Namibian independence movement.[63] SWAPO had the additional advantage of UN and international recognition, was able to garner arms, funding, and support from other African nations and the Soviet Union, and was soon able to establish military bases in the newly independent Zambia.

The military conflict between SWAPO and the South African government began in 1966 when PLAN established a base camp in Ovambo territory in northern South West Africa. In August 1966, a police unit destroyed the camp. Other skirmishes took place during 1966 and 1967 in the Caprivi Strip and northern Namibia. However, in May 1967 SWAPO suffered a setback when its military commander, Tobias Hanyeka, was killed in a skirmish by the Zambesi River.[64]

SWAPO's insurgency began at a low level, mostly mining the roads, killing Ovambo tribal chiefs reckoned friendly to the government, and conducting small attacks on white farms, and stayed that way through the 1960s. SWAPO units were well armed and well trained in camps in Zambia, but in order to get to the population in northern South West Africa, SWAPO units had to cross the heavily defended Caprivi Strip or cross through the hostile Portuguese colony of Angola. Even though southern Angola was largely in the hands of rebel groups fighting the Portuguese, the Portuguese government had no objection to South African police and military units crossing the border and intercepting SWAPO units in Angola. In short, Angola was no safe sanctuary for SWAPO. Under such conditions, the only effort that SWAPO could maintain was at a low level — mining roads, assassinating pro-government tribal leaders, and conducting ambushes by ten-man squads.

During the first years of the SWAPO insurgency, the South African government handled the situation largely as a police matter. In Namibia the South African army had the Windhoek Regiment (six battalions) and well-trained and equipped reserve forces enlisted from the white population in South West Africa. The South West Africa Police created elite and heavily armed counterinsurgency units. South African forces were sent to garrison and patrol the twenty-kilometer-wide Caprivi Strip in order to block SWAPO infiltration into the northern part of South West Africa. In 1967 the SAAF deployed helicopters to support the Portuguese fighting the UNITA rebel movement along Angola's southern border. Understanding that the UNITA rebels were allies of SWAPO, the SAAF established the First Air Component, a helicopter and liaison unit, at the air base at Runda in northern South West Africa in order to coordinate border reconnaissance with the Portuguese.

THE WAR INTENSIFIES

The low-level conflict intensified in January 1972 when a SWAPO-initiated workers' strike affected the economy of much of South West Africa and sent the white community and South African government a message about the strong support that SWAPO enjoyed among the overwhelmingly black population. The northern section of South West Africa was placed under a legal state of emergency, and more South African Defence Forces were dispatched to the region to support the police.[65] Increased activity by SWAPO units against the police, government facilities, and settlers led to further troop deployments of the South African Defence Forces, which had largely taken over the counterinsurgency campaign. The SWAPO campaign was encouraged by political support from the UN. In 1968 the UN Security Council endorsed the termination of the old League of Nations mandate for South African rule of South West Africa. In 1971 the World Court ruled that the South African presence in Namibia was illegal. In the early 1970s, PLAN, bolstered by the support from the international community, intensified its campaign of political activism, intimidation of native chiefs friendly to the government, ambushing police patrols, and attacking white settlers.

In the 1960s and early 1970s the primary form of airpower used in support of police and army operations against SWAPO was the Alouette III helicopter, one of the most popular helicopters in counterinsurgency operations from the 1960s to 1980s. The French-designed and South African–built (under license) helicopters carried four soldiers and could be modified as deadly light gunships with rockets, machine guns, or a 20 mm cannon. From 1966 on, Alouette IIIs worked with specially trained trackers of the South West Africa Police special counterinsurgency (Koevoet) teams. The helicopters usually operated in pairs in support of ground trackers to find and fix SWAPO guerrilla bands. Puma helicopters were used as troop transports to bring in sections of infantry to be set down to box in any band of SWAPO guerrillas found by the air/ground reconnaissance forces of the police. Several varieties of light aircraft, often operated by SAAF reserve pilots, served in the reconnaissance role, flying over large stretches of the desolate country looking for signs of guerrilla movement. The Cessna 185 and the Bosbok, a light monoplane built in South Africa, operated as sky scouts and could drop flares to mark guerrilla units. From the first major clash between SWAPO and the police in 1966 the South African military and police forces expanded rapidly so that by 1974 there were approximately fifteen thousand South African military personnel serving in South West Africa.[66]

In 1971 the South African government began the process of building a group of overt and covert special force units specifically trained and equipped for counterinsurgency war against the African National Congress and also to support anti-insurgent operations in Rhodesia and Angola. By the late 1970s, the South Africans possessed a variety of elite forces that were capable of conducting raids against insurgents with support from SAAF helicopters and aircraft.[67]

When South Africa awoke to the fact of a serious insurgency in South West Africa, the army moved quickly to remedy years of neglect of education, medical support, and infrastructure building for the black population. A large-scale civil affairs program was initiated to improve the condition of the blacks. Veterinarians worked to improve the health of the native cattle herds. Military medical corps units opened clinics for the natives. SADF (South African

Defence Forces) found qualified personnel to staff agricultural schools for the populace.[68] The SADF relied heavily upon its reserve soldiers to conduct the civic action programs. The "hearts and minds" civic action campaign had some success in keeping some of the Namibian tribes loyal to the government. The South Africans recruited military forces from among some of the tribes, especially the Bushmen, who proved very effective in tracking down SWAPO guerrillas. One advantage that the South Africans had in conducting civil affairs was that after fifty years of South African rule, the lingua franca among the tribesmen was Afrikaans.[69]

THE SOUTH AFRICAN DEFENCE FORCES

SWAPO, although capably led, armed, and trained, operated at a disadvantage in fighting the South African military forces. South Africa, a wealthy and technically advanced nation, arguably had the finest military forces on the entire continent. South Africa had committed large ground and air forces to the British forces in World War II, where they had performed admirably. The South African Air Force had sent a squadron to support the Americans in the Korean War. Flying at first F-51 fighters and later F-84 jet fighter-bombers, the South Africans performed very capably in the close air support role. South Africans, as already noted, had sent air and ground units to support the Rhodesians in their counterinsurgency war. By any standard, the South African forces had a strong military tradition, a lot of experience at war, and plenty of well-trained officers and soldiers. South Africa, which had conscription for its white population and voluntary enlistment for blacks in the forces, had a large and modern military establishment. Moreover, unlike Rhodesia or Portugal, South Africa had the economic resources to mount a large-scale counterinsurgency campaign.

South Africa had an impressive array of military and air force resources to bring to the conflict. In the 1950s the SAAF had developed into a small but capable air force equipped with modern fighter jets such as the American Sabrejet and the British Vampire. In the 1960s, the SAAF underwent a major expansion and modernization. Aircraft acquired for the SAAF included four versions of the Mirage III fighter from France (Mirage III models CZ, EZ, RZ, and BZ), British Canberra bombers, and Buccaneer S-50 strike aircraft. Two of the best transports available, the American C-130 and the French C-160 Transall, were obtained for the transport squadrons of the SAAF. From France the SAAF acquired a large number of helicopters including the Alouette III and Super Frelon, then the largest transport helicopter in the world. The British Wasp helicopter was also obtained. By the early 1970s the SAAF operated several helicopter squadrons (No. 15, 16, 19, and 22 Squadrons; in the early 1980s No. 30 and 31 Squadrons were added). The Impala Mark I jet trainer, a licensed version of the Italian Aeromacchi 326, went into production in South Africa.

With trouble on the Rhodesian and Angolan borders and an insurgency by the African National Congress (ANC) at home, the SAAF continued to modernize and expand into the 1970s. In the first half of the decade, the SAAF acquired more Mirage IIIs and bought Mirage F-1Azs and F-CZs from France, as well as additional Alouette helicopters and the Puma helicopter, a first-rate medium transport capable of carrying a 2.5-ton load or sixteen to twenty troops. The South African aircraft industry had matured and was able to produce a light strike fighter version of the Impala, the Mark II.[70] When the UN announced an arms embargo on the Republic of South Africa in 1977, the country was ready to provide for its own defense needs. Since the mid-1960s, the South African government had encouraged the development of an indigenous aircraft industry, relying on building foreign models under license. The South African army also developed a defense and munitions industry of high quality. South Africa was able to produce a superb family of armored vehicles and artillery pieces as well as a full range of munitions. By the late 1970s, the South Africans were even able to assemble their own Mirage F-1 fighters, a fairly sophisticated piece of equipment, from components imported from France. [71]

The conventional cutting edge of the SAAF during the hottest parts of the war in Angola and Namibia in the late 1970s to late 1980s consisted of sixteen Mirage IIIs (No. 2 Squadron) and fourteen F-1Azs for air-to-air combat (No. 3 Squadron), one Canberra bomber squadron (No. 12 Squadron), thirty-two Mirage F-1 AZs, and a squadron of Buccaneers (No. 24 Squadron) as well as three squadrons of Impala IIs (No. 4, 7, 8 Squadrons) in the ground attack role.[72] The South Africans also fielded four transport squadrons (C-130s, Transalls, C-47s) and three squadrons of light aircraft especially suitable for the counterinsurgency operations in Namibia: No. 11 Squadron equipped with Cessna 185s, No. 41 Squadron with Kudus, and No. 42 Squadron with Bosboks. To improve its light transport and reconnaissance capability, the army had created "Air Commando" squadrons in 1963, comprising volunteers with a private pilot's license and five hundred hours of flight time and their own aircraft or access to an aircraft. Twelve squadrons of the Air Commandos were turned over to the SAAF in 1978 and renamed the Volunteer Air Squadrons. Essentially their task was to relieve regular SAAF pilots from many of the routine support activities, such as flying reconnaissance, transport, and liaison missions in support of the counterinsurgency forces in South West Africa. This freed the regular air forces for conventional combat and support operations — which would become a major effort in what would be called the Angolan War.

THE ANGOLAN WAR

When Portugal granted Angola independence in 1975, the three rebel factions immediately fell into a savage civil war for control of the country. Within months the MPLA had emerged as the most powerful faction in the country, thanks to generous arms shipments and military aid from the Soviet bloc. MPLA controlled most of the country, including the oil-producing areas and the capital, Luanda, by the end of 1975. However, the other parties, UNITA and FNLA, still maintained significant forces and were capable of carrying on the war. UNITA was especially important to South Africa, as it controlled the southeastern third of Angola and much of the area bordering South West Africa. Since SWAPO had allied itself with the dominant MPLA, UNITA's territory, the best base area for attacks into South West Africa, was off limits to SWAPO's forces.

South African army commander General Jannie Geldenhuys developed a policy of forward defense by defending South West Africa in Angola. If the MPLA gained control of the entire border region, their SWAPO allies would have secure bases from which to attack Namibia, and South Africa would be at a strategic disadvantage. Only a massive South African military presence on the border could hope to provide any security for South West Africa. So the South Africans entered into an alliance with UNITA to keep the MPLA and their SWAPO allies away from the border. The forward defense strategy required a small South African force to be stationed within Angola. The Thirty-second Battalion — Angolan troops with South African officers — attacked SWAPO bases and conducted deep-penetration operations to gather intelligence and locate targets. These troops, often operating deep in Angola, were supplied by SAAF helicopters.[73] Generous military and logistics aid for UNITA offset the vast quantities of Soviet equipment and thousands of

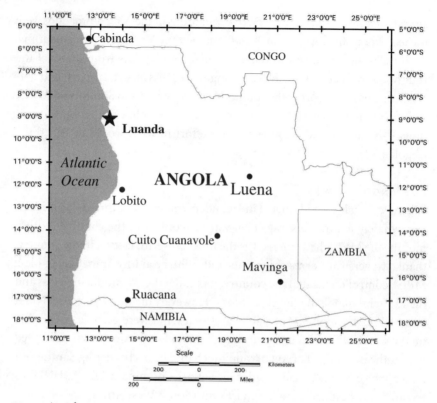

Angola, ca. 1971

Cuban troops sent to the MPLA. South Africa also set up a training and supply base for UNITA at Grootfontein.[74] On numerous occasions South African forces (never more than three thousand strong), and including armor and artillery units, actually deployed inside Angola to support UNITA during powerful MPLA/Cuban offensives.

For thirteen years the MPLA with Cuban and SWAPO support fought a mostly conventional war against UNITA and South Africa throughout southern Angola. The conventional war that South Africa fought inside Angola was extremely successful. South African troops and aircraft, operating in support of UNITA, were able to stop several major MPLA/Cuban offensives against the UNITA-controlled territory, even though the Cubans fielded powerful forces including five hundred tanks, more than thirty thousand troops, and

Mig-21 and Mig-23 squadrons in support of their MPLA allies.[75] South African troops, with SAAF Mirages, Impalas, Canberras, and Buccaneers flying cover and support, repeatedly inflicted heavy casualties upon the Cuban/MPLA forces in some of the largest conventional battles seen in Africa since World War II. In the late 1980s, the SAAF also employed No. 60 Squadron's Boeing 707 EW (electronic warfare) aircraft to provide their air units with an edge in intelligence and command and control in the Angolan battles. The story of the conventional war in Angola has already been told in several books and will not be covered in any detail in this book.[76]

In 1978, the SAAF and army demonstrated their capability for using airpower and conducting joint operations in one of the most decisive operations of the Angola War. The South Africans identified a large SWAPO base at Cassinga, 250 kilometers deep into Angola. In May 1978, in a superbly planned, well-executed raid, the South Africans dropped a paratroop battalion on Cassinga in an operation that included cover and air support from Mirages, Buccaneers, and Impalas. At the same time, South African light armored units struck other SWAPO bases inside Angola closer to the border. The South African paratroop force overran the SWAPO camp and killed one thousand SWAPO troops for a loss of less than thirty of their own troops. Once the base was destroyed, the paratroops were evacuated by SAAF Puma helicopters. Although the attack deep inside Angola caused an international outcry, it also proved to be a major blow to SWAPO by showing the insurgents that they were vulnerable even far from South West Africa's border.[77]

To support UNITA and South African forces in Angola, the SAAF rotated aircraft and aircrew through Grootfontein and Rundu, their major air bases in northern Namibia. A variety of air operations were conducted, including strikes by Buccaneers using laser-guided weapons. In major battles in 1987, the SAAF's No. 10 Squadron deployed RPVs (remote piloted vehicles — unmanned aircraft) as reconnaissance platforms to find enemy targets.[78] The SAAF demonstrated a high degree of skill in inflicting heavy losses on their MPLA and Cuban opponents while losing few aircraft.[79] As operations in Angola intensified, South African forces and their UNITA allies could not have held on without airlifted supplies from South Africa. Since the distances were great and there were no railroads and few roads (none of them good) connecting Angola with South Africa, the only practical means of supply and troop deployment was by transport aircraft flying into small dirt strips carved by UNITA out of the brush. During the second half of 1987, SAAF C-130s flew 412 sorties into Angola carrying 5,448 tons of materiel and 4,730 men. The Transalls flew 169 sorties carrying 1,435 tons of supplies and 2,097 men. The flying was done under the most primitive and hazardous conditions at night with few navigation aids and required the highest level of skill and training by the transport crews. To avoid being spotted by Cuban radar and to avoid any SWAPO and MPLA antiaircraft fire, SAAF transports usually flew into Angola at the extremely low altitude of 100 to 150 meters.[80]

COUNTERINSURGENCY OPERATIONS IN SOUTH WEST AFRICA
While the South Africans were engaging the Cuban, MPLA, and SWAPO inside Angola, SWAPO continued to infiltrate small groups of guerrillas into the populous areas of Namibia. With most of Angola in the hands of the MPLA after 1975, SWAPO had a friendly base of operations, albeit not a fully secure one. In the Angolan base areas SWAPO was able to organize, train, and equip its guerrilla forces. The SWAPO bands that infiltrated into northern Namibia were no ragtag revolutionaries, they were well-led, trained, and equipped forces.

In order to counter the guerrillas within South West Africa, the South African government in 1979 formed an elite police unit in June 1979 with the mission of tracking down and destroying the SWAPO squads. The unit, originally with only seventy-four policemen (ten security policemen and sixty-four white and black special constables), was called *Koevoet* (Afrikaans for "crowbar"). By 1980 the Koevoet had a fire force of armed Alouette III helicopters attached for support and light armored vehicles that were specially designed for protection against land mines. The Koevoet fought in small, usually platoon-sized units. Mounted in light armored vehicles, they would range deep into the thick brushland of northern Namibia for as long as a week at a time looking for traces of SWAPO guerrilla movement.[81] Airpower was important for Koevoet operations. Light reconnaissance airplanes such as the Cessna 185s and Bosboks flew reconnaissance for the Koevoet teams and could cover large areas flying at treetop level. As in Rhodesia, the airplane pilots and observers became adept at spotting people and tracks from the air. Once a SWAPO band was spotted, the Koevoet unit would call in a helicopter-mounted reaction force that was on constant standby status. The reaction force was usually provided from one of South Africa's three paratroop battalions. The reaction force could take over the guerrillas' spoor and follow up contacts, or be dropped off in the bush to act as a "stopper group" to block any guerrilla retreat.[82] If a guerrilla force was chased back over the Angolan border, "hot pursuit" was authorized. The South African army also had some special "Koevoet"-type units that specialized in tracking guerrillas on horseback and even motorcycle. The 101 Battalion, created in 1974 of mostly Ovambo tribesmen, also had special tracking teams on the Koevoet pattern.

The Koevoet was an elite light unit that proved extremely effective in counterinsurgency warfare. By the end of 1980 the Koevoet force had killed 511 guerrillas for a loss of 12 of their own.[83] The Koevoet, however, was just one step in establishing a comprehensive security program for South West Africa. In August the government of South West Africa established its own defense department. All local security, local military, and reserve forces were to be known as the South West African Territory Force (SWATF), which had its own headquarters. Coordination with the South African military forces was carried out efficiently through a joint committee. The SWATF consisted largely of part-time soldiers and some regular units recruited mostly from the bushmen and black inhabitants of South West Africa. At its peak in the late 1980s, the SWATF consisted of eight full-time battalions, twenty-seven area force units (manned by reserves), a reaction force brigade, a logistics brigade, and numerous special units — a force of thirty thousand men. By this time, about two-thirds of the combat units in northern Namibia were composed of SWATF units.[84] An important part of the SWATF was an air commando squadron of light aircraft manned by reservists with pilot's licenses.

One of the consistent strengths of the South Africans in countering insurgency was a very efficient intelligence system that combined human intelligence, signals intercepts, and aerial reconnaissance. As in most colonial wars, the greater part of the local defense forces was composed of loyal natives who knew the terrain and people of the region.[85]

By 1987, with major battles going on inside Angola, the South African forces along the Angolan border were strongly reinforced. The South African Tenth Division, made up of three mechanized battalions, a tank regiment, three armored car squadrons, and an artillery group, covered the north and took part in counterinsurgency operations in the Ovambo region.[86] With the north of Namibia fairly saturated with South African and local forces, the SWAPO guerrillas took a severe beating. By 1988 SWAPO activity in South West Africa had noticeably decreased. There had been 206 ambushes and contacts between security forces and SWAPO in 1987 but only 132 in 1988. Land mine incidents also decreased.[87] One of SWAPO's main goals had been to drive the white settlers and businessmen out of South West Africa by constant attack. Although some whites left the border region, for the most part the white population, especially those in the interior of the country, remained secure and prosperous.

THE END OF THE WAR

Although the South Africans took few casualties in their war in Angola and counterinsurgency campaign in South West Africa, the constant low-level attrition had a significant morale effect. The war was a financial drain on South Africa and imposed a heavy burden upon the white population, especially in South West Africa, which had to endure constant call-ups for reserve duty. By the late 1980s South African generals were openly complaining that the war in Angola had become "South Africa's Vietnam." The South African government looked for a politically acceptable way out of the mess. SWAPO, the Angolan factions, and the Cubans were also exhausted by the attrition war in Angola and ready to agree to a compromise peace. After a long period of negotiations, the South Africans, SWAPO, and the Cubans came to a series of agreements between August 1988 and April 1989. First, the Cubans and South Africans were to withdraw from Angola. By January 1989 the first Cubans were on their way home, and South Africa had pulled out of Angola and reduced its forces in Namibia. South Africa accepted a cease-fire agreement with SWAPO and agreed to the UN resolution calling for independence and free elections in Namibia. A UN peacekeeping force was sent into the country, only to observe a renewed outbreak of fighting as SWAPO illegally infiltrated troops into Namibia. As the conclusion to the war, the few South African forces remaining in Namibia killed several hundred guerrillas for little loss in April and May 1989.[88]

In November 1989 Namibia had an internationally supervised free election in which SWAPO won 57 percent of the vote. While gaining a majority of seats in the new Parliament, SWAPO did not have the necessary two-thirds majority that would have enabled them to change the constitution and establish a single party state. In March 1990 Namibia became an independent country with a multiparty democracy and carefully entrenched rights, a rarity for Africa.[89] In this case, there were several winners of the war. The peace agreement and Namibian constitution ensured that the rights and property of the whites in Namibia, as well as South African business interests, were protected. South Africa also ensured a stable and peaceful western border. SWAPO gained its goal of full independence and took control of the government, although the constitution and an independent judiciary carefully restricted its power, and SWAPO would have to learn to share power with the other parties. UNITA and the MPLA maintained their respective positions and continued their war in Angola. Only Cuba was a big loser in the end. The Cubans announced to the world that they had won some grand victories on the battlefield (they hadn't — they had been badly defeated) and brought their troops home to face unemployment and poverty.

Conclusion

The insurgencies throughout southern Africa from the 1960s through the 1980s all took on the form of long-term attrition wars. With the exception of the war in Angola in the 1970s and 1980s, most of the combat operations on both sides were small unit affairs with rarely more than one hundred guerrillas or government forces involved in any one action. In most cases, platoon operations were the norm. In this kind of low-intensity war, highly mobile elite troops came into their own as the best means to fight insurgents. Aviation was key to providing mobile transport and firepower to back up the small elite light infantry and police units. Airpower, often in the form of light civilian-type aircraft, also proved to be a key tool in reconnaissance and intelligence gathering. Paralleling the war in Vietnam, the helicopter came into its own in this era as an indispensable weapon of war. Indeed, in the kinds of war faced in southern Africa, airpower in its many forms was even more important. Air transport, for example, was essential in keeping isolated outposts and forces supplied. In short, airpower was a tremendous asset to counterinsurgency operations and multiplied the military power of the government forces by several times.

The wars in southern Africa also bring several strategic issues to the forefront. The government forces of Portugal, Rhodesia, and South Africa won most of the battles and managed to inflict horrendous losses on the insurgents. For example, 11,335 SWAPO insurgents were killed between 1966 and 1989 for the loss of only a few hundred South African/SWATF forces.[90] Yet

the insurgents also won most of their goals in the end, either full independence for the Portuguese colonies or independence with a compromise peace
agreement in Namibia and Rhodesia. The burden of conducting a constant
low-level war eventually wore down the will and morale of the Portuguese,
Rhodesians, and South Africans. However, the Rhodesians and South Africans could, at the end, negotiate from a position of relative strength. Their
strategy, doctrine, and tactics had worked to keep their populations, especially the white settlers, relatively secure during the long war and their economies functioning fairly smoothly. The Rhodesian and South African strategy
of forward defense, taking the war across the borders, and striking the insurgent base camps and logistics centers was extremely effective. For little loss
the South Africans and Rhodesians were able on several occasions to inflict
shattering blows upon the insurgent forces.

For the most part, these were wars conducted on a shoestring with limited
resources and limited airpower assets — often converted civilian aircraft or
aircraft long regarded as obsolete by other Western powers, such as the C-47
transport and T-6 trainer. Little Portugal, with its small economy and population, was never in strategic position to even hope to hold on to its huge
African empire, and it is somewhat surprising that the Portuguese managed
to carry on for so long. A few highly competent military commanders made
most of the difference for Portugal's war. South Africa and Rhodesia waged
a far more effective war and set a high standard for effective counterinsurgency
operations. Both nations became very competent in planning and conducting highly complex joint operations combining airpower, light infantry, good
communications, and timely intelligence, although there was a fairly steep
learning curve at first. On the other hand, the Portuguese never reached a
high standard in conducting joint operations.

The South Africans and Rhodesians used their airpower resources with
great imagination and efficiency. Indeed, the nature of the war and the distances involved made aircraft central to the war effort of the governments.
The insurgents, as they usually do, learned to cope with the airpower of the
government forces and moved stealthily in small bands. Although the insurgents took heavy losses, they persisted and eventually won.

A Portuguese AF Fiat G.91R trainer. These 1950s jet trainers, acquired cheaply as German surplus, were deployed to Africa in 1966. They replaced the T-6s as the primary strike aircraft of the FAP. The Fiats, nicknamed "Ginas," carried four machine guns and two thousand pounds of bombs. They proved very effective as counterinsurgency aircraft. (Portuguese air force)

One of the B-26s bought clandestinely (to avoid the U.S. embargo) by the Portuguese in the mid-1960s to reinforce their handful of old PV-2 Harpoon bombers. Since the rebels did not have effective antiaircraft weapons until the early 1970s, the B-26 was able to operate as a strike aircraft. (Portuguese air force)

U.S.-built DC-6 transport of the Portuguese air force. The DC-6 could carry over fifty thousand pounds of cargo over long distances. The Portuguese were able to use the DC-6s to rush reinforcements from Portugal or from other colonies to meet crises. (Portuguese air force)

FAP C-47 transport. Since the C-47s could easily land on and operate from the hundreds of small, dirt airstrips the Portuguese built throughout Angola and Mozambique, the C-47s remained the primary short-distance transport of the Portuguese forces throughout the long conflict. (Portuguese air force)

T-6 "Harvard" of the SAAF. This World War II trainer was modified as patrol and light strike aircraft by the French and Portuguese air forces and proved very effective in that role. The T-6s flew in combat with the Portuguese until 1974. (Dean Wingrin, South African Air Force website; www.saairforce.co.za)

Member of Rhodesian army Grey's Scouts. The Rhodesians used mounted troops, backed up by helicopters, to patrol the long borders. (Tom Henshaw, Rhodesians at War website; www.geocities.com/ rhodesiansatwar)

First Rhodesian Light Infantry in a fireforce operation, 1973. The Alouette III helicopters, often flown by South African pilots, gave the small Rhodesian army tremendous mobility against the rebel forces. (Tom Henshaw, Rhodesians at War website; www.geocities.com/rhodesiansatwar)

Rhodesian fireforce deploying from an Alouette III. The helicopter-mounted Rhodesian fireforce units, backed by helicopter gunships, developed extremely effective tactics to track down and destroy insurgent bands. The Rhodesian fireforce units racked up a kill ratio of over fifteen to one. (Tom Henshaw, Rhodesians at War website; www.geocities.com/rhodesiansatwar)

SAAF Mirage F-1 CZ. The South African Mirage squadrons were able to engage and defeat the Cuban air force in several engagements in the 1980s. By holding on to air superiority over southern Angola, the South Africans were able to maintain forces north of their border and fight the guerrilla war mostly on Angolan territory. (Dean Wingrin, South African Air Force website; www.saairforce.co.za)

Sud Aviation Super Frelon helicopter of the SAAF. This was South Africa's heavy lifter in South West Africa and Angola. It could carry thirty soldiers or several tons of equipment. (Dean Wingrin, South African Air Force website; www.saairforce.co.za)

C-130 Hercules of the SAAF. South Africa maintained its forward bases on the Angolan border by airlift. C-130s flew in reinforcements and supplies, mostly by night, at treetop level to avoid rebel antiaircraft guns and missiles. (Dean Wingrin, South African Air Force website; www.saairforce.co.za)

SAAF "Bosbok" light utility plane. This Italian-designed plane proved useful in patrolling the remote bush country of South West Africa. (Dean Wingrin, South African Air Force website; www.saairforce.co.za)

SAAF "Impala" light strike fighter. Designed as a jet trainer, this is another example of a successful modification of a trainer into a light strike aircraft. This plane was used for attack missions in Angola and South West Africa. (Dean Wingrin, South African Air Force website; www.saairforce.co.za)

Because of international trade embargoes, South Africa was forced to develop a sophisticated arms and aircraft industry in order to fight in Angola and South West Africa. By the late 1980s, the South Africans had managed to develop a modern attack helicopter. The RVLK is shown here. (Dean Wingrin, South African Air Force website; www.saairforce.co.za)

Protracted Insurgencies
Latin American Air Forces in Counterguerrilla Operations

From the 1960s to the 1990s, Latin America experienced several major insurgencies in which airpower played a significant role. One of the most serious insurgencies, in Colombia, is ongoing at the time of this writing. Insurgency in Latin America has taken many forms. In South America, Uruguay and Argentina were rocked by largely urban-based Marxist insurgencies in the 1970s and 1980s. Peru faced a very powerful rural-based insurgency in the late 1980s and early 1990s; however, the arrest and imprisonment of the top rebel leaders largely ended the conflict. Colombia has faced insurgency problems of increasing severity for four decades.

Most of the countries of Central America have had insurgencies. A national uprising in 1979 overthrew the Nicaraguan dictatorship of the Somozas. The left-dominated Sandinista government that followed the Somozas was, in turn, opposed by the U.S.-supported "Contras," who carried on a guerrilla war until free elections were granted in 1990 — elections that a democratic coalition that included the Contras won. Honduras was plagued with some minor guerrilla troubles in the 1980s, and Mexico has seen revolts and low-level guerrilla war in its southern states since the mid-1990s.

There is not room in this chapter to cover all of the anti-insurgent campaigns in Latin America since the 1960s. Therefore, we have chosen to concentrate upon three large conflicts in the region: El Salvador, Guatemala, and Colombia. The civil war in El Salvador, which raged from 1980 to 1992, not only featured airpower in a leading role but also featured a large role for the United States, which supported the government against the insurgency. Guatemala was Central America's bloodiest and longest protracted war with a series of insurgencies from the early 1960s until a peace settlement in 1996.

Guatemala offers a case of a small country that refused more than token U.S. assistance and fought and defeated an insurgency mostly with its own resources. Colombia is very different from the Central American cases. It is a large and fairly prosperous South American nation with a strong democratic tradition and has faced a series of guerrilla insurgencies since the 1960s. At this time, the insurgent wars are threatening the fabric of the nation and beginning to spill over into the neighboring countries. Because of the large territory of Colombia and its relatively large resources and armed forces, airpower has played, and is likely to play, a central role in military operations against the two guerrilla forces plaguing the nation.

All of these wars have been important for the United States. In Latin America the success of Marxist/Maoist insurgent movements, as in Cuba and Nicaragua, has invariably caused a spillover effect and has encouraged economic disruption, violence, and insurgency in neighboring nations. Insurgency in Latin America means regional instability and becomes a strategic security problem for the United States. Indeed, Central America and the Caribbean is America's backyard, and trouble in this region affects the United States almost immediately — usually in the form of refugees fleeing to the United States and other Latin American nations. As one might expect, there has been a fair amount of interest in the U.S. government and military concerning insurgencies in this region. However, it is surprising that relatively little has been written in either English or Spanish on the operational military history of these civil wars or about the role of airpower in Latin American counterinsurgency. Part of the explanation is that these operations are recent, and there has not been enough time to analyze events and develop lessons from these conflicts. Another explanation for the lack of writing is the reluctance of the Central and South Americans to deal with their own recent military history. Some of these conflicts, especially Guatemala and El Salvador, were exceptionally cruel and bloody, and both sides committed human rights violations of the grossest nature. There is, understandably, a reluctance of the combatants of both sides to frankly describe the events of recent conflicts in order to avoid opening up deep political and social wounds. In Colombia the conflict is ongoing, and neither the government nor the rebels are likely to describe their doctrine, planning, and tactics in the course of an ongoing war. Much of the information about the air operations in this war is still classified by the U.S. military.

Faced with a general lack of documents concerning the conduct of these wars, this chapter mixes some journalism with history. Both of us have served in the U.S. armed forces in Latin America and been involved in training Latin American forces. Thus, the analysis in this chapter will be based partly upon our own experience as well as interviews and discussions with many of the participants in the conflicts who provided information and impressions but prefer not to be directly cited. However, when documents, books, and secondary sources are available, we have naturally used them.

El Salvador

The civil war in El Salvador, which lasted from 1980 to 1992, was one of the largest and bloodiest insurgencies that the Western Hemisphere has seen. During the twelve-year war, an estimated one hundred thousand people died — fairly horrendous losses for a country of only five million people.

The war in El Salvador saw significant involvement by the United States in the form of military and economic aid, advisers, and training. During the course of the war, the United States poured $4.5 billion of economic aid into the country and over $1 billion in military aid.[1] Almost a quarter of the U.S. military aid was provided to the Salvadoran air force.[2] Some aspects of the war in El Salvador and the U.S. involvement have been told in numerous books and publications.[3] Yet, although airpower played a major role in the conflict, its story has not been dealt with in any detail. Indeed, there are no books and only one major journal article specifically on the history of the Salvadoran air force during the war.[4] Considering that the Salvadoran war provides us with one of the most recent examples of the use of airpower in a counterinsurgency campaign, this is a significant gap in the literature about the use of airpower in modern warfare.[5]

BACKGROUND OF THE CONFLICT

In 1980, El Salvador was ripe for a major insurrection. It was a small, poor, and densely populated nation long dominated by a small oligarchy and ruled by a series of military governments that had little regard for civil rights. The infant mortality rate was high, and the lack of economic opportunity had pushed hundreds of thousands of Salvadorans across the border into Honduras in a search for land and jobs. Several Marxist and Maoist-oriented revo-

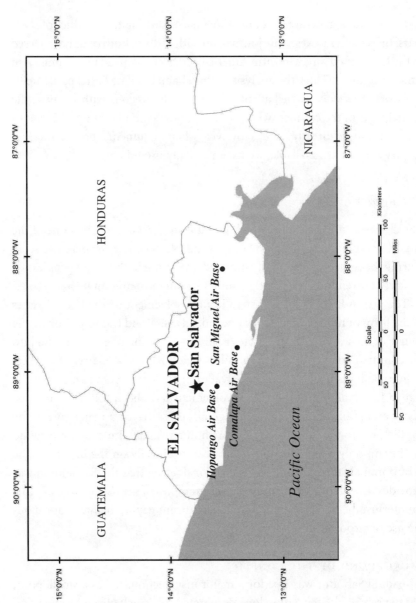

The War in El Salvador, 1980–1992

lutionary groups were already organized in the country. The events of 1979 would set the conditions for an open rebellion.[6]

The successful revolution by the Sandinistas against the Somoza regime in Nicaragua in 1979 provided encouragement to revolutionary movements in Central America. If such a powerful and oppressive regime could be brought down by a poorly equipped popular movement, then the oligarchy in El Salvador could also be brought down. Furthermore, the October 1979 coup that resulted in a new military government in El Salvador left that country in chaos. The Salvadoran armed forces were divided, with some officer factions favoring reforms and others violently opposed. As a result of chaos in the government and the unpopular state of the regime, guerrilla war broke out in 1980 and the major rebel factions amalgamated into one large alliance, the Marxist Farabundo Martí National Liberation Front (FMLN), which directed the insurgency. The various smaller factions, however, maintained their identity.

The rightist factions and parties in El Salvador, which included parts of the armed forces, reacted to the insurrection with a ruthless assassination program conducted by "death squads." Anyone suspected of leftist sympathies was liable to be abducted and shot. Dozens of murders by pro-government forces and militia were conducted nightly. Indeed, an estimated ten thousand people were killed in this manner in the first year of the war.[7] However, instead of suppressing the insurrection, the extreme violence by the regime pushed many more Salvadorans into open revolt. The violence escalated, and the Carter administration, in its disgust with the massive level of human rights violations, cut off U.S. economic and military aid. By January 1981, the rebels, who by this time numbered as many as ten thousand fighters, mounted a final offensive with the intent of occupying San Salvador and overthrowing the government. Alarmed at the very real possibility of insurgent victory, the Carter administration in its last days lifted the impounded military aid and authorized new aid.[8] As distasteful as the regime was in the U.S. view, it was preferable to another Marxist revolutionary government in Central America. The revolution in Nicaragua had alerted the United States and the other Central American nations who all feared a "domino effect." If El Salvador fell, then revolutions might also succeed in Guatemala and Honduras, and the Carter administration did not want Central America to collapse on its watch.

The rebel offensive in El Salvador made significant gains but failed to achieve victory in early 1981. The Carter administration was followed in that month by the conservative Reagan administration, which was ready to take a more active role against the expansion of communism in the hemisphere. In 1981 the Reagan administration made a commitment to assist El Salvador in defeating the most serious insurgency in the region.

THE STATE OF THE SALVADORAN ARMED FORCES IN 1981

El Salvador had small armed forces of approximately ten thousand military personnel and seven thousand paramilitary police in 1980 when the war began. The army, the largest part of the armed forces, had approximately nine thousand soldiers organized into four small infantry brigades, an artillery battalion, and a light armor battalion.[9] The level of training was low. The training that the army did have was all for conventional war — preparation for a replay of the short war with Honduras in 1969, where the army performed creditably. There was no training or preparation for fighting an insurgency.

The armed forces as a whole had severe leadership problems. The officer corps was disunited after the coup of October 1979. As in most armies in Central America, advancement and selection for command were based more upon political connections and sponsors than merit. In fact, there were no merit promotions in the Salvadoran army. All promotion was by seniority. While officers had gone through a cadet school and many had attended training in U.S. Army courses, they were not members of an especially capable officer corps. On the other hand, there was nothing even resembling a professional noncommissioned officer (NCO) corps in the Salvadoran forces. Most enlisted men were simply conscripted (or "press-ganged") young men, many of them in their midteens. If officer training was mediocre, the training of the enlisted men was minimal. In short, it was an army unready for a serious war. In comparison with the other branches of the armed forces, the Salvadoran air force — the Fuerza Aerea Salvadorena (FAS) — was the most professional service arm. It was a small force of under a thousand men consisting of a small paratroop battalion, a security force, a small antiaircraft unit, and four small flying squadrons with a grand total of sixty-seven aircraft. The main combat force of the FAS consisted of eleven Ouragan ground-attack fighters acquired from the Israelis, who had acquired them from the French in the 1950s, and four Fouga Magister trainers modified for combat (another 1950s aircraft). The combat squadrons also had six Rallye counterinsurgency aircraft. The rest of the air force consisted of a transport squadron with six

C-47s and four Arava transports. The training squadron consisted of a handful of T-34s, T-6s, T-41s, and four Magisters. The helicopter force amounted to one Alouette III, one FH-1100, one Lama, and ten UH-1s.[10]

The FAS had its primary air base at Ilopango on the outskirts of the capital, and there was a smaller base at San Miguel in the eastern part of the country that could handle light aircraft and helicopters. In 1982 a rotary-wing operating base (later concrete surfaced) was established at La Union in the east, and this became one of the most important bases in the war for the forward positioning of the air force and army. Another vital addition to the FAS infrastructure came on-line late in the war with the construction of a large new international airport at Comalapa, which also based military aircraft.

The training in the FAS was, like the army, geared for a conventional war. Unlike the army, the FAS had not done as well in the war with Honduras a decade before and had lost air superiority.[11] Since then, the only action the air force had seen was in the 1972 coup.[12] The air force had only a handful of pilots, and the pilot-training level was only fair. For a small and poor country like El Salvador, an air force is an expensive luxury. There were few funds for maintaining the obsolete aircraft of the force or for providing more than rudimentary combat training for the pilots. Things like joint training or practicing for close air support (CAS) were simply not part of the air force's repertoire.

THE REBELS HOLD THE INITIATIVE, 1981–1983

Although the rebel "final offensive" of early 1981 failed, the ten thousand rebels of the FMLN alliance held the initiative during the first three years of the war. Guerrillas held large areas of El Salvador's fourteen provinces (called departments).[13] The rebels were able to put significant forces into the field and fight an almost conventional war with battalion-sized columns. The insurgents were fairly well equipped and supplied with small arms (assault rifles and machine guns), as well as mortars, mines, and explosives. Cuba and Nicaragua supplied some FMLN weapons, but many of the rebels' weapons were captured from government troops. The rebels were, however, deficient in antiaircraft armament with only a few .50-caliber machine guns for protection against aircraft and helicopters.

Effective interdiction of supplies and arms to the rebels was not really possible. El Salvador shared a long land border with Honduras and Guatemala and was separated by only thirty miles of water from Sandinista Nicaragua at the Gulf of Fonseca. Light weapons and supplies could be brought in by land, sea, or air. The land borders were hard to seal, although the United States made a major effort in providing Honduran armed forces with aid and helicopters to help close the land border to gunrunners and rebel suppliers.[14] However, light aircraft could also bring arms and supplies into El Salvador at night from Nicaragua using small landing strips set up for crop dusters.[15] One of the FMLN leaders who later left the cause admitted the importance of the air routes from Nicaragua to El Salvador in supplying the insurgents.[16]

The whole country became the rebel infrastructure. Large areas of the mountains along the Honduran border were rebel territory in the early 1980s. The rebels also had several other strongholds under their control including the region around Mount Guazapa — only thirty miles from the capital of San Salvador. In the rural areas and small towns, the rebels could compel the local landowners and businessmen to provide food and pay taxes to the rebel forces — or face destruction of their property and assassination. In short, the rebels were largely self-sufficient for many of their needs.

Early in the war, the tendency of the El Salvadoran Armed Forces (ESAF) was to conduct sweeps in company and battalion strength. These tactics worked to the benefit of the rebels, who could pick an engagement with company-strength government units and then ambush the reinforcing column. Whole companies of the army were annihilated in this manner. The rebels also specialized in night operations — which nullified the Salvadoran air force and the firepower advantage of the army. In the early 1980s, relatively large rebel columns could even seize and hold towns for several days.

With the war going badly for the government, Brigadier General Fred Woerner, later commander of U.S. Southern Command, led a small group of U.S. military specialists to El Salvador for consultations with the Salvadoran government and military leaders. The result was eventually a national strategic plan for waging the war, which was approved by the United States and Salvadoran leadership.[17] Essentially, the U.S. policy was to emphasize land reform, political reform in the form of honest elections, economic development, and the end of human rights abuses. Most of the U.S. aid was to be civilian and financial aid. However, the military and economic aid to be provided to El Salvador would be dependent upon the willingness of the Salvadoran government and armed forces to go along with the reforms. If serious progress was not made on the issue of human rights, for example, then aid would be halted or delayed until satisfactory progress occurred.

The military strategy was to dramatically increase the size of El Salvador's armed forces and train the ESAF in counterinsurgency operations. Between 1980 and 1984, the ESAF more than tripled in size from twelve thousand troops to forty-two thousand troops.[18] The ESAF would be provided with modern weapons and equipment. Even basic equipment items, such as field radios for the army, were not available to government forces in 1980. Once the army was built up and retrained, a major portion of the counterinsurgency campaign would be carried out by specially trained "hunter" light infantry battalions. These light battalions would patrol aggressively and move quickly to keep the rebel columns under pressure.

Airpower was to have a major role in the national strategy for the El Salvadoran forces. The air force's planes were to be modernized and their numbers increased. Training and weaponry would be improved. However, the primary emphasis was to build up a large and capable helicopter force that could lift infantry companies and battalions for offensive operations and also provide helicopter gunship support. This type of mobility could provide a rapid reaction force to block and pin down rebel columns that engaged the ground troops.

The United States provided a total of $48,920,000 in military equipment sales, military equipment credits, and military aid to El Salvador in 1981.[19] In 1982, the military assistance and sales program for El Salvador grew to $82,501,000 with another $2,002,000 for the International Military Education and Training (IMET) program (officer and NCO training).[20] The portion of aid going to the Salvadoran air force was significant. A steady stream of new aircraft for the FAS flowed south throughout the conflict. In just the first six months of 1982, the United States delivered four O-2A aircraft for reconnaissance, six A-37B counterinsurgency fighters, and two C-123K transports. All of these aircraft had been fully modified and refurbished before being transferred. An additional $2 million worth of aerial munitions was provided for the FAS in 1982. As fast as equipment transfers were approved by the U.S. Congress, the U.S. Air Force (USAF) would rush the aircraft and munitions to El Salvador. In June 1982, the USAF sent twelve planeloads of munitions to the FAS while still more munitions went by sea.[21]

In 1982, the IMET program emphasized improving the Salvadoran air force. A total of $1.4 million was spent on pilot, aircrew, and technician training of Salvadorans in the United States.[22] The whole issue of training the Salvadorans, however, was complex and politically very sensitive. Because of strong opposition from liberals in the U.S. Congress who remembered how the United States had started in Vietnam with a small group of advisers, the administration imposed upon itself a strict limit to the number of military personnel that could be assigned to the U.S. Military Group (MilGroup) in El Salvador. Throughout the conflict, no more than 55 military personnel at any time could be assigned to the MilGroup.[23] With congressional committee acquiescence, additional U.S. military personnel could serve for brief periods on temporary assignment in El Salvador. Sometimes the total number of U.S. personnel in the country reached as high as 150. However, the nominal restriction of the MilGroup to only 55 meant that the permanent USAF contingent in El Salvador was only 5 people — 1 air force section chief who acted as the senior adviser to the FAS and 4 air force maintenance officers or instructor pilots.[24] The army also provided a few helicopter and munitions maintenance instructors to the Salvadoran air force, and some U.S. contract personnel (not on the MilGroup official strength) also assisted the FAS. However, this handful of Americans was not enough to make a serious impact on the training requirements of the FAS, so FAS personnel had to be trained outside their country in the United States or at the Inter-American Air Force Academy (IAAFA) at Albrook Field in Panama.

During the period from 1981 to 1984, as the ground and air forces of El Salvador were being retrained and reequipped by the United States, the FAS put in a combat performance that can be rated as fair. As small and poorly equipped as it was in 1981, it still represented the primary mobile firepower of the government. The FAS performed well in helping to stop the January 1981 offensive. However, it was limited in its ability to provide effective support to the army by the lack of training in the ESAF to effectively coordinate air/ground operations. The FAS was also essentially a daytime air force with a minimal ability to operate at night.

The FAS suffered a major blow in January 1982 when five Ouragans, six UH-1Bs, and three C-47s were destroyed and another five aircraft were badly damaged on the ground at Ilopango in a raid by one hundred rebel commandos. At one stroke, most of El Salvador's operational combat aircraft were knocked out of action.[25] It was a well-planned and -executed operation and demonstrated the tactical superiority of the FMLN guerrillas over the soldiers at this stage of the war. While this was counted as a major victory for the rebels, it was also something of a blessing for the FAS in the long term. The worn-out Ouragans destroyed by the commandos were quickly replaced by U.S.-provided A-37s, a far more capable and suitable aircraft for a counterinsurgency war. O-2 reconnaissance aircraft were also provided as well as twelve UH-1H helicopters to replace the losses.[26]

The FMLN strongholds along the Honduran border and in the south of El Salvador were simply too strong in the early 1980s for the government forces to attack directly. On the other hand, the Salvadoran forces were not about to allow the rebels' sanctuaries to operate freely within the borders of their own country. So in 1982 and 1983 the FAS began a program of bombing the rebel-held villages in the strongly FMLN regions of Chalatenango in the north and Mount Guazapa in the center of the country. What the air action amounted to was small harassment attacks in which flights of aircraft would regularly bomb and strafe the rebel areas in a desultory fashion. If no major military progress was made, at least the rebels were brought under some pressure.[27] Yet, the attacks seem to have made no real impact in terms of rebel morale, infrastructure, or combat capability. At the same time that the FAS began its bombing campaign — which it never actually acknowledged — the rebel forces managed to win a number of victories in the field, destroyed several army companies, and captured plenty of army weapons and ammunition.[28]

THE GOVERNMENT GAINS THE INITIATIVE, 1984–1988

By 1984, the U.S. military aid program was starting to pay off in terms of increased effectiveness of the government forces. While the rebel forces had not increased past ten thousand combatants, the Salvadoran army now outnumbered the rebels four to one. Moreover, new battalions had been formed and intensively trained by the U.S. Army in the United States, in Honduras, and in Panama, and then returned to El Salvador. These forces were ready to use a more aggressive strategy and take the war to the rebels. The FAS had also been strengthened, was better trained, and was ready to take on a larger role in airmobile operations and air support operations for the army.

Even so, 1984 started off badly for the government forces when a large rebel force managed to overrun and capture the army's Fourth Brigade headquarters at El Paraiso on New Year's Eve.[29] However, the army recovered from this setback, and throughout 1984 and 1985, government forces started to gain the initiative throughout the country. Airpower in the form of the A-37 fighters, helicopter gunships, and helicopter lift played a major role in the government's success. The FAS operational tempo increased notably. There had been a total of only 227 A-37 strikes in all of 1983. In June 1984 alone, there were 74 A-37 strikes.[30] The army went on the offensive in the spring of 1984 in order to protect the national elections from disruption by the FMLN. The UH-1H gunship missions were increased by three or four times their previous rate of operations during March to May 1984.[31] During 1984, U.S. military assistance enabled the FAS to increase its helicopter inventory from nineteen at the start of the year to forty-six by year's end.[32] The air attacks on the rebel strongholds surged throughout 1984 and 1985 despite stricter rules of engagement issued by President Jose Napoléon Duarte in September 1984.[33]

According to former FMLN leaders, the improvement of the FAS played a major role in turning the initiative over to the government forces. The U.S.-supplied O-2 light reconnaissance planes covered the country thoroughly, and the rebels could no longer operate relatively openly in large columns. Larger formations made lucrative targets that could be easily spotted from the air and then subjected to attacks by aircraft or heliborne troops.[34] Instead, rebel forces operated in smaller columns, which would combine for larger operations such as the attack on El Paraiso.[35] Rebel forces had to stay on the move, making it more difficult for them to coordinate several columns to participate in an operation. However, the rebels learned to adapt to the increased danger of aerial attack. After the FAS was able to successfully insert company-sized reaction forces to deal with FMLN attacks, the FMLN — like the Viet Cong before them — learned to spot likely helicopter landing zones and prepare them for ambush.[36]

The Salvadorans by the mid-1980s had built up a group of small, well-trained elite units. Some functioned as light infantry patrol forces that could be inserted by helicopter to search out the enemy and establish outposts deep in enemy territory. If contact with the rebels was made, the FAS could quickly transport company-sized forces to reinforce the light troops and block rebel units. The helicopter force was the only practical means of transporting troops in much of the country because of mountainous terrain and the bad roads. With effective reconnaissance and light heliborne forces, the government could, for the first time in the war, initiate combat at places of its own choosing.[37]

One of the U.S. advisers rated the FAS as "particularly effective" in the government operations of 1984 and 1985.[38] One of the most important events in the air war came in late 1984 to 1985, when the United States supplied two AC-47 gunships to the FAS and trained aircrews to operate the system.[39] The AC-47 gunship carried three .50-caliber machine guns and could loiter for hours and provide heavy firepower for army operations. As the FAS had long operated C-47s, it was easy for the United States to train pilots and crew to operate the aircraft as a weapons platform. By all accounts, the AC-47 soon became probably the most effective weapon in the FAS arsenal.

The tempo of aid to the FAS increased during 1984 and 1985. Five O-2A aircraft were delivered between September and November 1984. Two more O-2As and two O-2Bs along with three A-37s were prepared for delivery in early 1985, along with an additional five C-47 transports that had been modified and refurbished for the FAS at a cost of almost one million dollars each.[40] However, the increased flow of aircraft to the FAS in 1984 and 1985 did not result in a rapid increase in the number of aircraft available for combat, as the attrition rate from operational accidents was heavy. For example, in early 1994, an O-2A and one C-123K were lost to accidents.[41] However, the United States tried to replace aircraft as soon as they were lost. For example, a replacement C-123K was on the way from the United States within a month of the loss of the FAS C-123 transport.[42]

The United States also increased the training funds available to the FAS during 1984. In 1984, 117 FAS personnel took courses at the Inter-American Air Force Academy in Panama, in contrast to 98 personnel the year before. The IMET program funded training for 118 Salvadorans in the United States in 1984.[43] U.S. military aid was also committed to building up the infrastructure of the FAS. The FAS received $16.4 million in assistance funds in 1984, some of which went to building new hangars and repair shops at the main air base at Ilopango. By the mid-1980s, Ilopango had become a well-equipped air base.[44]

Despite all the training and expense, the FAS remained hampered by the exceptionally low operational readiness rate of its aircraft. While the FAS could muster well over one hundred aircraft by 1985, only 50 percent or fewer of the aircraft were operational at any time because of severe maintenance problems and a shortage of qualified pilots.[45] The helicopter readiness rate was lower than that of airplanes. The FAS was only able to maintain a small proportion of its helicopter inventory at any one time.[46] The FAS suffered continually from a lack of competent mechanics. Part of this is a cultural disdain for maintenance found in the Central American officer corps. The pay and conditions for the enlisted mechanics in the FAS were poor, and the most talented maintenance personnel would leave to find much higher-paying civilian jobs as soon as their term of enlistment was up. An even more serious problem was the pilot shortage. The pilot officers of the FAS had to be graduates of the military academy, and with the rapid expansion of the armed forces, there were not enough graduates to meet the needs of all the services. Even with a serious training effort by the United States, the FAS had only about half the pilots it needed. In 1987, the FAS had only seventy active pilots for 135 aircraft.[47]

With a slowly growing capacity to airlift troops by helicopter, the FAS and its airborne reaction force began to make a real impact in the war. In June 1984, an FMLN force attacked the Cerron Grande Dam, El Salvador's largest hydroelectric plant. Two companies were quickly airlifted to reinforce the small garrison at Cerron Grande. The rebel attack was successfully beaten back, albeit with heavy losses.[48] However, the FMLN also proved that it would not be easily cowed by the FAS's firepower. In October 1984, six hundred FMLN insurgents attacked an army "hunter" battalion. The guerrillas were attacked by aircraft that inflicted heavy casualties on the rebels. Still, the FMLN troops persisted in the attack, and by afternoon, the army battalion had simply disintegrated.[49]

The wider use of helicopters in support of the ground campaigns also resulted in heavy losses for the FAS. In the October 1984 fighting, one UH-1 was shot down. In November of that year, three more UH-1s were shot down and four heavily damaged in the fighting around Suchitoto.[50] While the A-37s and the AC-47 gunships proved to be relatively safe from enemy ground fire, the small arms of the FMLN proved to be lethal against helicopters.

Throughout 1985 and 1986, ground and air operations increased, while the competence of the army in counterinsurgency warfare continued to improve. In 1985 and early 1986, the FAS aircraft and helicopters supported several large army offensives, which finally reduced some of the FMLN's major strongholds in Guazapa and Chalatenango. The population and the rebel forces in these enclaves were bombed heavily as army troops swept in and forcibly evacuated thousands of civilians in FMLN areas and resettled them in refugee camps. It was a harsh campaign, but it succeeded in depriving the FMLN units of their civilian infrastructure in what had been their most secure strongholds.[51]

One of the FMLN leaders credits the greater airmobility of the army in the mid-1980s and the willingness of some army units to move by air deep into rebel country as having caused "a very significant turn in the war."[52] However, it should also be noted that the improvement of the air force's and army's tactics and firepower was not the primary cause for the demoralization of the FMLN alliance in the mid-1980s. The rebels were just as capable as the government of making major strategic and tactical mistakes. By 1984, the infighting within the FMLN groups became severe and, in true communist fashion, was resolved by purges and executions within the ranks of the FMLN. Soon FMLN leaders were ordering the killing of rival leaders. By 1984 and 1985, the membership of the FMLN began to decline as the rebel forces saw some of their own officers abandon the FMLN cause in disgust.[53] Yet, despite the internal dissension, being outnumbered six or seven to one, and under steady pounding by army and air force firepower, the FMLN was still a formidable force by the end of 1988 and could still field approximately seven thousand combatants throughout the country.

FROM STALEMATE TO PEACE, 1989–1992

By 1988, the government of El Salvador could bring a tremendous superiority of military power against the rebels. The army had grown to forty-three thousand troops organized into six brigades. There were twenty light infantry battalions and six counterinsurgency battalions that were able to take the war to the enemy. The artillery force had been tripled since the start of the war and communications and support improved. The tiny 1980 navy of three patrol craft had been expanded to a fifteen-hundred-man force by 1988 and included a marine battalion, marine commandos, and thirty patrol craft.

The FAS had more than doubled in size since the start of the war. By 1987, the FAS was a force of twenty-five hundred with an airborne battalion, a security group, five airplane squadrons, and a large helicopter force. The airplane force was organized into a fighter squadron, with eight Ouragans, a counterinsurgency squadron with ten A-37Bs, and two AC-47 gunships. A reconnaissance squadron of eleven O-2As supported the counterinsurgency squadron. The transport squadron consisted of five C-47s, one DC-6, three Aravas, and two C-123Ks. The training squadron had one T-41 and six CM-170 Magisters. The helicopter force had expanded into a force of nine Hughes 500MD attack helicopters, fourteen UH-1H gunships, thirty-eight UH-1H utility helicopters, three SA-315 Lamas, and three SA-316 Alouette IIIs, for a total of sixty-seven helicopters.[54]

Progress in El Salvador's internal political situation had been made since the mid-1980s after free elections and the election of a moderate reformer, José Napoleon Duarte, as president. Human rights abuses by the armed forces had been curbed. U.S. aid was continuing to flow. Throughout the mid-1980s, the direct U.S. military role had grown especially in the aviation side of the war. U.S. Army OV-1 Mohawk reconnaissance planes of the Twenty-fourth Military Intelligence Battalion stationed in Palmerola Air Base in Honduras conducted regular reconnaissance flights over El Salvador.[55] The counter-insurgency campaign progressed, and the election of the right wing Arena Party government in 1989, a party that ran on a "law and order" platform, indicated that there was considerable support among the populace for the counterinsurgency campaign.

This impression of progress was spoiled on 11 November 1989, when the FMLN guerrillas launched a surprise offensive against military and civilian targets across the nation. For three weeks, the guerrillas attacked military units and government installations in San Salvador, San Miguel, Santa Ana, and other cities. The entire northern arc of San Salvador was occupied and fortified by the rebels. In the fighting that followed, the military incurred heavy losses, but the FMLN sustained heavy losses as well. The FMLN re-portedly suffered 1,773 dead and 1,717 wounded by the end of the offensive on 5 December.[56] The rebels had hoped to demoralize the government in a grand show of strength right in the capital. They also hoped that the working-class Salvadorans would join the uprising. The rebels were surprised by the determination of the government when the air force employed helicopter gunships and attack aircraft against urban targets, causing heavy civilian ca-sualties. Even middle-class neighborhoods were not spared if resistance to government forces was met. In most respects, the 1989 offensive was a de-feat for the rebels. Working-class Salvadorans who might have felt sympa-thy for the FMLN were angry with the rebels for bringing the full force of the war to their doorsteps.[57] Ironically, the rebel offensive sped the peace process along. The government was made painfully aware that the FMLN still fielded a large and dangerous force even after years of government suc-cess on the battlefield. The rebels learned that the government had the ruthlessness necessary to fight the war and that it also had the forces and competence to indefinitely forestall a rebel takeover. With the war at a stale-mate, peace talks were renewed.

A further disturbing development for the air war in 1989 was the acquisition of handheld SAM-7 antiaircraft missiles by the rebels.[58] The attrition of FAS helicopters to the light weapons of the rebels had been heavy all through the war. However, until 1989, the A-37s and AC-47s had been relatively immune from the short-range ground fire of the FMLN. Now the guerrillas had a weapon that could knock down the best combat aircraft of the FAS.

The war continued into 1990, and the FMLN was still able to conduct numerous guerrilla attacks against the armed forces and economic targets despite the heavy losses of the 1989 offensive. In 1990, the FMLN forces inflicted over two thousand casualties on the Salvadoran armed forces and police, an almost 5 percent casualty rate.[59] By this time, the nation was simply exhausted by more than a decade of war. Both sides finally agreed to serious peace talks in 1990. A national cease-fire was agreed to in 1991, and peace accords were signed between the government and the FMLN in early 1992.

The war was ended by a compromise solution. The FMLN disarmed its forces and became a legal political party. Amnesty was granted to FMLN members. More than half of the army would be demobilized, and all of the paramilitary security forces — including the notorious Treasury Police, which operated under the Defense Ministry and was identified as having one of the worst human rights records — were disbanded. A new national police force was created, and former FMLN guerrillas were brought in. United Nations and Organization of American States observers remained in the country to help ensure that the disarmament was properly carried out and free and fair elections were held.[60]

Some of the American commentators would complain that the military strategy had failed and that the Salvadoran armed forces were never able to defeat the FMLN on the battlefield. That might be true, but in retrospect, the program of military aid to El Salvador was a genuine success for the United States. The primary objective of keeping El Salvador from becoming a communist state was realized. Moreover, El Salvador ended the war with a democratic government that remains friendly to the United States and committed to working peacefully with its neighbors. The peace accord may have been a compromise, but it has been recognized as fair by both sides and provides a solid basis for peacefully developing El Salvador — and a favorable peace is, after all, the primary objective in waging war.

THE PROBLEM OF INTERNAL POLITICS

The military culture of El Salvador was not only authoritarian and corrupt; it was also highly politicized. Despite training and advice from the United States, old habits were very hard to break. The internal politics of the armed forces played a large role not only in appointing officers to command, but also in the way the war was fought.

General Juan Rafael Bustillo, who served as the chief of the FAS from 1979 to 1989, was a competent pilot and probably one of the more capable senior officers in El Salvador when the war started. However, he also played a highly political role in the armed forces and used his position as air force commander to defy and even threaten the civilian government. In 1983, one of the most right wing of the army officers, Colonel Sigfrido Ochoa, demanded the firing of defense minister General José Guillermo Garcia and declared his military district to be in rebellion against the government. General Bustillo supported Ochoa and refused to fly in troops to oppose him. Eventually, a compromise was worked out that allowed Ochoa to remain but removed the defense minister.[61]

As was typical with the senior military leadership in El Salvador, the FAS under Bustillo was scarcely a meritocracy. An officer's politics and connections tended to count for more in promotions and gaining coveted assignments than competence on the battlefield. It was alleged by army officers that Bustillo often reserved the helicopter force for the air force paratroop battalion and tended to give air support to army units commanded by his friends while withholding air support from units commanded by his rivals.[62] There is also considerable evidence that U.S. military aid funds were diverted to an FAS slush fund. In 1989, the U.S. General Accounting Office found that the FAS had sold more than one hundred thousand dollars worth of U.S.-supplied aviation fuel to the Nicaraguan Contras in violation of U.S. rules.[63] For years, the FAS DC-6 that carried pilots and cargo to Howard Air Force Base, Panama, returned full of liquor and appliances, which were sold on the black market.[64]

Unfortunately, in a military culture such as El Salvador's, such behavior was to be expected. It is also argued that the United States tolerated this behavior and the diversion of funds because General Bustillo allowed the Ilopango Air Base to become the hub of the U.S. National Security Council's supply network for the support of the anti-Sandinista rebels in Nicaragua. Some 109 clandestine flights for Contra support shuttled in and out of

Ilopango.[65] In any case, Americans who become involved in supporting counterinsurgency campaigns need to be ready to face the political friction generated from within the armed forces of a Third World state.

THE BOMBING DILEMMA

The most controversial aspect of the air war in El Salvador was the bombing of civilians by the FAS. From 1981 to 1986, the FAS regularly bombed the rebel-controlled areas of the country, especially the strongholds of the Guazapa and Chalatenango regions. The bombing campaign was virtually the only means to keep the rebels under pressure in these areas until they were overrun and occupied by government troops in the campaigns of 1985 and 1986. The air attacks, carried out primarily by the A-37s, but also by helicopter gunships, were aimed at villages that supported the rebels. Civilian casualties were a consequence of the campaign. Sometimes the Salvadoran forces were open about the bombing campaign. Colonel Ochoa, commander in the Chalatenango district, told the U.S. press that he had declared a dozen free-fire zones in his area and that anything in those areas would be presumed hostile and bombed.[66]

Both the critics and supporters of the government of El Salvador provided testimony about the bombing of civilians to the U.S. Congress that was so propagandistic as to border on the absurd. On the left, American critics testified about the brutality of the FAS. For example, the mayor of Berkeley, California, testified in 1986 that sixty thousand civilians had already been killed by aerial bombardment in El Salvador — an extremely implausible figure.[67] On the right, Assistant Secretary of State Elliot Abrams rounded up testimony that was just as implausible. Abrams argued that there had been no indiscriminate bombing in El Salvador, despite the admissions made by Salvadoran officers.[68] Others supporting Abrams's view provided the U.S. Congress with anecdotes about FAS pilots complaining that they were denied permission to attack rebel troop concentrations because of the fear that civilians might be caught in the cross fire.[69] It was even argued that the AC-47 gunships were used so carefully in battle that in the course of the war they never fired a short round or even accidentally hit civilians.[70] If true, this is a record for accuracy in aerial warfare that far surpasses the competence of the United States or any other major air force.

In reality, the bombing campaign was neither so brutal as the critics alleged nor as careful of civilians as the U.S. State Department argued. The bombing campaign seems to have had no decisive results aside from harassing the insurgents and forcing the FMLN units to remain dispersed. According to witness accounts and U.S. journalists who traveled in the rebel-held areas, the air attacks caused relatively few civilian casualties. Civilians who lived in the free-fire zones quickly adapted to being the targets of aerial bombardment. They dug bomb shelters, learned to camouflage their homes, and took cover as soon as a helicopter, an A-37, or an O-2 reconnaissance aircraft was spotted.[71] The best casualty estimates are provided by Tutela Legal, the human rights office of the Catholic Church in El Salvador. This organization estimated that in 1985, a year of heavy combat, 371 civilians had been killed by air bombardment.[72] Since the air attacks in civilian areas were carried out between 1981 and 1986, an estimate of approximately two thousand civilians killed by air bombardment for the course of the war is probably close.

In El Salvador, both sides conducted campaigns designed essentially to assassinate, maim, and terrorize civilians. As for an assessment of the FAS's bombing campaign of civilian areas, it probably had some effect in harassing and disrupting the rebel strongholds, but it is doubtful that these benefits of the bombing campaign were greater than the considerable propaganda benefits that the rebels gained by being portrayed as victims of a repressive government in the international media.[73]

ASSESSMENT

Most insurgencies tend to last for years. In Malaya, the British faced a twelve-year-long insurgency (1948–1960). In the Philippines, the United States supported the Philippine government through an eight-year campaign (1946–1954). Colombia has faced an insurgency for more than twenty years. The twelve-year duration of the war in El Salvador fits the typical pattern. Mao's teachings notwithstanding, neither the insurgents nor governments that oppose them usually expect a campaign of many years' duration. The FMLN intended to win quickly in 1981. The government thought that the rebels could be crushed in a rapid campaign. General Woerner shocked the chairman of the Joint Chiefs of Staff and some members of the Reagan administration in his 1981 report when he outlined a five-year plan (the five-year time frame was used as an outline only, and Woerner was careful not to predict the length of the war) and estimated that defeating the rebels would cost three hundred million dollars in military aid. Woerner's analysis was seen as unduly pessimistic.[74]

Part of the problem in conducting a counterinsurgency campaign is the long lead time in creating and training military and police forces that can effectively wage a counterinsurgency campaign. As is typical with countries that face insurgencies, El Salvador was unprepared. Even with massive U.S. support for a small country, it took three or four years before the Salvadoran armed forces could conduct operations effectively. Air forces in particular require a long time to build infrastructure, acquire equipment, and train pilots to operate in the kind of joint operations required by counterinsurgency campaigns. It did not help that the U.S. Army and Air Force, suffering from the effects of post-Vietnam syndrome, had largely dropped counterinsurgency operations out of their doctrine and training repertoire in the late 1970s. Despite the many Vietnam veterans in the force, the U.S. military was not ready to train the Salvadorans in unconventional warfare. The bureaucratic requirements of the U.S. military system also got in the way of a timely response to El Salvador's situation. The requirement that foreign pilots training with the U.S. Air Force first take a six-month language course slowed down the pilot training program for the Salvadorans. Finally, when the shortage of helicopter pilots became truly severe, the U.S. Army conducted a one-time effort at Fort Rucker, Alabama, to train Salvadoran pilots with Spanish-speaking flight instructors.[75] Ideally, the FAS pilots and technicians should have been fluent in English, if only to read the technical manuals for the equipment. However, the immediate needs of the war overruled this requirement.

For various reasons, U.S. military schools were slow to create the courses that the Salvadoran military urgently needed. For example, the U.S.-run Inter-American Air Force Academy in Panama only initiated an advanced training course for the A-37B in 1985 — three years after that model aircraft had been supplied to the FAS.[76]

Most commentators on the war in El Salvador agree that by the mid-1980s, the FAS could operate fairly effectively. However, the ability to conduct more complex joint operations came very slowly. It was not until the period from 1986 to 1987 that the FAS intelligence section was reorganized for the needs of the counterinsurgency operations and a special analysis center was set up at the FAS headquarters at Ilopango. The center was able to integrate reconnaissance, area intelligence investigations, aerial photography, and special intelligence into one coherent system. This had much to do with the improvement of FAS combat capabilities.[77]

THE EFFECT OF U.S. AID RESTRICTIONS

At the start of the war, human rights abuses by the Salvadoran armed forces and government were so bad, and the government so mired in its traditional authoritarian culture, that the U.S. government had no realistic choice but to use a carrot-and-stick approach in providing military and economic aid to El Salvador. The military and the government would be encouraged to reform by the offer of generous aid. If reforms were not enacted quickly enough, the aid would be withheld or delayed. Thus, the aid to El Salvador was made contingent upon a program of national land reform, fair elections, and judicial reforms.[78] This approach by the United States caused constant friction between the two governments, but in the end, it pushed the government to make necessary reforms.

However, aid restrictions and the strong objections of many U.S. congressmen toward aid to El Salvador's armed forces resulted in unpredictable funding in the military aid program. This, in turn, inhibited long-term planning and resulted in many inefficiencies in the military aid.[79] Fiscal year 1983 began with no congressional appropriations for El Salvador. A $25 million continuing resolution was provided instead of the $60 million that the U.S. military support program required. Without adequate funds in the ammunition account, the army and FAS cut back operations and maintained a policy of hoarding ammunition and supplies until a continuation of the aid flow was assured.[80]

In the case of a small and poor country like El Salvador, such funding disputes had a major impact upon operations and doctrine. El Salvador's leaders were encouraged to look on an expensive asset such as the air force as too valuable to risk in combat if replacements, munitions, and funds were not assured. In the first half of the war, the attitude existed that the FAS was an "insurance policy" for the government. One might not win the war with airpower, but airpower would keep one from losing. Therefore, the air force was sometimes held back as a reserve for use only in emergencies.[81] Although a practical doctrine from the view of the Salvadorans, this was not a way to conduct effective joint operations in the field or keep the rebels under constant pressure.

The most problematic restrictions on the U.S. military aid program for El Salvador were those governing the military trainers and advisers in the country. The MilGroup throughout the war was limited to a total of only fifty-five advisers in order to deflect disapproval of a Congress worried about another Vietnam. With so few advisers and trainers in the country, the U.S. military had to create numerous expensive and inefficient work-arounds to train the Salvadoran army and air force outside the country. Some troops were trained, at enormous expense, at Fort Bragg, North Carolina. A new training center had to be built in Honduras, where U.S. Army trainers could train whole battalions of the Salvadoran army.[82] Salvadoran air force pilots had to do virtually all their training outside their country. However, when the pilots returned, there was virtually no infrastructure to enable them to maintain proficiency or develop advanced skills. Because of the shortage of pilots and the variety of aircraft models flown by the FAS, each pilot had to be able to fly three or four types of aircraft. As a result, the FAS pilots could not become truly proficient in any one aircraft.[83] Another serious problem was the lack of qualified instructor pilots in the FAS to oversee individual and unit training. This translated into a high accident rate and only a fair level of competence for the average FAS pilot.[84]

One very clear lesson from the war in El Salvador is the need for a far larger number of U.S. trainers and advisers to be present in the country in order to effectively support a country at war. An adviser/instructor group sent in early to support the FAS would have been far more effective in improving the combat efficiency of the force and would have been far less expensive than all of the training work-arounds that the United States had to improvise to train the FAS. An early commitment of instructor pilots and maintenance instructors would have improved the operability rate of the FAS and brought it to a respectable level of combat capability in one to two years instead of the three to five years that it actually took.

THE OPERATIONAL EFFECTIVENESS OF AIRPOWER IN EL SALVADOR

Airpower played an important role in the Salvadoran civil war. The air force was used primarily as an army support force, and certain weapon systems proved very successful for this mission. The low-tech O-2 spotter aircraft and the AC-47 gunships were used effectively by the FAS in close support operations. The slow, easy-to-fly A-37, a modified trainer, carried a moderate bomb load and machine-gun armament. It was not a heavy weapons system, but it still gave the army a major firepower advantage in battle with the lightly armed rebels. It proved very survivable in the low-threat counterinsurgency environment.[85] The AC-47 was one of the real success stories of the war. These easy-to-operate weapons were probably about as much as the Salvadoran pilots, aircrew, and support personnel could effectively handle at the time.

Of the aircraft supplied by the United States to the FAS during the war, the most effective was probably the UH-1 helicopters used for medevac and troop-lift. Even though the operability rate was low, the limited lift was essential for transport in a mountainous country with few roads. The next most useful aircraft were the O-2 light reconnaissance planes, which forced the rebels to operate in smaller columns and start a move out of the rural strongholds and back to the cities. The third most useful aircraft of the war was the AC-47, the only truly accurate and reliable CAS weapon. The A-37 fighter comes way down on the list of useful aircraft simply because it was hard to bomb accurately with it, and the training levels of the FAS pilots were rarely up to where they could reliably and accurately provide close air support.[86]

Probably the most effective single air unit in the war was the five medevac helicopters of the FAS, coupled with the improved medical care for the Salvadoran army made possible through the U.S. aid program. The availability of rapid medevac as well as good medical care cannot be underestimated as a major factor in improving the morale and fighting ability of the army. Soldiers fight much harder if they know they are likely to survive their wounds. Even though the army took more casualties thanks to the increased level of combat in 1985, there were fewer fatalities due to helicopter medevac operations.[87]

However, airpower in a low-intensity conflict has its downside. Air forces are very expensive for small countries to man and operate. The FAS soaked up a disproportionate share of the aid and defense budget, yet its real capabilities were very limited due to the low operational rate of aircraft, the shortage of pilots, and the deficiencies in training. Certainly through most of the war, the FAS was not employed very efficiently against the enemy. An array of U.S. Army officers who served in El Salvador, as well as a USAF-sponsored RAND study, all expressed misgivings about the large number of helicopters as well as the heavy equipment provided to the Salvadorans. These military critics of our military policy argued that the Salvadoran army and air force were trying to become a mini U.S. Army and Air Force and were trying to substitute airpower for basic military skills — a very dangerous strategy for a poor country with few resources. The large airmobile force that the United States supplied to El Salvador was likely to make the army behave much as the United States had done in Vietnam, with the army flying over the population rather than working on the ground and operating closely with the civilian population. What was needed, it was argued, was a greater emphasis on training more ground troops and saturating the country with light infantry forces that are always patrolling and always present. If one has limited resources to allocate, the counterinsurgency experience of the last fifty years would tend to support a policy of greater numbers of ground troops and a pervasive presence over a smaller army with more technology.

Of course, the U.S. military is not alone in preferring high-tech solutions. The FAS, which could barely operate and maintain the A-37s, AC-47s, and UH-1Hs it was equipped with, requested that the United States provide F-5 fighters and AH-1 Cobra gunships.[88] So enamored was the Salvadoran army with the airmobility concept that its leaders insisted on buying the much more expensive air-transportable 105 mm howitzers from the United States instead of the very capable — and much cheaper — heavier and older model. It was probably a blessing for the Salvadoran forces that their plans for a relatively high-tech airmobile force never came to fruition. By the mid-1980s, they hoped to have a helicopter force large enough to airlift at least a battalion anywhere in the country. However, the low operational rate and the pilot shortage ensured that the high command never could deploy more than a company or two at a time. Like it or not, the Salvadoran army had to learn to be an infantry force.

Guatemala's Protracted War

Guatemala, Central America's largest and most populous nation, experienced a series of major insurgencies from the 1990s to 1996 when a peace accord was signed between the government and the major guerrilla groups. Guatemala is a classic case of revolutionary warfare. From the early days of independence Guatemala had been ruled by a small and powerful oligarchy of landowners and businessmen. The social divisions were enormous and exacerbated by the fact that about half of the population was ethnically Indian, lived in a tribal society, spoke Indian languages, and maintained a culture highly distinct from the Ladino half of population. The Ladinos, usually a mix of Indian and Spanish blood but European in culture, religion, and language, had been the ruling caste in Guatemala since the days of the conquistadors

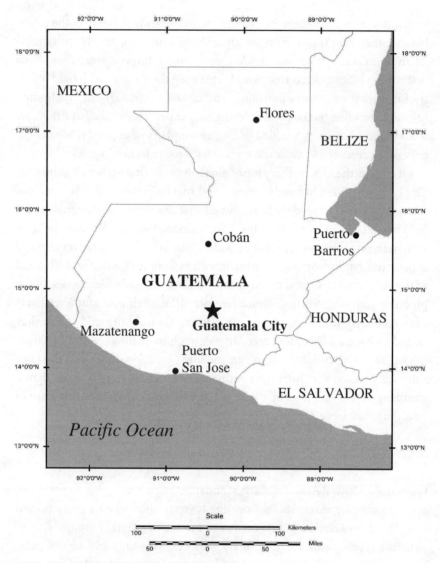

The War in Guatemala, 1960–1996

and looked down on the Indian population, with the great landowners often keeping the Indian villages in virtual peonage.[89]

Guatemala's revolutionary history rightly begins in 1954 when a left wing government that wanted to initiate land reform was overthrown in a coup sponsored by the American CIA. The United States viewed the reform program of the Arbenz government as the harbinger of communist revolution in the region. In 1960 a coup by leftist army officers was quickly suppressed and the culprits kicked out of the army. The ex-officers who had participated in the 1960 coup reorganized themselves into a revolutionary party in 1962 and sought assistance from Fidel Castro. In January 1963 they initiated a rebellion as the Revolutionary Armed Forces (Fuerza Armada Revolucionario — FAR) and began a rebellion in three departments (in Central America a department is a political region — something like an American county): San Marcos in the northwest and Izabal and Zacapa in the northeast.

In the 1960s the guerrilla war in Guatemala caught the attention of the U.S. government, which poured considerable military aid into Guatemala to support the rightist government. Guatemala became the focus of the U.S. military counterinsurgency operations in Central America in the 1960s. Hundreds of U.S. Special Forces soldiers were brought into the country to train and advise the army. By the mid-1960s Guatemala's small armed forces had been retrained as a light infantry, counterinsurgency force. The Guatemalan air force (Fuerza Aerea Guatemala — FAG) was also trained and organized to fight the counterinsurgency effort. Despite the reorganization and retraining of the army under American supervision, Guatemala retained a military culture much like that of El Salvador at the outbreak of its civil war. Guatemala was an authoritarian and highly polarized society, and rule by a military-led oligarchy had been the normal means of government for decades. As with El Salvador, and in common with most of Central and South America at the time, the officer corps was highly politicized and promotion was usually more a matter of belonging to the right faction rather than demonstrated professionalism. Another attitude in common with El Salvador was the deep-seated contempt for human rights in the military and a military tradition of suppressing dissent with a harsh hand rather than allowing for political debate and compromise. It should have been no surprise that political dissidents in the 1960s and 1970s turned to violence rather than attempt peaceful means to change their society. Nor is it surprising

that such insurgencies enjoyed a high degree of support from the population — especially the rural poor.

THE GUATEMALAN AIR FORCE

In the early 1960s, Guatemala had a small air force of a few hundred men and
a few dozen aircraft composed of World War II surplus trainers, P-51 Mus-
tang fighters, B-26 bombers, and some C-47 transports — pretty much the
usual force for Central America in those days.[90] As with El Salvador, the
Guatemalan air force was the most professionally competent of all the services. Still, throughout the course of the conflict from the 1960s until the peace
agreement of 1996, the training of the Guatemalan air force pilots and personnel can only be described as barely adequate. When the insurgency began
in 1963 the air force supported the army with its P-51s and B-26s. At the same
time, the United States supplied four T-33 jet trainers as part of a comprehensive modernization program for the FAG. The P-51s of the FAG were rapidly wearing out and becoming a maintenance nightmare, and the T-33s, based
on the F-80 fighter that had seen action as a fighter-bomber in the Korean
War, were seen as suitable aircraft for a low-level insurgency. By late 1963 the
new T-33s were put into service as attack aircraft. At this stage of the war, the
T-33 pilots were not trained as attack pilots and had to learn to conduct rocket,
bomb, and strafing attacks literally "on the job."[91] At the outset of the rebellion, against the counsel of American advisers, the FAG acquired two more
P-51s from an American dealer to serve as fighter-bombers. Despite the maintenance problems, the old propeller fighters were still excellent aircraft for
counterinsurgency, able to carry a lot of ordnance and to loiter over a battle
area for a long time. The major disadvantage of the T-33, aside from it being
thoroughly mediocre as a fighter-bomber, was that it was relatively expensive to operate. However, in 1964, the FAG received two more T-33s from the
U.S. military aid program.

By 1965 the insurgency had expanded and now covered several departments. The United States delivered another pair of T-33s as well as four armed
Sikorsky UH-19B helicopters, the first military helicopters in Central America.
This provided the Guatemalan forces with an air assault capability.[92] The
Sikorskys were soon equipped with two .30-caliber machine guns and two
2.7-inch rocket pods for gunship support.[93] By 1966, a rearmed and now well-
trained Guatemalan army was ready to undertake major operations against

the insurgents. Under the guidance of U.S. advisers, the FAG reorganized its combat aircraft into "Special Warfare Composite Squadrons" composed of two to three Mustangs, one to two T-33s, a B-26, a UH-19B, and a pair of C-47 transports with their own contingent of pilots and ground crews.[94] The Guatemalan air force, with considerable U.S. assistance, initiated a large-scale bombing campaign against rebel-held areas in addition to supporting the army ground operations.

In 1967 the FAG acquired five Bell UH-1B and UH-1D helicopters from the United States to reinforce its helicopter force.[95] By this time the Guatemalan armed forces were a formidable force. From 1966 to 1968 the greatly enlarged army and police forces conducted an all-out offensive against the few hundred rebels based primarily in the northeast. In addition to going after the rebels, the army attacked the rebel infrastructure and demolished villages providing support. Aerial bombing was common and napalm was used. By 1968 the rebellion had been largely stamped out at the cost of an estimated eight thousand rebels and civilians killed.[96]

Low-level insurgency continued in Guatemala, but the country was largely quiet during the early 1970s. One reason that the government had been able to mobilize and counter the guerrillas was the rapid economic growth of the 1960s and early 1970s. Guatemala had attracted a considerable amount of foreign industrial investment and diversified its agricultural exports.[97] Moderate prosperity took some of the sting out of the rural grievances. However, the oil crisis of 1973, falling agricultural prices, and a major earthquake that devastated Guatemala City in 1976, killed twenty-five thousand, and left more than a million homeless put the Guatemalan economy in poor shape by the late 1970s and made the position of Guatemala's rural poor even more tenuous.[98] Leftist rebel groups that had been operating since the early 1970s found a welcome home in the overwhelmingly Indian western highlands of the country. By the late 1970s the insurgency had been reborn as a mostly Indian rebellion organized around four Maoist-oriented rebel groups, the largest group of insurgents known as the EGP (Guerrilla Army of the Poor).[99]

The generals leading Guatemala replied to increased guerrilla activity in the highlands with the usual brute force methods. Death squads, which had made an appearance in the 1960s, resumed as the military and landowners tried to stamp out dissent in the rural areas. As the insurgency grew, the U.S. government, under the Carter administration, became critical of the Guatemalan junta for its appalling human rights record. Rather than modify its approach to dealing with the insurgency and shut down the murder squads and brutal methods tolerated and supported by the army and police, the Guatemalan government took an opposite tack. To forestall the embarrassment of a congressionally mandated cutoff of U.S. aid, in 1977 the Guatemalans declared they would forgo all U.S. military assistance rather than accept reforms that would be the price of U.S. support. Guatemala would go it alone and handle the insurgency in its own way.[100]

THE PEAK OF THE INSURRECTION — CUTOFF OF U.S. AID

Going without U.S. aid was especially hard on the Guatemalan air force, which was almost completely equipped with U.S.-made aircraft provided under military aid programs. In 1971 the FAG had been modernized with the arrival of eight Cessna A-37B fighter-bombers under the U.S. military aid program. Guatemala was the first nation in Central America to receive this very capable counterinsurgency aircraft. Seven more A-37s were supplied in 1974 and 1975, which enabled the FAG to establish a full-strength fighter-bomber squadron and retire the P-51s and pull from service some of the T-33s.[101] When the U.S. aid was cut off, Guatemala had a fairly capable small air force of about 650 officers, NCOs, and airmen with its principal combat squadron the A-37 unit. In all, the FAG constituted five flying squadrons (the fighter bombers, a reconnaissance squadron with light observation aircraft, two transport squadrons, and a helicopter squadron) operating out of four major bases: La Aurora (at Guatemala City and the headquarters of the FAG), San Jose on the coast, Santa Elena, and Puerto Barrios. The FAG's mission was to support the army, which had grown to about twenty-seven thousand men by the early 1980s.[102]

Cutting loose from dependence on U.S. aid was a bold move for the government but hurt the air force's ability to conduct operations. The FAG lost three A-37s to operational accidents in the 1970s and these could not be replaced.[103] With the T-33s worn out, Guatemala searched the world aviation market for affordable aircraft to replace losses and retirements. A deal was made in 1979 to import twelve Swiss Pilatus PC-7 turboprop trainers, which could also be modified as very capable counterinsurgency fighters.[104] Guatemala was able to reinforce its small helicopter fleet during 1981 and 1982 by purchasing at least eight Bell 206B helicopters as well as at least three Aroespatiale Alouettes. Four Fokker 27 light transport planes were acquired in 1982.[105]

While U.S. aid was cut off, Guatemala was not entirely without foreign support. Argentina provided arms, spare parts, and training for Guatemala and other Latin American nations facing insurgencies in the 1970s and early 1980s. Unfortunately for Guatemala, the replacement of the Argentine military regime with a democratic government after the defeat in the Falklands in 1982 resulted in a major reduction in Argentine aid. However, the Israelis stepped in to also play an important role in Latin America, selling and providing arms and assistance in this period. Between 1975 and the early 1980s, Israel supplied eleven Arava IAI-201 twin-engine transports. Indeed, the Aravas are ideal transport aircraft for combating an insurgency — able to bring several tons of people or equipment into small, rough landing fields and also easily modified as gunships with the addition of rocket pods and side-mounted machine guns.[106] The FAG acquired a variety of other surplus aircraft in this period, including a variety of civilian helicopters and three ex–French air force Fouga Magister CM-170 trainers — another aircraft suitable for conversion into a counterinsurgency craft.[107]

THE GOVERNMENT'S STRATEGY

Despite a large-scale commitment of government troops to saturate the Guatemalan highlands, the insurgency grew quickly. By 1981 much of the rural areas of the west and south were firmly in rebel hands. Guerrilla groups were active daily in nine of the nation's twenty-two departments and carried out occasional actions in another nine departments. The guerrillas were able to take over small towns and cut major roads, including the Pan-American Highway, almost at will. The rebels even conducted terrorist attacks in the capital, Guatemala City. It appeared that the rebels might soon be in full control of most of the countryside.[108] The rebel groups at this point amounted to approximately 10,000 to 12,000 active combatants with at least 100,000 active civilian sympathizers ready to supply and assist the rebels. Another 260,000 people were estimated to live in areas under rebel control.[109] The rebels were armed with light weapons bought on the black market or smuggled in through Mexico. In early 1982 the various guerrilla forces, the largest being the Guerrilla Army of the Poor, organized themselves as the Guatemalan National Revolutionary Unity Party, or URNG. By this time, the rebels were inflicting 250 casualties a month on the army.[110]

In 1981 the army initiated a strategy to deny the rebels the support of the rural population by simply depopulating the areas where the rebels were popular. In the first of a series of major campaigns, each lasting two to three months, villages in two central departments were attacked and destroyed. Several massacres of civilians resulted in thousands of peasants abandoning their villages and fleeing combat areas. This created the enormous refugee problem that characterized the Guatemalan civil war. By the late 1980s an estimated 1 million Guatemalans had been displaced within their own country, and another 250,000 had fled to Mexico and settled in refugee camps there.

In early 1982 the war was not going well for the government, and the regime of General Lucas Garcia was perceived as corrupt and inefficient. Garcia was thrown out of power in a coup in March 1982 and General Efrain Rios Montt, a former army chief of staff, took the reins of power. Unlike Garcia and his predecessors, Montt had a comprehensive concept for a counterguerrilla strategy and quickly unleashed it upon the country. Montt mobilized all the resources of the country into a ruthless, all-out war upon the rebels. Montt's strategy was very brutal and fairly effective. He realized that simply depopulating the rebel areas would not shut down support for the URNG, so he came up with a plan to put the rural population under tight government control. Between 1982 and 1984 hundreds of selected villages (one estimate is 440) were cleared out and destroyed by the army. While many rural inhabitants simply fled, thousands of others were resettled under Montt's strategy in model villages called "poles of development," carefully controlled by the army.[111] On the military side of Montt's counterinsurgency program, five task forces were created and a series of offensives was launched throughout the western and southern highlands of the country to clear whole departments of rebels.[112] The army saturated the country with troops and placed garrisons in all the major towns and even in the smaller villages. A new program of "civil guards" was created as another means of social control. Rural residents were armed with an assortment of old rifles and shotguns and placed under command of an army NCO or officer and directed to carry out patrols against the guerrillas and to mount guard in the villages. Refusal to support the civil patrols or to shoot rebel prisoners was seen as defiance of the government and was likely to invite a visit from a death squad for the offender. In this manner, the whole country was coerced into supporting the army.

The air force saw considerable combat in this period. Rebel villages were bombed, and if the rebels engaged the army in battle, they could expect attack from a flight of A-37s or attack helicopters to retaliate. In the campaigns of 1981 to 1983 the Arava and C-47 transports of the air force dropped paratroop units to seize territory deep in rebel country or to set up blocking positions. Although the fighting was sustained, it was generally on a low level with squad and platoon actions. The small Guatemalan air force was simply not capable of mounting anything resembling a large operation. A lack of modern maintenance facilities and personnel, coupled with the shortage of spare parts caused by the U.S. military aid cutoff, meant that no more than 50 percent of the air force was operational at any time. This meant that the FAG usually had no more than four attack or troop-lift helicopters available to support operations — scarcely enough to support a single platoon or company in action. Shortage of aircraft required keeping air operations on a small scale, and the company and battalion airmobile operations carried out in El Salvador were not possible in Guatemala.

THE AIR FORCE RESERVE

One means of maximizing the military capabilities of Guatemala was to engage all of the nation's civilian pilots and aircraft in a program to support the war effort. Civilian pilots were enlisted in a new force called the "Commando Especial Reserva Aerea" in 1982 under government decree 14-82. A regular air force colonel was put in command of the one hundred to two hundred civil pilots, who were given the rank of lieutenant in the air force reserve, provided with a bit of military instruction, and issued uniforms and sidearms. Aircraft owners provided aircraft, usually light single or twin-engine planes of the Piper, Beech, and Cessna variety, for a few days at a time. Pilots were not paid, but the air force provided the fuel. Pilots reported voluntarily to fly missions when they had time or were occasionally ordered to duty to fly in support of a major operation.

The air force reserve took over much of the routine, noncombat flying operations of the air force, which allowed the small FAG to concentrate on combat operations. The light civilian aircraft flew observation missions and personnel and supplies to small rural airstrips. It was an efficient and simple means of moving people and getting mail and supplies to isolated garrisons in a country where road movement was routinely ambushed. There are a few reports of combat with the light aircraft with FN or M-60 machine guns fired from the side doors of Cessna 182s and 206s. The mobilization of the nation's civil air fleet and pilots was an imaginative stroke and generally regarded as very successful.[113]

GOVERNMENT SUCCESS

General Rios Montt was relieved of the presidency in a coup after only sixteen months in power, but the strategy that he mapped out continued from 1983 to 1986. Several more major campaigns were mounted, and the western highlands of Guatemala, the hotbed of revolt and dissent, were systematically cleared and largely depopulated. By 1986 the rebellion was considered to be generally under control, and the military regime was able to turn over power to a civilian president and loosen some of the tight controls of the Montt era. The improvement of the political climate also meant the resumption of U.S. military assistance.[114] However, by this time, the military power of the rebellion was broken — but it was done at a tremendous cost, with estimates of seventy thousand to one hundred thousand dead. In most cases, the dead were rural civilians simply caught in the war.

Despite its small size and lack of modern equipment, the Guatemalan air force played an important role in the war. Throughout the war, the air force saw a high attrition due to operational accidents — probably caused by deficiencies in maintenance and pilot training. For example, of thirteen A-37B fighter-bombers supplied to the FAG, only one is known to have been lost as a result of combat, shot down by ground fire in a close support operation in 1988. Four A-37s were lost to accidents in the 1970s and one withdrawn from service in 1986 due to wing spar and bolt problems. It remained on the "dead line," as there were not enough parts and funds to fix the airplane.[115] Maintenance for an air force with less than one thousand personnel flying an assortment of fifteen different fixed-wing aircraft and several helicopter models, coupled with U.S. aid cutoffs and a shoestring budget, must have been close to impossible. Indeed, given the problems that Guatemala faced and the restrictions on U.S. aid caused by the government policies, it was a significant accomplishment to have kept the air force going as an effective force.[116]

As in most counterinsurgency operations, the primary role of the aircraft was in reconnaissance. The morale and psychological effect of patrolling aircraft was noted by the guerrillas. In the memoirs of one of the guerrilla leaders who helped organize the Guerrilla Army of the Poor in the 1970s, he spoke of helicopters and aircraft being constantly over his band and aircraft "thundering" over isolated villages.[117] At one point, he spoke of "the sky dark with helicopters and military planes" and "hundreds" of soldiers parachuting into Indian villages.[118] Of course, the small Guatemalan air force never had the capability to provide anything resembling constant air coverage, nor could it have ever dropped more than 150 paratroopers. Certainly, the psychological effect of airpower against the lightly armed insurgents, who had few weapons to oppose aircraft such as heavy machine guns or shoulder-fired SAMS, seems to have been significant and played an important role in demoralizing the insurgents.

The war continued in a desultory fashion for another ten years until 1996 when the URNG signed a peace agreement with the government and agreed to disarm and operate openly as a political party. The peace was made generally on the government's terms with a promised investigation of human rights abuses, a few land reforms, and the promise to accept and protect the Indian culture of much of the population. The army was reduced in size but, in contrast to El Salvador (where 108 senior officers were retired when peace was concluded), only a few officers lost their jobs and the military still held much of the power. Guatemala had evolved into a democracy, but a democracy where the armed forces still hold a privileged position and have enormous influence behind the scenes.

Colombia

Colombia is very different from Central American states such as El Salvador with their traditions of military governments, rule by small oligarchies, and deep-seated rural poverty. Colombia is a large nation, larger than Texas, New Mexico, and Arizona combined, and has a population of over thirty million people, a diverse and fairly modern economy, and considerable mineral resources, including significant oil reserves. Colombia has one of Latin America's strongest traditions of democratic government, and its armed forces have traditionally been respectful of civilian political authority. The government and military, while having serious problems with corruption, do not have a record of wholesale abuse of the population as was common in El Salvador and Guatemala.

The roots of Colombia's current insurgencies lie back in the 1940s. In 1948 a civil war broke out between the leftist and rightist factions, which is now

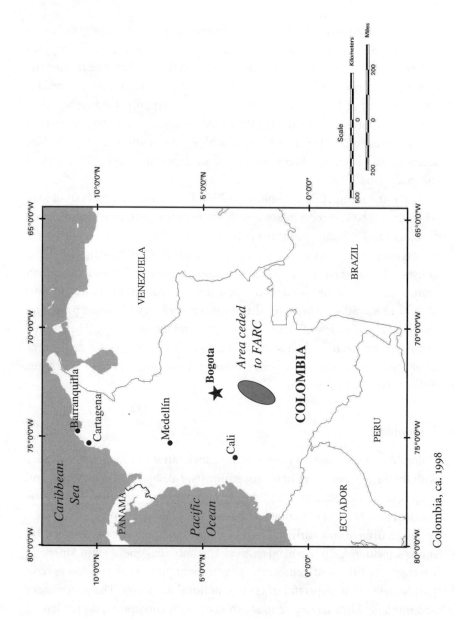

Colombia, ca. 1998

called simply "La Violencia." Between 1948 and 1956 an estimated 250,000 people lost their lives in riots, killings, and small-scale actions. In 1953 the military seized power and in 1956 brokered a political settlement between the factions that led to power sharing and a return of democratic government.[119] While most of the nation welcomed the peace agreement, some of the leftist guerrilla forces established during the civil war moved to the mountains and isolated rural areas and carried on a low-level insurgency with a few hundred followers. The main insurgent force in Colombia today, the Revolutionary Armed Forces of Colombia (FARC), was founded in 1950 during "La Violencia." Other groups carried on minor guerrilla campaigns into the 1960s.[120]

During the low-level guerrilla operations of the 1950s and 1960s, the Colombian army demonstrated a high level of professionalism and leadership. Rather than employ the usual strong-arm tactics of dealing with a Latin American insurgency, the army trained and employed a large number of civil affairs officers and fielded a fairly large engineer force. When the army moved into disaffected rural areas, it was not to cut a swath of destruction and create refugees but to build new roads, schools, and water wells. The army set up local self-defense militias and conducted internal peacekeeping and encouraged the government to grant amnesties to rebels who turned in their guns. Only occasionally did the army resort to all-out military offensives. This approach proved very successful in tamping down the smoldering fires of "La Violencia" in the 1950s and 1960s. Indeed, at this time, the Colombian army was considered to be a model counterinsurgency force.[121] The Colombian army also proved its competence in conventional operations by sending an infantry battalion to fight with the U.S. Army in the Korean War, where it compiled a solid combat record. As peacekeepers for the UN and for the U.S.-led peacekeeping operation in the Sinai, Colombian infantry battalions proved to be competent and effective. In general, the Colombian armed forces have a fairly strong record of military competence and professionalism — in strong contrast to the Central American armed forces that faced insurgencies.

During the 1970s and 1980s Colombia, like other nations in South America, experienced problems with urban-based Marxist terrorists. Small groups of disaffected middle-class intellectuals formed violent groups. The most dramatic action was by a small faction, M-19, which seized the Colombian Supreme Court in 1985 and held the justices and court personnel hostage. In the army's counterattack, half of the supreme court justices were killed, but the M-19 force was wiped out. Eventually, after a long series of negotiations, M-19 laid down its arms in the 1980s and became a legal political party.

The most important development for the insurgency and for the stability and prosperity of Colombia came in the 1980s with the rise in popularity of cocaine as the preferred illegal drug in the United States and Europe. The Andean region of South America became the world's center for growing the coca plants, from which cocaine is extracted, and Colombia became the center for the marketing and trafficking of the drug. The cocaine trade of the 1980s, controlled by powerful criminal cartels based in the Colombian cities of Cali and Medellín, was enormously lucrative for many, and the vast profits of the illegal trade had a tremendously corrupting influence at all levels of the Colombian government and society. In the 1980s Latin American experts discussed the devolution of Colombia into a "narco state." Numerous programs and military operations were carried out to destroy coca fields and to intercept the hundreds of light aircraft employed to fly cocaine from Colombia to Mexico or other locations for transshipment to the United States. The drug war was also a major problem for Peru and Bolivia, countries that produced a large proportion of the coca crop. The military and police operations of the drug war were relatively ineffective in inhibiting the transport of illegal drugs from Colombia. Cocaine was so profitable and so easy to grow and process that the loss of 10 to 20 percent of the drugs intercepted in transit, and the destruction of hundreds of coca fields and processing plants (easily constructed and hidden in rural areas), had little impact on the power and profits of the drug cartels. The level of violence in Colombia increased dramatically as the drug cartels killed off any threat to their interests in the form of honest politicians, journalists, policemen, and judges. Competitors in the drug trade were also snuffed out in record numbers. In short, Colombia, which had enjoyed fairly strong economic growth and relative prosperity in the 1970s, became demoralized, destabilized, and terribly violent.

The drug war of the 1980s came to a climax in 1989 when the popular Liberal Party politician Luis Carlos Galán, widely regarded as the probable next president of Colombia, was brutally assassinated by the drug cartels.[122] The government retaliated with new laws, closer cooperation with the U.S. antidrug agencies, and creation of elite police units, specially cleared to ensure police honesty. In the early 1990s the Colombian National Police scored some notable victories and arrested and killed the leading members of the Cali and

Medellín drug cartels. However, these victories did not serve to diminish drug cultivation or trafficking. Mexican cartels and small independent gangs stepped in and took over the illegal drug marketing and smuggling operations. More ominously, the two main Marxist insurgent groups in Colombia, FARC and ELN (National Liberation Army), became heavily involved in the drug trade. The insurgent groups, especially the larger and better-armed FARC, were very strong in large areas of the countryside and encouraged farmers to grow coca as a cash crop. FARC took a percentage of the farmers' profits as "taxes" to support its insurrection. The drug trade is so lucrative that in the 1990s FARC had an estimated income of $100 to $200 million (mostly from drugs but much from robbery, kidnapping, and extortion) per year and could afford to buy first-rate weaponry and high-tech equipment, such as night vision devices and state-of-the-art communications equipment, on the world arms market. FARC also had the money to pay and support its soldiers well. Unlike most insurgencies in Latin America, the Colombian insurgents are as well equipped as (sometimes better equipped than) the army opposing them.[123] U.S. and Western counterinsurgency doctrine has normally dealt with insurgencies that were largely dependent upon funds and support from communist nations. With the collapse of communism in the Soviet bloc in the early 1990s and the end of generous military aid to communist movements around the world, one might have thought that any future Marxist insurgency would be put at a severe disadvantage. In Colombia, however, the rebels have learned to support a major insurrection with their own resources.

During the 1990s the two main Marxist groups grew rapidly in size and power and operated in 40 percent of Colombia's territory. FARC virtually owns the sparsely settled southern and Amazon regions of Colombia and has strongholds in the central mountains.[124] The ELN, which has about four thousand to five thousand fighters and operates in Colombia's northeast, has targeted Colombia's oil industry, after coffee the nation's top foreign exchange earner. The five-hundred-mile-long pipelines carrying crude oil from the Cano Limon oil field to the port of Covenas are vital to Colombia's economy. In 1999 ELN attacked and sabotaged the oil pipelines seventy-seven times, often shutting down Colombia's crude oil shipments for days at a time.[125] FARC, which had grown to fifteen thousand to twenty thousand well-trained soldiers by late 2000, carried out an increasing number of raids against military and government posts. FARC stuck to traditional guerrilla tactics of swiftly striking small military and police outposts in night attacks and wiping them out — often beheading or mutilating the bodies of the servicemen and government sympathizers (landowners and businessmen). Occasional victories have been claimed by the armed forces, but generally the war had not gone well for the military prior to 2002.

COLOMBIAN ARMED FORCES

Colombia, a fairly prosperous country with a population of thirty million, can afford to have relatively large armed forces. The Colombian army has a personnel strength of over one hundred thousand men and a well-trained professional officer corps. Yet numbers can be very deceiving. In reality, the Colombian army can field no more than thirty thousand men against the rebels — thus making the odds of rebels versus soldiers about one to one. Colombian law forbids assigning high school graduates to combat duty, so 30 percent of the army is kept in the rear on garrison duty. Colombia has conscription, and as much as 25 to 35 percent of the army is being trained or is supporting the training establishment at any time.

As of this writing, the Colombian air force has about seven thousand personnel and is organized into the Air Combat Command with two squadrons of conventional fighter planes (eleven Dassault Mirage Vs and twelve IAI Kfir fighters) and two groups of fixed-wing aircraft organized for counterinsurgency and counterdrug operations (fifteen OV-10s, twenty-six A-37s, three IA-58A Pucaras, five T-37s, two AC-47 gunships, and six Embraer Tucanos). The Air Tactical Support Command has two helicopter groups, one primarily for training and five squadrons equipped with a variety of helicopters including sixteen UH-60 A/L Blackhawks, seven Hughes 500 HM attack helicopters, five Hughes 500 MDs, six UH-1s, four McDonnell Douglas MD 500 MG night attack helicopters, and fifteen other helicopters of various models.[126] The Air Transport Command is a small force with seven C-130 Hercules transports, nine CASA 212s, two Fokker F-28s, five C-47s, one IAI Arava, and several other craft.[127]

The army built up its air assets in the 1990s and operates some helicopter squadrons for troop transport including twenty refurbished UH-1 helicopters, seven Sikorsky UH-60s, and ten Mi-17 utility helicopters acquired from Russian surplus in 1987. The army and navy also have a small number of light Piper, Beech, and Cessna fixed-wing aircraft for utility and liaison work.[128] Colombia's much greater resources provide for much larger, better maintained, and more competent air units than any found in Central America. For example, Colombia is able to carry out its own pilot training at all levels and conduct avionics and maintenance upgrades on its aircraft. However, much of the Colombian air force budget is siphoned off to provide for the Mirage and Kfir fighter squadrons maintained for conventional air defense. For Latin American air forces, maintaining a high-tech conventional fighter unit is often a matter of national prestige and sometimes a matter of strategic necessity. In 1989 Colombia acquired a squadron of twelve Kfir fighters and one trainer from Israel at a cost of $200 million. Added to the fifteen Dassault Mirage 5CO fighters and two trainers acquired from France in the 1970s, and currently being upgraded, this gives Colombia a formidable conventional fighter force.[129] While such a unit is generally unsuited for counterinsurgency operations, the Colombians require modern air-to-air fighters because of the conventional threat posed by neighboring Venezuela and its squadron of F-16s. While chances of a war between the nations are low, there have been border clashes over the years, and neither nation wants to be unprepared for a conventional conflict. The problem is that Colombia does not have the resources to support both a conventional and counterinsurgency air force.

The Colombian emphasis upon conventional air defense has resulted in a very weak transport capability for the air force, a very important requirement in such a large nation with so few roads. Colombia's small transport force is overworked and rapidly wearing out and there is little relief in sight. Seeing this weakness, the FARC rebels have placed towns in southern Colombia under a land blockade that forces the government to airlift food and vital supplies in. The blockade of Puerto Asís, a city of thirty-eight thousand in southern Colombia, required an air force airlift effort in late 2000.[130] Further blockades could easily stretch the small transport force well beyond its capabilities and require the government to cede more territory to rebel control.

COUNTERDRUG OPERATIONS AND U.S. AID

Although Colombia is a nation with strong democratic traditions, a government chosen in free and fair elections, an armed forces with a good human rights record (for the region), and has committed troops with America in Korea and to serve under U.S. command in the Sinai peacekeeping operation, the U.S. government was reluctant to provide military and economic aid during the 1990s. Part of the problem has been strong opposition to aid among liberals in the U.S. Congress. Aid to Colombia is seen as engaging in another Vietnam in which the United States could be sucked into an unpopular war. Another aspect of the U.S. reluctance to support Colombia was the general lack of interest in Latin American issues and problems during the Clinton administration (1993–2001). There were no senior figures in the Clinton inner circle who expressed much knowledge of, or interest in, Latin American affairs. Indeed, many aspects of the Clinton administration seem inexplicable in terms of a rational foreign policy. During the Clinton years, U.S. troops were repeatedly committed to conflicts around the world in countries in muddled causes where U.S. national interests were, to put it charitably, marginal. For example, U.S. troops were committed to fight an internal conflict in Somalia — a country where no U.S. interests were at stake. The United States carried out an air war in Bosnia in 1995 and a major campaign against Serbia in 1999 and committed large U.S. forces to occupy Balkan provinces for the foreseeable future — all in a region where U.S. interests were again minimal. Yet, in Colombia, a large country with significant U.S. investments and whose instability affects the whole region, the United States has failed to provide more than a small fraction of the aid and support as has been given to the Albanians or Bosnians.

Despite tough talking about the war on drugs in the Clinton administration, U.S. assistance to nations on the front line of the drug war declined for several years under Clinton.[131] In other cases, the U.S. assistance amounted to small batches of completely worn-out equipment such as decades-old two-and-a-half-ton trucks, .50-caliber machine-gun ammunition made in 1952 and deemed unsafe for the U.S. military, and several dozen worn-out UH-1 "Huey" helicopters requiring a complete rebuild before they could be of any use.[132]

In 1998 the United States ended air surveillance of the Andean Region with USAF AWACS aircraft that served to identify drug trafficking light aircraft flying out of remote airstrips in Peru and Colombia for those nations to intercept. The U.S. State Department halted the surveillance support to the Latin Americans on the grounds that the Peruvians and Colombians might shoot down the drug-carrying aircraft. Indeed, that was precisely the point. The Peruvian air force, in particular, mounted an aggressive campaign through the 1990s to shoot down drug trafficking light aircraft with their Tucano fighters. Between 1992 and 1998 the Peruvians, often with U.S. surveillance assistance, shot down over one hundred drug planes and halved the amount of cocaine grown in Peru by interdicting transport and lowering the profits of the coca growers.

Officially, all of the U.S. military–type aid that goes to Colombia has to be for the campaign against drugs. U.S. aid is not allowed to go to the campaign against the insurgents. Both nations agree to this polite but absurd fiction that the drug war is somehow separate from the guerrilla war — even though the guerrillas receive their support from the drug trade. For years one of the major U.S. programs in the Colombian counterdrug operations has been the aerial spraying of herbicides on coca crops. U.S. DEA (Drug Enforcement Agency) personnel have been deployed to work with Colombian National Police and U.S.-financed crop dusters, and U.S.-supplied helicopters (manned and maintained with U.S.-contracted personnel) have made constant raids in the isolated hinterlands of southern Colombia to eradicate the coca crop.[133] While this program gives the impression that "something is being done," coca production has increased dramatically during the spraying campaign.[134] Indeed, this airpower approach to the cocaine production looks good in reports to Congress but has engendered resentment among rural Colombians who do not believe that the herbicides used are harmless and attribute non–coca crop destruction, cattle sickness, and so on to the U.S. spraying program.[135] As with the aerial bombing campaign in El Salvador, the propaganda value to the rebels of the U.S. crop spraying program in Colombia probably far outweighs the benefits of reducing the coca crop.

A NATIONAL STRATEGY — OR LACK OF ONE

Conservative Andrés Pastrana was elected president in 1998 and pledged to personally negotiate an end to the conflict with the guerrilla forces and with the paramilitaries. Pastrana followed through in his promise to seek a peaceful, negotiated end to Colombia's long conflict. In November 1998 Pastrana ordered all Colombian forces and police out of a ten-thousand-square-kilometer region in central Colombia and allowed FARC to operate openly in the region as a "demilitarized neutral zone." In general, Pastrana has been reluctant to order any major military offensives against the rebels, hoping that through compromise he can bring the FARC to the negotiating table and arrange a peace settlement. The strategy failed. Virtually ceding a large sanctuary to FARC simply strengthened the rebels, convinced them of the government's weakness, and encouraged them to pursue the war. The FARC leadership carried on the war as violently as before and used the opportunity to create a solid military base in "FARCland," as the Colombians nicknamed the demilitarized zone. FARC conscripted young men in its sanctuary and has increased its forces.[136]

The relative impotence of the regular armed forces in its fight against the rebels led to the rapid rise of large mercenary forces to fight the rebels in the late 1990s. The "paramilitary" forces, raised and financed by Colombia's landowners, businessmen, and middle class, are well armed and equipped and as willing as the FARC and ELN rebels to kill anyone perceived as an opponent. The first few months of 2001 saw some fairly large offensives of paramilitary units of up to one thousand men to clear strategic towns and regions of rebels. Victories against the rebels are often followed up by mass executions of the rebel sympathizers while the military is unwilling or incapable of intervening.[137]

A very worried Colombian government is quite willing to meet numerous conditions as a requirement for U.S. military aid. The Colombian army has set up a massive program to train its soldiers in international law and human rights and has set up a special committee with the power to remove officers involved in human rights abuses — a model that was implemented by the National Police and resulted in the firing of eleven thousand police officers under the seven-year tenure of National Police Chief General José Serrano.[138] In 2000 the U.S. Congress finally took serious action on Colombia and voted a multiyear $1.3 billion aid program for Colombia. Much of the aid is economic in nature, but funding has been provided to equip and train two specialist counterdrug battalions in addition to the U.S.-trained and -equipped counterdrug battalion already employed. U.S. Special Forces soldiers have been deployed to Colombia to train its forces. The new Colombian units will be equipped with the Sikorsky UH-60 "Blackhawk" helicopters for air mobility. The UH-60 is ideal for Colombian conditions as it is fast (160 knots cruising speed), can carry a heavy load (twelve fully loaded troops or a sling-loaded 105 howitzer), and can operate well at high altitudes — the most important factor, as most of Colombia is mountainous and counterdrug or counterguerrilla operations will often take place at eight-thousand-feet elevation.[139] Whether three elite battalions, along with the small elite forces of the Marine Corps and army, can suffice against the heavily armed FARC forces defending their sanctuaries is doubtful. Given the weakness of the Colombian forces in transport, a much larger number of transport aircraft and helicopters will be required to take on FARC and the ELN on favorable terms. The army will also need several more battalions of highly trained infantry capable of conducting airmobile operations. Any major military offensive against the rebels is likely to be costly, protracted, and result in a fairly heavy attrition rate of helicopters. However, given the current strength of FARC and the ELN, a sustained military offensive against the FARC strongholds is likely to be the only means by which the government can gain the upper hand. In the current conditions, the government's best military option is to conduct sustained mobile operations against the rebels to wear them down. At the same time, amnesties for rebels coupled with land resettlement and jobs programs for the ex-rebels are needed to encourage defections. Such methods, coupled with aggressive military action, have worked well in many other counterinsurgency campaigns.

Up until 2001 the Colombian government lacked any comprehensive strategy to fight the insurgents except to promote a series of peace negotiations. The lack of a clear military strategy on the part of the Colombian government, coupled with a very cautious U.S. attitude toward providing military aid, could lead to a situation where the government loses effective control of the nation.[140] While FARC and the ELN have relatively little support among the population — it is estimated that no more than 5 percent of Colombians would support FARC in an election — the rebel forces are formidable because of their size and armament. Until 2002 President Pastrana was reluctant to directly engage FARC as long as there is some chance of a negotiated peace. In the meantime, the paramilitaries have taken the war into their own hands and the end result might be a country literally out of control.

By 2001 the political/military situation in Colombia was deteriorating. However, the "Plan Colombia" for strengthening the Colombian forces provided a basis for the government to take a more aggressive policy toward the rebels. Indeed, the situation might now (2002 at the time of writing) be turning in the government's favor. In August the army carried out a fairly large joint operation against a FARC stronghold in north central Colombia with more than two battalions of troops employed. Paratroops were successfully dropped to seize key terrain, and the Colombian air force Kfir fighters were reported to have used precision-guided bombs against the rebel bases. Large joint operations of this nature are difficult to manage, and the success of the operation signals that the Colombians have reached the point of being capable of effectively coordinating joint operations. The use of precision munitions (laser-guided bombs) indicates a new level of competence on the part of the Colombian air force.

In February 2002 the war reached a major turning point. After three years of unsuccessful negotiations, President Pastrana canceled the peace talks and moved to restore government authority in the FARC sanctuary zone after FARC guerrillas hijacked a domestic airliner and murdered a senator on the flight. The Colombian government launched the largest military operations of the war as army and marine units moved into the rebel zone. Air force transports flew army counterinsurgency units into the southern city of Florencia, which became a major base for the ground operations. Air force fighters and helicopter gunships struck eighty-five strategic points within the FARC zone as the offensive commenced on the night of 20 February.[141] During the next ten days, air force aircraft relentlessly bombed any clearly identifiable FARC targets. FARC suffered a setback in the February 2002 government offensive, but the guerrilla organization showed its teeth by carrying out a wave of terrorist attacks throughout the country, setting up roadblocks, kidnapping civilians, and attacking electric lines and water reservoirs.[142]

The current rebel strategy of aggressively pursuing the war is proving to be counterproductive. In March 2002 Colombians went to the polls for the national congressional elections. Although FARC ordered the population to boycott the election and even disrupted the polling in several rural areas, there was a large turnout of voters. In areas where FARC is strong, people defied the FARC boycott in order to vote. The major winners in the congressional elections were the independent candidates who want the government to take a harder line against the rebels.[143] The desire of the Colombian people to defeat the insurgents was again expressed in the May 2002 presidential election. Alvaro Uribe, the candidate favoring a hard line against the FARC and ELN rebels, was elected by 52.8 percent with only 31.8 percent for his closest challenger. Uribe, whose father was murdered by FARC in 1983, has called for a major expansion of the military and a more aggressive approach to the war, in contrast to President Pastrana's peace strategy. The strong support for Uribe indicates that the average Colombian wants the war that kills 3,500 people a year to end — and not to end with a muddled political compromise.[144] Another factor working against the rebels is a new Bush administration in the

United States, which, in contrast with the Clinton administration, is much more engaged in Latin American issues. In the aftermath of the terror attacks against America, President Bush's top defense officials are making the case to the U.S. Congress for dramatically increasing U.S. aid to Colombia and lifting restrictions on U.S. aid going to the Colombian armed forces.[145]

As the war continues, it is clear that the Colombian air force will play a major role in the fighting. The Israelis have long been active in training and helping maintain the Colombian air force, which is partly equipped with Israeli aircraft. The adaptation of the Kfir from air-to-air combat to use as a precision munitions platform and training the pilots for the new mission were done with Israeli help. Using precision munitions against FARC is a wise move, as it will limit collateral damage to civilians and the consequent public backlash that occurs whenever guerrilla targets located near population centers are bombed. However, numerous airpower issues need to be addressed soon. Colombia's OV-10s and A-37s, fine counterinsurgency planes for their day, are wearing out and are becoming ever more difficult to maintain. Colombia will soon need a new light strike plane to replace the old U.S. planes. The Embraer EMB-314 Super Tucano is being considered.[146]

Summary

More than a few lessons are to be learned about the role of an air force and the employment of airpower in counterinsurgency from the wars in El Salvador, Guatemala, and Colombia. Considered as case studies, most of the operational, tactical, and political problems that one finds in supporting a counterinsurgency campaign are found. All three insurgencies are fairly classic conflicts in their nature — rebellions based on a long history of social discontent. In the case of El Salvador and Colombia, the United States has been faced with the problem of providing the right kind of aid, training, and assistance while avoiding the open commitment of U.S. forces that Congress would never tolerate. Since improving the human rights situation in a nation is important in conducting a successful opposition to an insurgency, the United States has had to use a carrot-and-stick approach in rewarding reform while withholding aid in cases of abuse. Guatemala rejected U.S. military aid for part of its counterinsurgency campaign to avoid having to submit to U.S. pressure on reform and human rights. Guatemala won its war with a "go it alone policy" — but at a higher cost in lives, refugees, and property destroyed than if a less aggressive military policy had been followed.

In helping the air forces of all three nations, the United States has had to understand the usual problems of Third World air forces and armies: a politicized and often corrupt officer corps, poor training levels, inadequate and obsolete weapons, and a lack of interest in logistics and maintenance. In the case of El Salvador, the U.S. commitment did dramatically change the military culture and competence — but it took a long time. Perhaps the biggest lesson to be learned is that transforming a Third World air force and army to fight a successful counterinsurgency campaign takes a long time and requires a major effort. Even if the United States had responded to the crisis in El Salvador in 1981 with massive aid, coupled with the right kinds of training programs given in a timely fashion, it still would have taken the FAS two to three years to become a capable force.

The three civil wars all highlight the importance of the government forces establishing a comprehensive military/political strategic plan to fight the insurgency. The turning point for the government in El Salvador's civil war was in 1981 when General Woerner and a team from the Pentagon met with El Salvador's military leadership for a week to craft a long-term program to oppose the rebels. From 1981 to 1983 the State Department helped the Salvadoran government create a long-term plan for political and economic reform. In general, the strategy was successful. In Guatemala support for the rebels was growing quickly until Rio Montt's regime crafted a national strategy to control the countryside and systematically clear regions of the rebels. The problem in Colombia is that it has lacked a clear and comprehensive national strategy to oppose the insurgency. Hopefully, that situation is changing, but if history is any guide, it will be a long process to develop a strategy.

In 1989 an aircraft carrying several dozen Soviet-made SA-18 antiaircraft missiles for the FMLN from Nicaragua's Sandinista government crashed in El Salvador. The availability of light antiaircraft missiles inhibited FAS operations somewhat in the last part of the war. Two FAS aircraft may have been lost to FMLN missiles. (Latin American Aviation Historical Society [Mario Overall])

Author James Corum in front of an FAS AC-47 gunship. The AC-47s, which carried three .50 caliber machine guns, were the most accurate and effective close support aircraft of the war. (James Corum)

O-2A "Super Skymaster" twin engine (fore and rear) reconnaissance plane. This aircraft was introduced in the mid-1960s and first used by the USAF in Vietnam. The O-2s saw extensive service in Central American air forces during the counterinsurgency operations of the 1970s through 1990s. By providing constant reconnaissance the O-2s played a major role in El Salvador's war by forcing the rebels to move and operate at night. (USAF)

FAS UH-1 helicopter modified as rocket-carrying gunship, Ilopango airfield, the main base of the Salvadoran air force. (James Corum)

A-37B counterinsurgency strike fighter of the FAS. This plane was the primary strike aircraft of the FAS during the civil war of 1980 to 1992. Because of the poor training level of the FAS pilots at the start of the conflict, the A-37s were not very effective until the mid-1980s. (James Corum)

Ouragan fighter-bomber of the FAS. Worn-out, obsolete equipment like this was typical of the Salvadoran and Guatemalan air forces in fighting insurgents in the early 1980s. (James Corum)

The UH-60 Blackhawk's two General Electric T-700 turboshaft engines provide enough power for the helicopter to operate at Colombia's high altitudes. The UH-60 is fast (160 kts cruise) and can carry fourteen troops and over a ton of cargo internally. It can sling load (as shown here) eight thousand pounds. Blackhawks used to equip the police and army counterinsurgency forces are the most important item of military aid for the Colombians. (U.S. Army)

A-37 attack plane of the FAG. The A-37s, modified U.S. trainers, became the main attack craft of the Guatemalan air force in the 1970s. (Latin American Aviation Historical Society)

Colombian Kfir fighter-bomber bought from Israel. The Colombian Kfirs have reportedly been used to make precision attacks on FARC bases in 2001 and 2002. (Colombian air force)

Colombian A-37 attack planes. The Colombians have been using the A-37s for years as their primary counterinsurgency aircraft. But the A-37s are getting old and are increasingly harder to maintain. (Colombian air force)

U.S. State Department contract crop duster (Ayers Turbo Thrush) spraying a coca field in northeastern Colombia in 2001. The aerial spraying of drug crops by U.S. pilots has caused some protest—but is strongly supported by the Colombian National Police. (U.S. Army)

Intervention in the Mideast, 1962–2000
Three Counterinsurgency Campaigns

Between 1962 and 2000 the Mideast saw three protracted and bloody campaigns waged by major military powers against insurgents and terrorists. Despite the commitment of large, well-equipped ground forces and the deployment of considerable air forces in each conflict, the insurgent and terrorist forces all won in the end. The Egyptian intervention in Yemen in 1962, the Soviet invasion in Afghanistan in 1979, and the Israeli invasion of southern Lebanon were all intended as short-term operations. All initially succeeded in attaining most of their short-term tactical objectives. However, none of the intervening powers anticipated that their actions would trigger protracted guerrilla wars.

In each intervention the intervening power had a limited political goal to be achieved by military force. The Egyptian and Soviet objectives were to intervene to support coups that would put friendly regimes into place. In those cases, neither power expected much military resistance, and forces were initially committed to provide an impressive show of force intended to psychologically overwhelm any factions likely to oppose the new regime. In contrast, the Israeli invasion of south Lebanon had a very limited goal of ending the constant terrorist attacks against northern Israel and eliminating the Palestine Liberation Organization (PLO) as a serious military threat to Israel. There was no intention of establishing a long-term presence, nor did the Israelis intend to change the Lebanese regime.

Although each intervention initially succeeded in its short-term military and political objectives, each intervention also set off a series of political reactions that the initiating powers had never envisioned. The Egyptian and Soviet interventions inspired popular insurgencies that carried on a war with heavy losses for the insurgents. The insurgents also lost most of the major engagements, a common occurrence in guerrilla warfare. Yet, through sheer persistence, the insurgents eventually compelled the Egyptians and Soviets to withdraw and leave their client states to their fate. The Israeli intervention succeeded in annihilating a fairly conventional military force (the PLO), but then also inspired a very unconventional force (Hizbullah) to take its place as the leading threat to northern Israel. In a guerrilla and terrorist campaign against the Israelis occupying southern Lebanon, the Hizbullah terrorists forced Israel into a war of attrition in a country where the Israeli government had no wish to maintain a permanent occupation. Although the Israelis inflicted heavy losses on Hizbullah, they were unable to defeat Hizbullah's attrition strategy. As in Afghanistan and Yemen, insurgent persistence and the willingness to take heavy casualties paid off when Israel acknowledged the inevitable and pulled its forces out of southern Lebanon in 2000.

Egypt in Yemen, 1962–1967

The 1952 coup that put General Abdul Gamal Nassar at the head of Egypt and threw out the corrupt monarchy of King Farouk triggered a fundamental change in the politics of the Arab world. Farouk's regime had been backward and corrupt, but it had generally been friendly to the interests of the major Western powers. Nassar came to power with a revolutionary ideology of Arab nationalism, a preference for socialism and a strong anti-Western bias. Even though the Egyptian armed forces suffered a major defeat at the hands of the Israelis, British, and French during the 1956 war that led to the British/French seizure of the Suez Canal, Nassar's popularity in the Arab world increased. Even though Nassar lost militarily in the short term, he had gained great prestige by standing up to the Israelis and the great powers of Britain and France. Nassar's efforts to modernize Egypt and his call for a revolutionary unity and a nationalist republican government was attractive to the educated classes throughout the Arab world, most of whom lived under the rule of repressive and reactionary monarchies.

One nation ripe for Nassar's brand of revolution was northern Yemen. Yemen was a small, miserably poor desert nation of approximately 4.5 million people. The monarch, Imam Ahmed, had steadfastly resisted any serious modernization of his country. When he died in 1962 Yemen was, in every sense, one of the most backward nations on earth, where most of the popu-

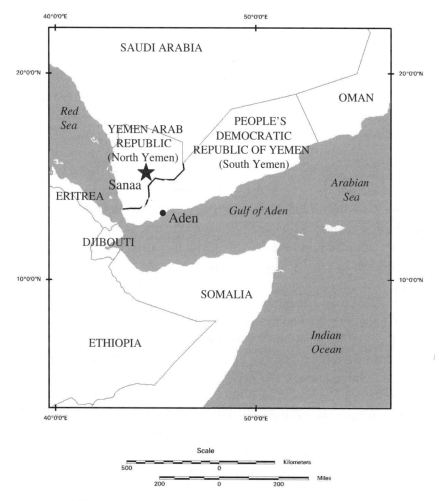

North Yemen, ca. 1962

lation was illiterate and slavery still quietly practiced. Most Yemenis took little notice of the national government, such as it was, and the average person gave his primary allegiance to his tribe or clan — an aspect of social organization that took on great importance during the insurgency.

In Yemen's small regular army (fifteen thousand to twenty thousand men) there was considerable sentiment in favor of Nassar's ideology of Arab revolution. By 1961 four hundred to five hundred Yemenis were enrolled in Egyptian schools and exposed to a strong dose of Egyptian propaganda. Yemenis living in Egypt were encouraged by Nassar to call for an end to the Yemeni monarchy. Nassar made a point of openly attacking the old-style Arab monarchies such as Yemen and Saudi Arabia and called for the formation of revolutionary governments throughout the Mideast.[1]

When Imam Ahmed died on 18 September 1962, his son, Mohamed al-Badr, succeeded him. The new Imam announced a series of reforms, but a group of Egyptian-influenced army and government leaders saw the chance to replace the old order entirely. On 26 September, a group of army officers, led by Colonel as-Sallal, carried out a coup and announced the formation of a new revolutionary republic. Egypt immediately announced its support of the new government, and the first act of the revolutionaries was to appeal to Egypt for aid. On 28 September the first contingent of Egyptian troops arrived by airlift, and the next day Egyptian ships carrying troops and equipment docked in Yemen. There was little resistance from the army, which largely melted away during the coup. The only problem for the revolutionaries and Egyptians is that Imam Mohamed al-Badr had quietly disappeared in the chaos of the first hours of the coup.[2]

Colonel as-Sallal became Yemen's new president and instituted a new republican government on the Egyptian model. Egypt quickly provided teachers, administrators, and health officials — as well as soldiers — to bolster the new regime and carry out a thorough modernization of Yemen. The new regime gradually extended its control over Yemen, and by March 1963 most of the country was in the hands of the new government. However, within a few weeks a resistance movement surfaced and coalesced around the deposed Imam al-Badr — who had survived the coup and fled to the refuge of friendly desert tribesmen living along the border of Saudi Arabia. Saudi Arabia, one of the conservative monarchies that Nassar constantly decried, had no desire to see a hostile, Egyptian-backed revolutionary government on its southern border, so the Saudis allowed the deposed Imam to set up a government in exile just inside the Saudi border. Jordan and Saudi Arabia supplied and equipped the rapidly growing Yemeni monarchist army, which, by early 1963, numbered about twenty thousand tribal warriors.[3] In one respect, raising an insurgency in Yemen was fairly simple. Since Yemen resembled a medieval feudal state more than a modern nation, there was no such thing as a national army aside from a small, poorly equipped force that functioned mostly as a royal bodyguard. Most Yemeni men counted themselves as warriors, and each of the many tribes in Yemen maintained its own small army.

The insurgency initially broke down on tribal and sectarian lines. The Imam rallied the Zaydi tribes of the north to oppose the revolutionary republic while most of their traditional rivals, the Shafii tribesmen, supported the republic. However, the war was not fought along clear tribal or ethnic lines. Many of the dozens of tribes and clans, to whom each Yemeni owed his primary loyalty, managed to change sides during the war on the basis of tribal interest and ancient rivalries and enmities.[4] In short, in this, as in so many revolutionary wars, it was never clear as to who was a friend and who was a foe.

EARLY EGYPTIAN OPERATIONS

Nassar set a high priority on the success of the Yemeni revolution and sent large forces to quickly overwhelm any Royalist opposition. By the end of 1962 Egypt had deployed over fifteen thousand troops to Yemen, supported by over two hundred aircraft.[5] The Yemeni government and the Egyptians soon initiated a plan to control all of northern Yemen with a priority of controlling all of the large towns and keeping the few main roads open. In addition, the Yemenis and Egyptians tried to close the rugged Saudi/Yemeni border in order to cut off Jordanian and Saudi aid to the rebels.

The Egyptian plan was far too ambitious for the forces available. Yemen is a very mountainous country with few roads — conditions ideal for small guerrilla forces to ambush and harass heavy, road-bound conventional armies such as the Egyptian. The first major operations against the Royalists were carried out in October and November of 1962. The Egyptian Air Force bombed several Saudi border towns that served as Royalist bases and supply depots.[6] On 22 October the Egyptians dropped a paratroop company east of the town of Sirwah in order to set up a blocking position as a mechanized battalion advanced to trap the Royalist forces. The operation turned into a disaster. The Egyptians had few maps of the area, and the paratroops soon became lost in the mountainous terrain. The rebels quickly hunted down and wiped out most of the paratroops. The mechanized unit acting as the hammer to the paratroop anvil was caught in an ambush on the road and suffered heavy losses.[7] In response to this first major engagement the Egyptians sent out armored columns in brigade strength, heavily supported by artillery and fighter-bombers, and tried to bring the rebels to battle. The rebels had the sense not to get sucked into a conventional battle they had no chance of winning and responded to the Egyptian offensive by traditional guerrilla tactics. They conducted harassment raids of Republican/Egyptian garrisons, mined roads, and ambushed mechanized Egyptian columns.[8]

In early 1963 the Egyptians, having failed in their ambitious campaign to overrun the whole country, adopted an enclave strategy of garrisoning and holding the most populated areas of Yemen. A large enclave was set up to include the capital city of Sana, the cities of Hodeidah and Taiz, as well as the port of Mocha. A small Republican national army was formed, and the Egyptians began to train it. By 1963 the Egyptian army presence in Yemen had grown to thirty-six thousand troops.[9] With their reinforcements, the Egyptians carried out some successful airborne/mechanized operations against the rebels. In February and March 1963 the Egyptians dropped a paratroop battalion at Sadah, a rebel stronghold in the north, and supplied it by airdrop. The paratroops then built an airstrip so that an infantry brigade could be flown in. At the same time, a mechanized column forced its way up the two hundred kilometers of road from Sana. A large Royalist force became trapped between the two Egyptian columns and suffered heavy losses. The Egyptian commander in Yemen believed he had won a decisive victory and that future operations would be nothing more than a mopping-up campaign.[10] Through 1963 the Egyptian forces strengthened their hold on the center of the country. As part of a strategy to secure their enclaves and to hold down rebel movements, the Egyptians established numerous small outposts and used helicopters and air transport to keep them supplied.[11]

The apparent success of the Egyptians in early 1963 proved an illusion. Although they had taken some conventional defeats, there were still plenty of Yemenis willing to fight the Egyptians. Organized into small guerrilla bands, the Royalist forces were able to roam the country virtually at will and generally controlled the rural areas. The effort to build a Yemeni national army to defend the new republic also failed, as the Yemeni soldiers generally had little enthusiasm for fighting their countrymen on behalf of a government that was, to all intents and purposes, run by the Egyptians. Thus, virtually the whole burden of fighting the war now fell upon the Egyptians and the call went for still more Egyptian forces.

While carrying out a ruthless military campaign in the countryside, which routinely included the carpet bombing of suspected rebel villages, the Egyptians also conducted an extensive civic action program to win the hearts and minds of the Yemenis. The Egyptians built schools and hospitals and provided aid to farmers — all in a country with almost universal illiteracy, no modern health care, and farming methods closer to the stone age than to the twentieth century.[12] Yet this expensive program to modernize and improve Yemen failed to win many hearts and minds. Indeed, it probably increased the resistance of most Yemenis toward their new revolutionary government and its Egyptian sponsors. Simply put, most Yemenis preferred their traditional way of life to the modern improvements offered by the Egyptians. Yemenis preferred their fairly anarchic tribal system to rule by a strong central government in Sana. Desert and mountain chieftains had no desire to disarm their tribal armies, lest an enemy tribe gain an advantage over them. Many Yemeni warriors were happy in their illiteracy and saw no need to build schools or to provide education and rights to women. Yemen was a society that saw little need to change or adapt the ways of the modern world beyond acquiring better guns and more firepower for the tribal armies. Contrary to most counterinsurgency theories, the Egyptian efforts represent a case in which governmental reforms and civic action programs had the effect of increasing the opposition to the government.

From June to August 1964 the Egyptians conducted a series of major offensives against the Royalists. Egyptian mechanized columns supported by squadrons of air force Yak 11, Mig 16, and Mig 17 fighters as well as Ilyshin 28 bombers pushed the Royalists out of several areas that they had won in 1963. There were heavy casualties on both sides.[13] The 1964 operations also saw the extensive use of Soviet-supplied Mi 4 helicopters in counterinsurgency operations — the first major use of helicopters in combat by a Third World power. The Egyptians maintained at least five squadrons of combat aircraft in Yemen with their main bases at Sana and Hodeidah. Egyptian Air Force (EAF) bombers based in Egypt provided additional air support.[14] At no time did the Egyptians suffer from any shortage of airpower. Yet, as long as the Royalists operated in fairly small guerrilla bands, the EAF rarely spotted Royalist forces from the air. Weapons and supplies for the Royalists were brought in by pack mule and camel train across the desert and through mountain paths from Saudi Arabia. The Egyptian Air Force had little success at spotting or interdicting this kind of rebel supply system.[15]

ATTRITION WAR AND A PEACE SETTLEMENT

The Egyptian commitment to the Yemen war peaked in 1965 when Egypt had seventy thousand troops stationed in Yemen — one-third of the Egyptian regular army. Yet, despite this large force, the Royalists had a number of minor victories that year. The rebel forces were also able to routinely cut the major roads and put small Egyptian garrisons under siege — requiring a constant effort by the Egyptians to supply their forces by air and to relieve besieged garrisons by mechanized columns. It was a classic case of a modern conventional army trapped in a war against unconventional insurgent forces. By mid-1965 it was clear that Egypt could not win the war. Nassar, desperate for a solution, threatened to invade Saudi Arabia to end Saudi support for the Yemeni Royalists. The Saudis replied by massing their forces, such as they were, along the Yemeni border to repel any Egyptian invasion attempt.[16] These steps toward war resulted in an intense diplomatic effort and, after a series of negotiations between Egypt and Saudi Arabia, the Jeddah Agreement was signed on 24 August 1965. It was an agreement that allowed the major foreign players in the conflict an opportunity for a face-saving withdrawal from a protracted war. King Faisal of Saudi Arabia agreed to stop supplying the Yemeni Royalist forces, and Nassar promised to withdraw his forces from Yemen. By mid-1966 the Egyptian forces in Yemen were down to twenty thousand men.[17]

However, the complete Egyptian withdrawal from Yemen was based on a comprehensive peace agreement between the Yemeni factions — and this did not occur. So Nassar announced that the Egyptian forces would remain in Yemen. The Egyptians withdrew to the enclave around Sana and the port cities and continued the war in a desultory manner. During the latter part of the conflict, the EAF regularly bombed the Saudi border towns, which still served as rebel bases. The EAF also carried out punitive bombing raids against rebel tribes as the Royalists continued to ambush and harass the Egyptian forces.[18] Some Egyptian forces were still in Yemen when the Egyptians fought the disastrous war against Israel in June 1967, and the last of the Egyptian forces were finally pulled out of Yemen in December 1967.

The war between the Royalists and Republicans carried on into 1968. The Royalists drove almost the whole way to Sana before being stopped by the Republican defense. Both the Egyptians and Saudis lost interest in the war, and the

Saudis cut off military aid to the royalists. By 1970 the Saudis brokered an agreement to end the war by creating a compromise Royalist/Republican government that would not be hostile to Saudi interests. Colonel as-Sallal was removed in 1967 as the Egyptians pulled out, and in 1970 Imam al-Badr was given a pension and shipped off to exile in Britain while most of his family was excluded from the government. Egypt had lost as many as twenty-six thousand soldiers killed in Yemen, while the Royalist rebels had lost approximately forty thousand.[19]

The Soviet War in Afghanistan

The Russians had long experience in the affairs of neighboring Afghanistan. Throughout the nineteenth century, as the Russian Empire annexed the neighboring regions of Uzbekistan, Turkmenistan, and Tajikistan, the Russians also had an interest in controlling Afghanistan as a gateway to the Indian Ocean and India. The Russians followed Afghani politics carefully, kept representatives and agents in the country, and passed large bribes to tribal leaders to buy influence. The British, to protect India, the crown jewel of the colonial empire, also kept agents in Afghanistan, paid bribes, and occasionally sent troops in to put pro-British factions into power and to keep down the Russian influence. When the communists inherited the Russian Empire, interest in Afghanistan did not wane. For decades the Soviets were heavily engaged in Afghani affairs and worked to put pro-Soviet socialist regimes in power and to arm and support a series of Afghani regimes.[20]

In the late 1970s Afghanistan was a chaotic and complicated scene of violent power struggles within the government while several parts of the country were in a state of rebellion. This was, of course, a perfectly normal state of affairs for Afghanistan. The large country (over 252,000 square miles) of seventeen million people was, and remains, one of the poorest and most backward nations on earth. The country of mostly barren desert and high mountains has little industry, only nineteen thousand kilometers of roads, and 85 percent of the population ekes out a living as subsistence farmers. Almost all Afghani women and most of the men are illiterate, and opium serves as the most lucrative cash crop. Afghanistan, while 100 percent Muslim, is divided into more than twenty national and ethnic groups (Pushtuns, Uzbeks, Tadjiks, Turkmen), none of which have any liking for the others. There is no tradition of a strong central

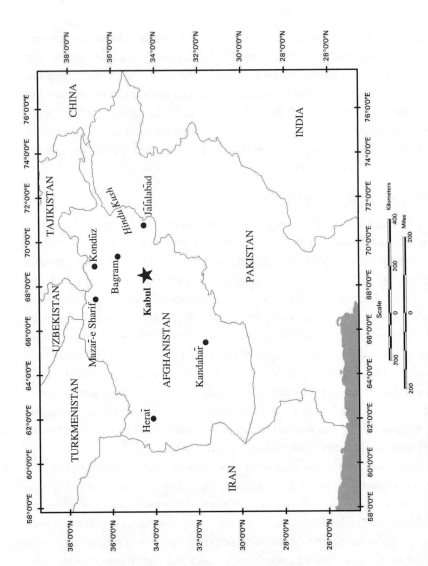

The Soviet Invasion of Afghanistan, 1979–1989

government in Afghanistan. As in Yemen, the primary loyalty of an Afghani is to his clan and tribe. Most of the men count themselves as warriors and are armed with a variety of small arms, from modern AK 47s to venerable (and still very lethal) old British .303 Lee Enfields. War between the ethnic groups and tribes has always been a routine factor in Afghani politics.

Throughout the 1970s the Soviet Union increased its influence in Afghanistan. A left wing, pro-Soviet government under Nur Mohammed Taraki seized power in 1978. Soviet military aid and a few hundred Soviet advisers were brought in to help Taraki's government hold on to power. The leftist Afghani government faced a serious rebellion by Muslim fundamentalists (Mujahideen), who controlled much of the country by 1979. Taraki also faced a threat from within his own party in the form of a faction leader, Hafizullah Amin. Through 1979 Amin's influence grew, and in October he led a coup that resulted in Taraki's murder and his appointment as prime minister. Although a leftist, Amin was seen as unreliable by the Soviets, so military intervention was planned in order to put a more reliably pro-Soviet leader into power — a leader who would more effectively combat the Mujahideen rebels.[21] In a carefully planned operation, the Soviet Fortieth Army, with over forty-five thousand men, crossed the border and invaded Afghanistan with large armored and mechanized forces. A Soviet airborne division landed in Kabul and seized the capital with little resistance. Prime Minister Amin was killed and a former deputy prime minister, the pro-Soviet Babrak Karmal, put into power. Within days all the major cities were under Soviet control. The Soviet plan had met all of its initial goals. The old government was out and a new pro-Soviet government was in. The new government was dedicated to defeating the Mujahideen rebels, and with the overwhelming firepower of the Soviet Fortieth Army and the Red Air Force to help out, there was little doubt that the mission would be accomplished in a few weeks and the Soviets could withdraw their forces, leaving a stable and orderly satellite state behind them.[22]

EARLY OPERATIONS, 1979–1981: THE SOVIET
ARMY TRANSFORMS

From the start, the Soviets miscalculated the political realities of Afghanistan. The pro-Soviet governments of Taraki and Amin had enjoyed little popular support — which is why the Mujahideen insurgents were making rapid gains. Karmal's new government had even less popular support. The large (eighty thousand men in 1980) but ill-equipped and ill-paid Afghani army had little desire to fight the insurgents before the Soviet invasion. After the Soviets invaded there was even less interest in fighting on behalf of an atheist foreign power that was fighting their own countrymen. While most army units remained officially loyal, entire companies and even battalions deserted en masse with all their equipment, often going directly to join the Mujahideen. Throughout the war, the rate of individual desertions in the Afghani government forces was very high, as many as ten thousand deserters a year in the mid-1980s.[23] With such a clearly unreliable force, the Soviets soon realized that they would have to take on the burden of defeating the rebels. The assumption was that the poorly trained and equipped Mujahideen would be no match for the large, well-equipped Soviet army backed by the largest air force in the world. Of course, if it had been a conventional war, then the Soviet assumptions would have been quite sound. However, the Afghani way of war has traditionally been a guerrilla war of ambush and mountain fighting, and the Soviet forces had no doctrine or training for the counterinsurgency war they had just embarked on.[24]

Within a few months the Soviet forces in Afghanistan had increased to about 110,000 men.[25] The Soviet forces that fought from 1979 to 1981 were primarily armored/mechanized units, equipped with the T-72 main battle tank and BMP armored personnel carrier. The Soviet soldiers assigned to the three motorized rifle divisions, two separate motorized rifle brigades, and two separate motorized rifle regiments in Afghanistan in 1980 had been trained to fight from their armored vehicles in a European environment.[26] Unfortunately for the Russians, Afghanistan is one of the worst countries in the world for armored/mechanized warfare. The Soviets soon learned the disadvantages of being a heavy, road-bound army in a mountainous country with few roads. The Mujahideen fell back from the first Soviet ground offensives in March 1980 and simply returned and reoccupied the country as soon as the Soviets left.[27] The Afghani insurgents were soon equipped with antitank rockets (RPGs), supplied by deserters from the government forces or smuggled in through Pakistan, and were ready to take on the heavy Soviet forces. In June the rebels ambushed and destroyed an entire Soviet battalion on the Gardez-Khost road.[28] The Mujahideen became very adept at carrying out ambushes of the Soviet armored and supply columns bound to the roads in the steep mountain country or narrow valleys. The insurgents employed fairly standard ambush tactics with blocking forces and mine barriers. The rebels would normally allow the armored security element of a convoy to pass without incident before opening fire on the supply vehicles. The rebels, who wore no uniform and operated in small bands, could inflict heavy damage and slip away and easily hide within the population.[29]

The Fortieth Army had, at first, deployed to Afghanistan with full air support. Stationed in Afghanistan were the 115th Fighter Regiment at Bagram Airfield and the 136th Fighter-bomber Regiment based at Shindand and Kandahar Airfields (a Soviet air force regiment is about the size of a fighter group in the USAF — about seventy to eighty aircraft). This amounted to over 150 modern fighter-bombers.[30] Longer-range aircraft were also available on call at nearby Soviet air bases across the border. However, the Soviet high command soon realized that their clumsy, armor-heavy force was simply unsuitable for the tactical conditions of Afghanistan. The initial Soviet invasion force had no more than sixty helicopters for reconnaissance, troop transport, and gunship support. During 1980 and 1981, the Soviets quickly reinforced their helicopter forces while withdrawing some of the armored vehicles. By early 1981, the Soviets had deployed three hundred helicopters of all types in Afghanistan.[31] As with the Americans fighting in the jungles of Vietnam, the Russians made the helicopter the primary transport and weapons system for the combat forces.

The Mi-8 and Mi-6 transport helicopters and Mi-24 helicopter gunships served the Soviet army well in Afghanistan. From 1980 to 1982 the Soviet forces made a transition from an armor-heavy force to a lighter, heliborne force. Motorized rifle battalions that had trained to go into battle in armored vehicles were detailed for air assault training and operated as helicopter-borne light infantry. The Soviets already had a paratroop division (103rd Paratroop Division) whose troops had been trained in the light infantry role, and the Fifty-sixth Air Assault Brigade was deployed to Afghanistan. In addition, highly trained elite special forces units, to include a Spetsnaz (commando) brigade and separate battalion, were deployed to Afghanistan.[32] Faced with a new form of warfare, the Soviets moved to adapt their strategy and develop a tactical doctrine suitable for conditions in Afghanistan. The air assault troops, and heliborne infantry, paratroops, and Spetsnaz units were assigned the primary responsibility for conducting offensive operations, while the armored and mechanized units operated mostly in defensive roles such as base defense and convoy escort.[33]

The Soviet doctrine from 1979 to 1980 emphasized combined arms warfare with large armored and mechanized formations. In Afghanistan, in order to catch elusive bands of insurgents that numbered anywhere from ten to eighty men (it was rare when more than one hundred rebels concentrated for one operation), standard Soviet tactics were generally unworkable. In order to seek out and destroy the small rebel bands, the Soviets had to deploy platoons or companies. The number of helicopters available often determined the deployable force. Since the Afghanis usually had the advantage of the high ground when firing on Soviet vehicles moving along valley or mountain roads, the Soviet air assault troops would seize the high ground via helicopter lift and set up blocking positions on strategic ground in order to trap Afghani rebels retreating from mechanized columns conducting sweep operations. Soviet operations came to closely resemble the American search-and-destroy tactics of Vietnam.

In many respects, the Soviets had to learn a whole new kind of war. Going into Afghanistan, Soviet procedures for coordinating air support were highly centralized at the battalion level or above. Few junior officers had the authority to request air strikes. Indeed, the Soviets discovered that few officers were able to effectively coordinate combined arms warfare. Company commanders could not request support from the mortar platoons without going through the battalion commander. This type of strictly centralized command and control might have been appropriate for a high-intensity conventional war in Europe, but was completely ineffective in a largely small unit war against Afghani insurgents.[34] Since the heliborne infantry, which became the primary offensive force for the Soviets, possessed only light firepower the Soviets learned to decentralize their fire and air support procedures and deploy forward air controller teams (FACs) to accompany even small units engaged in operations and allow junior officers to directly request air support without going through several higher headquarters. Although the Soviets deployed a considerable artillery force to Afghanistan, its relatively short range limited its effectiveness away from the Soviet base camps. Often, the most responsive and effective firepower for the air assault troops came from the helicopter gunships — especially the armored and heavily armed Mi-24 "Hinds," which carried a lethal mix of cannon, rockets, and Sagger guided missiles into combat.[35] Red Air Force fighter bombers, most notably the Su 25 attack planes, often worked in conjunction with the helicopter gunships to provide close air support for Soviet troops.

The air assault operations employing light infantry, gunship and fighter-bomber support, artillery support, and perhaps a mechanized reinforcing force, was a considerably more complicated form of war than the conventional armored warfare that the Soviets had trained for. For combined arms/air assault operations against small rebel bands to be effective, the Soviets first needed thorough reconnaissance and intelligence. Careful planning was required to bring several air assault teams down in the right locations at the right time. Moreover, the nature of the country made heliborne operations more difficult. Most of the airfields were located at 1,000 to 1,800 meters above sea level, and many of the operations were carried out in mountains at an altitude of 3,000 meters. The mountain conditions greatly limited the effectiveness of the helicopters. The tough Mi-8 Hip helicopter, the workhorse troop transport of the Soviet army, could carry over twenty fully loaded men at sea level, but less than half that load at 2,500 meters. The Mi-6 transport helicopter, which could carry up to twelve metric tons at sea level, also found its performance halved in Afghanistan's conditions. In summer, the temperatures often rise to over one hundred degrees Fahrenheit, another factor that limited helicopter performance. Airfields and heliports were dusty and parts of the country regularly experienced dust storms, which not only made flying dangerous but also made Afghanistan a maintenance nightmare for the airmen.[36]

The best aircraft for supporting combat operations in Afghanistan was the Sukhoi Su 25 fighter-bomber. The Su 25 was designed as an attack plane for supporting ground troops, and it did this quite well in Afghanistan. The Su 25 is a jet but much slower than the main fighter jets of the Red Air Force such as the Mig 29 and Mig 31. Its slow speed is actually an advantage in counterinsurgency flying, as the pilot has more time to observe and acquire the target. The Su 25s, like the American A-10, were armored to protect the pilot and engine and had a considerable loiter time, another important factor in providing effective close support to ground troops. It could carry a large amount of ordnance in the forms of bombs and its 23 mm aircraft cannon. The biggest complaint about the Fortieth Army's use of airpower is that it overtasked the pilots. Too many missions resulted in pilot fatigue, which caused the loss of many aircraft in accidents.[37]

THE MUJAHIDEEN REBELS

True to their Afghan culture, the Mujahideen rebels never managed to present a unified front against the Soviet invaders and the Soviet-supported Afghani government. While Mujahideen leaders often met, they met as peers negotiating to cooperate for a short-term operation or agreeing to divide up an aid or weapons shipment. There was no single body of national leadership or a command structure for an insurgent army. All of the Mujahideen forces were regionally and ethnically based and owed their allegiance not to any national movement but to their commander and the local tribal chiefs and elders. In one sense, this gave the Soviets an advantage because they never had to face a coordinated insurgent strategy. On the other hand, it also made the war very difficult for the Soviets because winning a battle in one sector had no impact whatsoever on the morale or fighting capabilities of other rebel groups in other sectors. There was no single Mujahideen government or council to single out for attack, nor was there any single body with whom one might negotiate if military victory was unattainable. In short, the Soviets faced not one enemy but many different groups spread all throughout the country.

In many cases, this might have worked to the advantage of a government carrying out a counterinsurgency policy. The "divide and conquer" approach is one of the oldest and most successful counterinsurgency techniques. However, the Soviets trapped themselves at the start of the intervention by picking a figurehead to control the Afghani government who had little popularity or following. The Afghani army, on paper three hundred thousand strong, could not be counted upon to support the war effort. The Afghani army resented being used as "cannon fodder" by the Soviets (at least that was their perception), and the Soviets had little trust in the Afghani army's fighting abilities. In fact, the Soviets rightly suspected that the Afghani government and army was riddled with informants and sympathizers of the Mujahideen. Essentially, from the beginning the Soviets were forced to shoulder the burden of fighting a war in a vast territory virtually alone. Finally, the heavy-handed approach to using military force, especially airpower, ensured that however much the Afghanis might dislike each other, they could all agree that they disliked the Russians even more.

There were ten different major Mujahideen groups, which ranged from fundamentalist Muslims to supporters of the Afghan monarchy, that took the field against the Russians.[38] The Mujahideen had the benefit of strong support from the Pakistani government and people throughout the war. The insurgent groups could operate openly in Pakistan and raise money and international support. More than a million Afghanis fled the devastation of the war and crossed into Pakistan, where most lived in squalid refugee camps. With large numbers of Afghanis within Pakistan, the entire border area became a secure base camp for the Mujahideen, who could cross the border to rest, rearm, and refit their forces. The long and mountainous border with Pakistan is exceptionally rugged country, but there were innumerable paths by which the Afghani rebels could bring people, arms, and supplies into the country. Between the arms captured from the Russians and the Afghani government forces and the arms smuggled across the Pakistani border, the Mujahideen rebels became fairly well equipped with small arms, rockets, and mortars. At first, the rebels used the SA-7 Grail handheld antiaircraft missiles against Soviet helicopters and aircraft but, by the mid-1980s, supplies of the much more lethal American "Stinger" light antiaircraft missiles were smuggled into Afghanistan with the cooperation of the American CIA.

Since the Mujahideen was a loose coalition of groups and warriors, no one then or now has any clear idea of how many took up arms against the Soviets. Estimates range from 90,000 active fighters to 250,000 fighters, and even one estimate of 744,000 if one were to include everyone who took an active role in the resistance.[39] In any case, the Afghan resistance to the Soviet invasion can fairly be described as a "people in arms." In contrast to most insurgencies, which are organized politically, the basic organization of the insurgents was through village and regional Islamic committees. The Islamic committees, many of which sought to create an Islamic republic in Afghanistan, carried on recruitment and propaganda campaigns and encouraged the village people to support the "holy war" against the Soviets. Although political and ethnic differences divided the major Mujahideen groups, they were all united by a common religion that provided a motivation to fight and resist even more powerful than any political ideology.[40]

ATTRITION WAR

From 1982 on the war was characterized by the concentration of Soviet forces and firepower to "sweep" the main centers of Afghan resistance. Air assault units were committed to seize high ground and to establish blocking positions. Soviet mechanized forces supported by artillery would attempt to push forward and drive the insurgents into a trap. The scene of some of the heaviest fighting in Afghanistan was the Panjsher Valley in northern Afghanistan near the major Soviet air base at Bagram. The Soviets carried out large offensives that included battalion-sized air assaults in April and May 1982 and again in September, yet failed to destroy the guerrilla stronghold in the rugged terrain.

For a while in 1983 the Soviets established a de facto truce with the insurgents in the Panjsher region. However, the truce did not last and the Soviets mounted further large operations in the Panjsher region again in 1984 and 1985. While the Mujahideen took heavy losses, the Soviets failed repeatedly in their attempts to trap and exterminate the rebels.[41] The Mujahideen strategy was fairly simple: trap the Soviets in an attrition war and continue to inflict casualties until the enemy gave up and went home. Fired by their religious devotion and hatred for the infidel invader, the Afghanis, for whom warfare was considered a normal way of life, were quite willing to take massive casualties to win.

Understanding that they were now facing a long-term attrition war, the Soviets embarked on a ruthless program of bombing the rebels into submission. Since the insurgent fighters relied on the strong support of the rural populations, the Red Air Force fighter-bombers and helicopter gunships selected areas of strong Mujahideen resistance for depopulation. Rebel villages were ruthlessly bombed in order to eliminate the Mujahideen bases.[42] No one can be sure of the casualty toll of the Soviet bombing campaign in Afghanistan, but it probably inflicted tens of thousands of casualties. Although the bombing succeeded in driving many Afghanis into Pakistan as refugees, the morale of the Mujahideen fighters was not seriously shaken. The Mujahideen developed tactics to fight the Soviet helicopters. For example, once the insurgents learned how the Soviets normally fought, they became adept at spotting probable helicopter landing zones. The landing zones were covered by well-camouflaged hidden heavy machine guns and rocket launchers ready to take down a helicopter at its most vulnerable moment and also to allow the Russians to land and then pin them down at the landing site. When the rebels fought at close range, the Soviets would be unable to bring down artillery fire or air support onto the rebels for fear of hitting their own troops. The emergence of U.S. supplied "Stinger" missiles, which could hit an aircraft at a distance of 4,800 meters, in the mid-1980s had a major effect on the Soviet employment of airpower. The increased lethality of the Stingers was a serious problem for the Soviets. As the Stingers appeared, the Soviets were forced to fly their aircraft at higher altitudes to avoid the light surface-to-air missiles. Red Air Force fighter-bombers bombed less accurately from higher altitudes. Helicopters had to be used much more cautiously, and employment was limited in daylight hours.[43] The Russians claim that aircraft losses did not increase noticeably with the deployment of Stingers, but this claim is very doubtful. The Russians do admit that the increased lethality of the rebels' antiaircraft missiles seriously affected the Soviet ability to provide effective air support.[44] For example, out of fear of the Stingers, the Soviets were forced to curtail helicopter operations during their 1987 offensive in the Paktia Province.[45]

The Mujahideen became skilled at hiding from Soviet airpower and developed an intricate system of bringing weapons and supplies into Afghanistan by vehicle or mule train along the mountain roads. Soviet air interdiction operations and attempts to ambush Mujahideen supply convoys along the Pakistani border failed to seriously impede rebel supplies.[46] The insurgents also made deals with the Afghan government forces to allow them unimpeded access through border areas in return for an unofficial local truce or perhaps bribes paid to the Afghan army commanders.

By April 1985 the Soviets understood that they were hopelessly bogged down in an attrition war and making little headway in defeating the insurgents. In fact, the number and intensity of Mujahideen raids on the Soviets and the Afghan government forces increased from 2,400 incidents in 1985 to 2,900 in 1986 and 4,200 in 1987.[47] The official Soviet casualties for the war were given as 13,833 dead. However, other sources argue that the Soviets incurred at least 26,000 deaths in Afghanistan.[48] By any reckoning, the losses incurred by the Afghanis were many times the Soviet figures, running into the hundreds of thousands killed. Yet, however many Mujahideen the Soviets killed, there were plenty of volunteers to replace losses. By the mid-1980s the Mujahideen training camps in Pakistan were filled with men who often got a fairly thorough training in small unit tactics and the use of weapons, mines, and explosives before going into battle — so the insurgents evolved into a more formidable fighting force even though losses were heavy. In 1985 the Soviets understood that the war was unwinnable and started to withdraw some forces from Afghanistan, six motorized rifle regiments at first. The Soviets began a process of turning over the major share of the fighting to the Afghan army. However, the Soviets continued to conduct numerous small-level helicopter operations by the air assault units and ambushes conducted by Spetsnaz. By early 1987 the Soviets disengaged from almost all ground combat operations and began pulling out their remaining forces.[49] By early 1989 the Soviets had evacuated Afghanistan and left their satellite government to fend for itself.

Israel's War in Lebanon

In 1982 Israel mounted a large-scale invasion of Lebanon with the intention of effectively destroying the Palestine Liberation Organization as a military force that could threaten the Israeli population. The offensive against the PLO was remarkably successful. In a rapid blitzkrieg drive to Beirut, the Israeli army swept the PLO forces aside and cornered the PLO in the city of Beirut. After a several-week siege, the PLO evacuated Lebanon in a clear Israeli victory. In the aftermath of victory, the Israelis slowly withdrew from most of southern Lebanon while continuing to occupy a ten-mile-wide strip of southern Lebanon as a "security zone." Israeli forces in southern Lebanon soon found themselves at war with an enemy even more dangerous than the PLO. For the next eighteen years Israel waged a constant battle in southern Lebanon with the Hizbullah (Party of God), a terrorist organization that very capably fought a war of attrition against Israeli forces until Israel finally withdrew from southern Lebanon in 2000.

The Israelis are superb practitioners of the military art and excellent strategists. They have to be. This small western and democratic nation surrounded by a violently hostile Arab world would be quickly exterminated if it ever lost a war. Military excellence and sound strategy means national survival for Israel, so Israel has built a formidable military machine. Israel ranks just after the United States in the quality of its military technology. In training and combat experience, Israel probably has the best forces in the world. Having fought and won four major conventional wars between 1948 and 1973, the Israeli Defense Forces (IDF) contain a high proportion of experienced combat leaders. Only a few Western nations have armed forces with training equal to Israeli standards. The large Israeli Air Force (IAF), equipped with some of the most modern U.S.-built warplanes, is superbly trained and capable of employing the latest precision munitions. The IAF played a central role in the campaign against Hizbullah, and its operations are the main subject of this section. Yet, despite these several advantages, Israel was eventually forced to admit the failure of its strategy in Lebanon and withdraw its forces. The story of the Israeli conflict against the Hizbullah terrorists is the story of how an exceptionally capable military can become embroiled in a war that it neither planned nor trained for and lose the conflict.

The immediate cause of Israel's 1982 invasion of Lebanon was a series of PLO terrorist actions coupled with the shelling of towns and settlements in

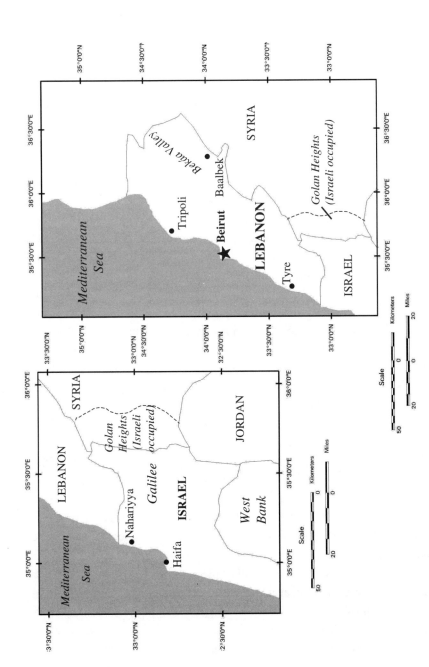

Northern Israel and Lebanon, ca. 1982

northern Israel. Of course, the origin of the conflict goes back much further. The PLO was founded in 1964 from several groups of Palestinian refugees and grew rapidly with financial support and subsidies from the Arab world. From the start, the PLO took the form of a government in exile representing the Palestinian refugees, and those living under Israeli occupation in the West Bank and Gaza Strip territories won by Israel in the 1967 war. The PLO acquired businesses and investments and created a formal government infrastructure. It received formal diplomatic recognition from Arab states and maintained offices and accredited representatives in the Arab nations. The PLO also established its own regular army with an infrastructure of military installations, training camps, and a professional military cadre. The PLO's political ideology was primarily nationalistic and the political objective of the PLO, stated in its charter, was the destruction of the Israeli state and the establishment of a Palestinian state. Although almost all of the PLO members were Muslim, religious views were not central to the PLO ideology, as the organization also had Arab Christian members and sympathizers.

From the 1960s through the 1980s, well-trained and -equipped PLO military teams carried out numerous major terrorist attacks against Israel, Israeli businesses, and citizens abroad and attacked Jewish synagogues and organizations in Europe and the Americas. Terrorist attacks by the PLO included the massacre of Israeli athletes at the 1972 Olympic games in Munich, the hijacking and destruction of numerous aircraft, and terror bombings of Israeli consulates and embassies and attacks on Israeli businesses in Europe. In addition to attacks on Jews and Israeli interests outside of Israel, the PLO regularly sent teams to carry out terrorist attacks within Israel. Some of the PLO terrorist attacks were especially brutal. In March 1978 a sea-landed PLO raiding party captured a bus on the Tel Aviv–Haifa Highway and massacred thirty-four civilians — mostly women and children.[50] During the 1970s and early 1980s, the PLO also attacked Israel by means of artillery and rocket barrages from PLO bases in southern Lebanon against civilian settlements in northern Israel.

The Israeli Defense Forces (IDF) had a policy of replying to every terrorist attack by force. In the 1950s, *fedayeen* terrorists, the forerunners of the PLO who raided Israeli settlements from bases in Egypt and Jordan, were the target of Israeli raids carried out by small commando teams. By the late 1960s both the PLO terrorism and the Israeli reprisals had grown in scope and scale.

In March 1968 the IDF crossed the Jordanian border with an entire brigade to destroy the PLO base at Karameh. However, the Israelis came to use air strikes for retaliation more and more in order to bring maximum firepower down upon terrorist bases while minimizing any potential Israeli losses. The first major air attack against a PLO base was carried out in August 1968 when the PLO camp in Salt (Jordan) was bombed.[51]

The PLO had maintained its primary government and military bases in the kingdom of Jordan up to the early 1970s. However, the PLO presence in Jordan became so strong that the Jordanian government rightly came to fear the establishment of a state within a state that could destabilize Jordan. In a series of military clashes in the early 1970s, the Jordanians overran the PLO military installations and forced the PLO to evacuate its organizational and military infrastructure to southern Lebanon, where it already had a presence. Due to the chaotic nature of Lebanese politics, the PLO was able to establish a large presence in Lebanon without fear of being expelled or bothered by the Lebanese government.[52] In short order, the PLO built a large military infrastructure in southern Lebanon, which had a large Palestinian refugee population, and effectively become a state within a state in Lebanon. The PLO Supreme Military Council, headquartered in Beirut, in 1982 commanded a military force of over fifteen thousand regular troops in southern Lebanon. The regular PLO forces were organized into units of battalion strength and were better trained and equipped than many armies of Third World nations. In addition the PLO had thousands of militia forces organized among the Palestinian refugee communities, which in Lebanon numbered several hundred thousand people.[53]

Although the PLO used terrorist attacks by small, well-trained teams as its primary means of waging war against Israel, it was well armed with conventional heavy weapons to include Soviet supplied T-54 and T-55 tanks, BTR-60 armored personnel carriers, and a variety of antiaircraft guns (23 mm, 37 mm, 57 mm) and SAM-7 and SAM-9 surface-to-air missiles. From the Israeli perspective the most dangerous weapons of the PLO were its 122 mm and 130 mm Soviet-made artillery pieces, 122 mm multiple launch rockets (katyushas), and its 82 mm, 120 mm, and 160 mm mortars. The PLO also possessed modern antitank weapons to include "Sagger" missiles.[54] PLO artillery and rockets were capable of firing from deep inside Lebanon at targets inside Israel. The 130 mm howitzers of the PLO had a range of over twenty-seven kilometers.

ISRAEL REARMS, 1973–1982

While Israel won the 1973 Yom Kippur War, its forces initially suffered some tactical defeats and took heavy losses. Israel already had a large and very modern armed forces in 1973, but the Yom Kippur War demonstrated the greatly increased lethality of antiaircraft and antitank weapons. The lessons learned from the war motivated Israel to embark on a major program to modernize and improve its armed forces and capabilities.

Between 1973 and 1982 Israel increased its standing armed forces (not counting reserves) from 75,000 men to 172,000. The tank force went from 1,225 tanks to 3,825 tanks, and Israel introduced a new main battle tank of its own design, the Merkava. Armored personnel carriers were increased from 500 to 4,800, and the army increased its numbers of self-propelled guns from 300 to 958.[55] In addition to enormous improvements in firepower and armor protection for the army, the IDF also acquired a large quantity of state-of-the-art communications and intelligence collection equipment.

The improvements in the Israeli Air Force (IAF) capabilities in this period were even more impressive than the army's program. The Phantom F-4E fighter-bomber first entered Israeli service in 1969, and between 1969 and 1977 the IAF received 204 F-4Es, each capable of carrying 16,000 pounds of ordnance, and 12 RF 4E reconnaissance airplanes from the United States. The IAF acquired 117 A-4Ns, advanced versions of the Douglas A-4 Skyhawks, between 1972 and 1976.[56] The Israeli Aircraft Industries introduced the Kfir CZ fighter-bomber in 1977. The Kfir, a derivative of the license-built Mirage 5 fighter with a General Electric J-79 engine, is a nimble aircraft that can carry 9,470 pounds of munitions.[57] The United States supplied Israel with sophisticated air-to-air fighters that gave the IAF a considerable edge over any other Mideast nation. The United States sold a batch of F-15 Eagles in 1976 and additional aircraft from 1981 to 1982. F-16 fighters began to arrive from the United States in July 1980.[58] In 1982 the quality of the IAF's U.S.-supplied aircraft, avionics, and air-to-air missiles proved their worth when more than 50 Syrian Mig 21s, 23s, and 25s were shot down over Lebanon without loss to Israel.[59]

One of the most significant changes in the IAF between 1973 and 1982 was the creation of a large and capable helicopter force. Up to the Yom Kippur War, the IAF had maintained a small helicopter force for troop-lift, but this force played only a minor role in Israeli combat doctrine. This changed in the mid-1970s when the IAF acquired AH-1G Cobra attack helicopters. The Cobra was equipped with a 20 mm Gatling-type cannon, rockets, and TOW missiles that made it a fearsome and highly accurate weapon against ground targets.[60] Another new helicopter in the IAF inventory was the Hughes 500-MD Defender, equipped with four antitank missiles.[61] Bell 212 helicopters, similar to the UH-1s of the U.S. Army, were acquired for troop-lift and special operations. Sikorsky CH-53 helicopters equipped the IAF search-and-rescue units.[62] In addition, the IAF's French-built Super Frelon helicopters were upgraded.[63]

By 1982 the IAF possessed over 600 combat aircraft, including 75 F-16s, 150 Kfirs, 138 F-4s, 130 A-4s, and 30 Mirage IIIs. The IAF also had a sophisticated aerial intelligence and electronic warfare capability with the purchase of OV-1E Mohawks and E-2C Hawkeyes for airborne intelligence collection and EC-130Es and EC-707s for electronic warfare. The IAF's helicopter force included 30 AH-1Gs (Cobras) and 20 Hughes 500s as gunships, along with 38 Bell 206s and 212s for transport and liaison.[64]

By 1982 the IAF was organized, equipped, and trained to carry out a wide variety of conventional and unconventional warfare operations. The first priority of the IAF was to win the air superiority battle against enemy fighters and antiaircraft defenses. This part of an air campaign required Israel's most advanced fighters supported by the intelligence and EW aircraft. Once air superiority was won, Israel could commit its fighter-bombers and attack aircraft to the destruction of enemy forces. Finally, the IAF's helicopter force enabled the Israelis to conduct large (battalion-size) air assault operations as well as raids by small commando forces. As the PLO would discover in the mid-1980s when a PLO headquarters in Tunisia was bombed by Israeli fighters in retaliation for a PLO attack on Israelis in Cyprus, the IAF also had developed the capability to conduct precision strikes against targets over fifteen hundred miles from Israel.

THE 1982 INVASION OF LEBANON

From 1981 through the spring of 1982, the PLO dramatically increased the scale of its attacks on Israel from its Lebanese bases. From May to July 1981 the PLO made 1,230 artillery and rocket attacks that hit twenty-six northern Israeli towns, killing 6 and wounding 26 civilians.[65] Israel retaliated with air strikes and commando raids. A cease-fire was arranged in July 1981 but like most Mideast truces, it didn't hold for long. Between July 1981 and May 1982 the PLO made 290 attacks on Israel from Lebanon that killed 29 and wounded 271 Israelis.[66]

In 1982 PLO artillery and rocket attacks on northern Israel increased. The PLO in 1981 and 1982 had received twenty tanks, one hundred 120 and 160 mm mortars, and forty heavy Katyusha rocket launchers from the Soviets and were eager to try their new equipment. The PLO had also significantly increased its artillery forces in southern Lebanon.[67] As tensions increased, on 3 June 1982 the Israeli ambassador in London was shot by three PLO terrorists. The next day artillery barrages between the PLO and Israel erupted all along the Israel/Lebanon border. Israeli air units struck PLO targets as far north as Beirut.[68] The Israeli cabinet decided on a full-scale invasion of Lebanon by Israeli forces to begin on 6 June.

On 6 June 1982 a force of six Israeli divisions, over seventy thousand men and one thousand tanks supported by the IAF, rolled forward into Lebanon. In a conventional war campaign, Israel rapidly drove the PLO out of its defensive positions and into headlong retreat toward Beirut and to the cover of two Syrian army divisions stationed in the Bekaa Valley in eastern Lebanon. Using effective combined arms tactics and well supported by the IAF, the Israeli army's left flank drove north with few losses and was on the outskirts of Beirut in four days. The PLO mounted its most serious defensive effort at Beaufort Castle, an old Crusader fortress. The IAF fighter-bombers and helicopters pounded the fort into rubble before PLO forces surrendered to the Israeli army. Four IAF helicopters were lost during the assault on the fortress.[69]

The heaviest fighting of 1982 was on the Israeli right flank in the Bekaa Valley against the Syrian forces occupying the eastern third of Lebanon. In order to have the ability to fly freely over Lebanon, the IAF had to deal with the extensive and sophisticated air defense system set up by the Syrians in eastern Lebanon. On 9 June, in a carefully planned and coordinated campaign, the IAF destroyed seventeen of nineteen SAM batteries in the Bekaa Valley. The IAF used a combination of deception, electronic warfare, and Harm missiles to systematically take out the Syrian SAMs, radars, and communications systems. That day twenty-nine of the Syrian fighters sent up to oppose the IAF were shot down without loss. The next day the IAF shot down a further thirty-five Syrian planes. The campaign against the Syrians in the Bekaa Valley eliminated any serious threat from the Syrian air force and assured the IAF complete air superiority over southern Lebanon.[70]

By 11 June the Israelis had trapped the PLO in Beirut. From there until August the IDF put the PLO-occupied sectors of Beirut under siege rather than attempting a costly house-to-house battle. The IAF carried out numerous attacks against PLO positions and heavy weapons. On 12 August, after a heavy Israeli air and artillery bombardment, the PLO agreed to a cease-fire and to withdraw its forces from Lebanon. Yassar Arafat, the PLO chairman, and thousands of PLO members were forced into exile in Arab nations. The Israeli invasion of Lebanon had effectively destroyed the PLO as a military force in Lebanon, although some Palestinian forces had found refuge under Syrian protection in eastern Lebanon. The PLO suffered thousands of casualties in the campaign. The PLO equipment captured by the Israelis included 80 tanks, 202 mortars, 56 Katyusha rocket launchers, and 70 heavy artillery pieces ranging in size from 122 mm to 155 mm guns. One hundred fifty three antiaircraft guns were also captured.[71] Israeli losses through the campaign had been light. Fighting the PLO in southern Lebanon had cost the Israelis only 25 dead and 96 wounded. The clash with the Syrians cost Israel 255 dead and 1,537 wounded. During the siege of Beirut, Israel lost 88 killed and 750 wounded.[72]

The IAF had performed brilliantly in the campaign. The IAF flew thousands of sorties and brought accurate fire upon the PLO and Syrians.[73] The attack helicopters proved their worth as highly lethal and precise weapons systems. The AH-1 Cobras and MD 500 Defenders fired 137 TOW missiles with ninety-nine reported hits — killing twenty-nine tanks, fifty-six vehicles, four radar sites, and other targets.[74] In addition to employing attack helicopters and precision munitions, the IAF used a variety of RPVs (remote piloted vehicles — also commonly called unmanned aerial vehicles, i.e., pilotless aircraft) as intelligence platforms. The RPVs performed very effectively to provide real-time intelligence on Syrian and PLO defenses to the IAF commanders. The RPVs were also used as laser designators so that fighter-bombers could drop precision munitions.[75] IAF losses in the campaign were low. In addition to the four helicopters lost in the battle at Beaufort Castle, an A-4 Skyhawk and AH-1 Cobra were lost to ground fire in the first two days of the campaign.[76] In July an RF-4 was lost.[77]

INTERNATIONAL CRITICISM OF ISRAELI AIR OPERATIONS

One of the things that the Israeli government must continuously contend with is widespread and vigorous criticism and disapproval from the United Nations, the Third World, and many Western nations whenever Israel uses force against terrorists. Normal policy for the Arab nations is to conduct a permanent propaganda war against Israel and accuse the Israeli government and military with every manner of war crime and human rights abuse in the fight against PLO and Hizbullah terrorists. In addition, Israel faces another propaganda front. Israel routinely faces condemnation from many European and American academics and in much of the Western media for its military actions. The UN and the left/liberal politicians and media in the Western nations view Israel's war with terrorists with a double standard, much the same as any military action of Western nations in the Third World is viewed. What this simply means is that Israel is held to the highest possible standards of international law and behavior, while Third World "liberation" movements are allowed to violate international law and norms with impunity and with little criticism. This double standard allows insurgent and terrorist movements a considerable propaganda advantage when Israel or any democratic Western nation uses military force in self-defense. Claims of war crimes committed by the Israelis or Americans are routinely presented with little or no evidence and will be faithfully repeated in the Third World media as fact. Even the Western media, with supposedly higher journalistic standards, tend to take reports from Third World movements known for bending the truth with considerable respect. On the other hand, when Israel brings forward concrete proof of gross violations of international law on the part of the PLO, Hizbullah, and other terrorist organizations, the story is routinely ignored or downplayed by the Western governments and media.

Because Israel has a free press and a democratic government, which maintains the principle of civilian control of the military, the IDF is held to a high standard of behavior for the conduct of its military operations. In suppressing the Palestinian "intifada" (rebellion) in the occupied territories of the West Bank in the late 1980s and early 1990s, IDF ground forces repeatedly violated their strict rules of engagement and used excessive force against Palestinian suspects and civilians. Between 1987 and 1994 the IDF initiated investigations, trials, and disciplinary action against three hundred officers and soldiers serving in the

West Bank for using excessive force.[78] During the battles in Lebanon in 1982 the IAF, for the first time, had to conduct large-scale operations in urban areas heavily populated by civilians and also had to deal with the issues of excessive force and civilian casualties. In the initial advance, the IDF cleared out the Palestinian camps around Tyre and Sidon with ground troops. It was more costly in lives and time to clear resistance methodically than to simply send the air force in and turn all the centers of resistance into rubble. However, the IDF decided that bombing the camps would cause heavy civilian losses.[79]

When the Israelis reached Beirut and cornered most of the PLO there, their government faced a dilemma. They had three choices. They could withdraw, after having handed a humiliating defeat to the PLO, they could send the ground troops in and finish the PLO, or they could put Beirut under siege and use artillery and airpower to pound the PLO into submission. Faced with the opportunity to totally defeat the PLO, the Israeli government did not want to abandon the fight and return to Israel. The second option, that of going in on the ground, would have cost many Israeli casualties as well as heavy losses to civilians. The Israelis took the third option, that of putting Beirut under siege. The use of artillery and air attacks necessarily caused several hundred, perhaps several thousand, civilian casualties and inspired strong criticism and open protest from many Israelis who argued that Israel's siege of Beirut was far too heavy-handed.[80]

The strategy of using artillery and fighter-bombers to destroy the PLO in Beirut, with the consequence of high civilian losses, resulted in a military victory and a political defeat for Israel. Although the IAF operated under fairly strict rules of engagement and tried to avoid civilian targets, there was bound to be heavy collateral damage in a siege campaign. The PLO was soon seen by much of the world's press as the victims of the ruthless and powerful Israeli war machine and emerged from the military defeat with considerably more sympathy than they had when the siege began. In short, the Israelis handed the PLO a propaganda victory by its use of firepower in Beirut.

An example of the propaganda advantage gained by the PLO and terrorist groups in their war against Israel is seen in the siege of Beirut (June to August 1982). A group of liberal Western European jurists came together to collect and publish findings of war crimes committed by the Israeli forces in its battle against the PLO. The Israeli Air Force came under especially harsh criticism. The "International Commission," chaired by Irish jurist Seán

MacBride, presented a case that appealed to the anti-Israel, pro-terrorist bias in European liberal academic circles. With little hard evidence the International Commission repeatedly accused the IAF of violations of international law in the conflict in Lebanon. For example, the Israeli bombing of PLO targets in Beirut was referred to as "terror bombing" and "indiscriminate bombing of Muslim civilians."[81] Partially refuting the International Commission's charges are the relatively low casualty figures for Beirut civilians incurred during the Israeli siege — a figure estimated in the hundreds. If Israel had actually wanted to carpet bomb Beirut with the intention of slaughtering civilians, it certainly had the means to do so with more than six hundred combat aircraft in the IAF inventory. In fact, Israel took considerable care to bomb only legitimate and carefully identified military targets and use precision munitions to limit collateral damage. If the IAF had not used any restraint in the air campaign, civilian casualties in Beirut would have run into the many thousands.

Yet, while criticism of the Israeli strategy in Lebanon in 1982 was certainly justified, the bias of the jurists against Israel was remarkably blatant. In numerous cases clear violations of international law on the part of the PLO were ignored or explained away by the International Commission. For example the commission criticized Israel for bombing an antiaircraft gun mounted on the roof of an apartment building. When the IAF bombed the gun, as many as twenty civilians were killed. Although international law allows for the bombing of clearly military equipment such as antiaircraft guns, the commission nevertheless condemned the Israelis because antiaircraft guns were "completely ineffective against the Israeli Air Force."[82] The last statement is especially absurd, as the IAF lost several aircraft to ground fire during the campaign.

After the fight in southern Lebanon and Beirut, the Israeli Defense Forces published aerial photos proving that the PLO had routinely violated international law by placing rocket launchers and antiaircraft guns on tops of hospitals and placing tanks and heavy weapons in civilian neighborhoods, often close to foreign embassies. If the Israelis had struck such weapons, as they had the right to, the bombs would have resulted in heavy civilian casualties and a propaganda coup for the PLO.[83] In the atmosphere of frustration with Israel, even from its friends, and with the help of many in Western media and academic circles that are sympathetic to the PLO and Islamic terrorists, such behavior by the PLO became a win-win situation. If the Israelis had refrained from bombing military targets in order to spare civilian lives, then the PLO preserved its weapons and personnel. If the Israelis bombed weapons and personnel that posed a threat to its troops, and consequently killed civilians, then the PLO got to document a new Israeli "war crime" and win sympathy in the international community.

WAR WITH HIZBULLAH STARTS

With the withdrawal of the main PLO forces from Beirut in August 1982, the PLO organization in Lebanon was reduced to a shadow of its former strength. Some factions of the PLO, as many as five thousand fighters, took refuge under Syrian protection in the Bekaa Valley. Some of the Palestinians organized themselves into even more radical groups and vowed to continue a terror campaign against Israel. Such groups, often closely allied with the PLO, included the Democratic Front for the Liberation of Palestine (DFLP), Popular Front for the Liberation of Palestine (PELP), and the Abu Nidal Organization.[84] In the fall of 1982 there were several attacks upon the Israeli forces in Lebanon that prompted Israeli air strikes against Palestinian group bases.[85] However, the PLO had been so badly beaten in the summer battles and the threat so reduced that the Israeli government felt confident in removing most of its forces in Lebanon by late 1983. Israel began a phased withdrawal from Lebanon with the intention of permanently occupying only a small strip of land along the southern border of Lebanon to ensure that PLO forces could not attack Israeli settlements in northern Israel. The Israeli strategy of keeping only a small force in Lebanon (one thousand men by the mid-1980s) required an alliance with the Christian militia in southern Lebanon. Israel began to arm and subsidize the Christian forces that became known as the South Lebanon Army (SLA) in return for their cooperation in keeping the PLO out of southern Lebanon. What the Israelis had not reckoned with in 1982 was the rise of a new threat that was more dangerous than the PLO.

When the Israelis invaded Lebanon, a group of Shiite Moslems organized a group known as Hizbullah (the Party of God). Hizbullah began a guerrilla war against the Israeli forces in Lebanon in late 1982, and the war between Hizbullah and allied terrorist groups lasted until Israel's withdrawal from Lebanon in 2000.

Shiite Muslims constitute the third largest religious group in Lebanon, after Sunni Muslims and Maronite Christians. In 1982 the Shiites were about 30 percent of the population. Shiites were poorer than the other groups in Lebanon and were underrepresented in Lebanese politics — which had always been dominated by the Sunnis and the Christians. One important aspect of the Shiites was their close tie to Iran. The leading Shiite clerics in Lebanon had long had a close relationship to leading Iranian clerics and many had studied in religious schools in Iran. Several of the top Lebanese Shiite leaders were old friends of Iran's Ayatollah Khomeini.[86] When the Shah was deposed and Iran became an Islamic republic under Khomeini in 1979, Lebanese Shiites rejoiced. The Lebanese Shiites tended to be deeply devout and looked at an uncompromising Islamic republic as the ideal government for Muslims. Shiites in Lebanon formed a militia (AMAL) in 1975 when civil war broke out, but many Shiites left that movement, as it was too secular in its views. Hizbullah, motivated by a radical Muslim vision, had far greater appeal to Lebanon's Shiites than AMAL.[87]

In 1982, during the Israeli invasion, as many as fifteen hundred (some figures go much higher) Iranian Revolutionary Guards were sent to Lebanon to help train and organize the military forces of Hizbullah to fight Israel.[88] From 1982 to today Iran has consistently and generously supported Hizbullah with money, arms and supplies, and advisers. For their part, the Syrians allowed the Iranians to bring personnel, supplies, and arms for Hizbullah into Lebanon through the territory occupied by its army, and Hizbullah was allowed to set up training camps and arms depots inside Syrian territory.

Founded by Muslim clerics, Hizbullah was especially secretive in its command structure and operations. The central authority of Hizbullah is a Supreme Consultative Council of eight to seventeen Shiite clerics. However, Hizbullah tends to be fairly loosely organized and does not possess the clear hierarchy of the PLO. Several groups associated with Hizbullah soon appeared in Lebanon and include the Jund Allah (Army of God) and Al-Jihad (Islamic Jihad). The politics of Hizbullah and the Shiites are not laid out as a clear charter or platform, but Hizbullah members believe that an Iranian model Islamic republic is the best form of statehood. Two other principles guide Hizbullah: a vicious anti-Americanism and the desire to destroy Israel. A Hizbullah manifesto of February 1985 describes America as "the root of vice" and argues that "fighting America is defending Islam." Israel is seen as an agent of the United States and it is therefore necessary to obliterate it. The Hizbullah ideology generally reflects the Iranian Islamic Republic's view of the United States.[89]

In the summer of 1982, many of the Shiites enjoyed seeing the defeat of the PLO by the Israelis as the Palestinians, outsiders from the Lebanese point of view, had acquired too much power in Lebanon. However, relations with the Shiites and the new outsiders, the Israelis, quickly soured. Within weeks, Hizbullah organized some small guerrilla units and began a small-scale war against the Israelis. The conflict with the Shiites was hardly noticed, as Israel was still mopping up PLO centers of resistance in Lebanon. However, by 1984 Shiites were starting to be viewed by Israel as the more dangerous of their enemies in Lebanon. One of the sources of Hizbullah strength and one of the things that alarmed the Israelis was the high degree of popular support Hizbullah enjoyed from the Shiite population.

Hizbullah did not make the mistake of the PLO in trying to oppose the Israelis with a conventional military force. Hizbullah consistently operated with small units that employed guerrilla and terrorist tactics. Thanks to Iranian trainers, Hizbullah terrorists became masters of bomb making.[90] One of the primary weapons of Hizbullah against the Israeli forces in Lebanon was the car bomb. In addition to hit-and-run guerrilla attacks and ambushes against small Israeli outposts, Hizbullah employed suicide bombers who would strap explosives to themselves or drive a car laden with explosives and detonate themselves close to Israeli troops.[91] A suicide attack is one of the most effective terrorist tactics, as it is especially difficult to defend against. Israeli forces stopping a Hizbullah car would be killed or wounded when the driver sets off a bomb and himself with it. Israelis found that conventional concepts of deterrence did not work against people who were willing and eager to die if it meant taking an Israeli along with him. The effectiveness of Hizbullah suicide terror tactics was amply demonstrated in October 1983 when a Hizbullah truck bomber killed almost three hundred U.S. Marines when he rammed his vehicle, packed with tons of explosives, into the U.S. headquarters in Beirut. The truck bombing not only created enormous damage, it showed that Hizbullah was capable of careful intelligence gathering and planning. Hizbullah had observed the Americans for weeks before hitting them at the most vulnerable time and place. Since Hizbullah enjoyed the support of much of the population, it and allied groups could easily collect information on Israeli troops, equipment, outposts, convoy schedules, and so on, and then strike. On the other hand, Israel did not have the same level of intelligence as it had enjoyed against the PLO. In the battle against the PLO,

Israeli intelligence had become expert at infiltrating Palestinian groups in the occupied West Bank and in Lebanon, and often used Israelis who had been born in Yemen and could pass as Arabs as agents. Hizbullah, however, was much smaller than the PLO and far more secretive and difficult to infiltrate. In Lebanon the Israelis did not have the same intelligence network of agents and informers in the Shiite community as it had in the Palestinian community.[92]

AIRPOWER AGAINST HIZBULLAH

Through 1983 the number of small raids and terrorist attacks against the IDF in Lebanon increased. From October 1982 to 1983 Israel refrained from bombing the PLO and Shiite groups as Israeli forces withdrew to the Awali River Line. Israel followed a "wait and see" strategy in dealing with the Arab response to the Israeli forces in southern Lebanon. As Arab violence increased the IAF began striking PLO and Shiite targets in Lebanon in October 1983.[93] Between October 1983 and October 1985, the IAF carried out twenty-eight air strikes against PLO and Shiite groups.[94] Of these, twenty-five were directed against the PLO bases and only three against the Hizbullah camps.[95] The standard Israeli response to PLO attacks was to use fighter-bombers to strike terrorist bases in the Syrian-occupied Bekaa Valley. Each air strike was a complex affair that took considerable planning. First the Israelis had to locate and photograph the site with air reconnaissance. Aircraft sent to bomb the site had to be covered by F-14 and F-15 fighters flying cover in case the Syrian fighters intervened. Other fighters carrying HARM antiradar missiles flew escort to take out Syrian air defense radar in case the Syrians activated their SAM missiles. Search-and-rescue helicopters stayed on alert in case a pilot was shot down. Electronic warfare aircraft also might accompany each mission. It was a difficult and expensive means to respond to Hizbullah terrorism, but it was the best way to inflict maximum damage with the least risk to Israeli lives.

The IAF strikes concentrated on the PLO and allied groups largely because the Israelis had better intelligence on the PLO and the PLO had a larger number of clearly identified bases, depots, and headquarters. In contrast, Hizbullah had a much smaller number of active fighters, never more than a few hundred, and these were easily hidden within the Shiite population. There were some known Hizbullah camps and headquarters, but not many. Another thing that worked to Hizbullah's advantage was the strict rules of engagement that limited the IAF's ability to strike at known terrorist cells if those cells were located in a town or village. Israel's system of Western democracy and respect for traditional humanitarian rules of war would not allow its forces to conduct operations that were likely to inflict heavy civilian casualties.[96] On the other hand, Hizbullah did not play by the same rules. For example, Hizbullah would routinely fire mortars or rockets from a site next to a school or village. Sometimes the Hizbullah guerrillas would set rockets with timers so that when they fired at Israeli settlements or military positions, the terrorists would be long gone. If IDF artillery fired a counterbattery barrage against the rockets, the Israeli rounds were more likely to hit Lebanese civilians than Hizbullah fighters. If the Israelis killed Lebanese civilians, even inadvertently and with just cause, it still ended up as a propaganda victory for Hizbullah.

By the mid-1980s Israel had become engaged in a low-level attrition war in southern Lebanon and had no clear strategy to extricate itself. The objective of Hizbullah's attrition strategy was to exert pressure on the Israeli government to pull out of Lebanon. Hizbullah understood that, as a democratic nation, the Israeli government was highly vulnerable to public opinion and by the mid-1980s there was considerable criticism of the government over its Lebanon policy. The policy of air strikes on Hizbullah targets had no discernible effect. As the Israelis increased their raids, Hizbullah ratcheted up the level of its attacks. Hizbullah's deputy secretary general, Shaykh Na'im Kassem, outlined the nature of the Hizbullah attrition war strategy. "When an Israeli soldier is killed, senior Israeli officials begin crying over his death. . . . Their point of departure is preservation of life, while our point of departure is preservation of principle and sacrifice."[97]

By 1987 the IDF had withdrawn to a ten-mile-wide buffer zone along Lebanon's southern border, which was jointly occupied by the South Lebanon Army and one thousand to two thousand Israeli troops.[98] As the Israelis pulled back, Hizbullah's campaign intensified. Hizbullah and Palestinian groups could again target northern Israeli settlements, firing rockets over the occupied buffer zone into Israeli territory. The ever-ingenious Hizbullah terrorists found innovative ways to use modern technology to attack Israel. In November 1987 two terrorists flying in powered hang gliders crossed over the Israeli buffer zone and landed in Israel. One was killed at Metla and the other landed near an army camp and killed six IDF soldiers and wounded eight more before being gunned down.[99]

In response to the guerrilla war in Lebanon, the Israeli high command turned to the IAF's helicopter force as the best means of striking Hizbullah with pinpoint accuracy.[100] In 1987, in a carefully planned operation, Hizbullah leader Sheikh Abdul Karim Obeid was taken prisoner in Lebanon by helicopter-borne commandos. Obeid was captured to facilitate negotiations with Hizbullah about Israeli prisoners. In February 1992 the Israelis conducted a brilliant raid that killed the secretary general of Hizbullah, Abbas Mussawi. Acting on intelligence, an RPV followed Mussawi's convoy of automobiles during a nighttime move (Hizbullah leaders, knowing the IDF's capabilities, drove at night, changed cars en route, moved in convoy, and took other actions to minimize the chance of ambush). The RPV gave the location of Mussawi's moving car to nearby Israeli Apache attack helicopters, which scored a direct hit with Hellfire missiles on the Hizbullah leader. In another brilliantly executed operation, a Hizbullah training camp in the Bekaa Valley was struck by helicopter-borne commandos and gunships in a nighttime raid that killed forty terrorists.[101] Several similar operations by IAF helicopter units exacted a toll on the Hizbullah leadership and cadre.

Yet Hizbullah was scarcely affected by these Israeli raids. When Mussawi was killed in 1992, Hizbullah soon found another leader. When terrorists were killed in training camps, plenty more volunteers were eager to join Hizbullah's ranks. Major operations into southern Lebanon that featured air and ground attacks such as "Operation Accountability" in 1993 and "Operation Grapes of Wrath" in 1996 inflicted a few casualties upon the terrorists but far more on civilians that were caught in the cross fire.[102] In the meantime, Hizbullah raids and terror actions exacted a steady toll on the Israelis. Between May 1993 and May 1997, 105 IDF soldiers were killed in Lebanon and another 221 wounded. These totals do not include the loss of 73 IDF soldiers when two helicopters accidentally crashed in the buffer zone in 1997.[103] While the Hizbullah and Palestinian terrorists lost 10 or more fighters for every Israeli killed, the attrition war still worked against Israel. Successive Israeli governments tried a variety of strategies including large-scale joint operations, air strikes against the Hizbullah infrastructure, and "regime targeting" that took out selected senior leaders and officers of Hizbullah. Nothing seemed to work. Finally, in mid-2000 the Israeli forces pulled out of their occupied zone in south Lebanon. The Israelis brought some of their SLA allies with them and resettled them in Israel to protect them from Hizbullah retaliation.

The border has been fairly quiet since then, although a few rocket attacks have occurred against northern Israel since the outbreak of Palestinian/Israeli violence in late 2000. It is likely that since Israel could not defeat the Hizbullah by direct attacks, it will probably hold Syria, and perhaps the Lebanese government, responsible for future attacks carried out by Hizbullah against northern Israel. Hizbullah exists and flourishes only because the Lebanese and Syrian governments allow arms and supplies to be imported through their territory for the terrorists. Without the passive support of the Lebanese and Syrian regimes, Hizbullah would not be as effective as it is. Since Syria and Lebanon have more to lose in IAF air attacks than Hizbullah, it will be interesting to see if Syria and Lebanon act to restrain Hizbullah operations on their territory rather than face IAF attacks.

A New Terror Campaign

In September 2000 Israel and the occupied territories erupted in violence after Likud Party leader Ariel Sharon visited a Muslim holy site, the Temple Mount, in Jerusalem. Riots by Arabs started and escalated as police and paramilitary forces of the Palestinian Authority joined the fray. In October 2000 the IDF began employing attack helicopters with precision weapons to strike Palestinian Fatah Party headquarters and known Palestinian terrorist groups.[104] Through 2001 violence continued throughout the occupied territories as Palestinian suicide bombers, usually members of Hamas and Islamic Jihad groups, drove bomb-laden cars into Israeli checkpoints. Many of the terrorists, including teenage girls, strapped bombs to themselves and detonated the bombs where they would inflict maximum Israeli civilian casualties in cafés, discos, restaurants, schools, buses, and markets. The Palestinian suicide terrorists, supposedly acting without the approval of the Palestinian Authority leader Yassar Arafat, have carried out a sustained campaign of terror aimed almost exclusively against Israeli civilians. Over four hundred civilians had been killed by April 2002.

Unlike Hizbullah's desultory campaign in south Lebanon, the Palestinian terror campaign against Israel is considered to be a major threat to the security of Israel and the government and people have responded accordingly. In March 2002 the Israeli government ordered a partial mobilization. Over twenty thousand reservists were called up, and Israeli mechanized forces, supported by the IAF, initiated a large-scale invasion of Palestinian towns and cities on the West Bank that serve as headquarters for the major terrorist groups (Hamas, Islamic Jihad, etc.) attacking Israel. Former defense minister Ariel Sharon, known for his hard-line views and as architect of Israel's invasion of Lebanon in 1982, was elected prime minister. He insisted that Israel was fighting for its survival and vowed to smash the Palestinian militants.[105] By mid-April 2002 more than sixteen hundred Palestinians had been killed and more than one thousand arrested and detained. In contrast to the Palestinian offensive against Israel, Palestinian civilian casualties have been low. The targets of the Israeli offensive into the Palestinian Authority in the West Bank have been terrorist groups and Arafat's police and militia forces, not the civilian population.

In contrast to the restrained response to the intifada of the 1980s, the Israeli government under Sharon has been very aggressive in seeking out and attacking the Palestinian terror network in the West Bank. Sharon authorized the use of attack helicopters and even F-16s using precision bombs to strike at the Palestinian Authority security forces and at known terrorist group headquarters, bomb factories, and weapons storage sites. The Israeli strategy is to hold Arafat's regime responsible for the Hamas and Al Jihad suicide attacks and to pressure the Palestinian Authority with air strikes and military action to coerce the Palestinian Authority to arrest the Hamas and Islamic Jihad terrorist leadership. Israel insists that the Palestinian Authority must take action to shut down the allegedly independent terrorists as the first condition before opening up negotiations.[106]

As in Lebanon, Israel has fared poorly in the world media in the propaganda war. The United Nations, predictably, took a strongly anti-Israeli stance when UN Secretary General Kofi Annan loudly condemned Israel's incursions into the West Bank to break down the Palestinian terror network.[107] Much of the Western media tends to equate the violence employed by the two sides in an attempt to be "evenhanded." In practice, the Israelis have been careful to use precision weapons such as Hellfire missiles and laser-guided bombs in striking military targets such as Palestinian police compounds and Fatah Party offices in order to minimize collateral damage. Palestinian terrorists, on the other hand, have intentionally struck primarily civilian targets such as restaurants that contain a maximum number of women and children. As with Hizbullah in southern Lebanon, there is no shortage of Palestinians willing to commit suicide in order to kill Israelis. In the current conflict the Palestinians acknowledge no rules or limits, and established norms of international law are blatantly ignored. Israel, which has followed the traditional rules of war and norms of international law in fighting the Palestinians, continues to receive most of the blame for the conflict in the Western media. For example, Israel has been roundly criticized in the European and American media for practices such as stopping and searching ambulances at checkpoints — an action seen as a human rights abuse in the West. However, in March 2002 the Israeli tactics were found to be quite reasonable when a Palestinian Red Crescent ambulance was stopped and found to be carrying twenty-two pounds of explosives packed into a suicide bomb.[108] As of early 2002, the conflict between the Israelis and the Palestinians continues to escalate.

In the current conflict, Israel has used airplanes and helicopters extensively in a mostly urban campaign. The IAF's ability to employ precision munitions and guided missiles allows Israel to use heavy firepower in built-up areas with less risk of collateral damage to civilians. The IAF helicopter force has also played a major role in the campaign, allowing the Israelis to hit terrorist centers with surprise raids and enabling the Israelis to set up blocking positions in Palestinian territory. The efficient Israeli medevac helicopters ensure that wounded Israeli soldiers are rushed to a hospital within minutes — another reason for the low fatalities suffered by the Israeli army. It is certain that airpower will play an ever larger role in combating the Palestinian terrorists.

Summary

The stories of the military campaigns in this chapter illustrate the difficulty of conducting a successful counterinsurgency campaign, even with the most modern weapons. One of the primary lessons learned is just how powerful religion can be in motivating people to fight. Muslims that wage a jihad (holy war) against infidels — Russians, Jews, or Americans — can expect a reward in paradise if they kill the enemy and die in the attempt. Since the early 1980s in Lebanon, suicide attacks have become a standard tactic used by Muslims in fighting Jews and Americans. Religion also served as a primary motivator for the Mujahideen in Afghanistan who endured great hardship and losses in their ultimately successful fight against the Soviets.

Airpower has been repeatedly used with decisive effects in conventional warfare, and the Israelis were tremendously successful in their conventional war against the PLO in 1982. However, against an unconventional enemy such as the insurgents in Yemen and Afghanistan and the terrorists in Lebanon, airpower proved far less effective simply because the insurgents and terrorists had no clear central organization to attack. The resistance to the Soviets in Afghanistan was a loose coalition of forces; the insurgency in Yemen was also a shifting coalition of tribes. Hizbullah has a fairly loose organization with autonomy for its many smaller cells. Attacks on the leadership have much less effect than attacks on a highly centralized organization — such as the PLO had in 1982.

The Egyptians tried a classical civic action campaign in Yemen, bringing material improvements, medical care, and schooling to that primitive country to win the "hearts and minds" of the tribesmen. The Egyptian campaign backfired. Aside from a tiny number of Egyptian-educated intellectuals, the vast majority of Yemenis didn't want any modernization that included things like modern medical care, the education of women, or the elimination of slavery. Yemenis, like most Afghanis, preferred their tribal society and distrusted *any* central government. Despite the poverty and misery of their countries, many in the Third World resist change of any type — even when that change is urged upon them by their brethren. The Israelis were criticized in southern Lebanon for not carrying out any extensive civic action campaign.[109] However, one wonders if Israel could have done anything to win the hearts and minds of the Shiites when the major motivation of the Shiites was the extermination of the Israeli state.

One of the most interesting strategies has been to strike at the governments that host terrorists. If it is difficult to find and strike terrorists, it is fairly simple to pressure governments that grant the terrorists refuge and support — such as the Syrians gave to Hizbullah in Lebanon and the Palestine Authority is providing for terrorist groups in communities under its authority. Established governments have much more to lose than terrorists and insurgents, and helicopters and precision weapons are easy to employ and avoid risk to one's own forces. Whether this form of coercion works to reduce or eliminate the support granted by governments to terrorist groups remains to be seen.

Afghan Mujahideen fighters, early 1980s. These tribal warriors, armed mostly with light weapons, managed to fight the Soviets to a standstill in Afghanistan.

The Mi-8 Hip was the primary transport helicopter of the Soviet army in Afghanistan. It was an effective aircraft for the time. In fact, the Mi-8s are still operating in many of the world's air forces. However, the conditions in Afghanistan (high altitudes and hot summer temperatures) cut its considerable lift capability in half.

The Soviet army Mi-24 Hind was designed to fight NATO tanks on the European battlefield. Instead, it saw its major action in Afghanistan. The partially armored and heavily armed helicopter (here with rocket pods and a twin 23 mm cannon) was a highly lethal close support aircraft. The Soviets built much of their airmobile tactics around the Hinds. However, the arrival of U.S.-supplied Stinger antiaircraft missiles in Mujahideen hands in 1985 and 1986 inflicted heavy casualties on the Hinds and forced the Soviets to restrict the use of helicopters on the front lines.

Israeli F-4 fighter-bomber. The F-4, capable of carrying sixteen thousand pounds of bombs, has been the workhorse attack plane of the IAF since the late 1960s. The F-4s played a major role in supporting the Israeli army during the 1982 invasion of Lebanon. (Israeli Air Force)

Israeli F-16. Since the F-16s were acquired by the IAF in the 1980s they have been employed in fighter-bomber and air defense roles. F-16s using precision munitions were employed against Hizbullah and the PLO in the 1990s and in the West Bank rebellion of 2000 to 2002. (Israeli Air Force)

IAF AH-1 Cobra helicopter gunship. This has been the IAF's primary helicopter gunship since the 1970s. Its ability to fire precision antitank weapons and to operate at night has made it a major support weapon of the Israeli forces in south Lebanon. Cobras have been used to ambush and pick off Hizbullah leaders with far more accuracy than an airplane. The Cobra is being supplanted by the U.S.-built Apache attack helicopter. (Israeli Air Force)

10

Conclusion

During the first half of the twentieth century, the most common form of insurgency was a rebellion against a colonial power, sometimes motivated by
nationalist aspirations but often by some local grievance. After World War II,
anticolonial insurgencies motivated by far more coherent nationalist ideologies swept through Africa and Asia. Many other insurgencies were led
by various brands of Marxists (later Maoists) trying to overthrow established
pro-Western governments such as in Greece, the Philippines, El Salvador, and
Guatemala. Other insurgencies, for example in Indochina and southern Africa,
combined the two. By the mid-1970s, with the fall of the Portuguese empire,
there were few colonial states left to rebel against and indigenous Marxist insurgencies, such as the one plaguing Colombia today, became the norm.

With the fall of the Soviet Union and with it the demise of communism as
a major political force in the early 1990s, many observers concluded that the
era of Marxist insurgencies was over. Communist states had played an important role in fomenting and supporting insurgencies in Asia, Africa, and
Latin America. Without generous assistance from the Soviet Union and its
satellites, the chance for a Marxist insurgent victory in a Third World country
seemed minimal. For example, the fall of the Soviet Union and the victory of
democratic parties over the Marxist Sandinista regime in Nicaragua in 1990
brought enormous pressure on the Marxist FMLN rebels in El Salvador to
make peace on essentially the government's terms as outside aid from the
Soviet bloc and Nicaragua would no longer be forthcoming.

However, the fall of communism as a major force in world politics did
not mean that Marxist insurgencies ended. Marxist rebels in Colombia soon
learned that the drug trade could provide a lucrative source of income. In

addition, Colombia's porous borders made it possible to obtain arms on the world market and, combined, these two factors permit the FARC to continue its rebellion in the absence of help from friendly states. Marxism retains a great appeal throughout the so-called Third World. Despite the failure of Marxism to bring about anything but dictatorship and misery to every country that has adopted it, Marxist ideology still remains attractive to many intellectuals in the developing world. Moreover, some intellectuals in the developed world similarly remain infatuated with Marxist theory and can be expected to encourage and support Marxist insurgencies as a result. While few if any intellectuals in the West would actually ever fight in a guerrilla war to create a Marxist society, they can be counted upon to provide moral and other support to self-styled revolutionaries, no matter how brutal. In short, Marxist ideology can be expected to inspire insurgents of various stripes in the future as well as provide the basis for support from external agents.

Irrespective of the general Marxist hue of postcolonial insurgencies, many internal conflicts today are motivated less by ideology than by ethnicity. Numerous countries have witnessed bloody insurgencies as well as irredentist terrorist movements made up primarily of ethnic minorities seeking autonomy or independence. Insurgents and terrorists in Africa, Asia, and Latin America are motivated as much by ethnic animosity toward the governing majority population than any ideology. Indeed, since the end of the Cold War the forces that have held many ethnic rivalries in check have fallen, resulting in more conflicts than ever before.

The Soviet war in Afghanistan prefigured some of the insurgencies and terrorist movements that we face today. The prime motivation for those who fought the Soviets was, in addition to a traditional xenophobia regarding foreign intrusion, a resurgent and fundamentalist Islam. Since then, Islamic movements engaged in terrorism or insurrection against non-Islamic states or against pro-Western states have benefited from generous funding and support from certain Islamic regimes, including but not limited to the Islamic Republic of Iran, as well as a large network of supporters throughout the Muslim world. Even during its heyday, Marxism never had the moral force or ideological clarity to motivate people to turn themselves into suicide bombers. But fundamentalist Islam has the moral force to do just that. The challenge this poses is immense: how does one deter a man who chooses a martyr's death in which he goes to Paradise, and after which his family is congratulated and supported by the community for having produced a martyr?

In light of religious fanaticism as the prime mover for many terrorists, as well as the ability of some rebel groups to sustain themselves in the absence of popular or external support (e.g., the FARC in Colombia), much of counterinsurgency theory as it currently exists may no longer be appropriate. In the colonial period, insurgents in Africa and Asia provided aid and sanctuary to each other in the limited aim of overthrowing their own governments. Now we see diverse groups across the globe cooperating against a common enemy — that is, the United States, Israel, and the West. Although the Soviet Union has ceased to be a major supplier to these groups, some Muslim states have stepped up their support to these selfsame insurgents and terrorists. In that regard, although insurgency and terrorism have been around since biblical times, modern insurgency and terrorism have evolved to new and deadlier forms.

Likewise, airpower has also evolved as a major player in fighting against insurgents and terrorists. We believe that the twenty-first century will likely see as many insurgencies and terrorist movements as the previous century, and airpower must continue to adapt and keep pace. The experience of airpower in small wars outlined in this book provides some useful lessons to guide the employment of airpower against insurgents and terrorists in the future. In this concluding chapter, we offer eleven of the most important lessons that we have drawn from history as a guide for future doctrine, technology, and organization. We believe that these lessons are useful not only for U.S. armed forces but also to any Western military that must contend with insurgency and terrorism. Future counterinsurgency and counterterrorism operations will mostly be by coalition forces involving several nations. Hopefully, the United States and its allies can use the historical record of airpower in small wars to arrive at a common framework and doctrine for its employment.

The Lessons

1. *A comprehensive strategy is essential.* The first lesson is a very simple one but, as Carl von Clausewitz noted, in war even the simple things are difficult. In order to defeat insurgents and terrorists, a state or coalition of states must start with a comprehensive strategy.

Strategy is defined as the allocation of military, political, economic, and other resources to attain a political goal. In a conventional war the military role in strategy is normally paramount, as the primary goal is usually the destruction of the enemy's military capability. In contrast, when fighting an insurgency the political and economic aspects of the strategy are often as important if not more important to victory as the military contribution. In conventional war states can realistically aim for full military victory. However, in an insurgency one cannot expect the unconditional surrender of the insurgents. In many cases, a compromise political settlement to end the insurgency becomes the most realistic end state for the government. In such a case, a compromise settlement is not a defeat. As Clausewitz noted, a "favorable state of peace" is the true goal of any state involved in a conflict.

The employment of military power and airpower in counterinsurgency is not an end in itself. The final political goal is always paramount, and the political repercussions of the use of military power must always be considered. The heavy-handed application of military force might lead to a short-term military advantage yet prove to be counterproductive in the long run if military action turns popular sentiment against the government. In successful counterinsurgency campaigns, military operations have been conducted in coordination with government reforms, education and propaganda campaigns, and economic programs that addressed the needs of the population and, as a result, won over the people. In the successful Malayan and Philippine campaigns, military operations were often secondary to the government's political and economic programs. In El Salvador, land and political reforms played a central role in winning the majority of the population over to the government side and gaining a favorable settlement for the government.

Unsuccessful counterinsurgency campaigns such as the Portuguese operations in Africa, the French in Algeria, the Rhodesian Republic, and the Soviets in Afghanistan were characterized by a strategy that viewed the war almost solely as a military operation and ignored the political and economic dimensions of the conflict.

Crafting a strategy that properly addresses the military, social, and economic aspects of a conflict is extremely difficult. In El Salvador a military strategy emerged in 1981, but a comprehensive political/economic strategy was not crafted until 1983 and 1984. In the decades-old insurgency in Colombia, it was not until 2000 and 2001 that anything resembling a national strategy began to emerge to guide the government's counterinsurgency efforts. However, Colombia is still in the early stages of crafting a comprehensive political/military strategy. Although developing a comprehensive strategy is a very difficult task, it is also an absolutely necessary first step in effectively combating insurgency. The failure of the French in Indochina and Algeria, as well as the Russians in Afghanistan, can be attributed largely to the lack of a comprehensive strategy. In the case of the Israeli failure in Lebanon and the U.S. failure in South Vietnam, an overarching strategy was present, but it was deeply flawed in terms of wrong assumptions about enemy behavior and motivation.

2. *The support role of airpower (e.g., reconnaissance, transport, and so on) is usually the most important and effective mission in a guerrilla war.* In opposing insurgents and terrorists conducting a low-level guerrilla war, the indirect application of airpower, that is, the support role of aviation, often proves the most important contribution. In numerous counterinsurgency campaigns the ability to airlift army and police units to remote locations and to keep them supplied by airdrop and helicopter has proven decisive. Such was the case during the U.S. Marines' intervention in Nicaragua in the late 1920s. Marine Corps transports and other aircraft sustained deep-penetration patrols and remote outposts as well as moved government forces to concentrate against guerrilla formations. During the Malayan Emergency, the RAF inserted light infantry units deep into the jungle and kept them supplied for weeks, thus playing a key role in defeating the communist insurgents there. Helicopter airlift in El Salvador enabled the army to garrison strategic points and to carry the war deep into insurgent-held territory without being vulnerable to road ambush. In addition, the availability of helicopters for medical evacuation of wounded soldiers greatly enhanced the morale of the Salvadoran army troops who knew that they were within an hour's flight time from hospital treatment. At the time of this writing, the UH-60 Blackhawk, a superb machine for transporting men and supplies, is proving to be the most important single weapon of the war in Colombia. Since their arrival from the United States, the Blackhawks have enabled the Colombian army to react quickly to guerrilla raids and have allowed government forces to take the offensive in 2002.

3. *The ground attack role of airpower becomes more important when the war becomes conventional.* The lethal application of airpower, primarily air strikes performed by ground attack aircraft, bombers, helicopter gunships, and so on — what the British call "direct action" — has a relatively small role in an

insurgency when enemy combat operations are characterized by acts of terrorism and small hit-and-run raids against government forces and infrastructure. However, when insurgents concentrate in large forces and aspire to conventional or positional warfare, they become especially vulnerable to air attack. Conventional military operations require heavy weapons, logistical bases, lines of communication, and headquarters elements to coordinate operations. All of these are excellent targets for airpower.

As was the case at Dien Bien Phu, when insurgent forces can deploy more firepower than the government forces, transitioning from guerrilla warfare to a conventional campaign may be a wise strategic decision. However, generally speaking, government forces — especially air forces — accrue the advantage when insurgents attempt positional warfare. When Augusto Sandino attempted to hold ground in Nicaragua in 1928, Marine Corps aviation mauled the guerrillas and on one occasion forced the Sandinistas to abandon their position due to aerial fires alone. The decision by the Greek communists to consolidate their forces and openly challenge the Greek army in the Granmos Mountains in 1949 was a disastrous strategic error, as the Royal Hellenic Air Force conducted attacks that broke the will of the insurgents. When the Huk insurgents in the Philippines attempted to "regularize" and fight a positional campaign, the combined efforts of the Filipino army and air force exacted a tremendous toll. Similarly, when the PLO attempted to fight conventionally in Beirut in 1982, this worked to the advantage of the Israelis, who were able to employ massive airpower against the PLO's heavy forces. Today, the FARC rebels in Colombia have built up a logistics and support infrastructure in the cease-fire zone created in Colombia between 1998 and 2002. The FARC infrastructure is now vulnerable to attack by Colombia's air force.

4. *Bombing civilians is ineffective and counterproductive.* Aerial campaigns that target insurgents and terrorists located in or very near population centers are generally counterproductive. Bombing civilians as punishment for supporting guerrillas has proven to be consistently counterproductive.

Although colonial powers that waged punitive aerial campaigns in the pre–World War II era could claim some success in their efforts against rebel tribesmen and bandits, air attacks directed against civilians have repeatedly failed in the post–World War II era. If anything, bombing insurgent-held towns and villages tends to make the population more hostile to government forces and any claims they make to represent a just cause. The French bombed Viet

Minh towns in Indochina and insurgent villages in Algeria and gained no military advantage thereby. The Egyptians conducted ruthless attacks against civilians in Yemen — which only increased the resentment toward the revolutionary government that the Egyptians were trying to support. The massive bombing campaign mounted against the Afghan population by the Soviets inflicted heavy civilian casualties and served to strengthen the resolve of the Afghans to drive the Soviets out of the country.

Bombing civilians, or targeting insurgents and terrorists in urban areas with resulting civilian casualties, generally works to the propaganda advantage of the rebels. In El Salvador, any military benefits gained as a result of bombing FMLN-held villages were greatly offset by the political losses brought about by the international outcry that it provoked. Moreover, the FMLN was able to portray the Salvadoran government as ruthless villains and human rights abusers. In addition, every time bombs were dropped, monetary contributions from sympathetic leftists around the world flowed to the FMLN. Finally, the government bombing campaign made it exceptionally difficult to obtain military aid for El Salvador from the U.S. Congress.

Likewise, Israel has been forced to be very careful in carrying out air attacks against PLO and Hizbullah targets, as these are normally located in or near villages and towns in southern Lebanon and in the occupied territories. Even when precision weapons are employed, there is still no such thing as a truly "surgical strike." Weapons often miss their intended targets and kill civilians. On those occasions where the weapons strike the intended target, shrapnel and debris often cause civilian casualties. Civilian casualties that have resulted from IAF strikes have produced considerable sympathy for Islamic terrorist groups, not only in Arab states but also in large segments of the Western media and among political groups in the United States and Western Europe. While it is unrealistic for Israel to forego striking legitimate terrorist targets when it has the opportunity to do so, the possibility, indeed the probability, of civilian casualties must be carefully weighed in order to assess the inevitable political fallout.

In much of the world, as terrorism is seen as the unique weapon of the poor and fanatic, airpower is seen as the symbolic weapon of the West — the means by which the wealthy and advanced countries can bully the poor and weak countries. Thus, bombing is automatically viewed in the Third World as cruel and heavy-handed. This creates a paradox that policymakers today do not seem willing to deal with. While airpower is often the most effective means to strike at insurgents and terrorists, its use will immediately provoke outcry and protest in many quarters of Western society and throughout most of the Third World. In short, there is a political price to pay when airpower in the form of air strikes is used. Of course, in fighting terrorists and insurgents, it may certainly be in the national interest to pay a political price for using airpower. However, national leaders must think hard and consider the long-term political effects when employing airpower in the strike role.

Similarly, indirect air actions that affect civilians must also be carefully considered. For example, the usefulness of the U.S.-supported aerial spraying program intended to eradicate the coca crop in Colombia must be weighed against the propaganda value it presents to the FARC. Leftist groups in Colombia and elsewhere have had some success in portraying the Colombian and U.S. governments as insensitive to the rural population by their use of aerial spraying. In short, the FARC has managed to divert media attention away from its own brutality toward the rural population by pointing to and emphasizing the alleged health consequences of aerial-delivered herbicides. Thus, even in the indirect application of airpower, governments must determine whether and to what extent the impact on civilians is truly worth the political costs, and they must also have a credible and clear justification ready to present to the media and be ready to conduct an effective public relations campaign to support their position.

5. *There is an important role for the high-tech aspect of airpower in small wars.* Recent conflicts have demonstrated that there is a very important role for high technology weapons and other equipment in small wars. Since 1982, Israel has extensively used remote piloted vehicles (RPVs) in its campaigns against the PLO and Hizbullah and with considerable success. RPVs are not only useful for collecting real-time intelligence, they also minimize the possibility of losing more expensive aircraft and pilots. In addition to RPVs, night vision devices and modern avionics used by U.S., Israeli, and other air forces have largely taken away the cover of darkness from insurgents and terrorists. Presently, Western forces fighting insurgents have an advantage in night operations, whereas before this was the best time for insurgents to move and attack.

Space-based reconnaissance and precision weapons guided by Global Positioning System (GPS) satellites have played a major role in the successful U.S. operations against Taliban irregulars and al-Qaeda terrorists in Afghanistan. The ability to bomb with precision through clouds and bad weather has enabled U.S. and coalition forces to inflict heavy losses on the enemy. Moreover, the fact that they can be bombed day and night and in any weather is a powerful psychological weapon that has proved useful against enemy morale.

While high-tech weaponry is not the whole answer to fighting terrorists and insurgents, it certainly makes for an efficient force multiplier. With cutting-edge communications technology and laser range finders and other targeting devices, lightly armed and highly mobile ground forces can bring devastating, immediate, and highly accurate firepower upon insurgents and terrorists. While small nations generally cannot afford the sophisticated technology employed by the United States in fighting a small war, a fairly modest investment in handheld GPS devices, improved communications equipment, some simple RPVs, better avionics, and night vision devices can dramatically improve the effectiveness of a small air force. In that regard, a small nation need not have an air force capable of the sort of large-scale precision bombing of the U.S. Air Force. Whereas in Malaya and in South Vietnam the debate was whether propeller-driven aircraft were better suited to counterinsurgency than fast-moving jets in terms of precisely delivering World War II–era "dumb" bombs, the appropriateness of the platform is no longer the issue, as the precision of modern "smart" weapons has made the question moot. It is now possible for a small air force to equip existing aircraft with precision munitions, whether they are sophisticated jet aircraft or not. There is some evidence, for example, that the Israeli Air Force has provided equipment and training to the Colombian air force in terms of using precision munitions in the war against FARC and that these weapons have been employed since late 2001. This is a positive development that should be promoted in other small countries facing insurgency and terrorism.

6. *There is an important role for the low-tech aspect of airpower in small wars.* In many cases, a "low-tech" approach has proven to be a highly useful and cost-effective means of employing airpower in counterinsurgency and counterterrorism operations. Air forces with limited resources have often devised new and ingenious uses for civilian and obsolete military equipment in small wars. One example of an effective low-tech approach to counterinsurgency has been the use of two-seat trainers in the reconnaissance and strike roles. World War II–era T-6 "Harvard" trainers proved their worth as superb counterinsurgency aircraft in French, British, Portuguese, and South African hands for decades

after World War II. The T-6s were cheap and readily available. Their slow speed and long loiter time made them excellent aircraft for observing artillery fire or for spotting small terrorist bands from the air and marking targets for strike aircraft.

Many other trainers have proven to be just as useful and adaptable as light strike aircraft, able to accurately hit a target with bombs, rockets, machine guns, and cannon. The propeller-driven T-28 trainer and the T-37 jet trainer were easily modified for the strike role, and many continue to serve in small air forces today. Such aircraft are especially useful for small Third World air forces because of their ease of operation, simple maintenance, and their ability to operate from short and rough airfields — something that cannot be done with more sophisticated and expensive jet fighter-bombers. One of the most effective light strike aircraft available today is the Brazilian-manufactured Tucano two-seat turboprop trainer. This aircraft has been adopted by many air forces and has been modified as a strike fighter that can carry up to a ton of munitions.

Old transport aircraft, such as the venerable DC-3/C-47, have been modified to serve in a variety of roles. The Greek air force used C-47 "Dakotas" as improvised bombers during the civil war. C-47s have often been used in psychological operations and as gunships employing heavy machine guns or automatic cannon, providing considerable firepower with precise accuracy at minimal cost. First used by the U.S. Air Force in the Vietnam War, the AC-47 gunship proved to be the most effective close air support aircraft during the war in El Salvador and has acquitted itself quite well in Colombia. New avionics and turboprop engines have given new life to the DC-3, and numerous turbo-modified DC-3s operate around the world performing a variety of roles, including maritime surveillance, command and control, transport, agricultural support, rodent and pest control, medical evacuation, and so on.

A variety of light turboprop civilian transports are in production today, such as the Spanish Casa 212 and the Pilatus Porter, which are very efficient at transporting small numbers of troops or a few tons of cargo to remote locations. Due to their short takeoff and landing characteristics and ability to use rough, forward airfields, these civilian transports are ideal for counterinsurgency operations, as they can go where the heavy and expensive transports cannot go.

One of the more innovative low-tech approaches to airpower in small wars in recent times was the creation of an air force reserve in Guatemala. The reserve was recruited from private pilots, and the Cessna 172s and Piper Arrows and other light planes making up the reserve proved a very useful support service in patrolling roads and rural areas from the air and flying personnel and supplies to remote airfields. Sometimes they were used in the artillery-spotting role. The Guatemalan air force reserve was an inexpensive and simple means of carrying out many of the routine missions of the air force and allowed the regular air force to concentrate on high-priority and more complex combat missions.

7. *Effective joint operations are essential for the effective use of airpower.* We cannot emphasize enough that successful counterinsurgency and counter-terrorism operations are joint operations. Airpower is most effective when it is carefully coordinated with ground forces. Moreover, jointness in the counterinsurgency and counterterrorism context means much more than just the ground, sea, and air forces working in close coordination. Police forces, intelligence agencies, and military and civilian "civic action" teams are also an integral and very important part of fighting against insurgents. Planners must understand the proper role of each of these organizations and employ them fully.

The idea that airpower can "go it alone" or be the primary focus of effort in counterinsurgency and counterterrorism has been proposed by several military writers who have been noted. We believe that such an approach is fundamentally irresponsible. All of the historical studies that we have provided here have taught the lesson that the best approach to combating insurgency is a joint approach with coordination between military and civilian agencies. From a military point of view, combating insurgents and terrorists is even more complex than fighting a conventional war and requires a broader understanding of jointness. One useful model of jointness for counter-terrorism operations is offered by the U.S. government's Joint Interagency Task Force–East (JIATF-E) located in Key West, Florida, with the responsibility for monitoring and coordinating counterdrug operations in Central America and the Caribbean. The joint task force is headed by a Coast Guard admiral and includes members of all the U.S. military services. It also includes personnel and staff officers from the FBI, DEA, CIA, Customs, and the State Department. Because the task force collects intelligence over a broad region and coordinates its efforts with other nations, the JIATF-E also includes liaison officers from Great Britain, France, the Netherlands, and several Latin

American countries. Intelligence is collected from many sources and is analyzed in a single joint intelligence center. The JIATF-E in Key West, created in 1994, proves that military and civilian agencies can effectively and efficiently share intelligence, coordinate operations, and pool their capabilities.

8. *Small wars are intelligence intensive.* A critical requirement in fighting insurgents and terrorists is intelligence. For example, following the Malayan Emergency every major military and civilian public official stated that intelligence was the key to victory against the communist insurgents. Success in small wars requires comprehensive all-source intelligence and analysis that in some respects exceed the intelligence requirements in a conventional war. In a conventional conflict, it is not difficult to locate and target an enemy army and its supporting infrastructure if one has air superiority. On the other hand, in small wars finding and identifying small guerrilla bands that can blend in with a sympathetic population is exceptionally difficult. In conventional war, space-derived imagery has become one of the best intelligence sources. In a small war, the old-fashioned human intelligence derived from agents, informers, and prisoner interrogations is still the best means to obtain accurate information about the enemy. One can determine from overhead imagery that a group of peasants have left their village to travel to a neighboring village, but overhead imagery cannot explain why.

A consistent problem in small wars operations has been in coordinating intelligence and information from all the various military and civilian agencies. The problem is almost never a lack of data but rather the sharing of data and analysis between military services and between police and other civilian agencies. Unfortunately it is in the nature of military services and government agencies to jealously guard their turf and their information even in a dire emergency. Overcoming the lack of intelligence sharing has been a lesson that has had to be learned again in every conflict. The Rhodesians were several years into their insurgency before they established a joint intelligence center that shared information and analysis from the military, police, and civilian agencies. El Salvador only established a joint intelligence center four years into its insurgency. In every case, the performance of the counterinsurgency forces quickly and noticeably increased due to better intelligence.

9. *Airpower provides the flexibility and initiative that is normally the advantage of the guerrilla.* In the era before airpower, insurgents had many advantages over regular police and military forces. Insurgents could move quickly,

live off the land, and, if the population was supportive, usually had much better intelligence than the government forces. Guerrillas could take the initiative and could carefully select each point to strike, as the government forces usually reacted to insurgent attacks by futile chases in pursuit of a long-gone foe.

Airpower restored the initiative and flexibility to government forces in counterinsurgency operations. Reconnaissance aircraft dramatically increased the intelligence capability of the regular forces. A few airplanes could do the work of several cavalry battalions — faster, cheaper, and better. With paratroops and helicopters in the post–World War II era, regular forces could achieve surprise by striking deep into rebel-held areas at will, attacking "strategic" targets even in remote locations. Government forces brought by air into remote areas could be supplied by air instead of a long and vulnerable land supply line. Airpower allowed government forces to take the offensive more easily than was done in the colonial era of punitive expeditions. Airpower allowed government forces to relentlessly harry guerrillas and, when guerrillas were cornered, airpower could bring to bear devastating and accurate firepower.

Before the advent of airpower, the common belief was that government forces needed a ten-to-one advantage over the insurgents in order to defeat them. In that earlier era, when the normal job of government troops was one of static defense, this was probably an accurate figure. However, such a ratio does not apply to a force that has effective air support. With adequate air support capable of providing reconnaissance, transport, and firepower, a relatively small counterinsurgency force can be employed against insurgents and terrorists and win. Simply put, airpower is a vital force multiplier. Airpower does not take away the need for ground forces in counterinsurgency and counterterrorism operations, but it certainly makes those forces much more effective. Moreover, it permits government forces to take the initiative and achieve surprise against an enemy that normally enjoys these advantages.

10. *Small wars are long wars.* In fighting an insurgency or terrorist movement, one must intellectually and militarily prepare to fight a long war. This is one of the most important differences between current conventional state-to-state war and a small war. Most of the major conventional wars of the last few decades have been decisively concluded in a matter of days or weeks, per the Gulf War of 1991, the Arab-Israeli wars of 1967 and 1973, and the Falkland's War of 1982. It is part of the nature of military leaders, and especially airmen,

to seek a quick and decisive victory in war. The search for a quick, decisive victory is an integral part of the Western military culture.

In that regard, regular armies and air forces generally dislike thinking about fighting insurgents and terrorists because a conflict against a nonstate entity does not lend itself to quick, decisive victory. In fact, small wars are almost always long wars. The insurgency in Guatemala lasted for over thirty years. The current war in Colombia began in the 1960s. All of the African insurgencies lasted for more than a decade. Israel fought Hizbullah in southern Lebanon for eighteen years.

Long wars are especially frustrating for airmen. Because of the highly complex and technical nature of an air force and the technical expertise required to manage even routine air operations, it takes many years for a country to develop an effective air force. Even a modern and capable air force can require a period of months or years to adapt its training, equipment, and doctrine to effectively fight insurgents and terrorists. Despite considerable outside aid and support, the air forces of many developing nations still require years of training and infrastructure development before they can be truly effective in counterinsurgency and counterterrorism. In El Salvador it took some four years of aid and training before the Salvadoran air force was able to make a truly effective contribution to the military effort.

Even when a state possesses a large and highly capable air force, as Israel had against the PLO and Hizbullah in Lebanon, the opportunity to employ such an impressive force against decisive targets generally does not exist. Small wars air operations consist of years of small strikes, heliborne commando raids, close air support missions, and troop transport and resupply flights. Success, if measured at all, comes in small, incremental steps and after months of air operations that may pass with little noticeable effect upon the enemy. Therefore, when a state engages in a counterterrorism or counterinsurgency effort, or decides to help another state in such a conflict, then that state can expect to be engaged for years, perhaps decades, and should plan its long-term strategy accordingly. Insurgents are not defeated quickly. Even in the highly successful counterinsurgency campaign in Malaya, it took the British twelve years to suppress the rebellion. Often an insurgency will end with no formal peace agreement at all. The insurgency will simply dissolve, with former guerrillas often turning to banditry.

Similarly, counterterrorism campaigns do not lend themselves to a final or conclusive victory. As long as a few terrorist cells remain active and funds and support from outside powers are available and people remain willing to commit suicide for a cause, terrorism will continue. In counterterrorism, success might be best defined as inflicting crippling losses upon the terrorist organization and infrastructure and reducing their capability to conduct major operations.

11. *The United States and its allies must put more effort into small wars training.* The historical experience of combating insurgencies shows that countries essentially have to fight and win against insurgents on their own. Popular support is the center of gravity for both sides in internal conflict. The legitimacy of the government in the eyes of the people is the most important factor in an insurgency. Even with the best of intentions, if another state intervenes to take over the fight against an indigenous insurgency, as was the case with U.S. intervention in South Vietnam, a majority of the population will come to resent the intervening power and the legitimacy of the government will erode. In the end, the insurgents will benefit politically from foreign intervention and will be able to credibly present themselves as the true representatives of the people while characterizing the national government as a "foreign puppet." For this reason alone it would be a mistake for the United States military to conduct direct combat operations against the FARC or ELN rebels in Colombia.

On the other hand, helping a friendly nation to combat insurgents and terrorists by providing equipment, training, intelligence, and economic and other aid does not delegitimize the central government. U.S. military aid and equipment played a key role in helping win the battle against communist insurgents in Greece, against the Huks in the Philippines, and in bringing the FMLN to the negotiating table in El Salvador. Unfortunately, the U.S. military currently puts very little emphasis on military aid and training to friendly and allied nations fighting insurgents and terrorists. The U.S. Air Force probably emphasizes foreign assistance the least among the armed services. Much of the reluctance stems from the fact that specific legislation exists that limits and often proscribes direct training of foreign military forces by the U.S. military. U.S. special operations forces are exempted from this legislation to some degree, but even then Air Force Special Operations Command fields a single squadron, the Sixth Special Operations Squadron, to conduct this complex and demanding mission. In short, although training, aid, and advice play a key role in combating terrorists and insurgents, the U.S. effort has been ghettoized in one small segment of the total force. In most respects, training foreign personnel has become a stepchild of special operations.

In the years to come, a much greater effort by the United States and other developed Western nations will have to be made to help friendly and allied states in the developing world combat internal as well as unconventional transnational threats. For the U.S. Air Force, a sensible solution might be to form several squadrons specially tailored for training foreign aviation forces in what is generally termed "foreign internal defense." However, current law largely restricts training of foreign forces to the special operations community, and legislation must be promulgated to rescind this limitation if the pool of available trainers is to be enlarged. Service efforts ought not to be "stovepiped" but rather coordinated through one joint training command for foreign training to oversee the training curriculum and program. Officers with experience in training the forces of developing nations know that even if a foreign military has well-trained individuals and small units, the ability to conduct joint operations that employ air, sea, and ground forces as well as police forces is usually poor. These skills are especially important for winning a small war and ought to have a strong training priority. Interagency operations are relatively new to the U.S. military and the United States is learning to make interagency operations work effectively. This is a skill that also needs to be taught to the officers of friendly and allied nations.

Revamping the organization and system for training of foreign armed forces by the U.S. military need not detract from the primary mission of fighting and winning conventional wars. The U.S. Army, Navy, Air Force, and Marine Corps all have large reserve forces with tens of thousands of experienced personnel with the technical skills, language skills, and experience that can support the mission of training foreign forces.

The United States military and other Western forces require an adequate doctrine for training foreign armed forces. Currently, there is little doctrine to guide personnel in that mission. Training is organized and carried out on an ad hoc basis with little in the way of long-term strategic planning or vision. Small wars can be won with ad hoc planning, and training programs thrown together can still work — El Salvador proves that. However, the job can be done much more effectively and efficiently. The biggest obstacle that faces the United States in developing an adequate training program for allied and friendly nations is our own enormous and sclerotic defense bureaucracy, where any sensible initiative must pass through the system with glacial speed. Aside from reforming the bureaucracy in toto, lesser reforms in the training system could be instituted in a matter of months and show some positive results in a short period.

Finally, the U.S. military education system, especially the staff colleges and senior service schools, need to spend a good deal more time addressing the issue of small wars. Currently, U.S. military schools are mired in curricula better suited for conventional war than for the types of unconventional wars likely to be fought in the next decades. There is very little history, theory, or doctrine on counterinsurgency and counterterrorism taught in the U.S. military staff colleges today. Again, this is something that can be remedied very quickly but will require a commitment from the Defense Department to devote personnel and funds to the mission.

INTRODUCTION

1. It is interesting to note that the U.S. Air Force has never published a history of the Seventh Air Force in World War II, the air force that fought the most joint campaign of all alongside navy and USMC air units. The Fifteenth Air Force, the other great strategic air force in the European history, has no major operational history written. The U.S. Ninth Air Force, the largest tactical air force in history, has only a short summary report as its published history. Such a gap in army history would be like leaving out the Italian campaign from historical consideration, or like the navy to ignore the role of the United States in the Battle of the Atlantic.

2. For an excellent critique on the U.S. Air Force's lack of doctrine for small wars, see Dennis Drew, "U.S. Airpower Theory and the Insurgent Challenge: A Short Journey to Confusion," *Journal of Military History* (October 1998): 809–32.

3. For examples of this school of airpower thought and history, see David Dean, *Airpower in Small Wars: The British Air Control Experience* (Maxwell AFB: CADRE Paper, August 1985), and Carl Builder, "Doctrinal Frontiers," *Airpower Journal* (winter 1995): 6–13.

4. *Small Wars Manual* (1940; reprint, Washington, D.C.: Department of the Navy, 1987), 1-7-11.

5. The first major theoretical work on this subject, and still a classic in the field, is Col. C. E. Callwell, *Small Wars: Their Principles and Practice* (Lincoln: University of Nebraska Press, 1996; reprint, originally published 1896), 21–22.

6. Keith Bickel, *Mars Learning: The Marine Corps' Development of Small Wars Doctrine, 1915–1944* (Boulder, Colo.: Westview Press, 2001).

7. Wray Johnson, *Vietnam and American Doctrine for Small Wars* (Bangkok: White Lotus, 2001).

8. *Joint Low Intensity Conflict Report*, vol. 1: *Analytical Review of Low Intensity Conflict* (Ft. Monroe, Va.: U.S. Army Training and Doctrine Command, August 1, 1986), 1–2.

9. On Summers and Cohen's views, see Harry Summers, "A War Is a War Is a War Is a War," in *Low Intensity Conflict: The Pattern of Warfare in the Modern World,* ed. Loren Thompson (Lexington, Ky.: Lexington Books, 1989), 45.

1. BIPLANES AND BANDITS: THE EARLY U.S. AIRPOWER
EXPERIENCE IN SMALL WARS

1. There is a significant body of work on the Punitive Expedition. See, for example, Halden Brady, *Pershing's Mission into Mexico* (El Paso: Texas Western College Press, 1966), and Clarence Clendenen, *Blood on the Border: The United States and the Mexican Irregulars* (New York: Macmillan, 1969). A worthwhile Mexican examination, albeit sympathetic to Villa, can be found in Federico Cervantes, *Francisco Villa y la revolución* (Mexico, D.F.: Ediciones Alonso, 1960).

2. Captain Benjamin Foulois, *Report of the Operations of the First Aero Squadron, Signal Corps, with Punitive Expedition, USA for Period March 15 to August 15, 1916* (Max-

well Air Force Base: Historical Research Agency, n.d.). Hereafter cited as Foulois, *Report of Operations*.

3. *Small Wars Manual* (1940; reprint, Washington, D.C.: Department of the Navy, 1987), 1-7-11.

4. Ian Beckett, "The United States Experience," in *The Roots of Counterinsurgency: Armies and Guerrilla Warfare, 1900–1945*, ed. Ian Beckett (London: Blandford Press, 1988), 105–6.

5. For a full treatment, see Robert Heinel Jr., *Soldiers of the Sea: The United States Marine Corps, 1775–1962* (Annapolis: United States Naval Institute, 1962), 147–290, passim.

6. For an in-depth examination of this period, see Robert Miller, *Mexico: A History* (Norman: University of Oklahoma Press, 1985), chap. 8–10, passim. Also see Peter Calvert, *Mexico* (New York: Praeger, 1973), 32–201, passim.

7. Friedrich Katz, *The Life and Times of Pancho Villa* (Stanford: Stanford University Press, 1998), 552.

8. Herbert Mason, *The Great Pursuit* (New York: Random House, 1970), 69.

9. Katz, *Pancho Villa*, 568.

10. Benjamin Foulois and C. V. Glines, *From the Wright Brothers to the Astronauts: The Memoirs of Major General Benjamin D. Foulois* (New York: McGraw-Hill, 1968), 108–22.

11. Mauer Mauer, "The 1st Aero Squadron," *The Air Power Historian* (October 1957): 209. The JN-3s were actually an upgrade of the JN-2s flown by the squadron up to that point. While at Fort Sill, Oklahoma, and performing border patrol duties near Brownsville, Texas, the underpowered, fragile, and largely unstable JN-2s were involved in a series of accidents (including several fatalities) and were often grounded due to engine problems and lack of spare parts. According to Foulois, the manufacturer of the JN-2, Glenn Curtiss, became concerned about the reputation of his airplanes and "promised to send new upper wings, stabilizing fins, rudders, and new engines to remodel completely the JN2's and remove the reported defects. He kept his word, and the planes at Fort Sill and Brownsville were modified into new JN3's." Although an improvement over the JN-2, the JN-3 would nevertheless prove ill-suited to the rigors of the Punitive Expedition. Foulois and Glines, *Memoirs*, 121.

12. Alfred Goldberg, *History of the U.S. Air Force, 1907–1957* (Princeton: D. Van Nostrand, 1957), 9. When the First Aero Squadron was directed to support the Expedition, it had eight of the thirteen planes commissioned in the United States Army. Calvin Hines, "First Aero Squadron in Mexico," *American Aviation Historical Society Journal* (fall 1965): 190.

13. Foulois and Glines, *Memoirs*, 123.

14. Hines, "First Aero Squadron in Mexico," 191.

15. Juliette Hennessy, *The U.S. Army Air Arm, April, 1861–April, 1917* (Maxwell Air Force Base: Air University, Historical Research Agency, USAF Historical Study 98, May 1958), 167. Hereafter cited as USAF Historical Study 98. See also Foulois, *Report of Operations*.

16. James Crouch, "Wings South: The First Foreign Employment of Air Power by the United States," *Aerospace Historian* (spring, March 1972): 28.

17. Foulois and Glines, *Memoirs*, 124.

18. Mason, *The Great Pursuit*, 108.

19. Ibid.

20. USAF Historical Study 98.

21. *History of the 1st Bombardment Squadron, 1913–1916* (Maxwell Air Force Base: Air University, Historical Research Agency, n.d.).

22. Mason, *The Great Pursuit,* 109–15.

23. Hines, "First Aero Squadron in Mexico," 192.

24. USAF Historical Study 98. See also Mason, *The Great Pursuit,* 145–46.

25. Frank Tompkins, *Chasing Villa* (Harrisburg, Pa.: Military Publishing Service, 1934), 242. See also Mason, *The Great Pursuit,* 221–22.

26. Foulois, *Report of Operations,* 10–11.

27. Ibid.

28. Goldberg, *History,* 10.

29. *Selected Case Histories* (Maxwell Air Force Base: Air University, Historical Research Agency, USAF Historical Study 491, 1953), cited in David Mets, *Master of Airpower: General Carl A. Spaatz* (Novato, Calif.: Presidio Press, 1988), 19.

30. Edwin McClellan, "The Birth and Infancy of Marine Aviation," *Marine Corps Gazette,* May 1931, 13.

31. Ibid., 11. See also Robert Sherrod, "Marine Corps Aviation: The Early Days," part 1, "The Beginning," *Marine Corps Gazette,* May 1952, 52.

32. Alfred Cunningham, "Aviation in the Navy," *Marine Corps Gazette,* December 1916, 333.

33. U.S. Marine Corps, Historical Reference Pamphlet, *Marine Corps Aircraft: 1913–1965* (Washington, D.C.: Headquarters U.S. Marine Corps, Historical Branch, 1967), 5.

34. Sherrod, "The Beginning," 54–55.

35. Ibid., 57–61.

36. For a full treatment, see Guy Poitra, *The Ordeal of Hegemony: The United States and Latin America* (Boulder, Colo.: Westview Press, 1990).

37. The irregular forces in the Dominican Republic generally lumped together as "bandits" actually comprised professional highwaymen known as *gavilleros,* ordinary criminals, discontented politicians who used banditry to advance their own ambitions, unemployed laborers, and peasants, the latter generally impressed into service. "Operating in bands that rarely exceeded 200 men and usually numbered less than 50, these brigands robbed and terrorized rural communities. . . . At all times, their armed presence in the countryside threatened the security of the rural population and challenged the authority of the central government. The gangs usually coalesced around a leader noted for his dynamic personality, ferocity, or physical strength. Many of these men were little more than hoodlums, but a few had the character of local political chiefs or warlords. . . . Whether to reinforce their local prestige or to assert territorial dominance, these major leaders were responsible for most bandit attacks on American Marines and civilians." Stephen Fuller and Graham Cosmas, *Marines in the Dominican Republic: 1916–1924* (Washington, D.C.: Headquarters United States Marine Corps, History and Museums Division, 1974), 35.

38. Ibid., 7–28, passim.

39. The Marines first used airplanes for medical evacuation in the Dominican Republic and Haiti in 1922. Captain Francis T. Evans modified a DH-4 with a "turtle-back

fuselage," mounting a Stokes stretcher, which could accommodate one reclining patient and another sitting in one of the two open cockpits. Two airplanes were modified in this fashion at the Naval Aircraft Factory in Philadelphia and were subsequently used by the First Squadron in Santo Domingo City and also by the Fourth Squadron in Haiti. These air ambulances "could cut evacuation time from three days by muleback, cart, and truck to two hours' round trip." Robert Sherrod, "Marine Corps Aviation: The Early Days," part 2, "Between Wars," *Marine Corps Gazette,* June 1952, note 5, 55.

40. Major General Ford O. Rogers, USMC (Ret.), (Washington, D.C.: History and Museums Division, Headquarters U.S. Marine Corps, 3 December 1970, Oral History Collection, transcript), 25, cited in Edward Johnson, *Marine Corps Aviation: The Early Years, 1912–1940* (Washington, D.C.: History and Museums Division, Headquarters U.S. Marine Corps, 1977), 49.

41. Hans Schmidt, *The United States Occupation of Haiti, 1915–1934* (New Brunswick: Rutgers University Press, 1995), 19–21. From 1888 to 1915, no Haitian president ever completed his full seven-year term. Most were murdered while in office, seven of whom died between 1911 and 1915. Ibid., 42.

42. *Caco* armies were generally raised in the rugged hills of northern Haiti. Mostly peasants, these mercenary soldiers would hire themselves out to presumptuous revolutionary leaders. "Organized in bands under local chiefs, their hierarchy ran up in theory to a supposed 'Chief of the *cacos,*' or at least to a small group of top-level generals. This loosely hierarchical organization made it possible for the aspiring presidential candidate to secure the services of an entire *caco* army by striking an agreement with only a few men. The revolutionary leader normally promised a lump-sum payment in case of success, to be distributed by the *caco* chiefs to their followers according to rank. Everyone understood that a certain amount of looting would also swell the profits of the campaign. When the successful revolutionist was installed in the presidency, he paid off his army and it returned to its northern haunts, to await the bidding of the next plotters against the incumbent regime." David Healy, *Gunboat Diplomacy in the Wilson Era: The U.S. Navy in Haiti, 1915–1916* (Madison: University of Wisconsin Press, 1976), 20–21.

43. Ibid., 61.

44. Sherrod, "Between Wars," 55.

45. Peter Mersky, *Marine Corps Aviation: 1912 to the Present,* 3d ed. (Baltimore: Nautical and Aviation Publishing Company of America, 1997), 20. See also Edward Johnson, *Marine Corps Aviation,* asterisk note, 53.

46. David Mets, "Dive-Bombing Between the Wars," *Airpower Historian* (July 1965): 86.

47. Letter, Brigadier General Lawton H. Sanderson to David Mets, 22 February 1953, cited in ibid.

48. Thomas Wildenberg, *Destined for Glory: Dive Bombing, Midway, and the Evolution of Carrier Airpower* (Annapolis: Naval Institute Press, 1998), 12–13.

49. Johnson, *Marine Corps Aviation,* 53.

50. In 1920, the secretary of the navy directed the creation of a formal system of designation for navy aircraft and squadrons, including Marine Corps Aviation. Before that time there was no regulated system of designating aircraft or squadrons. Squad-

rons were generally numbered according to the order in which they were raised, and airplanes were assigned letters and numbers mostly at random, which did not clarify the type nor the manufacturer. For example, the HS-2L flying boat, which saw action in Haiti, was manufactured by Curtiss as well as several other manufacturers. But the designation did not reveal the type of aircraft or the manufacturer and, not surprisingly, this led to confusion. By 1922, a lettering system was adopted whereby the first letter designated the manufacturer, the second letter the type of aircraft, and a number appended to denote the modification. For example, a UO-1 was a Vought (U) observation airplane (O), first modification. A second number inserted between the manufacturer and the type indicated the order or model number of the designer's aircraft in the same class (beginning with number 2). Thus, a U2O-1 was a Vought observation airplane, second model of its class, first modification. In 1923, the system was revised again so that the manufacturer and type letters were reversed (*Marine Corps Aircraft: 1913–1965*, 1–2). This system remained largely intact up to the 1960s when the Department of Defense directed that a system across all of the armed services be created to identify aircraft by type. In addition, beginning in 1920, squadrons were designated according to their principal mission. The first letter indicated whether the squadron operated heavier than air machines (V) or airships (Z). The following letter denoted the mission, e.g., fighter (F) or observation (O). Marine squadrons were distinguished by the addition of an "M." Thus, VO-1M designated Marine Observation Squadron One. This system remained intact until 1937 when the designation "VMO" was established. Mersky, *Marine Corps Aviation*, 16.

51. Wildenberg, *Destined for Glory*, 15.
52. In 1855, the American William Walker had attempted to establish a slaveholding state in Nicargua and at one point served as president and was recognized by the U.S. government. However, he was driven out in 1857. In 1860 he landed in Honduras and prepared to invade Nicaragua, but was captured by a British warship, was handed over to Honduran authorities, and was shot at Trujilla, Honduras, on 11 September 1860. Bernard Nalty, *The United States Marines in Nicaragua* (Washington, D.C.: History and Museums Division, Headquarters U.S. Marine Corps, 1968), 2–3.
53. "Protection of American Interests," *Marine Corps Gazette*, September 1927, 176–77.
54. Johnson, *Marine Corps Aviation*, 55.
55. "Protection of American Interests," 177.
56. Nalty, *The United States Marines in Nicaragua*, 15.
57. Johnson, *Marine Corps Aviation*, 55–56.
58. "Protection of American Interests," 178. An additional company at Rama, not part of the Second Brigade, included three officers and seventy-five men. Ibid.
59. Francis MulCahy, "Marine Corps Aviation in Second Nicaraguan Campaign," *United States Naval Institute Proceedings* (August 1933): 1122.
60. Johnson, *Marine Corps Aviation*, 56.
61. Lejeune Cummins, *Quijote on a Burro: Sandino and the Marines, A Study in the Formulation of Foreign Policy* (Mexico City: Distrito Federal: La Impresora Azteca, 1958), 54.
62. *Annual Report of the Secretary of the Navy, Fiscal Year 1928* (Washington, D.C.: 1929), 50, cited in ibid., 54.

63. Ibid., 55.

64. During the battle of Muy Muy, the homemade bombs used by Mason and Brooks failed to explode and their aircraft suffered severe damage from ground fire. "In fact, they were barely able to flutter back to an emergency air strip in deferred forced landings." Vernon Megee, "The Genesis of Air Support in Guerrilla Operations," *United States Naval Institute Proceedings* (June 1965): 50–51.

65. Ross Rowell, "The Air Service in Minor Warfare," *United States Naval Institute Proceedings* (October 1929): 871–72.

66. Ibid., 872.

67. Ibid.

68. John Gray, "The Second Nicaraguan Campaign," *Marine Corps Gazette*, February 1933, 36.

69. "Protection of American Interests," 179.

70. Rowell, "The Air Service in Minor Warfare," 873. For this action, Rowell became the first Marine aviator to receive the Distinguished Flying Cross. See Joseph Alexander, *A Fellowship of Valor: The Battle History of the United States Marines* (New York: Lou Reda Productions, 1997), 57.

71. According to one account, at least one hundred of the guerrillas that had laid siege to Ocatal were killed by the air attack, and according to another, some three hundred guerrillas had been killed.

72. The two-seat Vought Corsair was powered by a Pratt and Whitney Wasp radial engine. The airplane had a top speed of over 150 miles per hour, but a low landing speed of only 50 miles per hour, which proved crucial to operations from unimproved airstrips. Christian Schilt, who was awarded the Medal of Honor in Nicaragua, called the Corsair "an outstanding combat plane. . . . When we got that down in Nicaragua we were very happy to get it because of outstanding performance, ease in handling, quick takeoffs and landings." General Christian F. Schilt, USMC (Ret.), (Washington, D.C.: History and Museums Division, Headquarters U.S. Marine Corps, 17 and 20 November 1969, Oral History Collection, transcript), 57, 74, cited in Johnson, *Marine Corps Aviation,* 42.

73. Message transcript quoted by Ross Rowell in "Annual Report of Aircraft Squadrons, Second Brigade, U.S. Marine Corps, July 1, 1927, to June 20, 1928," *Marine Corps Gazette,* December 1928, 254.

74. C. Frank Schilt, "Marines in Nicaragua Saved by Airplanes," *Aero Digest* (February 1928): 173, 295.

75. Mersky, *U.S. Marine Corps Aviation,* 22.

76. Rowell, "Annual Report," 254.

77. Ibid.

78. "News of the Air Services: Aircraft in Nicaragua," *Aero Digest* (May 1928): 760.

79. Rowell, "Annual Report," 253. Also see Rowell, "Air Service in Minor Warfare," 875.

80. "News of the Air Services: Aircraft in Nicaragua," 760.

81. Rowell, "Annual Report," 253.

82. Cummins, *Quijote on a Burro,* 54.

83. MulCahy, "Marine Corps Aviation in Second Nicaraguan Campaign," 1127.

84. Alexander, *A Fellowship of Valor,* 60.

85. Johnson, *Marine Corps Aviation,* 57.

86. "News of the Air Services: First Non-Stop Flight U.S. to Nicaragua," *Aero Digest* (February 1928): 204; and "News of the Air Services: 2nd Non-Stop Flight U.S. to Nicaragua," *Aero Digest* (March 1928): 384.

87. Rowell, "Annual Report," 252.

88. MulCahy, "Marine Corps Aviation in Second Nicaraguan Campaign," 1129.

89. "Up to the end of 1928, aviation had 84 contacts in which the planes were struck 82 times by fire from the ground; in 1929, the number of contacts dropped to 26; in 1930, there were but 5; in 1931, 7; in 1932, 9; and from July 1 to December 15, 1932, 1. Consequently, it was impossible to relax the vigilance of aërial patrols, but, of course, the necessity of aërial transport was continuous." MulCahy, "Marine Corps Aviation in Second Nicaraguan Campaign," 1128–9.

90. Rowell, "The Air Service in Minor Warfare," 876.

91. MulCahy, "Marine Corps Aviation in the Second Nicaraguan Campaign," 1131.

92. Cummins, *Quijote on a Burro,* 45.

93. Ross Rowell, "Aircraft in Bush Warfare," *Marine Corps Gazette,* September 1929, 180.

94. During the final months of the war, the First Squadron operated B-29 bombers in the Pacific and participated in the firebombing of Japanese cities and aerial mining of Japanese waters in 1945. Mauer, "The 1st Aero Squadron," 210–12.

95. Charles Chandler and Frank Lahm, *How Our Army Grew Wings: Airmen and Aircraft Before 1914* (New York: Ronald Press Company, 1943), 244–50.

96. Edwin McClellan, "American Marines in Nicaragua," *Marine Corps Gazette,* March 1921, 48.

97. The story of Marine Corps aviators who attended the Air Corps Tactical School warrants treatment in and of itself and is beyond the scope of this work. Nevertheless, for Rowell's monograph, see Manuscript, "Aircraft in Bush Warfare" (Maxwell Air Force Base: Historical Research Agency, 1 January 1931), 248.211-81. See also Air Corps Tactical School, The Air Force, Minor Wars, 1930–1931, 248.2013A-7; Air Corps Tactical School, The Air Force, sec. VII, Minor Wars, January 1931, 248.101-1; and Air Corps Tactical School, The Air Force, Air Operations, Minor Wars, May 1930, 248.2011A-8. Also see General Vernon E. McGee, USMC (Ret.), (Washington, D.C.: Oral History Unit, G-3 Division, Headquarters U.S. Marine Corps, 10 April 1967, Oral History Collection, transcript).

98. Ross Rowell rose to become director of Marine Corps Aviation from 1 April 1936 to 10 March 1939 and as a major general was at one point the senior Marine aviator in the Pacific during World War II. But following a disagreement with the commandant of the Marine Corps and Admiral Nimitz regarding the use of Marine aircraft on escort carriers (as opposed to supporting Marines on the ground), he was relieved and sent to Lima, Peru, as the chief of the Naval Air Mission. It was a sorry end to the career of an otherwise illustrious and dedicated Marine aviator. See MulCahy, "Marine Corps Aviation," 1122; *Marine Corps Aircraft, 1913–1965,* 49; and Peter Mersky, *U.S. Marine Corps Aviation,* 98.

99. *Small Wars Manual,* 9-1-1 to 9-36-24.

100. Vernon McGee, "The Evolution of Marine Aviation," part 1, *Marine Corps Gazette,* August 1965, 24. The first Marine aviator, Alfred Cunningham, similarly claimed:

"It is fully realized that the only excuse for aviation in any service is its usefulness in assisting the troops on the ground to successfully carry out their operations." Alfred Cunningham, "Value of Aviation to the Marine Corps," *Marine Corps Gazette,* September 1920, 222.

101. J. N. Rentz, "Marine Corps Aviation — An Infantryman's Opinion," *United States Naval Institute Proceedings* (November 1949): 1278.

102. Ibid.

103. Megee, "The Genesis of Air Support in Guerrilla Operations," 59.

2. COLONIAL AIR CONTROL: THE EUROPEAN POWERS DEVELOP NEW CONCEPTS OF AIR WARFARE

1. See Philip Towle, *Pilots and Rebels: The Use of Aircraft in Unconventional Warfare, 1918–1988* (London: Brassey's, 1989), 9–55, for a good overview of the RAF and air control program in the interwar era.

2. Flight-Lieutenant F. A. Skoulding, "With 'Z' Unit in Somaliland," *RAF Quarterly* 2, no. 3 (July 1931): 387–96.

3. David Omissi, *Air Power and Colonial Control: The Royal Air Force, 1919–1939* (Manchester, England: Manchester University Press, 1990), 25–27.

4. A. Kearsey, *Notes and Lectures on the Campaign in Mesopotamia* (London: Hugh Rees, 1927). This work provides a useful summary of the World War I campaign in Iraq.

5. Alfred Burne, *Mesopotamia: The Last Phase* (Aldershot: Gale and Olden, 1936), 109.

6. Howard Sachar, *The Emergence of the Middle East 1914–1924* (New York: Alfred Knopf, 1969), 368–70.

7. Sachar, *Emergence of the Middle East,* 366–68.

8. David McDowell, *A Modern History of the Kurds* (London: I. B. Tauris, 1996), 152.

9. Sachar, *Emergence of the Middle East,* 377–82.

10. Omissi, *Air Power and Colonial Control,* 123. Of the 131,000 armed rebels in 1920 the British estimated that 17,000 had modern small bore magazine rifles and 43,000 had "old but serviceable rifles." By 1921, in the aftermath of the rebellion, nearly 63,000 rifles had been collected.

11. Sachar, *Emergence of the Middle East,* 369–72.

12. Mark Jacobsen, "Only by the Sword: British Counter-Insurgency in Iraq, 1920," *Small Wars and Insurgencies* 2, no. 2 (August 1991): 351–52, 358.

13. Jacobsen, "Only by the Sword," 356.

14. Ibid., 357.

15. Omissi, *Air Power and Colonial Control,* 31.

16. Omissi, *Air Power and Colonial Control,* 31.

17. Major General H. Rowan-Robinson, "Iraq," *RUSI Journal* 77 (November 1932): 384.

18. In summer 1923 there were six Indian army infantry battalions in Iraq. See Air Force Notes, *RUSI Journal* 472 (November 1923): 730.

19. Lieutenant Colonel R. H. Beadon, "The Iraqi Army," *RUSI Journal* (May 1926): 343–54.

20. For a good example of a typical nineteenth- and early twentieth-century punitive operation in the British Empire, see Winston Churchill, *The Story of the Malakand Field Force* (New York: W. W. Norton, 1989; reprint, originally published 1898). The book is Churchill's personal account of an expedition that he took part in.

21. Wing Commander J. A. Chamier, "The Use of Air Power for Replacing Military Garrisons," *RUSI Journal* 66 (February/November 1921): 205–12, see 210.
22. Cited in Towle, *Pilots and Rebels*, 20.
23. Ibid., 20.
24. Ibid., 20–21.
25. Ibid., 19–20; see also Omissi, *Air Power and Colonial Control*, 182.
26. Omissi, *Air Power and Colonial Control*, 182.
27. Basil Liddell Hart, *The British Way in Warfare* (London: Faber and Faber, 1932), 155.
28. Major General Sir Charles Gwynn, *Imperial Policing* (London: Macmillan, 1936), 114.
29. Robin Cross, *The Bombers* (New York: Macmillan, 1987), 70.
30. Military Notes, *RUSI Journal* 66 (February–November 1921): 545.
31. Air Notes, *RUSI Journal* 79 (February 1934): 194.
32. Omissi, *Air Power and Colonial Control*, 174.
33. McDowell, *A Modern History of the Kurds*, 155–63.
34. Lieutenant Colonel G. P. MacClellan, "Air Co-Operation in Hill Fighting: Kurdistan 1923," *RUSI Journal* 72 (May 1927): 318–26, see 319–20.
35. Ibid., 321–23.
36. Ibid., 324–25.
37. McDowell, *A Modern History of the Kurds*, 176.
38. Group-Captain A. G. R. Garrod, "Recent Operations in Kurdistan," *RUSI Journal* 78 (May 1933): 231–51.
39. Ibid. See also Lt. H. M. Curtis, "Shaikh Ahmed of Barzan and the Iraqi Government," *RUSI Journal* 77 (May 1932): 397–402.
40. Flight-Lieutenant C. J. Mackay, "The Influence in the Future of Aircraft Upon Problems of Imperial Defence," *RUSI Journal* 67 (May 1922): 274–310, see 299.
41. Air Marshal Sir John Salmond, "The Air Force in Iraq," *RUSI Journal* 70 (August 1925): 483–97.
42. Omissi, *Air Power and Colonial Control*, 57.
43. See Squadron-Leader E. J. Kingston-McCloughry, *Winged Warfare: Air Problems of Peace and War* (London: Jonathan Cape, 1937). In his chapter "Policing by Air," there is scant mention of the role of the ground forces in numerous operations, such as the campaign to expel the Turks from Kurdistan in 1923. See 201–57.
44. Hilary St. George Saunders, *Per Ardua: The Rise of British Air Power, 1911–1939* (London: Oxford University Press, 1945), 288–93.
45. Omissi, *Air Power and Colonial Control*, 165.
46. Towle, *Pilots and Rebels*, 40–43.
47. Omissi, *Air Power and Colonial Control*, 153.
48. Ibid., 155.
49. Ibid., 166.
50. Ibid., 167.
51. See Neville Jones, *The Beginnings of Strategic Air Power* (London: Frank Cass, 1987), 111–17, 146–48. Although the RAF had a doctrine centered on strategic bombing, the force's basic navigation and bombing skills were very poor at the outbreak of World War II.
52. Ibid. See also Towle, *Pilots and Rebels*, 18.

53. See Basil Liddell Hart, "Air and Empire: The History of Air Control," in *The British Way in Warfare* (London: Faber and Faber, 1932), 139–61. Liddell Hart accepted all of the RAF's positions on air control and was an enthusiastic supporter. As military correspondent for the *Daily Telegraph*, Liddell Hart was in a good position to influence the public and politicians.

54. Towle, *Pilots and Rebels*, 45–50.

55. Ibid., 48.

56. Cited in Bruce Hoffman, *British Air Power in Peripheral Conflict, 1919–1976* (Santa Monica: Rand, 1989), 32–33.

57. Towle, *Pilots and Rebels*, 50.

58. José Warleta, "Los comenzon bélicos de la aviación española," *Revue Internationale d'Histoire Militaire* 56 (1984): 239–62.

59. José Gomá Orduña, *Historia de la Aeronáutica Española* (Madrid, 1950), 36–39.

60. Orduña, *Historia de la Aeronáutica Española*, 25, 36–41.

61. Orduña, *Historia de la Aeronáutica Española*, 66–67.

62. David Woolman, *Rebels in the Rif* (Stanford: Stanford University Press, 1968), 74.

63. George Hills, *Franco: The Man and His Nation* (New York: Macmillan, 1967), 123–24; see also Woolman, *Rebels in the Rif*, 96.

64. Hills, *Franco: The Man and His Nation*, 135.

65. Rudibert Kunz and Rolf-Dieter Müller, *Giftgas gegen Abd el Krim* (Freiburg: Verlag Rombach, 1990), 17–18.

66. Kunz and Müller, *Giftgas gegen Abd el Krim*, 18.

67. Omissi, *Air Power and Colonial Control*, 185.

68. Orduña, *Historia de la Aeronáutica Española*, 147–49.

69. Orduña, *Historia de la Aeronáutica Española*, 237.

70. Bundesarchiv/Militärarchiv Freiburg. Doc. BA/MA RM 20/284 Document Annex 6. Captain Grauert and Lt. Jeschonnek, "Geheimer Bericht über die Reise nach Spanien von April–Juli 1925."

71. Kunz and Müller, *Giftgas gegen Abd el Krim*, 145.

72. Ibid., 147.

73. Orduña, *Historia de la Aeronáutica Española*, 214.

74. Paul Preston, *Franco: A Biography* (New York: HarperCollins, 1994), 45–46.

75. Hills, *Franco: The Man and His Nation*, 137.

76. Stephen Ryan, *Pétain the Soldier* (New York: A. S. Barnes, 1969), 182.

77. Hills, *Franco: The Man and His Nation*, 138; Preston, *Franco: A Biography*, 45.

78. Hills, *Franco: The Man and His Nation*, 47–48.

79. Kunz and Müller, *Giftgas gegen Abd el Krim*, 138.

80. Ibid., 149–65.

81. Ibid., 150–60.

82. François Pernot and Marie-Catherine Villatoux, "L'aéronautique militaire au Maroc avant 1914," *Revue Historique des Armées* [henceforth *RHDA*] 218 (March 2000): 89–97, see 92.

83. Ibid., 96.

84. Tony Geraghty, *March or Die* (New York: Facts on File, 1986), 157–58.

85. Omissi, *Air Power and Colonial Control*, 186.

86. Douglas Porch, *The French Foreign Legion* (New York: HarperCollins, 1991), 398–99.
87. Porch, *French Foreign Legion*, 399.
88. Omissi, *Air Power and Colonial Control*, 186.
89. Ibid.
90. S. Lainé, "L'aeronautique militaire français au Maroc, 1911–1939," *RHDA* 4 (1978): 107–20, see 112–18.
91. On French aerial mapping, see Charles Christienne and Pierre Lissarague, *A History of French Military Aviation* (Washington, D.C.: Smithsonian Institution Press, 1986), 231. See also "La photo-topographie par avion au Maroc," *Aeronautique* 24 (May 1921): 209–12.
92. Christienne and Lissarague, *History of French Military Aviation*, 231–33.
93. Captain Plantey and Major Vincent, "Les avions sanitaires," *Aeronautique* 29 (October 1921): 398–400.
94. Captain W. Breyton, "L'aviation sanitaire au Maroc en 1933," *Revue de L'Armée de L'Air* 56 (March 1934): 243–64. Descriptions of the aircraft are found in 246–48.
95. Ibid., 251–55.
96. S. Lainé, "L'aéronautique militaire français au Maroc (1911–1939)," *RHDA* 4 (1978): 107–20, see 118.
97. Jérôme Millet, "L'aviation militaire française dans la guerre du rif," *RHDA* 166 (March 1987): 46–58, see 54.
98. Kunz and Müller, *Giftgas gegen Abd el Krim*, 142.
99. "French Morocco: Summary of Events, Summer 1925," *RUSI Journal* 479 (August 1925): 762.
100. A good description of the French army campaign in Morocco is found in Porch, *French Foreign Legion*, 398–406.
101. Christienne and Lissarague, *History of French Military Aviation*, 233.
102. See Major T. E. Compton, "The French Campaign of 1920–21 in Cilicia," *RUSI Journal* 465 (February 1922): 68–79.
103. A description of the disorder in the Near East and the Allied politics in the region is found in Alan Palmer, *The Decline and Fall of the Ottoman Empire* (New York: Barnes and Noble, 1992), 247–65.
104. Arnaud Teyssier, "L'aviation contre les insurrections: L'expérience français au levant au lendemain de la première guerre mondiale," *RHDA* 169 (December 1987): 48–54, see 50–54.
105. Teyssier, "L'aviation contre les insurrections," 48–54, see 52.
106. Ibid., 54.
107. "Army Notes," *RUSI Journal* 479 (August 1925): 579.
108. Teyssier, "L'aviation contre les insurrections," 55.
109. Omissi, *Air Power and Colonial Control*, 193–95.
110. Ibid., 193–94.
111. Ibid., 195.
112. Ibid., 196.
113. "Army Notes," *RUSI Journal* 479 (August 1925): 795–801.
114. Ibid., 797.
115. Ibid., 800–801.

116. Omissi, *Air Power and Colonial Control,* 199–200; see also "Operations of the Italian Air Force in North Africa, 1929–31," *RUSI Journal* 510 (May 1933): 374–80.

117. For a good description of the 1929–1931 campaign, see "Operations of the Italian Air Force in North Africa, 1929–31," *RUSI Journal* 510 (May 1933): 377–80.

118. Omissi, *Air Power and Colonial Control,* 200–201.

119. Ibid., 199.

120. On British counterinsurgency doctrine in this era, see T. R. Moreman, "Small Wars and Imperial Policing: The British Army and the Theory and Practice of Colonial Warfare in the British Empire, 1919–1939," *Journal of Strategic Studies* 19, no. 4 (December 1996): 105–31, see 120–21.

121. Lt. Gen. Sir Aylmer Haldane, "The Arab Rising in Mesopotamia, 1920," *RUSI Journal* 68 (February 1923): 65.

122. Flight-Lieutenant C. J. Mackay, "The Influence in the Future of Aircraft Upon Problems of Imperial Defence," *RUSI Journal* 68 (February 1923): 299.

123. Omissi, *Air Power and Colonial Control,* 193–96.

124. Scott Robertson, "The Development of Royal Air Force Strategic Bombing Doctrine between the Wars: A Revolution in Military Affairs?" *Airpower Journal* (spring 1998): 44.

125. Omissi, *Air Power and Colonial Control,* 119–21.

126. Lt. Col. David Dean, "Airpower in Small Wars: The British Air Control Experience," *Air University Review* (July/August 1983): 24–31; Lt. Col. David Dean, *The Air Force Role in Low Intensity Conflict* (Maxwell AFB: Air University Press, 1986), 19–27; Maj. Mark Dippold, "Air Occupation: Asking the Right Questions," *Airpower Journal* 9, no. 4 (winter 1997): 78; Bruce Hoffman, *British Air Control in Peripheral Conflict, 1919– 1976* (Santa Monica: Rand Corporation, 1989) (A Project Air Force Report); Major Michael Longoria, *A Historical View of Air Policing Doctrine: Lessons from the British Experience between the Wars, 1919–1939* (Maxwell AFB: Air University Press, 1992). For a favorable view from Norway, see Nils Naastad, "Policing the British Empire from the Air," in *Use of Air Power in Peace Operations,* ed. Carsten Rønnfelt (Oslo: Norwegian Institute of International Affairs, 1997), 19–37.

127. Carl Builder, "Doctrinal Frontiers," *Airpower Journal* (winter 1995): 1–6.

128. For an overview of the debate on air control, see James S. Corum, "Air Control: Reassessing the History," *RAF Air Power Review* (summer 2001): 15–36. Another excellent critique of air control is Group Captain Peter Gray, "The Myths of Air Control and the Realities of Imperial Policing," *RAF Air Power Review* (summer 2001): 37–52.

129. Robert Pape, *Bombing to Win: Air Power and Coercion in War* (Ithaca, N.Y.: Cornell University Press, 1996), 333–34.

130. Salmond, "The Air Force in Iraq," 492.

3. THE GREEK CIVIL WAR AND THE PHILIPPINE ANTI-HUK CAMPAIGN

1. Edgar O'Ballance, *The Greek Civil War, 1944–1949* (New York: Praeger, 1966), 27–29.

2. For a definitive examination of Axis occupation of Greece, see Mark Mazower, *Inside Hitler's Greece: The Experience of Occupation, 1941–44* (New Haven: Yale University Press, 1993).

3. Lawrence Wittner, *American Intervention in Greece, 1943–1949* (New York: Columbia University Press, 1982), 3.

4. Ole Smith, "'The First Round' — Civil War During the Occupation," in *The Greek Civil War, 1943–1950*, ed. David Close (London: Routledge, 1993), 58.

5. British military memorandum, dated April 1943, cited in C. M. Woodhouse, *The Struggle for Greece: 1941–1949* (London: Hart-Davis, McGibbon, 1976), 38.

6. O'Ballance, *The Greek Civil War*, 72–73.

7. G. M. Alexander, "The Demobilization Crisis of November 1944," in *Greece in the 1940s*, ed. John Iatrides (Hanover, N.H.: University Press of New England, 1981), 156–66.

8. W. H. McNeill, *The Greek Dilemma: War and Aftermath* (New York: Lippincott, 1947), 152.

9. Woodhouse, *The Struggle for Greece*, 169.

10. D. G. Kousoulas, "The Guerrilla War the Communists Lost," *U.S. Naval Institute Proceedings* (May 1953): 68.

11. Unspecified document, cited in Tim Jones, "The British Army, and Counter-Guerrilla Warfare in Greece, 1945–1949," *Small Wars and Insurgencies* (spring 1997): 93. See note 38 for document list.

12. Ibid., 94. See note 36 for documents pertaining to air support.

13. *Loose Minute*, British Air Ministry, 21 June 1947, PRO, AIR 46/30, 7, cited in Amikam Nachmani, "Civil War and Foreign Intervention in Greece: 1946–49," *Journal of Contemporary History* (October 1990): 505.

14. *Peak Organized Strength of Guerrilla and Government Forces in Algeria, Nagaland, Ireland, Indochina, South Vietnam, Malaya, Philippines, and Greece* (Washington, D.C.: Special Operations Research Office, American University, June 7, 1965), 18.

15. David Close and Thanos Veremis, "The Military Struggle, 1945–9," in Close, *The Greek Civil War*, 102.

16. Memo to the British Royal Air Force (RAF) Delegation, Greece, 10 September 1947, PRO, AIR 46/35, 4, cited in Nachmani, "Civil War and Foreign Intervention in Greece," 508.

17. Close and Veremis, "The Military Struggle," 108.

18. Jones, "The British Army, and Counter-Guerrilla Warfare in Greece," 95.

19. CINCME/COS in, COS(48)127(0), 10 June 1948, DEFE5/11, cited in ibid., 100, 101.

20. Kousoulas, "The Guerrilla War the Communists Lost," 69.

21. Ibid., 69–70.

22. Close and Veremis, "The Military Struggle," 118.

23. *Peak Organized Strength of Guerrilla and Government Forces in . . . Greece*, 18.

24. J. C. Murray, "The Anti-Bandit War," part 2, *Marine Corps Gazette*, February 1954, 53.

25. Nachmani, "Civil War and Foreign Intervention in Greece," 513. "In December 1946, there were 9,285 guerrillas, and their casualties amounted to 285. A year later, the figures were 20,350 and 1,630, respectively, and in December 1948, 24,985 and 2,560. In the January–March quarter of 1949, total guerrilla losses amounted to 12,240 killed in action, captured or surrendered. In April 1949, there were 19,880 guerrillas, and their casualties amounted to 3,269. In the August 1949 Grammos battle that effectively ended the civil war, GDA losses were 922 dead, 765 captured and 179 surrendered, whereas the GNA had 245 dead and 1,452 wounded. In July, the GDA still had 16,400

names on its rolls; at the end of August, there were only 3,710. Figures issued by the Greek government indicated that between June 1945 and March 1949, guerrilla losses had totalled more than 70,000 (29,000 killed, 13,000 captured and 28,000 surrendered). . . . The GNA casualty figures for the same period were given as 11,000 killed, 23,000 wounded and 8,000 missing. Close to 4,000 civilians were reported executed or killed by the guerrillas. The tide had definitely turned against the GDA." Ibid., 514–15.

26. Theodossios Papathanasiades, "The Bandits' Last Stand in Greece," *Military Review* (February 1951): 23–26.
27. Ibid., 28–31.
28. Nachmani, "Civil War and Foreign Intervention in Greece," 507.
29. Close and Veremis, "The Military Struggle," 108.
30. J. C. Murray, "The Anti-Bandit War," Conclusion, *Marine Corps Gazette*, May 1954, 52.
31. M. Campbell, E. W. Downs, and L. V. Schuetta, *The Employment of Airpower in the Greek Guerrilla War, 1947–1949*. Project No. AU-411-62-ASI. (Maxwell Air Force Base: Concepts Division, Aerospace Studies Institute, Air University, December 1964), 8.
32. Murray, "The Anti-Bandit War," Conclusion, 55.
33. Ibid., 53.
34. Nachmani, "Civil War and Foreign Intervention in Greece," 507.
35. Ibid., 508.
36. HQ, RHAF, Report No. 4, *Activities of Airforce During August*, 27 September 1948, 3, PRO, AIR 46/46, cited in ibid., 508–9.
37. Nachmani, "Civil War and Foreign Intervention in Greece," 509.
38. Murray, "The Anti-Bandit War," Conclusion, 54.
39. D. M. Condit, Bert Cooper et al., *Challenge and Response in Internal Conflict*, vol. 1, *The Experience in Asia* (Washington, D.C.: American University, February 1968), 475.
40. A. H. Peterson, G. C. Reinhardt, and E. E. Conger, eds., *Symposium on the Role of Airpower in Counterinsurgency and Unconventional Warfare: The Philippine Huk Campaign*, RM-3652-PR (Santa Monica: Rand Corporation, July 1963), 6–7.
41. Condit et al., *Challenge and Response in Internal Conflict*, vol. 1, 475–76.
42. *Peak Organized Strength of Guerrilla and Government Forces in . . . Philippines*, 16.
43. Benedict Kerkvliet, *The Huk Rebellion* (Berkeley: University of California Press, 1977), 72.
44. A *datu*'s status was not determined by the productive capacity of the land, but by the number of *tau* who were sustained by the land and loyally supported the *datu*. Although a direct correlation existed between productivity and the number of *tau*, the heart of the *datuk* was the paternalistic relationship. In exchange for a percentage of the *tau*'s harvest (usually 50 percent) and corvee labor, the *datu* provided the land and protection from bandits and rival claimants and demonstrated a genuine concern for the welfare of his *tau* through specific deeds. The *datu* presided over weddings and provided pigs for holidays and ceremonies. He also paid a portion of the *tau*'s start-up costs (tools and seed) and provided interest-free loans or outright gifts following poor harvests. Those *datus* who failed to offer similar support were labeled *wayang hiya*, that is, unscrupulous or disrespectful, and would lose their *tau*

and consequently their status to nearby *datus* who had *utang na loob* — obligation. But by the 1930s, landlords (*datu* becoming archaic at this point) did not even bother to maintain the image of a patron let alone perform as one. With emphasis now on the product and associated profit, instead of the producer and his loyalty, the landlord's concern for the social welfare of his tenants evaporated (the term *tau* also being inappropriate at this point). Although occurring late relative to the remainder of Southeast and Northeast Asia, Philippine society was enduring the shock of transforming from an economy resting on internal consumption to an export-led capitalistic economy. The attendant social upheaval reinvigorated long-standing peasant unrest, particularly with respect to distribution of land. The failure of the Philippine government to intervene with appropriate land reforms, or at least the appearance of intervening on behalf of the peasants, is one of the more conspicuous aspects of this chapter of Philippine history. Kerkvliet, *The Huk Rebellion*, 8–16.

45. For example, a tenant-farmer who had attended a speech given by a PKP leader recalled the following: "It was a large demonstration. I remember one of us carried red flags with KPMP emblems. . . . We had heard about [the speaker] and knew he was a labor leader in Manila. . . . You know, I don't understand why he went on that night about how good things were in Russia. It wasn't relevant to our problems. It was also dangerous. The police could have thought we were a bunch of Communists and arrested us." Kerkvliet, *The Huk Rebellion*, 50–51.

46. Tomás Tirona, "The Philippine Anti-Communist Campaign," *Air University Quarterly Review* (summer 1954): 42–44.

47. The wartime Philippine Constabulary collaborated with the notorious Japanese secret police, the Kempei Tai, which raised an auxiliary of indigenous terrorists known as the Makapili, which brutally intimidated Filipino peasants thought to be sympathetic to the anti-Japanese guerrillas. Robert Smith, *The Hukbalahap Insurgency: Economic, Political, and Military Factors* (Washington, D.C.: Department of the Army, 1963), 22.

48. Condit et al., *Challenge and Response in Internal Conflict*, 483.

49. Rupert Selman, *What Operational Concepts Should Govern the Use of Tactical Air Forces in Guerrilla War?* (Air War College Thesis No. 2345, Maxwell Air Force Base: Air University), 25.

50. Luis Taruc, *He Who Rides the Tiger* (New York: Praeger, 1967), 6, as cited in Robert Asprey, *War in the Shadows: The Guerrilla in History*, vol. 2 (Garden City, N.Y.: Doubleday, 1975), 751.

51. Dana Dillon, "Comparative Counter-insurgency Strategies in the Philippines," *Small Wars and Insurgencies* (winter 1995): 284.

52. Smith, *The Hukbalahap Insurgency*, 70.

53. John Ellis, *From the Barrel of a Gun: A History of Guerrilla, Revolutionary and Counter-Insurgency Warfare, from the Romans to the Present* (London: Greenhill Books, 1995), 205.

54. Smith, *The Hukbalahap Insurgency*, 28.

55. Ellis, *From the Barrel of a Gun*, 206.

56. *Peak Organized Strength of Guerrilla and Government Forces in . . . Philippines*, 16.

57. Smith, *The Hukbalahap Insurgency*, 85.

58. Parker Borg, "The United States, the Huk Movement, and Ramon Magsaysay," *Government* 644 (26 April 1965): 6–8.

59. Lansdale wrote an autobiographical account of his experience in the Philippines in his book, *In the Midst of Wars: An American's Mission to Southeast Asia* (New York: Harper and Row, 1972).

60. Bohannan coauthored a book with Napoleon Valeriano, a senior Philippine army officer, entitled *Counter-Guerrilla Operations: The Philippine Experience* (New York: Praeger, 1962).

61. Department of State, Office of Intelligence Research, report no. 5209, *The Hukbalahap* (27 September 1950), as quoted in Daniel Schirmer and Stephen Shalom, eds., *The Philippines Reader* (Boston: South End Press, 1987), 71–73.

62. Schirmer and Shalom, *The Philippines Reader*, 107.

63. Ibid., 110.

64. Broadly speaking, the Filipino army cleared unsettled land far removed from the center of the insurgency, constructed roads, built houses, and laid out the basic infrastructure of a self-sufficient agricultural community. Settlers, preferably former Huks, but also other elements of Filipino society, were provided a loan as start-up capital, the repayment of which was according to very liberal terms.

65. Borg, *The United States, the Huk Movement, and Ramon Magsaysay*, 10–13.

66. Smith, *The Hukbalahap Insurgency*, 104.

67. Ibid., 21–22.

68. Figures vary for 1946 between ten thousand and fifteen thousand guerrillas. The Philippine government considered the fifteen thousand figure to be exaggerated but also conceded that it was entirely possible. Peterson, Reinhardt, and Conger, *Symposium*, 8.

69. *Peak Organized Strength of Guerrilla and Government Forces in . . . Philippines*, 16.

70. Dillon, "Comparative Counter-insurgency Strategies," 291.

71. Ellis, *From the Barrel of a Gun*, 206–7.

72. Napoleon Valeriano and Charles Bohannan, *Counter-Guerrilla Operations — The Philippines Experience* (New York: Praeger, 1962), cited in Asprey, *War in the Shadows*, 752.

73. Smith, *The Hukbalahap Insurgency*, 121–22.

74. Taruc, *He Who Rides the Tiger*, as cited in Ellis, *From the Barrel of a Gun*, 207–8.

75. Official History of the Philippines Air Force website. Available from *www.paf.mil.ph*.

76. Peterson, Reinhardt, and Conger, *Symposium*, 53.

77. Taruc, *He Who Rides the Tiger*, in Asprey, *War in the Shadows*, 752.

78. Peterson, Reinhardt, and Conger, *Symposium*, 44.

79. Ibid., 54.

80. Ibid., 23.

81. There seems little doubt that the Japanese used airpower in the Philippines in a destructive manner, but the extent to which U.S. airpower "devastated" the Philippines during the liberation campaign is questionable. General MacArthur restrained his more aggressive air commanders in the Philippines and denied a request to bomb Manila even though such bombing would have greatly assisted in expelling Japanese troops (see Conrad Crane, *Bombs, Cities, and Civilians: American Airpower Strat-*

egy in World War II [Lawrence: University Press of Kansas, 1993], 122–23). Filipino officials were loath to employ airpower against the Huks nonetheless.

82. Peterson, Reinhardt, and Conger, *Symposium,* 24.

83. Ibid.

84. Tirona, "The Philippine Anti-Communist Campaign," 49–50.

85. Peterson, Reinhardt, and Conger, *Symposium,* 26.

86. William Thorpe, "Huk Hunting in the Philippines," *Airpower Historian* (April 1962): 99.

87. Condit et al., *Challenge and Response in Internal Conflict,* vol. 1, 500.

88. Ibid., 37.

89. Ibid., 36.

90. Ibid., 326–37.

91. "Counter-Guerrilla Operations in the Philippines, 1946–1953," a seminar on the Huk Campaign, Fort Bragg, N.C., 15 June 1961. See also Peterson, Reinhardt, and Conger, *Symposium,* 39–42.

92. Peterson, Reinhardt, and Conger, *Symposium,* 44.

93. Smith, *The Hukbalahap Insurgency,* 96–97.

94. Peterson, Reinhardt, and Conger, *Symposium,* 36.

95. Ibid., 49. Regrettably, little information is available about PAF helicopters, the types, or details about their use. Nevertheless, as the British had done in Malaya, what few helicopters were available were used extensively when operable, including "picking up wounded and taking them to the base hospital in Manila within an hour." Filipino officers and their American advisers lamented the lack of helicopters during the Huk insurgency but attributed the unwillingness of the United States to provide more machines to the pressing needs of the Korean War. Ibid., 37, 45.

96. Ibid., 46.

97. Ibid., 46–47.

98. Ibid., 49–50.

99. Ibid., 47–48.

100. Ibid., 49.

101. Ibid., 46.

102. Dimitrios Kousoulas, "The Crucial Point of a Counterguerrilla Campaign," *Infantry* (January–February 1963): 19.

103. U. S. Baclagon, *Lessons from the Huk Campaign* (Manila: M. Colcol, 1960), 4.

104. Jones, "The British Army, and Counter-Guerrilla Warfare in Greece," 92–93.

105. Ibid., 99–100.

106. Joe Taylor, "Air Support of Guerrillas on Cebu," *Military Affairs* (fall 1959): 149–52.

4. THE FRENCH COLONIAL WARS, 1946–1962:
INDOCHINA AND ALGERIA

1. Jacques Fremeaux, "Troupes blanches et troupes de couleur," *RHDA* 218 (March 2000): 19–30, see 22–24.

2. Martin Thomas, *The French Empire at War, 1940–45* (Manchester, England: Manchester University Press, 1998), 31.

3. Ibid., 210–11.

4. Douglas Pike, *PAVN — People's Army of Vietnam* (Novato, Calif.: Presidio Press, 1986), 32.

5. Pike, *PAVN*, 190.

6. A good account of the French and Vietnamese politics of the immediate postwar period is found in David Marr, *Vietnam 1945: The Quest for Power* (Berkeley: University of California Press, 1995).

7. Thomas, *The French Empire at War*, 213–14.

8. J. Vernet, "Les progrès de réorganisation de l'armée de terre française de 1945–1946," *Revue Historique des Armées (RHDA)* 3 (1979): 205–29.

9. Christienne and Lissarague, *History of French Military Aviation*, 450.

10. James Dunnigan and Albert Nofi, *Dirty Little Secrets of the Vietnam War* (New York: Thomas Dunne Books, 1999), 38–39.

11. Pike, *PAVN*, 39.

12. See Martin Windrow and Mike Chappell, *The French Indochina War 1946–54* (Oxford: Osprey, 1998), 24. By the end of 1945 the Viet Minh had about sixty thousand rifles, three thousand light machine guns, some mortars, and a few field guns as well as a large stock of hand grenades.

13. Michael Maclear, *The Ten Thousand Day War. Vietnam: 1945–1975* (New York: St. Martin's Press, 1981), 24.

14. Ibid., 24.

15. Philippe Vial, "De l'impuissance à la renaissance: Le général léchères à la tête de l'Armée de l'air (1948–1953)," *Revue Historique des Armées* 192 (September 1993): 43–51.

16. For an overview of the French aviation industry from 1945 to 1950, see Emmanuel Chadeau, "Volume et emploi des dépenses aéronautiques, 1945–1950," *Revue Historique des Armées* 148 (1982): 28–39. See also Chadeau, "Notes sur les problèmes industriels de l'aéronautique nationale," *RHDA* 148 (1982): 40–49.

17. General Charles Christienne, "L'Armée de l'air de 1945 à 1949," *Revue Historique des Armées* 148 (1982): 4–15.

18. Vial, "De l'impuissance," 47.

19. Marcellin Hodeir, "Doctrine d'emploi et mission de l'Armée de l'air, 1946–1948," *RHDA* 148 (1982): 60–69.

20. Patrick Facon, "Les néo-douhétiens français de l'après — Seconde guerre mondiale," *Revue Historiques des Armées* 177 (December 1989): 100–110.

21. Hodeir, "Doctrine d'emploi," 64–65.

22. Ibid.

23. Christienne and Lissarague, *History of French Military Aviation*, 450–51.

24. Ibid.

25. Raymond Barthélemy, "L'aviation de transport militaire français de 1945 à 1949," *RHDA* 148 (1982): 70–79.

26. For a detailed overview of the French air force establishment in Indochina in 1945 and 1946, see Patrick Facon, "Reconstitution de l'Armée de l'air en Indochine, 1945–46," *RHDA* 148 (1982): 82–89.

27. Ibid., 89.

28. Ibid., 88–89.

29. Maclear, *Ten Thousand Day War*, 21.

30. Barthémy, "L'aviation de transport militaire français," 78.

31. Christienne and Lissarague, *History of French Military Aviation*, 452.

32. Ibid., 452.

33. Ibid., 452. See also Jim Mesko, *VNAF: South Vietnamese Air Force, 1945–1975* (Carrollton, Tex.: Squadron/Signal Publications, 1987), 5.

34. Christienne and Lissarague, *History of French Military Aviation*, 453–54.

35. Barthélemy, "L'aviation de transport militaire française," 70–79, see 75.

36. Christienne and Lissarague, *History of French Military Aviation*, 452–53.

37. Bernard Fall, *Street without Joy* (New York: Schocken Books, 1962), 27–29.

38. Ibid., 29–31.

39. Fall, *Street without Joy*, 262.

40. For a detailed overview of French air force reconnaissance operations in Indochina, see Alexander Zervoudakis, "Le renseignement aérien en Indochine (1950–1954)," *RHDA* 178 (March 1990): 69–84.

41. Christienne and Lissarague, *History of French Military Aviation*, 454–56.

42. Mesko, *VNAF*, 6.

43. Pike, *PAVN*, 39.

44. François Pernot, "L'Armée de l'air en Indochine et le probléme chinois," *RHDA* 194 (March 1994): 100–109, see 107.

45. Christienne and Lissarague, *History of French Military Aviation*, 454–56; see also Mesko, *VNAF*, 8.

46. André Delaporte, "L'effort de la marine à la fin de la guerre d'Indochine (fin 1953–début 1954)," *RHDA* 194 (March 1994): 110–22, provides an excellent overview of French naval air operations in the war.

47. Christienne and Lissarague, *History of French Military Aviation*, 457.

48. Windrow and Chappell, *French Indochina War*, 11.

49. Fall, *Street without Joy*, 32–33.

50. Ibid., 110–11.

51. Ibid., 36–40.

52. See Col. R. Trinquier, "Témoignage les maquis d'Indochine," *RHDA* 2 (1979): 169–90, for a full account of the French guerrilla operations in Indochina; see also Fall, *Street without Joy*, 267–79.

53. Fall, *Street without Joy*, 269.

54. John Everett-Heath, *Helicopters in Combat: The First Fifty Years* (London: Cassell, 1992), 22; see also Paul Gaujac, "Du parachute à l'hélicoptère de combat," *RHDA* 178 (March 1990): 63–73.

55. Fall, *Street without Joy*, 48–60.

56. Bernard Fall, *Hell in a Very Small Place* (Philadelphia: Lippincott, 1966), 24–25.

57. On the French air force at Dien Bien Phu, see Patrick Facon, "L'Armée de l'air et Dien Bien Phu," *RHDA* 158 (March 1985): 79–87; Hubert Ruffat, "Le ravitaillement par air de Dien Bien Phu," *RHDA* 157 (December 1984): 52–57; Patrick Facon, "L'Armée de l'air et Dien Bien Phu: Preparation de la bataille," *RHDA* 157 (December 1984): 58–64.

58. Fall, *Hell in a Very Small Place*, 2–3. Even with a significant number of new aircraft made available for Indochina by the Americans after 1950, between 1952 and 1953

the total strength of French air force personnel in Indochina only increased from 9,700 to 10,657. See Patrick Facon, "L'Armée de l'air et la guerre d'Indochine (1945–1954)," *RHDA* 177 (December 1989): 95–107, see 106.

59. For troop strength at Dien Bien Phu, see Fall, *Hell in a Very Small Place*, 479–82.

60. Ibid., 104–5.

61. Robert Scales, *Firepower in Limited War* (Washington, D.C.: National Defense University Press, 1990), 58–59.

62. Porch, *French Foreign Legion*, 559.

63. At least seven aircraft were lost to ground fire, including two C 119s, two MS 500s, and an F6F Hellcat fighter-bomber. See Victor Flintham, *Air Wars and Aircraft*, 259–61.

64. Fall, *Street without Joy*, 260.

65. The whole story is recounted in detail in Fall, *Street without Joy*, 185–250.

66. Alistair Horne, *A Savage War for Peace: Algeria, 1954–1962* (London: Penguin Books, 1977). See Anthony Clayton, "The Sétif Uprising of May 1945," *Small Wars and Insurgencies* 3 (spring 1992): 1–21, for a detailed account of the 1945 rebellion and its political effects.

67. Horne, *A Savage War for Peace*, 69–73.

68. For a very thorough overview of the FLN, see Abder-Rahmane Derradji, *The Algerian Guerrilla Campaign: Strategy and Tactics* (Lewiston, N.Y.: Edwin Mellen Press, 1997).

69. Horne, *A Savage War for Peace*, 113.

70. The Wilayas were organized as follows: Wilaya 1: Aurès Mountains, Wilaya 2: Constantine, Wilaya 3: Kabylia Mountains, Wilaya 4: Algiers region, Wilaya 5: Oran region, Wilaya 6: Sahara.

71. Horne, *A Savage War for Peace*, 118–22.

72. Martin Windrow and Mike Chappell, *The Algerian War 1954–62* (London: Osprey, 1997), 17.

73. Patrick Facon, "L'Algérie et la politique générale de l'Armée de l'air (1954–1958)," *RHDA* 187 (June 1992): 76–85, see 84.

74. Windrow and Chappell, *Algerian War*, 20.

75. Phillippe Vial and Pascal Tanchoux, "Les archives Algérie: De l'Armée de l'air," *RHDA* 187 (June 1992): 66–75, see 67.

76. Ibid.

77. Vial and Tanchoux, "Les archives Algérie," 68.

78. Lt. Col. Claude Carré, "Aspects opérationnels du conflit algérien, 1954–1960," *RHDA* 166 (May 1987): 82–91, see 89.

79. John Talbot, "The War Without a Name — France in Algeria, 1954–1962," in *The Chopper Boys: Helicopter Warfare in Africa*, ed. J. Ventner (London: Greenhill Books, 1994), 37–44, see 44.

80. Flintham, *Air Wars and Aircraft*, 80.

81. For a full account of French units and equipment in Algeria, see Flintham, *Air Wars and Aircraft*, 80–84; see also François Pernot, "La rébellion et le fait aérien," *RHDA* 187 (June 1992): 86–93, for a good overview of the tactics and equipment of French military aviation in Algeria.

82. Ibid.
83. Capitaine de vaisseau Daguzan, "Les hélicoptères de la marine en Algérie, 1955–1962," *RHDA* 187 (June 1992): 118–24.
84. The French air force raised a force of seven hundred elite airborne commando troops for service in Algeria (five companies). Units such as these also supported the "General Reserve" operations. See Henri Féraud, "1956–1986: Les commandos de l'air ont trente ans," *RHDA* 170 (March 1988): 104–11.
85. A good description of the small-scale combat action in the mountains of Algeria and action in the paratroop units was written by a veteran of the campaign. See Pierre Leulliette, *The War in Algeria* (New York: Houghton Mifflin, 1964).
86. Frédéric Guelton and Geneviève Errera, "Transmissions et guerre subversive en Algérie," *RHDA* 178 (March 1990): 74–83.
87. Christienne and Lassarague, *History of French Military Aviation,* 463–65.
88. John Everett-Heath, *Helicopters in Combat: The First Fifty Years* (London: Arms and Armour, 1992), 54–55.
89. Christienne and Lissarague, *History of French Military Aviation,* 464–65.
90. Horne, *A Savage War for Peace,* 265–66.
91. Talbot, "The War Without a Name," 44.
92. See Lt. Col. Claude Carré, "Aspects opérationnels du conflit algérien, 1954–1960," *RHDA* 166 (March 1987): 82–111.
93. Horne, *A Savage War for Peace,* 335–38.
94. Ibid., 249–50.
95. For an overview of French psychological operations in Algeria, see François Pernot, "La guerre psychologique en Algérie vue à travers les archives de l'Armée de l'air," *RHDA* 190 (March 1993): 90–99.
96. Pernot, "La rébellion et la fait aérien," 91.
97. Horne, *A Savage War for Peace,* 538.

5. THE BRITISH COLONIAL WARS, 1945–1975: MALAYA, SOUTH ARABIA, AND OMAN

1. The original goal was a postwar National Service Army of only 305,000, but the figure was raised by roughly 100,000 in 1951 due to the exigencies of the Korean War (Michael Dewar, *Brush Fire Wars: Minor Campaigns of the British Army since 1945* (New York: St. Martin's Press, 1984), 14.
2. David Lee, *Eastward: A History of the Royal Air Force in the Far East, 1945–1972* (London: Her Majesty's Stationery Office, 1984), 93.
3. It is beyond the scope of this chapter to treat in detail every small war in which the RAF played a role between 1945 and the middle of the 1970s. Many of these conflicts were more or less conventional in nature, e.g., the major Anglo-French operation that seized the Suez Canal in 1956. During that conflict, RAF and Royal Navy aircraft virtually destroyed the Egyptian Air Force as a viable combat force, enabling the airborne insertion of ground troops to take place. Such a conventional operation reveals little about the relevancy of RAF operations to counterinsurgency and counterrevolutionary warfare. Other conflicts, for a variety of reasons, provided few lessons regarding the role of airpower in small wars. For example, RAF operations

against Mau Mau "terrorists" in Kenya between 1952 and 1956 were too limited to draw any real conclusions. In March 1953, only four North American Harvard trainers fitted with a single Browning machine gun in the starboard wing, and capable of dropping only eight twenty-pound antipersonnel bombs, comprised the entire tactical strike force of No. 1340 Flight based in Thornhill, Rhodesia. Later, Bomber Command Lincolns, Fighter Command Vampires, and a collection of aging Dakotas performing psychological operations missions rounded out the air effort. But their impact was arguably negligible (Robert Jackson, *The RAF in Action: From Flanders to the Falklands* [Poole, Dorset: Blandford Press, 1985], 144–45). Other minor conflicts, e.g., the so-called Borneo confrontation between 1962 and 1966, offered lessons not unlike those detailed in the small wars treated in this chapter.

4. See K. Jeffrey, "Colonial Warfare, 1900–1939," in *Warfare in the Twentieth Century*, ed. C. McInness and G. D. Sheffield (London: Unwin Hyman, 1988), 31; and Ian Beckett, "The Study of Counter-Insurgency: A British Perspective," *Small Wars and Insurgencies* (April 1990): 49.

5. Douglas Porch, introduction to C. E. Callwell, *Small Wars: Their Principles and Practice* (Lincoln: University of Nebraska Press, 1996), xii.

6. Ibid., 41, 76.

7. A. D. English, "The RAF Staff College and the Evolution of British Strategic Bombing Policy," *Journal of Strategic Studies* (September 1993): 420, cited in T. R. Moreman, "'Small Wars' and 'Imperial Policing': The British Army and the Theory and Practice of Colonial Warfare in the British Empire, 1919–1939," *Journal of Strategic Studies* (December 1996): 110.

8. See, for example, Wing Commander R. H. Peck, "Aircraft in Small Wars," *Journal of the Royal United Service Institution* (February 1928): 542–54, hereafter cited as *RUSI*.

9. Lucian Pye, "The Roots of Insurgency and the Commencement of Rebellions," in *Internal War*, ed. Harry Eckstein (New York: Free Press of Glencoe, 1964), 159–60.

10. Callwell, *Small Wars*, 40.

11. Ibid., xvi–xvii.

12. Wing Commander C. N. Foxley-Norris, "The Use of Air Power in Security Operations," *RUSI* (November 1954): 554.

13. Beckett, "The Study of Counterinsurgency," 49.

14. Moreman, "'Small Wars' and 'Imperial Policing,'" 110.

15. *Notes on Imperial Policing 1934* (London: War Office, 1934), cited in ibid.

16. Beckett, "The Study of Counterinsurgency," 49.

17. Peck, "Aircraft in Small Wars," 537.

18. James Cross, *Conflict in the Shadows* (New York: Doubleday, 1963), 77.

19. Fall, *Street without Joy*, 267.

20. David Schwartz, *NATO's Nuclear Dilemmas* (Washington, D.C.: Brookings Institution, 1983), 27–28. As the Cold War developed, however, nuclear cooperation between the United States and Great Britain improved greatly.

21. In the immediate aftermath of World War II the Avro Lincoln Bomber, an improved version of the Lancaster, was the mainstay of RAF Bomber Command (along with over eighty U.S.-provided B-29s) until the early 1950s when new jet bombers were acquired. The first of these was the English Electric Canberra, one of the great suc-

cess stories of British aviation history. But the short-ranged Canberra was limited as a strategic bomber, and the Vickers Valiant soon entered service as the first truly strategic bomber of the nuclear V-Force. Two other bombers rounded out the V-Force, the Avro Vulcan and the Handley Page Victor. These three bombers served as the principal nuclear deterrent for Great Britain until 1969 when that role was assumed by Royal Navy Polaris submarines. Jackson, *The RAF in Action*, 133–37.

22. Group Captain G. G. Barnett, "The Role of the Royal Air Force in the Preservation of Peace," *RUSI* (February–November 1946): 77, 79.

23. Marshal of the Royal Air Force Sir John Slessor, "Air Power and the Future of War," *RUSI* (August 1954): 351. Slessor took pains in his lecture to point out that the criticism that airmen were wedded to the idea of victory in war by airpower alone was an unfortunate caricature: "All we early RAF officers were alleged to sit up late every night learning the works of General Douhet by heart. We may have had his book in the Staff College library, but, if so, I never saw it. But when I was a student at a Staff College in 1924, we were not taught that the RAF could win wars by itself, and when I was a teacher at a Staff College 10 years later, I certainly never taught that." Ibid., 344.

24. Ibid., 355.

25. Air Marshal Sir Robert Saundby, "Air Power in Limited Wars, *RUSI* (August 1958): 383.

26. For example, even after having subordinated the air effort to the ground effort, Air Marshal Saundby claimed, "We have had many years of experience of the system of air control of undeveloped countries and we know that aircraft of the suitable type, used promptly and in accordance with well-tried principles, are of the greatest value for this purpose" (ibid.). Others would lament the fact that air control was no longer a viable strategy in modern counterinsurgency, and hoped it could be restored as "the most efficient and economic way of controlling territory and peoples." See Foxley-Norris, "Air Power in Security Operations," 556.

27. Brigadier General F. H. Brooke, "Infantry and Air Power in Malaya," *Australian Army Journal* (December 1954): 15.

28. Thomas Marks, *The British Acquisition of Siamese Malaya, 1896–1909* (Bangkok: White Lotus, 1997).

29. Victor Purcell, *Malaysia* (New York: Walker and Company, 1965), 80–105.

30. Lee, *Eastward*, 94. Although the Chinese population is invariably described as the minority in Malaya, it was in fact very nearly half of the total population, and when Singapore is included in the figures the Chinese were slightly in the majority. Nevertheless, the British and native Malays controlled the political machinery, and the Chinese were not allowed to hold civil service posts and were subjected to other discriminatory measures.

31. Guy Arnold, *Wars in the Third World since 1945*, 2d ed. (London: Cassell, 1995), 99–100. See also Robert Jackson, *The Malayan Emergency: The Commonwealth's Wars, 1948–1966* (London: Routledge, 1991), 1–8.

32. John Coates, *Suppressing Insurgency: An Analysis of the Malayan Emergency, 1948–1954* (Boulder, Colo.: Westview Press, 1992), 10.

33. Jackson, *The Malayan Emergency*, 9.

34. Ibid.

35. Ibid., 10.

36. The communist movement in Malaya was very sensitive to external communist initiatives. At the time of the MCP decision, the Chinese communists were on the verge of victory in their battle with the Chinese nationalists and communist movements were emerging throughout the whole of Asia. At an international youth conference in Calcutta in February 1948, the communists called upon the peoples of Asia to turn from agitation to violent overthrow of the colonial powers. The MCP declared war on the colonial government of Malaya the following May. Noel Barber, *War of the Running Dogs: The Malayan Emergency, 1948–1960* (New York: Weybright and Talley, 1972), 28.

37. Brigadier General K. R. Brazier-Creagh, "Malaya," *RUSI* (May 1954): 177.

38. Barber, *War of the Running Dogs*, 64.

39. The impact of the Burma campaign in World War II on British military thinking regarding the Malayan Emergency warrants additional research. Field marshal the Viscount W. J. Slim employed the little airpower he had at his disposal in a masterful fashion against the Japanese. Moreover his experience with deep-penetration missions, along with that of Wingate, undoubtedly influenced British operations in the mountains and jungles of Malaya. See Slim, *Defeat into Victory: The Magnificent Account of a Great Campaign of the Second World War* (New York: David McKay Company, 1961).

40. Henry Probert, "Malaya: The Start of the Emergency," *Royal Air Force Historical Society Journal* 21 (2000): 10–11.

41. Air Vice Marshal Sir Francis Mellersh, "The Campaign Against the Terrorists in Malaya," *RUSI* (August 1951): 406.

42. John Cloake, *Templer: Tiger of Malaya* (London: Harrap Limited, 1985), 196.

43. Mellersh, "The Campaign Against the Terrorists in Malaya," 406.

44. Anthony Short, *The Communist Insurrection in Malaya, 1948–1960* (New York: Crane, Russak, and Company, 1975), 376–77. Robert Tabor, an American reporter who had fought alongside Fidel Castro's forces in repelling the Bay of Pigs invasion, pointed out that the food denial program targeted the "Achilles' heel" of the insurgency. Ultimately, "the jungle in which [the guerrillas] necessarily found refuge was inhabited not by farmers, but by tribal aborigines scarcely able to grow enough food to support themselves. Consequently, the food on which the rebels relied had to be smuggled in from the villages . . . and this was soon halted by vigilant police activity." The resettlement program — the "New Villages" — had already cut off direct contact between the guerrillas and their principal means of support. "Lacking the material support of even the Chinese community on which they relied, [the guerrillas] were . . . slowly starved into submission or lured into ambushes in which they were reduced piecemeal." Robert Tabor, *War of the Flea: A Study of Guerrilla Warfare Theory and Practice* (New York: Citadel Press, 1970), 123–24.

45. Dennis Duncanson, *Government and Revolution in Vietnam* (London: Oxford University Press, 1968), chap. 5 and 6, passim, as quoted in Douglas Blaufarb, *The Counterinsurgency Era: U.S. Doctrine and Performance, 1950 to the Present* (New York: Free Press, 1977), 44–45.

46. Short, *The Communist Insurrection in Malaya,* 185.

47. Larry Cable, *Conflict of Myths: The Development of American Counterinsurgency Doctrine and the Vietnam War* (New York: New York University Press, 1986), 88–89.

48. Royal Air Force, *The Malayan Emergency, 1948–1960* (London: Ministry of Defence, 1970 [Restricted]), declassified, n.d.), 4. This official document was reissued as Ministry of Defence, Air Historical Branch (RAF), *Operation Firedog: Air Support in the Malayan Emergency, 1948–1960* (London: Her Majesty's Stationery Office, 1992).

49. Brazier-Creagh, "Malaya," 179.

50. Blaufarb, Douglas, *The Counterinsurgency Era* (New York, The Free Press, 1977), 46.

51. Brigadier General Richard Clutterbuck, who served in Malaya from 1956 to 1958, asserted that intelligence was of greater importance than military tactics — "not high-level military intelligence on maps, but basic police intelligence at the Communists' own grass roots." Only good intelligence could enable government forces to find the elusive guerrillas. According to Clutterbuck, "when our soldiers made contact with the guerrillas, the soldiers nearly always won [owing to superior training and firepower]. . . . The problem was putting the forces in contact, and this depended on getting information from the people on whom the guerrillas relied for support." Brigadier Richard Clutterbuck, *The Long, Long War: Counterinsurgency in Malaya and Vietnam* (New York: Praeger, 1966), 4–5.

52. Group Captain Kingsley Oliver, "The Ground War in Malaya, 1948–1960," *Royal Air Force Historical Society Journal* 21 (2000): 16.

53. However, Tim Jones states that the "small-unit approach" has been overstated. See "The British Army, and Counter-Guerrilla Warfare in Transition, 1944–1952," *Small Wars and Insurgencies* (winter 1996): 279–80.

54. Julian Paget, *Counterinsurgency Operations: Techniques of Guerrilla Warfare* (New York: Walker and Company, 1967), 52.

55. In a semifictionalized account of his experiences in Malaya, Arthur Campbell described the Dayak trackers as courageous and tenacious, if not savage in their contributions to the British counterinsurgency effort. Arthur Campbell, *Jungle Green* (London: George Allen and Unwin, 1953), 38–39.

56. "The RAF Task Force, Malaya," *Royal Air Force Quarterly and Empire Air Forces Journal* (April 1949): 86.

57. A worthwhile discussion of the Spitfire as a counterinsurgency aircraft in Malaya can be found in Air Vice Marshal John Nichols, "Spitfires and Guerrillas," in Alfred Price, *Spitfire* (London: Promotional Reprint Company, 1991), 146–49.

58. Air Vice Marshal Micahel Robinson, "Offensive Air Operations, Beaufighter/Brigand," *Royal Air Force Historical Society Journal* 21 (2000): 22.

59. "The RAF Task Force, Malaya," 87.

60. Jackson, *The Malayan Emergency,* 68.

61. Robinson, "Offensive Air Operations," 23.

62. J. R. Burgess, "Lincolns — 100 Squadron Malaya 1950," *Royal Air Force Historical Society Journal* 21 (2000): 27, 28.

63. Air Commodore G. S. Cooper, "Venoms and Canberras," ibid., 31.

64. Ibid.

65. "RAF Action Overseas," in Jackson, *The RAF in Action,* 143.

66. "The air forces of the United Kingdom, Australia and New Zealand were represented by an average of over a dozen different types of aircraft at any one time. . . . During the first two years . . . Lincolns, Sunderlands, Beaufighters, Brigands, Spitfires, Tempests, Mosquitos, Yorks, Dakotas, Ansons, Devons, Austers, Harvards and Tiger Moths were flown . . . while the flypast at Kuala Lumpur on 1 August 1960 that marked [the end of the Emergency] included Canberras, Sabres, Meteors, Seahawks, Valettas, Bristol Freighters, Beverleys, Pioneers, Austers and Sycamores. To this list can be added Hornets, Venoms, Vampires, Shackletons, Hastings, Pembrokes, Chipmunks, Whirlwinds and Dragonflies." Royal Air Force, *The Malayan Emergency*, 31.

67. Ibid., 30.

68. Ibid.

69. Jackson, *The RAF in Action*, 142.

70. John Fricker, "Flying Against the Malayan Bandits — I," *Aeroplane* (5 January 1951), 6.

71. Lee, *Eastward*, 100.

72. Foxley-Norris, "Air Power in Security Operations," 555.

73. Ibid.

74. Mellersh, "The Campaign Against the Terrorists in Malaya," 407.

75. Group Captain K. R. C. Slater, "Air Operations in Malaya," *RUSI* (August 1957): 382.

76. Ibid., 378.

77. Brooke, "Infantry and Air Power in Malaya," 16.

78. Wing Commander John Dowling, *RAF Helicopters: The First Twenty Years* (London: Her Majesty's Stationery Office, 1992), 44.

79. Lieutenant Commander T. Blore, "The Queen's Copters," *Marine Corps Gazette*, July 1954, 54.

80. Dowling, *RAF Helicopter*, 44.

81. Slater, "Air Operations in Malaya," 383.

82. Dowling, *RAF Helicopter*, 65.

83. "The amount of cargo dropped on each sortie ranged from 1 to 3¼ tons and covered all provisions to sustain life and armaments to perpetuate the war. Live chickens were dropped on one occasion and cats to combat a rodent problem." Flight Lieutenant Maurice Rogers, "Air Transport Operations — Valetta's," *Royal Air Force Historical Society Journal* 21 (2000): 44.

84. Helicopters were in limited supply and were overtasked. Consequently, once a jungle fort was established, it was quickly followed by the construction of a short airstrip from which Prestwick Pioneer and Auster light liaison aircraft could operate. The Pioneer could take off in seventy-five yards with four passengers or an equivalent load of supplies. The venerable Auster had been employed during World War II as an Air Observation Post (AOP). AOP squadrons were intended to support the artillery of a Corps and throughout their operational history employed some type of Auster aircraft (Major P. W. Mead, "Air O.P. Squadrons, Royal Air Force," *Royal Air Force Quarterly and Empire Air Forces Journal* [April 1953]: 141, 143–44). Austers were therefore under the direct operational control of the British army. In addition to spotting in Malaya, Austers performed yeoman service in a variety of other roles such as reconnaissance, communications, and aerial resupply.

85. W. Courtenay, "Army Aviation in Malaya," *Canadian Aviation* (May 1956): 31–32.

86. Blore, "The Queen's Copters," 53.

87. Brooke, "Infantry and Air Power in Malaya," 16.

88. Brazier-Creagh, "Malaya," 179.

89. Slater, "Air Operations in Malaya," 385, 384.

90. Foxley-Norris, "Air Power in Security Operations," 557.

91. Slater, "Air Operations in Malaya," 379.

92. Arguably, the "jet-prop" controversy experienced by the United States during the Vietnam War was a continuation of the earlier controversy during the Korean War. See Conrad Crane, *American Airpower Strategy in Korea, 1950–1953* (Lawrence: University Press of Kansas, 2000), chap. 2, passim.

93. Lee, *Eastward*, 157.

94. Ibid. The figures pale in comparison to the cost of American involvement in Southeast Asia, but for the British Empire, at a time when the country was trying to recover from World War II and the British economy was at low ebb, the cost of the Emergency in Malaya was enormous.

95. Brazier-Creagh, "Malaya," 185.

96. Ibid., 185–86.

97. Slater, "Air Operations in Malaya," 387.

98. *Project Control Report PCR 1* (Maxwell Air Force Base: Historical Research Agency). See also Lieutenant Colonel David J. Dean, *Project Control: Creative Strategic Thinking at Air University* (Maxwell Air Force Base: Center for Aerospace Doctrine, Research, and Education, August 1985).

99. *Project Control Report PCR 1*, figure 6.

100. Ibid., Preface.

101. Wing Commander S. G. Walker, "Imperial Strategy and the Middle East," *RUSI* (February 1947): 17.

102. Ibid., 19–21.

103. R. J. Gavin, *Aden under British Rule, 1839–1967* (New York: Harper and Row, 1975), 1–26.

104. Ibid., 276.

105. Ibid., 281. Chapter 11, "Airpower and Expansion," is an excellent discussion of the promotion and execution of air control in the Aden Protectorate between the world wars.

106. Ibid., 333.

107. "Aden: Outpost of Empire," in Arnold, *Wars in the Third World since 1945*, 88–89.

108. Major M. E. Bransby-Williams, "Gold Medal and Trench Gasciogne Prize Essay, 1952," *RUSI* (May 1953): 231.

109. Walker, "Imperial Strategy and the Middle East," 25, 26.

110. "Aden: Outpost of Empire," 87.

111. Dewar, *Brush Fire Wars*, 117.

112. Gavin, *Aden under British Rule*, 346.

113. "Aden: Outpost of Empire," 90.

114. Gavin, *Aden under British Rule*, 350.

115. Jackson, *The RAF in Action*, 146–47. See also Air Chief Marshal Sir David Lee, "The Radfan Campaign," *Royal Air Forces Quarterly* (winter 1977): 355.

116. Bruce Hoffman, *British Air Power in Peripheral Conflict, 1919–1976* (Santa Monica: RAND Corporation, October 1989), 88.

117. Air Chief Marshal Sir David Lee, *Flight from the Middle East: A History of the Royal Air Force in the Arabian Peninsula and Adjacent Territories, 1945–1972* (London: Her Majesty's Stationery Office, 1980), 203. Also see Karl Pieragostini, *Britain, Aden, and South Arabia: Abandoning Empire* (New York: St. Martin's Press, 1991), 71.

118. "Britain's Warning Over Yemen," *The Times of London*, 25 March 1964, 11.

119. Dewar, *Brush Fire Wars*, 119–20.

120. "British Attack on Yemen Fort: Denial of Civilian Casualties," *The Times of London*, 30 March 1964, 7.

121. "Britain Denies Accusation by Yemen: 'Leaflet Warning Ignored,'" ibid., 3 April 1964, 12.

122. Dewar, *Brush Fire Wars*, 120.

123. Ibid., 120–25. See also Jackson, *The RAF in Action*, 146–47.

124. Wing Commander S. Hitchen, "Theatre Transport," ibid., 59–61.

125. Wing Commander Martin Sharp, *Evolution of Helicopter Forces in the United Kingdom*, Paper No. 60 (Royal Australian Air Force: Air Power Studies Centre, November 1997), 23.

126. Lieutenant Colonel Sir Julian Paget, "The Radfan Campaigns and Internal Security in Aden," *Royal Air Force Historical Society Journal* 18 (1998): 40.

127. Group Captain C. A. E. Simons, "Helicopter Operations," ibid., 56.

128. Dowling, *RAF Helicopters*, 138–40, 273–306.

129. "Oman: British Trucial Obligations," in Arnold, *Wars in the Third World since 1945*, 84, and Colonel D. de C. Smiley, "Muscat and Oman," *RUSI* (February–November 1960): 29.

130. Smiley, "Muscat and Oman," 30–35, 40.

131. "Oman: The Dhofar Rebellion," in Arnold, *Wars in the Third World since 1945*, 491–93.

132. Ibid., 19.

133. Ibid., 492.

134. John Akehurst, *We Won a War: The Campaign in Oman, 1965–1975* (The Chantry: Michael Russell [Publishing], 1982), 54.

135. According to General Akehurst, the paramilitary tribesmen known as *firqats* were "indispensable." Their "knowledge of the ground and their influence with the civilians" made them of value to the counterinsurgency in Dhofar far greater than their small numbers, and "worth all the time, trouble and money spent to secure and retain their goodwill and allegiance." Akehurst, *We Won a War*, 42–43.

136. Colonel Victor Croizat, "Oman and the Dhofar Rebelliuon," *Marine Corps Gazette*, February 1975, 21.

137. Douglas Blaufarb and George Tanham, *Who Will Win: A Key to the Puzzle of Revolutionary War* (New York: Crane Russak, 1989), 65.

138. Akehurst, *We Won a War*, 32–38.

139. Ibid., 42.

140. Ibid., 39.

141. Blaufarb and Tanham, *Who Will Win*, 66.

142. Dewar, *Brush Fire Wars,* 170–74.

143. Ibid., 177.

144. F. A. Clements, *Oman: The Reborn Land* (London: Longman, 1980), 101.

145. Mellersh, "The Campaign Against the Terrorists in Malaya," 407, and Air Marshal Sir John Kemball, "Air — The Essential Element," *Royal Air Force Historical Society Journal* 18 (1998), 47–50.

146. Lieutenant Colonel Sir Julian Paget, *Last Post: Aden, 1964–1967* (London: Faber and Faber, 1969), 104.

147. Akehurst, *We Won a War,* 38.

148. E. D. Smith, *Counter-Insurgency Operations: 1, Malaya and Borneo* (London: Ian Allen, 1985), 37.

149. Wing Commander I. M. Pedder, "The Rôle of Air Power in Guerrilla Warfare," *Royal Air Forces Quarterly* (winter 1965): 270.

150. Paget, *Last Post: Aden,* 53.

151. Dewar, *Brush Fire Wars,* 125.

152. Kemball, "Air — The Essential Element," 47.

6. AIRPOWER IN SOUTH VIETNAM, 1954–1965

1. For an in-depth treatment, see Edgar O'Ballance, *The Indo-China War, 1945–54* (London: Faber and Faber, 1964), and Bernard Fall's classic, *Street without Joy.*

2. Volume 1, written in 1954 by the Education Bureau of the Commander-in-Chief, Indochina, was entitled *Notes on Combat in Indochina.* Volumes 2 and 3, written in 1955 and 1956 by the French Supreme Command, Far East, were entitled *Lessons from the Indo-China War.* The first volume was classified "top secret" and was not made widely available. All three volumes were translated into English in the 1960s, and the U.S. Defense Documentation Center received its copies on 3 January 1967. Dennis Drew, "U.S. Airpower Theory and the Insurgent Challenge: A Short Journey to Confusion," *Journal of Military History* (October 1998): 813–14, nn. 16–19.

3. *Notes on Combat,* 34, ibid.

4. Fredric Smith, "Posture of the USAF: Statement to the Committee on Armed Services, House of Representatives," *Airman* (May 1962): 20, 22. Reflecting on World War II, the Korean War, and the French experience in combating communist insurgents in Indochina, General Smith advocated using nuclear weapons for "situation control," that is, exploiting nuclear fires to obviate enemy assembly, movement, and combat operations. For example, a low-yield nuclear bomb could be used to block enemy movement through a "rain-forest corridor." Nuclear weapons could be used to interdict choke points in mountain ranges. Finally, nuclear weapons could be used to support ground forces in close contact with the enemy — although General Smith did point out that friendly forces should be forewarned of the nuclear strike in order that adequate safety precautions could be taken. Frederic Smith, "Nuclear Weapons and Limited War," *Air University Quarterly Review* (spring 1960): 3–27, passim.

5. Ibid., 5.

6. "The Role of Airpower in Viet-Nam," address by General John P. McConnell, Chief of Staff, U.S. Air Force, before the Dallas Council on World Affairs, Dallas, Texas, 16 September 1965.

7. Bernard Fall, *The Two Vietnams*, rev. ed. (New York: Praeger, 1964), 3–8.

8. Stanley Karnow, *Vietnam: A History* (New York: Viking Press, 1983), 101.

9. Fall, *The Two Vietnams*, 20, 24.

10. Karnow, *Vietnam*, 107.

11. Timothy Lomperis, *The War Everyone Lost — and Won: America's Intervention in Vietnam's Twin Struggles*, rev. ed. (Washington, D.C.: CQ Press, 1993), 44.

12. The classic account of the battle is Bernard Fall's *Hell in a Very Small Place*.

13. Born in a small village in the southern Red River delta province of Nam-Dinh, Truong Chinh was reared in the spirit of resistance to foreign occupation and became an ardent revolutionary in his early teens. In 1928 he joined the Revolutionary Youth League. Like General Vo Nguyen Giap and South Vietnamese President Ngo Dinh Diem, Truong Chinh was educated at the French-run Lycée Albert Sarraut in Hanoi. There, Truong Chinh joined the Indo-Chinese Communist Party, created by Ho Chi Minh in 1930. After imprisonment by the French for radical activities, Truong Chinh gained a reputation as one of the best theoreticians in the party. Following World War II, Truong Chinh was named a member of the Central Committee of the Communist Party and came into his own as a "party philosopher" through serialized publication of *The August Revolution* and *The Resistance Will Win* in the newspaper *Su-That* ("The Truth"). The latter was written at the lowest ebb of the Viet Minh struggle against the French. Following the defeat of France, Truong Chinh became secretary-general of the Communist Party and vice premier of the Democratic Republic of Vietnam (Truong Chinh, *Primer for Revolt: The Communist Takeover in Vietnam*, a facsimile edition of *The August Revolution* and *The Resistance Will Win* by Truong Chinh [originally published in 1962 and 1960 respectively by the Foreign Languages Publishing House, Hanoi, Democratic Republic of Vietnam] [New York: Praeger, 1963], xi–xxii). General Giap specifically attributed his own military strategy to Truong Chinh in his book, *People's War, People's Army*. See Vo Nguyen Giap, *People's War, People's Army* (New York: Praeger, 1962), 102.

14. According to Mao, the "destruction of the enemy is the primary object of war [and] attack is the chief means of destroying the enemy. . . . To transform guerrilla units waging guerrilla warfare into regular forces waging mobile warfare, two conditions are necessary: an increase in numbers, and improvement in quality. . . . To raise the quality of the guerrilla units it is imperative to raise their political and organizational level and improve their equipment, military technique, tactics and discipline, so that they gradually pattern themselves on the regular army and shed their guerrilla ways." *Selected Military Writings of Mao Tse-tung* (Peking: Foreign Language Press, 1963), 238, 179–81.

15. "Truong Chinh on Revolutionary Warfare," SRAP1969 (Office of the Assistant Chief of Staff, Intelligence: Headquarters U.S. Military Assistance Command, Vietnam, 31 December 1969), 1, 10.

16. Perhaps the best examination of the Viet Cong in terms of its structure and strategy is Douglas Pike, *Viet Cong: The Organization and Techniques of the National Liberation Front of South Vietnam* (Cambridge: MIT Press, 1966). Also see Truong Nhu Tang, with David Chanoff and Doan Van Toai, *A Vietcong Memoir* (New York: Random House, 1986).

17. Oakah Jones, *Organization, Mission and Growth of the Vietnamese Air Force, 1949–1968* (Headquarters Pacific Air Forces, Directorate of Tactical Evaluation, CHECO Division [Contemporary Historical Evaluation of Combat Operations], 8 October 1968 [Secret], declassified 21 November 1991), 1; hereinafter cited as *Organization of the VNAF*.

18. Mesko, *VNAF*, 14.

19. Ibid., and Jones, *Organization of the VNAF*, 2.

20. Jones, *Organization of the VNAF*, 2–3.

21. Mesko, *VNAF*, 14.

22. A Ministry of Defense headed by a secretary of state for national defense was established on 19 September 1949. The Vietnamese army was created that same year. The Vietnamese navy was established on 6 March 1952, and the Vietnamese marine corps was established on 13 October 1954. James Collins, *The Development and Training of the South Vietnamese Army, 1950–1972* (Washington, D.C.: Department of the Army, 1975), 9.

23. Jones, *Organization of the VNAF*, 3–4; and Mesko, *VNAF*, 14–15.

24. Mack Secord, "Air Operations in Vietnam: The Viet-Nam Air Force," *Air University Review* (November–December 1963): 61.

25. Jones, *Organization of the VNAF*, 4; and Donald Ward, *VNAF A-1 Operations: 1962–1968* (Maxwell Air Force Base: Air Command and Staff College, Corona Harvest Designated Study, AUC-42–68–ACSC, May 1969) [Secret], declassified 29 October 1998), 1.

26. Jones, *Organization of the VNAF*, 4–5; and Mesko, *VNAF*, 19.

27. For a more detailed discussion of events during this period in terms of American interests in Indochina, see Ellen Hammer, *The Struggle for Indochina, 1940–1955* (Stanford: Stanford University Press, 1955) and the firsthand account by former Office of Strategic Services head, Archimedes Patti, in *Why Vietnam?* (Berkeley: University of California Press, 1980). See also volume 1 of the U.S. Army in Vietnam series, specifically, Ronald Spector, *Advise and Support: The Early Years, 1941–1960* (Washington, D.C.: Center of Military History, United States Army, 1983).

28. See, for example, John Gaddis, "Was the Truman Doctrine a Real Turning Point?" *Foreign Affairs* (January 1972): 386–402, and "Containment: A Reassessment," *Foreign Affairs* (July 1977): 873–87. See also John Gaddis, *Strategies of Containment* (Oxford: Oxford University Press, 1982). For an opposing view, see Eduard Mark, "The Question of Containment," *Foreign Affairs* (January 1978): 430–41.

29. *The Pentagon Papers: The Defense Department History of United States Decisionmaking in Vietnam*, Senator Gravel ed., 4 vols. (Boston: Beacon Press, 1971), vol. 1, 194–95.

30. For the full text, see *Foreign Relations of the United States, 1950*, vol. 6 (Washington, D.C.: GPO), 745–47.

31. *Foreign Relations of the United States, 1950*, vol. 6, 812. Responding to the communist victory in China, Secretary of State Dean Acheson wrote: "You will please take it as your assumption that it is a fundamental decision of American policy that the United States does not intend to permit further expansion of communist domination on the continent of Asia or in the Southeast Asia area" (memorandum to Ambassador-at-Large Philip Jessup, cited by Michael Morrow in *Asia Mail*, January 1977,

as quoted in James Harrison, *The Endless War: Fifty Years of Struggle in Vietnam* [New York: Free Press, 1982], 6).

32. For the complete text of this speech, see *Vietnam: Anatomy of a Conflict*, ed. Wesley Fishel (Itasca, Ill.: F. E. Peacock, 1968), 142–47.

33. W. V. McBride, "USAF Responsibilities and Operations in the Cold War," *Air University Quarterly Review* (summer 1962): 85, quoted in Charles Hildreth, *USAF Counterinsurgency Doctrines and Capabilities, 1961–1962* (USAF Historical Division Liaison Office, February 1964 [Secret], declassified 7 November 1983), 1.

34. As early as 1954, Kennedy had warned about the problem of insurgency (Roger Hilsman, *To Move a Nation* [Garden City, N.Y.: Doubleday, 1967], 423) and had read the works of Mao and Ché Guevara, as well as studied the successful counterinsurgency efforts in the Philippines and Malaya. Douglas Blaufarb, *The Counterinsurgency Era: U.S. Doctrine and Performance, 1950 to the Present* (New York: Free Press, 1977), 55, 88.

35. "Urgent National Needs: Special Message of the President to the Congress," *Department of State Bulletin* 44 (12 June 1961): 906, and Blaufarb, *The Counterinsurgency Era*, 55.

36. Presentation to Lieutenant General D. A. Burchinal, Deputy Chief of Staff for Plans and Programs, Headquarters United States Air Force, the Pentagon, June 1962, in Hildreth, *USAF Counterinsurgency*, 4–5. The briefing was prepared by the Counterinsurgency Operations Division, Deputy Chief of Staff for Operations, subject: "Air Force Role in Counterinsurgency." The briefing was presented by Colonel W. V. McBride, USAF, chief of the Cold War Division.

37. Blaufarb, *The Counterinsurgency Era*, 80.

38. Hildreth, *USAF Counterinsurgency*, 7. Official Air Force records contend that the Special Group for Counterinsurgency, created by *National Security Action Memorandum No. 124*, was an air force idea.

39. Hildreth, *USAF Counterinsurgency*, 8–10, 123.

40. Collins, *Development and Training of the South Vietnamese Army*, 2–3.

41. *Report on the War in Vietnam* (as of 30 June 1968), 75. Section I: "Report on Air and Naval Campaigns Against North Vietnam and Pacific Command-Wide Support of the War, June 1964–July 1968," by Admiral U. S. G. Sharp. Section II: "Report on Operations in South Vietnam, January 1964–June 1968," by General William C. Westmoreland.

42. As Truong Nhu Tang, the Viet Cong Minister of Justice, wrote: "Liberation" in South Vietnam "had always been tied to the Party — not because they were ardent communists, but because as far back as 1920, the only ally Vietnamese nationalism had even known was the Communist International. Ho Chi Minh had grasped this support . . . and he had woven the fabric of independence out of the twin fibers of nationalism and communism." Truong Nhu Tang, *A Vietcong Memoir*, 190.

43. *Report on the War in Vietnam*, 75.

44. Cao Van Vien and Dong Van Khuyen, *Reflections on the Vietnam War* (Washington, D.C.: U.S. Army Center of Military History, 1980), 2. The authors were former South Vietnamese general officers. They contended that the American emphasis on preparing the South Vietnamese army to face North Vietnamese invasion succeeded in preventing a repeat of the Korean War; however, communist leaders simply resorted to aiding the insurgency in the south. But had "popular forces" been empha-

sized from the outset, the Viet Cong could have been managed if not defeated outright. Nevertheless, the American Advisory Group did not appreciate the importance of countering the insurgents and the role played by paramilitary forces until 1961, but by then six years had been irretrievably lost and the insurgency alone threatened to overthrow the government of South Vietnam. Ibid., 3.

45. Collins, *Development and Training of the South Vietnamese Army*, 6.

46. Blaufarb, *The Counterinsurgency Era*, 252–53.

47. Robert Thompson, *Defeating Communist Insurgency: Experiences from Malaya and Vietnam* (London: Chatto and Windus, 1966), 60.

48. William Momyer, *The Vietnamese Air Force, 1951–1975: An Analysis of Its Role in Combat and Fourteen Hours at Koh Tang*, ed. Charles McDonald and A. J. C. Lavalle, new imprint, USAF Southeast Asia Monograph Series, vol. 3, Monographs 4 and 5 (Washington, D.C.: Office of Air Force History, 1985), 9.

49. Ibid., 9.

50. In a memorandum from Defense Secretary McNamara's assistant for special operations, the ubiquitous Edward Lansdale, to Maxwell Taylor, the recommendation was aired to declare a "sub-limited war" on the communists in Vietnam: "[The] U.S. needs a way of action short of war but more dynamic than merely the bolstering of peacetime measures. . . . This can be done by Presidential proclamation, a Congressional supporting act, and a new streamlined organization within the Executive." See *Foreign Relations of the United States, 1961–1963*, vol. 1, *Vietnam 1961* (Washington, D.C.: GPO), 522–32.

51. See Maxwell Taylor, *Swords and Plowshares* (New York: W. W. Norton, 1972). Also see U.S. President, *Public Papers of the President of the United States* (Washington, D.C.: Office of the Federal Register, National Archives and Records Service, 1953–), *John F. Kennedy* (1961).

52. Jacob Van Staaveren, *USAF Plans and Policies in South Vietnam, 1961–1963* (USAF Historical Division Liaison Office, June 1965 [Top Secret], declassified 11 July 1991), 16.

53. Ibid., 17. In April 1962, General LeMay complained vigorously about the dominant position of the U.S. Army in the American military mission to South Vietnam. Since the position of chief of staff had been filled with a U.S. Marine Corps officer, LeMay recommended a three-star U.S. Air Force officer be assigned as deputy commander under General Harkins. Although General Harkins agreed to the proposal and Admiral Felt and the Joint Chiefs supported the idea, Defense Secretary McNamara decided the post was unnecessary. The Air Staff continued to press for greater representation, but to no avail. When a deputy commander billet was created in January 1964, it was filled by U.S. Army Lieutenant General William Westmoreland. Moreover, by the end of 1963, two positions formerly held by airmen were filled with officers from the U.S. Navy and U.S. Marine Corps. When General Westmoreland arrived, the U.S. Army still held six of the nine top positions on the staff and the U.S. Air Force retained the one general officer billet. Ibid., 48.

54. Hildreth, *USAF Counterinsurgency*, 25–26.

55. Staaveren, *USAF Plans and Policies*, 39.

56. Hildreth, *USAF Counterinsurgency*, 26.

57. Hildreth, *USAF Counterinsurgency*, 28–29.

58. Jones, *Organization of the VNAF*, 9.

59. Ibid.

60. Hildreth, *USAF Counterinsurgency*, 12.

61. Staaveren, *USAF Plans and Policies*, 49.

62. Ibid.

63. Ibid., 49–53.

64. Ibid., 54.

65. The shoulder-wing, twin-engine de Havilland-Canada DHC-4 first flew in 1958 and was ordered by the U.S. Army as the CV-2. The CV-2 was designed to have the payload of the C-47 and the short-field capability of the de Havilland-Canada "Beaver" (DHC-2) and "Otter" (DHC-3) aircraft. Operational use of the CV-2 included airlift of troops and light-wheeled vehicles to forward airstrips. CV-2s saw considerable action in South Vietnam but were ultimately transferred to the U.S. Air Force in 1967 and redesignated the C-7A.

66. William Momyer, *Airpower in Three Wars* (Washington, D.C.: Department of the Air Force, January 1978), 9.

67. Ibid., 9.

68. The original T-28 was a trainer, but the T-28D attack version could carry three thousand pounds of ordnance, was armed with fixed forward-firing .50 caliber machine guns, and boasted a 1,300 hp engine (as opposed to the original 800 hp engine). The T-28D could be used for close support and reconnaissance missions as well as for training. More important, the simplicity and reliability of the T-28 made it particularly well suited for developing countries with limited technical capabilities. A proposed "growth model" of the T-28 included the installation of an R-1820-26 engine rated at 1,425 hp, a greater payload, and a photoreconnaissance capability for intelligence collection. In fact, a turboprop version was envisioned and a prototype constructed, the YAT-28E, equipped with a T-55 turboprop engine rated at 2,450 hp. Robert Solomon, *United States Security Assistance to Thailand: Case Studies in Military Interaction*, WN-7257-1-ARPA (Washington, D.C.: Advanced Research Projects Agency, November 1971 [Secret]), declassified 31 December 1980, 100. Also see Charles Hildreth, *USAF Special Air Warfare Doctrines and Capabilities 1963* (USAF Historical Division Liaison Office, August 1964 [Secret]), declassified 7 November 1983, 51.

69. Robert Johnston, "The Invader Returns," *Air University Review* (November–December 1963): 9–12.

70. Hildreth, *USAF Special Air Warfare*, 2.

71. Assistant director for Joint Matters, Directorate of Operations, Headquarters United States Air Force, *Book of Actions in Southeast Asia*, item IV-B (Washington, D.C.: Office of Air Force History), 961–64.

72. Arthur O'Neill, *Fifth Air Force in Southeast Asia (a Sequel)* (Washington, D.C.: Office of Information, 30 January 1962), 30, and Philip Chinnery, *Any Time, Any Place: Fifty Years of the USAF Air Commando and Special Operations Forces, 1944–1994* (Annapolis: Naval Institute Press, 1994), 68. See also Hildreth, *USAF Special Air Warfare*, 2. Regarding the performance of missions beyond the capability of the Vietnamese, see M. M. Doyle, Commander, Detachment 2 (Farm Gate), transcript of oral interview

by J. Grainger, 16 February 1963, Bien Hoa Air Base, Republic of South Vietnam (History, Second Air Division, 15 November 1961–8 October 1962, vol. 3, Supporting Documents), 23.

73. The designation RB-26 was sleight-of-hand. The Geneva agreement of 1954 prohibited the introduction of tactical bombers into Vietnam. The redesignation as RB-26 was intended to convey the impression that these aircraft were not bombers, but rather reconnaissance aircraft. Van Staaveren, *USAF Plans and Policies*, 18. See also Hildreth, *USAF Special Air Warfare*, 14.

74. The requirement that a Vietnamese crew member be present in Farm Gate combat aircraft provides an interesting metaphor for the American airpower experience in South Vietnam. In the beginning, South Vietnamese pilots received air-to-ground training and the American instructors often flew in the rear seat of the aircraft. But as time went by, the Americans moved permanently to the front seat and the South Vietnamese pilots realized that they were merely "cover" for the Americans to conduct strike missions. Soon afterward, enlisted South Vietnamese airmen, more often than not administrative and other nonflying personnel, flew with the Americans on these missions. Farm Gate veterans recalled afterward having to incarcerate these Vietnamese passengers (for that is all they were) to ensure that they would not run away before missions. Before long, however, the pretense of training was dropped and Farm Gate aircraft replaced their South Vietnamese markings with American markings and conducted strike missions with no South Vietnamese crewmen aboard the aircraft. Thus, in less than five years, Vietnamese pilots moved literally and figuratively from the front seat to the rear seat to being pushed aside altogether.

75. Hildreth, *USAF Counterinsurgency*, 14.

76. Message, TSC-PFOCC-S 61-170, Commander, Pacific Air Forces to Commander, Thirteenth Air Force (Headquarters Pacific Air Forces, Directorate of Tactical Evaluation, CHECO Division, Part V-A, Supporting Documents, October–December 1963, 4 December 1961).

77. Staaveren, *USAF Plans and Policies*, 24.

78. Rollen Anthis, Commander, Second Air Division, transcript of oral history interview by Dean Gausche and J. W. Grainger, 30 August 1963 (Maxwell Air Force Base: Historical Research Agency, Project CHECO Southeast Asia Report, appendix 2, Counterinsurgency Interviews, October 1961–December 1963).

79. Warren Trest, *Air Commando One: Heinie Aderholt and America's Secret Air Wars* (Washington, D.C., Smithsonian Institution Press, 2000), 123–24.

80. The First Air Commando Group traced its lineage to World War II when special U.S. Army Air Forces units were raised to support the Office of Strategic Services in Europe and General Orde C. Wingate's "Chindit" forces in Burma. The First Air Commando Group itself was specifically raised to provide air support for long-range penetration missions by Wingate's troops. During the latter stages of the war there were three air commando groups, but by the end of the war these had been absorbed into conventional units. See Monro MacCloskey, *Alert the Fifth Force: Counterinsurgency, Unconventional Warfare, and Psychological Operations of the United States Air Force in Special Air Warfare* (New York: Richards Rosen Press, 1969), 104–20. For a detailed treatment of the First Air Commando Group, see R. D. Van-Wagner, *1st*

Air Commando Group (Maxwell Air Force Base: Air Command and Staff College, Military History Series 86–1, 1986).

81. Hildreth, *USAF Counterinsurgency,* 2–3, 29–30.

82. Ibid., 31–34.

83. Staaveren, *USAF Plans and Policies,* 63.

84. Jones, *Organization of the VNAF,* 2.

85. Ibid., 65, 66–68; and Mesko, *VNAF,* 43–44.

86. Staaveren, *USAF Plans and Policies,* 67.

87. Jones, *Organization of the VNAF,* 16–17.

88. Ibid., 19–20.

89. Ibid., 23–24.

90. Ward, *VNAF A-1 Operations,* 39.

91. Jones, *Organization of the VNAF,* 24–25. Regarding night flying limitations, see Ward, *VNAF A-1 Operations,* 14–15.

92. Ward, *VNAF A-1 Operations,* 6–11.

93. Ibid., 19–20.

94. Ralph Rowley, *USAF FAC Operations in Southeast Asia, 1961–1965* (Office of Air Force History, January 1972 [Secret], declassified 5 December 1989), 13, 20.

95. Staaveren, *USAF Plans and Policies,* 44.

96. Ibid., 63.

97. For an in-depth discussion of the battle of Ap Bac and its impact on the war in Vietnam, see Neil Sheehan, *A Bright Shining Lie: John Paul Vann and America in Vietnam* (New York: Random House, 1988), 206–314.

98. John Morrocco, *The Vietnam Experience: Thunder From Above: Air War, 1941–1968* (Boston: Boston Publishing Company, 1984), 18. U.S. Army helicopter units arrived in South Vietnam in January 1962. They bore American markings and were flown by American crews but were used to airlift South Vietnamese forces in quick strikes against the Viet Cong. These initial units were followed by more U.S. Army units and a U.S. Marine squadron flying UH-34D Choctaws. With Farm Gate aircraft in limited supply and in great demand, the U.S. Army decided to arm several UH-1 "Hueys" with machine guns and rockets to provide close support. Ibid., 16–17.

99. Staaveren, *USAF Plans and Policies,* 39.

100. Morrocco, *The Vietnam Experience,* 18.

101. Ibid.

102. Staaveren, *USAF Plans and Policies,* 39–42, 48.

103. Morrocco, *The Vietnam Experience,* 18.

104. For a detailed examination of air operations between 1961 and 1965, see Robert Futrell, *The United States Air Force in Southeast Asia: The Advisory Years to 1965* (Washington, D.C.: Office of Air Force History, 1981).

105. Staaveren, *USAF Plans and Policies,* 58–59.

106. Ibid., 60.

107. Ibid., 60–61.

108. Momyer, *The Vietnamese Air Force,* 10.

109. Staaveren, *USAF Plans and Policies,* 25, 27.

110. Ibid., 27.

111. Futrell, *The Advisory Years to 1965*, 141.

112. Ibid., 137.

113. Ibid., 136.

114. Ibid., 139.

115. Ibid., 139–40.

116. Futrell, *The Advisory Years to 1965*, 167.

117. Ibid., 110–11, 167.

118. Staaveren, *USAF Plans and Policies*, 35–36.

119. Ibid., 36.

120. Ibid., 33.

121. W. C. Porter and W. G. von Platen, "Reconnaissance in COIN," *Air University Review* (March–April 1964): 65.

122. Carl Berger, ed., *The United States Air Force in Southeast Asia, 1961–1973* (Washington, D.C.: Office of Air Force History), 17. See also Ward, *VNAF A-1 Operations*, 19.

123. James Sunderman, "Air Escort — A COIN Air Technique," *Air University Review* (November–December 1963): 72. The L-19 served as a spotter and a "radio-relay station" between the strike aircraft and the convoy. The L-19 would fly low, "essing," or circling over the convoy and ranging out ahead to inspect likely ambush sites (ibid). The presence of these aircraft dissuaded the Viet Cong from attacking and, although 462 attacks had occurred against convoys in the first eight months of 1962, afterward the communist guerrillas did not attack a convoy that was covered by tactical aircraft through the end of 1963. Andrew Chapman, "Air Operations in Viet Nam: Employment of Tactical Air Power in COIN Operations," *Air University Review* (March–April 1964): 58. See also Berger, *The United States Air Force in Southeast Asia*, 17.

124. Although the U.S. Air Force had claimed around twenty-five thousand, General Harkins's staff claimed thirty-three thousand. Staaveren, *USAF Plans and Policies*, 36.

125. Mack Secord, "Air Operations in Viet Nam: The Viet Nam Air Force," *Air University Review* (November–December 1963): 66. See also Staaveren, *USAF Plans and Policies*, 36.

126. Secord, "Air Operations," 66.

127. James Cross, *Conflict in the Shadows* (New York: Doubleday, 1963), 77. Bernard Fall, perhaps the most astute observer regarding the nature of the conflict in Vietnam as it continued to unfold, expressed similar reservations. "In South Viet-Nam, where the enemy hardly offers conventional aerial targets . . . the use of massive bomb attacks and napalm drops on villages is not only militarily stupid, but it is inhuman and is likely to backfire very badly on the psychological level." Fall noted that in 1963, officials claimed over 23,000 Viet Cong had been killed, some 7,500 of whom were killed by fixed-wing strike aircraft of the South Vietnamese Air Force. "One might want to ponder the question," he wrote: "How many of those 7,500 were innocent bystanders?" Bernard Fall, *Street without Joy*, 266–67.

128. Staaveren, *USAF Plans and Policies*, 37–38.

129. Message, CSAF to JCS, 8 February 1963, PACAF to to CSAF, 20 February 1963, and Second Air Division to PACAF, 18 February 1963; *History of the Special Air Warfare Center* (January–June 1963): 166.

130. The number identifying the unit type was as follows: 1, liaison aircraft; 2, helicopters; 3, special missions; 4, transports; 5, fighters; 7, reconnaissance aircraft; 8, gunships; and 9, training units. Mesko, *VNAF*, 30.

131. The South Vietnamese air wings were numbered and based as follows: Bien Hoa, Twenty-third Tactical Wing; Tan Son Nhut, Thirty-third Tactical Wing; Da Nang, Forty-first Tactical Wing; Pleiku, Sixty-second Tactical Wing; and Can Tho, Seventy-fourth Tactical Wing. Mesko, *VNAF*, 38, 35.

132. Fall, *Street without Joy*, 266.

133. Staaveren, *USAF Plans and Policies*, 38.

134. End of tour reports, Major John Schmitt, 18 September 1963, and Lieutenant Colonel David Mellish, 15 January 1964 (Maxwell Air Force Base: Historical Research Agency).

135. "Combat Operations, Nineteenth TASS," 31 December 1963, in *History, Thirteenth Air Force*, July–December 1963, III, Document 80; Message, Second Air Division to PACAF, 5 October 1963.

136. Staaveren, *USAF Plans and Policies*, 42. As Harriman pointed out, the French experience should have proved instructive. According to Bernard Fall, many French air force officers claimed that a greater concentration on interdiction would have "helped the war effort more than a constant 'babying' of ground troops." But critics of this notion countered that "the Korean War had amply proved how ineffectual even the heavy B-29s were against the rudimentary efficiency and invulnerability of a supply system built largely on human carriers and that even a moderate road cut . . . cost about 70 tons of bombs. . . . How ineffectual aerial interdiction, at least with non-nuclear weapons, can be in jungle warfare is best evidenced by the fact that the French Air Force never succeeded in shutting off the Viet Minh's major road artery, Road 41, leading to Dien Bien Phu, no matter how hard it tried." Fall, *Street without Joy*, 264–65. In the end, the U.S. Air Force was no more successful than l'Armée de l'air.

137. Staaveren, *USAF Plans and Policies*, 42.

138. Mesko, *VNAF*, 39.

139. *Book of Actions in Southeast Asia*, VI-1.

140. Berger, *The United States Air Force in Southeast Asia*, 29.

141. Ibid.

142. It is important to bear in mind that all of these frontline jet aircraft were designed with nuclear war in mind, not guerrilla warfare. For a useful discussion of this aspect of the air war, see Earl Tilford, *Setup: What the Air Force Did in Vietnam and Why* (Maxwell Air Force Base: Air University Press, June 1991).

143. Futrell, *The Advisory Years to 1965*, 229; *Book of Actions in Southeast Asia*, III-P.

144. At Binh Gia, southeast of Saigon, the South Vietnamese Thirty-third Ranger and Fourth Marine battalions were virtually wiped out by communist forces. Afterward, the Viet Cong boasted that Binh Gia "marked the end of the insurgency phase of its campaign and the start of conventional field operations." Berger, *The United States Air Force in Southeast Asia*, 35.

145. André Beaufre, "Military Opinion Abroad: Reflections on Vietnam," trans. Joseph Annunziata, *Air University Review* (March–April 1966): 70.

146. Ibid., 69, 71. Beaufre described "big guerrilla warfare" in terms that reflected Truong Chinh's "war of interlocking." It was warfare dominated by the "strategy and tactical procedures of guerrilla warfare but which [employed] relatively large and well-armed forces." Traditional guerrilla warfare manifests itself in small unit raids and ambushes, using surprise, exploitation of local advantage, and the refusal to fight a pitched battle unless the prospects of victory are overwhelmingly in favor of the guerrilla. "Big guerrilla warfare retains this line of conduct, but instead of doing so by sections, companies, or battalions it does it with regiments and whole divisions which, like patrols, advance and take cover in the forests. It is still guerrilla warfare but enlarged to the dimensions of classical warfare." Ibid., 71.

147. Perhaps the best exposition of Mitchell's thinking with respect to airpower can be found in his book, *Winged Defense: The Development and Possibilities of Modern Air Power, Economic and Military* (New York: G. P. Putnam's Sons, 1925). Also see Alfred Hurley, *Billy Mitchell, Crusader for Airpower* (Bloomington: Indiana University Press, 1975).

148. For example, Douhet believed that, when it came to airpower, "clinging to the past will teach us nothing useful for the future." Giulio Douhet, *The Command of the Air*, new imprint (Washington, D.C.: Office of Air Force History, 1983), 26. In a similar vein, Mitchell wrote: "A new set of rules for the conduct of war will have to be devised and a whole new set of ideas of strategy learned by those charged with the conduct of war." Mitchell, *Winged Defense*, 6.

149. Richard Clutterbuck, *The Long, Long War: Counterinsurgency in Malaya and Vietnam* (New York: Praeger, 1966), 156.

150. Charles Maechling, "Our Internal Defense Policy: A Reappraisal," *Foreign Service Journal* (January 1969), 27.

151. Clutterbuck, *The Long, Long War*, 156.

152. Drew, "U.S. Airpower Theory and the Insurgent Challenge," 816, 815.

153. Ibid. Indeed, U.S. Air Force Brigadier General Jerry D. Page, deputy director of aerospace plans, rejected the distinction between limited war and general war as an exaggerated premise. In a position paper presented on 24 April 1962, he asserted that "limited war against communist forces is not a separate entity from general war," therefore "our strategy and forces for limited war should not be separated from our overall strategy and force structure." He went on to assert, "The artificial distinction of limited war forces for this war and general war forces for that war destroys the inter-acting strength [sic] of our forces that will provide force superiority and continuous deterrence at any level of conflict." Futrell, *Ideas, Concepts, and Doctrine*, vol. 2, 56–57.

154. Staaveren, *USAF Plans and Policies*, 46.

155. Memo, Director of Plans, HQ USAF, for Deputy Commander for Support, Plans and Operations, HQ USAF, 17 December 1962, cited in Futrell, *The Advisory Years to 1965*, 148. See also Staaveren, *USAF Plans and Policies*, 70.

156. "Are We Using or Abusing Technology?" *Air Force-Space Digest* (October 1961), 45.

157. Hildreth, *USAF Counterinsurgency*, 8–10, 123.

158. AFM 2-5, *Tactical Air Operations, Special Air Warfare* (Washington, D.C.: Department of the Air Force, 10 March 1967).

159. "Worthless residue." The Latin term *caput mortuum* literally means "death's head," or a skull. The term originated with medieval alchemists, referring to the residue left after distillation was complete. Since then it has been used to refer to any worthless residue. Although the description is unfair to the dedicated air commandos who remained in the U.S. Air Force after American defeat in South Vietnam, the fact remains that the U.S. Air Force dismantled the air commando wings and the air commandos were but a shadow of their former selves.

160. *AFSOC Foreign Internal Defense* (Hurlburt Field: Headquarters Air Force Special Operations Command, July 1990), 5.

161. Clutterbuck, *The Long, Long War*, 164.

162. Carl von Clausewitz, *On War*, trans. Michael Howard and Peter Paret (Princeton: Princeton University Press, 1976), 154.

163. Maurice Comte de Saxe, *Mes rêveries; or Memoirs Upon the Art of War* (Westport, Conn.: Greenwood Press, 1971; reprint, originally published 1757), 162.

7. AIRPOWER AND COUNTERINSURGENCY IN SOUTHERN AFRICA

1. Anthony Clayton, *Frontiersmen: Warfare in Africa Since 1950* (London: UCL Press, 1999), 35–37.

2. Ibid., 37–38.

3. Dott Riccardo Niccoli, "Atlantic Sentinels," *Air Enthusiast* 73 (January/February 1998): 20–35, see 29–30.

4. Eng. Mario Canongia Lopes, "Latin Harpoons: the Lockheed V-2 in Brazilian and Portuguese Service," *Air Enthusiast* 40 (1989): 31–42, see 37–38.

5. Flintham, *Air Wars and Aircraft*, 114.

6. Clayton, *Frontiersmen*, 39.

7. A good overview of the Portuguese war in Africa is found in John Cann, *Counterinsurgency in Africa: The Portuguese Way of War, 1961–1974* (Westport, Conn.: Greenwood Books, 1997), 13–35.

8. Cann, *Counterinsurgency in Africa*, 6.

9. Ibid., 10–11, 37–55, 61–81.

10. Ibid., 63–65.

11. Cann, *Counterinsurgency in Africa*, 172–73.

12. A. J. Venter, "Portugal's Forgotten War," *Air Enthusiast* 2, no. 2 (February 1972): 59–62, 74, and Mario Canongia, "Portugal's 'Ginas,'" *Air Enthusiast* 36 (May–August 1988): 61–78, see 65.

13. Canongia, "Portugal's 'Ginas,'" 65–69.

14. Niccoli, "Atlantic Sentinels," 20–35, see 30.

15. Ibid., 31.

16. Ibid., 31–32.

17. Clayton, *Frontiersmen*, 42–47.

18. Ibid.

19. A useful overview of the insurgency in Mozambique is found in Thomas Henriksen, *Revolution and Counterrevolution: Mozambique's War of Independence, 1964–1974* (Westport, Conn.: Greenwood Press, 1983).

20. Ibid., 47–51.

21. Clayton, *Frontiersmen,* 51–56.
22. Cann, *Counterinsurgency in Africa,* 95.
23. The best general overview of the African forces that fought for Portugal is found in Cann, *Counterinsurgency in Africa,* 95–106.
24. Cann, *Counterinsurgency in Africa,* 72–73.
25. Ibid., 134–40.
26. Flintham, *Air Wars and Aircraft,* 115.
27. Ibid., 121.
28. For numerous critiques of the Portuguese armed forces performance in Mozambique, see Henriksen, *Revolution and Counterrevolution,* esp. 46–69.
29. For a useful critique of the Portuguese tactics and operations see A. J. Venter, *The Chopper Boys: Helicopter Warfare in Africa* (London: Greenhill Books, 1994), 66–72.
30. Ibid., 120.
31. Niccoli, "Atlantic Sentinels," 32.
32. Flintham, *Air Wars and Aircraft,* 115, 121, 98.
33. For an overview of the FAP organization in Guinea, see Flintham, *Air Wars and Aircraft,* 97–98.
34. Canongia, "Portugal's 'Ginas,'" 68.
35. Ibid., 69.
36. Lewis Gann and Thomas Henriksen, *The Struggle for Zimbabwe: Battle in the Bush* (New York: Praeger: 1981), 47–48.
37. Ibid., 48–50.
38. Ibid., 48.
39. See also J. R. T. Wood, "Fire Force: Helicopter Warfare in Rhodesia: 1962–1980," 7. From "Rhodesia and South Africa Military History" website, maintained by Richard Allport Wood. Available from *http://home.wanadoo.nl/rhodesia.*
40. On the Rhodesian Air Force, see Flintham, *Air Wars and Aircraft,* 123–30. See also Wood, "Fire Force," 8–10.
41. Venter, *The Chopper Boys,* 90–91.
42. Dudley Cowderoy and Roy Nesbit, *War in the Air: Rhodesian Air Force 1935–1980* (Alberton, South Africa: Galago, 1987), 26–27. See also Wood, "Fire Force," 7.
43. Michael Hamence, "Cyclone Five: The Canberra in Rhodesian and Zimbabwean Service," *Air Enthusiast* 52 (winter 1993): 28–42, see 41.
44. Roy Braybrook, "Air Lessons from a COIN War," *Defence* (February 1983): 82–86, see 83–84.
45. Venter, *The Chopper Boys,* 90–91.
46. Ibid., 98.
47. On Rhodesian counterinsurgency strategy, see J. R. T. Wood, "Rhodesian Insurgency — Part I and Part II," 2–10. From Rhodesia and South Africa Military History website, maintained by Richard Allport Wood. Available from *http://home.wanadoo.nl/rhodesia.*
48. Clayton, *Frontiersmen,* 62–63.
49. Ibid., 63.
50. For an excellent and highly detailed overview of fireforce operations and tactics see Wood, "Fire Force: Helicopter Warfare in Rhodesia," part 1, 18–22, and part 2.

51. Wood, "Fire Force: Helicopter Warfare in Rhodesia," part 1, 22.

52. Flintham, *Air Wars and Aircraft*, 125.

53. A full account is provided by Richard Wood, "Counter-Punching on the Mudzi: D Company, 1st Rhodesian African Rifles on Operation 'Mardon,' 1 November 1976," *Small Wars and Insurgencies* 9, no. 2 (autumn 1998): 64–82.

54. Flintham, *Air Wars and Aircraft*, 126; also Allport, "A Brief History of the Rhodesian Army," 3.

55. Flintham, *Air Wars and Aircraft*, 127.

56. Alex Binda, "Operation Uric — Gaza, Mozambique, 1–7 September 1979: A Reconstruction," *Lion and Tusk* 5, no. 2 (February 1994): 1–8. From Rhodesia and South Africa Military History website. Available from *http://home.wanadoo.nl/rhodesia*.

57. Col. C. J. Nöthling, "Military Chronicle of South West Africa (1915–1988)," 2. From Rhodesia and South Africa Military History website. Available from *http://home. wanadoo.nl/rhodesia*. See also Patricia Hayes, ed., *Namibia under South African Rule: Mobility and Containment, 1915–46* (Oxford: James Curry, 1998), 25.

58. Hayes, *Namibia under South African Rule*, 274.

59. Ibid., 3.

60. Ibid., 263.

61. The OPO (Ovambo People's Organization) was founded in 1957. Its name was changed to SWAPO in 1960 to make the group more inclusive. SWAPO started mainly as a labor organization — aimed at destroying the migrant labor system operated by the white regime. A number of the early members were also part of the South African Communist Party. Violence began in December 1959 when a black township next to Windhoek was to be relocated. The inhabitants declined to be moved and confronted the police. Police ended up shooting and killing eleven and wounding fifty-four. At this point SWAPO decided to confront guns with guns. See W. Steenkamp, *South Africa's Border War, 1966–1989* (Gibraltar: Ashanti Publishing, 1989), 18.

62. Steenkamp, *South Africa's Border War*, 20.

63. Donald L. Sparks and December Green, *Namibia: The Nation after Independence* (Boulder, Colo.: Westview Press, 1992), 28–29.

64. Nöthling, "Military Chronicle of South West Africa," 4.

65. Ibid., 5.

66. Sparks and Green, *Namibia*, 33.

67. For a good overview of South African special forces and operations, see Kevin O'Brien, "Special Forces or Counter-Revolutionary Warfare: The South African Case," *Small Wars and Insurgencies* (summer 2001): 79–109.

68. Nöthling, "Military Chronicle of South West Africa," 5–6.

69. James Corum has interviewed several former South African soldiers who served as reservists in South West Africa during the conflict. All were proud of the fact that the South Africans had used their reserve forces extensively and that the reserves had supported a fairly effective large-scale civic action program.

70. Helmoed-Römer Heitman, *South African War Machine* (Novato, Calif.: Presidio Press, 1985), 58–60.

71. Dora Alves, "The South African Air Force in the Early Eighties," *Air University Review* 34, no. 5 (July–August 1983): 72–79.
72. Alves, "The South African Air Force in the Early Eighties," 76; Heitman, *South African War Machine,* 68–71.
73. Steenkamp, *South Africa's Border War,* 231.
74. Clayton, *Frontiersmen,* 122.
75. By the end of 1985 there were 31,000 Cubans in Angola as well as 3,250 Soviet and East German advisers. The MPLA and Cubans were equipped with thirty Mig-23s, eight Sukhoi-22 fighter-bombers, fifty Mig-21s, sixteen MI-17 helicopters, and thirty-three MI-24 helicopters. See Helmoed-Römer Heitman, *War in Angola: The Final South African Phase* (Gibraltar: Ashanti Publishing, 1990), 14–15.
76. For some thorough accounts of the Angola War, see Heitman, *War in Angola,* and Fred Bridgeland, *The War for Africa* (Gibraltar: Ashanti Publishing, 1990); Willem Steenkamp, *Borderstrike! South Africa into Angola* (Durban/Pretoria: Butterworths Publishers, 1983). See also Keith Somerville, *Foreign Military Intervention in Africa* (New York: St. Martin's Press, 1990).
77. Clayton, *Frontiersmen,* 123.
78. Heitman, *War in Angola,* 322–25.
79. For a good overview of airpower in the latter phase of the Angolan War, see Heitman, *War in Angola,* 319–30.
80. Ibid., 321.
81. Venter, *The Chopper Boys,* 153–62, provides a detailed account of Koevoet operations and tactics.
82. Steenkamp, *South Africa's Border War,* 202.
83. Venter, *The Chopper Boys,* 154.
84. Col. C. J. Nöthling, "Military Chronicle of South West Africa (1915–1988)," originally published in *South African Defence Force Review,* 1989, 8–9. From Rhodesia and South Africa Military History website. Available from *http://home.wanadoo.nl/rhodesia.*
85. Clayton, *Frontiersmen,* 142.
86. Heitman, *War in Angola,* 307–8.
87. Nöthling, "Military Chronicle of South West Africa," 17.
88. Ronald Dreyer, *Namibia and Southern Africa: Regional Dynamics of Decolonization, 1945–90* (London: Kegan Paul International, 1994), 188–93.
89. Sparks and Green, *Namibia,* 54–58.
90. Nöthling, "Military Chronicle of South West Africa," 17.

8. PROTRACTED INSURGENCIES: LATIN AMERICAN AIR FORCES IN COUNTERGUERRILLA OPERATIONS

1. Benjamin Schwarz, *American Counterinsurgency Doctrine and El Salvador: The Frustrations of Reform and the Illusions of Nation Building,* RAND Report R-4042 (Santa Monica, Calif.: RAND, 1992), 2.
2. Charles Lane, "The Pilot Shark of El Salvador," *New Republic,* 24 September 1990, 27.
3. For very useful works that cover both sides of the conflict, see Marvin Gettleman ed., *El Salvador: Central America in the New Cold War* (New York: Grove Press, 1986).

See also Max Manwaring and Courtney Prisk, eds., *El Salvador at War: An Oral History* (Washington, D.C.: National Defense University Press, 1988).

4. The one detailed article on the Salvadoran air force in the war is James Corum, "The Air War in El Salvador," *Airpower Journal* (summer 1998): 27–44.

5. For the background to the revolution in El Salvador, see Tommie Sue Montgomery, *Revolution in El Salvador: Origins and Evolution* (Boulder, Colo.: Westview Press, 1982). See also Liisa North, *Bitter Grounds: Roots of Revolt in El Salvador* (Toronto: Between the Lines, 1982).

6. I was fortunate to have some valuable assistance and advice in writing this chapter from Gen. Fred Woerner, USA (Ret.), former CINC SOUTHCOM; Ambassador David Passage, deputy chief of the U.S. Mission in El Salvador, 1984–1986; and Dr. Judy Gentleman of the Air War College faculty, who has interviewed former FMLN leaders. Comments and interviews with these three experts were tremendously helpful in conducting research.

7. Schwarz, *American Counterinsurgency Doctrine*, 23.

8. North, *Bitter Grounds*, xxii–xxiii.

9. *The Military Balance, 1981–1982* (London: International Institute for Strategic Studies, 1982), 101.

10. Ibid.

11. Flintham, *Air Wars and Aircraft*, 359–60.

12. Steffen Schmidt, *El Salvador: America's Next Vietnam?* (Salisbury, N.C.: Documentary Publications, 1983), 82.

13. Schwarz, *American Counterinsurgency Doctrine*, 85.

14. Donald Schulz and Deborah Schulz, *The United States, Honduras, and the Crisis in Central America* (Boulder, Colo.: Westview Press, 1994), 60.

15. John Waghelstein, *El Salvador: Observations and Experiences in Counterinsurgency* (Carlisle Barracks, Pa.: U.S. Army War College, 1985), 21–22.

16. Miguel Castellanos and Courtney Prisk, eds., *The Commandante Speaks: Memoirs of an El Salvadoran Guerrilla Leader* (Boulder, Colo.: Westview Press, 1991), 36–38.

17. Schwarz, *American Counterinsurgency Doctrine*, 2–5; and Waghelstein, *El Salvador*, 36.

18. Gettleman et al., *El Salvador*, 230.

19. History, U.S. Southern Command 1981, USAF Historical Research Agency (HRA), Maxwell AFB, AL, 10–11.

20. Ibid., 1982, 50–54.

21. History, Directorate of International Programs, 1 January–30 June 1982, USAFHRA, K145.01, 5–6.

22. History, Programs and Evaluation, DCS, July–December 1982, USAF HRA, K 145.01, 181.

23. Gen. Fred Woerner, former CINC SOUTHCOM, interview with author, 26 January 1998.

24. Waghelstein, *El Salvador*, appendix F.

25. Flintham, *Air Wars and Aircraft*, 365.

26. Ibid.

27. A good description from the rebel viewpoint of these operations in 1982 and 1983 is found in Charles Clement's *Witness to War* (New York: Bantam Books, 1984).

28. Manwaring and Prisk, *El Salvador at War*, 132–41.

29. Ibid., 145–46.
30. Gettleman et al., *El Salvador*, 233.
31. Ibid.
32. Ibid., 234.
33. Ibid.
34. Dr. Judy Gentleman, Air War College Faculty, interview with author, 19 January 1998.
35. Lt. Col. Edward King, USA (Ret.), *Testimony before House Committee on Foreign Affairs*, 99th Cong., 1st sess., 31 January 1985, 21–22.
36. Colonel Duryea, U.S. defense attaché to El Salvador, cited in Manwaring and Prisk, *El Salvador at War*, 316–19.
37. Ambassador David Passage, deputy chief of U.S. Mission in El Salvador, 1984–1986. Interview with author, 10 January 1998.
38. Col. James Steele, USA, cited in Manwaring and Prisk, *El Salvador at War*, 145–46.
39. *History, Directorate of International Programs*, July–December 1984, USAF HRA K 14.01, 6–7.
40. Ibid.
41. *History, U.S. Southern Command*, 1985, USAF HRA, K463.ol, 6.
42. Ibid.
43. *History, U.S. Southern Command*, 1984, USAF HRA, K463.01, 46–47.
44. A. J. Bacevich, ed., *American Military Policy in Small Wars: The Case of El Salvador* (Washington, D.C.: Pergamon-Brassey's, 1998), 29.
45. Ibid., 32.
46. Vance Bateman, "Tactical Air Power in Low Intensity Conflict," *Airpower Journal* 5, no. 1 (spring 1991): 77.
47. Bacevich, *American Military Policy in Small Wars*, 32.
48. Joseph Cirincione, "Latin America: Regional Threats to Western Security," *International Security Yearbook*, ed. Barry Blechman (Boulder, Colo.: Westview Press, 1984/85), 183–210, especially 188.
49. Col. Joseph Stringham, cited in Manwaring and Prisk, *El Salvador at War*, 148–51.
50. Flintham, *Air Wars and Aircraft*, 366.
51. For an account of this campaign from the rebel viewpoint, see Joe Fish and Cristina Sganga, *El Salvador: Testament of Terror* (New York: Olive Branch Press, 1988), 88–89.
52. Castellanos and Prisk, *The Commandante Speaks*, 88–89.
53. Ibid., xvii–xix.
54. *The Military Balance 1987/1988* (London: International Institute for Strategic Studies, 1987). A good description of El Salvador's helicopter force is Julio Montes, "Las Fuerzas Aéreas Salvadorñas: Antaño, la mayor flota de helicopteros en América Central," *Revista Aérea* (December 2000/January 2001): 52–55.
55. Schulz and Schulz, *The United States, Honduras, and the Crisis in Central America*, 153; and Barry Blechman and Edward Luttwak, eds., *International Security Yearbook* (Boulder, Colo.: Westview Press, 1984/85), 189, 192.
56. Leroy Thompson, *Ragged War: The Story of Unconventional and Counterrevolutionary Warfare* (London: Arms and Armour, 1994), 79.
57. Saul Landau, *The Guerrilla Wars of Central America* (New York: St. Martin's Press, 1993), 139–41.

58. Thompson, *Ragged War*, 79.
59. Ibid.
60. For a useful overview of the final stages of the peace process, see Tommie Sue Montgomery, "Getting to Peace in El Salvador: The Roles of the United Nations Secretariat and ONUSAL," *Journal of Interamerican Studies and World Affairs* (winter 1995): 139–72.
61. Lane, "The Pilot Shark of El Salvador," 27; and *History, U.S. Southern Command, 1983*, USAFHRA, K463.01, 85.
62. Lane, "The Pilot Shark of El Salvador," 28.
63. Ibid.
64. *Congressional Record*, 14 May 1986, 121.
65. Ibid.
66. *Dallas Morning News*, 21 January 1985.
67. Statement of Gus Newport, Mayor of Berkeley, House Committee on Foreign Affairs, *Congressional Record*, 14 May 1986, 17, 20, 21.
68. Ibid., 23, 41, 51.
69. Statement of Samuel Dickens, American Security Council Foundation, House Committee on Foreign Affairs, *Congressional Record*, 31 January 1985, 29–31.
70. Ibid.
71. "El Salvador's Guerrillas," *Washington Post*, 7–8 November 1985.
72. *Congressional Record*, 14 May 1986, 121.
73. General Woerner, interview by author, 19 January 1998.
74. Schwarz, 2–3.
75. Waghelstein, *El Salvador*, 46–47.
76. *History, U.S. Southern Command, 1985*, USAFHRA, K463.01, 50.
77. Col. Orlando Seeped, cited in Manwaring and Prisk, *El Salvador at War*, 310.
78. See Edwin Corr and Courtney Prisk, "El Salvador: Transforming Society to Win the Peace," in *Low Intensity Conflict: Old Threats in a New World*, ed. Edwin Corr and Stephen Sloan (Boulder, Colo.: Westview Press, 1992), 223–53.
79. Bacevich et al., *American Military Policy in Small Wars*, 13.
80. Waghelstein, *El Salvador*, 42–45. See also Col. Joseph Stringham, cited in Manwaring and Prisk, *El Salvador at War*, 148–51.
81. Col. John Ellerson, cited in Manwaring and Prisk, *El Salvador at War*, 86–87.
82. The cost of building the training facilities in Honduras in FY 83 was fourteen million dollars. *History, Programs and Evaluation, DCS*, July–December 1982, USAF HRA, K145.01, 181.
83. Bacevich et al., *American Military Policy in Small Wars*, 32.
84. Ibid.
85. Bateman, "Tactical Air Power in Low Intensity Conflict," 77.
86. Woerner, interview.
87. Elliot Abrams, *Congressional Record*, 14 May 1986, 31.
88. Bacevich et al., *American Military Policy in Small Wars*, 32.
89. Several books provide a detailed background to Guatemala's civil war. These include Beatriz Manz, *Refugees of a Hidden War* (Albany: State University of New York Press, 1988); Richard Nyrop, ed., *Guatemala: A Country Study* (Washington, D.C.: Department

of the Army, 1983); and Victor Perera, *The Unfinished Conquest: The Guatemalan Tragedy* (Berkeley: University of California Press, 1993). For a leftist/Marxist perspective on the war, see Tom Barry, *Inside Guatemala* (Albuquerque: Inter-Hemispheric Education Resource Center, 1992); and Marlene Dixon and Susanne Jones, eds., *Revolution and Intervention in Central America* (San Francisco: Synthesis Publications, 1983).

90. For a general overview of the Guatemalan air force history, see Dan Hagedorn, *Central American and Caribbean Air Forces* (Tonbridge, U.K.: Air Britain Publications 1993), 47–59.

91. Mario Overall, "The Lockheed T-33 in Guatemalan Air Force Service," 2000, 2–5. From LAAHS website. Available from *www.LAAHS.com*.

92. Ibid., 6–7.

93. Hagedorn, *Central American and Caribbean Air Forces,* 56.

94. Overall, "The Lockheed T-33," 7.

95. Hagedorn, *Central American and Caribbean Air Forces,* 56.

96. George Black, *Garrison Guatemala* (New York: Monthly Review Press, 1984), 22.

97. Susanne Jonas, *The Battle for Guatemala* (Boulder, Colo.: Westview Press, 1991), 45–53.

98. Jonas, *The Battle for Guatemala,* 79–83, 95–96.

99. Documents of the EGP are found in Dixon and Jones, *Revolution and Intervention,* 126–89.

100. Richard Nyrop, ed., *Guatemala: A Country Study* (Washington, D.C.: U.S. Army, 1984), 210–11.

101. Kev Darling, Mario Overall, Tulio Soto, and Dan Hagedorn, "Cessna A-37B in Latin America, Part 1: The Guatemalan A-37Bs," October 2000, 1–2. From LAAHS website. Available from *www.LAAHS.com*.

102. Nyrop, *Guatemala,* 194–95.

103. Darling et al., "Cessna A-37B," 2.

104. Hagedorn, *Central American and Caribbean Air Forces,* 57. A good overview of the FAG is also found in *World Airpower Journal* 32 (spring 1998): 150–51.

105. Ibid., 56–57.

106. Ibid.

107. Ibid.

108. Manz, *Refugees of a Hidden War,* 15.

109. Jennifer Schirmer, *The Guatemalan Military Project: A Violence Called Democracy* (Philadelphia: University of Pennsylvania Press, 1998), 41.

110. Manz, *Refugees of a Hidden War,* note 15, 238.

111. Susanne Jonas, *The Battle for Guatemala: Rebels, Death Squads, and U.S. Power* (Boulder, Colo.: Westview Press, 1991), 150–56; see also Schirmer, *Guatemalan Military Project,* 1.

112. Ibid., XIV; Schirmer, *Guatemalan Military Project,* 23–25.

113. Information provided by a veteran of the FAG Reserve Command.

114. Between 1978 and 1984 Guatemala received no U.S. military aid. Aid resumed in 1985 with $500,000 allocated to military training. In 1986, with the resumption of a civilian government and an improvement in human rights, the Guatemalan government received $400,000 in military training funds and $5 million in equipment. In 1988 and 1989

Guatemala received $9.4 million in U.S. military aid. See Victor Perera, *Unfinished Conquest: The Guatemalan Tragedy* (Berkeley: University of California Press, 1993), 272.

115. Darling et al., "Cessna A-37B," 2.

116. In 1983 the FAG consisted of eight to ten A37s, five T-33s, twelve Pilatus PC-7s, three Fouga Magisters as combat and training aircraft, a transport force of one DC-6, one DC-4, nine C-47s, ten IAI Arava's, ten Aerotec T-23 Trainers, and some Cessna 172s, 180s, and 206s, and a Beech King Air as utility and VIP craft. See Christopher Chant, *Air Forces of the World* (New Jersey: Chartwell Books, 1983), 20.

117. Mario Payeras, *Days of the Jungle: The Testimony of a Guatemalan Guerrillero* (New York and Havana: 1983), 29, 77–79, 82, 88.

118. Ibid., 76.

119. Russell Ramsey, *Guardians of the Other Americas: Essays on the Military Forces of Latin America* (Lanham, Md.: University Press of America, 1997), 88. On "La Violencia" and for a good summary of Colombian history, see David Bushnell, *The Making of Modern Colombia* (Berkeley: University of California Press, 1993), esp. 201–22.

120. Ibid., 89–92, for an overview of the groups and their tactics.

121. Ramsey, *Guardians of the Other Americas*, 114–24. See also Russell Ramsey, "Internal Defense in the 1980s: the Colombian Model," *Comparative Strategies* 4, no. 4 (1984): 349–67. Some accounts of the Colombian army's civic action successes in the 1950s are noted in Dennis Rempe, "The Origin of Internal Security in Colombia: Part 1 — A CIA Special Team Surveys *la Violencia,* 1959–60," in *Small Wars and Insurgencies* 10 (winter 1999): 36.

122. Bushnell, *The Making of Modern Colombia,* 264.

123. "Colombia's Rebels Keep the Marxist Faith," *New York Times,* 25 July 2000, A1, A8.

124. Ibid.

125. "Rebels Blow Up Pipeline in Colombia," *Washington Post,* 2 January 2000, 18.

126. Information from unofficial Colombian air force website, April 2001. Available from *www.airpower.maxwell.af.mil/almanac/english/Colombia.*

127. The best general work on the Colombian air force and military air units is "Air Power Analysis: Colombia," in *World Air Power Journal* 30 (autumn 1997): 132–37.

128. Ibid.

129. Ibid., 132.

130. "To Make a Point, the Rebels Are Strangling a Town," *New York Times,* 3 November 2000.

131. In 1992 U.S. international counterdrug spending was $660 million. The Clinton administration cut funds in 1993, 1994, 1995, and 1996. In 1996 international counterdrug spending was $290 million. U.S. drug interdiction funding under Clinton dropped from $1.96 billion in 1992 to $1.28 billion in 1995.

132. "U.S. Criticised for Obsolete Equipment Aid," *Janes' Defence Weekly,* 5 January 2000. See also "U.S. Sends Colombia 'Unsafe' Shells from 1952," *Washington Times,* 11 May 2000.

133. "Stepped-Up Coca Battle Ignites Debate," *Miami Herald,* 16 April 2000.

134. "CIA: Colombia Cocaine Production Up," *Associated Press,* 17 February 2000. Colombian cocaine production hit 520 metric tons in 1999, up from 435 tons in 1998 and 230 tons in 1995 according to CIA figures.

135. The U.S. Conference of Catholic Bishops, Social Development and World Peace Committee, Statement: Colombia Update, February 2002, 3. From United States Conference of Catholic Bishops website. Available from *www.nccbuscc.org*. The bishops condemned the U.S. government herbicide program for drug eradication in Colombia, arguing that the herbicide used, a common one used in the United States, is damaging to the environment.

136. "Colombia Rebel Group Plans Mass Recruitment," *San Diego Union-Tribune*, 29 April 2000.

137. "Colombian Massacre Large, Brutal," *Washington Post*, 21 April 2001, 14; "Dozens of Colombians Reported Massacred by Paramilitaries," *New York Times*, 20 April, 2001; "Rightist Forces Thwart Leader in Colombia," *Washington Post*, 19 April 2001.

138. "Colombia Vows to End Abuses," *Washington Post*, 22 July 2000, 15.

139. "Colombia to Order Fourteen Black Hawks," *Janes' Defence Weekly*, 12 April 2000.

140. A good overview of the strategic situation in Colombia in 2001 is found in Max Manwaring, "United States Security Policy in the Western Hemisphere: Why Colombia, Why Now, and What Is to Be Done?" *Small Wars and Insurgencies* (autumn 2001): 67–96.

141. Andrew Selsky, "Colombia Bombs Rebel Territory," *Associated Press*, 21 February 2002.

142. Susannah Nesmith, "Colombian Rebels Step Up Violence," *Associated Press*, 6 March 2002.

143. "Defying Threats, Colombians Cast Ballots," *Washington Post*, 10 March 2002, A18.

144. "Colombia Elects Uribe: Rebels Face Crackdown," *Washington Times*, 27 May 2002.

145. "FARC Triggers Concern in U.S.," *Washington Times*, 11 February 2002.

146. Jose Higuere, "Latin American Air Forces," *Janes' Defence Weekly*, 13 March 2002, 21.

9. INTERVENTION IN THE MIDEAST, 1962–2000: THREE COUNTERINSURGENCY CAMPAIGNS

1. David M. Witty, "A Regular Army in Counterinsurgency Operations: Egypt in North Yemen, 1962–1967," *Journal of Military History* 65 (April 2001): 401–40. See pages 401–5 for a good summary on the state of Yemen before the Egyptian intervention.

2. Edgar O'Ballance, *The War in Yemen* (Hamden, Conn.: Archon Books, 1971), 65.

3. Ibid., 79–80.

4. Ibid., 406–9.

5. Ibid., 97.

6. Witty, "A Regular Army in Counterinsurgency Operations," 411.

7. Ibid., 411–12.

8. Ibid., 412.

9. Ibid., 414.

10. Ibid.

11. Dana Schmidt, *Yemen: The Unknown War* (London: The Bodley Head, 1968), 168–69.

12. Ibid., 83–85.

13. O'Ballance, *The War in Yemen*, 125–26.

14. Schmidt, *Yemen: The Unknown War*, 168–69.

15. For a good overview of the Egyptian Air Force operations in Yemen, see Flintham, *Air Wars and Aircraft*, 162–64.

16. Witty, "A Regular Army in Counterinsurgency Operations," 426.

17. Ibid., 426–27.

18. Ibid., 428.

19. Ibid., 431–32.

20. The best work available on the Russian view of the Afghanistan War is: Russian General Staff, ed. and trans. W. Grau and Michael Gress, *The Soviet Afghan War: How a Superpower Fought and Lost* (Lawrence: University Press of Kansas, 2002). On Soviet aid to Afghanistan before 1979, see 10–11.

21. For a good overview of the Afghanistan War, see Lester Grau, ed., *The Bear Went over the Mountain: Soviet Combat Tactics in Afghanistan* (Washington: National Defense University Press, 1996). See also David Isby, *Russia's War in Afghanistan* (London: Osprey Press, 1986).

22. Russian General Staff, 8–14. On Soviet troop strength, see Scott McMichael, "Soviet Tactical Performance and Adaptation in Afghanistan," *Journal of Soviet Military Studies* 3 (March 1990): 73–105, see 79–80.

23. Isby, *Russia's War in Afghanistan*, 18.

24. McMichael, "Soviet Tactical Performance and Adaptation," 76–79.

25. Ibid., 79–80.

26. For the Table of Organization and Equipment of the Soviet forces in 1980, see Russian General Staff, 315–17.

27. Flintham, *Air Wars and Aircraft*, 204.

28. Ibid.

29. Russian General Staff, 58–79, offers an excellent overview of Afghani rebel tactics.

30. Ibid., 317.

31. Flintham, *Air Wars and Aircraft*, 204.

32. Russian General Staff, 314–18.

33. Ibid., 208.

34. Stephen Blank, "Imagining Afghanistan: Lessons of a 'Small War,'" *Journal of Soviet Military Studies* 3 (September 1990): 468–90. For a discussion of command and control and air support, see 477–79.

35. The Mi-24 Hind D and E models used in Afghanistan had some titanium armor protection for the belly of the aircraft. It carried a 12.7 mm Gatling gun supported by infrared imaging equipment with a range of two to four kilometers. Other models carried twin 23 mm automatic cannon. The Hinds carried antitank missiles, rockets, and AS-8 surface-to-air missiles. See David Isby, *Weapons and Tactics of the Soviet Army*, rev. ed. (London: Janes', 1988), 450–54.

36. For an overview of Soviet aviation operations in Afghanistan, see Russian General Staff, 200–222.

37. Ibid., 222.

38. For an overview of the Mujahideen groups and their political orientation, see Russian General Staff, 53–61.

39. Isby, *Weapons and Tactics of the Soviet Army*, 23.

40. On Mujahideen organization and the Islamic committees, see Russian General Staff, 53–61.

41. Isby *Weapons and Tactics of the Soviet Army*, 7, 13.
42. Ibid.
43. Russian General Staff, 212–13.
44. Ibid., 222.
45. Isby, *Weapons and Tactics of the Soviet Army*, 86.
46. Ibid., 70–72.
47. Ibid., 68–69.
48. Ibid., xix.
49. Ibid., 13–14.
50. Lon Nordeen, *Fighters over Israel* (New York: Orion Books, 1990); see 153–61 for an overview of PLO terror incidents against Israel.
51. On the Israeli counterinsurgency campaigns against the PLO, see Stuart Cohen and Efraim Inbar, "Varieties of Counter-Insurgency Activities: Israel's Military Operations against the Palestinians, 1948–90," *Small Wars and Insurgencies* 2 (April 1991): 41–60, see 48–50.
52. On the state of Lebanon in the 1970s, see Guy Arnold, *Wars in the Third World Since 1945*, 2d ed. (London: Cassell, 1995), 483–90.
53. On PLO strength and organization in southern Lebanon, see David Eschel, *The Lebanon War: 1982* (Hod Hasharon, Israel: Eschel Dramit, 1982), 3–5.
54. Ibid., 26.
55. Richard Gabriel, *Operation Peace for Galilee: The Israel-PLO War in Lebanon* (New York: Hill and Wang, 1984), 21.
56. Yehuda Borovik, *Israeli Air Force: 1948 to the Present* (London: Arms and Armour, 1984), 31, 33.
57. Ibid., 46–47, 33–34.
58. Ibid., 36–37, 39.
59. Ibid., 37.
60. Ibid., 56.
61. Ibid., 18.
62. Ibid., 54.
63. Nordeen, *Fighters over Israel*, 153.
64. For a table of organization of the IAF in 1982, see Flintham, *Air Wars and Aircraft*, 71.
65. Gabriel, *Operation Peace for Galilee*, 56.
66. Ibid.
67. Ibid., 8–59.
68. Ibid.
69. Nordeen, *Fighters over Israel*, 180.
70. Mathew Hurley, "The Bekaa Valley Air Battle, June 1982: Lessons Mislearned?" *Airpower Journal* (winter 1989): 60–70, see 61. See also Gabriel, *Operation Peace for Galilee*, 99–100.
71. Gabriel, *Operation Peace for Galilee*, 113.
72. Ibid., 182.
73. An overview of the air operations is found in Flintham, *Air Wars and Aircraft*, 68–74.
74. Nordeen, *Fighters over Israel*, 180.

75. Hurley, "The Bekaa Valley Air Battle," 65. On Israeli RPVs, see John F. Kreis, "Unmanned Aircraft in Israeli Air Operations," *Air Power History* (winter 1990): 46–60.
76. Nordeen, *Fighters over Israel*, 169.
77. Hurley, "The Bekaa Valley Air Battle," 61–62.
78. Martin van Creveld, *The Sword and the Olive: A Critical History of the Israeli Defense Force* (New York: Public Affairs, 1998), 348–49.
79. Ze'ev Schiff, *A History of the Israeli Army: 1874 to the Present* (New York: Macmillan, 1985), 254–55.
80. Criticism of the siege of Beirut was very intense in Israel. See Schiff, *History of the Israeli Army*, 255–57. See also van Creveld, *The Sword and the Olive*, 296–99.
81. Chair Seán MacBride, *Israel in Lebanon: Report of the International Commissions to Enquire into Reported Violations of International Law by Israel during its Invasion of Lebanon* (London: International Commission, 1983), 104, 146, 190–91.
82. Ibid., 147.
83. See Eschel, *The Lebanon War*, 52–53, for aerial photos of PLO weapons emplaced on hospitals and near civilian residences and foreign embassies.
84. Ephraim Segoli, Brig. Gen. IAF (Ret.), *The Israeli-Lebanese Dilemma*, monograph published by the USAF School of Advanced Airpower Studies: Maxwell AFB AL 1998, 25–26.
85. Eschel, *The Lebanon War*, 70.
86. A very useful and detailed summary of Hizbullah and its ideology is found in Andrew Schad, *Lebanon's Hizbollah Movement: The Party of God* (Wright Patterson AFB: Air Force Institute of Technology, 1999), 15–20.
87. Ibid., 14.
88. Ibid., 18.
89. The Hizbullah manifesto is reproduced whole in Augustus Norton, *AMAL and the Sh'ia: Struggle for the Soul of Lebanon* (Austin: University of Texas Press, 1987), 72.
90. Shmuel Gordon, *The Vulture and the Snake: Counter-Guerrilla Air Warfare: The War for Southern Lebanon*, Study 39. Mideast Security and Policy Studies: Begin-Sadat Center for Strategic Studies: Bar-Ilan University, Israel, July 1998, 19.
91. Schad, *Lebanon's Hizbollah Movement*, 40–44.
92. On Israeli intelligence in Lebanon, see Ian Black and Benny Morris, *Israel's Secret Wars* (New York: Grove Weidenfeld, 1991), 363–99.
93. Kenneth Schow, *Falcons Against the Jihad*, SAAS thesis, Air University Press: Maxwell AFB, November 1995, 9–12.
94. Ibid., 21.
95. Ibid., 34.
96. Gordon, *The Vulture and the Snake*, 22.
97. Clive Jones, "Israeli Counter Insurgency Strategy and the War in South Lebanon, 1985–97," *Small Wars and Insurgencies* (winter 1997): 82–108, see 89.
98. Ibid., 73.
99. Ibid.
100. Segoli and Gordon provide a good overview of Israel's use of helicopters in southern Lebanon. On Israeli helicopters and tactics, see Simon O'Dwyer-Russell, "Helicopters Over the Lebanon," *Defence Helicopter World* (June–August 1984): 42–43;

Roni Daniel, "Israeli Assault," *Defence Helicopter World* (October/November 1987): 29–30; Martin Streetly, "Helicopter EW from Israel," *Defence Helicopter World* (August/September 1986): 17–18, 22.

101. Segoli, *The Israeli-Lebanese Dilemma,* 32–40.
102. Jones, "Israeli Counter Insurgency Strategy," 99.
103. Ibid., 90.
104. "Israel's Helicopter Attacks Raise Fears of Heightened Violence," 31 October 2001. Available from *www.cnn.com.*
105. "Sharon Says Israel 'at War,'" *Washington Times,* 1 April 2002.
106. "Israeli F-16s Attack Nablus," *Washington Times,* 6 February 2002; "Israeli Helicopters Strike Nablus," *Washington Times,* 7 February 2002.
107. "Annan Blasts Israel's 'Illegal Occupation,'" *Jerusalem Post,* 13 March 2002.
108. "Israel Catches Weapons-Smuggling Ambulance," *Washington Times,* 27 March 2002.
109. Jones, "Israeli Counter Insurgency Strategy," 95–97.

The study of airpower in small wars is essentially a subset of the study of small wars and irregular warfare in general. Before approaching the subject of airpower in these wars, we recommend that the reader become familiar with the general history and theory of small wars. A good starting point for a review of the literature on small wars is Anthony Joes's *Guerrilla Warfare: A Historical, Biographical, and Bibliographical Sourcebook* (Westport, Conn.: Greenwood, 1996). Joes has also written two other useful general histories, *Modern Guerrilla Insurgencies* (Westport, Conn.: Praeger, 1996) and *Guerrilla Conflict Before the Cold War* (Westport, Conn.: Praeger, 1992). One of the classic works on the history of guerrilla and irregular warfare is Robert Asprey's two-volume *War in the Shadows: The Guerrilla in History* (Garden City, N.Y.: Doubleday, 1975).

On the theory of small wars we have already noted the nineteenth-century classic, C. E. Callwell's *Small Wars: Their Principles and Practice* (Lincoln: University of Nebraska Press, 1996; reprint, originally published 1896). It is striking that many of the basic principles of counterinsurgency have not changed in over a century. The Marine Corps' *Small Wars Manual* (1940; reprint, Washington, D.C.: Department of the Navy, 1987), also already noted, is another classic work concerning counterinsurgency theory. Soldiers engaged in a counterinsurgency or peacekeeping campaign today can get far more practical operational and tactical guidance from this work than from most of the current doctrine manuals of the U.S. military. Another highly recommended although rather obscure book on the theory of irregular warfare is Friedrich von der Heydte's *Modern Irregular Warfare, In Defense Policy as a Military Phenomenon* (New York: New Benjamin Franklin House, 1986).

More recent American theorists of small wars deserve some mention. Max Manwaring, who has written many works on counterinsurgency, provides some useful models for analyzing insurgencies and counterinsurgency campaigns in *Uncomfortable Wars: Towards a New Paradigm of Low Intensity Conflict* (Boulder, Colo.: Westview Press, 1991). Edwin Corr and Stephen Sloan's *Low Intensity Conflict* (Boulder, Colo.: Westview Press, 1992) provides some case studies of counterinsurgency campaigns and some recommendations for creating an effective counterinsurgency strategy. Larry Cable has written several books, including *Conflict of Myths: The Development of American Counterinsurgency Doctrine and the Vietnam War* (New York: New York University Press, 1986), and numerous articles with some valuable insights on the American way of conducting counterinsurgency. Finally, Wray Johnson's book *Vietnam and American Doctrine for Small Wars* (Bangkok: White Lotus, 2001) addresses the extent to which theory informed and shaped the development of U.S. military doctrine for foreign internal conflict and why the United States has had, at best, a poor record in small wars.

General Airpower Books

Counterinsurgency and counterterrorism operations have received relatively little attention in the general literature on military aviation, primarily because there is rarely any opportunity for airpower to act in a *decisive* role, at least in the sense either of the lethal application of airpower or unilaterally. As previously stated, although the military plays an important part in small wars it is usually in a supporting role. In that airpower is usually additionally adjunctive within this role, airmen find little inspiration from the experience, and airpower historians similarly are disinclined to explore the same. Ironically, however, as this volume shows, airpower can be decisive in its own fashion, if only indirectly. For example, virtually every senior official involved in the Malayan Emergency claimed afterward that the Royal Air Force played a crucial if not decisive role in the successful British effort. An account of the Marines' successful intervention in Nicaragua from 1927 to 1933 declared that it could not have been accomplished without Marine Corps aviation. Nevertheless, airpower's primary contribution to the military effort in a small war is likely to be in the very important but less dramatic support roles of reconnaissance and transport, and the result is less exciting than "fire and steel on target."

Only a few books provide more than a very cursory mention of airpower in small wars. Victor Flintham's *Air Wars and Aircraft: A Detailed Record of Air Combat, 1945 to the Present* (New York: Facts on File, 1990) is an extremely useful general work that briefly covers airpower's role in dozens of small wars and provides an overview of the air units and aircraft employed in the wars since 1945. For the period before 1945, David Omissi's superb *Air Power and Colonial Control: The Royal Air Force, 1919–1939* (Manchester, England: Manchester University Press, 1990) provides a comprehensive history of the Royal Air Force's colonial air campaigns as well as discusses the colonial air operations of the other colonial powers (Italy, France, and Spain) in considerable detail. Omissi's book is indispensable for anyone looking at the evolution of airpower doctrine in small wars. Philip Towle's *Pilots and Rebels: The Use of Aircraft in Unconventional Warfare, 1918–1988* (London: Brassey's, 1989) is a brief but useful look at the Royal Air Force's small wars operations from the colonial era to recent times. Charles Christienne and Pierre Lissarague's *A History of French Military Aviation* (Washington, D.C.: Smithsonian Institution Press, 1986), while a general history, discusses the French colonial air operations from Morocco in the 1920s to the Algerian War in some depth.

Some good histories have been written about airpower operations in specific small wars. The Royal Air Force wrote a very good critical history of its airpower operations in Malaya during that conflict that lasted from 1947 to 1960; however, this work remained classified for years after it was published in 1970 and therefore had little impact on scholarly thinking about the topic. Fortunately, it is now available to the general public (Royal Air Force, *The Malayan Emergency, 1948–1960* [London: Ministry of Defence, 1970]). Other good books on airpower operations in small wars have recently appeared. One that covers the U.S. Air Force's operations in counterinsurgency in the 1950s and 1960s is Warren Trest's *Air Commando One: Heinie Aderholt and America's Secret Air Wars* (Washington, D.C.: Smithsonian Institution Press, 2000). A variety of other official histories and other works deal with airpower operations in small wars, but rarely in any detail. Considering that airpower has been employed in counterinsurgency operations for almost a century, the literature on the subject is quite thin.

INDEX

Abd el Krim, 68–77
Abrams, Elliot, 343
Abu Nidal Organization, 409
Acheson, Dean, 236
Aden, 60, 84, 199, 201–03, 207
  Communications Squadron, 207
  insurrection, 203–08
  National Liberation Front, 204–05
  Radfan, 204, 207–08, 211, 216–17
  RAF in, 203–08
Aderholt, Harry C. "Heinie" (Gen.), 247
Afghanistan, 2, 10, 379, 380, 430–31
  Mujahideen, 389–97, 419–20
  Soviet air force in, 389–97
  Soviet army aviation in, 392–93, 395
  Soviet army in, 389–97
  Soviet special forces in, 391
  War with Soviets, 387–97
Africa, 1
Air Corps Tactical School, 42, 269
Akehurst, John (Brig. Gen.), 211, 213, 214, 216
al-Badr, Mohamed, 382, 383
Albania, 93, 98, 100
Algeria, 426
  Algerian Assembly, 163
  Algerian War, 161–74, 284, 289
  FLN (Front de Libération Nationale), 164–66, 170–74
  French air force in, 165–74, 178
  French army in, 165–66
  harkis, 166
  psychological operations in, 173
  troops of, 141
Algiers, 161
Alhuremas Bay, 72
al-Jihad, 410, 415, 416
al-Qaeda, 2, 430
Amritsar, India, 59
Angola, xiii
  FNLA, 286, 287, 309
  MPLA, 286, 287, 309–11

South African War, 305–06, 309, 310, 311, 312, 313, 314, 316, 318, 321, 322, 324
UNITA, 286, 287, 309–11
UPA (União das Populações de Angola), 281
  war of independence, 279–92
Annam, 148, 152
Annual (Spanish Morocco), 69–71
Anthis, Rollen (Gen.), 244, 246, 253–54, 257–59, 265, 271
Arab Covenant, 201
Arafat, Yassar, 405, 415, 416
Argentina, 325
Armeé de l'air (French air force)
  in Indochina, 139, 141, 144–61, 227
  in Morocco, 74–76, 83
  in Syria, 77–79, 83
Army Air Forces School of Applied Tactics, 41
Army of God (Jund Allah), 410
as-Sallal, 382
Athens, 94, 96–98
Aurès Mountains, 165, 170, 173
Atlas Mountains, 74, 172
Ayatollah Khomeini, 410

Babrak Karmal, 389, 390
Badoglio, Prieto (Marshal), 80
Baghdad, 54
Bagram air base, Afghanistan, 395
Baker, Newton (Secretary of War, U.S.), 16, 19
Bao Dai, 152
Beaufre, André (Gen.), 268, 269
Beirut, 398, 401, 404, 405, 407, 408
Bekaa Valley, Lebanon, 404, 409, 412
Bobo, Rosalvo, 27
Bohannan, Charles "Bo," 119, 138
Bolivia, 362
Bosnica, 6
Boxer Rebellion, 11

Briggs, Sir Harold (Lt. Gen.), 188–89
Britain, 1, 2, 8, 29, 51
    Colonial Ministry, 58, 61, 82
    Parliament, 58, 64–65
    War Ministry, 57, 59
British army, 52–56, 61–63
    aviation, 207–08
    British Army Staff College, 182
    Gurkhas, 191, 221
    Special Air Service, 191, 204–05, 217
British Middle East Command, 205
Bryan, William Jennings (Secretary of
    State, U.S.), 12
Builder, Carl, 85
Burma, 9
Bush, George W. (President, U.S.):
    administration of, 371
Bustillo, Juan Rafael (Gen.), 342

Cabral, Amilcar, 287, 288
Cairo Conference, 54
Callwell, C. E. (Maj. Gen.), 180, 181, 182
Cambodia, 139, 143, 146
Carranza, Venustiano (President,
    Mexico), 12, 14
Carter, James E. (President, El
    Salvador): administration of, 329,
    353–54
Casas Grandes, Mexico, 18
Castaneda, Mariano (Maj. Gen.), 121
Challe, Maurice (Gen.), 170–73
Chamorro, Emiliano (President,
    Nicaragua), 32
China, 143, 151, 153–54, 186–87, 228–29,
    236
    civil war, 11
Chinandega Province, Nicaragua, 39
    battle of, 34
Chindits, 9
Churchill, Sir Winston (Prime Minister,
    Britain), 54, 189
CIA, 395
Clark Air Force Base, 265
Clausewitz, Carl von (Gen.), 7, 180, 274,
    425–26

Clinton, William Jefferson (President,
    U.S.): administration of, 366, 371
Cohen, Eliot, 7
Colombia
    air force of, 364–65, 367–71, 377, 428, 431
    army of, 361, 364, 367–71, 376
    drug trafficking in, 362–63, 366–67,
        378, 423, 430
    ELN (National Liberation Army), 363,
        368–70
    FARC (Revolutionary Armed Forces
        of Colombia), 361, 363–70, 424–
        25, 430–31
    insurgency in, xiv, 2, 325–26, 423, 426–
        27
    La Violencia, 361
    M-19, 361–62
    National Police of, 368, 378
    Plan Colombia, 369
    U.S. aid to, 366–71
Columbus, New Mexico, 14, 16–17, 19–20
Communist International, 115
Congo, 10, 279, 281, 283, 286
Constantine, Algeria, 161, 163, 172
Corinto, Nicaragua, 33
Cox, Sebastian, xiii
Crane, Conrad, xiii
Cuba, 2, 11, 326, 331
    in Angola, 309–12, 314–15
    armed forces of, 281
Cummins, Lejeune, 34

Damascus, 79
Decker, George (Gen.), 238
De Gaulle, Charles, 142, 145–46, 154,
    157–60, 170, 173–75
DFLP (Democratic Front for the
    Liberation of Palestine), 409
Dhofar, 210–12, 216
Diaz, Adolfo (President, Nicaragua), 32
Diem, Ngo Dinh, 232, 241–42, 257–58,
    263
Dien Bien Phu, 225, 230–32, 428
Dominican Republic, 1, 3, 11–12, 24–26, 28
Douhet, Giulio, 269–70

Down, E. Eric (Maj. Gen.), 136
Druze Rebellion, 78–79
Duarte, Jose Napoleón, 336, 340
Dulles, John Foster, 237
Duong Van Minh, 263

Eglin Air Force Base, 238, 277
Egypt, xii, 164, 179, 400
    air force of, 383–86
    armed forces of, 380–86
    Yemen war, 379–82
Eisenhower, Dwight D. (President,
    U.S.), 236
El Chipote, Nicaragua, 37–38
El Salvador, xiv, 2, 4
    civil war in, 325–49, 426–27
    ESAF (El Salvador Armed Forces),
        330–49
    FAS (El Salvador air force), 327–49,
        373–75
    FMLN (Farabundo Martí National
        Liberation Front), 329, 331–32,
        334, 335, 336, 338, 339, 340, 341,
        344, 373, 423
    MilGroup (U.S. Military Group), 334,
        346–47
    U.S. Air Force in, 333–34, 338–43
    U.S. military aid to, 333–34, 335, 336
    See also Ilopango Air Base (El
        Salvador)
Esteli Province, Nicaragua, 39

Fall, Bernard, 157, 229
Feland, Logan (Gen.), 33
Fez, Morocco, 72
Fletcher, Jack (Brig. Gen.), 211
Foulois, Benjamin D., 11, 16, 18–19
France, 51, 54, 380
    army of, 1, 44, 72, 77–79, 83, 166, 172
    Foreign Legion, 146, 168
    National Assembly, 161
    naval aviation of, 152
    Vichy regime, 229–30
    See also Armeé de l'air (French air
        force)

Franco, Francisco, 70, 72
French Morocco, 72–77, 79, 83
French Union, 143, 152, 161
Funston, Frederick (Gen.), 15

Gaza Strip, 2
Geldenhuys, Jannie (Gen.), 309
Geneva Accords, 225, 229, 233–34, 239
German army: use of poison gas by,
    70–71
Giap, Vo Nguyen, 141–42, 146, 156, 158–
    60, 230, 232
Graziani, Rodolfo (Gen.), 80
Greece
    British army in, 97, 98, 99
    British military mission to, 96, 102–03,
        108, 134, 136
    civil war in, 93–110, 133–34, 227
    EAM (National Liberation Front),
        96, 98
    EDES (National Republican Greek
        League), 96–98
    ELAS (National Popular Liberation
        Army), 96–100
    GDA (Greek Democratic Army), 98,
        100, 104, 106–07, 109, 134
    GNA (Greek National Army), 97,
        99–110
    Grammos Mountains, 106, 134
    KKE (Greek Communist Party), 95–
        97, 100, 103
    National Defense Corps, 104
    RHAF (Royal Hellenic Air Force), 93,
        101–02, 107–10, 134, 428
    Royalists, 94–95
    U.S. military mission to, 102–03, 107,
        109, 110
    Vitsi, 106, 134
Grootfontein Air Base, 310
Guantánamo Bay (U.S. military base), 27
Guatemala, 2
    air force reserve of, 357–58, 432–33
    civil war in, 325, 329, 349–59, 371, 377
    EGP (Guerrilla Army of the Poor),
        353, 355, 358

Guatemala *(continued)*
  FAG (Fuerza Aerea Guatemala:
    Guatemalan air force), 351–59
  FAR (Fuerza Armada Revolucionario:
    Revolutionary Armed Forces),
    351
  Guatemala City, 353, 354
  URNG (Guatemalan National
    Revolutionary Unity Party),
    355, 359
  U.S. aid to, 352–355
Guevara, Ernesto "Ché," 8
Guinea-Bissau
  insurgency in, 279, 281, 283–85, 287,
    288, 291
  PAIGC (the revolutionary party in
    Guinea), 287, 288, 291
Gulf of Tonkin, 152
  Gulf of Tonkin Resolution, 266
Gurney, Sir Henry, 188
Gwynn, Sir Charles (Maj. Gen.), 182

Haiti, 1, 11, 24, 26–29, 32
  Haitian gendarmerie (police force),
    28
  See also Port-au-Prince, Haiti
Hamas, 9, 415–16
Hanoi, 149, 156
Hargroves, Louis (Gen.), 206
Harkins, Paul (Gen.), 242, 254, 256, 259,
  271
Harris, Arthur (Air Commodore), 65
Hart, Basil Liddell, 59, 61
Hays-Pauncefote Treaty of 1901, 31
Hizbullah, 9, 380, 398, 406, 409–15, 421,
  429–30
Ho Chi Minh, 141, 143, 145–46, 149, 160,
  225, 230, 233
Honduras, 325, 327, 329–32, 335, 347
Huerta, Victoriano (Gen.), 12, 14
Hukbalahap-Huks, 1, 93, 110–38, 227
Hussein, King (Jordan), 212

Ilopango Air Base (El Salvador), 331,
  334, 337, 342, 343, 345

IMET (International Military Education
  and Training) Program, 333–34
India, 60, 63–64, 76, 88
  Indian army, 53, 55, 57, 61, 82
  Indian army in Iraq, 61
  Indian Civil Service, 54
Indochina, 139–161, 169
  French army in, 230–31
  See also Vietnam
IAAFA (Inter-American Air Force
  Academy), 334, 337, 345
International Commission, 407–08
Iran, 424
  air force of, 212
  Revolutionary Guards of, 410
  support for terrorism, 2
Iraq, 52–56, 66, 85, 61–62
  army of, 56–57
  RAF in, 85–87
Islam, 424–25
  Islamic Jihad. *See also* al-Jihad
  Islamic terrorism, 2, 9
Israel, 2, 9, 379–80, 421
  IAF (Israeli air force), 398, 402–05,
    407
  IDF (Israeli defense forces), 398,
    400–05, 407–08, 413–14, 416–17,
    422
  Lebanon War, 398–415
  West Bank conflict, 415–17
Israeli aircraft industries, 402
Italian army, 80–81
Italian air force, 84
  in Libya, 80–81, 89
  in North Africa, 90–91
Italian military archives, xiii
Italy, 1, 51, 80–81

Japanese armed forces, 141, 143, 229–30
Jeddah Agreement, 386
Jiminez, Juan Isidro, 25
Johnson, Lyndon B. (President, U.S.),
  265–67
Joint Interagency Task Force–East, 433–34
Jordan, Transjordan, 54, 60, 382, 400–01

Kabylia Mountains, 170, 172
Kangleon, Ruperto, 121, 127
Karch, Frederick (Gen.), 267
Kennedy, John F., 237, 241–42, 263, 270, 273
Kenya, 63, 284, 292
Khormaksac Airfield, 205
Khrushchev, Nikita, 237
King's African rifles, 53
Kuala Lumpur, Malaya, 188, 191, 195
Kurds, Kurdistan, 54–55, 61–62, 82–84
Ky, Nguyen Cao, 248, 275

Lansdale, Edward, 119–20, 122, 138, 237
Laos, 139, 143, 255
Latin America, 1, 3, 4, 29
Latin America Aviation Historical Society, xiv
Laurel, José, 118
League of Nations, 59, 77, 305
Lebanon, 2, 9, 54, 77
    AMAL militia, 410
    conflict, 398–415, 422
    Israeli operations in, 379–415
    Maronite Christians, 409–10
    Shiite Moslems, 409–10, 411, 418
    Southern Lebanon Security Zone, 398, 413
    South Lebanon army, 409, 413–14
    Syrian Forces in, 404–05, 410, 415
Léchères, Charles (Gen.), 144
LeMay, Curtis (Gen.), 243–45, 262
Leon Province, Nicaragua, 39
Libya, 80–81, 89
Long Son, 154
Low-intensity conflict, 6
Lunt, J. D. (Brig. Gen.), 206
Lyautey, Louis-Hubert, Marshal, 73–75

MacArthur, Douglas (Gen.), 115, 121, 126, 137
Macedonia, 100
Madero, Francisco I. (President, Mexico), 12

Magsaysay, Ramon, 112, 119, 121–24, 128, 132, 135
Malaya, 3, 8, 167
    battle of Tasek, 188
    British army in, 184
    Butterworth airfield, 188
    Chinese community of, 186
    emergency, 179–99, 227, 256, 274, 284, 290, 296
    emergency directives, 216
    Home Guard of, 190
    Kota Bharu airfield, 189
    Malaya police, 190–91
    MCP (Malayan Communist Party), 186, 190
    Min Yuen (People's Movement), 188
    MPAJA (Malayan People's Anti-Japanese Army), 186
    MRLA (Malayan Races Liberation Army), 187, 190–91, 196, 198
    RAF Task Force Malaya, 191
    Special Constabulary of, 190
    Tengah airfield, 193
    See also Kuala Lumpur, Malaya
Managua, Philippines, 33
Manila, Philippines, 123
Mao Tse-tung, 151, 231, 236, 280, 287
    Mao's theory of war, 8
Marine Corps Gazette, 42, 43
McBride, Seán, 407–08
McGee, Vernon (Gen.), 42–44
McHugh Airdrome, Nicaragua, 46, 49
McNamara, Robert S., 237, 242, 244–46, 255, 258–59
Mekong Delta, 261
Melilla (Spanish Morocco), 66, 69, 71
Mexico: punitive expedition, 11–21, 41, 44, 45
Mitchell, Billy (Gen.), 20, 44
Mohammed bin Adullah Hassan ("Mad Mullah"), 53
Moncada, José (Gen.), 32, 33, 34
Mondlane, Eduardo, 287
Monroe Doctrine, 24

Montt, Efrain Rios, 356, 358, 372
Morocco, 1, 141, 161, 164, 170
Moslems
    Shiites, 54, 55
    Sunni, 54, 55
Mosul, 85
Mozambique, 279, 281–92, 297–99, 300,
    318
    FRELIMO, 287, 297, 298
Mugabe, Robert, 294, 300, 302
Mulcahy, Francis (Capt.), 40, 42
Muzorewa, Abel, 300–01

Namibia, xiii. See also Rhodesia; South
    West Africa
Nassar, Abdul Gamal, 164, 380, 382, 383,
    386
NATO (North Atlantic Treaty
    Organization), 144, 166, 282
Navarre, Henri (Gen.), 157
Nicaragua, 1, 3, 11–12, 24, 31–40, 373
    battle of Muy Muy, 34
    Contras, 325
    National Guard of, 32, 35, 39
    Sandinista government, 329
    Sandinista Revolution, 325, 329, 331–
        32, 342
    Sandinistas, 423
    Somoza regime, 329
    U.S. intervention in, 37–43, 48
    See also Chamorro, Emiliano
        (President, Nicaragua);
        Chinandeya Province,
        Nicaragua; Corinto, Nicaragua;
        Diaz, Adolfo (President,
        Nicaragua); El Chipote,
        Nicaragua; Esteli Province,
        Nicaragua; Leon Province,
        Nicaragua; McHugh Airdrome,
        Nicaragua; Ocotal, Nicaragua;
        Puerto Cabezas, Nicaragua;
        Quilalí, Nicaragua
Nolting, Frederick (Ambassador), 242
Northern Rhodesia, 279, 292, 295
    See also Zambia

North Korea: partisans, 9
North Vietnam, 268–69
    North Vietnam army, 240–41
Nur Mohammed Taraki, 389

OAS (Organization of American States),
    341
Obregón, Álvaro (Gen.), 12
Ocotal, Nicaragua, 35–36
Oman
    army of, 210
    British Army Training Team, 212
    insurgency, 208–18
    Omon Liberation army, 210
    RAF base in, 211
    Sultan of Oman Air Force, 212, 213,
        216, 221
Omissi, David, 83
Oran, 161
OSS (Office of Strategic Services), 141–
    42, 143
Ottoman Empire, 51–52, 54–55, 77–79,
    94–95
Overall, Mario, xiv

Pakistan, 390, 394–97
Palestine, 2, 9, 54, 65–66, 84, 179,
    201
    Palestinian Authority, 415, 416
    Palestinian terrorists, 2, 9
    PELP (Popular Front for the
        Liberation of Palestine), 409
    West Bank conflict, 415–17
    See also PLO (Palestine Liberation
        Organization)
Panama Canal, 23, 26
Panjsher Valley, Afghanistan, 395, 396
Paoletti, Ciro, xiii
Papagos, Alexander (Marshal), 103, 135
Papandreou, George, 98
Pape, Robert, 85
Pastrana, Andrés, 367, 370
Pershing, John J. (Gen.), 11, 15–18, 45
Peru, 2, 325, 362
    Peruvian air force, 366–67

Pétain, Philippe, Marshal, 77
PFLOAG (People's Front for the Liberation of the Occupied Arabian Gulf), 210–11, 215
Philippeville, Algeria, 165
Philippines, 1–3, 11, 110–14
  air force of, 93, 123–34, 136
  BCTs (armed forces of), 124–25, 128, 130–31
  BUDC (Barrio United Defense Corps), 117
  constabulary of, 116–17
  Democratic Alliance, 116
  EDCOR (Economic Development Corps), 120–22
  JUSMAG (Joint United States Military Advisory Group), 119, 126
  Liberal Party of, 116
  Luzon, 110, 113
  Military Academy of, 127
  Military Police Command, 116–17
  Mindanao, 110
  People's Home Defense Guard, 118
  Philippine Trade Act of 1946, 119
  PKO (Philippine Communist Party), 114–15, 123–24
Pike, Douglas, 228–29
PLAN (People's Liberation Army of Namibia), 304–06
PLO (Palestine Liberation Organization), 379–80, 418, 421
  in Lebanon, 398–409, 411–12
  Supreme Military Council of, 401
Poison gas, 73
  See also German army: use of poison gas by
Porch, Douglas, 181
Port-au-Prince, Haiti, 27
Portugal
  army of, 281–92
  colonial wars of, 279–92
  FAP (Portuguese air force), 280, 282–92, 315–19
Puerto Cabezas, Nicaragua, 38

Quantico, Virginia, 28
Quezon, Manuel (President, Mexico), 120
Quilalí, Nicaragua, 36–37
Quirino, Elpido, 118, 121

RAAF (Royal Australian Air Force), 193, 219
RAF (Royal Air Force)
  in Aden, 203–08
  Air Command Southeast Asia, 179
  Bomber Command, 192
  in Egypt, 92
  Far East Communications Command, 194
  in India, 63, 64, 76, 81–83
  in Iraq, 52–57
  in Malaya, 179–99
  in Somaliland, 53–54, 84
  Staff College, 180
Ramos, Albert, 121
Ramsey, Russell, xiv
Reagan, Ronald (President, U.S.):
  administration of, 330, 344
Red Army Fraktion (Germany), 8
Red Brigades (Italy), 8
Red River Delta, 147, 151, 155
Rhodesia, xii, 2, 279–80, 292–302, 306, 426
  army of, 290, 295–301, 319–21
  police in, 296, 299, 307, 320
  RhAF (Rhodesian Air Force), 295–301
Rhodesian war, rebel groups, 292–302
  ZANLA, 297, 300, 301
  ZANU, 294–95, 297–99
  ZAPU, 294–95, 297
  ZIPRA, 300–01
Rif Republic, 70–77, 84
Roberto, Holden, 281
Roosevelt, Theodore (President, U.S.), 24
Rowell, Ross "Rusty," 29–40, 42
Roxas, Manuel, 116–18, 120, 123
Royal Marines, 191, 196, 204, 206

RN (Royal Navy), 207
  Coastal Command, 194
  Fleet Air Arm, 193–96
RNZAF (Royal New Zealand Air Force),
  193
Rundu air base, 311
Rusk, Dean, 236, 256
Russia, 3

SAAS (U.S. Air Force School of
  Advanced Airpower Studies), xi
Sacasa, Juan, 32
Sahara, 163, 173
Saigon, 145, 234, 252, 268–69
Sakiet, Tunisia, 172
Salmon, Sir John (Air Marshal), 62
Sanderson, A. C. (Air Vice Marshal),
  192
Sandino, Augusto, 428
Santa Isabel, Mexico, 14
Santo Domingo, Dominican Republic,
  25–26, 32
SAS (Special Air Service), British army,
  196, 210
Saudi Arabia: in Yemeni War, 382–83,
  385, 386
Saundby, Sir Robert (Air Marshal),
  184
Schilt, Christian (Lt.), 36–37, 42, 46
Serbia, 6
Sétif, Algeria, 163
Sharon, Ariel, 415, 416
Sharp, Ulysses S. Grant (Admiral),
  239–40
Sheik Admed of Barzan, 62
Sheik Mahmud, 61, 84
Sherman, William C., 20–21
Sierra Madre, Mexico, 16–18, 33–38, 47
Singapore, 185, 187
Slessor, Sir John (Air Marshal), 184
Smith, Frederic (Gen.), 227
Smith, Ian, 300
Somalia, 6
Somaliland, 53, 55, 89
Soto, Tullio, xiv

South Africa, xii–xiii, 2, 279–81
  police, 305
  SAAF (South African Air Force), xiii–
    xiv, 302, 305–13, 316, 321–24
  SAAF reserve, 306, 308–09
  SADF (South African Defense
    Forces), 305–07, 309–13, 315–16
South Arabia, 200–02, 204, 210, 217
South Vietnam, 3, 225–78
  army of, 235, 240–43, 245, 257–59, 261–
    62, 267, 269, 271–73, 275
  Civil Guard, 243
  French air force training of, 233–35
  VNAF (air force), 177, 233–35, 243–58,
    260–67, 271–72, 275–77
South West Africa, Namibia, 279–80,
  302–24
  police, 305–06, 312–13
  SWAPO (South West African People's
    Organization), 280, 304–09, 311–15
Soviet Union, 1, 2, 9, 379–80, 423
  air force of, 389–93, 396–97
  army of, 3, 89, 390–93, 395–97
  army aviation of, 392–93, 395
  in Afghanistan, 379
  special forces of, 391
Spain, 1, 51
  air force of, 68–73, 83
  army of, 69–73
  colonial wars, 66–73
  Foreign Legion, 70, 72
Spinola, Antonio de (Gen.), 288
Sultan Qaboos, 211
Summers, Harry (Col.), 7
Syria, 78–79, 161
  Druze tribes of, 78–79
  French air force in, 77

Taft, William Howard, 12, 24
Taliban regime, 2, 10, 430
Tampico, Mexico, 14
Tanganyika, 63
Tan Son Nhut Airfield, Vietnam, 145,
  235, 250–51, 255, 260, 265–66,
  276, 278

Tanzania, 279, 287, 294–95
Taruc, Luis, 112, 115–16, 123, 127
Tassigny, de Lattre de (Marshal), 154, 157
Taylor, Maxwell (Gen.), 241
Tetuan (Spanish Morocco), 68
Tito, Josef Broz (Marshal), 105, 106
Transjordan, 201
Trenchard, Hugh (Air Marshal), 52, 54, 63, 72, 189–90, 224
Truman, Harry (President, U.S.), 120, 183, 236
    Truman Doctrine, 102
Truong Chinh, 231–32
Tunisia, 164, 170, 171, 172
Turkey, 61–62, 80, 85

Uganda, 63
United African National Council, 300–01
United Nations, 10, 172, 280, 293–94, 305, 341, 406, 416
Uribe, Alvaro, 370
Uruguay, 325
USAF (U.S. Air Force), 4, 137, 199
    Air University, 271
    in Colombia, 366
    in El Salvador, 333–49
    in Vietnam (Farm Gate), 257–60, 262, 264, 266, 271–72, 277
    Pacific Air Forces, 246, 257, 260
    special operations, 225, 247
USAFFE (United States Armed Forces Far East), 116
USAF Historical Research Agency, xiii
U.S. Army: in Vietnam, 267–69
U.S. Army Air Corps, 9, 17, 29, 41
U.S. Army Air Service, 15–21, 29, 45
U.S. Army Aviation, 1
U.S. Coast Guard, 433
U.S. Congress, 334, 354, 366, 429
U.S. Defense Department, 6
U.S. Defense Intelligence Agency, 260
USMC (United States Marine Corps), 1, 3, 4, 11
    aviation, 12, 21, 23–27, 29
    in Nicaragua, 31–44, 46, 48–49, 228, 427

in Vietnam, 261, 267
Small Wars Manual, 5–6, 43, 82
U.S. Military advisory mission, Vietnam, 268–69, 271–72
U.S. Military Assistance Command Vietnam, 231–32
U.S. National Security Council, 342
U.S. Navy, 3, 238, 242
U.S. Southern Command, 332
U.S. State Department, 285, 343, 366, 372

Vapheiades, Markos, 100, 105
Veracruz, Mexico, 14
Vietnam
    AVN (Vietnamese National Army), 153, 233
    Communist Party of, 141
    Democratic Republic of, 142, 230
    Diem government, 241–42
    NLF (National Liberation Front: Viet Cong), 233, 240–42, 258–61, 263–65, 268–70, 272, 278
    PAVN (People's Army of Vietnam), 143, 151
    U.S. Air Force in, 238, 242–50, 252, 255–57
    U.S. Army in, 244–45, 252–53, 260–63, 272
    U.S. Marine Corps in, 238, 242
    U.S. Military Assistance Advisory Group, 239–40
    U.S. Navy in, 242
    Viet Minh, 141–43, 145–46, 149–51, 153–61, 225, 230–33
    See also Indochina
Villa, Francisco "Pancho," 11–21, 45, 47

Weygand, Maxime (Gen.), 78
Westmoreland, William (Gen.), 240
WHINSEC (Western Hemisphere Institute for Security Cooperation), xiv
Wilbur, Curtis D., 34

Wilson, Woodrow (President, U.S.), 11,
12, 14–15
Woerner, Fred (Gen.), 332, 344, 372
World Court, 305–06
World Trade Center, 2

Xauen (Spanish Morocco), 72

Yemen, 201, 203, 205–06
civil war, 380–87
NLF (National Liberation Front), 203

Yemen Arab Republic, 204
Yemen army, 381–82
Yemen Republican army, 383–85, 387
Yemen Royalist army, 382–87
Yom Kippur War, 402
Yugoslavia, 9, 93, 98, 105–06

Zachariades, Nikos, 100, 105
Zambia, 286, 300–01, 304
Zapata, Emiliano, 12
Zelaya, José Santos, 31

Both of the authors have some practical experience in small wars operations. Wray Johnson is a retired U.S. Air Force colonel with a Ph.D. in history who served for many years in the Air Force Special Operations Command and advised Latin American and other air forces in the employment of aviation resources in counterinsurgency, counterdrug operations, and the civil development use of military airpower. He also taught courses on small wars topics at the U.S. Air Force Special Operations School and at the U.S. Army John F. Kennedy Special Warfare Center and School. He currently teaches about airpower, among other subjects, at the Marine Corps Command and Staff College.

James Corum served as an Army Intelligence officer in Central America from 1987 to 1988 and has taught graduate courses on airpower and small wars for more than a decade at the U.S. Air Force School of Advanced Airpower Studies (SAAS). He holds a Ph.D. in military history and is a lieutenant colonel in the U.S. Army Reserve. He also teaches at the Army War College.

Both authors have written extensively on the subject of airpower and small wars. Johnson is the author of *Vietnam and American Doctrine for Small Wars* (Bangkok: White Lotus, 2001); "Whiter Aviation Foreign Internal Defense?" *Air Power Journal* (spring 1997): 67–86; "Airpower and Restraint in Small Wars: Marine Corp Aviation in the Second Nicaraguan Campaign, 1927–1933," *Aerospace Power Journal* (summer 2001); and with Paul Dimech, "Foreign International Defense and the Hukbalahap: A Model Counterinsurgency," *Small Wars and Insurgencies* (spring/summer 1993): 29–52. James Corum has written extensively on airpower and peace operations, including "Airpower and Peace Enforcement," *Airpower Journal* (winter 1996): 10–26; and on small wars history in "The Air War in El Salvador," *Airpower Journal* (summer 1998): 27–44; and "The Myth of Air Control: Reassessing the History," *Aerospace Power Journal* (winter 2000): 61–77. He is also the author of *The Luftwaffe: Creating the Operational Air War, 1918–1940* (Lawrence: University Press of Kansas, 1997) and *The Roots of Blitzkrieg: Hans von Seeckt and German Military Reform* (Lawrence: University Press of Kansas, 1992).